DESIGN FOR SIX SIGMA FOR GREEN BELTS AND CHAMPIONS

APPLICATIONS FOR SERVICE OPERATIONS — FOUNDATIONS, TOOLS, DMADV, CASES, AND CERTIFICATION

Howard S. Gitlow, Ph.D.
David M. Levine, Ph.D.
Edward A. Popovich, Ph.D.

PEARSON
Prentice
Hall

An Imprint of PEARSON EDUCATION
Upper Saddle River, NJ • New York • London • San Francisco • Toronto • Sydney
Tokyo • Singapore • Hong Kong • Cape Town • Madrid
Paris • Milan • Munich • Amsterdam

www.ft-ph.com

Publisher: Tim Moore
Executive Editor: Jim Boyd
Editorial Assistant: Susan Abraham
Associate Editor-in-Chief and Director of Marketing: Amy Neidlinger
Cover Designer: Nina Scuderi
Managing Editor: Gina Kanouse
Project Editor: Kayla Dugger
Copy Editor: Water Crest Publishing
Compositor: Jake McFarland
Proofreader: Laurel Road Publishing
Manufacturing Buyer: Dan Uhrig

Prentice Hall offers excellent discounts on this book when ordered in quantity for bulk purchases or special sales. For more information, please contact U.S. Corporate and Government Sales, 1-800-382-3419, corpsales@pearsontechgroup.com. For sales outside the U.S., please contact International Sales, 1-317-581-3793, international@pearsontechgroup.com.

Printed in the United States of America

First Printing

ISBN 0-13-185524-7

Pearson Education LTD.
Pearson Education Australia PTY, Limited.
Pearson Education Singapore, Pte. Ltd.
Pearson Education North Asia, Ltd.
Pearson Education Canada, Ltd.
Pearson Educatión de Mexico, S.A. de C.V.
Pearson Education—Japan
Pearson Education Malaysia, Pte. Ltd.

Library of Congress Cataloging-in-Publication Data

Gitlow, Howard S.
  Design for six sigma for green belts and champions : applications for service operations—foundations, tools, DMADV, cases, and certification / Howard S. Gitlow, David M. Levine, Edward A. Popovich.
    p. cm.
  ISBN 0-13-185524-7 (hardback : alk. paper) 1. Six sigma (Quality control standard) 2. Quality control—Statistical methods. 3. Production management—Statistical methods. I. Levine, David M., 1946- II. Popovich, Edward A. III. Title.
  TS156.G535 2006
  658.4'013—dc22
                                    2005034259

Dedicated to our families:

Ali Gitlow

Sharyn Levine Rosenberg

Daniel Rosenberg

Edward Dylan Popovich

Shelly Gitlow

Marilyn Levine

Nadine Hoffenden Popovich

Beatrice Gitlow (in loving memory)

Abraham Gitlow

Lee Levine (in loving memory)

Rueben Levine (in loving memory)

Colette Popovich

Edward J. Popovich

CONTENTS

PART II: THE DESIGN FOR SIX SIGMA (DFSS) MODEL 75

6 ANALYZE PHASE 157

PART III: DESIGN FOR SIX SIGMA TOOLS AND METHODS   283

ACKNOWLEDGMENTS AND THANKS

We would like to thank the American Society for Testing and Materials for allowing us to use their statistical tables in this book. The authors would also like to thank Louis Schultz and Rip Stauffer of Process Management International (Minneapolis, MN) for their substantial support in the development of this Design for Six Sigma book—Jordan Ledford, Ameena Shrestha, and Qun (Amy) Zuo for contributing the case study in Chapter 17, and Scott Widener and Adam Johnson for contributing the dormitory example.

We would especially like to thank our editor, Jim Boyd, of Prentice Hall for his insights and encouragement. We would also like to thank Sarah Kearns for her copy editing, Kerry Reardon for her proofreading, and Kayla Dugger for her work in the production of the book.

ABOUT THE AUTHORS

Howard S. Gitlow, Ph.D. is Executive Director of the University of Miami Institute for the Study of Quality in Manufacturing and Service and a Professor of Management Science, University of Miami, Coral Gables, Florida. He was a Visiting Professor at the Science University of Tokyo in 1990, where he studied Quality Management with Dr. Noriaki Kano. He received his Ph.D. in Statistics (1974), M.B.A. (1972), and B.S. in Statistics (1969) from New York University. His areas of specialization are Six Sigma Management, Dr. Deming's theory of management, Japanese Total Quality Control, and statistical quality control.

Dr. Gitlow is a Six Sigma Master Black Belt, a Fellow of the American Society for Quality, and a member of the American Statistical Association. He has consulted on quality, productivity, and related matters with many organizations, including several major universities and Fortune 500 companies.

Dr. Gitlow has co-authored several books. These include: *Six Sigma for Green Belts and Champions*, Financial Times Prentice Hall (2005); *Quality Management, 3rd ed.*, McGraw-Hill-Irwin (2005); *Quality Management Systems*, CRC Press (2000); *Total Quality Management in Action, 2nd ed.*, Prentice Hall (1994); *The Deming Guide to Quality and Competitive Position*, Prentice Hall (1987), 15th printing; *Planning for Quality, Productivity, and Competitive Position*, Dow Jones-Irwin Publishers (1990); and *Stat City: Understanding Statistics Through Realistic Applications, 2nd ed.*, Richard D. Irwin Publishers (1987). He has published over 50 academic articles in the areas of quality, statistics, management, and marketing.

While at the University of Miami, Dr. Gitlow has received awards for Outstanding Teaching, Outstanding Writing, and Outstanding Published Research Articles.

David M. Levine, Ph.D. is Professor Emeritus of Statistics and Computer Information Systems at Bernard M. Baruch College (City University of New York). He received B.B.A. and M.B.A. degrees in Statistics from City College of New York and a Ph.D. degree from New York University in Industrial Engineering and Operations Research. He is nationally recognized as a leading innovator in business statistics education and is the co-author of such best-selling statistics textbooks as *Statistics for Managers Using Microsoft Excel, Basic Business Statistics: Concepts and Applications, Business Statistics: A First Course,* and *Applied Statistics for Engineers and*

Scientists Using Microsoft Excel and Minitab. He also recently wrote *Even You Can Learn Statistics*, published by Financial-Times Prentice Hall. He is co-author of *Six Sigma for Green Belts and Champions*, Financial Times-Prentice Hall (2005), and *Quality Management, 3rd ed.*, McGraw-Hill-Irwin (2005). He has published articles in various journals, including *Psychometrika, The American Statistician, Communications in Statistics, Multivariate Behavioral Research, Journal of Systems Management, Quality Progress*, and *The American Anthropologist.* While at Baruch College, Dr. Levine received numerous awards for outstanding teaching.

Edward A. Popovich, Ph.D. is former Vice President of Enterprise Excellence at Boca Raton Community Hospital, brought on board to introduce Six Sigma as it began its planning for a new community-affiliated teaching hospital and medical center. Previously, he worked with clients focusing on Organizational Effectiveness, Quality Systems including Six Sigma, Customer Support, Service Leadership, Business Improvement/ Reengineering, Total Quality/Organizational Change, and Statistical/Technical Analysis. The industries Ed has been involved with include large manufacturing companies, financial services companies, medical services organizations, state and county government, foreign armed services, and overseas organizations. Clients have included GE, Motorola, Lockheed Martin, Johnson & Johnson, Intuit, Sony, Bell South, First Data, Singapore Air Force, Hanley Hazelden Center at St. Mary's, NCR, J.P. Morgan, Intuit, Wachovia, A & P, and Samsung, among others.

Dr. Popovich began his corporate career at Corporate Headquarters of Harris Corporation, a diversified Fortune 500 electronics and communication company. At Harris, he helped facilitate the development of a corporate-wide process improvement and quality transformation strategy based on Dr. Deming's management principles including coordination of the PEOPLE Program. While at Harris, he also facilitated the joint University of Florida—Harris Masters degree program in Statistics, which resulted in several associates obtaining their degrees.

After Harris Corporation, Dr. Popovich joined Process Management International, a consulting firm specializing in consulting and training in quality principles in keeping with the teachings of Dr. W. Edwards Deming. In this position, process improvements in research and development; marketing; operations, and support areas within client companies, along with organizational quality management assessments, were provided, including to the board of Jaguar Cars Limited based in Coventry, England.

In the late 1980s, Dr. Popovich joined Motorola Corporation, the creators of Six Sigma. He started IMPACT, the quality action team process within the Paging Group that successfully addressed problems and opportunities in Sales, Manufacturing, and Engineering. Dr. Popovich often represented Motorola as a keynote speaker on Six Sigma. As the business operations manager, Dr. Popovich helped Motorola create a new subsidiary that introduced wireless e-mail messaging to PDAs, laptops, and other roaming devices.

Since 1994, Dr. Popovich has served as President of Sterling Enterprises International, Inc., a member of the RMC group. This organization has provided services directly and as an affiliate of several major consulting firms that provide Six Sigma consulting and training.

Dr. Popovich earned his Ph.D. in Statistics (1983), his M.B.A. (1979), and his B.S. in Mathematics (1977) at the University of Florida. He has taught at the University of Florida, University of Central Florida, Florida Atlantic University, and Nova Southeastern University, and guest lectured at several other universities.

PREFACE

INTRODUCTION

I'll bet at some point in your life you had a great idea for a new product, service, or process. All your friends agreed that it was a great idea. Well, that great idea was the beginning of the invention and innovation processes.

Invention is the process of creating new products, services, or processes that are usable in accomplishing human objectives that were formerly difficult or impossible. The first club used by a caveman to kill animals to feed his family is an example of an invention. Some of the most significant inventions were created before recorded history—for example, crude tools, weapons, speech, cultivation of plants, domestication of animals, building techniques, production and control of fire, pottery, political systems, and the wheel. The period of recorded history began with the invention of cuneiform script by the Sumerians of Mesopotamia around 3000 B.C.

Innovation is the process by which invention is put to use for the betterment of humanity. Thomas Edison was both an inventor (of the electric light bulb) and an innovator because he was critical to the electrification of New York City and the establishment of the General Electric Company.

All inventions and innovations do not have to be generated from complex, theoretical, and radical ideas. Sometimes they come from the simplest of ideas. For example, whoever thought it was possible to create an improved corkscrew? Yet, in the last decade or two, a new corkscrew was invented. This corkscrew has wings or handles that allows the corkscrew to pull the cork out of the bottle. Another example of a product that you might not think could be improved is the teabag. Surprise! Lipton invented a teabag with two strings that allows the user to squeeze the last drops of tea out of the bag without burning his or her fingers. Ingenious!

DESIGN FOR SIX SIGMA (DFSS)

Design for Six Sigma (DFSS) is the method used by a Six Sigma project team to invent and innovate products, services, and processes. DFSS can be used to design entirely new products, services, and processes, or major new features of existing products, services, or processes that are *consistently* reliable and able to be manufactured, and *uniformly* surpass customer requirements. Additionally, DFSS creates designs that are: (1) based on stakeholder needs and wants; (2) resource efficient; (3) minimal in complexity; (4) capable of generating high yields; (5) robust to process variations; and (6) quick to generate a profit.

An organization can reap many benefits from employing the DFSS methodology. The list of benefits includes: launching projects on time and on budget; reaping additional incremental revenues sooner; achieving greater market share; minimizing problems uncovered at launch; improving rolled throughput yield (RTY) significantly; ensuring quality and efficient production through data-driven scorecards; and differentiating products, services, and processes due to a customer focus.

DFSS is a method that embodies several principles. The first principle is for all areas within an organization to simultaneously design the product, service, and/or process to minimize future problems. The second principle is to design the product, service, and/or process to minimize variability in critical to quality characteristics (CTQs) important to customers and maximize customer satisfaction. The third principle is to design a process capable of delivering the quantity and quality of products or services desired by customers in a timely fashion. The fourth principle is to include suppliers early in the design process. These four principles are the bedrock of the DFSS method.

It is not always apparent, but more businesses in the United States today are actually engaged in providing "services" rather than products. They are providing work, information, or some other less tangible utility. In order to compete in those markets, service providers must "design" their service(s) to meet and surpass the needs and expectations of those using or consuming those services. Design principles here do not very readily tie into traditional engineering disciplines, and the DFSS tools and methods must be adapted accordingly.

Finally, whether you are preparing to manufacture a new product or deliver a service, you must establish supporting business processes to produce, deliver, and support those products and/or services. In the case where you are putting in place processes that previously did not exist, then you must "design" those processes.

THE DMADV MODEL

There are at least three very distinct flavors of DFSS, and no one of these can be universally applied to any design effort. To be more descriptive, it may be helpful to more precisely designate them as DFSS–Product, DFSS–Service, and DFSS–Process. Although it is helpful for organizations to have a simple, standard design methodology, the specific techniques employed and the deliverables produced will vary by DFSS flavor.

DMADV is a five-phase process for progressing through a design project. Even though there may be at least three flavors of DMADV, there are some common themes across all flavors. However, variation exists at the tool level.

The "**D**" or "Define" Phase is essentially a good conventional program management phase to set the stage for success. You can think of this phase as verifying that the project is ready to move forward with a reasonable chance of success. The key output of the Define Phase is the project charter. A good charter will contain several key elements. It will clearly articulate the purpose of the project, both specifically and how it integrates with other relevant projects. Specific and measurable project goals (both functional and administrative) will be identified. You identify the scope of the project—what will be included, and what will be excluded from consideration and delivery for the project. You identify the key players and other resources, and ensure their availability for the project. You create a formal project plan with schedule and milestones. Finally, you obtain written approval and commitments from all key players to demonstrate acceptance and support.

The "**M**" or "Measure" Phase is primarily concerned with defining the requirements for the project by considering the perspectives of all the relevant stakeholders of the project's outcome(s)—for example, the Voice of the Customer (market segments), the Voice of the Business (employee segments), and the Voice of the Process. Each will have concerns that will differ from the others, and sometimes occur in conflict. The key Measure phase activities are to capture those voices and then translate them into measurable project requirements. At this stage, you are talking about higher-level considerations that will ultimately be distilled down to specifications for the final design. A requirement can be achieved in several different ways. Only after one design alternative has been chosen can you develop exact specifications that deliver on the requirements.

The "**A**" or "Analyze" Phase is concerned with generating high-level design alternatives, which in the judgment of experts, are likely to be able to meet the defined requirements. In truth, all design efforts are faced with contradictory requirements and constraints that must be coordinated. Compromises are always required. The tools used in this phase are designed to sift through the requirements in a methodical manner to discover the combination(s) of compromises that offer the best overall benefit and value for the imposed constraints. The various design alternatives are then checked against these refined requirement sets to determine which design approach offers the most desired results.

The "**D**" or "Design" phase is concerned with developing the detailed design requirements for the product, service, or process. This is where exact specifications are developed for the actual elements that will combine to make the desired result. It may be helpful to use a familiar analogy. If the project was to design a house, then you would partition the activities into two major components. The first would be the selection of the site, the foundation, and the building design. The second would be the details concerning style, colors, appearance, etc. The raw building is the "architecture," while the design details make it specifically your house. Similarly, you have a design concept completed at the end of the Analyze Phase, but it doesn't become usable and specific until you complete the (Detailed) Design Phase. The key outputs from the Design Phase include all analyses, detailed specifications (which, if achieved, will deliver the requirements), and often several prototypes or models. Frequently, what is known as Alpha-Testing is performed at the end of this stage. This testing is done to ensure that the prototype (or model) does meet the specifications.

The "**V**" or "Verify/Validate" Phase is used to verify that the detailed design is acceptable and desirable to all of the stakeholders of the design. This is often the first opportunity for each of the stakeholder groups to see the result and evaluate its fitness for use. It is during this stage that Beta-Testing often occurs. This testing is done to ensure that the design does meet the requirements in addition to the specifications. In the field of commercial products and services, this is sometimes known as "test marketing."

DMADV is not a magic bullet, and is never meant to supplant good engineering judgment. It is intended to bring some discipline to organizing design information often neglected or forgotten, as well as augment reliable, time-proven design methods. The overhead of DMADV does not always bring significant design improvements worth the time and cost, so DMADV must be used only when it can add net benefit.

COMPLEXITY

A discussion about design is not complete without considering complexity factors. It is one thing to go about designing the next new wooden pencil, but quite another to design a moon-bound spacecraft. As a new product, service, or process becomes more complex, you need to partition the effort into tractable elements. There is a common hierarchy employed by designers that is useful to consider with DFSS.

At the highest level, there is the "system." It is the totality of all that is to be created in the final design. Systems are composed of two or more "subsystems," each of which are elements that can be designed more or less separately from each other. In order for subsystems to integrate into the complete systems, it is usually necessary to develop specifications for integration as part of the system architecture. Specifications within a subsystem are often left to more detailed design stages. Subsystems are composed of two or more "modules," and like subsystems, are relatively independent design elements. Usually you need to develop specifications for module integration as part of the subsystem design. The final level in the hierarchy is called the "component" level. This is the smallest design unit relative to the system available. In the case of product design, the component level may be a single part or an assembly of just a handful of parts. The designations "system," "subsystem," "module," and "component" are relative terms. A design unit that is called "subsystem" may still be rather complex, and to that unit's design team may still be viewed as a "system" from that perspective. For example, the Apollo moon vehicle was a system composed of three elements: the Command Module, the Service Module, and the Lunar Module. The entire system was made up of these three subsystems. However, to Grumman Aerospace, the designers of the Lunar Module, they were only concerned with this one incredibly complex unit. To them, it alone was worthy of "system" designation. On the other hand, to NASA, an Apollo spacecraft was not a "moon vehicle system." The Apollo craft cannot go anywhere by itself. To NASA, the "system" may be the assembly of an Apollo craft with a Saturn V rocket.

The practical reality is that complex design projects must be dissected into tractable elements, each worthy of the formalisms of project management and DFSS. One engineer can easily design a component, but it takes teams of talented people to manage large-scale projects and complete them in reasonable periods of time. You need to have a way to logically partition large jobs into "bite-sized" pieces and spread the work around to a larger number of people. The trick is to find a portioning scheme that is sound and practical, and then manage the interfaces between pieces to make sure that the fully integrated system works as designed.

DFSS principles can be applied at any level in this hierarchy. However, different levels may require different parts of the DFSS toolsets. DMADV, for example, does not necessarily apply to all design levels. Although the full DMADV process can be used at the component, and probably module levels, the A-D-V phases have less utility at the system and subsystem levels. The following chart illustrates that "DMADV" and the tools used at each phase apply differently to each level in the design hierarchy.

DFSS Phases

	Define	Measure	Analyze	Design	Verify/Validate
System	A	A	N	N	A
Subsystem	N	A	O	N	O
Module	N	O	A	A	O
Component	N	N	N	A	N

A—Always Used
O—Often Used
N—Not Often Used

For example, if you apply DMADV to the design of a cardiovascular facility at Boca Raton Community Hospital, in Boca Raton, Florida, you can see how the hierarchy forms, and how you can employ DFSS. BRCH can view the "system" as the entire, functional facility—on site, built, staffed, equipped, and operating. The system, however, will have several key "subsystem" elements, including but not limited to parking, landscaping, and building. These subsystems may be composed of several "modules." For example, "building" may be composed of electrical system, water system, heating ventilation and air conditioning (HVAC) system, space allocation, elevator system, etc. In fact, there are dozens upon dozens of functional modules for something as complex as a hospital building. Each of those modules will be composed of several (or many) components. The cardiovascular facility will be primarily providing "services," but will use tangible assets, information, skilled and semi-skilled professionals, and dozens of primary and supporting business processes. Not only will BRCH have to be judicious in where to apply DFSS in the system hierarchy, but the right flavor of DFSS must be applied to a design element that is judged to benefit from the DFSS discipline. One size of DMADV does not fit all, and designing the cardiovascular center is not a single DMADV project.

It is the sincere hope of the authors that you, the reader, will find this book a valuable and practical guide in your design efforts. Good luck with your design!

UNIQUE ASPECTS OF THIS BOOK

Design for Six Sigma for Green Belts and Champions—Foundations, DMADV, Tools, Cases, and Certification has numerous features that make this book unique:

- **Contains coverage of the foundation of management necessary for professional Design for Six Sigma Management.** This includes how to deploy an organization's mission statement throughout an organization through a cascading and interlocking system of key objectives and key indicators called a *dashboard*, which is illustrated with many practical and relevant examples.

- **Presents a thorough and detailed anatomy of the Design for Six Sigma Management improvement model, called the DMADV model.** DMADV is an acronym for Define—Measure—Analyze—Design—Verify/Validate. The DMADV model is a well-tested vehicle for guiding a Six Sigma team through the maze of a complex design or redesign project.

- **Integrates coverage of Design for Six Sigma Management with detailed coverage of those statistical methods that are appropriate for Champion and Green Belt certification.** Each statistical method is explained and applied to an example involving actual data in a design or redesign context. Coverage of statistics assumes familiarity with those statistical methods used in Six Sigma and focuses on design of experiments, multiple regression, and simulation from an applied design or redesign perspective. Outputs from the Minitab and JMP statistical software packages and the Sigma Flow simulation software package, widely used in Design for Six Sigma Management, are illustrated.

- **Includes chapter-ending appendixes that provide step-by-step instructions for using the latest version of Minitab and JMP for the statistical methods covered in each chapter.**

- **Includes a detailed case study in Design for Six Sigma Management that provides a "how to" examination of all the steps involved in using the Define—Measure—Analyze—Design—Verify/Validate (DMADV) Design for Six Sigma approach.** The case is from a service industry (higher education).

- **Includes information on Champion and Green Belt certification exams along with sample test questions.**

CONTACTING THE AUTHORS

We have gone to great lengths to make this book both pedagogically sound and error-free. If you have any suggestions or require clarification about any of the material, or if you find any errors, please contact us at:

`HGITLOW@MIAMI.EDU`

or

`DAVID_LEVINE@BARUCH.CUNY.EDU`

Howard S. Gitlow, Ph.D.
David M. Levine, Ph.D.
Edward A. Popovich, Ph.D.

DESIGN FOR SIX SIGMA BASICS

FOUNDATIONS OF SIX SIGMA MANAGEMENT

SECTIONS

Introduction
1.1 Successful Applications of Six Sigma Management
1.2 Key Ingredients for Success with Six Sigma Management
1.3 Benefits of Six Sigma Management
1.4 Fundamentals of Improving a Product, Service, or Process
1.5 Fundamentals of Inventing–Innovating a Product, Service, or Process
1.6 What Is New about Six Sigma Management?
1.7 Six Sigma in Non-Manufacturing Industries
Summary
References

LEARNING OBJECTIVES

After reading this chapter, you will be able to:

* Present strong evidence of the value of Six Sigma style of management.
* Understand the key ingredient for success with Six Sigma management.
* Appreciate the benefits of Six Sigma management.
* Review the fundamentals of improving a product, service, or process.
* Appreciate the DMAIC model for improvement.
* Introduce the fundamentals of inventing and innovating a product, service, or process.
* Appreciate the DMADV model for invention and innovation.
* Know what is new about Six Sigma management.
* Appreciate the significance of Six Sigma management in non-manufacturing industries.

INTRODUCTION

This chapter is about getting you comfortable with Six Sigma management. We accomplish this objective by providing you with strong anecdotal evidence that Six Sigma is a very successful style of management, explaining how it must be emphatically led from the top of the organization, and, finally, introducing you to the Six Sigma models for improving and inventing/innovating products, services, or processes. This chapter could serve as a brief introduction to Six Sigma management for any stakeholder of your organization.

1.1 SUCCESSFUL APPLICATIONS OF SIX SIGMA MANAGEMENT

Manufacturing organizations have experienced great success with Six Sigma management. Selected manufacturing organizations that use Six Sigma management include the following:

Asea-Brown-Boveri

AT&T

Bombardier

Eli Lilly

Foxboro

General Electric

Honeywell/Allied Signal

IBM–UK

Lockheed Martin

Motorola

Raytheon

Seagate

Texas Instruments

Additionally, non-manufacturing organizations have had excellent results with Six Sigma management. A few non-manufacturing organizations using Six Sigma management include the following:

Allstate Insurance

Amazon.com

American Express

Bank of America

Bankers Life and Insurance

Capital One Services

Intuit

J. P. Morgan Chase

Merrill Lynch

Microsoft

United Health Group

University of Miami

Jack Welch, Chairman emeritus and CEO of General Electric, was so committed to and impressed with Six Sigma that he stated:

"Six Sigma GE Quality 2000 will be the biggest, the most personally rewarding, and, in the end, the most profitable undertaking in our history."

"…we plunged into Six Sigma with a company-consuming vengeance just over three years ago. We have invested more than a billion dollars in the effort and the financial returns have now entered the exponential phase." (GE's letter to share-owners, February 12, 1999)

1.2 Key Ingredients for Success with Six Sigma Management

The key ingredient for a successful Six Sigma management process is the commitment of top management. Executives must have a burning desire to transform their organizations. This means total commitment from the top of the organization to the bottom of the organization. An executive's commitment is shown in part by how she or he allocates time and resources, and by the questions she or he asks of others. Many Six Sigma executives spend at least 25% of their time on Six Sigma matters and allocate major organizational resources to drive the Six Sigma style of management. If an executive asks: "What was yesterday's production volume?," she or he is saying: "I care about quantity, not quality." If an executive asks: "What is happening with the Production Department's Six Sigma projects to increase production volume?," she or he is saying: "I care about quality *and* quantity."

1.3 BENEFITS OF SIX SIGMA MANAGEMENT

There are two types of benefits from Six Sigma management: benefits to the organization and benefits to stakeholders. Benefits to an organization are gained through the continuous reduction of variation and, where applicable, the centering of processes on their desired (nominal) levels. The benefits are as follows:

Improved process flows

Reduced total defects

Improved communication (provides a common language)

Reduced cycle times

Enhanced knowledge (and enhanced ability to manage that knowledge)

Higher levels of customer and employee satisfaction

Increased productivity

Decreased work-in-progress (WIP)

Decreased inventory

Improved capacity and output

Increased quality and reliability

Decreased unit costs

Increased price flexibility

Better designs

Decreased time to market

Faster delivery time

Increased ability to convert improvements and innovations into hard currency

In essence, Six Sigma is a roadmap for an enterprise to become more effective and efficient. An "effective" enterprise is one that does the "right" things "right" the first time, and an "efficient" enterprise is one that uses minimum resources to accomplish the "right" thing. The "right" thing is judged by the perception of customers and the marketplace. Simply put, the Six Sigma enterprise focuses on providing a value-added experience to current and future customers through its processes, products, and services. Processes that do not add value to the customer's experience are candidates for elimination by management. A value-added process is a process that the customer is willing to pay for, does not involve rework or fixes, is done "right" the first time, and is not wasteful to the enterprise.

Louis Schultz, President of Process Management International, a consulting firm in Minneapolis, Minnesota, states that:

"The perception and performance of an enterprise determines its value. Six Sigma management focuses on driving effective and efficient performance across the total enterprise to increase the perception of the marketplace of its ability to deliver value-added processes, products, and services. The perception of the marketplace of the value of an enterprise is indirectly measured by market share, shareholder value, and the willingness of customers to recommend these processes, products, and services to other potential customers."

Benefits to stakeholders are a by-product of the organizational benefits. The benefits to stakeholders include the following:

- Shareholders receive more profit due to decreased costs and increased revenues.
- Customers are delighted with products and services.
- Employees experience higher morale and more satisfaction from joy in work.
- Suppliers enjoy a secure source of business.

1.4 FUNDAMENTALS OF IMPROVING A PRODUCT, SERVICE, OR PROCESS

Process Basics (Voice of the Process [VoP])

Definition of a Process

A **process** is a collection of interacting components that transform inputs into outputs toward a common aim, called a *mission statement*. The job of management is to optimize the entire process toward its aim. This may require the sub-optimization of selected components of the process. Sometimes a particular department in an organization may have to give up resources in the short run to another department to maximize profit for the overall organization. This is particularly true when one department expends effort to correct the failings or omissions of another department working on the same process. Inspection, signature approvals, rework areas, complaint-resolution areas, etc. are all evidence that the process was not done effectively and efficiently the first time. The consumption of resources utilized in correcting the failings and omissions would have been avoided if the process was done "right."

The transformation, as shown in Figure 1.1, involves the addition or creation of value in one of three aspects: time, place, or form. An output has "time value" if it is available when needed by a user. For example, you have food when you are hungry. Or material inputs are ready on schedule. An output has "place value" if it is available where needed by a user. For example, gas is in your tank (not in an oil field), or wood chips are in a paper mill. An output has "form value" if it is available in the form needed by a user. For example, bread is sliced so it can fit in a toaster, or paper has three holes so it can be placed in a binder.

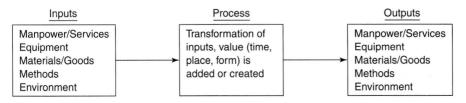

FIGURE 1.1 Basic Process

Processes exist in all facets of organizations, and our understanding of them is crucial. Many people mistakenly think only of production processes. However, administration, sales, service, human resources, training, maintenance, paper flows, interdepartmental communication, and vendor relations are all processes. Importantly, relationships between people are processes. Most processes can be studied, documented, defined, improved, and innovated.

An example of a generic assembly process is shown in Figure 1.2. The inputs (component parts, machines, and operators) are transformed in the process to make the outputs (assembled product).

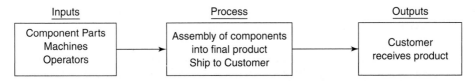

FIGURE 1.2 Production Process

An organization is a multiplicity of micro sub-processes, all synergistically building to the macro process of that organization. All processes have customers and suppliers; these customers and suppliers can be internal or external to the organization. A customer can be an end user or the next operation downstream. The customer does not even have to be a human; it could be a machine. A supplier could be another organization supplying sub-assemblies or services, or the prior operation upstream.

Variation in a Process

The outputs from all processes and their component parts may be measured; the measurements invariably fluctuate over time, creating a distribution of measurements. The distribution of measurements of the outputs from a process over time is called the "Voice of the Process (VoP)." Consider a process such as getting ready for work or for class in the morning. Some days you are busier than usual, while on other days you have less to do than usual. Your process varies from day to day to some degree. This is common variation. However, if a construction project begins on the highway you take to work or school, you might drastically alter your morning routine. This would be special variation because it would have been caused by a change external to your "driving to work or school" process. If the traffic patterns had remained as they were, your process would have continued on its former path of common variation.

The design and execution of a process creates common causes of variation. In other words, common variation is due to the process itself. **Process capability** is determined by inherent common causes of variation, such as hiring, training, or supervisory practices; inadequate lighting; stress; management style; policies and procedures; or design of products or services. Employees working within the process cannot control a common cause of variation and should not be held accountable for, or penalized for, its outcomes. Process owners (management) must realize that unless a change is made in the process (which only they can make), the capability of the process will remain the same. Special causes of variation are due to events external to the usual functioning of the process. New raw materials, a drunken employee, or a new operator can be examples of special causes of variation. Identifying the occurrence of special and common causes of variation is discussed extensively in References 2 and 3.

Because unit-to-unit variation decreases the customer's ability to rely on the dependability and uniformity of the outputs of a process, managers must understand how to reduce and control variation. Employees use statistical methods so that common and special causes of variation can be differentiated; special variation can be resolved and common variation can be reduced by management action, resulting in improvement and innovation of the outputs of a process.

The following fictionalized case history demonstrates the need for management to understand the difference between common and special causes of variation to take appropriate action. In this case history, an employee comes to work intoxicated. His behavior causes productivity, safety, and morale problems. You, as the supervisor, speak to the employee privately, try to resolve the situation, and send the employee home with pay. After a second instance of intoxication, you speak to the employee privately, try to resolve the problem again, and send the employee home without pay. A third instance causes you to refer the employee to an Employee Assistance Program. A fourth offense results in you terminating the employee. As a good manager, you document the employee's history to create a paper trail in case of legal action. All of the above is necessary and is considered to be good management practice.

The thought process behind the preceding managerial actions assumes that the employee is the problem. In other words, you view the employee's behavior as the special cause of variation from the desired sober state. However, this is true only if there is a statistically significant difference between the employee in question and all other employees. If the employee's behavior is part of a process that allows such behavior to exist, then the problem is not a special cause, but rather a common cause; it requires a different solution. In the latter case, the employee must be dealt with as before; but, additionally, organizational policies and procedures (processes) must be changed to prevent future incidents of intoxication. This new view requires a shift in thought. With the new thought process, if existing organizational policies and procedures allow employees with drinking problems to be present in the workplace, an intoxicated employee must be dealt with according to the original solution, and policies and procedures must be improved to prevent future incidents of such behavior on the job.

Feedback Loops

An important aspect of any process is a **feedback loop**. A feedback loop relates information about outputs from any stage(s) back to other stage(s) to make an analysis of the process. Figure 1.3 depicts the feedback loop in relation to a basic process.

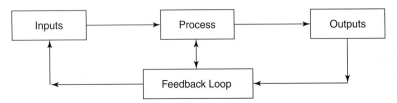

FIGURE 1.3 Feedback Loop

The tools and methods discussed in this book provide vehicles for relating information about outputs to other stage(s) in the process. Decision making about processes is aided by the transmission of this information. A major purpose of quality management is to provide the information (flowing through a feedback loop) needed to take action with respect to a process.

There are three feedback loop situations: no feedback loop, special cause only feedback loop, and special and common cause feedback loop. A process that does not have a feedback loop is probably doomed to deterioration and decay due to the inability of its stakeholders to rejuvenate and improve it based on data from its outputs. An example of a process without a feedback loop is a relationship between two people (manager and subordinate, husband and wife, or buyer and seller) that contains no vehicle (feedback loop) to discuss issues and problems with the intention of establishing a better relationship in the future. A process in which all feedback information is treated as a special cause will exhibit enormous variation in its output. An example of a process with a special cause only feedback loop could be a relationship between two people; but in this case, the relationship deteriorates through a cycle of successive overreactions to problems that are perceived as special by both members of the relationship. In fact, the problems are probably repetitive in nature due to the structure of the relationship itself and to common causes of variation. Finally, in a process in which feedback information is separated into common and special causes—special causes are resolved and common causes are reduced—products, services, or processes will exhibit continuous improvement of their output. For example, the relationship problems between a superior and a subordinate can be classified as either due to special and/or common causes; statistical methods are used to resolve special causes and to remove common causes, thereby improving the relationship in the future.

Consider the following example. Paul is a 40-year-old, mid-level manager who is unhappy because he wants his boss to give him a promotion. He thinks about his relationship with his boss and wonders what went wrong. He determines that over a period of 10 years, he has had about 40 disagreements with his boss (one per quarter).

Paul thinks about what caused each disagreement. Initially, he thought each disagreement had its own special cause. After studying the pattern of the number of disagreements per year, Paul discovered that it was a stable and predictable process of common causes of variation. Subsequently, he wrote down the reason for as many of the disagreements as he could remember (about 30). However, after thinking about his relationship with his boss from the perspective of common causes, he realized his disagreements with his boss were not unique events (special causes); rather, they were a repetitive process, and the reasons for the disagreements could be classified into common cause categories. He was surprised to see that the 30 reasons collapse down to four basic reasons—poor communication of a work issue, a process failure causing work not to be completed on schedule, unexcused absence, and pay-related issues—with one reason, poor communication of a work issue, accounting for 75% of all disagreements. Armed with this insight, he scheduled a discussion with his boss to find a solution to their communication problems. His boss explained that he hates the e-mails that Paul is always sending him and wished Paul would just talk to him and say what is on his mind. They resolved their problem; their relationship was greatly improved, and, eventually, Paul received his promotion.

Definition of Quality (Voice of the Customer [VoC])

Goal Post View of Quality   Quality is a concept whose definition has changed over time. In the past, *quality* meant "conformance to valid customer requirements." That is, as long as an output fell within acceptable limits (called **specification limits**) around a desired value or target value (also called the **nominal value,** denoted by "**m**"); it was deemed conforming, good, or acceptable. We refer to this as the "goal post" definition of quality. The nominal value and specification limits are set based on the perceived needs and wants of customers. Specification limits are called the **Voice of the Customer**. Figure 1.4 shows the "goal post" view of losses arising from deviations from the nominal value. That is, losses are minimum until the **lower specification limit (LSL)** or **upper specification limit (USL)** is reached. Then, suddenly, losses become positive and constant, regardless of the magnitude of the deviation from the nominal value.

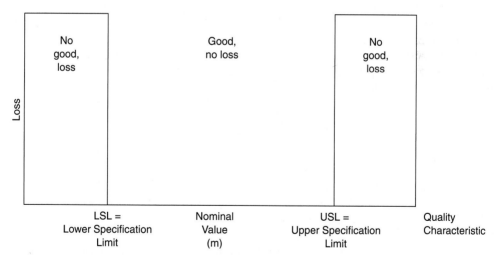

FIGURE 1.4   Goal Post View of Losses Arising from Deviations from Nominal

An individual unit of product or service is considered to conform to a specification if it is at or inside the boundary (USL or LSL) or boundaries (USL and LSL). Individual unit specifications are made up of a nominal value and an acceptable tolerance from the nominal. The nominal value is the desired value for process performance mandated by the customer's needs and/or wants. The tolerance is an allowable departure from a nominal value established by designers that is deemed non-harmful to the desired functioning of the product or service. Specification limits are the boundaries created by adding and/or subtracting tolerances from a nominal value; for example:

USL = upper specification limit = nominal + tolerance

LSL = lower specification limit = nominal – tolerance

A service example of the goal post view of quality and specification limits can be seen in a monthly accounting report that must be completed in 7 days (nominal), no earlier than 4 days (lower specification limit—not all the necessary data will be available), and no later than 10 days (upper specification limit—the due date for the report at the board meeting). Therefore the "Voice of the Customer" is that the report must be completed ideally in 7 days, but no sooner than 4 days or no later than 10 days.

Another example of the goal post view of quality and specification limits is to insert a medical device into the chest of a patient that is 25 mm in diameter (the nominal value). A tolerance of 5 mm above or below the nominal value (25 mm) is acceptable to the surgeon performing the operation. Thus, if a medical device's diameter measures between 20 mm and 30 mm (inclusive), it is deemed conforming to specifications. It does not matter if the medical device is 21 mm or 29 mm; they are both conforming units. If a medical device's diameter measures less than 20 mm or more than 30 mm, it is deemed as not conforming to specifications and is scrapped at a cost of $1,000.00 per device. Therefore, the "Voice of the Customer" states that the diameters of the medical devices must be between 20 mm and 30 mm, inclusive, with an ideal diameter of 25 mm.

In this section, you assumed that there is a reasonable target from which deviations on either side are possible. For situations in which there is only one specification limit—such as time to deliver mail in hours, with the target of 0 hours and an upper specification limit of 5 days—the objective is not to exceed the upper specification, and to deliver the mail on a very consistent basis (little variation) to create a highly predictable mail delivery process. In other words, whether there are two-sided specifications or a one-sided specification, the goal is to have increased consistency, implying minimal variation in performance and, thus, increased predictability and reliability of outcomes.

Continuous Improvement View of Quality A more modern definition of *quality* states that: "**Quality** is a predictable degree of uniformity and dependability, at low cost and suited to the market" [see Reference 1, p. 229]. Figure 1.5 shows a more realistic loss curve in which losses begin to accumulate as soon as a quality characteristic of a product or service deviates from the nominal value. As with the "goal post" view of quality, once the specification limits are reached, the loss suddenly becomes positive and constant, regardless of the deviation from the nominal value beyond the specification limits.

The continuous improvement view of quality was developed by Genichi Taguchi [see Reference 10, pp. 7-11]. The **Taguchi Loss Function**, called the *Loss curve* in Figure 1.5, expresses the loss of deviating from the nominal within specifications: the left-hand vertical axis is "loss" and the horizontal axis is the measure, y, of a quality characteristic. The loss associated with deviating $(y - m)$ units from the nominal value, m, is:

$L(y) = k(y - m)^2 =$ Taguchi Loss Function   (1.1)

where

y = the value of the quality characteristic for a particular item of product or service.

m = the nominal value for the quality characteristic.

k = a constant, A/d^2.

A = the loss (cost) of exceeding specification limits (e.g., the cost to scrap a unit of output).

d = the allowable tolerance from the nominal value that is used to determine specification limits.

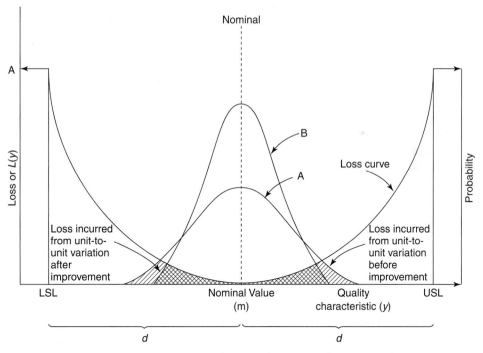

FIGURE 1.5 Continuous Improvement View of Losses of Deviations from Nominal

Under this Taguchi Loss Function, the continuous reduction of unit-to-unit variation around the nominal value is the most economical course of action, absent capital investment (more on this later). In Figure 1.5, the righthand vertical axis is "Probability" and the horizontal axis is the measure, y, of a quality characteristic. The distribution of output from a process before improvement is shown in Curve A, while the distribution of output after improvement is shown in Curve B. The losses incurred from unit-to-unit variation before process improvement (the lined area

under the loss curve for Distribution A) is greater than the losses incurred from unit-to-unit variation after process improvement (the hatched area under the loss curve for Distribution B). This
definition of quality promotes continual reduction of unit-to-unit variation (uniformity) of output
around the nominal value, absent capital investment. If capital investment is required, then an
analysis must be conducted to determine if the benefit of the reduction in variation in the process
justifies the cost. The capital investment for a process improvement should not exceed the single
lined area under the Taguchi Loss Function in Curve A, but not in Curve B, in Figure 1.5. This
modern definition of quality implies that the Voice of the Process should take up a smaller and
smaller portion of the Voice of the Customer (specifications) over time, rather than just being
inside of the specification limits. The logic here is that there is a loss associated with products or
services that deviate from the nominal value, even when they conform to specifications.

To illustrate the continuous definition of quality, return to the example of the medical
device that is to be inserted into a patient's chest. Every millimeter higher or lower than 25 mm
causes a loss that can be expressed by the following Taguchi Loss Function:

$$L(y) = k(y - m)^2 = (A/d^2)(y - m)^2 = (\$1,000/[5^2])(y - 25\text{mm})^2 = (40)(y - 25\text{mm})^2$$

$$if\ 20 \leq y \leq 30$$
$$L(y) = \$1,000 \qquad if\ y < 20\ or\ y > 30$$

Table 1.1 shows the values of $L(y)$ for values of the quality characteristic (diameter of the
medical device).

TABLE 1.1   Loss Arising from Deviations in Diameters of the Medical Device

Diameter of the Medical Device (y)	Value of Taguchi Loss Function (L[y])
18	1,000
19	1,000
20	1,000
21	640
22	360
23	160
24	40
25	0
26	40
27	160
28	360
29	640
30	1,000
31	1,000
32	1,000

Under the loss curve shown in Table 1.1, it is always economical to continuously reduce the unit-to-unit variation in the diameter of medical devices, absent capital investment. This will minimize the loss of surgically inserting medical devices.

If a Taguchi Loss Function has only one specification limit, such as an upper specification limit, the preceding discussion applies without loss of generality. For example, if in the opinion of customers, 30 seconds is the maximum acceptable time to answer phone calls at a customer call center and the desired time is 0 seconds, any positive deviation will result in loss to the customer. Moreover, the greater the process variation (above the nominal time of 0), the greater the loss to the customer. In the case where there is no natural nominal value (e.g., 0 seconds), deviation between the process average and the desired time results in a process bias. The loss function can be used to show in these cases that the loss is a function of the bias squared plus the process variation. This implies that the goal is to eliminate the bias (i.e., move the process average toward the desired time) and to reduce process variation. For example, customer call centers not only wish to reduce their time to answer phone calls from their customers, but they want to have uniformly short answer times. Why? When management determines staffing requirements for the customer call center, it needs to be able to have enough staff to meet its specification for time-to-answer. The more variation in the time-to-answer per call, the more unpredictable the process, and the less confidence management will have in its staffing model. Management may actually overstaff to ensure it meets its specifications. This introduces more cost to the customer call center, which is indirectly passed on to the customer.

Definitions of Six Sigma Management (Relationship Between VoC and VoP)

Non-Technical Definitions of Six Sigma Management

Six Sigma management is the relentless and rigorous pursuit of the reduction of variation in all critical processes to achieve continuous and breakthrough improvements that impact the bottom line and/or top line of the organization and increase customer satisfaction. Another common definition is that Six Sigma management is an organizational initiative designed to create manufacturing, service, and administrative processes that produce a high rate of sustained improvement in both defect reduction and cycle time (e.g., when Motorola began its effort, the rate it chose was a 10-fold reduction in defects in two years, along with a 50% reduction in cycle time). For example, a bank takes an average of 60 days to process a loan with a 10% rework rate in 2004. In a Six Sigma organization, the bank should take no longer than an average of 30 days to process a loan with a 1% error rate in 2006, and no more than an average of 15 days to process a loan with a 0.10% error rate by 2008. Clearly, this requires a dramatically improved/innovated loan process.

Technical Definitions of Six Sigma Management

The Normal Distribution. The term Six Sigma is derived from the normal distribution used in statistics. Many observable phenomena can be graphically represented as a bell-shaped curve or a normal distribution [see Reference 3], as illustrated in Figure 1.6.

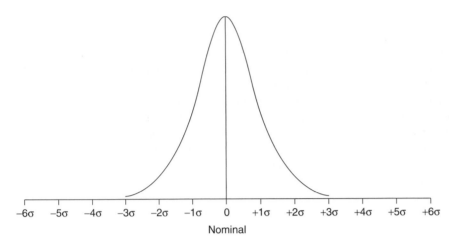

-6σ -5σ -4σ -3σ -2σ -1σ 0 +1σ +2σ +3σ +4σ +5σ +6σ

Nominal

FIGURE 1.6 Normal Distribution with Mean (μ) and Standard Deviation (σ)

When measuring any process, its outputs (services or products) vary in size, shape, look, feel, or any other measurable characteristic. The typical value of the output of a process is measured by a statistic called the *mean* or *average*. The variability of the output of a process is measured by a statistic called the *standard deviation*. In a normal distribution, the interval created by the mean plus or minus 2 standard deviations contains 95.44% of the data values; 45,600 data values per million are outside of the area created by the mean plus or minus 2 standard deviations (45,600 = 1,000,000 × [4.56% = 100% – 95.44%]). In a normal distribution, the interval created by the mean plus or minus 3 standard deviations contains 99.73% of the data; 2,700 defects per million opportunities are outside of the area created by the mean plus or minus 3 standard deviations (2,700 = 1,000,000 ×[0.27% = 100% – 99.73%]). In a normal distribution, the interval created by the mean plus or minus 6 standard deviations contains 99.9999998% of the data; 2 data values per billion data values are outside of the area created by the mean plus or minus 6 standard deviations (2 = 1,000,000,000 × [0.0000002% = 100% – 99.9999998%]).

Relationship Between VoP and VoC. Six Sigma promotes the idea that the distribution of output for a stable normally distributed process (Voice of the Process) should be designed to take up no more than half of the tolerance allowed by the specification limits (Voice of the Customer). Although processes may be designed to be at their best, you assume that the processes may increase in variation over time. This increase in variation may be due to small variation with process inputs, the way the process is monitored, changing conditions, etc. The increase in process variation is often assumed to be similar to temporary shifts in the underlying process mean. In practice, the increase in process variation has been shown to be equivalent to an average shift of 1.5 standard deviations in the originally designed and monitored process. If a process is originally designed to be twice as good as a customer demands (i.e., the specifications representing the customer requirements are 6 standard deviations from the process target), then even with a shift in the Voice of the Process, the customer demands are likely to be met. In fact, even if the process mean shifted off target by 1.5 standard deviations, there are 4.5 standard deviations between the process mean and closest specification limit, resulting in no more than 3.4 defects per million opportunities (DPMO). In the 1980s, Motorola demonstrated that in practice, a 1.5 standard deviation shift was what was observed as the equivalent increase in process variation for many processes that were benchmarked.

Figure 1.7 shows the "Voice of the Process" for an accounting function with an average of 7 days, a standard deviation of 1 day, and a stable normal distribution. It also shows a nominal value of 7 days, a lower specification limit of 4 days, and an upper specification limit of 10 days. The accounting function is referred to as a **3-sigma process** because the process mean plus or minus 3 standard deviations is equal to the specification limits; in other terms, USL= $\mu + 3\sigma$ and LSL = $\mu - 3\sigma$. This scenario will yield 2,700 defects per million opportunities, or one early or late monthly report in 30.86 years [(1/0.0027)/12].

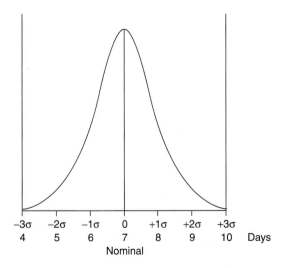

FIGURE 1.7 Three Sigma Process with 0.0 Shift in the Mean

Figure 1.8 shows the same scenario as in Figure 1.7, but the process average shifts by 1.5 standard deviations (the process average is shifted down or up by 1.5 standard deviations [or 1.5 days] from 7.0 days to 5.5 days or 8.5 days) over time. This is not an uncommon phenomenon. The 1.5 standard deviation shift in the mean results in 66,807 defects per million opportunities at the nearest specification limit, or one early or late monthly report in 1.25 years [(1/.066807)/12], if the process average moves from 7.0 days to 5.5 days or from 7.0 days to 8.5 days. In this discussion, only the observations outside the specification nearest the average are considered.

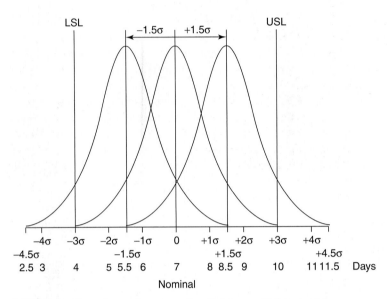

FIGURE 1.8 Three Sigma Process with a 1.5-Sigma Shift in the Mean

Figure 1.9 shows the same scenario as Figure 1.7, but the Voice of the Process takes up only half the distance between the specification limits. The process mean remains the same as in Figure 1.7, but the process standard deviation has been reduced to one half-day through application of process improvement. In this case, the resulting output will exhibit two defects per billion opportunities, or one early or late monthly report in 41,666,667 years [(1/.000000002)/12].

Figure 1.10 shows the same scenario as Figure 1.9, but the process average shifts by 1.5 standard deviations (the process average is shifted down or up by 1.5 standard deviations [or 0.75 days = 1.5 × 0.5 days] from 7.0 days to 6.25 days or 7.75 days) over time. The 1.5 standard deviation shift in the mean results in 3.4 defects per million opportunities at the nearest specification limit, or one early or late monthly report in 24,510 years [(1/.0000034/12]. This is the definition of 6-sigma level of quality.

Another Look at the 1.5-Sigma Shift in the Mean. The engineer responsible for creating the concept of Six Sigma at Motorola was Bill Smith. Bill Smith indicated that product failures in the field were shown to be statistically related to the number of product reworks and defect rates observed in production. Therefore, the more "defect and rework free" a product was during production, the more likely there would be fewer field failures and customer complaints. Additionally, Motorola had a very strong emphasis on total cycle time reduction. A business process that takes more steps to complete its cycle increases the chance for changes/unforeseen events, and the opportunity for defects. Therefore, reducing cycle time is best accomplished by streamlining the process, removing non-value added effort, and as a result, reducing the opportunities for making mistakes (defects). What a concept! Reducing cycle time by simplifying a process will result in fewer defects, lower remediation/warranty/service costs, and ultimately increased customer satisfaction with the results. This last concept is not new to those who are familiar with Toyota production system concepts, Just-In-Time philosophy, or what many call "Lean Thinking." Six Sigma practitioners concern themselves with reducing the defect or failure rate while Lean practitioners concern themselves with streamlining processes and reducing cycle time. Defect reduction and lean thinking are "flip sides" of the "same coin." The integrated strategy of considering both sides at the same time was the basis of the original work in Six Sigma.

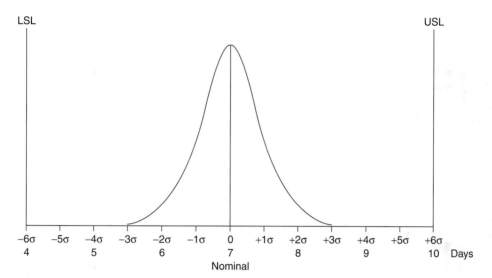

FIGURE 1.9 Six Sigma Process with a 0.0 Shift in the Mean

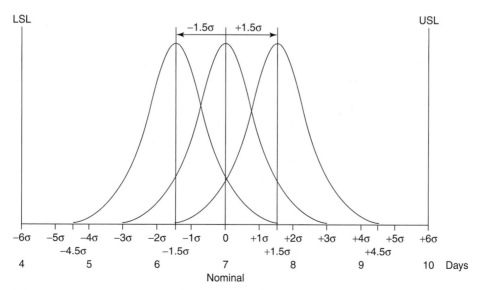

FIGURE 1.10 Six Sigma Process with 1.5-Sigma Shift in the Mean

Some proof of this was gained in the period from 1981 to 1986 when Bob Galvin (CEO of Motorola) set a goal of a tenfold improvement in defect rates over those five years. During those five years, positive results were demonstrated in field failures and warranty costs. However, some of Motorola's key competitors improved at a faster rate. In 1987, Motorola indicated it would increase the rate of improvement to tenfold improvement every two years rather than five years. What was the target? The target was called *Six Sigma* quality (which was defined to be 3.4 defects per million opportunities) by 1992.

Of course, the key question was whether there was a tradeoff between reducing defect rates and implementation cost. Bill Smith and others were not advocating increasing costs by increasing inspection, but rather that engineers design products and production processes so that there would be little chance for mistakes/defects during production and customer usage. The focus was on the upstream X variables that would be indicators of future performance and process problems that were observed. The Y variables were the downstream defect rates, rework rates, and field failures that were observed and measured.

Motorola's strict focus on the rate of improvement challenged engineering, supply management, and production to develop materials, production equipment, and products that were more robust to variation, and as a result, less sensitive to processing variation. Hence, the focus was on understanding the X variables.

What is interesting about the preceding two paragraphs is that often the initial focus of Statistical Process Control (SPC) was limited to monitoring Y variables or average/target values of process variables. Six Sigma did not really change the tools, but instead focused the tools on their usage upstream on X variables; in particular, on understanding the relationship of the variation in the X variables on the variation of the Y variables, and finally, using the tools in such a sequence as to uncover the relationships and be able to improve and control the results of the Y variables.

Studies did show that Bill Smith's insights were valid: defects per million opportunities (DPMO) and defects per unit (DPU) measures calculated in production facilities did predict field performance, customer complaints, and warranty costs. Therefore, DPMO and DPU became metrics of emphasis at Motorola.

Around the same time that these studies were done, employees at Motorola gathered empirical evidence that even when the Y variables were in statistical control, the X variables might not be in statistical control. Additionally, SPC as practiced in many operations was more of a monitoring method on the Y variables with the only "out of control" indicator being a point beyond a control limit. Consequently, run tests[1] were not used as indicators of "out of control." Empirical evidence indicated that a process could shift within the 3-sigma control limits as much as 2 standard deviations and stay there for some run of points before a point outside 3 standard deviations was observed. In fact, if a process with stable variation shifts 1.5 standard deviations, there is an average run of 16 points that would be observed before one point was beyond the 3 standard deviation control limits.

---

1 A *run* is a consecutive series of similar items that are preceded or followed by items of a different type. For example, in tossing a coin eight times, the sequence Head Head Head Head Tail Tail Tail Tail contains two runs—a run of four heads followed by a run of four tails. A *runs test* is a statistical test that determines whether a particular sequence has a random pattern.

In addition to DPMO and DPU measures, Motorola was also concerned about upstream X variables that could be measured (rather than attribute variables). To control measurement data, a focus on means (i.e., targets) and spreads (i.e., standard deviations) was needed. If the Voice of the Process (VoP) is equal to the Voice of the Customer (VoC), the process's mean output plus or minus 3 standard deviations equals the specification limits; about 0.27% of the process output is "defective" given a normal distribution. If SPC were utilized to track that variable, and the mean shifted halfway to the control limits (i.e., this assumes an individual—moving range type control chart that is discussed in References 2 and 3), then there could be an average run of 16 observations before a point beyond a control limit would be noted. Another way of saying this is there could be an increase in dpmo from 2,700 to 66,807 with no points being beyond a control limit. If various run tests were conducted, then the shift in the mean would be detected; but in practice, production personnel rarely shut down a process for failure of a run test, if no points were outside the control limits.

So, why does Six Sigma often reference a 1.5 standard deviation shift in the mean of a process? Studies of various production lines at Motorola Corporation showed that even in a state of control, where the only out-of-control condition to be checked was observations outside the 3 standard deviation control limits, there often would be uncontrolled shifts of between 1 to 2 standard deviations. For example, for some manual assembly processes, the shift averaged between 1.2 and 1.8 standard deviations at the time an out-of-control observation was recorded. Of course, for automated processes, this degree of shift is frequently not allowed.

A statistical purist would argue that the genesis of the sigma metric is flawed because it is based on a shift factor. The engineers viewed the metric as a worst-case DPMO for a process because they assumed that any shift factor significantly larger than 1.5 would be caught by the common usage of statistical process control (a point beyond a 3-sigma control limit). If there is a shift less than 1.5 sigma, that is all to the good since the dpmo is less.

From a practical standpoint, Six Sigma seems to be an effective form of management. Moreover, the argument against the 1.5-sigma shift in the mean seems similar to the claim that a yard is not really three feet. Some say a yard was based on the distance from the tip of the nose to the tip of the middle finger on an outstretched arm for an average male. What is an "average" male? Is that similar to knowing an "average" shift? It turns out that eventually everyone accepted the definition that a yard is equal to three feet, and few remember the original definition. At Motorola, the story is similar in that only a few folks remember the original reason for the definition of the sigma levels, and it is accepted that the DPMO levels can be equated with sigma levels.

Interestingly, many of those who continue to argue about the derivation of sigma levels are those who have learned about Six Sigma in the last seven years. It seems that they are trying to understand the "legend" of Six Sigma rather than seeing the upside and benefit. We can continue to argue about this, but practitioners are continuing to improve their organizations regardless of any technical flaws in the derivations of the methods.

Does Six Sigma Matter? The difference between a 3-sigma process (66,807 defects per million opportunities at the nearest specification limit) and a 6-sigma process (3.4 defects per million opportunities at the nearest specification limit) can be seen in a service with 20 component steps. If each of the 20 component steps has a quality level of 66,807 defects per million opportunities, assuming each step does not allow rework, then the likelihood of a defect at each step is 0.066807 (66,807/1,000,000) or 6.68 percent. By subtraction, the likelihood of a defect-free step is 0.933193 (1.0 – 0.066807) or 93.3 percent. Consequently, the likelihood of delivering a defect-free final service is 25.08 percent. This is computed by multiplying 0.933193 by itself 20 times ($[1.0 – 0.066807]^{20}$ = 0.2508 = 25.08%). However, if each of the 20 component parts has a quality level of 3.4 defects per million opportunities (0.0000034), then the likelihood of delivering a defect-free final service is 99.99932% ($[1.0 – 0.0000034]^{20}$ = 0.99999966^{20} = 0.9999932 = 99.99932%). A 3-sigma process generates 25.08% defect-free services, while a 6-sigma process generates 99.99932% defect-free services. The difference between the 3-sigma process and the 6-sigma process is dramatic enough to certainly believe that 6-sigma level of performance matters, especially with more complex processes with a greater number of steps or components.

The DMAIC Model for Improvement

The relationship between the Voice of the Customer, the Voice of the Process, and the DMAIC model is explained in Figure 1.11. DMAIC is an acronym for Define, Measure, Analyze, Improve, and Control. The left side of Figure 1.11 shows an old flowchart with its 3-sigma output distribution. The right side of Figure 1.11 shows a new flowchart with its 6-sigma output distribution. The method utilized in Six Sigma management to move from the old flowchart to the new flowchart through improvement of a process is called the DMAIC model.

The **Define Phase** of a Six Sigma DMAIC project involves identifying the quality characteristics that are critical to customers (called CTQs) using a SIPOC analysis and a Voice of the Customer analysis, and for preparing a business case for the project with a project objective. SIPOC is an acronym for Supplier, Input, Process, Output, and Customer. The **Measure Phase** involves operationally defining the CTQs, conducting studies of the validity of the measurement system of the CTQ(s), collecting baseline data for the CTQs, and establishing baseline capabilities for CTQs. The **Analyze Phase** involves identifying input and process variables that affect each CTQ (called Xs) using process maps or flowcharts, creating a cause-and-effect matrix to understand the relationships between the Xs and the CTQs, conducting an FMEA analysis (Failure Mode and Effects Analysis) to identify the critical Xs for each CTQ, operationally defining the Xs, collecting baseline data for the Xs, establishing baseline capabilities for the Xs, conducting studies of the validity of the measurement system of the Xs, identifying the major noise variables (MNVs) in the process, and generating hypotheses about which Xs affect which CTQs. The **Improve Phase** involves designing appropriate experiments to understand the relationships between the Xs and MNVs that impact the CTQs, generating the actions needed to implement optimal levels of critical Xs that minimize spread in CTQs, and conducting pilot tests of processes with Xs set at their optimal levels. The **Control Phase** involves avoiding potential problems in Xs with risk management and mistake proofing, standardizing successful process changes, controlling the critical Xs, developing process control plans for the critical Xs, documenting the control plans, and turning over the control plan to the process owner.

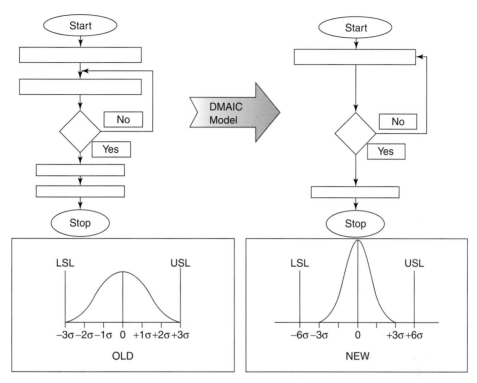

FIGURE 1.11 Relationship Between the VoC, the VoP, and the DMAIC Model

1.5 FUNDAMENTALS OF INVENTING–INNOVATING A PRODUCT, SERVICE, OR PROCESS

Invention

Introduction

I'll bet at some point in your life you had a great idea for a new product or service. All your friends agreed that it was a great idea. Well, that great idea was the beginning of the invention and innovation processes.

Lee Kaplowitz of Los Angeles had a great idea. His was to invent a litmus paper test for the presence of caffeine in decaffeinated coffee. Lee noticed that most decaffeinated coffee drinkers ask of the waitperson, "Is that decaf?" Lee had an inspiration that could lead to an invention and innovation.

Definition

Invention is the process of creating new products, services, or processes that are usable in accomplishing human objectives that were formerly difficult or impossible. The first club used by a caveman to kill animals to feed his family is an example of an invention.

Inventions and History

Some of the most significant inventions were created before recorded history; for example, crude tools, weapons, speech, cultivation of plants, domestication of animals, building techniques, production and control of fire, pottery, political systems, and the wheel. The period of recorded history began with the invention of cuneiform script by the Sumerians of Mesopotamia in about 3000 B.C.

Innovation

Definition

Innovation is the process by which invention is put to use for the betterment of humanity. Thomas Edison was both an inventor (of the electric light bulb) and an innovator because he was critical to the electrification of New York City and the establishment of the General Electric Company.

Reasons for Innovation

Innovations are created for five reasons. They are discussed next.

- **Reason 1:** Build competitive advantage in target markets, and increase market share by offering products, services, or processes that are preferred above those of competitors. Innovation offers an organization the opportunity to take a step ahead of its competitors for the customer's positive attention and resources.

- **Reason 2:** Increase profitability by introducing more profitable lines. Innovation aids organizations in creating products, services, and processes that yield higher profit margins than those of their competitors.

- **Reason 3:** Build a reputation for technological excellence by introducing state-of-the-art products. Innovation provides an opportunity for organizations to enhance their image of being a provider who is on the frontier of their core discipline.

- **Reason 4:** Counteract the effects of downsizing on stakeholders by creating new employment opportunities through upsizing [see Reference 7]. **Downsizing** is a term used to describe an organizational layoff policy whose purpose is to reduce costs. **Upsizing** is a term used to describe an organizational product creation focus whose purpose is to create new employment opportunities to mitigate the uncertainties caused by downsizing. Innovation provides an organization with the opportunity to create products, services, and processes, and hence, upsize.

- **Reason 5:** Creating exportable products for developing countries. Frequently, developing countries experience great economic difficulties due to unstable governments, an uneducated work force, variable and poor quality raw materials, and rampant inflation. In the face of such unfavorable conditions for economic health, developing countries need to export products that enjoy a non-competitive marketplace. They need protection from industrialized countries that do not suffer from the same economic woes. This can be accomplished by creating, producing, and selling innovative products, services, and processes that enjoy the legal protection of patents, copyrights, and trademarks.

Eight Methods for Invention and Innovation

There are eight methods available for creating inventions and innovations.

- **Method 1:** Exploit core technologies; for example, using excellence in electrical engineering and physics to create new electronic products.
- **Method 2:** Capitalize on particularly excellent common operating elements; for example, using unusually excellent repair service or unusually short delivery times.
- **Method 3:** Pray for an inspiration; for example, luckily thinking to put an eraser on the end of a pencil.
- **Method 4:** Conduct scientific research; for example, studying computer science to develop a laptop computer.
- **Method 5:** Use expertise in specialized functional areas; for example, using excellence in quality control to create dependability and reliability (e.g., McDonald's or Marriott).
- **Method 6:** Identify the unmet needs of known customers; for example, conducting market research to provide faster delivery time of office supplies or longer battery life for laptop computers.
- **Method 7:** Study "lead users" to identify the unknown needs of customers. *Lead users* are consumers of a product, service, or process who are months or years ahead of regular users in their use of the item and who will benefit greatly by the innovation. For example, a lead user of a hair dryer may attach a portable battery pack and use it as a body warmer at football games played in cold weather. In this example, studying lead users resulted in the invention of a "personal body warmer."
- **Method 8:** Study the unstated (or unknown) problems of existing users through observational studies. Ideas to surpass customers' unknown needs and wants do not come from direct queries to customers, but rather from the manufacturer's observations of the problems customers encounter while using products and services. An example of a product created using this method is a camera with automatic load [see Reference 8].

In 1974, the camera market was saturated with cameras that satisfied customers' current needs; cameras were reliable, relatively inexpensive to use, and produced good pictures. This created a nightmare for the camera industry. Consequently, Konica decided to ask consumers: "What else would you like in a camera?" Consumers replied that they were satisfied with their cameras. Unfortunately, asking consumers what else they would like in a camera did not yield the information Konica needed to create a breakthrough. In response to this situation, Konica studied negatives at film-processing laboratories and discovered that the first few pictures on many rolls were overexposed, indicating that users had difficulty in loading film into the cameras. This presented an opportunity to innovate camera technology. The customer could not have been expected to think of this innovation. In response to this analysis, Konica developed the automatic-loading camera. This is an excellent example of the eighth method for innovating current products, services, or processes.

Simple Examples of the Invention and Innovation Process

All inventions and innovations do not have to be generated from complex, theoretical, and radical ideas. Sometimes, they come from the simplest of ideas. For example, whoever thought it was possible to create an improved corkscrew? Yet, in the last decade or two, a new corkscrew was invented. This corkscrew has wings or handles that allows the corkscrew to pull the cork out of the bottle.

Another example of a product that you might not think could be improved is the teabag. Surprise! Lipton invented a teabag with two strings that allow the user to squeeze the last drops of tea out of the bag without burning his or her fingers. Ingenious!

Design for Six Sigma (DFSS)

Design for Six Sigma (DFSS) is the method used by a Six Sigma project team to invent and innovate products, services, and processes. DFSS can be used to design entirely new products, services, and processes, or major new features of existing products, services, or processes that are *consistently* reliable and able to be produced, delivered, or carried out and *uniformly* surpass customer requirements. Additionally, DFSS creates designs that are: (1) based on stakeholder needs and wants; (2) resource efficient; (3) minimal in complexity; (4) capable of generating high yields; (5) robust to process variations; and (6) quick to generate a profit.

An organization can reap many benefits from employing the DFSS methodology. The list of benefits includes: launching projects on time and on budget; reaping additional incremental revenues sooner; achieving greater market share; minimizing problems uncovered at launch; improving rolled throughput yield (RTY) significantly; ensuring quality and efficient production; and differentiating products, services, and processes due to a customer focus.

Fundamental Principles of "Design for Six Sigma"

DFSS is a method that embodies several principles. The first principle is for all areas within an organization to simultaneously design the product, service, and/or process to minimize future problems. The second principle is to design the product, service, and/or process to minimize variability in CTQs and maximize customer satisfaction. The third principle is to design a process capable of delivering the quantity and quality of products or services desired by customers in a timely fashion. The fourth principle is to include suppliers early in the design process. These four principles are the bedrock of the DFSS method.

Leverage from Professional Design Methods

Research has shown [see Reference 5 (p. 153)] that 70% of the cost influence (or total cost) of a product or service (including warranty costs and insurance costs) incurred by a producer or supplier is due to poor design. This cost is largely avoidable if producers and suppliers would invest more resources into designing their products and services. In other words, if suppliers and producers would increase their actual cost expenditures in the design function, then their total costs would decrease. Table 1.2 shows the relationships between actual costs and total costs for the different components of products and services.

TABLE 1.2 Cost Comparisons

	Actual Cost	**Cost Influence (Total Cost)**
Overhead	30%	5%
Labor	15%	5%
Material	50%	20%
Design	5%	70%
Total	**100%**	**100%**

The DMADV Model for Invention and Innovation

The DMADV model is the Six Sigma method for innovating existing products, services, or processes; or for creating entirely new products, services, or processes. DMADV is an acronym for Define, Measure, Analyze, Design, and Verify/Validate.

The **Define Phase** of a Six Sigma DMADV project involves developing a business case with a project objective and establishing a schedule and guidelines for the design review process. The **Measure Phase** involves identifying the market segments for potential designs, developing critical parameters for high-level designs, developing targets and tolerances for the critical parameters, preparing design scorecards for the critical parameters, and reviewing intellectual property. The **Analyze Phase** involves generating high-level conceptual designs, evaluating the high-level conceptual designs, and selecting the best design. The **Design Phase** involves developing detailed designs. This requires that team members construct detailed specifications, schematics, and blueprints for processes, services, and products. Additionally, team members develop detailed designs for ancillary processes (i.e., Human Resources and Information Technology, to name a few). Finally, the **Verify/Validate Phase** involves conducting a pilot test of the detailed design; confirming the design outputs will yield product or service specifications;

reviewing designs with respect to all potential users and possible uses, and, if necessary, improving designs; establishing appropriate control and monitoring systems to ensure designs meet and maintain goals throughout production or ongoing service life; and transferring the design to the process owner with a functioning control plan.

1.6 WHAT IS NEW ABOUT SIX SIGMA MANAGEMENT?

Many people think that Six Sigma management is an "old wine in a new bottle." This notion is both false and true. It is false for several reasons. First, it is false because Six Sigma projects are far more structured and formatted than projects in most previous Quality Management processes. Second, it is false because Six Sigma management provides metrics for discussing the quality of processes that can transcend ownership of the processes (i.e., finance, human resources, engineering, and service processes can be compared). It creates "apples to apples" metrics for understanding process improvements. Other Quality Management approaches do not have such metrics. Third, it is false because Six Sigma is very focused on impacting the bottom line or top line of an organization, and it has a specific method for accomplishing this objective. Most other Quality Management approaches do not have such a clear financial focus. The cost of poor quality and other similar concepts have been investigated by the quality profession, but they have not been well utilized outside the quality profession until Six Sigma management. Fourth, it is false because Six Sigma is focused on ongoing rapid improvement of the enterprise. Most other Quality Management processes are focused on incremental continuous improvement, whereas Six Sigma demands breakthrough improvement. Fifth, it is false because past Quality Management efforts were initially spurred on by quality professionals, consultants, or academics, while Six Sigma is being promoted by executive managers such as George Fisher (Motorola) and Jack Welch and Jeffrey Immelt (General Electric). Finally, it is false because Six Sigma is facilitated by an infrastructure of Six Sigma experts overlaying the current organizational structure. Other Quality Management approaches use supervisors, managers, or workers to facilitate teams. Expert facilitation of teams is a big step forward in rapid process improvement that impacts the bottom line of an organization.

On the other hand, it is true that Six Sigma management is an "old wine in a new bottle" because most of the tools, methods, and theories were borrowed from the Quality Management predecessors of "Six Sigma." The authors believe that Six Sigma is more an example of evolutionary management than revolutionary management. The founders of Six Sigma management stood on the shoulders of the giants who preceded them in the quality movement, such as W. Edwards Deming, Joseph Juran, and Kaoru Ishikawa.

1.7 SIX SIGMA IN NON-MANUFACTURING INDUSTRIES

Six Sigma management is equally applicable in manufacturing and service industries, education, and government. Most people in manufacturing organizations are employed in service functions such as Human Resources, Payroll, Food Services, and Risk Management. General Electric has been very successful utilizing Six Sigma theory and methods in its non-manufacturing functions such as GE Capital. Additionally, service organizations such as American Express, HSBC, and the University of Miami have successfully used Six Sigma management.

Granted, service transactions are frequently "one-of-a-kind" transactions that take place on demand (zero inventories) in the presence of the customer (zero time between production and use of service) with subjective service quality characteristics. Still, Six Sigma is appropriate in this type of environment. For example, a subjective quality characteristic in a restaurant is how patrons feel about the taste of cheesecake. One way to measure this is to ask patrons how they feel about the taste of cheesecake on a 1 to 5 scale, where 1 = very dissatisfied, 3 = neutral, and 5 = very satisfied. This type of measurement is subject to inaccuracies caused by factors such as embarrassment at telling the "truth." Another way to determine how a patron feels about the taste of cheesecake is to instruct one busboy to collect the first cheesecake dessert eaten by a patron each of the six evening hours each day, and to weigh the cheesecake left on the plate. All cheesecake slices are 4 ounces, so 4 ounces minus the weight of cheesecake returned is the weight of cheesecake eaten by the patron. With the preceding information, the chef can estimate the average ounces and range (maximum–minimum) of cheesecake eaten by patrons each day. Consequently, the chef can modify the recipe for preparing cheesecake and determine from the statistics if the patrons eat more cheesecake (higher average) with less variation (smaller range) per day. If they do, the chef assumes that the patrons like the taste of the cheesecake better with the new recipe than with the old recipe.

SUMMARY

A **process** is a collection of interacting components that transform inputs into outputs toward a common aim, called a *mission statement*. Two kinds of variation exist in a process: special variation and common variation. Common causes of variation are due to the process itself. Special causes of variation are due to events external to the usual functioning of the process. A feedback loop relates information about outputs from any stage(s) back to other stage(s) so that an analysis of the process can be made.

The goal post view of quality states that as long as a unit of output falls within acceptable limits (called *specification limits*) around a desired value (called the *nominal* or *target value*), the process is deemed conforming, and there is minimum cost. The continuous improvement view of quality states that quality is a predictable degree of uniformity and dependability, at low cost and suited to the market. This is a more realistic view in that losses begin to occur as soon as a quality characteristic of a product or service deviates from the nominal value, even within specification limits. The pursuit of quality requires that organizations globally optimize their process of interdependent stakeholders.

Six Sigma management is the relentless and rigorous pursuit of the reduction of variation in all critical processes to achieve continuous and breakthrough improvements that impact the bottom line and top line of the organization, and to increase customer satisfaction. Another common definition of Six Sigma management is that it is an organizational initiative designed to reduce defects tenfold while simultaneously reducing processing time by 50% every two years.

Finally, the objective of Six Sigma management is to create processes that are twice as good as the customer demands so that if the process mean shifts down, the process will not generate more than 3.4 defects per million opportunities.

The methodology utilized in Six Sigma management to lead to breakthrough improvement in current existing processes is the DMAIC model. DMAIC is an acronym for Define, Measure, Analyze, Improve, and Control. The methodology used to create new products, services, or processes or to substantially innovate broken processes is Design for Six Sigma (DFSS). DFSS uses the DMADV model. DMADV is an acronym for Define, Measure, Analyze, Design, and Verify/Validate. The key ingredient for a successful Six Sigma management process is the commitment of top management.

Six Sigma management is equally applicable in manufacturing and service industries, education, and government.

REFERENCES

1. W. E. Deming, *Quality, Productivity, and Competitive Position* (Cambridge, MA: Massachusetts Institute of Technology Center for Advanced Engineering Study, 1982).

2. H. Gitlow, A. Oppenheim, R. Oppenheim, and D. Levine, *Quality Management*, 3rd ed. (New York: McGraw-Hill-Irwin, 2005).

3. H. Gitlow and D. Levine, *Six Sigma for Green Belts and Champions* (Upper Saddle River, NJ: Financial Times-Prentice Hall, 2005).

4. G. Hahn, N. Dogannaksoy, and R. Hoerl, "The Evolution of Six Sigma," *Quality Engineering*, 12, 2000, pp. 317–326.

5. M. Harry and R. Schroeder, *Six Sigma: The Breakthrough Management Strategy Revolutionizing the World's Top Corporations* (New York, NY: Currency/Doubleday, 2000), p. 153.

6. K. Ishikawa and D. Lu, *What Is Total Quality Control? The Japanese Way* (Englewood Cliffs, NJ: Prentice-Hall, 1985).

7. N. Kano, "Quality in the Year 2000: Downsizing Through Reengineering and Upsizing Through Attractive Quality Creation," *ASQC Annual Quality Conference* (Las Vegas, NV: May 24, 1994).

8. N. Kano and H. Gitlow, "The Management of Innovation: Predicting the Products and Services of Tomorrow," *The Kano Program* (Miami, FL: 1995).

9. R. D. Snee, "The Impact of Six Sigma on Quality," *Quality Engineering*, 12, 2000, pp. ix–xiv.

10. G. Taguchi and Y. Wu, *Introduction to Off-Line Quality Control* (Nagoya, Japan: Central Japan Quality Control Association, 1980).

SIX SIGMA ROLES, RESPONSIBILITIES, AND TERMINOLOGY

SECTIONS

LEARNING OBJECTIVES

After reading this chapter, you will be able to:

* Understand the various roles and responsibilities required by Six Sigma management.
* Understand the technical terminology of Six Sigma management.

INTRODUCTION

Six Sigma management is replete with jargon. You might think that the sheer volume of jargon in Six Sigma management would make it too confusing for some or possibly deter others from using it, but that does not seem to have happened. However, to understand Six Sigma management, you need to know the terminology. The aim of this chapter is to get you familiar and comfortable with the terms specific to Six Sigma management. If you decide to begin a Six Sigma journey, you will need a roadmap for getting started.

This chapter presents such a roadmap. People in all sectors of the economy can use this roadmap; for example, people in manufacturing and services industries, as well as people in government and education. If you decide to take this journey, you begin with learning the language of the land.

2.1 ROLES AND RESPONSIBILITIES IN SIX SIGMA MANAGEMENT

There are several positions in an organization that are critical to the Six Sigma management process. These positions are: senior executive (CEO or President), executive committee, champion, process owner, master black belt, black belt, and green belt. The roles and responsibilities of each position are described as follows.

Senior Executive

The **senior executive** provides the impetus, direction, and alignment necessary for Six Sigma's ultimate success.

The senior executive should:

- Lead the executive committee in linking strategies to Six Sigma projects using a dashboard (see Chapter 3, "Macro Model of Six Sigma Management (Dashboards)").
- Participate on appropriate Six Sigma project teams.
- Maintain an overview of the system to avoid sub-optimization.
- Maintain a long-term view.
- Act as a liaison to Wall Street, explaining the long-term advantages of Six Sigma management.
- Constantly and consistently, publicly and privately, champion Six Sigma management.
- Conduct project reviews.

The most successful, highly-publicized Six Sigma efforts have had one thing in common: unwavering, clear, and committed leadership from top management. There is no doubt in anyone's mind that Six Sigma is "the way we do business." Although it may be possible to initiate Six Sigma concepts and processes at lower levels, dramatic success will not be possible until the senior executive becomes engaged and takes a leadership role.

Executive Committee

The members of the **executive committee** are the top management of an organization. They should operate at the same level of commitment for Six Sigma management as the senior executive.

The members of the executive committee should:

- Deploy Six Sigma throughout the organization using dashboards (see Chapter 3).
- Prioritize and manage the Six Sigma project portfolio.
- Assign champions, black belts, and green belts to Six Sigma projects.
- Conduct reviews of Six Sigma projects with the senior executive, and within their own areas of control.
- Improve the Six Sigma process.
- Identify strategic improvement initiatives.
- Remove barriers to Six Sigma management and projects.
- Provide resources for the Six Sigma management process and projects.

Champion

Champions take a very active sponsorship and leadership role in conducting and implementing Six Sigma projects. They work closely with the executive committee, the black belt assigned to their project, and the master black belt overseeing their project. A champion should be a member of the executive committee, or at least a trusted direct report of a member of the executive committee. He or she should have enough influence to remove obstacles or provide resources without having to go higher in the organization.

Champions have the following responsibilities:

- Identify their project's impact on the organizational dashboard (see Chapter 3).
- Develop and negotiate project objectives and charters with the executive committee.
- Select a black belt (or a green belt for a simple project) to lead the project team.
- Remove any political barriers or resource constraints to their Six Sigma project (run interference).
- Provide a link between their project team(s) and the executive committee.
- Help team members manage their resources and stay within the budget.
- Review the progress of their project with respect to the project's timetable.
- Keep the team focused on the project by providing direction and guidance.
- Ensure that Six Sigma methods and tools are being used in the project.

Process Owner

A **process owner** is the manager of a process. He or she has responsibility for the process and has the authority to change the process on her or his signature. The process owner should be identified and involved immediately in all Six Sigma projects relating to his or her own area.

In some organizations, it is difficult to determine an appropriate process owner. For example, in many banks, the "obtaining new customers process" is the responsibility of both the marketing department (e.g., publicity) and branch management (e.g., registering and servicing new customers). It is possible that the CEO of the bank is the only common process owner under which there is ownership for both marketing and branch operations. In this case, it may be more convenient to have a virtual process owner who will take ownership and have decision-making authority for projects dedicated to obtaining new customers. In some cases, the process owner will be a team of leaders who jointly have responsibility for the process. If the team effort is used, it requires that the joint process owners establish a good working relationship with frequent communication and cooperation regarding projects.

A process owner has the following responsibilities:

- Be accountable for the monitoring, managing, and output of his or her process.
- Empower the employees who work in the process to follow and improve the best practice method for the process.
- Focus the project team on the project objective.
- Assist the project team in remaining on schedule.
- Allocate the resources necessary for the project (people, space, etc.).
- Accept, manage, and sustain the improved process after completion of the Six Sigma project.
- Ensure that process objectives and indicators are linked to the organization's mission through the dashboard (see Chapter 3).
- Understand how the process works, the capability of the process, and the relationship of the process to other processes in the organization.

Master Black Belt

A **master black belt** takes on a leadership role as keeper of the Six Sigma process and advisor to senior executives or business unit managers. He or she must leverage his or her skills with projects that are led by black belts and green belts. Frequently, master black belts report directly to senior executives or business unit managers. A master black belt has successfully led many teams through complex Six Sigma projects. He or she is a proven change agent, leader, facilitator, and technical expert in Six Sigma management. Becoming a master black belt is a career path. It is always best for an organization to grow its own master black belts. Unfortunately, sometimes it is impossible for an organization to grow its own master black belts due to the lead time required to become a master black belt. It takes years of study, practice, tutelage under a master, as well as project work. Ideally, master black belts are selected from the black belts within an organization. However, circumstances sometimes require hiring master black belts external to the organization.

Master black belts have the following responsibilities:

- Help identify, prioritize, and coordinate key project areas in keeping with strategic initiatives using a dashboard (see Chapter 3).
- Teach black belts and green belts Six Sigma theory, tools, and methods.
- Mentor black belts and green belts.
- Continually improve and innovate the organization's Six Sigma process.
- Be able to apply Six Sigma across both operations and transaction-based processes such as sales, human resources, information technology, facility management, call centers, finance, etc.

Senior master black belts have ten years of ongoing leadership experience and have worked extensively with mentoring the organizational leaders on Six Sigma management.

Black Belt

A **black belt** is a full-time change agent and improvement leader who may not be an expert in the process under study [see Reference 3].

The ideal candidate for a black belt is an individual who possesses the following characteristics:

- Has technical and managerial process improvement/innovation skills, including mastery of the DMAIC and DMADV models (see pages 22 and 27).
- Has a passion for statistics and systems theory.
- Understands the psychology of individuals and teams.
- Understands the PDSA cycle (see page 43) and learning.
- Has excellent communication and writing skills.
- Works well in a team format.
- Can manage meetings.
- Has a pleasant personality and is fun to work with.
- Communicates in the language of the client and does not use technical jargon.
- Is not intimidated by upper management—process owner or champion.
- Has a customer focus.

The responsibilities of a black belt include:

- Help to prepare/refine a project charter.
- Communicate with the champion about progress of the project.
- Lead the project team.
- Schedule meetings and coordinate logistics.
- Help team members design experiments and analyze the data required for the project.
- Provide training in tools and team functions.
- Help team members prepare for reviews by the champion and executive committee.
- Recommend additional Six Sigma projects.
- Lead and coach green belts leading projects limited in scope.

A black belt is a full-time quality professional who is mentored by a master black belt, but who may report to a manager for his or her tour of duty as a black belt.

An appropriate time frame for a tour of duty as a full-time black belt is two years. Black belt skills and project work are critical to the development of leaders and high potential people within the organization.

Green Belt

A **green belt** is an individual who works on projects part-time (25%), either as a team member for complex projects or as a project leader for simpler projects. Green belts are the "work horses" of Six Sigma projects. Most managers in a mature Six Sigma organization are green belts. Green belt certification is a critical prerequisite for advancement into upper management in a Six Sigma organization. Managers act as green belts for their entire careers, as their style of management.

Green belts leading simpler projects have the following responsibilities:

- Refine a project charter for the project.
- Review the project charter with the project's champion.
- Select the team members for the project.
- Communicate with the champion, master black belt/black belt, and process owner throughout all stages of the project.
- Facilitate the team through all phases of the project.
- Schedule meetings and coordinate logistics.
- Analyze data through all phases of the project.
- Train team members in the basic tools and methods through all phases of the project.

In complicated Six Sigma projects, green belts work closely with the team leader (black belt) to keep the team functioning and progressing through the various stages of the Six Sigma project.

Roles Are Not Mutually Exclusive

An individual can satisfy more than one role in Six Sigma management. For example, senior executives, members of the executive committee, and champions can also be green belts. In fact, because senior leaders typically control large budgets, they can typically lead or participate in projects as green belts having great financial impact on the organization. Furthermore, in some organizations, black belt training and project completion is seen as a good way to enhance leadership skills or "groom" future leaders.

Roles Are Not Necessarily Related to Position in the Organization

Six Sigma roles are not necessarily driven by position within an organization. For example, senior executives who are green belts might have master black belts and black belts reporting to them. Roles are more related to the level of training and expertise than to position within the organization.

Green Belt Versus Black Belt Projects

Black belt and green belt Six Sigma projects differ on the basis of five criteria. Green belt projects tend to be less involved (e.g., they have one CTQ (see page 22) and few Xs), do not deal with political issues, do not require many organizational resources, do not require significant capital investment to realize the gains identified during the project, and utilize only basic statistical methods. On the other hand, black belt projects tend to deal with more complex situations that may involve two or more CTQs and many Xs, may involve substantial political issues, may be cross-functional in nature, require substantial organizational resources, may need substantial capital investment to realize the gains made during the project, and utilize sophisticated statistical methods. One exception occurs in organizations where executives act as green belt team leaders because they control large budgets and are responsible for major systems/issues. In these cases, the executives get assistance from black belts or master black belts.

Another exception is where a process owner with great area expertise takes on the mantle of team leader. This occurs if area expertise is more critical than Six Sigma expertise in the conduct of a project. In this situation, the black belt takes more of a non-voting, facilitator role, while the process owner/team leader is a voting member and more involved in the content. Black belts take more of a formal leadership role early in the project, when the team is forming and storming and needs a lot of direction and support. As the team becomes more self-directed and comfortable with the tools, and begins to implement things, the process knowledge of the team leader becomes more important to success, and the black belt can become more of an observer, coach, and mentor to the team.

Supervision Ratios Between the Different Levels of Six Sigma Certification

Table 2.1 shows the percentage of an organization needing each level of Six Sigma belt certification. Additionally, the table shows the supervision ratios between the different levels of belts. For a small organization of 100 people, an organization needs 1 master black belt, between 6 and 12 black belts, and between 25 and 50 green belts. For a large organization of 100,000 people, an organization needs 1,000 master black belts, between 6,000 and 12,000 black belts, and between 25,000 and 50,000 green belts. These supervision ratios demonstrate that Six Sigma must be a strategic initiative in an organization and must represent a critical key to advancement up the organization hierarchy.

TABLE 2.1   Supervision Ratios for Six Sigma Belts

Certification Level	Percentage of Organization Needing Certification Level*	Supervision Ratios
Master Black Belt (MBB)	1% of organization	A MBB can mentor about 10 BB at a time, but if the MBB is skilled and several skilled BBs are available, then there can be one senior MBB managing many BBs.
Black Belt (BB)	6% to 12% of organization	A BB can mentor about 4 to 8 GBs at a time.
Green Belt (GB)	25% to 50% of organization (includes executives as GBs)	

*Approximations depend on level of general knowledge in the organization and expertise of those individuals who are certified.

2.2 TECHNICAL TERMINOLOGY OF SIX SIGMA MANAGEMENT

Six Sigma practitioners use a lot of jargon. You must know the language of Six Sigma management in order to use it.

CTQ—CTQ is an acronym for critical-to-quality characteristic for a product, service, or process. A CTQ is a measure or proxy (i.e., related measure predictive of what is desired by customers) of what is important to a customer. Examples of CTQs are the mean and range of the waiting times in a physician's office for four patients selected each day at 10:00 A.M., noon, 2:00 P.M., and 4:00 P.M., the percentage of errors in ATM transactions for a bank's customers per month, and the number of car accidents per month on a particular stretch of highway. Six Sigma projects are designed to improve CTQs.

Unit—A unit is the item (e.g., product or component, service or service step, or time period) to be studied with a Six Sigma project.

Defective—A nonconforming unit is a defective unit.

Defect—A defect is a nonconformance on one of many possible quality characteristics of a unit that causes customer dissatisfaction. For a given unit, you define each quality characteristic by translating customer desires into specifications. Each defect for a unit needs to be operationally defined. For example, if a word in a document is misspelled, that word may be considered a defect. A defect does not necessarily make a unit defective. For example, a water bottle can have a scratch on the outside (defect) and still be used to hold water (not defective). However, if a customer wants a scratch-free water bottle, that scratched bottle could be considered defective.

Defect Opportunity—A defect opportunity is each circumstance in which a CTQ can fail to be met. There may be many opportunities for defects within a defined unit. For example, suppose a service has four component parts. If each component part contains three opportunities for a defect, then the service has 12 defect opportunities in which a CTQ can fail to be met. The number of defect opportunities generally is related to the complexity of the unit under study. Complex units usually experience greater opportunities for the occurrence of defects than simple units.

Defects per Unit (DPU)—Defects per unit refers to the average of all the defects for a given number of units; that is, the total number of defects for *n* units divided by *n*, the number of units. If you are producing a 50-page document, the unit is a page. If there are 150 spelling errors, DPU is 150/50 or 3.0. If you are producing ten 50-page documents, the unit is a 50-page document. If there are 75 spelling errors in all ten documents, DPU is 75/10 or 7.5.

Defects per Opportunity (DPO)—Defects per opportunity refers to the number of defects divided by the number of defect opportunities. In the previous service example, there are 12 defect opportunities per unit (service). If there are 20 errors in 100 services, DPU is 0.20. However, if there are 12 opportunities per unit, there are 1,200 opportunities in 100 units. In this case, DPO is 0.0167 (20/1,200). You can also calculate DPO by dividing DPU by the total number of opportunities.

Defects per Million Opportunities (DPMO)—DPMO equals DPO multiplied by one million. Hence, for the previous example, the DPMO is (0.0167) x (1,000,000), or 16,700 defects per million opportunities.

Yield—Yield is the proportion of units within specification divided by the total number of units. If 25 units are served to customers and 20 are good, then the yield is 0.80 (20/25).

Rolled Throughput Yield (RTY)—Rolled Throughput Yield is the product of the yields from each step in a process. RTY is the probability of a unit passing through each of *k* independent steps of a process the first time without incurring one or more defects at each of the *k* steps. RTY = $Y_1 * Y_2 * \cdots * Y_k$, where *k* = number of steps in a process or the number of component parts or steps in a product or service. Each yield *Y* for each step or component must be calculated to compute the RTY. For those steps in which the number of opportunities is equal to the number of units, $Y = 1 - \text{DPU}$. For those steps in which a large number of defects are possible but only a few are observed (e.g., number of typographical, grammatical, or spelling errors in a document), the yield Y (the probability of no defects in a unit) is found by $Y = e^{-\text{DPU}}$, where DPU is the defects per unit for the step. Table 2.2 shows the values of $Y = e^{-\text{DPU}}$ for DPU values from 1 through 10.

TABLE 2.2   Values of $Y = e^{-\text{DPU}}$

Row	DPU	$Y = e^{-\text{DPU}}$
1	1	0.367879
2	2	0.135335
3	3	0.049787
4	4	0.018316
5	5	0.006738
6	6	0.002479
7	7	0.000912
8	8	0.000335
9	9	0.000123
10	10	0.000045

For example, if a process has three independent steps and the yield from the first step (Y_1) is 99.7%, the yield from the second step (Y_2) is 99.5%, and the yield from the third step (Y_3) is 89.7%, the RTY is 88.98% ($0.997 \times 0.995 \times 0.897$).

Process Sigma

Process sigma is a measure of the process performance determined by using DPMO and a stable normal distribution [see Reference 2]. Process sigma is a metric that allows for process performance comparisons across processes, departments, divisions, companies, and countries, assuming all comparisons are made from stable processes whose output follows the normal distribution. In Six Sigma terminology, the sigma value of a process is a metric used to indicate the number of DPMOs, or how the process is performing with respect to customer needs and wants.

The left side of Table 2.3 is used to translate DPMO statistics for a stable, normally distributed process with no shift in its mean (0.0 shift in mean) over time into a process sigma metric, *assuming that defects occur at only one of the specifications* if there are lower and upper specifications. For example, in a short period of time, processes that are monitored closely should exhibit a high level of stability (i.e., consistency). For that short period of time, there should be greater likelihood of meeting customer requirements as indicated by the level of performance on the left side of the table. You use the right side of Table 2.3 to translate DPMO statistics for a stable, normally distributed process that has experienced a 1.5-sigma shift in its mean over time into a process sigma metric. You may wonder why a 1.5-sigma shift is allowed as this seems

TABLE 2.3   Process Sigma—DPMO Table

Assume 0.0-sigma shift in mean				Assume 1.5-sigma shift in mean			
Process σ Level	**Process DPMO**	**Process σ Level**	**Process DPMO**	**Process σ Level**	**Process DPMO**	**Process σ Level**	**Process DPMO**
0.10	460,172.1	3.30	483.5	0.10	919,243.3	3.10	54,799.3
0.20	420,740.3	3.40	337.0	0.20	903,199.5	3.20	44,565.4
0.30	382,088.6	3.50	232.7	0.30	884,930.3	3.30	35,930.3
0.40	344,578.3	3.60	159.1	0.40	864,333.9	3.40	28,716.5
0.50	308,537.5	3.70	107.8	0.50	841,344.7	3.50	22,750.1
0.60	274,253.1	3.80	72.4	0.60	815,939.9	3.60	17,864.4
0.70	241,963.6	3.90	48.1	0.70	788,144.7	3.70	13,903.4
0.80	211,855.3	4.00	31.7	0.80	758,036.4	3.80	10,724.1
0.90	184,060.1	4.10	20.7	0.90	725,746.9	3.90	8,197.5
1.00	158,655.3	4.20	13.4	1.00	691,462.5	4.00	6,209.7
1.10	135,666.1	4.30	8.5	1.10	655,421.7	4.10	4,661.2
1.20	115,069.7	4.40	5.4	1.20	617,911.4	4.20	3,467.0
1.30	96,800.5	4.50	3.4	1.30	579,259.7	4.30	2,555.2
1.40	80,756.7	4.60	2.1	1.40	539,827.9	4.40	1,865.9
1.50	66,807.2	4.70	1.3	1.50	500,000.0	4.50	1,350.0
1.60	54,799.3			1.60	460,172.1	4.60	967.7
1.70	44,565.4	**Process σ Level**	**Defects per Billion Opportunities**	1.70	420,740.3	4.70	687.2
1.80	35,930.3			1.80	382,088.6	4.80	483.5
1.90	28,716.5			1.90	344,578.3	4.90	337.0
2.00	22,750.1	4.80	794.4	2.00	308,537.5	5.00	232.7
2.10	17,864.4	4.90	479.9	2.10	274,253.1	5.10	159.1
2.20	13,903.4	5.00	287.1	2.20	241,963.6	5.20	107.8
2.30	10,724.1	5.10	170.1	2.30	211,855.3	5.30	72.4
2.40	8,197.5	5.20	99.8	2.40	184,060.1	5.40	48.1
2.50	6,209.7	5.30	58.0	2.50	158,655.3	5.50	31.7
2.60	4,661.2	5.40	33.4	2.60	135,666.1	5.60	20.7
2.70	3,467.0	5.50	19.0	2.70	115,069.7	5.70	13.4
2.80	2,555.2	5.60	10.7	2.80	96,800.5	5.80	8.5
2.90	1,865.9	5.70	6.0	2.90	80,756.7	5.90	5.4
3.00	1,350.0	5.80	3.3	3.00	66,807.2	6.00	3.4
3.10	967.7	5.90	1.8				
3.20	687.2	6.00	1.0				

contradictory to having a stable process. In practice, processes tend to shift over time. For example, the width of a typical automobile is about 6 feet, so that the distance from the center of the car to the sides of a car is plus or minus 3 feet. If a typical car is parked on a highway, it would take up only 6 feet of the lane. However, assuming you are not impaired by any chemical substance as you drive down the highway at posted highway speeds, your car will tend to drift slightly between the lane markers. There is evidence that drivers often vary 1 to 2 feet from the absolute center of the lane as they use the lane markers to guide their path. Therefore, over time, cars appear to take up from 8 to 10 feet of the highway lane (i.e., 6 feet for the car and a drift of 1 to 2 feet on both sides). In a similar fashion, as we "drive" our organizational processes, we tend to drift within our own "lane" markers or guidelines. If these guidelines represent the requirements of customers that must not be exceeded, we will tend to get closer to breaching these guidelines as we drift. If you assume a 1.5-sigma shift (i.e., the average of a 1 to 2 feet drift for the cars) in processes, the performance in terms of meeting the process guidelines will degrade, as represented on the right side of Table 2.3. The process level represents the distance to the guidelines (e.g., 3 would represent that the lane markers were 3 feet from the center of the automobile, meaning the car would fit snugly within the lane while it is parked). As the process variation increases over time due to drift, it will result in a process that is less likely to meet its guidelines or requirements.

For example, suppose a process has three independent steps. Each step has one defect opportunity and a 95% yield. The RTY for the process is 85.74% (0.95 x 0.95 x 0.95) and the DPO is 0.1426 (DPO = 1.0 – RTY = 1.0 – 0.8574), assuming each step has only one opportunity so that DPU and DPO are the same. The DPMO for the process is 142,600 (DPMO = DPO x 1,000,000). You find the process sigma metric, assuming a 1.5-sigma shift in the process mean over time, by looking down the DPMO column to the two numbers bracketing 142,600. The actual process sigma metric lies between the corresponding two bracketing process sigma metrics. In this example, 142,600 is bracketed by a DPMO of 135,666 and a DPMO of 158,655. The corresponding bracketing process sigma metrics are 2.60 and 2.50. Hence, the actual process sigma metric is approximately 2.55.

If green belts and black belts collect process data for a long enough period of time to provide a realistic view of process performance, they calculate the DPMO for the process and use the right side of Table 2.3 to determine the process sigma. If they collect data for a short period of time, the process may appear to be more stable or consistent than it actually is, and they can calculate the DPMO using the left side of Table 2.3 to determine the process sigma. As a result, in practice, you use the left side of the table when process performance data is collected over a short period of time, and you use the right side when process performance data is collected over a long period of time.

You need to realize that RTY represents the proportion of units that pass through the entire process without a single occurrence of any defect on any step. RTY is dependent on the number of steps and the yield at each step. Furthermore, RTY can be no greater than the lowest yield of any step in the process. Because RTY can decrease as the number of steps in the process increases, or as any yields for the steps in the process decrease, some organizations do not report RTY and the associated sigma levels to those outside the organization. In fact, many organizations only report the "average" sigma level for any step in the process or the sigma level for the last step in the process when they "tell the world" their sigma level. So, a 5-sigma company may mean that its "average" process step has a 5-sigma level of performance or its final step outputs are at a 5-sigma level of performance. If it reports the sigma level that is equivalent to the RTY, then it will likely be much lower if there are a large number of steps in the process for which it is reporting performance. On the other hand, internal reporting will have more impact if the RTY and associated sigma level is reported. This is due to the fact that the RTY and associated sigma level provide a means to track Six Sigma projects that seek to increase the yield of process steps with the lowest yield and to reduce the number of steps (especially by eliminating wasteful steps and replacing low-yielding steps with improved or redesigned new steps). RTY reporting drives reduction in number of process steps, often reducing process cycle time and eliminating, improving, or redesigning poorly performing steps.

SDSA Model

The **SDSA (Standardize–Do–Study–Act) model** is a method or roadmap that helps employees standardize a process [see Reference 1]. It includes four steps: (1) **Standardize:** Employees study the process and develop "best practice" methods with key indicators of process performance; (2) **Do:** Employees conduct planned experiments using the best practice methods on a trial basis; (3) **Study:** Employees collect and analyze data on the key indicators to determine the effectiveness of the best practice methods; and (4) **Act:** Managers establish standardized best practice methods and formalize them through training.

PDSA Model

The **PDSA (Plan–Do–Study–Act) model** is a method or roadmap that helps employees improve and innovate a process by reducing the difference between customers' needs and process performance [see Reference 1]. Initially, a revised flowchart is developed to improve or innovate a standardized best practice method (Plan). The revised flowchart is tested using an experiment on a small scale or trial basis (Do). The effects of the revised flowchart are studied using measurements from key indicators (Study). Finally, if the Study phase generated positive results, the revised flowchart is inserted into training manuals and all relevant personnel are trained in the revised method (Act). If the Study phase generated negative results, the revised flowchart is abandoned and a new Plan is developed by employees. The PDSA cycle continues forever in an uphill progression of never-ending improvement.

DMAIC Model

The DMAIC model has five phases: Define, Measure, Analyze, Improve, and Control. The relationship between the Voice of the Customer (nominal value and specification limits), the Voice of the Process (distribution of output), and the DMAIC model is illustrated in Figure 2.1. The left side of Figure 2.1 shows the flowchart for the existing system with its 3-sigma output distribution, assuming no shift in the system mean. The right side of Figure 2.1 shows the flowchart for a revised system with its 6-sigma output distribution, assuming no shift in the system mean. The method utilized in Six Sigma management to move from the existing system to the revised system is called the DMAIC model. DMAIC is an acronym for Define-Measure-Analyze-Improve-Control.

To illustrate the DMAIC model, return to the accounting report example discussed on page 12.

Define Phase. The **Define Phase** involves preparing a business charter (rationale for the project); understanding the relationships between Suppliers–Inputs–Processes–Outputs–Customers (called SIPOC analysis); analyzing Voice of the Customer data to identify the critical-to-quality (CTQ) characteristics important to customers; and developing a project objective. A Six Sigma team was assigned by top management to review the production of a monthly report by the accounting department as a potential Six Sigma project. This involved identifying the need for the project (relative to other potential projects), the costs and benefits of the project, the resources required for the project, and the time frame of the project. As a consequence of doing a SIPOC analysis and a Voice of the Customer analysis, the team determined that management wants a monthly accounting report completed in 7 days (the nominal time to complete is 7 days). The team also determined that the report should never be completed in less than 4 days (the relevant information is not available before then) and never more than 10 days (the report is required for decision-making purposes).

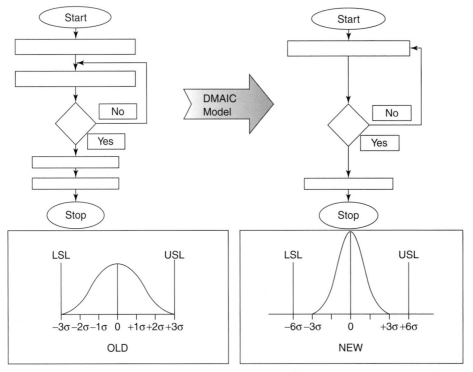

FIGURE 2.1 Relationship Between the Voice of the Customer, the Voice of the Process, and the DMAIC Model

Team members identified the project objective as follows:

Reduce (direction) the variability in the cycle time (measure) to produce an error-free accounting report (process) from the current level of 7 days plus or minus 3 days to 7 days plus or minus 1½ days (target) by January 10, 2006 (deadline).

Measure Phase. The **Measure Phase** involves developing operational definitions for each CTQ variable(s); determining the validity of the measurement system for the CTQs (see Chapter 5, "Measure Phase"); and establishing baseline capabilities for each CTQ.

First, the team members created an operational definition of variability in cycle time such that all relevant personnel agreed upon the definition. For example, they clearly identified the start and stop points needed to compute cycle time. Second, they performed a measurement systems analysis to determine the ability of the measurement system to properly measure "variability in cycle time." Finally, the members of the team collected baseline data about variability in cycle time and statistically analyzed it to get a clear picture of the current situation.

Analyze Phase. The **Analyze Phase** involves identifying the upstream variables (*X*s) for each CTQ using a flowchart. Upstream variables are the factors that affect the performance of a CTQ. This is restated quantitatively as:

$$CTQ = f(X_1, X_2, X_3, \ldots, X_k),$$

where

CTQ = the critical-to-quality characteristic important to customers identified in the define phase and clarified in the measure phase of the DMAIC model.

$X_i = i^{th}$ variable that is hypothesized to have an impact on the performance of the CTQ.

Additionally, the Analyze Phase involves operationally defining each *X*, collecting baseline data for each *X*, performing studies to determine the ability of the measurement system for each *X* to adequately reflect the behavior of each *X*, establishing baseline capabilities for each *X*, and understanding the effect of each *X* on each CTQ.

Referring to the example of the accounting report, team members identify all input and system variables, called the *X*s, that impact the CTQ ("variability in cycle time") using a flowchart (see Section 6.8).

These *X*s are:

X_1 = number of days from request to receipt for line item *A* data.

X_2 = number of days from request to receipt for line item *B* data.

X_3 = number of days from request to receipt for line item *C* data.

X_4 = number of days from request to receipt for line item *D* data.

X_5 = number of days to reformat the line item data to prepare the report.

X_6 = number of days to prepare the report.

X_7 = accounting clerk preparing the report (Mary or Joe).

X_8 = number of errors in the report.

X_9 = number of days to correct the report.

X_{10} = accounting supervisor performing the corrections to the report (Harry or Sue).

X_{11} = number of signatures required before the report is released.

For example, the number of signatures required before releasing the report (X_{11}) may affect the average time to process the report; or the accounting clerk preparing the report (X_7) may dramatically affect the variability in cycle time to produce the report. Next, team members operationally define the Xs and perform measurement systems studies to determine the validity of the measurement systems. Fourth, team members collect baseline data to determine the current status of each X using control charts [see Reference 2]. Finally, team members study the data and develop hypotheses about the relationships between the Xs and each CTQ. In this case, histograms of the CTQ for each level of each X indicated that X_1 (number of days from request to receipt for line item A data), X_3 (number of days from request to receipt for line item C data), X_7 [accounting clerk preparing the report (Mary or Joe)], and X_{10} accounting supervisor performing the corrections to the report (Harry or Sue) may be important to the reduction of variability in the cycle time (CTQ). The other Xs did not substantially affect the CTQ.

Many practitioners include the identification and operational definition of the Xs in the Measure Phase. This is common for well-monitored systems where the Xs have been studied using a dashboard and/or in previous DMAIC projects.

Improve Phase. The **Improve Phase** involves designing experiments to understand the relationships between the CTQs and the Xs; determining the levels of the critical Xs that optimize the CTQs; developing action plans to formalize the level of the Xs that optimize the CTQs; and conducting a pilot test of the revised process using the levels of the critical Xs that will hypothetically optimize the CTQs.

Team members conducted an experiment to identify the levels of the critical Xs identified in the Analyze Phase to minimize variation in the time to produce the accounting report. The experiment revealed that team members had to work with the personnel responsible for line items A and C to decrease the average and standard deviation of days to forward the line items to the department preparing the report. Further, the experiment revealed that there is an interaction between the clerk preparing the report and the supervisor correcting the report. The analysis showed that if Mary prepared the report, it was best for Sue to correct the report; if Joe prepared the report, it was best for Harry to correct the report. A pilot run of the revised system to produce the accounting report showed a predictable normal distribution of days to produce the report with a mean of 7 days and a standard deviation of 0.5 day.

Control Phase. The **Control Phase** involves avoiding potential problems with the Xs with risk management and mistake proofing; standardizing successful process revisions; controlling the critical Xs; documenting each control plan; and turning the revised process over to the process owner. Risk management involves developing a plan to minimize the risk of increasing variation in cycle time. Mistake proofing involves installing processes/methods that have a low probability of producing errors in the production of the accounting report, from incoming data to submitted report.

Team members identify potential problems and methods to avoid them with X_1, X_3, X_7, and X_{10} using risk management and mistake-proofing techniques. For example, they establish procedures to ensure the pairing of clerks and supervisors, as well as data collection methods to identify and resolve future problems in the reporting process. The new process is standardized and fully documented in training manuals. At this point, team members turn over the revised process to the process owner and celebrate their success. The process owner continues to work toward improvement of the revised process beyond its current improved level of output, in which the distribution of days to produce the report follows a predictable normal distribution, with an average of 7 days with a standard deviation of 0.5 day. This translates to a report being early or late about once every 24,500 years! The team chose not to wait around for an error to occur.

DMADV Model

The **DMADV (Define, Measure, Analyze, Design, Verify) model** is used to create major new features of existing products, services, or processes, or to create entirely new products, services, or processes.

The phases of the DMADV model are as follows:

- *Define Phase.* The **Define Phase** of the DMADV model has five components: establishing the background and business case; assessing the risks and benefits of the project; forming the team; developing the project plan; and writing the project objective.

- *Measure Phase.* The **Measure Phase** of a Design for Six Sigma project has three steps: segmenting the market; designing and conducting a Kano survey; and using the Kano survey results as Quality Function Deployment inputs to find critical-to-quality characteristics (CTQs).

- *Analyze Phase.* The **Analyze Phase** contains four steps: design generation; design analysis; risk analysis; and model design. The aim of these four steps in the Analyze Phase is to develop high-level designs. In addition to this, the designs will be evaluated per risk assessments. Finally, nominal values are established for all CTQs in the Analyze Phase for the "best" design.

- *Design Phase.* The **Design Phase** of a Design for Six Sigma project has three steps: constructing a detailed design of the "best" design from the Analyze Phase; developing and estimating the capabilities of the critical-to-process elements (CTPs) in the design; and preparing a verification plan to enable a smooth transition among all affected departments.

- *Verify/Validate Phase.* The intent of the **Verify/Validate Phase** is to facilitate buy-in of process owners, to design a control and transition plan, and to conclude the DMADV project.

SUMMARY

The senior executive provides the impetus, direction, and alignment necessary for Six Sigma's ultimate success. The members of the executive committee are the top management of an organization. They actively promote Six Sigma management throughout the organization. Champions take a very active sponsorship role with Six Sigma projects. A champion should be a member of the executive committee, or at least a trusted direct report of a member of the executive committee. A black belt is a full-time change agent and improvement leader who may not be an expert in the process under study. A green belt is a part-time (25%) team member for complex projects and acts as a team leader for simple projects. Green belts are the "work horses" of Six Sigma projects. Most managers should seek to attain green belt-level skills. A master black belt is a partner with the executive team in the success of the Six Sigma process. A master black belt is a staff job whose purpose is to teach, promote, and advise the members of an organization on Six Sigma management. A process owner is the manager of a process.

The following technical terminology is important to Six Sigma management. A unit is the item (e.g., product or component, service or service step, or time period) to be studied with a Six Sigma project. A nonconforming unit is a defective unit. A defect is a non-conformance on one of many possible quality characteristics of a unit that causes customer dissatisfaction. A defect opportunity is each circumstance in which a CTQ can fail to be met. There may be many opportunities for defects within a defined unit. Defects per Unit (DPU) refers to the total number of defects for n units divided by n, the number of units. Defects per Opportunity (DPO) refers to the number of defects divided by the number of defect opportunities. Defects per Million Opportunities (DPMO) equals the DPO multiplied by one million. Yield is the proportion of units within specification divided by the total number of units. Rolled Throughput Yield (RTY) is the product of the yields from each step in a process. It is the probability of a unit passing through all steps of a process correctly the first time with no rework and incurring no defects. Process sigma is a metric that allows for process performance comparisons across processes. The SDSA cycle is an acronym for Standardize–Do–Study–Act. The SDSA cycle is the Quality Management model for standardizing a process. The PDSA cycle is an acronym for Plan-Do-Study-Act. The PDSA cycle is the Quality Management model for improving a process. The DMAIC model is an acronym for Define-Measure-Analyze-Improve-Control. This model is the Six Sigma method for improving a process, service, or product. The DMAIC model is used as an alternative to the SDSA and PDSA cycles. The DMADV model is an acronym for Define-Measure-Analyze-Design-Validate. This model is the Six Sigma method for inventing and innovating entirely new or major features of processes, products, or services. The DMADV model is used as an alternative to the SDSA/PDSA cycle.

REFERENCES

1. H. Gitlow, A. Oppenheim, R. Oppenheim, and D. Levine, *Quality Management*, 3rd ed. (New York, NY: McGraw-Hill-Irwin, 2005).

2. H. Gitlow and D. Levine, *Six Sigma for Green Belts and Champions* (Upper Saddle River, NJ: Financial Times-Prentice Hall, 2005).

3. R. Hoerl, "Six Sigma Black Belts: What Do They Need to Know?" *Journal of Quality Technology*, 33, 4, October 2001, pp. 391–406.

4. N. Kano, "A Perspective on Quality Activities in American Firms," *California Management Review*, Spring 1993, pp. 14–15.

MACRO MODEL OF SIX SIGMA MANAGEMENT (DASHBOARDS)

SECTIONS

LEARNING OBJECTIVES

After reading this chapter, you will be able to:

- Begin Six Sigma management in your organization.
- Understand the interrelationships between the mission statement, key objectives, key indicators, and Six Sigma projects and tasks.
- Explain the different types of key objectives.
- Explain the different types of key indicators.
- Use a dashboard to manage an organization.
- Prioritize Six Sigma projects.

INTRODUCTION

If you decide to begin a Six Sigma journey, you will need a roadmap for getting started. This chapter presents such a roadmap. The journey is difficult, but worth the effort. People in all sectors of the economy can use this roadmap; for example, people in manufacturing and services industries, as well as people in government and education. If you decide to take this journey, it begins with the first step. Here we go!

3.1 BEGINNING SIX SIGMA MANAGEMENT

Starting Six Sigma Management

Six Sigma management begins the moment the senior executive and the executive committee of an organization begin to manage using Six Sigma theory and methods [see Reference 2]. The time required to obtain the benefits from Six Sigma management in an organization is a function of the resources allocated to the effort. Lack of top management commitment will stop a Six Sigma process before it can begin.

Energy for Transformation to Six Sigma Management

Top management creates and directs the energy necessary to promote Six Sigma management in its organization. There are only two known sources for this energy, a **crisis** or a **vision** [see Reference 5]. Many companies begin Six Sigma management as a reaction to crises.

Top management can uncover crises in at least two ways. First, management can highlight a crisis by asking a probing question such as "What are the characteristics of our products and/or services that are most important to our customers?" This question was stated by Dr. Noriaki Kano of the Science University of Tokyo in 1989. Frequently, top managers are not able to answer this question. This may create a crisis because top managers realize that they are out of touch with their customers. This can create a burning desire for transformation of an organization to Six Sigma management. Second, management can highlight a crisis by conducting a brainstorming session on the crises facing the organization and analyzing the data [see Reference 1]. This can also create a burning desire for transformation of an organization to Six Sigma management.

On the other hand, top management can initiate action for Six Sigma management through a provocative vision. A vision can stimulate top management to expend the energy needed to transform an organization. This idea is critical for organizations not facing a crisis. A vision can replace a crisis as a rallying point for the creation of quality.

An example of a vision that drove top management to transform an organization is a situation that occurred in a social service agency. The agency, a group home program for troubled teenagers, was achieving its mission—adequately providing temporary shelter and basic care for adolescents separated from their families. However, the top management of the agency knew, through surveys of clients and referral agents, what the program needed to change to provide other services. These services included individual, group, and family therapy; academic counseling; and an overall plan coordinated by the clients, along with social workers, psychologists, house parents, teachers, and other involved staff members.

Top management had a vision of transforming the agency to one in which the needs of the clients were met in a more professional manner, utilizing a team to carry out an integrated plan. There was no crisis that stimulated this transformation. Top management saw a need to change the organization to exceed the clients' needs, which were not being addressed by the program in its current state.

One technique that can be used to create a vision is to imagine the following scenario, in which the developer(s) of the vision personify the organization; that is, pretend the organization is a person:

> *Imagine it is 100 years in the future and your organization has just died. All the stakeholders of the organization are standing around the coffin and the clergyman reads the eulogy. The eulogy ends with these words: Here lies <u>insert the name of your organization</u>; it was known and loved for <u>insert the reason here</u>.*

The reason inserted above is the vision of your organization. A vision should be a noble statement of long-term purpose. It should inspire people to take action to transform their organization. It should be very short and easy to remember. Anecdotally, in the experience of the authors, organizations that are vision-driven stay with Six Sigma over the long haul, while organizations that are crisis-driven may revert back to preexisting behaviors once the crisis passes.

Initiating Action for Six Sigma Management

As stated previously, top management initiates action for Six Sigma management through a crisis and/or vision. Top management synthesizes, studies, and digests the crises facing the organization; it also formulates and articulates the vision of the organization. If top management feels it is warranted, it communicates the information about the crises and/or vision to relevant stakeholders. This process clarifies the need for Six Sigma management among top management.

Retaining Outside Counsel

After management has communicated the crises and/or vision, it needs to retain a master black belt. A master black belt is necessary for two reasons. First, expertise in Six Sigma management is not likely to be found within an organization. Second, organizations frequently cannot recognize their own deficiencies with respect to Six Sigma management; that is, they don't know what they don't know.

Window of Opportunity Opens

Once a master black belt has been retained, a **window of opportunity** for Six Sigma management opens. The window of opportunity has an unspecified time limit that varies from organization to organization. If signs of Six Sigma management do not become obvious to the stakeholders of an organization, they will not believe that top management is serious, and the window of opportunity will begin to close. This is a common reason for the failure of Six Sigma management in organizations. Another reason Six Sigma is not effective in some organizations is the failure to engage middle management. True, you can usually not engage middle management without commitment at the top. However, if all you get is commitment at the top and a lot of black belts running projects, the resulting middle management revolt will be a wall that cannot be breached from below or above.

Develop a Six Sigma Transformation Plan

The master black belt conducts a study to assess the desire of stakeholders to transform the organization into a Six Sigma organization. The study identifies the "**barriers against**" and the "**aids for**" a fruitful **transformation**, at all levels within an organization (see Table 3.1). Table 3.1 lists some generic barriers against, and aids for, transformation, and thematic groupings for those barriers. Thematic groupings are the underlying structure of the lists of barriers and aids. Thematic groupings are identified using brainstorming and an affinity diagram (see Chapter 12, "Additional Tools and Methods," for a detailed discussion of these techniques).

TABLE 3.1   Barriers and Aids for Transformation

Aids for Transformation			Barriers Against Transformation	
List	**Thematic Groupings of Aids**		**Thematic Groupings of Barriers**	**List**
Exceed customer requirements.	FOCUS ON CUSTOMER	OVERCOME	MANAGEMENT PROBLEMS	Inability to change the mindset of top management.
Improve the organization's image.				Lack of uniform management style.
Improve the design of processes, products, and services.				Lack of long-term corporate direction.
Increase market size.	FISCAL RESPONSIBILITY			Inability to change the culture of the organization.
Increase market share.				
Increase profits.				Lack of management commitment.

Aids for Transformation		OVERCOME	Barriers Against Transformation	
List	**Thematic Group- ings of Aids**		**Thematic Group- ings of Barriers**	**List**
Improve employee morale.	FOCUS ON EMPLOYEE		FEAR OF CHANGE	Fear of process standardization.
Create a common mission.	IMPROVE MANAGEMENT SYSTEM			Fear of loss of individualism.
Bridge responsibility gaps.				Fear of rigidity.
Standardize processes.	FOCUS ON PROCESS IMPROVEMENT		LACK OF RESOURCES	Lack of financial and human resources.
Create best prac- tices.				Lack of training and education.
Improve the physical environment.				
Improve the docu- mentation of processes, products, and services.				
Improve manufactur- ing and delivery of service.				
Produce uniform products at low cost and suited to the mar- ket (improve quality).				
Improve communication.	IMPROVE COMMUNICATION			

The executive committee and the master black belt develop a transformation plan that uses the thematic groupings in Table 3.1. For example, Table 3.1 would lead top management to create a four-point transformation plan. The first point is to improve the management system by: (1) creating the energy for transformation; (2) developing a uniform mission; (3) promoting a functional and uniform style of management that deals with accountability issues in resource allocation; and (4) improving the system of communication in the organization. The second point is to deal with the fear of change by management and employees. The third point is to focus on the customer when making decisions. The fourth point is to focus on process improvement to get results, not to only demand results.

Window of Opportunity Begins to Close

Once initial Six Sigma training of top management is complete, the window of opportunity for Six Sigma management begins to close unless the members of the executive committee take two actions. First, they must implement the transformation plan. Second, they must diffuse Six Sigma management theory and practice in the organization.

Implement the Transformation Plan

Six Sigma management begins the moment the senior executive and the executive committee begin to implement their transformation plan. The transformation plan includes a budget, training programs, an implementation schedule, and a dashboard. A **dashboard** is a tool used by management to clarify and assign accountability for: (1) the promotion of the transformation plan; (2) the diffusion of Six Sigma management throughout the organization; and (3) the pursuit of the key objectives needed to steer an organization toward its mission statement.

3.2 BENEFITS OF A DASHBOARD

Dashboards have both strategic and tactical benefits. The **strategic benefits** of dashboards include the following:

- Deploying the mission statement throughout all levels of an organization using a cascading and interlocking set of key objectives and key indicators.
- Pursuing key objectives through improving and innovating processes as measured by key indicators.
- Balancing management's attention between customer, process, employee, and financial key objectives as measured through key indicators.
- Increasing communication between, and within, the levels of an organization.
- Promoting the transformation plan to move an organization toward a Six Sigma style of management.
- Diffusing Six Sigma management throughout the organization by integrating Six Sigma issues into the organization's key objectives and key indicators.

The **tactical benefits** of a dashboard include the following:

- Linking all processes (jobs) to the mission statement.
- Improving each employee's comprehension of his/her job responsibilities and accountabilities and Six Sigma management tools and methods.
- Eliminating tampering with a process; each employee understands the effects of overreacting to random noise on their job, and on decision making in the organization.

Tampering is taking action on the random noise in a process. In other words, employees treat each departure from the desired state of a key indicator as a special event (crisis) needing special attention. This issue is discussed in detail in References 1 and 2.

- Developing and testing hypotheses about the effectiveness of potential improvements to a process.

3.3 STRUCTURE OF A DASHBOARD

The president's key objectives and key indicators emanate from the mission statement (see Row 1 and Columns 1 and 2 of Table 3.2). Direct reports identify their key objectives and indicators by studying the president's key indicators (Column 2 of Table 3.2) that relate to their area of responsibility. The goal of these studies is to identify the key objectives and indicators (see Columns 3 and 4 of Table 3.2) required to improve the president's key indicator(s) (see Column 2 of Table 3.2) to achieve a desirable state for presidential key objective(s) (see Column 1 of Table 3.2). This process is cascaded throughout the entire organization until processes are identified that must be improved or innovated with projects or tasks (see Column 5 of Table 3.2).

TABLE 3.2   Generic Dashboard

Mission Statement: —				
President		**Direct Reports**		**Potential Projects or Tasks**
Key Objectives	**Key Indicators**	**Area Key Objectives**	**Area Key Indicators**	
Key objectives must be achieved to attain the mission statement.	One or more key indicators show progress toward each key objective.	Area key objectives are established to move appropriate higher-level key indicators in the proper direction.	One or more area key indicators show progress toward each area key objective.	Projects are used to improve or innovate processes to move key indicators in the desired direction.

3.4 COMPONENTS OF A DASHBOARD

Mission Statement

A **mission statement** is a declaration of the reason for the existence of an organization. It should be short and memorable, as well as noble and motivational. It should be easily remembered by all stakeholders of the organization and should be used in decision making at all levels within the organization. State Farm Insurance Company has an excellent mission statement: "To help people manage the risks of everyday life, recover from the unexpected, and realize their dreams."

Or to restate this mission in terms of the State Farm philosophy statement: "Like a good neighbor, State Farm is there." This is a noble and memorable statement.

Mission statements are constructed using several methods. One method is for the president to develop a mission statement in the privacy of his or her own mind. Another method is for top management to go off on a retreat and come back with a mission statement. Yet another method is for top management to survey the organization's stakeholders to develop a mission statement. In the opinion of the authors, all three methods are correct in the right circumstances.

Key Objectives (as Measured by Key Indicators)

There are two kinds of **key objectives**: business objectives and strategic objectives [see Reference 6, p. 69]. **Business objectives** are the goals that must routinely be pursued within an organization if it is to function. Producing paper in a paper mill, answering customer inquiries in a call center, preparing paychecks in a payroll department, or doing return on investment calculations (ROI) in a finance department are examples of business objectives. **Strategic objectives** are the goals that must be accomplished to pursue the presidential strategy of an organization. For example, one of the strategic objectives of the University of Miami is to "gerontologize" the entire university. "Gerontologize" is a term used at the University of Miami to describe the strategic objective of creating a focus on human aging in all relevant processes and functions of an organization. Any objective, at any level, within the university that promotes "gerontologizing" the university is a strategic objective. Any other objective (as long as it doesn't support another of the president's strategies) is not a strategic objective; it is a business objective. Another example of a strategic objective is the implementation of Six Sigma management as the method for conducting business at General Electric. Any General Electric objective, at any level, that promotes Six Sigma management is a strategic objective. Any other objective (as long as it doesn't support another of the president's strategies) is not a strategic objective; it is a business objective.

There are four basic categories of key objectives: financial, process improvement and innovation, customer satisfaction, and employee growth and development [see Reference 6, p. 69]. Examples of each key objective category are shown next.

Financial Key Objectives

Examples of **financial key objectives** include: management's and stockholder's desire for more profit, market share, dominance, and growth; and the desire for less waste, turnover, financial loss, and customer defection.

Process Improvement and Innovation Key Objectives

Examples of **process improvement and innovation key objectives** include: (1) management's desire for consistency and uniformity of output; (2) high productivity; (3) products, services, and processes that exceed the needs and wants of current and future stakeholders; (4) products, services, and processes that are easy to create and low cost to provide; (5) products and services that meet technical specifications; (6) products and services that do not incur warranty costs; and (7) products that are easy to distribute throughout the channels of distribution.

Customer Satisfaction Key Objectives

There are four types of **customer satisfaction key objectives**: (1) customer's desired outcomes; (2) customer's undesired outcomes; (3) customer's desired product and service attributes; and (4) customer's desired process characteristics. Examples of customer desired key objectives include: joy, security, personal time, belonging, and health; customer's undesired outcomes include avoidance or elimination of death, taxes, discomfort, wasted time, and frustration. Examples of customer's desired product and service attribute key objectives include ease-of-use, accessibility, low cost of ownership, durability, and appeal. Examples of customer's desired process characteristic key objectives include timely arrival of product, no waiting time, and ease of acquisition.

Employee Growth and Development Key Objectives

Examples of **employee growth and development key objectives** include improving leadership skills, providing training opportunities, providing educational opportunities, and creating the opportunity to work on stimulating special assignments.

Leading and Lagging Indicators

It is interesting to consider that financial objectives are a result of customer satisfaction objectives, that customer satisfaction objectives are a result of process improvement objectives, and that process improvement objectives are a function of employee growth and development objectives.

Key Indicators

A **key indicator** is a measurement that monitors the status of a key objective. There are five types of key indicators:

- Attribute indicators
- Measurement indicators
- Binary indicators
- List by time period indicators
- Gantt chart indicators

Attribute Key Indicators

You use **attribute indicators** when a key objective is being monitored using attribute data (classification or count data) over time. Some examples of attribute classification indicators are the percentage of defective products produced by week, the percentage of customers complaining per month, and the percentage of accounts receivables over 90 days by quarter. Some examples of attribute count indicators are the number of industrial accidents per week, the number of customer complaints per month, and the number of thefts per quarter.

Measurement Key Indicators

You use **measurement indicators** when a key indicator is being monitored using measurement data. Measurement data can be displayed over time in a run chart, by mean and range by time period, and by mean and standard deviation by time period.

Binary Key Indicators

You use **binary indicators** (Yes/No by date) when a key indicator monitors whether an action has been accomplished by a given data. An example of a binary key indicator is: "Computer system operational by July 12, 2006? Yes or No."

List Key Indicators

You use **list indicators** when a key indicator monitors a group of people or items for compliance to some deadline or standard. Two examples of list key indicators are "List of employees not trained in the new safety standards by December 31, 2005" and "List of laboratories not up to federal code standards as of June 15, 2006."

Gantt Chart Key Indicators

You use **Gantt chart** indicators when a key indicator is a record-keeping device for following the progression in time of the tasks required to complete a project. A Gantt chart indicates which tasks are on or behind schedule. An example of a generic Gantt chart key indicator is shown in Table 3.3.

TABLE 3.3   Generic Gantt Chart

TASKS	Resp.	Month														Comments
		J	F	M	A	M	J	J	A	S	O	N	D	J	F	
Task 1	HG	B	...	E												
Task 2	HG				B	...	E									
Task 3	EP					B	...	...	...	E						
Task 4	EP									B	...	...	E			
Task 5	EP										B	E				
Task 6	HG													B	E	

Table 3.3 shows that Task 3 is planned to begin in May and end in September, while Task 4 begins in September and ends in December.

Flag Diagrams

A **flag diagram** [see Reference 4, pp. 3 and 34] is a tool used to track the contributions of subordinate key objectives to the pursuit of a superior key objective. There are two types of flag diagrams: additive flag diagrams and non-additive flag diagrams.

Additive Flag Diagram

Corporate indicators that are the summation of departmental indicators can be represented by additive flag diagrams. An example of an additive flag diagram is the case of burglaries on a university campus as a function of the buildings that the burglaries occurred in:

$$Y_i = (X_{1i} + X_{2i} + X_{3i} + X_{4i}),$$

where

Y_i = total burglaries on campus in month i

X_{1i} = burglaries in building 1 in month i

X_{2i} = burglaries in building 2 in month i

X_{3i} = burglaries in building 3 in month i

X_{4i} = burglaries in building 4 in month i

Non-Additive Flag Diagram

Corporate indicators that are *not* the summation of departmental indicators can be represented as non-additive flag diagrams. When departmental indicators are not additive, knowledge, experience, and statistical expertise are required to determine the relationships between corporate and departmental indicators. An example of a non-additive flag diagram in which the corporate indicator (Y) is not a linear combination of the departmental indicators ($Y = f[X_{11}, X_{12}, X_{21}, X_{22}, X_{31}, X_{32}, X_{41}, X_{42}]$) is the total number of burglaries on a university campus as a function of the number of doors left open (unlocked) and the number of hours of police patrol in the building the burglaries occurred in:

where

Y_i = total burglaries on campus in month i

X_{11i} = number of open doors in building 1 in month i

X_{12i} = number of hours police patrol in building 1 in month i

X_{21i} = number of open doors in building 2 in month i

X_{22i} = number of hours of police patrol in building 2 in month i

X_{31i} = number of open doors in building 3 in month i

X_{32i} = number of hours of police patrol in building 3 in month i

X_{41i} = number of open doors in building 4 in month i

X_{42i} = number of hours of police patrol in building 4 in month i

Tasks and Projects

A **task** is a process improvement activity in which the necessary process change is known by the process owner, but he or she has not yet had an opportunity to carry out the process change. The need for a task is determined by a chronic gap between the real and ideal value of a key indicator. A **project** is a process improvement activity in which the necessary process change is unknown by the process owner. Generally, the process owner forms a Six Sigma team to identify and test the necessary process change. The need for a project is determined by a chronic gap between the real and ideal values of a key indicator.

There are three categories of projects or tasks: zero projects or tasks, increase projects or tasks, and decrease projects or tasks [see Reference 5].

Zero Project or Task

In a **zero project or task**, the ideal value of a key indicator is zero or the optimal difference between the current value and ideal value of a key indicator is zero. The purposes of a zero project or task are: (1) to get the current value of a key indicator to be zero (the ideal value of the key indicator) by a given date; or (2) to reduce the gap to zero between the current value of a key indicator and the ideal value of a key indicator by a given date. Examples of zero tasks or projects are to reduce to zero the proportion of returned meals in a restaurant by day or to reduce unit-to-unit variation around the nominal value of waiting times in a physician's office.

Increase Project or Task

In an **increase project or task**, the ideal value of the key indicator is X units or Y percentage points higher than the current value of the key indicator. The purposes of an increase task or project are: (1) to get the real value of a key indicator to be X units or Y percentage points higher by a given date; (2) to raise the ideal value of the key indicator by a given date; or (3) to establish or clarify the ideal value for a key indicator by a given date. Examples of increase projects or tasks are to increase revenue or to increase profit.

Decrease Project or Task

In a **decrease project or task**, the ideal value of the key indicator is X units or Y percentage points lower than the current value of the key indicator. The purposes of a decrease task or project are: (1) to get the current value of a key indicator to be X units or Y percentage points lower by a given date; (2) to lower the ideal value of the key indicator by a given date; or (3) to establish or clarify the ideal value for a key indicator by a given date. Zero may not be a rational target for a decrease task or project. Most costs of doing business cannot be zero if the business is still operating. Examples of decrease tasks or projects are to reduce costs or to decrease cycle time.

There are two popular models for managing projects: the SDSA–PDSA model and the DMAIC–DMADV model. Both of these models were defined and discussed in Chapter 2, "Six Sigma Roles, Responsibilities, and Terminology." The DMADV model is discussed in detail in Chapters 4 through 8.

3.5 EXAMPLE OF A DASHBOARD

The University of Miami has a classic type of organizational structure. It is composed of several divisions; for example, Medical Affairs, Academic Affairs, Business and Finance, Governmental Relations, and Student Affairs. Each division is composed of several departments; for example, the Business and Finance division is composed of Business Services, Facilities Administration, Human Resources, Information Technology, Continuous Improvement, Treasurer, Controller, and Real Estate. Each department is composed of several areas. For example, the Business Services department is composed of Public Safety and Parking, Purchasing, Safety, and Environmental Health, to name a few.

An example of a dashboard between a third (Vice President of Business Services) and fourth (Chief of Campus Police) tier manager in Figure 3.1 is shown in Table 3.4.

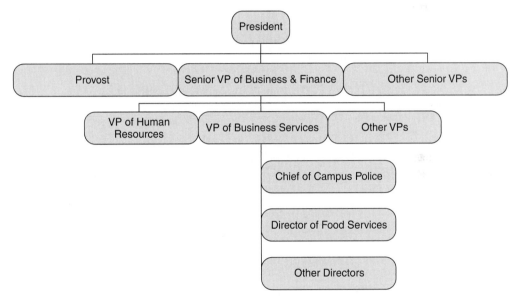

FIGURE 3.1 Partial Organizational Chart of the University of Miami

The mission of the Business Services Department is "Optimize SAS" (Security, Assets, and Services). The Vice President of Business Services promotes the Business Services Department's mission statement through three key objectives: (1) improve security on campus; (2) protect university assets; and (3) improve university services. The first key objective (improve security on campus) is measured through eight key indicators: (1) number of murders by month (SEC1); (2) number of rapes by month (SEC2); (3) number of robberies by month (SEC3); (4) number of aggravated assaults by month (SEC4); (5) number of burglaries by month (SEC5); (6) number of larcenies by month (SEC6); (7) number of auto thefts by month (SEC7); and (8) number of arsons by month (SEC8).

TABLE 3.4   Portion of a Dashboard from the Organizational Chart in Figure 3.1

Mission Statement for Business Services Department of the Business and Finance Division of the University of Miami: "Optimize SAS."*				
Vice President of Business Services		**Chief of Campus Police**		**Tasks or Projects**
Key Objectives	**Key Indicators**	**Key Objectives**	**Key Indicators**	
Improve Security on campus	SEC1: Number of murders, by month.	No murders. No objective other than to continue with current processes.	SEC1: List of murders, by month.	No murders. No task or project.
	SEC2: Number of rapes, by month	Detail not shown.		
	SEC3: Number of robberies, by month.	Detail not shown.		
	SEC4: Number of aggravated assaults, by month.	Detail not shown.		
	SEC5: Number of burglaries, by month.	Reduce number of open doors on campus.	SEC5A: Number of open doors, by department, by building, overall, by month.	The Police Chief established a team to study SEC5. Team members determined that most burglaries occurred when doors were left open (SEC5A).
	SEC6: Number of larcenies, by month.	Detail not shown.		
	SEC7: Number of auto thefts by month prior to September 1999 (see Figure 3.2).	Optimize deployment of police patrols in parking lots.	SEC7: Number of auto thefts by month before and after September 1999 (see Figure 3.3).	The Police Chief established a team to study SEC7. Team members determined that most auto thefts occur in two parking lots between 7:00 A.M. and 7:00 P.M. Consequently, the Police Chief redeployed

Mission Statement for Business Services Department of the Business and Finance Division of the University of Miami: "Optimize SAS."*				
Vice President of Business Services		**Chief of Campus Police**		**Tasks or Projects**
Key Objectives	**Key Indicators**	**Key Objectives**	**Key Indicators**	
				The police force to heavily patrol the two problematic lots between 7:00 A.M. and 7:00 P.M. during September 1999. SEC7 showed a dramatic reduction after redeployment of the police force.
	SEC8: Number of arsons, by month.	Detail not shown.		
Protect University Assets	Detail not shown.			
Improve University Services	Detail not shown.			

*NOTE: SAS = Security, Assets, and Services

An example of a key indicator can be seen in Figure 3.2. Figure 3.2 shows the number of auto thefts by month (SEC7) before September 1999. September 1999 is the month that a Six Sigma team implemented a change to the process for dealing with auto thefts.

The Chief of Campus Police promotes the mission statement of the Business Services Department by studying his superior's key indicator data to identify his key objectives. For example, the Police Chief established a Six Sigma team to study the number of auto thefts by month (SEC7) (as shown in Figure 3.2). The team members determined that the auto theft process is stable and predictable, and that most auto thefts occur in two campus parking lots between 7:00 A.M. and 7:00 P.M. The Police Chief redeployed the police force to heavily patrol the two problematic lots between 7:00 A.M. and 7:00 P.M. in September 1999. Subsequently, as shown in the chart in Figure 3.3, there was a drastic reduction in the number of auto thefts by month (SEC7).

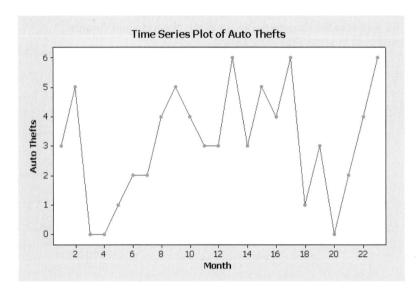

FIGURE 3.2   Minitab Line Graph of Auto Thefts on Campus Per Month Before September 1999

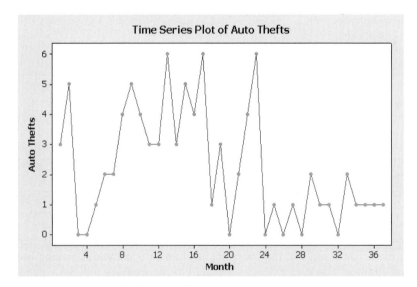

FIGURE 3.3   Minitab Line Graph of Auto Thefts on Campus Per Month Before and After September 1999

3.6 ANOTHER EXAMPLE OF A DASHBOARD

As stated earlier, you can use a dashboard to promote the strategic objectives of the president of an organization. For example, the president can use a dashboard to diffuse Six Sigma management throughout his/her organization (see Table 3.5).

TABLE 3.5 Partial Dashboard

Mission Statement: _____				
President		**Direct Reports**		**Projects or Tasks**
Key Objectives	**Key Indicators**	**Key Objectives**	**Key Indicators**	
Promote Six Sigma management throughout the stakeholders of the organization.	Adoption curve for departments (see Figure 3.4).			
	List of departments not yet adopting Six Sigma management as of xx/xx/xx.			
	Adoption curve for suppliers.			
	List of suppliers not yet adopting Six Sigma management as of xx/xx/xx.			
	Cumulative adoption curve and percent maximum profit by quarter (see Figure 3.5).			
	...			
Develop products and services of tomorrow.	List of new product-service concepts as of xx/xx/xx, with estimated revenues 1, 3, and 5 years out.			

(continued)

TABLE 3.5   Partial Dashboard (Continued)

Mission Statement:				
President		**Direct Reports**		**Projects or Tasks**
Key Objectives	**Key Indicators**	**Key Objectives**	**Key Indicators**	
	Is product concept "*i*" using DFSS methods in its innovation (Y/N) as of xx/xx/xx?			
Increase customer satisfaction.	Survey of customer opinion by quarter.	Decrease wait times for services calls.	Percentage of wait times for service calls in excess of 30 minutes by month (see Figure 3.6).	Potential DMAIC project: Identify key elements of customer dissatisfaction and reduce their effects on customers.

An adoption curve (see Figure 3.4) is an indicator that measures the diffusion of Six Sigma management. An adoption curve has the cumulative adoption rate of Six Sigma management plotted on the Y axis and time plotted on the X axis. The adoption curve must have a basic unit of measurement for adoption. In Figure 3.4, the basic unit of adoption is the department; that is, adoption of Six Sigma by the ith department = 1 if department "*i*" has adopted Six Sigma management, or adoption of Six Sigma by the ith department = 0 if department "*i*" has not yet adopted Six Sigma management. The cumulative adoption rate as of a given date is the number of departments with a "1" divided by the total number of departments in the organization. The criteria for adoption are varied and are determined by the users of the adoption curve. For example, a department could be considered adopting Six Sigma management if the CEO says the department has adopted Six Sigma management; or a department could be considered adopting Six Sigma management if the department has had at least one successful Six Sigma project completed within the last quarter; or a department could be considered adopting Six Sigma management if the Finance Department has recording hard currency savings in excess of $250,000 per quarter from Six Sigma management from the department. Adoption must be operationally defined so that all users of the adoption curve agree on the meaning of adoption.

Another indicator that directly measures the success of Six Sigma management is a simultaneous plot of organizational profit and the cumulative adoption curve by quarter (see Figure 3.5). Figure 3.5 shows the relationship between "Percent of Maximum Profit" and "Cumulative Adoption Rate of Six Sigma Management" by quarter. "Percent of Maximum Profit" is computed for a given time frame by dividing the profit amount for each time period by the maximum profit amount for the entire time frame. The purpose of this calculation is to put profit on the same Y axis scale as the adoption curve.

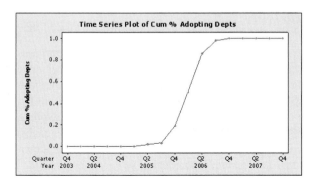

FIGURE 3.4 Adoption Curve for Six Sigma Management

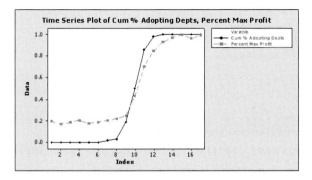

FIGURE 3.5 Relationship Between Percent of Maximum Profit and Cumulative Adoption Rate of Six Sigma Management

An indicator that indirectly measures the diffusion of Six Sigma management is a CTQ for a Six Sigma project. Observe from Figure 3.6, the Six Sigma DMAIC project achieved positive results in the 25th month when the proportion of customers waiting for 30 or more minutes for a service call dropped from about 30% to about 5%.

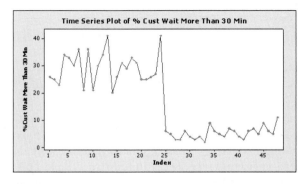

FIGURE 3.6 Percentage of Customers Waiting More than 30 Minutes for a Service Call by Month

3.7 MANAGING WITH A DASHBOARD

Top management uses a dashboard at monthly operations review meetings for several purposes. First, managers use dashboards to clarify key objectives and accountability among all personnel and areas. Second, managers use dashboards to promote statistical thinking to prevent overreaction to random noise in a process. The statistical methods used for this purpose are called **control charts** [see References 1 and 2]. Third, a manager uses dashboards to develop and test hypotheses concerning potential changes to processes. A hypothesis test analyzes the effect of a change concept on a key indicator (see Figure 3.3 on page 64 for the auto theft example). Fourth, a manager uses dashboards to ensure the routine and regular updating of key indicators. Fifth, a manager uses dashboards to diffuse and promote Six Sigma management.

Managers can use the following questions when conducting reviews of Six Sigma projects (called *tollgates*) to get the most out of their dashboard [see Reference 6]:

- Are the key objectives and key indicators on the dashboard the "best" set of objectives and indicators to attain the mission statement?

- Do appropriate key objectives and key indicators exist for the promotion of Six Sigma management? How are the Six Sigma key indicators doing with respect to the Six Sigma key objectives?

- Is the dashboard balanced with respect to customer, process, employee, and financial objectives? Do any areas have too much (or too little) representation on the dashboard?

- What products and/or services are most critical to your organization achieving its mission statement? List the top 5 or 10 products and services.

- Are targets being met in a timely fashion for all key objectives? Remember, targets are set to allocate resources to projects.

- What process is used to improve processes?

- Which key indicators on the dashboard are used to measure customer satisfaction and dissatisfaction? Are these measures operationally defined? Are these measures adequate?

- Does your organization have the ability to identify the return on investment from its dashboard? How is return on investment measured?

3.8 PROJECT PRIORITIZATION FOR A DASHBOARD

Once the projects and tasks required to pursue the presidential key objectives have been identified through the dashboard, the projects are prioritized for receiving resources using a project prioritization matrix. A **project prioritization matrix** (see Table 3.6) is constructed using the following method. First, the Office of the President creates the shell matrix shown in Table 3.6 by listing the presidential key objectives in the rows and the potential Six Sigma projects in the columns. (Be aware that there may be a lot of columns.) The rows in Table 3.6 come from the

TABLE 3.6 Shell Project Prioritization Matrix

Presidential Business Objectives (BO)			Potential Six Sigma Projects			
			Project 1	Project 2	...	Project k
BO1	**W**	W1				
BO2	**E**	W2				
	I					
	G					
BOm	**H**	Wm				
	T					
	S					
Weighted Average of Potential Projects (Benefits)						
Estimated Budget for Potential Project (Cost)						
(Benefit/Cost) Ratio for Potential Project						
Gantt Chart for Selected Project						

presidential key objectives column in a dashboard and the columns in Table 3.6 come from the projects/tasks column in a dashboard (see Table 3.4 for a dashboard). Second, the Finance Department weights the importance of the presidential key objectives to achieving bottom-line results. The weights are called W_i, where W_i indicates the weight of the ith presidential objective. The sum of the $W_i = 1.0$. Third, a committee is appointed by the Office of the President to document the relationships between potential projects (columns in Table 3.6) and the presidential objectives (rows in Table 3.6). The relationship values are recorded in the appropriate cells of Table 3.6. The relationship values are: 0 = no relationship; 1 = weak relationship; 3 = moderate relationship; and 9 = strong relationship. Cell values are determined by the committee members with the strong guidance of the Finance Department. Fourth, the committee members compute the weighted average relationship scores for each project in the "Weighted Average of Potential Projects (Benefits) row of Table 3.6. Fifth, the committee members estimate the budget for each potential project and record the values in the "Estimated Budget for Potential Project Costs" row of Table 3.6. Sixth, committee members compute the benefit cost ratio for each potential project and place the values in the "(Benefit/Cost) Ratio for Potential Project" row of Table 3.6.

Seventh, the potential projects with the highest benefit/cost ratios are funded by the Office of the President, up to the total budget available for projects. Eighth, project team members create a draft Gantt chart for the selected projects (see Chapter 12) and review the timelines with top management. The Gantt chart is rather rough at this stage of the project.

A portion of the project prioritization matrix for the University of Miami case study presented on pages 61–63 is shown in Table 3.7.

Table 3.7 shows that the "Open Door" project (resulting from analysis of Key Indicator SEC5 in Table 3.4) and the "Auto Theft" project had the highest benefit/cost ratios. Further, only $15,000 was available to finance projects, hence, making it possible to support both projects.

TABLE 3.7   Project Prioritization Matrix

Presidential Key Objectives			Potential Projects			
			Project 1: Open Door Project	**Project 2: Auto Theft Project**	**...**	**Project k**
KO1: Improve Security	**W**	W1 = .33	9	9		
KO2: Protect Assets	**E** **I**	W2 = .33	9	3	...	
KO3: Provide Services	**G** **H** **T** **S**	W3 = .33	9	3		
Weighted Average of Potential Projects (Benefits)			9.0	5.0		2.2
Estimated Budget for Project (Cost)			$5,000	$10,000		$100,000
(Benefit/Cost) Ratio for Project × 1,000,000			1,800	500		22
Gantt Chart for Project						

3.9 MANAGEMENT DECIDES IF A PROJECT TEAM IS NECESSARY

The process owner and champion decide "Does the potential Six Sigma project create a high-priority opportunity to positively impact customer's needs and wants and business objectives?" If the project receives a "No" to this question, the project is dropped, at least for now. If the project receives a "Yes" to the question, the project continues to the Define Phase so that the process owner and champion can charter the Six Sigma team.

3.10 TYPES OF SIX SIGMA PROJECTS

As stated in Chapter 1, "Foundations of Six Sigma Management," there are two types of Six Sigma projects. The first project type is DMAIC projects for improving a service, product, or process. The second project type is DMADV projects for inventing and innovating entirely new services, products, or processes, or for inventing or innovating major new features of existing services, products, or processes. Both types are critical to an organization's health. DMAIC projects deal with the issues of today, while DMADV projects deal with the issues of tomorrow.

DMAIC projects for improvement. As stated in Chapter 1, DMAIC is an acronym for Define, Measure, Analyze, Improve, and Control. A quick review of the DMAIC model is presented next.

Recall, the **Define Phase** of a Six Sigma DMAIC project involves identifying the quality characteristics that are critical to customers (called CTQs) using a SIPOC analysis and a Voice of the Customer analysis, and for preparing a business case for the project with a project objective. SIPOC is an acronym for Supplier, Input, Process, Output, and Customer. The **Measure Phase** involves operationally defining CTQs, conducting studies of the validity of the measurement system of the CTQ(s), collecting baseline data for CTQs, and establishing baseline capabilities for CTQs. The **Analyze Phase** involves identifying input and process variables that affect each CTQ (called Xs) using process maps or flowcharts, creating a cause and effect matrix to understand the relationships between the Xs and the CTQs, conducting an FMEA analysis (Failure Mode and Effects Analysis) to identify the critical Xs for each CTQ, operationally defining the Xs, collecting baseline data for the Xs, establishing baseline capabilities for the Xs, conducting studies of the validity of the measurement system of the Xs, identifying the major noise variables (MNVs) in the process, and generating hypotheses about which Xs affect which CTQs. The **Improve Phase** involves designing appropriate experiments to understand the relationships between the Xs and MNVs that impact the CTQs, generating the actions needed to implement optimal levels of critical Xs that minimize spread in CTQs, and conducting pilot tests of processes with Xs set at their optimal levels. The **Control Phase** involves avoiding potential problems in Xs with risk management and mistake proofing, standardizing successful process changes, controlling the critical Xs, developing process control plans for the critical Xs, documenting the control plans, and turning the control plan over to the process owner.

DMADV projects for invention and innovation. Again, as stated in Chapter 1, DMADV is an acronym for Define, Measure, Analyze, Design, and Verify/Validate. A quick review of the DMADV model is presented next.

The **Define Phase** of a Six Sigma DMADV project involves developing a business case with a project charter and establishing a schedule and guidelines for the design review process. The **Measure Phase** involves segmenting the market for the design concept, developing critical parameters for high-level designs, developing targets and tolerances for the critical parameters, preparing design scorecards for the critical parameters, and reviewing intellectual property. The **Analyze Phase** involves generating high-level conceptual designs, evaluating the high-level conceptual designs, and selecting the best design. The **Design Phase** involves developing detailed designs. This requires that team members construct detailed specifications, schematics, and blueprints for processes, services, and products. Additionally, team members develop detailed designs for ancillary processes (i.e., human resources and information technology). Finally, the **Verify/Validate Phase** involves conducting a pilot test of the detailed design; confirming the design outputs will yield product or service specifications; reviewing designs with respect to all potential users and possible uses, and, if necessary, improve designs; establishing appropriate control and monitoring systems to ensure designs meet and maintain goals throughout production or ongoing service life; and transferring the design to the process owner with a functioning control plan.

SUMMARY

Six Sigma management begins in an organization the moment top management realizes that it is the method that management will use to resolve crises or to promote a vision. Once Six Sigma has begun, top management retains a master black belt to develop a plan to transform the organization from its current style of management to a Six Sigma style of management. Next, top management is trained and a window of opportunity to diffuse Six Sigma throughout the organizations opens.

Dashboards are valuable tools that focus employee's efforts on the mission statement and the president's key objectives for his/her organization. Presidential key objectives include the promotion and diffusion of Six Sigma management throughout the organization. This is accomplished by developing a cascading and interlocking system of key objectives and indicators throughout all levels of the organization. Each employee can identify his or her key objectives by studying his or her superior's key indicators. This study identifies the projects and tasks needed to attain key objectives.

REFERENCES

1. H. Gitlow, A. Oppenheim, R. Oppenheim, and D. Levine, *Quality Management*, 3rd ed. (New York, NY: McGraw-Hill-Irwin, 2005).

2. Gitlow, H.S. and D. M. Levine, *Six Sigma for Green Belts and Champions* (Upper Saddle River, NJ: Financial Times-Prentice Hall, 2005).

3. H. Gitlow, *Quality Management Systems: A Practical Guide* (Boca Raton, FL: St. Lucie Press, 2000).

4. N. Kano, "Second Report on TQC at Florida Power & Light Company" (Miami, FL: October 1, 1986).

5. N. Kano, M. Yamaura, M. Toyoshima, and K. Nishinomiya, "Study on the Methods for Solving Increase, Reduction, and Zero Problems Encountered in the Promotion of TQC: Parts I and II" (unpublished paper).

6. R. Lawton, "Balance Your Balanced Scorecard," *Quality Progress*, 35, 2002, p. 66–71.

THE DESIGN FOR SIX SIGMA (DFSS) MODEL

DEFINE PHASE

SECTIONS

LEARNING OBJECTIVES

After reading this chapter, you will know how to:

- Prepare the business case for the project.
- Document the control system for the project.

- Activate the Product Development (PD) team.
- Present or conduct a management or tollgate review.
- State the project objective.

INTRODUCTION

The purpose of the Define Phase is to identify and clarify the worthiness of a Six Sigma DMADV project. Some DMADV projects do not survive the Define Phase. However, if they do survive it, generally, they make significant contributions to the bottom-line indicators and customer satisfaction indicators of the organization.

4.1 STEPS OF THE DEFINE PHASE

The Define Phase of the DMADV model has six steps:

1. Develop the business case.
2. Compute the benefits of the Six Sigma project.
3. Assess the risks to the project's success.
4. Activate the PD team.
5. Finalize the project objective.
6. Pass the Define Phase tollgate review.

If a Six Sigma project does not pass the Define Phase tollgate review, then it is revised and resubmitted for a future tollgate review, or it is abandoned as an unfruitful area of inquiry.

4.2 INPUTS TO THE DEFINE PHASE

The inputs to the Define Phase of the DMADV model are notification to a team leader and/or process owner from the executive committee, a champion, process owner, master black belt, or black belt about the need for a Six Sigma project. The project will have been highlighted for attention in the organizational dashboard (see Table 4.1) and will have a high weighted average importance score from the organizational Six Sigma project priority matrix (see Table 4.2).

4.3 DEVELOP THE BUSINESS CASE

As stated previously, the first step to preparing a business case for a Six Sigma project is to identify its location on the organizational dashboard (see Table 4.1) and to show its priority on the organizational project priority matrix (see Table 4.2). Dashboards and project priority matrices were discussed in Chapter 3, "Macro Model of Six Sigma Management (Dashboards)."

TABLE 4.1 Generic Organizational Dashboard

Mission Statement: –				
President		**Direct Reports**		
Business Objectives	**Business Indicators**	**Area Objectives**	**Area Indicators**	**Potential Six Sigma DMAIC and DMADV Projects**
Business objectives must be achieved to attain the mission statement.	One or more business indicators show progress toward each business objective.	Area objectives are established to move each business indicator in the proper direction.	One or more area indicators show progress toward each area objective.	Six Sigma projects are used to improve or innovate processes to move area indicators in the proper direction.

TABLE 4.2 Generic Project Priority Matrix

				Potential Six Sigma Projects			
				Project 1	**Project 2**	**...**	**Project k**
Business Objectives	BO_1	**W**	W_1				
	BO_2	**E**	W_2				
		I					
		G					
	BO_m	**H**	W_m				
		T					
		S					
Weighted Average of Potential Six Sigma Projects							

Example. The University of Miami has undergone a renaissance as an institution, building an image of a strong, private, doctoral-granting university with academic integrity. Student enrollment has flourished as a result of these efforts. Rapid growth and a presidential policy requiring all freshmen to live on campus (unless they live with their families) have created a demand for student housing that far exceeds the supply. Consequently, there is tremendous pressure to construct additional on-campus housing.

The Dean of the School of Business saw the need for additional on-campus housing as an opportunity. His desire to create a top-50 business school requires an executives-in-residence building. The new building could also serve as a high-end residential college for the University of Miami business students. On-campus housing would be available for MBA students for the first time, as space would no longer constrain the School of Business.

Table 4.3 shows the portion of the University's mission and dashboard.

TABLE 4.3 The Mission and Selected Portions of the Dashboard for the University of Miami

"Mission Statement: The University of Miami exists that human knowledge be treasured, preserved, expanded, and disseminated and that the human mind, body, and spirit be nurtured and strengthened through learning." *Content last modified on March 28, 2003*

President		Provost		Dean of the School of Business		*Projects*
Key Objectives	**Key Indicators**	**Key Objectives**	**Key Indicators**	**Key Objectives**	**Key Indicators**	
Improve student experiences	Number of students applying by semester	Increase the percentage of students living on campus	Percentage of students living on campus by semester	Increase the percentage of business students living on campus	Percentage of business students living on campus by semester	Create more on-campus housing for business students (New Housing)
	Percent of students returning by semester	Increase student/resident retention rate	Percentage of students retained each semester	Increase business student retention	Percentage of business students retained by semester	Improve on-campus housing options for business students (Housing Renovations)
Improve the national ranking of the university	I-MR chart of national ranking					
Improve interdisciplinary research	Number of interdisciplinary projects by year					
Increase the endowment	Total value of the endowment by year					

The potential projects that are shown in the rightmost column of Table 4.3 are prioritized for action in the columns of a project prioritization matrix (see Table 4.4). Additionally, the president's business objectives shown in the leftmost column of Table 4.3 are listed in the leftmost column of the project prioritization matrix (see Table 4.4).

TABLE 4.4 Business Prioritization Matrix

		Weight	Partial List of Potential Projects for Business School			
			Office Wing	New Housing	Housing Renovations	Business Library
President's Business Objectives	Improve National Ranking	0.40	9	3	3	1
	Improve Interdisciplinary Research	0.30	9	1	1	3
	Increase the Endowment	0.15	1	9	1	1
	Improve Student Experience	0.15	3	9	9	3
	Weighted Average	1.00	**6.9**	4.2	3	1.9

The project with the highest weighted average (bottom row of Table 4.4) is selected as a Six Sigma project because it has the most impact on the presidential business objectives. In this case, Office Wing Construction has the highest average score of 6.9. However, this project was already completed, so the Dean of the School of Business selected New Housing Construction as a Six Sigma project.

The second step to preparing a business case is to answer the following partially redundant questions:

Why do the highest project at all?

The New Housing Construction project should be conducted to satisfy the wishes of the President of the University for a live-on-campus university by increasing the limited supply of on-campus housing.

Why do the highest-priority project now?

The New Housing Construction project should be done now because the current housing supply is not adequate to meet the demand, and the University is spending large sums of money on local hotels to rectify the situation.

What are the consequences of not doing the highest-priority project?

Failing to do the New Housing Construction project would eventually create a student housing crisis with significant negative financial ramifications.

What business objectives are supported by the highest-priority project?

The New Housing Construction project is strongly related to the "Improve student experience" and "Increase the endowment" presidential objectives.

4.4 PREPARE THE OPPORTUNITY STATEMENT

The opportunity statement describes the current and desired states of the problem, opportunity, or objective in clear, concise, and measurable terms. It answers the question: "What is the pain?" A typical opportunity statement might read: "The competition has developed a product similar to our flagship product. Although it has a few minor new features, its quality is well-received by customers and its price is 15% lower than our price. This could lead to erosion of market share, making it difficult to achieve our business objective of 'Increasing Market Share by 2%.'" Desired state: "Marketing and sales estimate that a new version of our flagship product, with some significant new customer-desired features, could reverse the projected market share erosion. If it could be released by the end of the fiscal year and priced competitively, we could gain 2–3% market share beyond current levels."

In the dormitory example, the opportunity statement is shown next:

- The current state of the University of Miami is a strong and growing Carnegie V (doctoral-granting research) institution with increasing demands for on-campus housing. The Business School is rapidly advancing in national ranking.

- The desired state of the University of Miami is as follows: President Shalala made it known that she wishes to create a more residential campus to enhance the student experience (see the dashboard in Table 4.3). The Dean of the School of Business would like to establish the School of Business as a top-50 business school. Currently, there is a need to expand the facility and infrastructure to keep up with the escalating competition to become a top-50 business school.

4.5 DEVELOP THE INITIAL PROJECT OBJECTIVE

A project objective describes a team's design objective. It includes the product, service, or process being designed; the relevant market segment(s); and the measure(s) of success [market share, sales, ROI, etc.], direction, target, and deadline. Finally, it begins with a verb such as "Invent," "Innovate," or "Create." In the University of Miami case study, the project objective is: "To create a high-end living facility that encourages learning and community (service) aimed at executives in residence, MBAs, and junior and senior undergraduate business students (market segments). It should increase (direction) the number of on-campus residents (measure) by 200 students (target) no later than July 15, 2003 (deadline)."

4.6 DEVELOP THE PROJECT SCOPE

A Multi-Generation Product Plan (MGPP) is a method that is used to view the "entire picture of a project." It does not concern itself with details, but rather addresses the more significant strategic and tactical issues. There are three types of MGPPs that are described in Table 4.5.

There are four major benefits from using a Multi-Generation Product Plan. First, an MGPP helps focus the design team's energies on a manageable project that can be completed relatively quickly, without project scope creep. Project scope creep is a deadly disease to which many projects succumb. It occurs when team members start expanding the boundaries of the project to meet every new opportunity presented to them. Eventually, the project becomes

TABLE 4.5 Characteristics of Generation Plans

Generation	Generation 1	Generation 2	Generation 3
Vision	Stop bleeding in existing market(s).	Take offensive action by filling unmet needs of existing market(s).	Take leadership position in new market(s).
Product/Service Generations	Improved or less-expensive existing features.	New major features.	New products, services, or processes.
Product/Service Technologies and Platforms	Current technology.	Current technology with relevant technological enhancements, if any.	Current technology plus new technology, if possible.

completely unmanageable. An example of project scope creep would be expanding the new dormitory construction project to include a parking garage, which is a political hot potato. Second, an MGPP helps team members make decisions that are compatible with future generations of the product, service, or process. An example of a decision that is compatible with future generations of the dormitory is to require only standard-issue appliances (no special-order sizes) so they can be easily replaced in the future. Third, an MGPP creates a structure by which team members can add new ideas generated during the course of a project to a list of future modifications for the product, service, or process, instead of increasing the development time for the first generation. An example of an item on a list of future modifications might be adding self-cleaning glass windows to the dormitory building. Fourth, a MGPP promotes the development of new technologies needed for future generations of the product, service, or process while the first generation enters the market and establishes a presence. In the new dormitory project, the facility is a cross between Generations 1 and 2, as there is some bleeding in the housing market as students leave campus to seek off-campus housing. However, this is a concentrated effort to target just the students in the School of Business, including the previously neglected graduate students. It is also the wish to create something new, and far better, so this is an indication of trying to develop and incorporate new technologies into an on-campus living facility. As such, the project is a Generation 2 project and will be treated accordingly through the remainder of the project.

Additionally, the project scope focuses a Six Sigma project in light of all the constraints placed upon it, such as design boundaries and resource limitations. Design boundaries identify what is out-of-bounds for the project team in the conduct of the project. Out-of-bounds project elements are identified by answering the question: "What, if anything, is out-of-bounds?" The answer to this question is obtained using the following five-step method:

1. Brainstorm elements of the project.
2. Write each element on a self-stick note.
3. Draw a frame on a flipchart to indicate project boundaries.

4. Place the notes either inside or outside the frame's boundaries to show whether the element is within the team's scope or not.
5. Record the results in the worksheet table, as shown in Table 4.6.

Returning to the dormitory project, Table 4.6 lists a few selected in-scope and out-of-scope project elements.

TABLE 4.6   In-Scope and Out-of-Scope Elements

In-Scope	Out-of-Scope
Building design	Location of dormitory on-campus (see Figure 4.1).
Floor design	Budget for construction of dormitory.
Room design	Completion date for Certificate of Occupancy.
Services (e.g., concierge)	

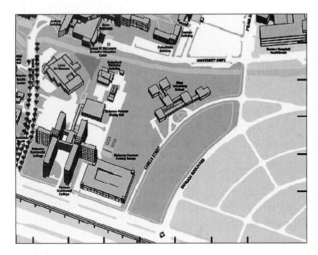

FIGURE 4.1   Proposed Location on the Coral Gables Campus

Another set of issues considered by the project scope are obstacles to the completion of the project. In the case of the dormitory project, obstacles such as confidentiality, politics, and a diverse population must be considered when designing the new facility.

Resource constraints must also be factored in when determining the scope of the project. They include budgetary issues such as planning, design, construction, and maintenance costs. Also, a project manager with fiscal responsibility must be determined early in the process. The project scope should clearly state the time commitments expected from team members and the acceptable impact on their normal jobs. These time commitments must be cleared with appropriate supervisors. Returning to the dormitory project, the initial planning budget was fixed at $1,000, of which $300 was dedicated strictly to a survey of stakeholder needs. All of the initial planning expenditures must be cleared through the project's black belt, then all expenditures and decisions are made by the project champion.

4.7 DEVELOP THE PROJECT PLAN

A **Gantt chart** is a simple scheduling tool. It is a bar chart that plots tasks and sub-tasks against time. Once a list of tasks and sub-tasks has been created for a project, then responsibilities can be assigned for each. Next, start and end dates can be scheduled for each task and sub-task. Finally, the milestones and resources relevant to a task or sub-task are indicated on the Gantt chart. A generic Gantt chart is shown in Table 4.7.

TABLE 4.7 Generic Gantt Chart

Tasks	Resp.	Timeline (Month)																	Mile-stones	Re-sources
		J	F	M	A	M	J	J	A	S	O	N	D	J	F	M	A	M	J		
Task 1	HG	B	E																		
Task 2	AO			B				E													
Task 3	DL			B	E																
Task 4	DL					B						E									
Task 5	RO					B								E							
Task 6	RO					B									E						
Task 7	RO																B		E		
Task 8	AO																	B	E		

Construction. A Gantt chart is constructed using the following method:

1. Identify the tasks of the project by answering the following questions:
   - What are the steps in the flowchart for completing this project?
   - Does this activity produce any outputs that are required in another activity?
   - What inputs does this activity require and where do they come from?
   - Can Activity A be completed independently of Activity B, etc.?
   - What activities must be completed so that this activity can be completed?
   - Where or how are the outputs of this activity used?

2. Identify the milestones for each task.
3. Identify individuals responsible for each task.
4. Identify the start and stop dates for each task (duration of task).
5. Identify the resources needed for each task and check against the budget.

Each task or subtask is listed on the vertical axis in Table 4.7, as are the person(s) or area(s) responsible for completion. The horizontal axis is time. It shows the anticipated and actual duration of each task by a bar of the appropriate length. The left end of the bar indicates the beginning time (B) for the task, and the right end indicates the ending time (E) for the task. For example, Table 4.7 shows that Task 3 begins in March and ends in April, while Task 4 begins in May and ends in November. The Gantt chart in Table 4.7 shows that three tasks begin in May.

Returning to the dormitory project, the portion of the Gantt chart is laid out in Table 4.8.

TABLE 4.8   Gantt Chart for the School of Business Housing Project

Task	Resp.	Month						
		Jan	Feb	Mar	Apr	May	Jun	Jul
Define	HG	██	██	██				
Measure	HG			██	██	██		
Analyze	HG						██	
Design	HG						██	
Validate	HG							██

4.8 Develop the Document Control System

A document control system is needed to manage design changes when individuals and sub-teams are working concurrently (Concurrent Engineering) on a Six Sigma project. The following checklist reflects suggested minimum requirements for a document control system.

- All documents are marked with creation date (Yes/No).
- All documents are assigned control numbers (Yes/No).
- All documents are backed up in a central repository (Yes/No).
- There is a system for assigning access to documents, and all documents have proper access controls (Yes/No).

You can add or replace items on the preceding checklist, or include references to currently used document controls within your organization, as deemed appropriate by your black belt. Each change document includes a valid reason(s) for the design change with reference to:

- The original design to prevent the design from mutating over time.
- The impact of the design change on the cost and schedule.
- The approval(s) appropriate for each design change.

For example, suppose part of the plan for a new dormitory includes a common area that can be used for meals, meetings, and relaxation. The blueprints or design layout is often maintained electronically in a central, password-protected file. Changes to the current design layout would not be included in the primary electronic file without the knowledge of the individuals having the password to the file. This requires that proposed changes are documented and approved prior to inclusion. All people would have access to the electronic file in "read-only" format, allowing them to edit, comment, or provide highlighted changes. These changes would be required to be saved electronically with a naming convention that includes the revision number or date and editor of the file. These can be saved in a central repository for others to review to generate feedback and additional edits, comments, or changes. As these "additional" electronic documents are developed, the Electronic Information System would also track the date of submission and the person submitting the file. Ultimately, these changes can be accepted or rejected by those who have password access to the one master electronic file. This process allows more individuals or teams to view the "master," contribute revisions or suggestions, and finally to allow the "master" to be updated as appropriate.

4.9 ASSESS THE BENEFITS OF THE SIX SIGMA PROJECT

Six Sigma projects have both **soft benefits** and **hard benefits**. Examples of soft benefits include improving quality and morale and decreasing cycle time. Examples of hard (financial) benefits include increasing revenues or decreasing costs. Project team members "guesstimate" the dollar impact of a Six Sigma project. This "guesstimate" will be refined through iterative learning over the life of the project.

There are two taxonomies for classifying the potential cost-related benefits that may be realized from a Six Sigma project. These taxonomies are discussed next.

Taxonomy 1: Cost Reduction Versus Cost Avoidance

Cost reduction includes costs that fall to the bottom of the profit and loss statement. A cost reduction can be used by management to offset price, increase profit, or reinvest elsewhere. Cost reductions are calculated by comparing the most recent accounting period's actual costs with the previous accounting period's actual costs. Cost avoidance includes those costs that can be reduced, if management chooses to do so; but until action is taken, no real costs are saved. Examples include reducing labor hours needed to produce some fixed volume of work. Unless the headcount that produced this fixed volume is reduced (e.g., through attrition) or unless there is an increase in volume of work completed with the same headcount, then there are no real savings realized. The impact of cost avoidance is not visible on the profit and loss statement and is difficult to define, but is still important in meeting organizational goals.

Taxonomy 2: Tangible Costs Versus Intangible Costs

Tangible costs are more easily identified; for example, the costs of rejects, warranty, inspection, scrap, and rework. Intangible costs are costs that are difficult to measure; for example, the costs of long cycle times, many setups, low productivity, engineering change orders, low employee morale, turnover, low customer loyalty, lengthy installations, excess inventory, late delivery, overtime, lost sales, and customer dissatisfaction. However, some intangible costs are not difficult to measure, such as express package delivery. It is important to realize that some of the most important benefits are measured through intangible costs. Hence, the "guesstimate" of benefits in the Define Phase often identifies a minimum estimate of intangible benefits.

The project team members develop a formula to "guesstimate" the potential benefits that the organization may realize due to the Six Sigma project. For example, a possible formula appears in Table 4.9.

TABLE 4.9   Cost-Benefits Formula

Cost Reductions _____
PLUS Cost Avoidance _____
PLUS Additional Revenue _____
LESS Implementation Costs _____
EQUALS Financial Benefits _____

The financial impact of a project is a best estimate that will be refined through iterative learning over the life of the project.

Dormitory Example

The benefits of the new housing construction are both tangible and intangible. The tangible benefits can be broken down into two groups: financial and nonfinancial. Examples of financial benefits include seminar fees collected from executives in residence and revenues from the rental of dormitory rooms to students. The vision of the Dean of the School of Business is to build high-end facilities for which the University could charge significantly more rent. Preliminary estimates are summarized in Table 4.10.

Intangible benefits would be realized; for example, potentially increased ratings from sources like *Business Week* and *U.S. News and World Report*. Another example is the positive feelings evoked from a physically apparent sign of growth, as the new building stimulates interest and excitement.

TABLE 4.10   Cost-Benefits Summary by Semester

Revenues: Undergrads and MBAs (150 rooms × 12 months for $12,000)	$1,800,000
Revenues: Execs in Residence (50 rooms × 5 days/week × 50 weeks/year × $200 per night) .... $1,500,000 × 60% occupancy	
Total Construction Cost	$25,000,000
40% of construction cost raised through donation	$10,000,000
60% of construction cost raised through debt	.$15,000,000
Annual servicing of the debt of construction	$1,500,000
Annual cost of maintenance	$200,000
Profit	$1,600,000

4.10 ASSESS THE RISKS TO THE PROJECT'S SUCCESS

Before we discuss risk, let's determine your attitude toward risk by using the following test:

> A million dollars is yours (tax free), but there is a 1 in a _____ chance you will experience a quick and painless death and your family will not get to keep the money. What risk would you accept for the opportunity to get the million dollars?
>
> 1 in a 1,000,000
>
> 1 in 100,000
>
> 1 in 10,000
>
> 1 in 1,000
>
> 1 in 100
>
> 1 in 10

Some people will not accept the 1 in a million chance, while a few accept the 1 in ten chance.

Technical Reasons for Risk

There are many technical reasons that can affect the risk of a step in a project or of an entire project. Some examples of technical sources of risk include the following:

1. Complex or hazardous (unsafe) design elements and/or functions.
2. Complex interactions between a design element(s) and one or more existing processes, products, or services.
3. Inappropriate design tools or methods that create problems.
4. New, unfamiliar, or inappropriate technology used in the design.
5. Inadequate consideration of failure modes and safety issues in design.

6. Functional capability requirements not appropriate for use.

Human Factors Affecting Risk

There are several human factors that can affect the risk of a step in a project or of an entire project. Some examples of human factors that create risk include the following:

1. Stakeholders resist design.
2. Design is not user-friendly (for example, it is difficult to use and expensive).
3. Political and cultural reasons affect attitudes about the design.
4. Variation in the mode of usage of the users (e.g., cell phones being used in hazardous places such as on top of tall buildings under construction, may have a greater risk for failure due to dropping a phone than those who work on the ground).
5. Managers not capable of explaining the design to their people.
6. Team members fail to achieve professional intimacy with potential adopters.

Team Dynamics Affecting Risk

There are several team factors that can affect the risk of a step in a project or of an entire project. Some examples of team factors that create risk include the following:

1. Unstable project team.
2. Low commitment to project by team members.
3. Project team unfamiliar with business area.
4. Poor or inexperienced project management skills.
5. Weak champion.
6. Distant process owner.

Planning Issues Affecting Risk

There are many planning issues that can affect the risk of a step in a project or of an entire project. Some examples of planning issues that can affect risk include the following:

1. Inadequate customer and competitive research on design.
2. Frequent changes to the scope of design (including scope creep).
3. Failure to identify stakeholders of design.
4. Failure to assess stakeholder attitudes about change(s) to a design.
5. Inadequate strategy for change.
6. Critical or unrealistic implementation date.

7. Inadequate project control procedures.
8. Too many people needed for the project over time.
9. Too many major new features required by the design.
10. Inadequate resources.
11. Unclear requirements or specifications of design element(s).
12. Failure to plan for additional resources (for example, people).
13. Inadequate document control system.

Business Sources of Risk

There are many business issues that can affect the risk of a step in a project or of an entire project. Some examples of business issues that can affect risk include the following:

1. Significant increase in anticipated costs of the project.
2. Change in business or customer requirements.
3. Incomplete definition of scope or requirements of the project.
4. Poorly defined benefits of the project.
5. Long ROI for project.
6. Project is critical to achievement of one or more strategic objectives.

Organizational and Political Sources of Risk

There are many organizational and political issues that can affect the risk of a step in a project or of an entire project. Some examples of organizational and/or political sources of risk include the following:

1. Too many decision makers required by the project.
2. Multiple geographic locations.
3. Unrealistic expectations by stakeholders.
4. Powerful stakeholders resist design.
5. Inadequate sponsorship.
6. Unavailable key users.
7. Significant changes required by organization.
8. Resistance to change by current organization.
9. Extensive education of users required.

External Sources of Risk

There are many external issues that can affect the risk of a step in a project or of an entire project. Some examples of external sources of risk include the following:

1. Too many vendors, contractors, or consultants.
2. Poor support by vendors, contractors, or consultants.
3. Project dependent on external suppliers.

Identify Risk Elements

Team members identify the risk elements for the process, service, or product being designed, as well as risk caused by or related to processes, using the following procedure. First, team members identify the process, product, or service under study, as well as all related processes that might cause or experience collateral damage from the design project. Second, team members identify risk elements for each process. Third, team members assign risk element scores for each process step using the following two scales.

The "Probability of Occurrence of Problem" scale uses the classifications in Table 4.11.

TABLE 4.11   Probability of Occurrence Scale

Classification	Scale Value	Definition
High	5	Uncertainties Remain No or Little Prior Experience Data, Infrastructure, and/or Resources not in Place
Medium	3	Some Uncertainties Remain Some Experience and Data Exist Infrastructure in Place but Under-Resourced
Low	1	Few Uncertainties Remain Significant Experience and Data Exist Infrastructure in Place and Fully Resourced

The "Impact of Problem on Project" scale used the classifications in Table 4.12.

TABLE 4.12   Impact of Problem Scale

Classification	Scale Value	Definition
High	5	Performance, Quality, Cost, or Safety Impacts Resulting in Major Redesign and Program Delay.
Medium	3	Performance, Quality, Cost, and/or Safety Impacts Resulting in Minor Redesign and Schedule Adjustment.
Low	1	Performance, Quality, Cost, and Safety Requirements Met Within Planned Schedule.

Fourth, team members multiply both scales for each risk element to compute a risk element score. Table 4.13 shows the resulting risk element scores that range from 1 = low risk to 25 = high risk.

TABLE 4.13   Risk Element Scores

	Impact of Problem on Project		
	Low (1)	**Medium (3)**	**High (5)**
Probability of Occurrence of Problem **High (5)**	Fix before production (5)	Reassess project (15)	Do not proceed (25)
Medium (3)	Proceed with caution (3)	Proceed with great caution (9)	Reassess project (15)
Low (1)	Proceed (1)	Proceed with caution (3)	Fix before production (5)

Fifth, team members prioritize the risk elements for all relevant processes, products, or services (see Table 4.14). Column 1 states the name of the process, product, or service. Column 2 lists the risk element(s) (for example, failure modes) for the process, product, or service. Column 3 lists the potential source(s) of harm (hazards) for each risk element. Column 4 lists the source(s) of actual injury or damage (harm). Column 5 shows the likelihood score. Column 6 shows the severity score. Column 7 shows the risk element score.

TABLE 4.14   Prioritization of Risk Elements

1	2	3	4	5	6	7
Process, Product, or Service Under Study	**Risk Element**	**Hazard (potential source of harm)**	**Harm (physical injury to person and/ or damage to property)**	**Likelihood 1 = low 5 = high**	**Severity 1 = low 5 = high**	**Risk Element Score 1 to 8 = low 9 to 15 = medium 16 to 25 = high**
Related process 1	Element A Element B Risk Element for the related process 1	Hazard (potential source of harm) for the related process 1	Harm (physical injury to person and/or damage to property) from the related process 1	Likelihood 1 = low 5 = high	Severity 1 = low 5 = high	Risk Element Score 1 to 8 = low 9 to 15 = medium 16 to 25 = high

(continued)

TABLE 4.14　Prioritization of Risk Elements (Continued)

1	2	3	4	5	6	7
Process, Product, or Service Under Study	Risk Element	Hazard (potential source of harm)	Harm (physical injury to person and/ or damage to property)	Likelihood 1 = low 5 = high	Severity 1 = low 5 = high	Risk Element Score 1 to 8 = low 9 to 15 = medium 16 to 25 = high
Related process 2	Element C Element D Risk Element for the related process 2	Hazard (potential source of harm) for the related process 2	Harm (physical injury to person and/or damage to property) from the related process 2	Likelihood 1 = low 5 = high	Severity 1 = low 5 = high	Risk Element Score 1 to 8 = low 9 to 15 = medium 16 to 25 = high

Sixth, team members construct risk abatement plans for risk elements with high- and medium-risk elements; that is, a risk element score of 16 to 25 (see Table 4.15). Seventh, team members identify changes to the process under study to reduce the risk for each high- and medium-risk element in the related processes identified in Table 4.15 (see Column 4 in Table 4.15). Eighth, team members estimate the risk element score after the risk abatement plan is set into motion (see Column 3 in Table 4.15). Ninth, team members identify the risk element owner and set a completion date for the risk abatement plan to become operational (see Columns 5 and 6 in Table 4.15). Tenth, team members document the risk abatement plans. Eleventh, team members carry out the risk abatement plan.

For example, when constructing a dorm, there is a risk that another local developer may decide to build a residency facility close to campus that has many amenities; for example, a 24-hour restaurant, gymnasium, etc. A risk abatement plan would examine the new construction permits in the immediate area of the dormitory and determine if there are any potentially threatening new development projects underway. Also, a study of open land or other potential residential sites may provide insight as to the existence of risk. Furthermore, a study of satisfaction levels of other similar facilities on or near other university campuses can help determine the opportunities to "delight" potential residents. These can be incorporated into the new design for a dorm.

TABLE 4.15 Format for a Risk Abatement Plan

1	2	3		4	5	6
Potential Risk Elements for Process *i*	Potential Harm for the Risk Elements from Process *i*	Risk Element Score		Counter-measure (Risk Abate-ment Plan)	Risk Owner	Completion Date for Counter-measure
		Before	After			

Reduce Risk with Risk Reduction Plans

Failure Mode and Effects Analysis (FMEA) is a tool used to identify, estimate, prioritize, and reduce the risk of failure in CTQs through the development of actions (process changes and innovations) and contingency plans based on *X*s. It is an alternative to the analysis discussed in Table 4.15.

You can use FMEA to redesign an existing unit, design a new unit, or make existing units more robust to environmental conditions; that is, less risky with respect to failure modes. In this phase of the DMADV model, you use FMEA (see Table 4.16) to reduce the high- and medium-priority risk elements (risk element score > 15).

There are 10 steps to conducting a FMEA. First, team members identify the critical parameters and their potential failure modes for each *X* identified through the type of analysis shown in Table 4.14, or a cause and effects matrix or diagram through brainstorming or other tools; that is, ways in which the process step (*X*) might fail (Columns 1 and 2 of Table 4.16). Second, team members identify the potential effect of each failure (consequences of that failure) and rate its severity (Columns 3 and 4 of Table 4.16). The definition of the **severity scale** is shown in Table 4.17. Third, team members identify causes of the effects and rate their likelihood of occurrence (Columns 5 and 6 of Table 4.16). The definition of the **likelihood of occurrence scale** is shown in Table 4.18. Fifth, team members identify the current controls for detecting each failure mode and rate the organization's ability to detect each failure mode (Columns 7 and 8 of Table 4.16). The definition of the **detection scale** is shown in Table 4.19. Sixth, team members calculate the **RPN (Risk Priority Number)** for each failure mode by multiplying the values in Columns 4, 6, and 8 (Column 9 of Table 4.16). Seventh, and very importantly, team members identify the action(s), contingency plans, persons responsible, and target completion dates for reducing or eliminating the RPN for each failure mode (Columns 10 and 11 of Table 4.16). Actions are the process changes needed to reduce the severity and likelihood of occurrence, and increase the likelihood of detection, of a potential failure mode. **Contingency plans** are the alternative actions immediately available to a process owner when a failure mode occurs in spite of process improvement actions. A contingency plan might include a contact name and phone number in case of a failure mode. Eighth, team members identify the date the action was taken to reduce or eliminate each failure mode (Column 12 of Table 4.16). Ninth, team members rank the severity (Column 13 of Table 4.16), occurrence (Column 14 of Table 4.16), and detection (Column 15 of Table 4.16) of each failure mode after the recommended action (Column 10 of Table 4.16) has been put into motion. Tenth, team members multiply the values in Columns 13, 14, and 15 of Table 4.16 to re-calculate the RPN (Risk Priority Number) for each failure mode after the recommended action (Column 12 of Table 4.16) has been put into motion.

TABLE 4.16 Format for a FMEA

1	2	3	4	5	6	7	8	9	10	11	12	13	14	15	16
Critical Para-meter	Potential Failure Mode	Potential Failure Effect	Severity	Potential Causes	Occurrence	Current Controls	Detection	BEFORE RPN	Recommended Action	Resp. and Target Date	Counter-measure (Action Taken)	Severity	Occurrence	Detection	AFTER RPN

TABLE 4.17 Definition of "Severity" Scale = Likely Impact of Failure

Impact	Rating	Criteria: A failure could...
Bad	10	Injure a customer or employee.
	9	Be illegal.
	8	Render the unit unfit for use.
	7	Cause extreme customer dissatisfaction.
	6	Result in partial malfunction.

Impact	Rating	Criteria: A failure could...
	5	Cause a loss of performance likely to result in a complaint.
	4	Cause minor performance loss.
	3	Cause a minor nuisance; can be overcome with no loss.
	2	Be unnoticed; minor affect on performance.
Good	1	Be unnoticed and not affect the performance.

TABLE 4.18 Definition of "Occurrence" Scale = Frequency of Failure

Impact	Rating	Time Period	Probability of occurrence
Bad	10	More than once per day	> 30%
	9	Once every 3–4 days	< = 30%
	8	Once per week	< = 5%
	7	Once per month	< = 1%
	6	Once every 3 months	< = .3 per 1,000
	5	Once every 6 months	< = 1 per 10,000
	4	Once per year	< = 6 per 100,000
	3	Once every 1–3 years	< = 6 per million (approx. Six Sigma)
	2	Once every 3–6 years	< = 3 per ten million
Good	1	Once every 6–100 years	< = 2 per billion

TABLE 4.19 Definition of "Detection" Scale = Ability to Detect Failure

Impact	Rating	Definition
Bad	10	Defect caused by failure is not detectable.
	9	Occasional units are checked for defects.
	8	Units are systematically sampled and inspected.
	7	All units are manually inspected.
	6	Manual inspection with mistake-proofing modifications.
	5	Process is monitored with control charts and manually inspected.
	4	Control charts used with an immediate reaction to out-of-control condition.
	3	Control charts used as above with 100% inspection surrounding out-of-control condition.
	2	All units automatically inspected or control charts used to improve the process.
Good	1	Defect is obvious and can be kept from the customer or control charts are used for process improvement to yield a no-inspection system with routine monitoring.

Table 4.20 shows a FMEA for a student accounts office process with four steps: student waits for clerk, clerk pulls record, clerk processes record, and clerk files record. In Table 4.20, X_2 (clerk pulls record) is a critical failure mode because it exhibits such a high risk priority number (RPN = 700), while X_3 (clerk processes record) is not a critical failure mode due to its low risk priority number (RPN = 42). In a brainstorming session, the clerks determined that the most likely reason for not locating a record is because another clerk was using it. Consequently, the recommended action (Column 10) was to "insert a note in a file if it is in use with the user's name." The department manager, Hiram, said that the revised best practice method would take effect no later than 1/31/03 (Column 11); in fact, it was in effect on 12/15/02 (Column 12). The calculation of the revised RPN number is shown in Columns 13 through 16. As you can see, the recommended action lowered the RPN number from 700 to 28.

TABLE 4.20 Partial FMEA Chart

1	2	3	4	5	6	7	8	9	10	11	12	13	14	15	16
Process Step (Xs) or Critical Parameter	Potential Failure Mode(s) for Each X	Potential Failure Effect	Severity	Potential Causes	Occurrence	Current Controls	Detection	RPN	Recommended Action	Resp. and Target Date	Action Taken	Severity	Occurrence	Detection	RPN
X_1 Cycle to student waits for clerk.															
X_2 Cycle time to pull record.	Record cannot be located.	Student leaves frustrated without processing record.	7	File misplaced.	10	Search for missing file.	10*	700	Clerks inserts note with his/her name in file when using a record.	Hiram 1/31/03	12/15/02	7	4	1	28

1	2	3	4	5	6	7	8	9	10	11	12	13	14	15	16
Process Step (Xs) or Critical Para-meter	Poten-tial Failure Mode(s) for Each X	Poten-tial Failure Effect	S e v e r i t y	Poten-tial Causes	O c c u r r e n c e	Current Con-trols	D e t e c t i o n	R P N	Recom-mended Action	Resp. and Target Date	Action Taken	S e v e r i t y	O c c u r r e n c e	D e t e c t i o n	R P N
X_3 Cycle time to process record.	Record cannot be processed.	Student leaves frustrated without process-ing record.	7	Record/ Clerk is missing informa-tion.	3	Clerks update best practice method.	2	4 2							
X_4 Cycle time to file record.															

(* = only can detect folders for students waiting)

Table 4.21 shows a Failure Modes and Effects Analysis (FMEA) for the new housing project. The two major risks, obsolescence (RPN = 560) and design team dynamics (RPN = 448), can be avoided by planning flexible interiors that can be easily updated (revised RPN = 210) and maintaining a team environment (revised RPN = 192), respectively.

TABLE 4.21   FMEA of the Proposed Project

Risk Elements	Failure Mode	Likelihood of Occurrence	Severity	Likelihood of Detection	RPN	Action	Likelihood of Occurrence	Severity	Likelihood of Detection	RPN
Executives Continue to Use Five-Star Hotels	Executive Rooms Empty	5	6	1	30	Market Research and Design Facilities to Better Suit Executives	2	6	1	12
Parking Required by Coral Gables Housing Code	Building Permit Not Issued	3	10	1	30	Add Parking to Design if Dictated by Code	1	10	1	10
Obsolescence	High Renovation Expenses	7	8	10	560	Plan a Flexible Interior That Can Easily Be Changed	7	3	10	210
Project Exceeds Budget	Other Sacrifices or Unfinished Construction	3	7	5	105	Strong Planning Effort	2	5	5	50
Design Team Dynamic Problems	Poor Design	7	8	8	448	Maintain a Team Environment	4	6	8	192
Technical Incompetence	Poor Design	4	8	4	128	Independent Consulting of Specifications	1	8	4	32
Construction Defects	Poor Workmanship/Broken Facilities	10	3	5	150	Allocate Time and Money to Fix Problems	10	1	5	50
Rushing to Decisions	Poor Design	1	8	8	64	Strong Planning Effort	1	6	8	48
Natural Disaster	Destruction or Damage to the Building	1	10	1	10	Properly Insure the Facility	1	3	1	3
Lack of Student Interest	Unfilled Rooms	4	7	2	56	Market Research and Design Facilities to Better Suit Students	2	7	2	28
Facilities Integration Problems	High Utility and Maintenance Costs	3	6	4	72	Specialists Create Specifications and Study Integration of Systems	1	6	4	24
Alienation of Business Students	Underclass Backlash	2	3	3	18	Market the Building Properly	1	3	3	9
Strained University Relationships	Political Turf Battles	5	5	2	50	Define the Purpose of the Building to the Presidential Dashboard	1	5	2	10

4.11 ACTIVATE THE DFSS DEVELOPMENT TEAM (DT)

Team Formation

The champion and process owner accept the Six Sigma project identified through a dashboard. Next, they select a green belt or black belt to be team leader. The team leader selects the team members. Then, the team leader and champion identify the Finance and IT representatives, and obtain all approvals for team activities (see Table 4.22).

TABLE 4.22   DFSS Development Team Table

Role	Responsibility	Signature	Date	Supervisor's Signature	Address	Phone #	Fax #	E-mail
Champion								
Process Owner								
Team Leader								
Team Member 1								
…								
Team Member n								
Green Belt								
Black Belt								
Finance Rep								
IT Rep								

Ground Rules

A large portion of the planning and leg work required for a Six Sigma project is accomplished in a team setting. Ground rules are important because they help team members experience effective, efficient, and productive meetings. Ground rules are placed in full view of all team members at each team meeting and are reviewed every few meetings. Some commonly used ground rules are as follows:

1. The team will meet *<enter meeting frequency (weekly, monthly, etc)>*.
2. The team will keep attendance records of all meetings.

3.   At least (*<enter x>* members) or (*<enter x>* % of members) must be present to convene a meeting.

4.   All meetings will begin and end on time.

5.   Team members who must be absent will inform the team leader in advance.

6.   Team members who must be late will inform the team leader in advance.

7.   Meeting interruptions are kept to a minimum.

8.   Consensus decision making will be used by team members, as much as is practical.

9.   One person speaks at a time.

10.   Team members attack an issue, not the messenger of the issue.

11.   Team members seek first to understand, then to be understood.

12.   The team leader keeps an action items list and a future item list.

13.   Agendas will be prepared and distributed by *<insert name>*.

14.   Minutes will be prepared and distributed by *<insert name>*.

15.   Insert name, date, and version number on all documents.

16.   Team members respect confidentiality, when it is requested by team members.

17.   Team members don't "beat a dead horse" when discussing an issue.

Returning to the dormitory project, the team is to be comprised of two members and one master black belt: Adam Johnson, Scott Widener, and Howard Gitlow, respectively. This information is summarized in Table 4.23.

TABLE 4.23   Composition of the Team

Role	Responsibility
Master Black Belt	Dr. Howard Gitlow
Champion	Dr. Paul Sugrue
Team Member	Scott Widener
Team Member	Adam Johnson

4.12 FINALIZE THE PROJECT OBJECTIVE

The next-to-last step in the Define Phase is to finalize the project objective. The project objective for the dormitory project is: "To create a high-class living facility that encourages learning and community (process) aimed at executives in residence, MBAs, as well as junior and senior undergraduate business students (market segments) to increase (direction) the number of on-campus residents (measure of success) by 200 students (target) by July 15, 2003 (deadline)."

4.13 CONDUCT TOLLGATE REVIEW

A master black belt establishes a schedule with deadlines for management and tollgate reviews of Six Sigma projects. There are four types of management reviews: daily, weekly, monthly, and tollgate reviews:

- **Daily** reviews are conducted by the team leader to assess and resolve problems with Six Sigma projects.

- **Weekly** meetings are held between the team members and their champion to resolve budget, resource, and scheduling issues; to evaluate project requests; and to remove barriers to the project.

- **Monthly** reviews are done by the top management of selected project teams to evaluate the status of projects, approve the scope of new projects, approve communications plans for lessons learned from projects, assess the risk for each project, and evaluate the quality management plan for each project.

- **Tollgate** reviews are conducted by the champion and process owner (of each project) after completion of each phase of the Six Sigma project.

4.14 DEFINE PHASE TOLLGATE REVIEW (CHECK SHEET)

The typical elements of a Define Phase tollgate review are as follows:

(1) Develop the Business Case

Dashboard completed. (Yes/No)

Project priority matrix completed. (Yes/No)

Answered partially redundant questions.

- Why do the highest priority project at all? (Good reason/Poor reason)

- Why do the highest priority project now? (Good reason/Poor reason)

- What are the consequences of not doing the highest priority project? (Listed Yes/No)

- What business objectives are supported by the highest priority project? (Listed Yes/No)

Opportunity statement completed. (Yes/No)

Project objective completed. (Yes/No)

Develop the project scope.

- Multi-Generation Product Plan (MGPP) completed. (Yes/No)

- Constraints (In-Scope and Out-of-Scope Elements) identified. (Yes/No)

Project plan (Gantt chart) completed. (Yes/No)

Document control system completed. (Yes/No)

(2) **Benefits of the Design for Six Sigma Project**

Soft benefits estimated. (Yes/No)

Hard benefits estimated. (Yes/No)

(3) **Assess the Risks to the Project's Success**

Risk elements identified. (Yes/No)

Risk reduction plan developed. (Yes/No)

(4) **DFSS Development Team (DT) Activated** **(Yes/No)**

(5) **Project Objective Finalized** **(Yes/No)**

(6) **Management and Tollgate Review Process Successful** **(Yes/No)**

4.15 KEY OUTPUTS OF THE DEFINE PHASE

The key outputs of the Define Phase are the inputs to the Measure Phase:

1. Project team [leader (BB or GB), members, champion, process owner, IT representative, finance representative].
2. Project business case.
3. Project objective.
4. Project plan (Gantt chart).
5. Document control system.
6. Risk reduction plan.

SUMMARY

This chapter discussed the Define Phase of a DMADV project. It was illustrated with a Six Sigma project concerning the design of a new on-campus dormitory at the University of Miami.

After reading this chapter, you will know how to:

- Develop a project plan.
- Document the control system for the project.
- Prepare a risk reduction plan for the project.
- Identify the process owner and champion.
- Select the project leader and members.
- Present or conduct a management or tollgate review.
- State the project objective.

Remember, all projects do not survive the Define Phase.

REFERENCES

1. H. Gitlow and D. Levine, *Six Sigma for Green Belts and Champions: Foundations, DMAIC, Tools and Methods, Cases and Certification* (Upper Saddle River, NJ: Financial Times Prentice Hall, 2005).

2. H. Gitlow, A. Oppenheim, R. Oppenheim, and D. Levine, *Quality Management*, 3rd ed. (New York, NY: McGraw-Hill-Irwin, 2005).

MEASURE PHASE

SECTIONS

LEARNING OBJECTIVES

After reading this chapter, you will be able to:

- Segment the market for an innovation.
- Survey each market segment using a Kano questionnaire.
- Identify the CTQs for the innovation in each market segment.

- Minimize the risks involved with the CTQs for the innovation.
- Consider the life-cycle issues for the innovation.
- Successfully pass a Measure Phase tollgate review.

INTRODUCTION

In the Measure Phase of a DMADV project, team members obtain a clear and concise understanding of the needs and wants of the market for a design. To understand the market for a design, team members segment the market and develop the CTQs for each segment. Once the CTQs are known, team members study the legal issues concerning the proposed design, assess the risks of the proposed design, and update the multigenerational plan developed in the Define Phase.

5.1 Steps of the Measure Phase

The Measure Phase has eleven steps:

1. Segmentation of the market and establishment of segmentation strategies.
2. Identify cognitive images using a Kano survey.
3. Convert cognitive images into CTQs using Quality Function Deployment.
4. Select final CTQs.
5. Develop and validate the measurement systems for each CTQ.
6. Develop a design scorecard.
7. Review intellectual property issues.
8. Develop a plan to manage risk among the CTQ characteristics from the customer and critical-to-process characteristics (CTPs) of the project (i.e., understand the conflicts between the requirements of the targeted "customer requirements," (CTQs) and the critical-to-process requirements (CTPs) of the project.
9. Revise the project objective, if necessary.
10. Revise the Multi-Generational Product Plan (MGPP), if necessary.
11. Passage through the Measure Phase tollgate review.

5.2 INPUTS TO THE MEASURE PHASE

There are several inputs to the Measure Phase:

- Project team [leader (BB or GB), members, champion, process owner, IT representative, finance representative].
- Project business case.
- Project objective.
- Project plan (e.g., Gantt chart with responsibilities and resources).
- Document control system.
- Risk reduction plan.

5.3 MARKET SEGMENTATION

Definition

Market segmentation is the process of dividing a market into homogeneous subsets of customers such that the customers in any subset will respond similarly to a marketing mix established for them and differently from the customers in another subset. A marketing mix is a combination of product, service, or process features; a price structure; a place (distribution) strategy; and a promotional strategy. For example, the market for soft drinks may be divided into several market segments. Two such segments are males 18–25 years old and females 50–65 years old. The male 18–25 years old segment may have a marketing mix that includes sales at a convenience store, while the marketing mix for the female 50–65 year old marketing mix might include sales in a supermarket. Market segmentation is extensively discussed in Chapter 14, "Articulating the Voice of the Stakeholder."

Dormitory Example. The Dean of the School of Business Administration identified three distinct market segments for the new business school housing construction. These market segments are: executives in residence, regular MBA students, and undergraduate business students.

Executives in Residence. The dormitory will have two floors dedicated to executives in residence. The Dean of the School of Business made this decision before the project began. Executives in residence are individuals who come to campus for one or two weeks to attend a concentrated class. They are a market segment that requires the amenities of a five-star hotel. Therefore, the marketing research effort for this segment focused on studying five-star hotels.

Regular MBA Students. It is proposed that the dormitory have two floors dedicated to regular Master of Business Administration (MBA) students. This is a diverse group. There is a lower age bound around 22 years old and an upper age bound around 45 to 50 years old. Many of the older students are also married with children. Currently, no regular MBA students live on campus, as no housing options are provided for them. However, over half of the regular MBA students are from outside the state of Florida, so they require local housing to attend classes. This segment presents a financially diverse group with some need-based financial aid, some merit-based scholarships, some receiving funding from their company, and others paying out of pocket.

Undergraduate Business Students. The undergraduate business students are more homogenous in respect to their age and marital status. The average age of full-time undergraduates is 20 years old, with only eight percent being above the age of 25, and most of these students are single. Over half of undergraduates are from outside the state of Florida, so they also require local housing. Current options on campus for the undergraduate students include: standard double rooms, suite-style double rooms, single rooms, and apartments. Five floors will be dedicated to undergraduate students. The Director of Residence Halls stated, "I have never had a student presented with the opportunity to live in a premium room be unable to find the money to pay for the room."

5.4 FINDING COGNITIVE IMAGES WITH KANO SURVEYS

Kano surveys embrace a set of market research tools used for three purposes:

1. To improve existing products, services, or processes or to create less expensive versions of existing products, services, or processes (called Level A surveys).
2. To create major new features for existing products, services, or processes (called Level B surveys).
3. To invent and innovate an entirely new product, service, or process (called Level C surveys). Kano surveys are extensively discussed in Reference 1 and Chapter 14.

Kano surveys are used to classify product, service, or process features into one of six categories.

One-Dimensional (O). User satisfaction is proportional to the performance of the feature; the less performance, the less user satisfaction, and the more performance, the more user satisfaction.

Must-Be (M). User satisfaction is not proportional to the performance of the feature; the less performance, the less user satisfaction to the feature, but high performance creates feelings of indifference to the feature.

Attractive (A). Again, user satisfaction is not proportional to the performance of the feature. However, in this case, low levels of performance create feelings of indifference to the feature, but high levels of performance create feelings of delight to the feature.

Reverse (R). The researcher's *a priori* judgment about the user's view of the feature is the opposite of the user's view.

Indifferent (I). The user is indifferent to the presence and absence of the feature.

Questionable (Q). The user indicates conflicting responses with respect to the feature. For example, the user desires that the feature is both present and absent.

Additionally, Kano surveys are used to determine how much regular users desire a new feature (cognitive image) by asking them what percentage increase in costs over current costs they would be willing to accept to have the new feature. There are three "tolerable cost increase" distributions in practice: uniform, triangular, and J-shaped.

Uniform distribution. The uniform distribution shows that 80% of a market segment will pay at least a 10% cost increase to obtain the feature described by the cognitive image under study. Cognitive images exhibiting this distribution can be used to develop ideas for completely new products.

Triangular distribution. The triangular distribution shows that 60% of a market segment will pay at least a 10% cost increase to obtain the product feature described by the cognitive image under study. Cognitive images exhibiting this distribution can be used to develop ideas for major new features of existing products.

J-shaped distribution. The J-shaped distribution shows that 10% of a market segment will only pay a 10% cost increase to obtain the product feature described by the cognitive image under study. Cognitive images exhibiting this distribution can be used to improve features of existing products.

Dormitory Example. Product development (PD) team members conducted a Kano survey to identify each cognitive image and its percentage increase in cost that is acceptable to each market segment. Figures 5.1 and 5.2 present the filtered, reduced set of cognitive images for the undergraduate and MBA market segments. For each market segment, the percentage increase in cost that is acceptable to consumers is shown as a horizontal bar. Please note the difference in the scale of the X-axis between Figures 5.1 and 5.2.

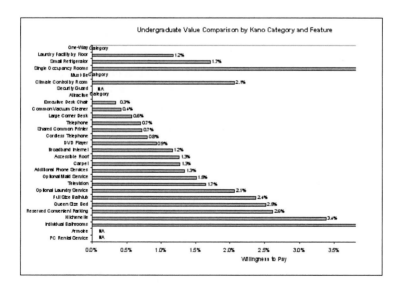

FIGURE 5.1 Undergraduate Filtered Features

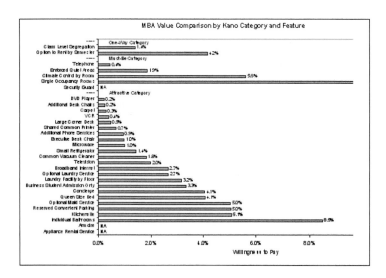

FIGURE 5.2   MBA Filtered Features

5.5 CONVERT COGNITIVE IMAGES INTO CTQS WITH QUALITY FUNCTION DEPLOYMENT

Introduction

Quality Function Deployment (QFD) is a method used to build the demands of customers into product and/or service features, characteristics, and specifications, as well as to select and develop process equipment, methods, and control systems. It is a series of matrices and charts that deploys customer's demands and technical requirements into critical-to-product, service, or process (CTP) characteristics, such as all phases of design, planning, production or service, and delivery. For example, QFD clarifies the relationships between the following dimensions:

1. Cognitive images and CTQs, called product planning.

2. CTQs and service steps and/or parts characteristics (CTPs), called parts deployment.

3. Service steps and/or parts characteristics (CTPs) and manufacturing operations (more detailed CTPs), called process planning.

4. Manufacturing operations (more detailed CTPs) and production requirements (even more detailed CTPs), called production planning.

The first QFD matrix (cognitive images by CTQs) is called the "House of Quality" (see Reference 2 and Table 5.1).

TABLE 5.1 House of Quality

CTQ A1
CTQ A2
CTQ A3
CTQ B1
CTQ B2
CTQ B3
CTQ B4
CTQ B5

Directional Objectives for CTQs

Kano Category

Tertiary Voice (cognitive image)

Secondary Voice (final focus point)

Primary Voice (initial focus point)

Segment Weights

Voice Segments

Voice Weights

Voice of the Stakeholder

Voice Sum
Voice %

Sum / %

CTQ A1 | CTQ A2 | CTQ A3 | CTQ A | CTQ B | CTQ B3 | CTQ B4 | CTQ B5

Importance Rating | Our Org. | Competitor A | Competitor B

Voice Sum
Voice %
CTQ Total
CTQ %
Target / Specification
Our Organization
Competitor A
Competitor B
Competitor C

1 2 3 4 5 6 7

Room 1 in the House of Quality

Room 1 is used to identify, list, and weight primary, secondary, and tertiary "Voice of the Stakeholder" data and benchmark data by stakeholder segment. Examples of stakeholder segments are:

- "Voice of the Customer" by market segment.
- "Voice of the Employee" by employee segment (top management, middle management, supervisors, employees).
- "Voice of the Investor" by investor segment.
- "Voice of the Supplier" by type of supplier.
- "Voice of the Sub-Contractor" by type of sub-contractor.
- "Voice of the Regulator" by regulator.
- "Voice of the Environment."
- "Voice of the Community."

First, team members list the cognitive images (features) for each stakeholder segment using a systematic (tree) diagram (primary voice, secondary voice, and tertiary cognitive image).

Dormitory Example. The rows of Room 1 (House of Quality) for the dormitory example are shown in the systematic diagram in Figure 5.3.

System	Component Level A	Component Level B	Component Level C	Feature or Service
Dormitory	Outside the Room	General	Occupancy	Single Occupancy Rooms
				Admissions for Business Students Only
				Segregate Residents by Class Level
			Control	Climate Control by Room
			Floor	Carpet
		Entertainment	Television	Television Unit
			Television Peripherals	DVD Player
				VCR
			Audible Communication	Telephone
				Cordless Telephone
				Additional Phone Services
	Inside the Room	Cleaning	Laundry	Laundry Facilities by Floor
				Optional Laundry Service
			Environment	Optional Maid Service
				Shared Common Vacuum Cleaner
		Common Area	Security	Security Guard
			Accessibles	Enforced Quiet Areas
				Accessible Roof

System	Component Level A	Component Level B	Component Level C	Feature or Service
Dormitory	Inside the Room	Office	Furniture	Large Corner Desk
				Executive Desk Chair
				Additional Desk Chairs
			Computer	Broadband Internet
				Personal Computer Rental Service
				Shared Common Printer
		Kitchen	Full Setup	Kitchenette
			Components	Microwave
				Small Refrigerator
				Appliance Rental Service
		Bathroom	Allocation	Individual Bathrooms
			Amenities	Full Size Bathtub
		Sleeping/ Living Room	Sleeping	Queen Size Bed
			Organizing	Armoire
		Other	Parking	Reserved Convenient Parking Place
			Administrative	Option to Rent by Semester
			Suggestive Advice	Concierge

FIGURE 5.3   Systematic Diagram of Cognitive Images for Dormitory Project

Second, team members identify the Kano category for each tertiary cognitive image. Third, team members weight each stakeholder segment on a 0.0 to 1.0 scale, such that the sum of the weights equals 1.00. Internal experts develop these weights based on revenue or other considerations. Fourth, team members establish 0.0 to 1.0 weights for the cognitive images within a stakeholder segment that sum to 1.0.

Parking Example. Table 5.2 shows an example of Room 1 (House of Quality) for the Parking Department at the University of Miami.

TABLE 5.2   Room 1 of the House of Quality for the Parking Example

Voice of the Stakeholder	Voice Weights	Voice Segments	Segment Weights	Primary Voice (initial focus point)	Secondary Voice (final focus point)	Tertiary Voice (cognitive image)	Kano Category
Students	0.60	Commuter	0.50	Riding shuttle bus is slow.	Shuttle bus can't guarantee on-time delivery.	Guaranteed arrival time at destination for shuttle bus service.	Attractive
		Sum					
		%					
		Residential	0.50				
		Sum					
		%					
	Voice Sum						
	Voice %						
Faculty and Administration	0.40	Faculty	.75				
		Sum					
		%					
		Admin.	.25				
		Sum					
		%					
	Voice Sum						
	Voice %						

Room 2 in the House of Quality

Room 2 compares your organization with best-in-class organizations with respect to each cognitive image. First, team members select a sample of stakeholders from each segment, administer a survey to the selected individuals or organizations in each segment using a rating scale for the importance of each cognitive image (1 = very unimportant, 3 = neutral, 5 = very important), and compute the average importance rating for each cognitive image for each stakeholder segment. Second, team members rate each competitor's performance on each cognitive image. Initially, team members list the "best of the competition" in the columns of Room 2 (list created by internal experts). "Best of the competition" organizations are market share leaders, innovative providers in respect to quality, cost, service, delivery, safety, environment, and more. Then, team members rate each "best competitor" on each cognitive image for each stakeholder segment. The same rating scale is used as the one in the stakeholder survey earlier. Third, team members compare and contrast all organizations on each cognitive image by stakeholder segment. Room 2 is not always appropriate in a House of Quality; for example, a new product, service, or process might not have any competition.

Table 5.3 shows Room 2 for the parking example.

TABLE 5.3 Room 2 of the Parking Example

Voice of the Stakeholder	Voice Weights	Voice Segments	Segment Weights	Primary Voice (initial focus point)	Secondary Voice (final focus point)	Tertiary Voice (cognitive image)	Kano Category	CTQ A			CTQ B					Importance Rating	Our Org.	Competitor A	Competitor B
								CTQ A1	CTQ A2	CTQ A3	CTQ B1	CTQ B2	CTQ B3	CTQ B4	CTQ B5				
				Riding shuttle bus is slow.	Shuttle bus can't guarantee on-time delivery.	Guaranteed 15-minute arrival time at destination for shuttle bus.										4.5	2.3	2.9	2.8
		Sum																	
		%																	

Voice of the Stakeholder	Voice Weights	Voice Segments	Segment Weights	Primary Voice (initial focus point)	Secondary Voice (final focus point)	Tertiary Voice (cognitive image)	Kano Category	CTQ A1	CTQ A2	CTQ A3	CTQ B1	CTQ B2	CTQ B3	CTQ B4	CTQ B5	Importance Rating	Our Org.	Competitor A	Competitor B
								CTQ A			CTQ B								
		Sum																	
		%																	
	Voice Sum																		
	Voice %																		
		Sum																	
		%																	
		Sum																	
		%																	
	Voice Sum																		
	Voice %																		

Room 3 in the House of Quality

Room 3 is used to translate each cognitive image into one or more product, service, or process CTQs. CTQs are identified using:

- Product, service, or process knowledge.
- Benchmark information.
- Data from existing QFD tables for similar designs.

Team members can ask: "How might we meet the need or want stated by this "Voice?" There are three basic types of relationships between cognitive images and CTQs:

- One cognitive image to one CTQ.
- One cognitive image to many CTQs.
- Many cognitive images to many CTQs.

Table 5.4 shows an example of each type of relationship.

TABLE 5.4 Examples of Relationships Among Cognitive Images and CTQs

Cognitive Image(s)	CTQ(s)
One-to-One Relationship	
Guaranteed on-time arrival at destination by shuttle bus.	Arrival at destination within 15 minutes of arrival to shuttle bus station (% of riders arriving at destination within 15 minutes of arrival to shuttle bus station).
One-to-Many Relationship	
Create a Visitor's Center in the Ponce de Leon parking garage.	CTQ1—Fifty additional parking spaces reserved for visitors (Y/N).
	CTQ2—Information Center to answer questions and provide directions (Y/N).
	CTQ3—Kiosk for bookstore (U of Miami paraphernalia) (Y/N).
	CTQ4—Kiosk for Admissions (U of Miami brochures and bulletins) (Y/N).
	CTQ5—Kiosk for food services (vending area) (Y/N).
	CTQ4—Shuttle car service for VIP visitors (Y/N).
Many-to-Many Relationship	
Cease using the services of a towing company. End the $80 towing fee.	Begin "booting" cars that were previously towed (Y/N).
	Charge a $50 booting fee (Y/N).

Room 3 encourages team members to ask the following set of questions about each CTQ, for each stakeholder segment:

- Can we measure this CTQ?

  If we can measure the CTQ, how will we measure it and how will we ensure data integrity? If there are different methods and people involved in collecting the measurements, can we perform a Gage R&R (i.e., a repeatability and reproducibility) study on this measure of how well we are achieving the CTQ requirement?

  Is this CTQ important to one or more stakeholder groups?

  Does it relate to one or more cognitive images?

Will improving this CTQ improve the product, service, or process?

Will the stakeholder pay to collect and analyze data on this CTQ?

- Is the CTQ easy to understand?

Can employees interpret the measurement associated with the CTQ?

Do employees understand why the CTQ is important to stakeholders?

- Does the CTQ have a direction?

Does the CTQ have a nominal value and specification limit(s)?

Does the CTQ assist in good, cost-effective, timely decision making?

Table 5.5 provides an example of Room 3 of the parking example.

TABLE 5.5 Room 3 of the Parking Example

Voice of the Stakeholder	Voice Weights	Voice Segments	Segment Weights	Primary Voice (initial focus point)	Secondary Voice (final focus point)	Tertiary Voice (cognitive image)	Kano Category	CTQ A Percentage of riders arriving at destination within 15 minutes of arrival to shuttle bus station.	CTQ B					
									CTQ B4	CTQ B5	Importance Rating	Our Org.	Competitor A	Competitor B
				Riding shuttle bus is slow.	Shuttle bus can't guarantee on-time delivery.	Guaranteed arrival time at destination for shuttle bus.	A				4.5	2.3	2.9	2.8
		Sum												
		%												
		Sum												
		%												
	Voice Sum													
	Voice %													

Room 4 in the House of Quality

Room 4 presents the relationships between the cognitive images in Room 1 and the CTQs in Room 3, and prioritizes the CTQs by stakeholder segment. A team of internal experts determines and presents the relationship between each cognitive image and CTQ using the following scale:

9 = strong relationship (positive or negative) between a cognitive image and a CTQ.

3 = moderate relationship (positive or negative) between a cognitive image and a CTQ.

1 = weak relationship (positive or negative) between a cognitive image and a CTQ.

0 = no relationship (blank cell) between a cognitive image and a CTQ.

It is important for the internal experts to document the logic for the cell relationship values. If this is not done, the entire analysis may collapse under scrutiny by management.

Room 4 employs the following procedure to prioritize the CTQs. First, team members calculate each weighted cell value by multiplying each cell relationship value by its appropriate row importance rating. Second, they compute the column totals for each stakeholder segment by adding the weighted cell values down the column for each CTQ. Third, team members compute the weighted column total for each CTQ overall stakeholder segment by multiplying the segment weight by the segment column total for each CTQ and summing over all segments. Fourth, team members calculate the relative percentage for each CTQ by dividing the weighted value of each CTQ overall segment by the total of all of the weighted values for all CTQs overall segment. Finally, team members study the empty rows and/or columns of Room 4. An empty row indicates a stakeholder voice that is not being serviced by any CTQ. This represents the opportunity to fill an unmet stakeholder need or want. An empty column indicates a CTQ that is not related to any stakeholder need or want. This represents an opportunity to eliminate an unnecessary CTQ.

Table 5.6 presents Room 4 of the parking example.

TABLE 5.6 Room 4 of the Parking Example

Voice Segments	Segment Weights	Primary Voice (initial focus point)	Secondary Voice (final focus point)	Tertiary Voice (cognitive image)	Kano Category	% of riders arriving at destination within 15 minutes of arrival at shuttle bus.	Fifty additional parking spaces in the parking garage.	Importance Rating
				Guaranteed on-time delivery.	A	9 (40.5)	3 (13.5)	4.5
						3 (11.1)	1 (3.7)	3.7
						0 (0)	0 (0)	2.9
						1 (3.5)	0 (0)	3.5
						0 (0)	0 (0)	3.1
						0 (0)	9 (42.3)	4.7
	Sum					55.1	59.5	
	%					0.48	0.52	
	Sum							
	%							

Room 5 in the House of Quality

Room 5 is used to compare your organization with the best-in-class organizations with respect to each CTQ (use internal experts and benchmarking to make the comparisons). It helps to uncover perceptual problems with your product, service, or process, rather than technical problems. Room 5 assumes that there is a benchmark product, service, or process. However, if no benchmark exists, as in the case of a new invention, then Room 5 is vacant. For example, RFID is a device that allows wireless identification of objects implanted in patients to track that their medications are appropriately applied, allergies are known, etc. If no one else uses RFID technology, then there is no benchmark.

Room 5 involves team members assessing the perceived or actual performance of your organization and best-in-class competitors for each CTQ. A "best" competitor is a market share leader, an innovator, or a channel captain. Internal experts use a 1 to 5 scale to score the performance of your product, service, or process using benchmark data. Additionally, the internal experts use another 1 to 5 scale to score the performance of your best-in-class competitor's products, services, or processes using benchmark data. Frequently, team members only benchmark 50% of all CTQs.

In the parking example, Room 5 shows that CTQ_{A2}, CTQ_{B2}, and CTQ_{B5} present potential perceptual and/or competitive problems because your organization has a lower rating than all 3 competitors (see Table 5.7).

TABLE 5.7   Room 5 of the Parking Example

Voice of the Stakeholder	Voice Weights	Voice Segments	Segment Weights	Primary Voice (initial focus point)	Secondary Voice (final focus point)	Tertiary Voice (cognitive image)	Kano Category	CTQ A			CTQ B				
								CTQ A1	CTQ A2	CTQ A3	CTQ B1	CTQ B2	CTQ B3	CTQ B4	CTQ B5
CTQ Total															
CTQ %															
Target/Specification				**ROOM 6**											
Your Organization								4	3	3	5	3	2	2	4
Competitor A								3	4	2	5	5	3	3	5
Competitor B								2	5	1	5	5	2	3	5
Competitor C								5	5	5	5	5	4	2	5

Room 6 in the House of Quality

Room 6 is used to set target (nominal values) and specification limits for each CTQ (see Table 5.1). Team members establish targets (nominal values) and specification limits for each CTQ using product, service, or process knowledge and technical expertise. Team members should not set specifications just to meet the performance levels of best-in-class competitors. Rather, they should be set to surpass the needs and want of relevant stakeholder segments.

Some Six Sigma professionals define CTQs as specifications and others define CTQs as general needs with specifications identified later. For example, a "quiet" riding car may be the CTQ or having ambient noise measured at less than 70 dB at highway speed may be the way the CTQ is defined.

Targets (nominal values) identify the ideal level of performance necessary to satisfy stakeholders, overall or by stakeholder segment. Targets define what the organization wants to do with respect to the product, service, or process. They are based on stakeholder needs and wants, not on company constraints. Targets are set to achieve a desired level of stakeholder perception of our product, service, or process; they are not set on current or projected process capability.

Specification limits are developed by determining the minimum (LSL = Lower Specification Limit) and/or maximum (USL = Upper Specification Limit) level of performance that will satisfy the customer. They identify the performance at which a product, service, or process is deemed nonconforming. Recall, this is called the "goal post" view of quality.

A one-sided specification limit is an upper or lower boundary on the acceptable performance of a quality characteristic (CTQ or CTP). In its simplest form, it is determined by constructing a questionnaire, as is shown in Table 5.8. This table shows how to identify the upper specification limit for acceptable waiting time in a hospital clinic from the perspective of patients.

TABLE 5.8 Questionnaire for Constructing a One-Sided Specification Limit for Waiting Time in a Hospital Clinic

Waiting Time	Very Satisfied (1)	Satisfied (2)	Neutral (3)	Dissatisfied (4)	Very Dissatisfied (5)
00<15 min.					
15<30 min.					
30<45 min.					
45<60 min.					
60<75 min.					
75 + min.					

Team members select a sample of patients waiting for service and administer the questionnaire in Table 5.8. The results of the survey are shown in Table 5.9.

TABLE 5.9 Survey Results for a Sample of 100 Patients Concerning Acceptable Patient Waiting Time

Waiting Time	Very Satisfied (1)	Satisfied (2)	Neutral (3)	Dissatisfied (4)	Very Dissatisfied (5)
00<15 min.	100	0	0	0	0
15<30 min.	95	5	0	0	0
30<45 min.	25	50	25	0	0
45<60 min.	0	0	0	75	25
60<75 min.	0	0	0	0	100
75 + min.	0	0	0	0	100

Figure 5.4 shows a bar chart of the percentage "Very Satisfied" versus "Waiting Time." The bar chart shows that an upper specification limit of 30 minutes is acceptable, if a 5% not "Very Satisfied" rating is acceptable (USL = 30). Consequently, if a 5% not "Very Satisfied" rating is not acceptable, the upper specification limit is 15 minutes (USL = 15).

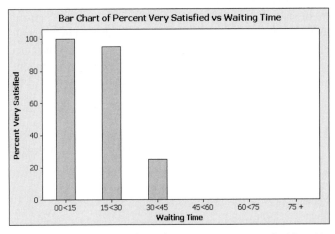

FIGURE 5.4 Minitab Bar Chart of Percentage Very Satisfied by Waiting Time

A two-sided specification limit is an upper and lower boundary on the acceptable performance of a quality characteristic (CTQ or CTP). In its simplest form, it is determined by constructing a questionnaire, as is shown in Table 5.10. This table shows how to identify the upper and lower specification limits for acceptable waiting times for the delivery of perishable materials.

TABLE 5.10 Questionnaire for Constructing a Two-Sided Specification Limit for Waiting Time for Perishable Materials

Waiting Time	Very Satisfied (1)	Satisfied (2)	Neutral (3)	Dissatisfied (4)	Very Dissatisfied (5)
4 days early					
3 days early					
2 days early					
1 day early					
On time					
1 day late					
2 days late					
3 days late					
4 days late					

Team members select a sample of patients waiting for perishable materials and administer the questionnaire shown in Table 5.10. The results are shown in Table 5.11.

TABLE 5.11 Survey Results for a Sample of 100 Customers Concerning Acceptable Waiting Time for Perishable Materials

Waiting Time	Very Satisfied (1)	Satisfied (2)	Neutral (3)	Dissatisfied (4)	Very Dissatisfied (5)
4 days early	0	0	0	0	100
3 days early	0	25	50	25	0
2 days early	60	40	0	0	0
1 day early	98	2	0	0	0
On time	100	0	0	0	0
1 day late	95	5	0	0	0
2 days late	50	50	0	0	0
3 days late	0	25	50	25	0
4 days late	0	0	0	0	100

The bar chart in Figure 5.5 indicates that 1 day early is the LSL and 1 day late is the USL on number of days a delivery can be off target before there is serious erosion in the level of customer dissatisfaction. A stricter interpretation may indicate that only on-time delivery (0 days early or late) is acceptable to customers. The specification depends on what the company is trying to achieve with the product, service, or process.

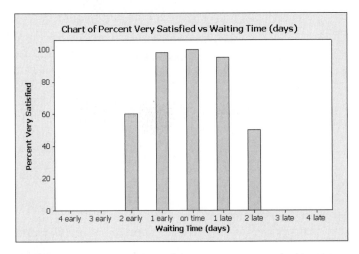

FIGURE 5.5   Minitab Bar Chart of Percentage Very Satisfied by Waiting Time for Perishable Materials

Room 7 in the House of Quality

Team members use Room 7 to quantify and study the relationships among the CTQs and to create tradeoffs among the CTQs (see Table 5.12).

First, internal experts establish the directional goals for each CTQ (see the "Directional Objectives for CTQs" row in Table 5.12), using the following scale:

(+) = customer satisfaction increases as we increase this CTQ.

(0) = customer satisfaction increases as we get closer to target for this CTQ.

(−) = customer satisfaction increases as we decrease this CTQ.

Second, internal experts state the strength of the relationship between CTQ pairs in the triangular portion of Table 5.12 using the following scale:

(++) = strong positive relationship between a pair of CTQs.

(+) = moderate positive relationship between a pair of CTQs.

(−) = moderate negative relationship between a pair of CTQs.

(− −) = strong negative relationship between a pair of CTQs.

TABLE 5.12 Generic Room 7

	c1	c2	c3	c4	c5	c6	c7
CTQ A1							
CTQ A2							
CTQ A3		− −					
CTQ B1			+				
CTQ B2							
CTQ B3	++						
CTQ B4			− −		+		
CTQ B5						++	
Directional Objectives for CTQs	+	−	0	−	0	−	−	+

								CTQ A			CTQ B								
Voice of the Stakeholder	Voice Weights	Voice Segments	Segment Weights	Primary Voice (initial focus point)	Secondary Voice (final focus point)	Tertiary Voice (cognitive image)	Kano Category	CTQ A1	CTQ A2	CTQ A3	CTQ B1	CTQ B2	CTQ B3	CTQ B4	CTQ B5	Importance Rating	Our Org.	Competitor A	Competitor B

Third, internal experts define tradeoffs between negatively related CTQs. This requires much time and thought to satisfy the conflicting needs and wants expressed by the CTQs. Customer's needs and wants, not organizational constraints, should be considered when creating tradeoffs between negatively related CTQs. For example, "speed of service" and "maintenance of service area" are negatively related. Increasing "speed of service" causes additional cost in "maintenance of service area." TRIZ is a helpful methodology for resolving such tradeoffs (contradictions). TRIZ is discussed in detail in Chapter 15, "Enhancing Creativity to Develop Alternative Designs."

Deploying Stakeholder Voices Beyond CTQs. Team members deploy the various "Voices of Stakeholders" beyond the CTQs into product parts or service steps, manufacturing or delivery operations, and production or service requirements. The construction of a cascading set of QFD matrices entails a significant amount of effort (see Table 5.13). It is important that the effort be justified by financial or customer satisfaction benefits.

TABLE 5.13 Cascading QFD Matrices

Dormitory Example. Tables 5.14 through 5.16 show excerpts from the QFDs in which one-to-one relationships dominated between the rows, or cognitive images, and the columns, or features. These strong one-to-one relationships between the cognitive images and the features occur because the cognitive images are the features needed to fulfill customer requirements. For example, the cognitive image associated with providing each room with individual climate controls requires rooms to be built with individual climate controls. This structure caused the features, now classified as CTQs, to be "present or not present" variables.

TABLE 5.14 Undergraduate QFD

	Features Used to Respond to Cognitive Images								
Customer Requirements	Single Occupancy Rooms	Individual Bathrooms	Queen-Size Bed	Broadband Internett	Television Unit	...	Reserved Convenient Parking	Armoire	Importance
Single Occupancy Rooms	9	9	0	0	0	...	1	1	4.28
Individual Bathrooms	9	9	0	0	0	...	0	0	4.61
Queen-Size Bed	3	0	9	0	0	...	0	0	4.50
Broadband Internet	0	0	0	9	1	...	0	0	4.42
Television Unit	0	0	0	1	9	...	0	3	4.40
Telephone Unit	0	0	0	3	0	...	0	0	3.92
Cordless Telephone Unit	0	0	0	0	0	...	0	0	4.00
Additional Phone Services	0	0	0	1	0	...	0	0	4.42
PC Rental Service	0	0	0	1	0	...	0	0	3.39
Shared Common Printer	0	0	0	0	0	...	0	0	4.15
Large Corner Desk	3	0	0	0	0	...	0	0	4.21
Executive Desk Chair	1	0	0	0	0	...	0	0	4.15
Climate Control by Room	0	0	0	0	0	...	0	0	4.33
Full-Size Bathtub	3	9	0	0	0	...	0	0	4.00
Small Refrigerator	0	0	0	0	0	...	0	0	3.90
Kitchenette	0	0	0	0	0	...	0	0	4.33
DVD Player	0	0	0	1	0	...	0	1	4.26
Carpet	0	0	0	0	0	...	0	0	3.56
Common Vacuum Cleaner	0	0	0	0	0	...	0	0	4.14
Accessible Roof	0	0	0	0	0	...	0	0	4.55
Security Guard	3	1	0	0	1	...	1	0	3.84
Laundry Facility by Floor	0	0	0	0	0	...	0	0	4.52
Optional Laundry Service	0	0	0	0	0	...	0	0	4.20
Optional Maid Service	1	1	0	0	0	...	0	0	4.11
Reserved Convenient Parking	0	0	0	0	0	...	9	0	4.57
Armoire	3	0	0	0	3	...	0	9	4.53
Unnormalized Weights	151.53	123.97	40.50	68.00	61.45	...	49.24	62.52	1779.46
Normalized Weights	8.52%	6.97%	2.28%	3.82%	3.45%	...	2.77%	3.51%	100.00%

TABLE 5.15   Graduate/MBA QFD

Features Used to Respond to Cognitive Images

Customer Requirements	Single Occupancy Rooms	Individual Bathrooms	Queen-Size Bed	Broadband Internet	Television Unit	...	Class-Level Segregation	Armoire	Option to Rent by Semester	Importance
Single Occupancy Rooms	9	9	0	0	0	...	0	1	3	4.30
Individual Bathrooms	9	9	0	0	0	...	0	0	1	4.56
Queen-Size Bed	3	0	9	0	0	...	0	0	0	4.33
Broadband Internet	0	0	0	9	1	...	0	0	0	4.58
Television Unit	0	0	0	1	9	...	0	3	0	4.50
Telephone Unit	0	0	0	3	0	...	0	0	0	4.12
Additional Phone Services	0	0	0	1	0	...	0	0	0	4.31
Shared Common Printer	0	0	0	0	0	...	0	0	0	4.19
Large Corner Desk	3	0	0	0	0	...	0	0	0	4.50
Executive Desk Chair	1	0	0	0	0	...	0	0	0	4.69
Additional Desk Chairs	1	0	0	0	0	...	0	3	0	3.81
Climate Control by Room	0	0	0	0	0	...	0	0	0	4.33
Microwave	0	0	0	0	0	...	0	0	0	4.29
Small Refrigerator	0	0	0	0	0	...	0	0	0	4.81
Kitchenette	0	0	0	0	0	...	0	0	0	4.38
Appliance Rental Service	0	0	0	0	0	...	0	0	0	3.60
VCR	0	0	0	3	0	...	0	3	0	4.24
DVD Player	0	0	0	1	0	...	0	1	0	4.71
Carpet	0	0	0	0	0	...	0	0	0	4.00
Enforced Quiet Areas	3	0	0	0	1	...	3	0	0	3.92
Common Vacuum Cleaner	0	0	0	0	0	...	0	0	0	3.92
Security Guard	3	1	0	0	1	...	0	0	0	4.16
Laundry Facility by Floor	0	0	0	0	0	...	1	0	0	4.04
Optional Laundry Service	0	0	0	0	0	...	0	0	3	3.85
Optional Maid Service	1	1	0	0	0	...	0	0	3	3.65
Concierge	0	0	0	0	0	...	1	1	3	3.88
Reserved Convenient Parking	0	0	0	0	0	...	1	0	0	4.57
Business Student Admission Only	0	0	0	0	0	...	1	3	1	3.83
Class-Level Segregation	1	0	0	0	0	...	9	0	0	4.13
Armoire	3	0	0	0	3	...	0	9	0	4.27
Option to Rent by Semester	1	0	0	0	0	...	0	0	9	4.48
Unnormalized Weights	164.11	87.60	39.00	79.85	66.67	...	65.26	100.70	95.75	2432.83
Normalized Weights	6.75%	3.60%	1.60%	3.28%	2.74%	...	2.68%	4.14%	3.94%	100.00%

TABLE 5.16 Overall QFD

	Features Used to Respond to Cognitive Images									
Customer Requirements	**Single Occupancy Rooms**	**Individual Bathrooms**	**Queen-Size Bed**	**Broadband Internett**	**Television Unit**	**. . .**	**Class-Level Segregation**	**Armoire**	**Option to Rent by Semester**	**Importance**
Single Occupancy Rooms	9	9	0	0	0	...	0	1	3	4.29
Individual Bathrooms	9	9	0	0	0	...	0	0	1	4.60
Queen-Size Bed	3	0	9	0	0	...	0	0	0	4.45
Broadband Internet	0	0	0	9	1	...	0	0	0	4.48
Television Unit	0	0	0	1	9	...	0	3	0	4.44
Telephone Unit	0	0	0	3	0	...	0	0	0	4.00
Cordless Telephone Unit	0	0	0	0	0	...	0	0	0	3.96
Additional Phone Services	0	0	0	1	0	...	0	0	0	4.39
PC Rental Service	0	0	0	1	0	...	0	0	0	3.43
Shared Common Printer	0	0	0	0	0	...	0	0	0	4.16
Large Corner Desk	3	0	0	0	0	...	0	0	0	4.32
Executive Desk Chair	1	0	0	0	0	...	0	0	0	4.36
Additional Desk Chairs	1	0	0	0	0	...	0	3	0	3.82
Climate Control by Room	0	0	0	0	0	...	0	0	0	4.34
Full-Size Bathtub	3	9	0	0	0	...	0	0	0	3.99
...	...	...	...	...	...	...	...	...	...	...
Accessible Roof	0	0	0	0	0	...	1	0	0	4.20
Security Guard	3	1	0	0	1	...	0	0	0	3.96
Laundry Facility by Floor	0	0	0	0	0	...	1	0	0	4.34
Optional Laundry Service	0	0	0	0	0	...	0	0	3	4.07
Optional Maid Service	1	1	0	0	0	...	0	0	3	3.94
Concierge	0	0	0	0	0	...	1	1	3	3.90
Reserved Convenient Parking	0	0	0	0	0	...	1	0	0	4.57
Business Student Admission Only	0	0	0	0	0	...	1	3	1	3.47
Class-Level Segregation	1	0	0	0	0	...	9	0	0	3.22
Armoire	3	0	0	0	3	...	0	9	0	4.45
Option to Rent by Semester	1	0	0	0	0	...	0	0	9	4.25
Unnormalized Weights	173.36	123.72	40.01	80.95	65.21	...	59.83	99.81	94.92	2684.77
Normalized Weights	6.46%	4.61%	1.49%	3.02%	2.43%	...	2.23%	3.72%	3.54%	100.00%

Table 5.14 indicates that Single Occupancy rooms are very important to the undergraduate business student stakeholder group. This is evidenced by the high normalized weight in the Single Occupancy Room column. This is an interesting result considering students ranked Individual Bathrooms higher when asked specifically about the features one at a time. This may result from the fact that when undergraduates think of a single occupancy room, they assume that it will have a separate bathroom.

Table 5.15 shows that, much like the undergraduate business students, the graduate business student stakeholder group's satisfaction hinges on the inclusion of Single Occupancy Rooms more than the other features.

Table 5.16 is the composite results of all stakeholder groups surveyed. There is a slight discrepancy between Tables 5.14 and 5.15, and Table 5.16. One and a half percent of the respondents did not answer the question on academic level. Consequently, these respondents were not included in Tables 5.14 and 5.15, but were included in Table 5.16. The implications of these results are further illustrated in the Analyze Phase.

5.6 SELECT FINAL SET OF CTQS

Team members select the final set of CTQs to be designed into the product, service, or process. These decisions require a benefit/cost analysis of each cognitive feature.

5.7 DEVELOP AND VALIDATE A MEASUREMENT SYSTEM FOR THE CTQS

Construct Operational Definitions for CTQs

Background

An **operational definition** promotes understanding between people by putting communicable meaning into words. Operational definitions are required to give communicable meaning to terms such as: late, clean, good, red, round, 15 minutes, or 3:00 P.M.

An operational definition contains three parts: a criterion to be applied to an object or group, a test of the object or group, and a decision as to whether the object or group met the criterion.

1. **Criteria**—Operational definitions establish "Voice of the Process" language for each CTQ and "Voice of the Customer" specifications for each CTQ.

2. **Test**—A test involves comparing "Voice of the Process" data with "Voice of the Customer" specifications for each CTQ, for a given unit of output.

3. **Decision**—A decision involves making a determination whether a given unit of output meets "Voice of the Customer" specifications.

Problems, such as endless bickering and ill will, can arise from the lack of an operational definition. A definition is operational if all relevant users of the definition agree on the definition.

Effect of No Operational Definition

The supervisor in charge of the Customer Complaint Department in a large chain of national retail stores was asked for a definition of a customer complaint. He stated that a customer complaint is the result of an unsatisfactory experience between a customer and the retail store. He also said, "The Customer Complaint Department has 5 employees. Each one has more than 15 years of experience on the job. They know a customer complaint when they see one."

A test was conducted to determine if the definition of a customer complaint was consistent among all 5 employees. In the test, 10 customer interactions were videotaped and each videotape was assigned a unique number between 0 and 9. Each of the employees was shown each videotape in random order and asked to determine which customer interactions exhibited complaints (see Table 5.17).

TABLE 5.17 Identification of Complaints on 10 Customer Interactions

	Employee				
Customer Interaction	**A**	**B**	**C**	**D**	**E**
1	0	1	1	1	0
2	0	1	1	0	0
3	1	1	1	1	0
4	1	1	1	0	0
5	0	1	1	1	0
6	0	1	1	0	0
7	1	1	1	1	0
8	1	1	1	0	0
9	0	1	1	1	0
10	0	1	1	0	0

Legend: 0 = No customer complaint in video. 1 = Customer complaint in video.

Although Employees B and C always agree, they always disagree with Employee E. Employee A agrees with Employees B and C forty percent of the time, with Employee E sixty percent of the time, and with Employee D fifty percent of the time. Employee D agrees with Employees B, C, and E fifty percent of the time.

The preceding example shows that the absence of an operational definition can create problems and confusion. The manager of the Customer Complaint Department (process owner) and employees have no consistent concept of their jobs.

Examples of an Operational Definition

Example 1. Mary lends Susan her coat for a vacation. Mary requests that the coat be returned clean. Clean is the CTQ. In Mary's opinion, Susan returns it dirty. Is there a problem?

Yes! What is it? The problem is failing to operationally define clean. Mary and Susan have different definitions of clean. Failing to operationally define terms can lead to problems.

A possible operational definition of a clean coat is that Susan will get the coat dry cleaned before returning it to Mary. This is an acceptable definition if both parties agree on the definition. This operational definition is shown next:

Criteria:	The coat is dry cleaned and returned to Mary.
Test:	Mary determines if the coat was dry cleaned.
Decision:	If the coat was dry cleaned, Mary accepts the coat. If the coat was not dry cleaned, Mary does not accept the coat.

From past experience, Mary knows that coats get stained on vacation and that dry cleaning may not be able to remove a stain. Consequently, the preceding operational definition is not acceptable to Mary. Susan thinks dry cleaning is sufficient to clean a coat and feels the preceding operational definition is acceptable. Because Mary and Susan cannot agree on the meaning of clean, Mary should not lend Susan the coat.

An operational definition of clean that is acceptable to Mary is shown next:

Criteria:	The coat is returned. The dry cleaned coat is clean to Mary's satisfaction or Susan must replace the coat, no questions asked.
Test:	Mary examines the dry cleaned coat.
Decision:	Mary states the coat is clean and accepts the coat. Or, Mary states the coat is not clean and Susan must replace the coat.

Susan doesn't find this definition of clean acceptable. The moral is: Don't lend things to people who don't accept your "Voice of the Stakeholder."

Example 2. An operational definition of a customer satisfied with certain aspects of service in a restaurant is shown next:

Criteria:	A customer in a restaurant is considered satisfied with certain aspects of service if the answers to *all* of the following questions are yes:

1. Was your waiting time to make a reservation less than 15 seconds?   (Y/N)
2. Was your reservation honored within 60 seconds of your arrival to the restaurant?   (Y/N)
3. Were any errors made during your time in the restaurant?   (Y/N)
4. Was your waiting time for your bill less than 120 seconds?   (Y/N)
5. Was your bill accurate?   (Y/N)
6. Was your gratuity made clear on your credit card receipt?   (Y/N)

Test:	Select a particular customer and ask the preceding six questions.
Decision:	If the answer to all of the questions is Yes, then the customer is a satisfied customer. If the answer to any of the questions is No, then the customer is a dissatisfied customer.

Example 3. An operational definition of the maid service in a hotel established the following operational definition for a clean shower drain in guest rooms:

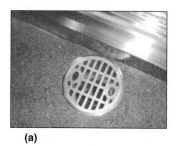 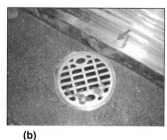

(a)   **(b)**

FIGURE 5.6   Operational Definition of a Clean Shower Drain

Criteria:	A shower drain is clean if it looks like the drain in Photo A in Figure 5.6 and is not clean if it looks like the drain in Photo B in Figure 5.6.
Test:	Select a particular shower drain and compare it to Figures 5.6a and 5.6b.
Decision:	If the selected shower drain looks like Figure 5.6a, then it is a clean drain. If the selected shower drain looks like Figure 5.6b, then it is not a clean drain.

Example 4. An operational definition of "concierge service" in the dormitory example is shown next:

Criteria:	An attendant in a lobby is providing "concierge service" if he or she provides at least one of the following services:
	1. Makes reservations at local restaurants.
	2. Makes reservations at local events.
	3. Provides advice on local activities.
	4. Takes messages.
	5. Accepts packages.

6. Provides liaison services between residents and local
   merchants.

Test:	Examine the job description of the attendant in the dormitory.
Decision:	If the attendant in the dormitory provides at least one of the preceding services to residents, then he or she is providing "concierge service." If the attendant in the dormitory does not provide at least one of the preceding services to residents, then he or she is not providing "concierge service."

Establish the Validity of the Measurement System for Each CTQ

Questions to Ask About a Measurement System

Process owners should ask themselves the following questions to better understand the capability of the measurement system for a particular CTQ to deliver the information needed for making decisions. Validity means that the measurements gathered reflect the "right" operational definitions represented in the project. You need to know if the measurements that will be used to monitor the product, service, and processes are as follows:

1. **Timely**—Are you able to detect changes as they occur?

2. **Accurate**—Does the average of the measurements represent the "true" representation of what is happening?

3. **Repeatability**—If the same person were to measure the same products, services, or processes at two different instances of time, would they yield the same measurements, assuming there was no change?

4. **Reproducibility**—If different people were to measure the same products, services, or processes at the same time without collaborating, would they yield the same measurements?

5. Do the methods of collecting the measurements match your need to know what is happening with the products, services, or processes?

6. Do the processes of data entry, transfer (e.g., between one computer application and another), processing of the data, and extraction of the data change the reliability of the data in any way (e.g., rounding of significant digits in the data, transcription errors, etc.)?

7. Are our methods reliable in that the measurement process is expected to maintain itself in a state of statistical control?

8. Can the measurement system be improved in the future?

The validity of a measurement system can be determined through designed studies, statistical analysis, and data integrity audits. For instance, the answers to questions 1, 5, and 6 are answered through system audits. The answer to question 2 is found through calibration and linearity studies. The answers to questions 3 and 4 are often determined through Gage R&R studies, which are designed studies conducted to measure the variation due to repeatability and reproducibility. Question 7 is only answered over time through the use of statistical tools such as run charts and control charts [see Reference 1]. In particular, the statistical tools needed to determine the validity of a measurement system are illustrated in this chapter using Minitab and JMP statistical software. These tools are discussed in depth in Chapters 9 through 11. Appendices at the end of Chapters 9 through 11 illustrate how to use Minitab and JMP with each of these statistical tools. The appendices at the end of this chapter show how to use Minitab and JMP for Gage R&R studies.

Measurement system design includes who will be responsible, what will be measured, when will it be measured, why is it being measured, how will the measurement process be monitored and improved if necessary, and where will the measurement data be hosted (i.e., which system(s) will hold the information), along with how will it be accessed.

Terminology. There are several terms and concepts that must be formally defined to discuss variation in a product, service, or process due to the measurement system (see Figure 5.7). In practice, additional sources such as data changes due to transcription, transfer between systems, and the methods of extraction or extrapolation of the data are sources of measurement error. This section does not address these concerns. Data integration and access is often a reason why data are not used because the data are not easily retrieved, interpreted, or well managed.

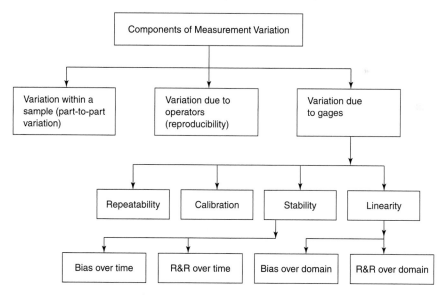

FIGURE 5.7 Components of Measurement Variation

1. **Part-to-part variation** is the variability created by the measurement of multiple parts per unit under identical conditions (e.g., same server, same store in chain). The ideal measurement system has 100% of variability due to part-to-part variation.

2. **Reproducibility** (e.g., variation due to servers) is the variability created by multiple conditions such as multiple operators or labs.

3. **Variation due to gages** is the variability created by repeatability, calibration, stability, and linearity.

     a. **Repeatability** (or precision) is the variability created by multiple measurements of the same unit under identical conditions (e.g., same server, same store in chain). This is called within group variation, or common variation.

     b. **Calibration** is the adjustment of a measurement instrument to eliminate bias. It is important that adjustment of a measurement instrument is not overreactive to noise in the system. For example, if a marksman adjusts his rifle sight every time he shoots by how far he is off target, as opposed to shooting six shots and adjusting the sight by how far the average of the six points is off the target, he will increase the variation of the shots from the target.

     c. **Stability** (or drift) is a change in the accuracy (bias), repeatability (precision), or reproducibility of a measurement system when measuring the same part for a single characteristic over time. **Bias over time (accuracy)** is the difference between the observed process average and a reference value over time.

     d. **Linearity** is the difference (bias) between the part reference value and the part average over the different values of the domain of the gage. **Bias over domain (accuracy)** is the difference between the observed process average and a reference value over the domain of a gage. An example of a linearity issue occurs when reading an automobile speedometer. If the speedometer has a 10% error rate, then the error of measurement in a school zone (20 mph with an error rate of 2 mph) is different than the error of measurement at highway speeds (70 mph with an error rate of 7 mph). If a constant error of measurement over the domain of a measurement system is desired, then different measurement instruments should be used at different speeds.

4. **Percent R&R** is the percentage of the process variation due to the repeatability and reproducibility of the measurement system. Percent tolerance is the percentage of the part tolerance due to the repeatability and reproducibility of the measurement system.

5. **Resolution** (discrimination or number of distinct categories) is the fineness of the measurement system (meters, centimeters, millimeters, etc.). At a minimum, the measurement system must be able to distinguish between excellent, good, fair, and poor units (four categories). Some researchers require at least 7 to 10 categories if the data represented is continuous. A gage scale (measurement tool) should be able to divide the tolerance (USL − LSL) into at least 10 parts measurable by significant digits. For example, a 12-inch ruler marked in whole inches yields 2 significant digits to the left of the decimal point and 1 doubtful digit to the right of the decimal point (10.7 inches yields 2 significant digits (1 and 0) and 1 doubtful digit (7)). If this is a sufficient resolution, then you can continue. If it is not, then the gage (measurement tool) is inadequate, and it must be replaced or fixed.

A sign of inadequate discrimination for a measurement system of a continuous variable is when a range chart (*R*-chart) exhibits three or fewer values within the control limits, or when the range chart exhibits four values within the control limits and more than 25% of the ranges are zero.

Variation due to the measurement process must be separated from variation due to the actual process to address variation due to the process.

Measurement System Studies

Measurement system studies are used to calculate the capability of a measurement system. There are three component parts to a measurement system study: (1) Measurement system analysis (MSA) checklist, (2) Test-retest study, and (3) Gage R&R study.

Measurement System Analysis Checklist. A **measurement system analysis checklist** involves determining whether the following tasks have been completed:

1. Description of the ideal measurement system (flowchart the process).
2. Description of the actual measurement system (flowchart the process).
3. Identification of the causes of the differences between the ideal and actual measurement systems.
4. Identification of the accuracy (bias) and precision (repeatability) of the measurement system using a test-retest study (see page 140).
5. Estimation of the proportion of observed variation due to unit-to-unit variation and R&R variation using a Gage R&R study (see page 142). R&R variation includes repeatability (e.g., within person variation), reproducibility (e.g., between person variation), and operator-part interaction (e.g., different people measure different units in different ways). A common rule of practice that has developed over the years is:

   - If R&R variation < 10% of observed total variation, then the measurement system is acceptable. R&R variation is called study variation in Minitab, but this is a misnomer because R&R variation is based on the standard deviation, not the variance. Because the variance is the square of standard deviation, then an R&R variation of 10% is equivalent to an R&R variance (called R&R contribution in Minitab) of 1%.

   - If $10\% \leq$ R&R variation < 30% of observed total variation, then the measurement system is borderline acceptable (acceptability depends on the situation). Alternatively, R&R variance is marginal between 1% (0.10^2) and 10% (approximately 0.30^2).

   - If R&R variation $\geq$ 30% of observed total variation, then the measurement system is unacceptable. Alternatively, R&R variance greater than 10% (approximately 0.30^2) is unacceptable.

Test-Retest Study. **Test-retest studies** are performed by repeatedly measuring the same item under the same conditions, operator, inspector, gage, location, etc. A general rule is to collect at least 20 observations and to calculate the mean and standard deviation of the repeated measurements. The resulting statistics are analyzed as follows:

1. If (standard deviation < [1/10] × Tolerance), then the measurement system has acceptable precision or repeatability. If (standard deviation ≥ [1/10] × Tolerance), then the measurement system has unacceptable precision or repeatability. In the later case, the measurement system must be improved or replaced before baseline data can be collected for a Six Sigma project.

2. A "**standard unit**" or reference value is required to determine the bias in a measurement system. Bias = (Standard value – Mean value). Without a "standard unit," it is impossible to determine the accuracy of the measurement system.

A test-retest study was conducted on a caliper (measuring device) used to test body fat content of a patient in a weight-loss clinic on a "standard unit" that is 40 centimeters thick. The allowable tolerance [(USL – Mean) and/or (Mean – LSL)] of the measurement system is 10 centimeters (± 5 centimeters). One hundred repeated measurements (across the rows of Table 5.18) were taken under the same conditions.

TABLE 5.18   100 Repeated Measurements on a Standard Unit

41	38	41	39	40	38	40	40	40	39
38	39	42	40	37	38	37	41	42	41
40	40	37	38	38	40	43	39	41	41
38	42	41	43	40	39	39	40	38	38
39	40	39	43	42	42	40	42	40	40
40	38	40	37	39	41	41	38	39	41
39	41	42	39	38	40	38	39	43	39
41	39	42	38	38	38	43	41	39	39
39	41	40	39	40	41	39	41	41	40
39	42	39	40	41	40	40	39	41	38

 THICKNESS

An I-MR chart of the 100 measurements using Minitab and JMP revealed a stable system of measurements (no trends or drifts in the measurement system over time) (see Figures 5.8 and 5.9).

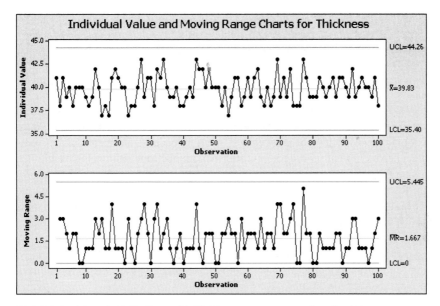

FIGURE 5.8 Minitab I-MR Chart of 100 Measurements on a Standard Unit

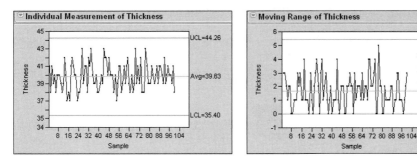

FIGURE 5.9 JMP I-MR Chart of 100 Measurements on a Standard Unit

A basic descriptive statistical analysis of the 100 measurements on a standard unit revealed a mean of 39.8 and a standard deviation of approximately 1.5 ($\overline{R}/d_2 = 1.667/1.128$). The following conclusions can be made from the test-retest study:

1. The measurement system is stable and predictable into the near future.
2. The standard deviation > [1/10] × Tolerance (1.5 > [1/10] × 10). Hence, the measurement system exhibits unacceptable precision.
3. The bias of the measurement system (Bias = Standard value – Mean value) = (40.0 – 39.8) = 0.2. If the bias remains constant over time, 0.2 should be added to all future measurements.

Conduct a Gage R&R Study. A **Gage R&R study** is used to estimate the proportion of observed total variation due to unit-to-unit variation and R&R variation. R&R variation includes repeatability, reproducibility, and operator-part interaction (different people measure different units in different ways). If R&R variation is large relative to unit-to-unit variation, then the measurement system must be improved before collecting data.

The data required by a Gage R&R study should be collected so that it represents the full range of conditions experienced by the measurement system. For example, the most senior individual and the most junior individual should repeatedly measure each item selected in the study. The data should be collected in random order to prevent individuals from influencing each other.

An example of a Gage R&R study follows. Two psychologists independently score a subjective psychological test to measure the assertiveness for each of five patients four separate times. This results in 40 measurements. The data to be collected by the two psychologists is shown in Table 5.19. Table 5.19 presents the "standard order," or the logical pattern, for the data to be collected by the psychologists.

Table 5.20 shows the random order used by the psychologists to collect the data required for the measurement study. Random order is important because it removes any problems induced by the structure of the standard order. Table 5.20 is an instruction sheet to the psychologists actually collecting the data.

TABLE 5.19 Standard Order for Collecting Data for the Gage R&R Study

Row	Patient	Psychologist	Measurement
1	1	Enya	To be collected
2	1	Enya	To be collected
3	1	Enya	To be collected
4	1	Enya	To be collected
5	1	Lucy	To be collected
6	1	Lucy	To be collected
7	1	Lucy	To be collected
8	1	Lucy	To be collected
9	2	Enya	To be collected
10	2	Enya	To be collected
11	2	Enya	To be collected
12	2	Enya	To be collected
13	2	Lucy	To be collected
14	2	Lucy	To be collected
15	2	Lucy	To be collected
16	2	Lucy	To be collected
17	3	Enya	To be collected
18	3	Enya	To be collected
19	3	Enya	To be collected
20	3	Enya	To be collected
21	3	Lucy	To be collected
22	3	Lucy	To be collected
23	3	Lucy	To be collected
24	3	Lucy	To be collected
25	4	Enya	To be collected

Row	Patient	Psychologist	Measurement
26	4	Enya	To be collected
27	4	Enya	To be collected
28	4	Enya	To be collected
29	4	Lucy	To be collected
30	4	Lucy	To be collected
31	4	Lucy	To be collected
32	4	Lucy	To be collected
33	5	Enya	To be collected
34	5	Enya	To be collected
35	5	Enya	To be collected
36	5	Enya	To be collected
37	5	Lucy	To be collected
38	5	Lucy	To be collected
39	5	Lucy	To be collected
40	5	Lucy	To be collected

TABLE 5.20 Random Order for Collecting Data for the Gage R&R Study

Random Order	Standard Order	Patient	Psychologist
1	36	5	Enya
2	5	1	Lucy
3	30	4	Lucy
4	29	4	Lucy
5	26	4	Enya
6	28	4	Enya
7	6	1	Lucy
8	8	1	Lucy
9	4	1	Enya
10	3	1	Enya
11	18	3	Enya
12	20	3	Enya
13	40	5	Lucy
14	9	2	Enya
15	31	4	Lucy
16	24	3	Lucy
17	38	5	Lucy
18	17	3	Enya
19	32	4	Lucy
20	11	2	Enya
21	27	4	Enya
22	19	3	Enya
23	10	2	Enya
24	33	5	Enya
25	37	5	Lucy
26	2	1	Enya
27	35	5	Enya
28	23	3	Lucy

(continued)

TABLE 5.20 Random Order for Collecting Data for the Gage R&R Study (Continued)

Random Order	Standard Order	Patient	Psychologist
28	23	3	Lucy
29	13	2	Lucy
30	7	1	Lucy
31	15	2	Lucy
32	22	3	Lucy
33	14	2	Lucy
34	34	5	Enya
35	1	1	Enya
36	12	2	Enya
37	16	2	Lucy
38	39	5	Lucy
39	21	3	Lucy
40	25	4	Enya

Table 5.21 shows the data collected in the Gage R&R study in random order.

TABLE 5.21 Data for Gage R&R Study

Random Order	Standard Order	Patient	Psychologist	Assertiveness Score
1	36	5	Enya	21.85
2	5	1	Lucy	21.19
3	30	4	Lucy	23.14
4	29	4	Lucy	23.09
5	26	4	Enya	23.28
6	28	4	Enya	23.23
7	6	1	Lucy	21.29
8	8	1	Lucy	21.24
9	4	1	Enya	21.24
10	3	1	Enya	21.33
11	18	3	Enya	22.28
12	20	3	Enya	22.34
13	40	5	Lucy	21.78
14	9	2	Enya	21.65
15	31	4	Lucy	23.02
16	24	3	Lucy	22.17
17	38	5	Lucy	21.84
18	17	3	Enya	22.31
19	32	4	Lucy	23.19
20	11	2	Enya	21.67
21	27	4	Enya	23.24
22	19	3	Enya	22.31
23	10	2	Enya	21.60
24	33	5	Enya	21.84
25	37	5	Lucy	21.76
26	2	1	Enya	21.29

Random Order	Standard Order	Patient	Psychologist	Assertiveness Score
27	35	5	Enya	21.93
28	23	3	Lucy	22.14
29	13	2	Lucy	21.50
30	7	1	Lucy	21.21
31	15	2	Lucy	21.51
32	22	3	Lucy	22.23
33	14	2	Lucy	21.55
34	34	5	Enya	21.89
35	1	1	Enya	21.34
36	12	2	Enya	21.56
37	16	2	Lucy	21.55
38	39	5	Lucy	21.81
39	21	3	Lucy	22.18
40	25	4	Enya	23.27

GAGER&R1

A visual analysis of the data in Table 5.21 using a Gage R&R run chart from Minitab revealed the results shown in Figure 5.10. In Figure 5.10, each dot represents Enya's measurements, and each square represents Lucy's measurements. Multiple measurements by each inspector are connected with lines. Good repeatability is demonstrated by the low variation in the squares connected by lines and the dots connected by lines, for each unit. Figure 5.10 indicates that repeatability (within group variation) is good. Good reproducibility is demonstrated by the similarity of the squares connected by lines and the dots connected by lines, for each unit. Reproducibility (one form of between group variation) is good. The Gage R&R run chart in Figure 5.10 shows that most of the observed total variation in assertiveness scores is due to differences between patients.

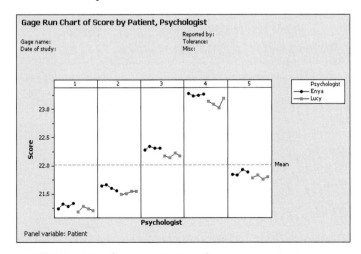

FIGURE 5.10 Minitab Gage R&R Run Chart

A statistical analysis using the Two-Way ANOVA method (see Section 10.2) of the data in Table 5.20 using a Gage R&R study (crossed) from Minitab yielded the results in Figure 5.11.

```
Two-Way ANOVA Table With Interaction

Source                 DF      SS       MS       F       P
Patient                 4  17.6209  4.40522  2005.79  0.000
Psychologist            1   0.1061  0.10609    48.31  0.002
Patient * Psychologist  4   0.0088  0.00220     1.23  0.319
Repeatability          30   0.0536  0.00179
Total                  39  17.7894
```

FIGURE 5.11   Minitab Gage R&R Study of Assertiveness Scores

Variation under identical conditions (same gage, inspector, and lab)—called within group variation, common variation, or repeatability—is used to test for the statistical significance of the part-to-part and reproducibility variance components. If it turns out the part-to-part variation is small relative to the repeatability component of variation, then the Gage R&R will be high relative to the part-to-part variation indicating that either the measurement system is poor or that the parts were chosen to be too close in measurement value to each other to distinguish them from each other. If the latter is the case, then the design of the measurement study (e.g., selection of the specific parts) is poor.

Figure 5.11 provides the following insights into the "goodness" of the measurement system. First, patient-to-patient variation accounts for most of the observed total variation (p-value[1] = 0.0001). This is a strong indicator of a good measurement system. Second, inspector-to-inspector (psychologist-to-psychologist) variation (gage-to-gage or lab-to-lab, called reproducibility) is a small, but a statistically significant, portion of the observed total variation (p-value = 0.002). Third, inspector * unit (psychologist * patient) variation is a small and not a statistically significant portion of the observed total variation (p-value = 0.319). This indicates that psychologists consistently apply inspection methods over different patients.

If the measurement system exhibits a low Gage R&R component of variation, it does not necessarily indicate a good measurement system. Why? If the tolerance range of the specifications [(USL – Mean) and/or (Mean – LSL)] is such that the measurement system cannot distinguish good from bad, then the measurement system is not capable of making decisions.

Figure 5.12 combines repeatability variation and inspector * unit variation because inspector * unit variation is not statistically significant. Again, part-to-part variation and inspector variation are statistically significant.

```
Two-Way ANOVA Table Without Interaction

Source         DF      SS       MS       F       P
Patient         4  17.6209  4.40522  2400.86  0.000
Psychologist    1   0.1061  0.10609    57.82  0.000
Repeatability  34   0.0624  0.00183
Total          39  17.7894
```

FIGURE 5.12   Minitab Two-Way ANOVA Table Without Interaction

---

[1] A ***p*-value** is a measure of the statistical significance of a population parameter(s) being studied using a hypothesis test. Smaller p-values are associated with greater statistical significance. Common values for considering a test statistically significant occur when a p-value is less than 0.05 or 0.01.

Figure 5.13 shows that the total effect of repeatability and reproducibility on the measurement system is 11.24% (see Total Gage R&R % Study Var in Figure 5.13). This indicates a marginal measurement system because Gage R&R variation is between 10% and 30% of total variation.

Additional indications of a good measurement system are as follows:

1. Part-to-part variation, as opposed to repeatability variation and reproducibility variation, is a large proportion of the observed total variation. The relative contributions to the observed total variation of the part-to-part variation, repeatability variation, and reproducibility variation are identified on a bar chart.

2. Inspectors (psychologists) assign the same measure to the same unit, in repeated measurements of the unit. This is called reproducibility. Reproducibility is identified by a stable R chart, where a subgroup contains the repeated measurements for a given unit and inspector.

```
Gage R&R

                                 %Contribution
Source              VarComp      (of VarComp)
Total Gage R&R      0.007048            1.26
  Repeatability     0.001835            0.33
  Reproducibility   0.005213            0.94
    Psychologist    0.005213            0.94
Part-To-Part        0.550423           98.74
Total Variation     0.557471          100.00


                                 Study Var   %Study Var
Source              StdDev (SD)   (6 * SD)      (%SV)
Total Gage R&R      0.083950       0.50370      11.24
  Repeatability     0.042835       0.25701       5.74
  Reproducibility   0.072199       0.43320       9.67
    Psychologist    0.072199       0.43320       9.67
Part-To-Part        0.741905       4.45143      99.37
Total Variation     0.746640       4.47984     100.00


Number of Distinct Categories = 12
```

FIGURE 5.13 Gage R&R Contribution to Observed Total Variation

3. Small ranges in the subgroups based on the repeated measurements for a given unit and inspector yield an $\bar{X}$ chart with extremely narrow control limits. If $\bar{R}$ is small, then the control limits will be narrow. Narrow control limits cause the subgroup averages on the $\bar{X}$ chart to be out of control. If the $\bar{X}$s are out of control, this indicates the major component of observed total variation is part-to part variation, not repeatability variation or reproducibility variation.

4. A run chart in which the subgroups are composed of all the repeated measurements for all inspectors by unit shows very little variation in the distribution of individual measurements by subgroup. However, the $\bar{X}$ for each subgroup can be very different from each other. This indicates large part-to-part variation.

5. A dot plot of all the repeated measurements for all units by inspector shows similar distributions of measurements for each inspector.

6. If the $\bar{X}$ charts for each inspector show parallel lines over all units, then most of the observed total variation is due to part-to-part variation.

Figure 5.14 shows the preceding additional analysis for the assertiveness scoring system. The left side of Figure 5.14 reveals that:

1. Part-to-part variation, as opposed to repeatability variation and reproducibility variation, is a large proportion of the observed total variation (see the Components of Variation panel in Figure 5.14). This is an indicator of a good measurement system.
2. Reproducibility exists when inspectors (psychologists) assign the same measurement to the same unit, in repeated measurements of the unit. Reproducibility is identified by a stable R chart of the range between the repeated measurements for each unit by each inspector (see the R Chart by Psychologist panel in Figure 5.14). The stable R chart is an indication of a good measurement system.

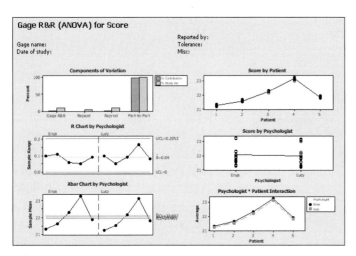

FIGURE 5.14   Minitab Gage R&R Study

3. Part-to-part variation is a large proportion of observed total variation, as opposed to repeatability variation or reproducibility variation, if the $\bar{X}$ chart by unit (patient) by inspector (psychologist) indicates many points beyond the control limits (see the $\bar{X}$ Chart by Psychologist panel in Figure 5.14). This is an indicator of a good measurement system because the major source of variation is unit to unit.

The right side of Figure 5.14 shows that:

1. Part-to-part variation is a large proportion of observed total variation, as opposed to repeatability variation or reproducibility variation, if the distribution of assertiveness scores by patient is very tight. In other words, most of the variation is due to patient-to-patient variation, not between psychologists (repeatability) or within a psychologist (reproducibility) (see the Score By Patient panel in Figure 5.14). This chart indicates a good measurement system.

2. Repeatability variation is a small proportion of observed total variation, as opposed to Part-to-part variation or Reproducibility variation, if the distributions of assertiveness scores by inspector (psychologists) are the same. The distributions of assertiveness scores are very similar by psychologist (see the Score By Psychologist panel in Figure 5.14). This is an indication of a good measurement system.

3. A low interaction between inspectors and units is indicated by parallel lines on the lower-right panel. Crossing lines indicate that inspector's ratings are dependent on the unit being inspected. This chart shows parallel lines—hence, no inspector-unit interaction (see the Psychologist * Patient Interaction panel in Figure 5.14). This is an indication of a good measurement system.

In conclusion, the assertiveness scoring system is adequate for the collection of baseline data.

5.8 DEVELOP A DESIGN SCORECARD

The purpose of a design scorecard is to formally state critical parameters (CTQs, Part Features (CTPs), etc.) in the Voice of the Customer and the Predicted Voice of the Process (see Table 5.22). This helps team members:

- Establish nominal values and specification limits for each CTQ, as well as the target for the process sigma (Part A of the scorecard).
- Predict output of the Voice of the Process with respect to stability, shape, mean, and standard deviation, as well as DPU and predicted process sigma (Part B of the scorecard).
- Highlight problems and risks of CTQs with respect to failure to meet desired process sigma levels.
- Track CTQs throughout the entire life of the product, service, or process.

TABLE 5.22   Generic Design Scorecard

Scorecard—Part A (Voice of the Customer)					Scorecard—Part B (Predicted Voice of the Process)					
CTQ	Target (Nominal)	LSL	USL	Sigma Target	Stable (Y/N)	Shape	Mean	Standard Deviation	DPU	Predicted Process Sigma

5.9 REVIEW INTELLECTUAL PROPERTY ISSUES

An **agreement** is a statement of the terms agreed upon by two or more entities. With respect to intellectual property, the terms generally focus on the control and ownership of intellectual property.

A **trademark** is a unique name or design that is used to distinguish a particular product or service from other products or services. If an entity (individual or organization) fails to properly apply a trademark, it can result in the loss of brand identity; for example, Kleenex, Corn Flakes, Cellophane, Nylon, and Aspirin are a few cases of lost brand identity.

A **patent** in the United States is a contract between the federal government and an inventor (individual or organization), such that the United States federal government grants the inventor the right to exclude others from making, using, or selling the invention, for a finite period of time, in exchange for the inventor teaching the public how to utilize the invention. Patents are important because they:

- Provide legal protection for an invention.
- Provide exclusive rights to an invention.
- Block competitors from benefiting from an invention.
- Obtain the maximum return for the research and development investment for the patent holder.
- Enable inventive entities to learn from the work of other inventive entities.
- Enable inventive entities to identify potential competitors.
- Enable inventive entities to identify potential strategic alliances.

It is critically important that team members seek the counsel of a competent patent attorney and/or trademark attorney. Patent law is a specialized area of the law with its own bar examination.

Dormitory Example. The dormitory example required study of intellectual property with respect to construction procedures, materials, and design similarities to the works of other architects. No conflicts or problems surfaced.

5.10 PLAN TO MANAGE THE RISK

Team members input the CTQs and CTPs into a **Failure Modes and Effects Analysis (FMEA)**. Recall from the Define Phase that FMEA is a tool used to identify, estimate, prioritize, and reduce the risk of failure in CTQs and CTPs through the development of risk abatement and contingency plans. Some Six Sigma experts consider managing risk part of the Analyze Phase of the DMADV model.

5.11 REVISE THE PROJECT OBJECTIVE, IF NECESSARY

PDT members update the project objective at this point based on any new information that has come to light due to the Measure Phase of the DMADV model.

5.12 UPDATE THE MULTI-GENERATIONAL PRODUCT PLAN (MGPP)

Recall that the Multi-Generational Product Plan (MGPP) is used to view the "entire picture of a project." It does not concern itself with details, but rather addresses the more significant strategic and tactical issues. The following questions are useful to determine if PDT members need to update the MGPP:

- Has scope creep created an unmanageable project from a manageable project? If no, fine. If yes, the scope of the project and its future implications must be reviewed and studied by product development team (PDT) members, the champion, and the process owner.

- Are PDT members making decisions that are compatible with future generations of the product, service, or process? If yes, fine. If no, PDT members must do a benefit/cost analysis of the future ramifications of their current design decisions.

- Have PDT members added new ideas generated during the course of the project to a list of future modifications? If yes, fine. If no, PDT members must justify their rationale for increasing the development time for the first generation.

5.13 CONDUCT TOLLGATE REVIEW (CHECK SHEET)

The typical elements of a Measure Phase tollgate review are as follows:

Markets Successfully Segmented   **(Yes/No)**

Market Strategy Selected   **(Differentiated/Undifferentiated/Concentrated)**

Type of Kano Survey Selected   **(Level A/Level B/Level C)**

If Level B Survey:

Step 1 – Selected an innovation as the subject of a DFSS project   (Yes/No)
and segmented the market for it.

Step 2 – Identified lead users and heavy users in each market segment.   (Yes/No)

Step 3 – Collected "VoU" and "VoC" data concerning circumstantial   (Yes/No)
issues from each market segment.

Step 4 – Classified "VoU" and "VoC" data as circumstantial or   (Yes/No)
product-related data in each market segment.

Step 5 – Determined the critical circumstantial issues to regular users   (Yes/No)
in each market segment.

Step 6 – Determined the focus point for each circumstantial   (Yes/No)
issue in each market segment.

Step 7 – Developed cognitive images for each focus point in each   (Yes/No)
market segment.

Step 8 – Classified cognitive images by Kano category and cost   (Yes/No)
distribution in each market segment.

Step 9 – Developed strategic themes for each cognitive image   (Yes/No)
for selected market segments.

If Level C Survey (Entirely New Designs):

Step 1 – Determined an aspect of people's behavior that will create new   (Yes/No)
product opportunities, which are congruent with the organization identity.

Step 2 – Conducted a survey of *opinion* leaders in the selected market   (Yes/No)
segment to collect "Voice of the People (VoP) data about the
behavior of interest.

Step 3 – Classified Voice of the People data as circumstantial issues   (Yes/No)
or product-related issues.

Step 4 – Used an affinity diagram to determine the underlying latent   (Yes/No)
categories of circumstantial issues.

Step 5 – Determined the focus point for each circumstantial issue.   (Yes/No)

Step 6 – Developed cognitive images for each focus point.   (Yes/No)

Step 7 – Classified each cognitive image into a Kano category and cost distribution.	(Yes/No)
Step 8 – Developed strategic themes.	(Yes/No)

Convert Cognitive Images into CTQs Using QFD

Room 1 completed.	(Yes/No)
Room 2 completed.	(Yes/No)
Room 3 completed.	(Yes/No)
Room 4 completed.	(Yes/No)
Room 5 completed.	(Yes/No)
Room 6 completed.	(Yes/No)
Room 7 completed.	(Yes/No)
Selected final set CTQs.	(Yes/No)
Developed a measurement system for each CTQ.	(Yes/No)
Validated the measurement system for each CTQ.	
Operational definition created for each CTQ.	(Yes/No)
Measurement system analysis for each CTQ.	(Yes/No)

Developed a Design Scorecard	**(Yes/No)**
Reviewed Intellectual Property Issues	**(Yes/No)**
Developed a Plan to Manage the Risk	
FMEA completed.	(Yes/No)
Contingency plans completed.	(Yes/No)
Revised the Objective, if Necessary	**(Yes/No)**
Update the MGPP, if Necessary	**(Yes/No)**
Pass Measure Phase Tollgate Review	**(Yes/No)**

5.14 OUTPUTS OF THE MEASURE PHASE

The outputs from the Measure Phase are as follows:

- Prioritized list of CTQs, part features (CTPs), etc. with plans to manage risk through contingency planning.
- Nominal values and specification limits for each CTQ, part feature (CTP), etc.
- Design scorecard for CTQs, part features (CTPs), etc.
- Report on the status of existing patents and trademarks.

SUMMARY

This chapter explained how to segment the marketplace for an innovation; survey each market segment using a Kano questionnaire; identify the CTQs for the innovation in each market segment using QFD; minimize the risks involved with the CTQs for the innovation; consider the life-cycle and legal issues for the innovation; and successfully pass a Measure Phase tollgate review. The work done in the Measure Phase pays large dividends as a DMADV project progresses into the Analyze Phase, where a high-level design is created for the innovation under study.

REFERENCES

1. H. Gitlow and D. Levine, *Six Sigma for Green Belts and Champions* (Upper Saddle River, NJ: Financial Times Prentice Hall, 2005).
2. J. Hauser and D. Clausing, "House of Quality," *Harvard Business Review*, May/June 1988, pp. 63–73.

A P P E N D I X   5.1

USING MINITAB FOR GAGE R&R STUDIES

Before using Minitab for the gage studies done in this chapter, refer to the Introduction to Minitab in Appendix 9.1.

Generating a Gage Run Chart

To generate the gage run chart in Figure 5.10 on page 145, open the **GAGER&R1. MTW** worksheet.

Select **Stat → Quality Tools → Gage Study → Gage Run Chart**. Then do the following:

1. In the Gage Run Chart dialog box (see Figure A5.1), enter **Patient** or **C3** in the Part numbers: edit box, **Psychologist** or **C4** in the Operators: edit box, and **Score** or **C5** in the Measurement data: edit box.

2. Click the **OK** button.

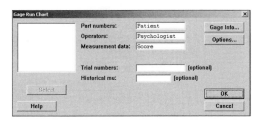

FIGURE A5.1 Minitab Gage Run Chart Dialog Box

Generating a Gage R&R Study (Crossed)

To generate the Gage R&R study (crossed) in Figures 5.11–5.14 on pages 146–148, open the **GAGER&R1** worksheet.

Select **Stat → Quality Tools → Gage Study → Gage R&R Study** (**Crossed**). Then do the following:

1. In the Gage R&R Study (Crossed) dialog box (see Figure A5.2), enter **Patient** or **C3** in the Part numbers: edit box, **Psychologist** or **C4** in the Operators: edit box, and **Score** or **C5** in the Measurement data: edit box. Under Method of Analysis, select the **ANOVA** option button.

2. Click the **OK** button.

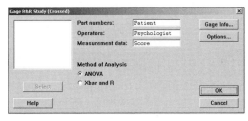

FIGURE A5.2 Minitab Gage R&R Study (Crossed) Dialog Box

APPENDIX 5.2

USING JMP FOR GAGE R&R STUDIES

Before using JMP for the gage studies done in this chapter, refer to the Introduction to JMP in Appendix 9.2.

To generate the Gage R&R study (see Figure A5.4), open the **GAGER&R1.JMP** data table.

1. Select **Graph → Variability/Gage Chart** (see Figure A5.3). Enter **Score** in the Y,Response edit box. Enter **Psychologist** in the X,Grouping edit box. Then enter **Patient** in the X,Grouping edit box. Click the **OK** button.

Analysis of Variance

Source	DF	SS	Mean Square	F Ratio	Prob > F
Psychologist	1	0.10609	0.10609	48.31	0.0023
Patient	4	17.62089	4.40522	2005.79	<.0001
Psychologist*Patient	4	0.008785	0.0022	1.23	0.3194
Within	30	0.0536	0.00179		
Total	39	17.78936	0.45614		

Variance Components

Component	Var Component	% of Total	20 40 60 80	Sqrt(Var Comp)
Psychologist	0.00519469	0.9318		0.07207
Patient	0.55037813	98.7		0.74187
Psychologist*Patient	0.00010240	0.0184		0.01012
Within	0.00178667	0.3205		0.04227
Total	0.55746188	100.0		0.74663

FIGURE A5.4   JMP Gage R&R Study Results

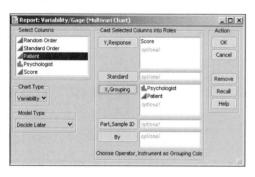

FIGURE A5.3   JMP Variability/Gage Dialog Box

2. Click the red triangle to the left of Variability Gage. Select **Variance Components**. In the JMP: Variability Model dialog box, select the **Crossed** button. Click the **OK** button.

ANALYZE PHASE

SECTIONS

LEARNING OBJECTIVES

After reading this chapter, you will know how to:

- Use de Bono's thinking habits and several of his thinking tools, TRIZ, and benchmarking to generate alternative high-level design concepts for the CTQs and CTPs.
- Investigate the alternative design concepts using a Pugh Matrix.
- Reduce the set of potential design concepts using FMEA, Hazard Analysis, or a risk abatement plan.

- Optimize the Total Life Cycle Cost of the best design.
- Develop a process model for the best design.
- Develop a discrete event simulation for the best design, if appropriate.
- Prepare design scorecards for the best design.
- Pass an Analyze Phase tollgate review.

INTRODUCTION

PD team members use the Analyze Phase of the DMADV model to generate and investigate alternative high-level design concepts for the critical parameters (CTQs and/or CTPs), with nominal values and tolerances, developed in the Measure Phase. Further, the set of alternative designs are compared and studied to identify the best design to move forward into the Design Phase of the DMADV model.

6.1 STEPS OF THE ANALYZE PHASE

The Analyze Phase has five steps:

1. Generate alternative high-level design concepts for each CTQ and high-level CTP.
2. Reduce the number of alternative high-level design concepts for each CTQ and high-level CTP.
3. Combine the best parts of the remaining design concepts to create two or three composite best design concepts for each CTQ and high-level CTP.
4. Study the resulting composite design concepts.
5. Select the best design concept for each CTQ and high-level CTP.

The first step of the Analyze Phase is to generate high-level design concept(s) for each critical parameter (CTQ and/or CTP). This requires that team members:

- Determine the level of difficulty of generating the design concept.
- Use creative methods to generate alternative design concepts, if appropriate.
- Employ the theory of inventive problem solving (called TRIZ), which utilizes physics, chemistry, and mathematics to generate alternative design concepts, if appropriate.
- Use any other methods to generate alternative design concepts, if appropriate.

The second step is to screen each critical parameter for every design concept to reduce the set of potential design concepts. Design concepts are screened using the following procedure:

- The team members select viable design concepts for each critical parameter.
- The team members develop high-level designs for two or three of the viable design concepts.
- The team members assess the risks relating to the "best high-level" design concepts.
- The team members conduct a risk/hazard analysis (hazards and harms) for the "best high-level" design concepts using one or more of the following techniques:
  - FMEA
  - Hazard Analysis
  - Fault Tree Analysis (FTA)
  - Basic Reliability Concepts to quantify the risks on a FTA
- The team members optimize the Total Life Cycle Costs for the "best high-level" design concepts.
- The team members develop a process model (e.g., flowchart, blueprint, etc.) of the "best high-level" design concepts.
- The team members perform a discrete event simulation of the "best high-level" design to study its performance, if appropriate.

The third step is to combine the best aspects of all the design concepts to create a limited set of potential high-level design concepts. The fourth step is to study the resulting potential high-level design concepts. The fifth step is to select the "best-fit" design concept for each critical parameter.

Dormitory Example. The aim of the Analyze Phase in the dormitory example is to develop several high-level dormitory design concepts for the School of Business Administration. In addition to this, risk assessments will be prepared for each design. Usually, nominal values are established for all CTQs and high-level CTPs; however, in this case, all the CTQs and high-level CTPs are either present or absent. For example, "inclusion of a kitchenette in a dormitory room" is either present or absent. Consequently, the nominal values are the "present" or "absent" targets. However, these are binary indicators, and as such, there is no variation or tolerance around them.

6.2 INPUTS OF THE ANALYZE PHASE

The Analyze Phase requires four inputs. They are as follows:

- Prioritized list of CTQs, part features, service steps (high-level CTPs), etc.
- Nominal values and specification limits for CTQs, part features, service steps (high-level CTPs), etc.

- Design scorecard for CTQs, part features, service steps (high-level CTPs), etc.

- Report on the status of existing patents and trademarks.

6.3 GENERATE HIGH-LEVEL DESIGN CONCEPTS FOR CRITICAL PARAMETERS

Effort Level Needed to Create Design Concepts

Product Development team members identify the level of effort required in design concept generation to understand time frames and resources required by the project. The effort required for design concept generation ranges from simple, fairly obvious solutions to an entirely new discovery and ensuing invention.

Simple, fairly obvious design concepts that require absolutely no invention require PD team members to expend the least design effort. These design efforts utilize existing and well-known design concepts with no "wrinkles" to the design concept. The original design concept is being tailored to a current need, and is not changed in any significant way. The PD team members can generate a design concept using personal knowledge and common sense. An example of this type of design effort is designing a water heater that answers the following question: "What size water heater should be installed at 155 Main Street, Minneapolis, MN?"

System modifications or small improvements, with no invention, require slightly more effort on the part of PD team members in generating a design concept. These design efforts require a minor modification (twist) of an existing design concept. An off-the-shelf design concept does not exist; the original design concept is being improved and slightly changed. These design concepts have contradictions that require tradeoffs and compromises between the components of the design concept. The PD team members must study dozens of design concept variants within their discipline to generate a design concept for the critical parameter. An example of this type of design effort is designing a water heater that answers the following question: "What size water heater should be installed at 155 Main Street, Minneapolis, MN, if the salinity of the water being heated is 150% above average?"

An inventive design concept or a major change to an existing design concept (invention within the current paradigm) requires more effort on the part of PD team members in generating a design concept. These designs require a major change to an existing design concept because a well-known available design concept does not exist. Design concept contradictions do exist and require tradeoffs and compromises between the components of the design concept. Designers must study hundreds of design concept variants inside and outside of their discipline to generate a design concept for the critical parameter. An example of this type of design effort is designing a water heater that answers the following question: "What size water heater should be installed at 155 Main Street, Minneapolis, MN, if the salinity of the water being heated is 150% above average, and it must cost 50% less than a typical water heater?"

A significant inventive design concept or a radical change to an existing design concept (invention outside the current paradigm) requires significant effort on the part of PD team members in generating a design concept. These designs require a new paradigm to create the critical design parameters. Design concept contradictions do exist and require tradeoffs/compromises between the components of the design concept. The original design concept is entirely changed, but the critical design parameters will perform the same function as the original critical parameter. PD team members must study thousands of design concept variants outside their discipline to generate a design concept for the critical design parameters. An example of this type of design effort is designing a water heater that answers the following question: "Can a water heating system be installed at 155 Main Street, Minneapolis, MN, that heats water of any salinity on demand?"

A new phenomenon or discovery (an entirely new invention) requires extremely high effort on the part of PD team members in generating a design concept. These designs require a new discovery (beyond current science) used to create the critical parameter; this discovery can create an entirely new industry. PD team members must study tens or hundreds of thousands of design concept variants outside current knowledge to generate a design concept for the critical design parameters. An example of this type of design effort is: "Install a system at 155 Main Street, Minneapolis, MN, that heats and cools water of any salinity on demand for ten percent of the cost of current water heaters."

Breaking Down CTQs into CTPs

PD team members use a **systematic (tree) diagram** to decompose each CTQ into its component parts or functions, called critical-to-product characteristics or critical-to-process characteristics (high-level CTPs). Examples of critical-to-process characteristics are the components of the design for a new process to quickly respond to requests for bedside assistance from patients in a hospital (CTQ). Specifically, when a patient pushes a call button (CTP1), an operator is notified and calls the patient on the telephone (CTP2), the need is discovered (CPT3), the appropriate person is paged (CPT4), and upon walking in the room, the employee's badge transmits a signal wirelessly to turn off the call light (CTP5).

Table 6.1 depicts three designs generated in the Analyze Phase of the dormitory example. "Undergraduate Preferences" depicts the design selected by undergraduate students via a questionnaire, "Graduate Preferences" depicts the design selected by graduate students via a questionnaire, and "Composite" depicts the design with all of the CTQs and high-level CTPs from a questionnaire (see Chapter 14, "Articulating the Voice of the Stakeholder," for a discussion of questionnaires).

TABLE 6.1   CTQ and High-Level CTP Relationships Between Target Markets

System	Component Level A	Component Level B (CTQ)	Component Level (High-Level CTP)	Feature or Service (High-Level CTP)	Undergrad Prefs	Grad Prefs	Composite
Dormitory	Inside the Room	General	Occupancy	Single Occupancy Rooms	X	X	X
				Admissions for Business Students Only		X	X
				Segregate Residents by Class Level		X	X
			Control	Climate Control by Room	X	X	X
			Floor	Carpet	X	X	X
		Entertainment	Television	Television Unit	X	X	X
			Television Peripherals	DVD Player	X	X	X
				VCR		X	X
		Office	Audible Communication	Telephone	X	X	X
				Cordless Telephone	X		X
				Additional Phone Services	X	X	X
			Furniture	Large Corner Desk	X	X	X
				Executive Desk Chair	X	X	X
				Additional Desk Chairs		X	X
			Computer	Broadband Internet	X	X	X
				Personal Computer Rental Service	X		X
				Shared Common Printer	X	X	X
		Kitchen	Full Setup	Kitchenette	X	X	X
			Components	Microwave		X	X
				Small Refrigerator	X	X	X
				Appliance Rental Service		X	X
		Bathroom	Allocation	Individual Bathrooms	X	X	X
			Amenities	Full-Size Bathtub	X		X
		Sleeping/Living Room	Sleeping	Queen-Size Bed	X	X	X
			Organizing	Armoire	X	X	X
	Outside the Room	Cleaning	Laundry	Laundry Facility by Floor	X	X	X
				Optional Laundry Service	X	X	X
			Environment	Optional Maid Service	X	X	X
				Shared Common Vacuum Cleaner	X	X	X
		Common Area	Security	Security Guard	X	X	X
			Accessibles	Enforced Quiet Areas		X	X
				Accessible Roof			X
		Other	Parking	Reserved Convenient Parking Place	X	X	X
			Administrative	Option to Rent by Semester		X	X
			Suggestive Advice	Concierge		X	X

Using Thinking Habits and Tools for Generating Design Concepts

Lateral thinking [see Reference 2] is used to move from established ideas and perceptions to new ideas and perceptions. It is required for creating the ideas and perceptions necessary to generate design concepts. Creative thinking can be used deliberately. It is not necessary to wait for an inspiration.

Thinking Habits

de Bono [see Reference 2] has developed the thinking habits required for creative thinking: focus and purpose, forward and parallel, perception and logic, values, and outcome and conclusion. Each habit is briefly discussed next.

The **focus and purpose** habit keeps a thinker aimed in the right direction. It stops drift, confusion, and inefficiency in thinking about a topic.

- What am I looking at (thinking about) right now?
- What am I trying to do?

The **forward and parallel** habit helps a thinker identify the next step in his or her thinking process. Is the next step forward or sideways?

- Forward—So what follows?
- Sideways—What else might there be?

The **perception and logic** habit helps the thinker see his or her world (perception) and how to utilize his or her perceptions (logic) about the world.

- Perception (Breadth)—How broad of a view am I taking?
- Perception (Change)—In what other ways is it possible to look at things?
- Logic—What follows from this?

The **values** habit determines the value of the thinking to real life.

- What are the values involved?
- Who are affected by these values?

The **outcome and conclusion** habit assists the thinker in harvesting the fruit of the thinking effort and feeling achievement in the outcome. It comes at the end of a thinking effort.
If you have not succeeded in reaching a conclusion:

- What have I found out?
- What is the sticking point?

If the thinker has succeeded in reaching a conclusion:

- What is my answer?
- Why do I think my answer will work?

Thinking Tools

de Bono [see Reference 2] has developed several tools to assist individuals or teams to think creatively about a problem—in this case, about a design parameter. Each thinking tool is discussed in detail in Chapter 15, "Enhancing Creativity to Develop Alternative Designs." One tool, Consider All Factors (CAF), is discussed below to illustrate its usefulness in generating alternative design concepts.

The **CAF (Consider All Factors)** tool is designed to increase the breadth of perception with respect to a topic. It adds to the list of factors relevant to a topic.

- What has been left out?
- Can you add another factor to the list we have?
- What else must be considered?

Exercise: You are redesigning the "paperwork for obtaining a bank loan." What things do you have to consider? Do a CAF. One of an infinite number of possible answers is: Hire high school students to be runners for quickly moving the paperwork required for a bank loan through the bank loan process.

Exercise: You are designing a "pill box" for frail elderly people. What things do you have to keep in mind? Do a CAF. One of an infinite number of possible answers is: Design a pill box that beeps when pills are to be taken by the pill box owner.

Dormitory Example

Consider All Factors (CAF) was employed in the dormitory example to generate two additional designs. It was determined that the simplest design considered should be the equivalent of the nicest room currently available on campus. Therefore, a study of the nicest room was performed. The design of the room is generalized in Table 6.2. It is referred to as "Eaton Hall," the name of the building housing the rooms. Another design was inspired by the revelation that one high priority of the Dean of the Business School is the academic success of the students. It is clear that some of the features and services will make larger contributions to "business activities" than will others. These features and services that constitute the "Business Suite" design are depicted in Table 6.2. All features not included in the "Business Suite" design were then deemed as luxury items, which led to the renaming of the "Composite" design as the "Luxury Suite" design.

TABLE 6.2 Room Designs

System	Component Level A	Component Level B (CTQ)	Component Level (High-Level CTP)	Feature or Service (High-Level CTP)	Eaton Hall	Business Suite	Luxury Suite
Dormitory	Inside the Room	General	Occupancy	Single Occupancy Rooms	X	X	X
				Admissions for Business Students Only			X
				Segregate Residents by Class Level			X
			Control	Climate Control by Room			X
			Floor	Carpet			X
		Entertainment	Television	Television Unit			X
			Television Peripherals	DVD Player			X
				VCR			X
		Office	Audible Communication	Telephone		X	X
				Cordless Telephone		X	X
				Additional Phone Services			X
			Furniture	Large Corner Desk		X	X
				Executive Desk Chair		X	X
				Additional Desk Chairs		X	X
			Computer	Broadband Internet	X	X	X
				Personal Computer Rental Service		X	X
				Shared Common Printer		X	X
		Kitchen	Full Setup	Kitchenette			X
			Components	Microwave			X
				Small Refrigerator		X	X
				Appliance Rental Service			X
		Bathroom	Allocation	Individual Bathrooms	X	X	X
			Amenities	Full-Size Bathtub			X
		Sleeping/Living Room	Sleeping	Queen-Size Bed			X
			Organizing	Armoire			X
	Outside the Room	Cleaning	Laundry	Laundry Facility by Floor	X	X	X
				Optional Laundry Service			X
			Environment	Optional Maid Service			X
				Shared Common Vacuum Cleaner			X
		Common Area	Security	Security Guard	X	X	X
			Accessibles	Enforced Quiet Areas	X	X	X
				Accessible Roof			X
		Other	Parking	Reserved Convenient Parking Place			X
			Administrative	Option to Rent by Semester			X
			Suggestive Advice	Concierge			X

In summary, there are five alternative high-level room designs:

- **Undergraduate Preferences**—This design includes only the features that are deemed as "One-Way," "Attractive," or "Must-Be" via the undergraduate responses in the Kano questionnaire. See Chapter 14 for a discussion of Kano questionnaires and categories of features (e.g. One-Way, Attractive, or Must-Be).

- **Graduate Preferences**—This design includes only the features that are deemed as "One-Way," "Attractive," or "Must-Be" via the graduate responses in the Kano questionnaire.

- **Eaton Hall**—This design includes only the features of the nicest dormitory rooms currently available on campus.

- **Business Suite**—This design includes only the features and services that have large contributions to business activities.

- **Luxury Suite**—This design includes all the features that were deemed as "One-Way," "Attractive," or "Must-Be" by any of the participating market segments via the Kano questionnaire.

Note that the five designs do not consider common area designs, just the rooms themselves. However, all designs will share the same common area design within the building.

Using TRIZ for Generating Design Concepts

Introduction

TRIZ is a method developed by Altshuller [see Reference 1] that uses physics, mathematics, and chemistry to create inventions and innovations to solve real-world problems. TRIZ is an acronym for "The Theory of Inventive Problem Solving," translated from Russian. It is a dramatic improvement over the "trial and error" method for solving problems. TRIZ significantly improves the abilities of PD team members to develop inventive and innovative design concepts. Altshuller studied thousands of patents from many industries and discovered that 90% of the problems have been previously solved elsewhere. He organized the information from the patents into an extensive knowledge base that is independent of industry.

TRIZ is most appropriate for small improvements, major changes, and significant inventions. It is not suitable for solving simple and obvious problems (known by most everyone) and discovering entirely new phenomena (not known in science literature).

TRIZ is discussed in detail in Chapter 15.

Benchmarking for Generating Creative Design Concepts

Benchmarking is "a structured approach for identifying the best practices from industry and government, and comparing and adapting them to your organization's operations. It counteracts the 'reinvent the wheel' syndrome. Such an approach is aimed at identifying more efficient and effective processes for achieving intended results, and suggesting ambitious goals for program output, product/service quality, and process improvement." Consequently, benchmarking is a technique that can be used to discover creative solutions to problems discovered by others. The solutions may be used in another organization or industry. Nonetheless, they may be very helpful for creatively solving problems in your organization or industry.

Many business processes are common throughout industry. For example, the University of Miami has similar basic Human Resources requirements for hiring and developing employees as ExxonMobil. Xerox has similar customer problem resolution needs as McDonald's. Business processes from many industries are similar and can be benchmarked.

The key to successful benchmarking is to compare your organization's flowchart or process map for the process under study to a best-in-class organization's flowchart or process map, called a "best practice." If its flowchart, or a section of it, makes sense in your organization, you have a potential process improvement or alternative design concept.

6.4 INVESTIGATE ALTERNATIVE DESIGN CONCEPTS FOR EACH CRITICAL PARAMETER

Reducing the Set of Potential Design Concepts

The PD team members need to reduce the list of potential concepts to no more than six concepts. Three simple rules can be used to eliminate less-worthy design concepts. First, team members can eliminate all "show-stopper" concepts. These are concepts that have some extremely negative aspect associated with them. For example, they are likely to increase accidents, they create political problems, they are very expensive, they break laws, or they are particularly unattractive. Second, team members can attempt to combine the concepts from different designs to create fewer designs with better features. For example, team members may combine simulation software, statistical software, and spreadsheet software to create an improved Six Sigma software package. Third, team members can eliminate concepts that don't fit with the organization's mission, values and beliefs, and strategic objectives or create stakeholder dissatisfaction.

Team members identify the criteria upon which they will base their decisions concerning which design concepts to drop and which to carry forward into the next phase of analysis. Examples of possible criteria for evaluating the worthiness of a design concept are the following:

- Benefit/cost of concept
- Time required to realize the concept
- Organization's ability to realize concept
- Effect of concept on organization's strategy
- Legal/regulatory impact of concept
- Safety impact of concept on stakeholders
- Political ramifications of concept

PD team members establish importance weights for the design criteria using the following weighting scale:

1 = Very unimportant
2 = Unimportant
3 = Neutral
4 = Important
5 = Very important

PD team members select the "best" design concept using a Pugh Matrix. Table 6.3 presents the structure of a Pugh Matrix.

TABLE 6.3 Structure of a Pugh Matrix

1	2	3	4	5	6	7	8
Criteria to Evaluate Concepts	**Concept 1 (Baseline Concept)**	**Concept 2**	**Concept 3**	**Concept 4**	**Concept 5**	**Concept 6**	**Concept 7**
Benefit/cost of concept.	All concepts are evaluated with respect to the baseline concept.	+	+	S	S	+	–
Time required to realize the concept.		S	+	S	–	–	S
Organization's ability to realize concept.		+	S	+	S	S	S
Effect of concept on organization's strategy.		+	–	S	+	S	S
Legal/regulatory impact of concept.		+	+	+	+	+	+
Safety impact of concept on stakeholders.		S	+	+	–	–	S
Political ramifications of concept.		+	–	–	–	+	+
Sum of "+"s		5	4	3	2	3	2
Sum of "–"s		0	2	1	3	2	1
Sum of "S"s		2	1	3	1	2	4

Column 1 of Table 6.3 lists the design criteria for assessing the alternative high-level design concepts shown in Columns 2 through 8. Additionally, Column 1 lists the summary statistic categories for each alternative design concept at the bottom of Table 6.3. Column 2 is intentionally left blank because it is the standard or baseline design concept with which all other design concepts are ranked with respect to each of the design criteria. Columns 3 through 8 list the rankings and summary statistics for each design concept. The cells in Columns 3 through 8 relating to the design criteria (rows) are assigned a plus (+), a same (S), or a minus (–) ranking with respect to the baseline design concept shown in Column 2. A plus (+) indicates that the alternative design concept in question is superior to the baseline concept with respect to the design criteria in question. A same (S) indicates that the alternative design concept in question is similar to the baseline concept with respect to the design criteria in question. A minus (–) indicates that the alternative design concept in question is inferior to the baseline concept with respect to the design criteria in question. Next, the cells in Columns 3 through 8 are summarized. For example, design concept 2 (in Column 3) received five "+"s, two "S"s, and zero "–"s when compared to the baseline design concept in Column 2. Clearly, design concept 2 (in Column 3) is the best alternative high-level design concept with the most positives and the least negatives.

Dormitory Example of a Pugh Matrix

Five alternative dormitory designs are analyzed via a Modified Pugh Matrix with Eaton Hall serving as a baseline. The Pugh Matrix grades the designs on criteria determined by the PD team. The criteria chosen to grade these designs are the following:

- **Willingness of Customer to Pay More**—Luxuries come at a price that must be evaluated with respect to customer price sensitivity. This information can be determined by a Kano questionnaire, see Chapter 14 for a discussion of Kano questionnaires. This information is included in Table 6.4.

- **Low Repair Frequency**—This is a general comparison to the baseline that answers the question: Will this design increase the frequency of needed repairs over that of the baseline?

- **Ease of Repair**—This is a general comparison to the baseline that answers the question: Will this design introduce CTQs and/or high-level CTPs that will unduly burden current campus employees in repair and maintenance work?

- **Replacement Frequency**—Does the design introduce many CTQs and/or high-level CTPs that need yearly replacement?

- **Ease of Clean and Common Maintenance**—Do any of the introduced CTQs and/or high-level CTPs require an inordinate amount of maintenance and cleaning? As an example of this criterion, fish tanks would score a low grade on this criterion as they require significant upkeep; in contrast, plastic plants would score high as they only require an occasional dusting.

- **Low Benefit/Cost Ratio**—This is the most subjective grade. It takes into consideration the cost of the design and tries to match the soft benefit of appreciation of current university students and the value as a selling point to future students.

TABLE 6.4   Willingness of Customer to Pay More

CTQ (Feature or Service)	Largest Kano Category	E(Percent Increase in Pay)	Dollars per Month (Based on $3500 per Semester)	Year Sum	"Grade"	Undergraduate	Graduate	Eaton	Business Suite	Luxury Suite
Single Occupancy Rooms	One-Way (25.6%)	6.6%	$57.54	$632.99	0.00	X	X	X	X	X
Individual Bathrooms	Attractive (37.5%)	5.8%	$50.31	$553.44	0.40	X	X	X	X	X
Queen-Size Bed	Attractive (56.8%)	3.0%	$26.16	$287.77	0.80	X	X			X
Broadband Internet	Attractive (36.4%)	1.6%	$14.43	$158.75	0.50	X	X	X	X	X
Television	Attractive (54.5%)	1.7%	$15.23	$167.50	0.80	X	X			X
Telephone	Attractive (34.2%)	0.6%	$5.28	$58.13	1.00	X	X		X	X
Cordless Telephone	Attractive (49.3%)	0.7%	$5.80	$63.75	0.00	X			X	X
Additional Phone Services	Attractive (60.0%)	1.2%	$10.40	$114.38	-0.60	X	X			X
Personal Computer Rental Service	Indifferent (61.8%)	NA	NA	NA	0.00	X			X	X
Shared Common Printer	Attractive (44.3%)	0.7%	$6.08	$66.88	1.00	X	X		X	X
Large Corner Desk	Attractive (54.8%)	0.5%	$4.61	$50.73	-0.20	X	X		X	X
Executive Desk Chair	Attractive (53.4%)	0.6%	$4.91	$53.98	0.00	X	X		X	X
Additional Desk Chairs	Indifferent (47.1%)	0.4%	$3.71	$40.77	-0.50		X		X	X
Climate Control by Room	Must-Be (43.7%)	3.1%	$27.11	$298.24	1.00	X				X
Full-Size Bathtub	Attractive (29.6%)	1.8%	$15.71	$172.84	1.00	X				X
Microwave	Attractive (31.0%)	1.2%	$10.23	$112.52	1.00		X			X
Small Refrigerator	Attractive (32.4%)	1.6%	$14.05	$154.54	0.20	X	X		X	X
Kitchenette	Attractive (45.1%)	3.8%	$33.52	$368.73	-0.40	X	X			X
Appliance Rental Service	Indifferent (47.8%)	NA	NA	NA	0.00		X			X
VCR	Attractive (40.0%)	0.7%	$6.00	$66.00	0.10		X			X
DVD Player	Attractive (60.3%)	0.5%	$4.25	$46.75	-0.20	X	X			X
Carpet	Attractive (33.3%)	0.7%	$6.00	$66.00	-0.60	X	X			X
Enforced Quiet Areas	Indifferent (46.4%)	0.7%	$6.44	$70.81	0.00		X	X	X	X
Shared Common Vacuum Cleaner	Attractive (39.1%)	0.6%	$5.50	$60.50	1.00	X	X			X
Accessible Roof	Attractive (42.6%)	1.4%	$11.88	$130.63	0.80	X				X
Security Guard	Must-Be (33.8%)	NA	NA	NA	0.00	X	X	X		X
Laundry Facility by Floor	One-Way (30.4%)	1.1%	$9.75	$107.25	-0.10	X	X	X		X
Optional Laundry Service	Attractive (47.8%)	1.4%	$11.94	$131.31	0.00	X	X			X
Optional Maid Service	Attractive (43.3%)	1.7%	$14.56	$160.19	0.00	X	X			X
Concierge	Attractive (35.3%)	1.0%	$8.94	$98.31	-0.80		X			X
Reserved Convenient Parking Place	Attractive (48.0%)	2.0%	$17.33	$190.60	0.00	X	X			X
Admissions for Business Students Only	Reverse (25.7%)	0.8%	$6.71	$73.79	1.00		X			X
Segregate Residents by Class Level	Indifferent (44.6%)	0.3%	$2.99	$32.93	1.00		X			X
Armoire	Attractive (43.8%)	NA	NA	NA	0.00	X	X			X
Option to Rent by Semester	One-Way (30.7%)	1.3%	$11.67	$128.33	1.00		X			X
Raw			Sum of Undergraduate Preferences		6.40					
			Sum of Graduate Preferences			7.40				
			Sum of Eaton Hall				0.80			
			Sum of Business Suite					2.40		
			Sum of Luxury Suite						9.20	
Standardized			Sum of Undergraduate Preferences		0.70					
			Sum of Graduate Preferences			0.80				
			Sum of Eaton Hall				0.09			
			Sum of Business Suite					0.26		
			Sum of Luxury Suite						1.00	

The willingness of a customer to pay more for a dormitory facility is first broken down by individual CTQs and/or high-level CTPs in Table 6.4. The calculations assume that the current cost of an Eaton Hall dormitory room is $875 per month. Given this cost structure, the expected values of the customers' willingness to pay additional money for CTQs and/or high-level CTPs can be determined from their input from the Kano questionnaire. PD team members graded each CTQ on a –1 to +1 scale. A zero can be assumed as a break-even value on the customers' willingness to pay more, while a –1 reflects that the university would lose money if it provided the CTQ and/or high-level CTP. This cost recovery is based on the Total Life Cycle Cost (TLCC) of the CTQs and/or high-level CTPs (features and services). While these TLCCs for the CTQs and/or high-level CTPs could not be precisely estimated, a general consensus regarding TLCC recovery was determined from expert advice. For instance, tenants are expected to be willing to pay approximately $63.75 per year for a cordless phone. The computation of $63.75 per year is as follows:

E(Percent increase in pay) $\times$ $875 $\times$ 11 months occupancy

$= 0.7\% \times \$875 \times 11 \approx \$5.80 \times 11 \approx \$63.75$
(numbers are off due to rounding error)

Cordless phones have a life expectancy of approximately one-year in a dormitory environment. Given that, the TLCC should be recovered on a yearly basis. In this example, the TLCC is very near the expected value of the amount tenants are willing to pay for that feature, meaning that it "graded out" at zero. The largest portion of the TLCC of a parking place would be the coupons paid on the bonds that finance the parking place. Therefore, the expected value of the amount customers are willing to pay should exceed the coupons needed to cover the 30-year bonds that would finance the parking places. By considering TLCC and the length of a lifetime for the feature or service, a perpetual recovery can be predicted. Any "grades" below zero are a prediction of an under-recovery and any "grades" above zero are a prediction of an over-recovery. The "grades" are not integer values and represent the likelihood of recovery and not the magnitudes of recovery, although there is a relationship between the two. For instance, a CTQ and/or CTP can be graded at 0.5 to indicate that the likelihood of over-recovery is positive but not as likely as another CTQ and/or CTP graded at 0.7. The opposite is true for negative grades. The sum of those grades are then standardized and used as an input into the Pugh Matrix for the different designs. To further illustrate this concept, consider the following example.

The Kano surveys indicate that students are willing to pay an additional 3% in rent if they are furnished a queen-size bed as opposed to a twin-size bed (see Table 6.4). This amounts to an estimated value of $287.77 per year. Now, the marginal TLCC of furnishing a queen-size bed as opposed to a twin-size bed should be considered. Given the conservative estimate of a three-year lifespan for the bed, an additional $863.31 (*3 × $287.77, ignoring interest effects for simplicity of example*) should be willingly generated by the patrons of the dormitory due to the added value of furnishing a queen-size bed. The additional cost incurred due to upgrading this provision from that of a twin-size bed should fall well below $861.31 and, therefore, the university stands a very favorable probability that they can fully recover the cost of the queen-size bed via rent. This favorable probability of cost recovery is represented with a score of 0.8 indicating that an over-recovery is actually likely. This score is also summed into the following raw values: "Sum of Undergraduate Preferences," "Sum of Graduate Preference," and "Sum of Luxury Suite." It is excluded from the other two summations because the Eaton and Business Suite designs do not include a queen-size bed. The summations are then standardized by dividing all sums by the value of the largest sum. These standardized sums are then used as inputs in the Modified Pugh Matrix (see Table 6.5 on page 173) in the row labeled "Willingness of Customer to Pay More" as a substitute for the usual +/S/− notation.

The column "Year Sum" assumes that the room is rented out for eleven months. All rental services are graded out at zero because, theoretically, the university can match the price and inventory to the demand. All CTQs and/or high-level CTPs come at a price of close to zero, yet the ones students are willing to pay for are graded out at positive one. An example of one of these features is admissions for business students only. The selective admissions have no direct cost, yet students are willing to pay for it.

The standardized values in the bottom of Table 6.4 provide the only calculated input for the Modified Pugh Matrix in Table 6.5. They are calculated by dividing the sum for each design by the sum for the Luxury Suite. For example, the standardized value for the sum of Undergraduate Preferences is calculated by dividing 6.40 by 9.20, producing the result of approximately 0.70. A traditional Pugh Matrix uses a series of plusses and minuses and "S"s ("Same") to distinguish between designs. However, in this case, a binary decision does not adequately discriminate between the designs due to their similarity. Instead of using the +/S/− system, all criteria were graded on a continuum ranging from −1 to +1. Also, the other criteria used to rate the designs (not "Willingness of Customer to Pay More") were established through brainstorming and were graded on a holistic level rather than one feature at a time. Eaton is considered a baseline for all criteria other than "Willingness of Customer to Pay More." As such, Eaton earned a score of zero for those respective criteria. The other designs were then compared to Eaton and comparatively graded against Eaton on the different criteria. For example, the cell Graduate/Low Repair Frequency has a value of -0.10 because the Graduate design included additional features that are expected to require repair more frequently than the features included in Eaton. Luxury graded out at -0.20 on this feature because it contained even more additional features that are expected to require frequent repair. Negative values indicate a problematic CTQ and/or high-level CTP. These criteria were then weighted to composite out a final series of differences between the designs. The weights shown were then standardized for multiplication back against the criteria to composite a final picture as to what would be perceived as the best design.

TABLE 6.5 Modified Pugh Matrix

Criteria to Evaluate Designs	Baseline	Designs					Standardized Criteria Weights
	Eaton	Undergraduate	Graduate	Business	Luxury	Criteria Weights	
Willingness of Customer to Pay More	0.09	0.70	0.80	0.26	1.00	5.00	0.24
Low Repair Frequency	0.00	−0.10	−0.10	0.00	−0.20	3.00	0.14
Ease of Repair	0.00	−0.10	−0.10	0.00	−0.20	2.00	0.10
Replacement Frequency	0.00	−0.50	−0.60	−0.40	−0.70	3.00	0.14
Ease to Clean and Common Maintenance	0.00	−0.30	−0.30	−0.10	−0.40	3.00	0.14
Low Cost/Benefit Ratio	0.00	1.00	1.00	1.00	1.00	5.00	0.24
Sum of Positives	0.09	1.70	1.80	1.26	2.00	21.00	1.00
Sum of Negatives	0.00	−1.00	−1.10	−0.50	−1.50		
Difference	0.09	0.70	0.70	0.76	0.50		
Weighted Sum of Positives	0.02	0.40	0.43	0.30	0.48		
Weighted Sum of Negatives	0.00	−0.14	−0.15	−0.07	−0.20		
Weighted Difference	0.02	0.27	0.28	0.23	0.27		

The Modified Pugh Matrix (see Table 6.5) indicates that the Graduate Preferences concept is the best concept, with Undergraduate and Luxury concepts being possible substitutes. Next, an analysis of the risk is required to refine the design(s).

6.5 CREATE A LIMITED SET OF POTENTIAL HIGH-LEVEL DESIGN CONCEPTS

Team members select the 2 or 3 highest ranked alternative design concepts from the Pugh Matrix for further testing and development. Team members test the selected concepts by surveying the stakeholders of the design concepts to obtain their feedback on the best concept. Finally, team members develop a design scorecard for the single best design concept.

In the dormitory example, the product to be delivered is a design concept, not the actual dormitory; as such, some detailed specifications will not be supplied. For example, whether a dormitory room is 19 feet long or 21 feet long is the concern of the architect. Other external restrictions such as available land area and building codes are not part of this project.

A common theme among all stakeholders of the dormitory was to create a generic design. Students, both undergraduate and graduate, wanted the freedom to design their own living spaces. Administrative stakeholders did not want to deal with the costs and pains associated with providing anything more than basic furniture and a concrete walled box to hold it all. This meant that given the wishes of the Dean of the School of Business, a design was needed that could be considered posh, yet plain. That way, the room could be modified, yet be distinct and classy.

The key constraint in the detailed design was the fact that most stakeholders wanted to use a poured concrete design. This is an ideal way to construct the building as it is inexpensive, durable, and able to withstand the ever-present threat of tropical storms and hurricanes prevalent in South Florida. Poured concrete technology has also evolved to the point where buildings can be manufactured offsite and delivered very quickly in pieces to the job site.

The detailed design merges the preceding two ideas to create a space that is not easily modified, given the rigidity of the concrete walls, but that could be modified internally to be distinct and classy. Consequently, a modular style room will be designed.

The Analyze Phase concluded with three modular styles: the Undergraduate design, the Graduate design, and the Luxury Suite. Before deciding to offer three separate designs, it is worthwhile to examine the differences between the designs and determine if the individual designs are actually different enough to justify offering three designs.

Table 6.6 shows the physical facilities requirements of the room, by design. These would be permanently placed into the room.

TABLE 6.6   Building Facilities Characteristics by Design Type

CTQ (Feature or Service)	Undergraduate	Graduate	Luxury Suite
Single Occupancy Rooms	X	X	X
Individual Bathrooms	X	X	X
Climate Control by Room	X	X	X
Full-Size Bathtub	X		X
Kitchenette	X	X	X
Carpet	X	X	X

Figure 6.1 shows the floor plan. It is going to be fixed into place once the concrete forms are poured.

This floor plan shows a bathtub in the bathroom, despite the fact that the graduates preferred not having a bathtub. Given that the single rooms, such as those in Eaton Hall, have bathtubs, this is not a significant change. Furthermore, the cost of a bathtub is not very high relative to the cost of tiling an entire shower. Therefore, to remain generic and standardized, all bathrooms will be fitted with bathtubs.

Given that the physical constraints of the building are not all that relevant in the design, the primary problem becomes that of furnishings, or in this case, high-level CTPs. The Kano survey determined the furnishings that belong in each room. Table 6.7 shows the listing of the furnishings that will be placed in each style of room.

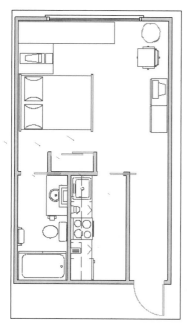

FIGURE 6.1 Revised Room Layout from Physical Constraints and Preferences

TABLE 6.7 Furnishings by Design Type

CTQ (Feature or Service)	Undergraduate	Graduate	Luxury Suite
Queen-Size Bed	X	X	X
Television Unit	X	X	X
Telephone Unit	X	X	X
Cordless Telephone Unit	X		X
Large Corner Desk	X	X	X
Executive Desk Chair	X	X	X
Additional Desk Chairs		X	X
Microwave		X	X
Small Refrigerator	X	X	X
VCR		X	X
DVD Player	X	X	X
Armoire	X	X	X

Furnishings are defined as "any permanent or semi-permanent object in the dormitory that is not fixed into the building itself." The Facilities Administration Director said: "Furnishings are the stuff that we provide that would fall out if you were to pick up the building, turn it upside down, and shake it." In this case, this list includes kitchen appliances, electronic devices, and furniture.

Table 6.7 shows that these furnishings are also very similar between all three of the available options. The same furniture goes into all three of the room types, with the exception of additional chairs into the Undergraduate rooms. The suggestion here is to give the Undergraduate rooms the extra chairs. The students could call to have them removed if they desired. This is a beneficial system in multiple respects. First, this is the current system used in the other dormitories on campus. For example, if students decide to construct a loft and no longer require their bed frames, they call the Facilities Offices to have movers come and pick up their unused furniture and return it to storage. This would also further standardize the rooms, and the set up process, as the furniture movers set up the same furniture in the same way in every room.

The only significant differences are in the electronics and the appliances. These decisions should be made by the stakeholders themselves using their expertise. This is especially true with the telephones, as theft was shown to be an issue in the Analyze Phase. However, the telecommunications system used by the university itself may dictate exactly what is supplied given the levels of telephone services and other wireless systems used in the building. This also has very little impact on the room design, as a corded or cordless telephone requires approximately the same amount of space.

The lack of a microwave in the Undergraduate design is a curiosity, especially given that the other two designs dictated microwaves were important. Digging back into the Kano survey shows that the microwave became classified as Indifferent. This kept microwaves off the Undergraduate QFD, but microwaves also appeared as the 15th most important item in the overall QFD. Based on the popularity of microwave cooking in the United States, and a desire for standardization across all rooms, a microwave will be placed in all of the designs, counter to the findings of the Kano survey.

The final difference relates to electronics, specifically in movie-viewing. Providing VCR and DVD players are attractive qualities. Providing separate units might make sense. However, one option the team found was to consider a VCR/DVD combination machine. These are readily, and cheaply, available on the market. Providing a combination machine could further standardize the room options. This is a relatively minor item that should be considered by the stakeholders when making all the other purchases. It does not significantly impact the design.

In summary, the difference among furnishings for the three designs is small, so a standardized room closely resembling the Luxury Suite appears to be the best option. However, there are additional considerations still to be made, as a dormitory is not comprised strictly of rooms; there are also common areas.

The final portion of the dormitory that must be designed are the common areas. Many of the common area CTPs were highlighted by the Kano survey and discussions with stakeholders. For example, there must be some sort of mail distribution facility, which is dictated by law.

Other design issues relating to the fact that the dormitory is to be a residential college were not considered by this project. For example, the team had no input regarding classrooms and other academic and social facilities. However, two common area design CTPs that were addressed are shown in Table 6.8.

The requirements here are clear and no further explanation is required.

The final area to be addressed concerns the services that the dormitory will provide. Table 6.9 shows a list of service CTPs by design option.

TABLE 6.8 Common Area Requirements by Design Type

CTP (Feature or Service)	Undergraduate	Graduate	Luxury Suite
Laundry Facility by Floor	X	X	X
Reserved Convenient Parking Place	X	X	X

TABLE 6.9 Services Desired by Design Type

CTP (Feature or Service)	Undergraduate	Graduate	Luxury Suite
Broadband Internet	X	X	X
Additional Phone Services	X	X	X
PC Rental Service	X		X
Shared Common Printer	X	X	X
Appliance Rental Service		X	X
Enforced Quiet Areas		X	X
Shared Common Vacuum Cleaner	X	X	X
Accessible Roof	X		X
Security Guard	X	X	X
Optional Laundry Service	X	X	X
Optional Maid Service	X	X	X
Concierge		X	X
Admissions for Business Students Only		X	X
Segregate Residents by Class Level		X	X
Option to Rent by Semester		X	X

Table 6.9 shows a distinct difference between the Undergraduate design and the other two designs, as the Undergraduate design does not require many services. However, this difference is not as significant as it might seem at first. The key factor here is that the marginal cost of providing many of the services demanded by the Graduate and Luxury designs approaches zero. For example, if a student in an Undergraduate room wanted to ask the concierge a question, there is not any significant marginal cost to this, as the concierge is getting paid regardless. The optional services also follow this line of reasoning, because the marginal cost of providing an optional service that is not used is zero. If a student elects to not use a maid or laundry service, then there is no charge to either the university or the student. This also applies to all of the rentals that could be administered by the university, although there are capital considerations to be made. As an example, purchasing one more computer to rent to a student only costs the value of the expenditure for the computer, as maintenance, administration, and capital cost recovery would be figured into the rental rate. Therefore, these rental services can scale themselves by demand.

The only two services (CTPs) not covered by the marginal cost problem are those dealing with the segregation of students. The Undergraduate design favors an open door policy, which is in strict opposition to the segregated views of the other two design types. Other stakeholders, including the Dean of the School of Business Administration, favor a segregated structure for the dormitory. Consequently, the building will be segregated.

The final design derived from the three significant Pugh designs will contain the detailed CTPs shown in Table 6.10.

TABLE 6.10 Final Design Features

System	Component Level A	Component Level B (CTQ)	Component Level (High-Level CTP)	Feature or Service (High-Level CTP)	Final Detailed Design
Dormitory	Inside the Room	General	Occupancy	Single Occupancy Rooms	X
				Admissions for Business Students Only	X
				Segregate Residents by Class Level	X
			Control	Climate Control by Room	X
			Floor	Carpet	X
		Entertainment	Television	Television Unit	X
			Television Peripherals	DVD Player	X
				VCR	X
		Office	Audible Communication	Telephone	X
				Cordless Telephone	X
				Additional Phone Services	X
			Furniture	Large Corner Desk	X
				Executive Desk Chair	X
				Additional Desk Chairs	X
			Computer	Broadband Internet	X
				Personal Computer Rental Service	X
				Shared Common Printer	X
		Kitchen	Full Setup	Kitchenette	X
			Components	Microwave	X
				Small Refrigerator	X
				Appliance Rental Service	X

			Allocation	Individual Bathrooms	X
		Bathroom	Amenities	Full-Size Bathtub	X
		Sleeping/Living Room	Sleeping	Queen-Size Bed	X
			Organizing	Armoire	X
	Outside the Room	Cleaning	Laundry	Laundry Facility by Floor	X
				Optional Laundry Service	X
			Environment	Optional Maid Service	X
				Shared Common Vacuum Cleaner	X
		Common Area	Security	Security Guard	X
			Accessibles	Enforced Quiet Areas	X
				Accessible Roof	X
		Other	Parking	Reserved Convenient Parking Place	X
			Administrative	Option to Rent by Semester	X
			Suggestive Advice	Concierge	X

6.6 Assess the Risks of the "Best" Design Concept

Sources of Risk

Examples of sources of risk associated with design of products, processes, or services include the following:

- Reliability
- Safety
- Complex functions
- Hazardous design elements
- Complex interactions with other services, processes, or products
- Unclear requirements or specifications
- Available products, services, or processes not properly evaluated
- Functional capability requirements not appropriate for use
- Inappropriate development tools or methods
- New or unfamiliar technology

- Unstable project team
- Project team unfamiliar with business area
- Project team skills inadequate for project
- Poor project management

Purpose of Risk Management

Risk management systematically and continuously identifies and quantifies risk elements in design concepts at tollgates and prevents them from occurring through risk abatement programs; it also communicates risk to management.

Method 1: Identifying Risk Elements Using FMEA

Recall from the Define Phase, Failure Modes and Effects Analysis (FMEA) can be used by team members to identify, estimate, prioritize, and reduce the risk of failure of the CTQs in the best design concept through the development of actions (process changes on the CTPs) and contingency plans (just-in-case plans based on CTPs).

Method 2: Identifying Risk Elements Using Hazard Analysis

Hazard Analysis is a tool that can be used by team members to identify corrective and or preventive measures for hazards and harms (risk elements). It is similar to FMEA analysis. Hazards and harms are quantified using the following measures:

- Hazard frequency—frequency of occurrence of a hazard over time.
- Hazard severity:
  - Class I: Negligible—Will not result in personal injury or property damage.
  - Class II: Marginal—Can be counteracted or controlled without personal injury or major property damage.
  - Class III: Critical—Will cause personal injury or major property damage.
  - Class IV: Catastrophic—Will cause death, severe personal injury, or severe property loss.

Hazard Analysis is accomplished by constructing a hazard matrix. A Hazard Analysis for the dormitory example is shown in Table 6.11.

TABLE 6.11 Hazard Analysis for the Dormitory Example

CTQ (Feature or Service)	Function	Hazard	Frequency	Cause	Effect	Hazard Severity	Corrective or Preventive Measure
Single Occupancy Rooms	Occupancy	Incapacitation in Isolation	Once every 6–100 years	No way to request help	Potentially alone if any disabling circumstances occur	Class IV	Accessible Telephones
Admissions for Business Students Only	Occupancy	Isolation from Diversity	More than once per day	Lack of diverse neighbors	Reclusive residents	Class I	Dormitory Programs
Segregate Residents by Class Level	Occupancy	Isolation from Diversity	More than once per day	Lack of diverse neighbors	Reclusive residents	Class I	Dormitory Programs
Climate Control by Room	Control	High Temperatures and Humidity	Once per month	Organically fostered reactions	Mildewing Occurs	Class II	Governor on thermostat
Carpet	Floor	Lack of Care	Once per month	Spillages and inappropriate contacts surfaces	Stains and/or unusual wear	Class II	Deposit on Provisions
Television Unit	Television	Nonpermanence	Once per month	Klepto-Tendencies	Thievery	Class II	Deposit on Provisions
DVD Player	Television Peripherals	Nonpermanence	Once per month	Klepto-Tendencies	Thievery	Class II	Deposit on Provisions
VCR	Television Peripherals	Nonpermanence	Once per month	Klepto-Tendencies	Thievery	Class II	Deposit on Provisions
Telephone	Audible Communication	Nonpermanence	Once per month	Klepto-Tendencies	Thievery	Class II	Deposit on Provisions
Cordless Telephone	Audible Communication	Nonpermanence	Once per month	Klepto-Tendencies	Thievery	Class II	Deposit on Provisions
		Privacy	More than once per day	Channel duplications	Confidential information may accidentally pass to unintended recipients	Class I	Provide High-end phones with many channels
Additional Phone Services	Audible Communication	.	.	.	.	.	.
Large Corner Desk	Office Furniture	Lack of care	Once per month	Inappropriate contact surfaces	Unusual wear	Class III	Deposit on Provisions
Executive Desk Chair	Office Furniture	Lack of care	Once per month	Inappropriate contact surfaces	Unusual wear	Class II	Deposit on Provisions
Additional Desk Chairs	Office Furniture	Lack of care	Once per month	Inappropriate contact surfaces	Unusual wear	Class II	Deposit on Provisions
Broadband Internet	Computer	Dedicated Connection	Once per day	Hacking	Computer Viruses	Class I	Provided Virus Protection and Firewall
Personal Computer Rental Service	Computer	Nonpermanence	Once per month	Klepto-Tendencies	Thievery	Class III	Deposit on Provisions
Shared Common Printer	Computer	.	.	.	.	.	.
Kitchenette	Full Kitchen Setup	Fire	Once every 1–5 years	Chemically fostered reaction	Burning of Room and/or buildings - Possible Fatalities	Class IV	High-end Fire Control System
		Water	Once every 1–5 years	Physically fostered reaction	Flooding - Damage to Furniture	Class III	Real-time Control Chart of Water Usage
Microwave	Kitchen Components	Fire	Once every 1–5 years	Chemically fostered reaction	Burning of Room and/or buildings - Possible Fatalities	Class IV	High-end Fire Control System
Small Refrigerator	Kitchen Components	.	.	.	.	.	.
Appliance Rental Service	Kitchen Components	Fire	Once every 1–5 years	Chemically fostered reaction	Burning of Room and/or buildings - Possible Fatalities	Class IV	High-end Fire Control System
		Nonpermanence	Once per month	Klepto-Tendencies	Thievery	Class II	Deposit on Provisions
Individual Bathrooms	Allocation	Incapacitation in Isolation	Once every 6–100 years	No way to request help	Potentially alone if any disabling circumstances occur	Class IV	Accessible Telephones
Full-Size Bathtub	Amenities	Incapacitation in Isolation	Once every 6–100 years	No way to request help	Potentially alone if any disabling circumstances occur	Class IV	Non-Slip Surfaces
Queen-Size Bed	Sleeping	.	.	.	.	.	.
Armoire	Organizing	Lack of care	Once per month	Inappropriate contact surfaces	Unusual wear	Class III	Deposit on Provisions
Laundry Facility by Floor	Laundry	Nonpermanence	Once per month	Klepto-Tendencies	Thievery	Class III	Security cameras and guards
Optional Laundry Service	Laundry	Accessibility	Once every 6 months	Klepto-Tendencies	Thievery	Class III	Extensive background checks
Optional Maid Service	Environment	Accessibility	Once every 6 months	Klepto-Tendencies	Thievery	Class III	Extensive background checks
Shared Common Vacuum Cleaner	Environment	Lack of care	Once per week	Inappropriate transportation and storage	Unusual wear	Class II	Check-in and Check-out requirement
		Nonpermanence	Once per month	Klepto-Tendencies	Thievery	Class II	Check-in and Check-out requirement
Security Guard	Security	Accessibility	Once every 6–100 years	Klepto-Tendencies	Thievery	Class III	Extensive background checks
Enforced Quiet Areas	Accessibles	.	.	.	.	.	.
Accessible Roof	Accessibles	Heights	Once every 6–100 years	Gravity	Falling - Possible Fatalities	Class IV	Guardrail
Reserved Convenient Parking Place	Parking	.	.	.	.	.	.
Option to Rent by Semester	Administrative	.	.	.	.	.	.
Concierge	Suggestive Advice	.	.	.	.	.	.

The Hazard Analysis of the dormitory design reveals seven Class IV hazards:

- **Single Occupancy Rooms**—Potential lack of help in disabling circumstances.
- **Kitchenette**—Potential fire.

- **Microwave**—Potential fire.
- **Appliance Rental Service**—Potential fire.
- **Individual Bathrooms**—Potential lack of help in disabling circumstances.
- **Full-Size Bathtub**—Potential lack of help in disabling circumstances.
- **Accessible Roof**—Potential falls.

There are two primary types of actions to counter these hazards. There are actions that reduce the potential of hazards occurring, and there are actions that remove the possibility of the hazards. It is believed that the fire hazards can be adequately controlled with a fire control system, and that single occupancy room hazards are bearable because it is common for universities to offer single occupancy rooms. However, the accessible roof hazard is harder to control. This "Graduate Preferences" design excludes this feature while "Undergraduate Preferences" and "Business/ Luxury Suite" designs do not. This is a continuation of the evidence revealed in the Pugh Matrix that the "Graduate Preferences" design may be the most suitable because it will eliminate the hazards of falls and suicide attempts. However, other solutions will continue to be considered, such as having a roof that is semi-accessible, as it could be used for various formal functions.

Method 3: Identifying Risk Elements Using a Risk Abatement Plan

Risk abatement plans can be developed by team members to prioritize and reduce elements of risk in a design concept. This is accomplished by team members assigning risk ratings to each risk element and prioritizing risk elements in a risk abatement plan.

Risk elements are prioritized in a Risk Element Score Matrix using a "likelihood of occurrence" score and a "severity of impact" score (see Table 6.12). The "likelihood of occurrence" score is determined by team members using a 1 (low) to 5 (high) scale. The "impact of occurrence" score is also determined by team members using a 1 (low) to 5 (high) scale. The "risk element" score is computed by multiplying the "likelihood of occurrence" score by the "impact of occurrence" score for each risk element. The "risk element" score is defined using a 1 (low) to 25 (high) scale.

TABLE 6.12   Risk Element Score Matrix

Risk Element Score		Severity		
		Low (1)	**Medium (3)**	**High (5)**
Likelihood	**High (5)**	5	15	25
	Medium (3)	3	9	15
	Low (1)	1	3	5

A risk element is considered to have high risk if the risk element scores are from 16 to 25. A risk element is considered to have a medium risk if the risk element score is from 9 to 15. A risk element is considered to have a low risk if the risk element score is from 1 to 8. Risk elements are prioritized in a Risk Element Matrix (see Table 6.13). Column 1 lists the CTQs or high-level CTPs under study. Column 2 lists the risk element(s) for the CTQ and/or high-level CTP. Column 3 shows the hazard for each risk element; that is, the potential source of harm associated with the risk element. Column 4 shows the harm for each risk element; that is, the physical injury to person and/or damage to property associated with the risk element. Columns 5, 6, and 7 show the "likelihood of occurrence," "severity of impact," and "risk element" scores respectively. Team members need to attend to all medium and high risks in a risk abatement plan.

TABLE 6.13　　Risk Element Matrix

1	2	3	4	5	6	7	8	9	10	11	12	13
CTQ or CTP	Potential Risk Element	Hazard (potential source of harm)	Harm (physical injury to person and/or damage to property)	Likelihood Before	Severity Before	Risk Element Score Before	Countermeasure Or Contingency Plan	Likelihood After	Severity After	Risk Element Score After	Risk Owner	Completion Date for Countermeasure of Contingency Plan

Team members use Table 6.13 to construct a risk abatement plan for risk elements with high and medium risk element scores. First, they identify countermeasures and/or contingency plans to reduce the risk element scores for each risk element with high and medium risk scores (see Column 8 of Table 6.13). Countermeasures are determined using brainstorming, creative thinking, TRIZ, process improvement methods based on data analysis, or some other technique. Second, team members estimate "likelihood" and "severity" scores, and compute the risk element score, for each risk element in the risk abatement plan (see Columns 9, 10, and 11 of Table

6.13). Third, team members identify the risk element owner and completion date for countermeasure being put into motion (see Columns 12 and 13 of Table 6.13). Fourth, team members document the risk abatement plan. Fifth, team members and the process owner carry out the risk abatement plan. Sixth, team members document the lessons learned and transfer to other relevant risk elements. Seventh, team members incorporate the risk abatement plan into the control plan before the product, service, or process is turned over to the process owner.

6.7 OPTIMIZE THE TOTAL LIFE CYCLE COST (TLCC) OF THE DESIGN

Definition of Total Life Cycle Cost (TLCC)

Total Life Cycle Cost (TLCC) identifies and quantifies all aspects of cost associated with the following:

- **Developing a product, service, or process concept.** This involves conducting research on the concept, designing the concept, and conducting marketing research on the concept.

- **Creating a product, service, or process prototype.** This involves performing functionality tests, usability tests, durability tests, safety tests, and destructive tests to determine appropriate modifications and changes to the design concept.

- **Producing a product or generating a service.** This usually involves pilot runs, initial production, scale-up runs, and full-scale production. These activities require raw materials and supplies, equipment and maintenance, safety policies, procedures, packaging, and logistics.

- **Using a product, service, or process in the field.** This involves sales and marketing, channels of distribution, service, warranty, repair and replacement, rebates, and safety.

- **Disposing of a product, service, or process (recycling and retirement).** This requires early consideration of facilities and equipment, logistics, environmental factors, and legal factors relevant to the disposal function in the Design Phase.

Relationship Between Design and Total Life Cycle Cost

Past experience with many products has determined that approximately 70% of total life cycle costs are directly due to the design function. Further experience has shown that early design decisions (the first 5%) can determine the lion's share of the 70% of total life cycle costs.

Some important downstream total life cycle costs that must be considered when designing a product, service, or process include: cost of quality, cost of manufacturability, cost of assembly, cost of maintainability, cost of disposal, and cost to the environment. These costs can come back and cause serious, even deadly, damage to the profitability of a product, service, or process if not properly attended to when designing a product, service, or process.

Using TLCC to Reduce the Set of Potential Designs

Total Life Cycle Costs (TLCCs) are usually applied to products. However, the concept of TLCCs can be generalized to services. For example, if a patient is cared for, and believes he has been diagnosed and treated properly, does this ensure that the patient knows how to best care for himself after departing a hospital? If the patient is not instructed in his own self-care, or choose not to follow his instructions, he may continue to exhibit dysfunctional habits, such as smoking, that will mean his TLCCs are higher than a patient who would follow the discharge instructions.

Potential designs should be eliminated if the price the customer is willing to pay (Pc) does not exceed the price required (Pr) to recover costs of goods sold (CGS) plus overhead plus profit; in quantitative terms:

$$P_c > \{Pr = CGS + Overhead + Profit\}.$$

Cost of goods sold (CGS) is a concept usually related to products. However, CGS can also be related to services. For example, what is the "cost of services sold" for a nurse providing service to a patient? What is the CGS for a nurse practitioner or a physician? Is there a difference in the willingness of a patient, or managed care provider, as to who should provide the service and how much it is worth?

The components of CGS and overhead are as follows:

- **Direct costs**—Direct costs are costs directly associated with the development, manufacture, distribution, maintenance, and disposal of a product, service, or process.

- **Residual costs**—Residual costs are potential costs attributable to producing a product or generating a service; for example, warranty costs, environmental clean-up costs, and corporate image costs.

- **Fixed costs**—Fixed costs are costs associated with the investment required to develop and produce/generate a product, service, or process. They do not change with the volume of production or service; for example, buildings and grounds, equipment, and insurance.

- **Variable costs**—Variable costs are the costs directly connected to producing each unit of product or rendering each unit of service (for example, materials, supplies, labor, and packaging).

Team members use Table 6.14 to keep track of costs for all TLCC stages.

TABLE 6.14   Total Life Cycle Costs

	Direct Costs	**Residual Costs**	**Fixed Costs**	**Variable Costs**
Concept				
Prototype				
Production				
Field Use				
Disposal and Environment				

6.8 DEVELOP A PROCESS MODEL FOR THE BEST DESIGN

Definition of a Model

A **model** is a representation or abstraction of an idea, object (product or service), or a process. It is used to understand the nature and/or behavior of the ideas, objects, or systems they represent. Examples of models are: mathematical equations ($E = mc^2$), prototypes (e.g., small-scale physical representation of a piece of furniture), blueprint of a motor mount, floor plan of a retail store, flowcharts/process maps, and verbal description of a service, to name a few.

Types of Models

There are three types of models: descriptive, predictive, and prescriptive. Each type of model is defined in this section.

Descriptive models are used to describe the "what is" condition of a product, service, or process. For example:

- Profit = Revenue – Cost
- $E = mc^2$

Predictive models are used to predict future events. For example:

- Demand = $a - b$(Unit Price) + Error
- Sales = f (version of the service, price of the service, promotional budget for the service, channels of distribution used for the service) + Error.

Prescriptive models are used to identify the best alternative to optimize a process to reach an objective. Examples of prescriptive models can be found in queuing (waiting line) theory, inventory theory, mathematical programming, and simulation. An application of a prescriptive computer simulation model is used to identify the alternative shuttle bus routes and schedules to minimize the percentage of people "waiting for and traveling on" a shuttle bus for 15 or more minutes.

Benefits of a Model

Models present several benefits to the people who use them to understand a product, process, or service. A list of the benefits follows:

- **Increases communication**—A model provides an easy way to convey ideas between engineers, managers, hourly personnel, vendors, and other stakeholders. It is a concrete, visual way of representing complex systems. It facilitates effective training of employees and other stakeholders.
- **Promotes standardization of "best practices"**—Many models require a flowchart that helps standardize a product, service, or process.
- **Enables benchmarking**—Benchmarking requires flowchart-to-flowchart comparisons of methods or theories to learn about and improve a design.
- **Promotes planning**—Models enable designers to visualize the elements of new or modified processes and their interactions while still in the planning stages.
- **Provides an overview of the system**—Flowcharts provide an easy way to view the critical elements and steps of the process. A model highlights unnecessary details and breaks down the system so designers and others get a clear, unencumbered look at what they're creating.
- **Defines roles**—A model demonstrates the roles of personnel, workstations, and sub-processes in a system. It also shows the personnel, operations, and locations involved in the process. This promotes more efficient design efforts.
- **Demonstrates interrelationships**—Models show how the elements of a process relate to, and possibly interact with, each other. This promotes more efficient design efforts.
- **Promotes logical accuracy**—Models enable the viewer to easily spot errors in logic. Planning is facilitated because designers have to clearly break down all of the elements and operations of the process.
- **Facilitates trouble-shooting**—Models are an excellent diagnostic tool. Problems in the process, failures in the system, and barriers to communication can be detected by using a model.
- **Documents a system**—The record of a system that a model provides enables anyone to easily examine and understand the system. Models facilitate changing a system because the documentation of what exists is available.

Steps for Developing a Process Model of a Design

There are nine steps for developing a process model of a design concept:

1. Identify the idea, object, or process for the design.
2. Identify the start and stop points, and any other boundaries.

3. Select the appropriate type of model (e.g., static or dynamic, etc.).

4. Construct initial high-level model.

5. Construct detailed-level model.

6. Validate the detailed-level model.

7. Optimize the model.

8. Perform a pilot test of the model.

9. Transfer the model to its proper user.

Static Process Models of a Design

Flowcharts

A **flowchart** is a pictorial representation of the steps, decisions, and flows that comprise a process. The American National Standards Institute, Inc. (ANSI) has approved a standard set of flowchart symbols that are used for defining and documenting a process (see Figure 6.2). The shape of the symbol and the information written within the symbol provide information about that particular step of the process.

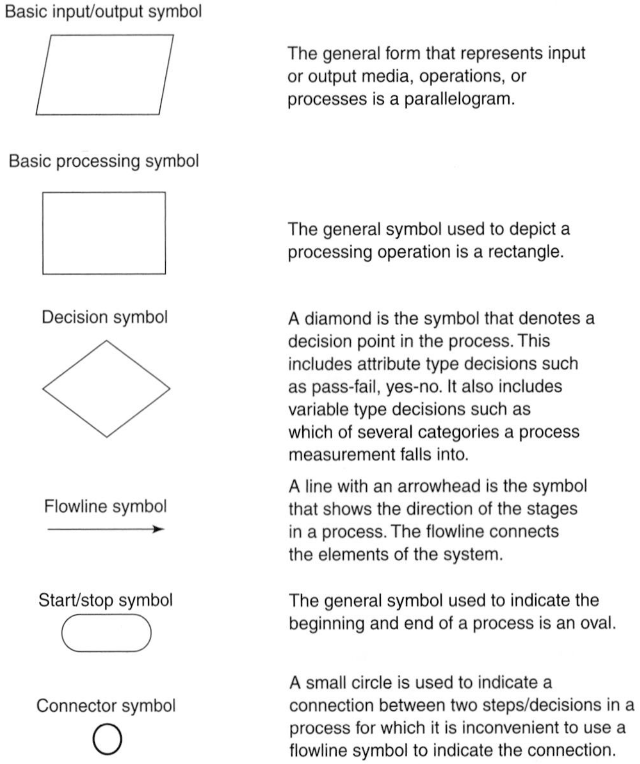

Basic input/output symbol

The general form that represents input or output media, operations, or processes is a parallelogram.

Basic processing symbol

The general symbol used to depict a processing operation is a rectangle.

Decision symbol

A diamond is the symbol that denotes a decision point in the process. This includes attribute type decisions such as pass-fail, yes-no. It also includes variable type decisions such as which of several categories a process measurement falls into.

Flowline symbol

A line with an arrowhead is the symbol that shows the direction of the stages in a process. The flowline connects the elements of the system.

Start/stop symbol

The general symbol used to indicate the beginning and end of a process is an oval.

Connector symbol

A small circle is used to indicate a connection between two steps/decisions in a process for which it is inconvenient to use a flowline symbol to indicate the connection.

FIGURE 6.2   Standard Flowcharting Symbols

Using the symbols in Figure 6.2 standardizes process definition and documentation.

Example of a Flowchart. Figure 6.3 shows a flowchart of a service design process. The process begins with team members developing the design of a trial service prototype, including specifications for the CTQs and high-level CTPs. Next, team members evaluate the prototype. A "bad" evaluation results in looping back to the design of the trial prototype specifications step for redesign of the service. A "good" evaluation results in a trial of the service. Next, team members evaluate the success of the trial service. A "bad" evaluation results in looping back to the design of the trail prototype specifications step. A "good" evaluation results in acceptance of the service design and the end of the service design process for the service under study.

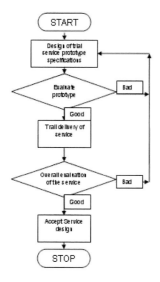

FIGURE 6.3 Service Design Process

Integrated Flowcharts (also called Deployment Flowcharts)

An **integrated flowchart** is a special type of flowchart that is used to highlight responsibility for the various steps and decisions in a process. A small circle on an integrated flowchart indicates a stakeholder of the process that must be kept informed about a certain step or decision in the process.

Figure 6.4 shows an integrated flowchart for a software development process. The columns of Figure 6.4 represent all the stakeholders of the proposed software product: programmers, a supervisor, a product manager, the customer service department, and customers. The process begins with a customer service representative identifying features that are required by customers. Next, the product manager, a customer service representative, and the programming supervisor decide which features to include in the next version of the software product; they keep the programmers informed about their decisions. Then, the product manager and programming supervisor develop the requirements and definition of the required features, while keeping the customer service department informed of their decisions. Then, the programmers and their supervisor plan the development of the new features into the software product. Next, the programmers develop the new features and keep their supervisor and the product manager informed of their progress.

Then, the product manager, supervisor, and programmers release the new version of the updated software to see if the customer's requirements are met, and they inform the customer service department and customers of their release decision. Next, the product manager decides if the customer's requirements have been met by the revised software product. If the answer is no, the programmers modify the new features and send them back to the "release new version" step. If the answer is yes, the product manager, the supervisor, and the programmers release the new version of the software and inform customer service and customers. Finally, the programmers and their supervisor support the new version of the software product. The design process terminates here for this software project.

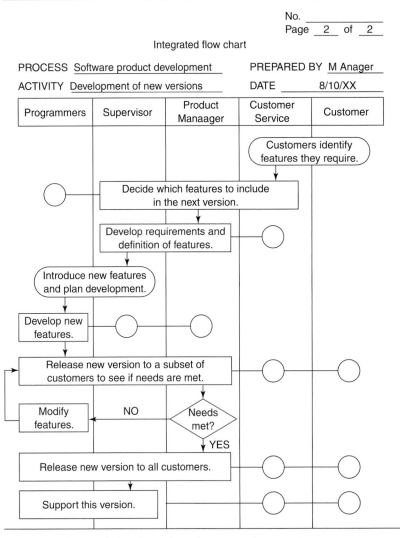

FIGURE 6.4   Integrated Flowchart of a Software Development Process

Value-Added/Non-Value-Added Flowcharts (VA/NVA)

A **VA/NVA flowchart**, also called an *opportunity flowchart*, is a special type of integrated flowchart in which there are only two columns: a value-added column and a non-value-added column. The value-added column contains the steps and decisions of a product, service, or process that customers are willing to pay for because they positively change the product, service, or process in the view of the customer. The non-value-added column contains the steps and decisions of a product, service, or process that:

1. Customers are not willing to pay for.
2. Do not change the product or service.
3. Contain errors, defects, or omissions.
4. Require preparation or setup.
5. Involve control or inspection.
6. Involve over-production, special processing, and inventory.
7. Involve waiting and delays.

Figure 6.5 shows a generic flowchart constructed to highlight value-added (VA) and non-value-added (NVA) steps in a process to identify non-value-added steps in a process for possible elimination or modification, thereby reducing the complexity of the process.

Imagine a flowchart for making a photocopy of a document. It might include the following steps: turn on the machine, wait for it to warm up, open the lid, insert the document, close the lid, press the copy button, wait for the copy, open the lid, remove the original document, close the lid, remove the copy, turn off the machine. Imagine how complex the photocopy process gets if the machine runs out of toner, jams, or runs out of paper, to name a few problems. All of the functions in the previous sentence are non-value-added functions that add an enormous amount of complexity to the process.

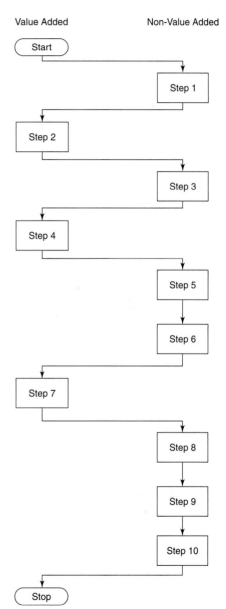

FIGURE 6.5 VA/NVA Generic Flowchart

Value Analysis Matrix

A **value analysis matrix** is a tool that assists in identifying the steps and decisions of a product, service, or process that are non-value added, and the nature of the non-value-added steps or decisions. Table 6.15 shows a VA/NVA matrix for the VA/NVA flowchart shown in Figure 6.5. In Figure 6.5, only Steps 2, 4, and 7 are value-added steps of the process. The value-added steps account for only 9% (9 minutes = 2 minutes + 5 minutes + 2 minutes) of the 100 minute total elapsed cycle time for the process. The remaining cycle time of 91 minutes is attributable to non-value-added steps such as fixing errors (4 minutes), prep/set-up (10 minutes), control/inspection (30 minutes + 7 minutes), and transportation/motion (10 minutes + 20 minutes + 10 minutes).

TABLE 6.15 Value Analysis Matrix

Process Step	1	2	3	4	5	6	7	8	9	10	Total	% Total
Time (minutes)	10	2	10	5	30	20	2	7	4	10	100	100%
Value-Added		X		X			X				9	9%
Non-Value-Added												
Fixing Errors									X		4	4%
Prep/Set-Up	X										10	10%
Control/Inspection						X		X			37	37%
Transportation/Motion				X			X			X	40	40%

Layout Flowchart

A **layout flowchart** depicts the floor plan of an area, usually including the flow of paperwork or goods and the location of equipment, file cabinets, storage areas, and so on. These flowcharts are especially helpful in visualizing and improving the layout to more efficiently utilize a space.

Figure 6.6 shows a layout flowchart before and after flowcharting analysis and flow improvement. The existing system is shown in Figure 6.6a; the new proposed system appears in Figure 6.6b. This flowchart includes the flow of work along with the floor plan and location of desks and files. Comparing the existing and proposed systems is easier when the process's flow is documented this way. Sometimes a flowchart that depicts the physical layout of the process and the flow through it is called a "spaghetti map," as it often highlights the convoluted flows of real processes.

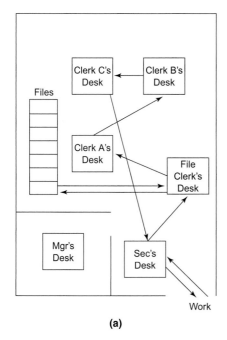
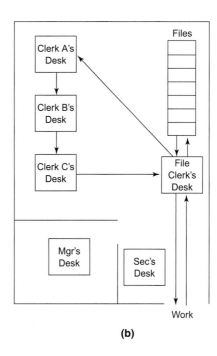

(a)   **(b)**

FIGURE 6.6   Office Layout Flowchart

Returning to the dormitory example, the "Graduate Preference" design is put forth as the leading design. A model for the "Graduate Preference" design was created with Broderbund's 3D Home Architect 4.0 and is depicted in Figures 6.7 through 6.10.

Recall, Figure 6.1 shows a floor plan with the dimensions intentionally not included. However, it is within range of what is expected to be available for a single room.

Figure 6.7 shows what you would see after you walked into a room through the front door. From this view, you can see an executive desk chair, entertainment center, large corner desk, and a queen-size bed.

FIGURE 6.7   View from Front Door

Figure 6.8 shows the view of the room if you were sitting at the desk and looking back over the room. From left to right, you can see the entrance hallway, the entrance to the kitchen, the closet, and the bathroom.

FIGURE 6.8   View of Desk and Entertainment Center

Figure 6.9 shows the bathroom. Notice that the bathroom has a full bathtub.

Figure 6.10 shows a closer view of the kitchen. Notice the compact refrigerator at the end of the countertop.

These illustrations provide a loose interpretation of the model put forth by the Analyze Phase, which will be further developed in the Design Phase.

FIGURE 6.9   View of Bathroom   **FIGURE 6.10**   View of Kitchen

Dynamic Process Models of a Design

Definition of Simulation

Simulation is a method for developing a model to numerically study and describe the alternative characteristics of an idea, product, service, or process over a pre-established time frame to select the best (optimal) alternative from the set of available alternatives. Simulation is discussed in detail in Chapter 13, "Discrete Event Simulation Models."

A quantitative statement of a simulation optimization model is:

Simultaneously optimize $\{CTQ_a, CTQ_b, CTQ_c, CTQ_d, CTQ_e\}$,
where

CTQ_a[center, spread, shape] $= f(X_{1a}$[center, spread, shape], $\dots, X_{na}$[center, spread, shape])
CTQ_b[center, spread, shape] $= f(X_{1b}$[center, spread, shape], $\dots, X_{nb}$[center, spread, shape])
CTQ_c[center, spread, shape] $= f(X_{1c}$[center, spread, shape], $\dots, X_{nc}$[center, spread, shape])
CTQ_d[center, spread, shape] $= f(X_{1d}$[center, spread, shape], $\dots, X_{nd}$[center, spread, shape])
CTQ_e[center, spread, shape] $= f(X_{1e}$[center, spread, shape], $\dots, X_{ne}$[center, spread, shape])

Advantages and Disadvantages of Simulation

The four main advantages of a simulation model are:

- Provides a method to study an extremely complex system.
- Allows experimentation on a system without disrupting the system.
- Promotes "what-if" analysis of a system with instant feedback.
- Conserves raw materials and resources.

The four major disadvantages of a simulation model are:

- Can consume much time and resources.
- Is only as reliable as the assumptions and data utilized in building the model.
- Provides only estimates of true system parameters.
- Provides no guarantee of the optimality of the result.

Types of Simulation Models

There are four common taxonomies of simulation models.

The first taxonomy is a static model versus a dynamic model. A **static model** is one in which events are studied for only one point in time and, if repeated, are independent of time frames. A **dynamic model** is one in which events are run over time. The second taxonomy is a deterministic model versus a probabilistic model. A **deterministic model** assumes constant values for each independent parameter of a set of one or more independent variables; for example, cycle time for steps in the process, which will yield a fixed and "determined" value of an outcome each and every time the independent variables are set at the same constant values. A **probabilistic model** exhibits a distribution for each parameter; for example, a stable and normally distributed cycle time with a mean of 30 minutes and a standard deviation of 5 minutes. The third taxonomy is a continuous model versus a discrete model. A **continuous model** continuously runs a clock representing time in which there is randomness of occurrence over all events. A **discrete model** advances a clock discretely according to the occurrence of the next event. Finally, the fourth taxonomy is a Monte Carlo simulation model versus a discrete event simulation model. **Monte Carlo simulation** advances time by a clock. A **discrete event simulation** advances time by events.

Steps to Performing a Discrete Event Simulation

There are nine steps in performing a discrete event simulation. Each step is described next with an example of simulating the shuttle bus system at the University of Miami [see Reference 7].

Step 1. The first part of Step 1 is for PD team members to specify the idea, product, service, or process to be simulated, as well as the purpose of the simulation. The University of Miami shuttle bus system is being developed with the purpose of promoting a campus perimeter parking culture. Research shows that a perimeter parking lot culture is supported by a combination of an appropriately priced parking policy, and an efficient and reliable shuttle bus system. Figure 6.11 shows a map of the University of Miami campus.

FIGURE 6.11   Map of the University of Miami

The second part of Step 1 is for team members to collect input from relevant stakeholders about the simulation concerning their perspective on the parameters needed for the simulation. For example, the stakeholders of the University of Miami shuttle bus system are passengers, parking department staff, and facilities planning staff.

The passengers include students, faculty, administration, staff, and visitors. An extensive survey was conducted at various parking lots where passengers were asked: "What would make you park at the perimeter parking lots?" The answers are summarized as follows:

- Overall time from arrival at shuttle stop to arrival at destination (subject of this simulation model).
- Comfortable shuttle bus stations.
- Sheltered shuttle bus stations.

The staff of the Parking Department was personally interviewed and asked, "In your opinion, what issues must be addressed to get passengers to park at perimeter lots?" The answers are summarized as follows:

- Adequate existing routes (defined by stops) to get passengers to their destinations quickly.
- Sufficient number of shuttle buses to get passengers to their destinations quickly.
- Procedures for controlling shuttle bus routes (e.g., dispatcher control) to eliminate inefficiencies.
- Appropriately equipped shuttle buses to deal with handicapped passengers.

Additionally, the Parking Department staff indicated that the preceding items require an understanding of the following aspects of the shuttle bus system:

- Arrival patterns for passengers to stops.
- Arrival patterns for shuttle buses to stops.
- Shuttle travel time between stops.
- Shuttle wait time at stops.

The staff of the Facilities Planning Department was personally interviewed and asked, "In your opinion, what issues must be considered to get passengers to park at perimeter lots?" The answers are summarized as follows:

- Location of existing and new roads.
- Location and size of existing and new parking lots.
- Location of decommissioned parking lots.

The third part of Step 1 is for team members to assign roles and responsibilities for building and experimenting with the discrete event simulation model. This step requires that team members prepare a Gantt chart for the simulation study. The Gantt chart for the simulation study is not shown here.

Step 2. The first part of Step 2 is to develop a conceptual model of the idea, product, service, or process. In the shuttle bus example, developing a conceptual model involves specifying the CTQ, which is the percentage of riders with 15-minute shuttle bus service from arrival point to destination point. The CTQ was established in the Measure Phase of a Six Sigma project. The second part of Step 2 is to study the real-world idea, product, service, or process. In the shuttle bus example, this involves mapping out the existing shuttle bus routes and stops. Figure 6.12 is a layout flowchart of one of the shuttle bus routes, with stop numbers indicated on it.

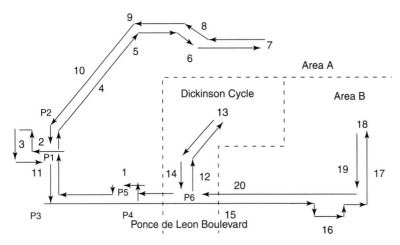

FIGURE 6.12   Existing Route Structures (Numbers Are Route Stops)

The third part of Step 2 is to identify the CTPs. The CTPs include the following:

- Item (entity or transaction) being processed.
- Activity being performed on the item.
- Resources needed to process the item.
- Connections between the activities being performed on the items.
- Properties (numerical characteristics) of the activities, entities, or resources.
- Control logic (rules) by which items are processed through activities using resources.

Items. The items (entities or transactions) being processed are introduced into a model using a generator. A generator issues items with attributes (individualized characteristics) at a specified rate and quantity. In the shuttle bus example, there are two types of items: shuttle buses and passengers. Shuttle buses are generated (enter the system) according to an arrival distribution for each shuttle bus stop, a service (time to load up or wait) distribution for each shuttle bus stop, and a travel time distribution between each connected pair of shuttle bus stops. Passengers are generated (enter the system) according to an arrival distribution for each shuttle bus stop.

Activities. The activities are the operations being performed on the items in the system. In the shuttle bus example, the activities are advancing each shuttle bus from stop to stop through its route.

Resources. Resources are the factors needed to process an item as it passes through a system. In the shuttle bus example, the resources are as follows:

- Number of shuttle buses.
- Capacity of each shuttle bus.
- Hours of operation for each shuttle bus (bus, driver, and dispatcher).

Connections. Connections are the links between the activities in a system. An entity enters and exits an activity through a connection line. Entities can split and reform while moving through connection lines (e.g., a three-part form is separated at one point in a process and reassembled at the end of the process). The connections in the shuttle bus example are shown by the arrows in Figure 6.13.

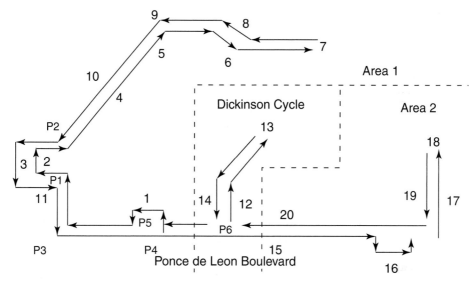

FIGURE 6.13   Connections in the Shuttle Bus System

Properties. Properties are the numerical characteristics of activities, items, or resources. In the shuttle bus example, one property of a passenger (item) is if the passenger is handicapped and requires wheelchair access to the shuttle bus (Yes = 1 or No = 0). One property of a shuttle bus (item) is if the shuttle bus is equipped with wheelchair access (Yes = 1 or No = 0) or the number of seats on the shuttle bus (n).

Control Logic. Control logic defines the rules by which items are processed through the activities in a system using the resources that help define the system. In the shuttle bus example, one instance of control logic is that a shuttle bus cannot move from a stop until a dispatcher knows the previous shuttle bus has left its stop. This prevents multiple shuttle buses at a given stop.

The fourth part of Step 2 is to develop a realistic model of the system under study that relates the CTPs to the CTQs; that is, to make a flowchart of the connections between activities of the system under study. This requires that team members create a description or graphic (e.g., flowchart) of the system under study that indicates how the items flow through the system. In the shuttle bus example, this involves developing a discrete event simulation model of the shuttle bus system using a simulation software package.

The fifth part of Step 2 is to compare the flows of the items from the model with flows from the real-world system to determine if the simulated system reflects reality. In the shuttle bus example, this is comparing the waiting time distributions for the passengers at each shuttle bus stop for each simulated and actual shuttle bus stop.

The sixth part of Step 2 is to revise the simulation model, if necessary, until its functioning adequately reflects the functioning of the actual system. In the shuttle bus example, the simulation model was revised until the waiting time distributions for passengers at each shuttle bus stop were not statistically different between the simulated system and the actual system.

Step 3. In Step 3, team members collect the data needed to define the parameters of the simulation model; for example, arrival and service time distributions, and attributes of the items.

The first part of Step 3 is for team members to collect data on the arrival patterns for the items (entities) in each activity. Generic questions and selected answers for the shuttle bus system for this part of Step 3 are shown next:

- How many items enter a given activity per unit of time? How many passengers arrive at each shuttle bus stop every 5 minutes?

- Is the rate constant or variable over time? The rate is variable with a mean of 9 passengers with a standard deviation of 3 passengers. We can identify this as one assumption that is not likely true. Why? Academic class schedules vary throughout the day, and consequently, so do the number of students and faculty. Also, separately, the time to arrival between bus stops is also likely to vary with the time of day due to traffic conditions.

- If the rate is variable, is it stable? The rate is a stable Poisson distribution [see Reference 6].

- Are the units batched (collect all ballots until they are processed)? Passengers are collected until the shuttle bus comes to the stop.

The second part of Step 3 is to estimate the processing times and resources (e.g., costs) for the items in each activity. Generic questions and answers for the shuttle bus system for this part of Step 3 are shown next:

- How long does it take to process an item in a given activity? This is the mean, standard deviation, and shape of the service time distribution, for a shuttle bus to load passengers at a stop.

- Are processing times stable distributions? The service time distributions for all shuttle stops are stable distributions.

- How much does it cost to process an entity in a given activity? It costs an average of $1.00 to process one passenger[1] for the shuttle bus system.

- What resources are used to process an entity by a given activity? In this example, these include shuttle buses, drivers, and dispatchers, to name a few resources.

-----

[1] $1.00 is a fictitious number.

The third part of Step 3 is to estimate movement (transfer) times for items between activities. Generic questions and answers for the shuttle bus system for this part of Step 3 are shown next:

- How long does it take to move between two linked activities? The inter-arrival time between stop A and stop B has a mean of 5 minutes.

- Are movement/transfer times stable? The inter-arrival time between stop A and stop B is a stable normal distribution with a standard deviation of 1/2 minute.

- Are the entities batched? Passengers are batched (collected) until they exit the shuttle bus at their destination.

The fourth part of Step 3 is to estimate storage and wait time statistics for items as they pass through the system. Generic questions and answers for the shuttle bus system for this part of Step 3 are shown next:

- How long is an entity stored in a given activity?

- Are the storage times constant or variable?

- Are the entities batched?

The fifth part of Step 3 is to determine the resources required by each activity. Generic questions and answers for the shuttle bus system for this part of Step 3 are shown next:

- What resources are required to process entities by each activity? Shuttle buses, drivers, and dispatchers are required to move passengers around the campus.

- What is the availability schedule for each resource for each activity?

The sixth part of Step 3 is to determine the control logic of the system. Generic questions and answers for the shuttle bus system for this part of Step 3 are shown next:

- What path does a particular entity take through the model? Passengers can select either the green, orange, or express lines.

- What percentage of the entities takes path A1 versus path A2 through the model? Each route has an identified percentage of the passengers selecting it.

To summarize, data for all the CTPs specified above were collected for the simulation model of the shuttle bus system.

Step 4. In the fourth step, team members develop a computer model for the system under study using a discrete event simulation software package—for example, SigmaFlow (see Reference 7 and Chapter 13). As stated previously, the computer model includes: entities, activities, resources, control logic, and properties of items. All of these elements of a simulation model were developed for the shuttle bus system.

Step 5. In the fifth step, team members run and validate the simulation model against the real system to determine its validity as a surrogate for the actual system. In the shuttle bus system, the CTQs and CTPs from the simulation model compared favorably with the statistics of the real system.

Step 6. In the sixth step, team members plan one or more experiments to identify the optimal configuration of the system (best levels for the CTPs to obtain the best statistics for the CTQs). In the shuttle bus system, this involves determining the route designs that yield the minimum percentage of passengers waiting for and arriving at their destination in more than 15 minutes. Team members examined many possible routes as part of the experiment to determine the optimal set of routes.

Step 7. In the seventh step, team members run, record, and analyze the experimental alternatives using the computer simulation model. In the shuttle bus example, each possible route structure was studied using the simulation model to minimize the percentage of passengers with more than 15-minute shuttle bus service from arrival point to destination point.

Step 8. In the eighth step, team members must study the results and select the best high-level route design. The configuration of the optimal route structure is shown in Figure 6.14.

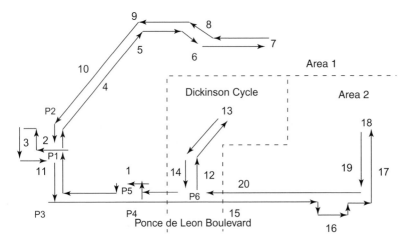

FIGURE 6.14 Optimal Route Structure

The optimal route yields 5% of passengers with more than 15 minutes between arrival and destination, while the existing route structure yields 35% with more than 15 minutes between arrival and destination. This is a significant improvement in the performance of the shuttle bus system.

Step 9. In the ninth step, team members make recommendations concerning the best high-level design concept by:

- Documenting assumptions concerning the best high-level design concept.
- Preparing report and presentation.
- Avoiding the use of technical jargon.

In the shuttle bus example, this involved presenting the finding for action by management. Management acted, and the shuttle bus system is much improved today.

6.9 TRANSFER HIGH-LEVEL DESIGN TO PROCESS OWNER WITH DESIGN SCORECARDS

Recall from the Measure Phase that the purpose of a design scorecard is to formally state critical parameters (CTQs, part features (CTPs), etc.) in the Voice of the Customer and the Predicted Voice of the Process (see Table 6.16). Design scorecards help PD team members:

- Establish nominal values and specification limits for each CTQ and CTP, as well as the target for the process sigma (Part A of the scorecard).
- Predict output of the Voice of the Process in respect to stability, shape, mean, and standard deviation, as well as DPU and predicted process sigma (Part B of the scorecard).
- Highlight problems and risks of CTQs and CTPs with respect to failure to meet desired process sigma levels.
- Track CTQs and CTPs throughout the entire life of the product, service, or process.

TABLE 6.16 Generic Design Scorecard

Scorecard—Part A (Voice of the Customer)					Scorecard—Part B (Predicted Voice of the Process)					
CTQ or CTP	Target (Nominal)	LSL	USL	Sigma Target	Stable (Y/N)	Shape	Mean	Standard Deviation	DPU	Predicted Process Sigma

6.10 ANALYZE PHASE TOLLGATE REVIEW (CHECK SHEET)

The typical elements of an Analyze Phase tollgate review are as follows:

Generate High-Level Design Concepts for Critical Parameters

Determine the effort level needed to create design concepts.	(Low/Medium/High)
Break down CTQs into CTPs using thinking tools.	(Yes/No)
Break down CTQs into CTPs using TRIZ.	(Yes/No)
Break down CTQs into CTPs using Benchmarking.	(Yes/No)

Reduce the Set of Potential Design Concepts Using a Pugh Matrix   **(Yes/No)**

Create a Limited Set of Potential Design Concepts:

Using FMEA.	(Yes/No)
Using Hazard Analysis.	(Yes/No)
Using a Risk Abatement Plan.	(Yes/No)

Optimize the Total Life Cycle Cost of the Design

Determine the total life cycle costs (TLCC) of the design.	(Yes/No)
Use TLCC to reduce the set of potential designs.	(Yes/No)

Develop a Process Model for the Best Design

Identify the start and stop points, and any other boundaries.	(Yes/No)
Construct initial high-level model using one of the following:	
Flowchart	(Yes/No)
Integrated flowchart	(Yes/No)
VA/NVA flowchart	(Yes/No)
Value analysis matrix	(Yes/No)
Layout flowchart	(Yes/No)
Simulation	(Yes/No)

Construct Detailed-Level Model; If a Discrete Event Simulation, then:

Specify the idea, product, service, or process to be simulated.	(Yes/No)
Collect input from relevant stakeholders about their perspective on the parameters needed for the simulation.	(Yes/No)

Assign roles and responsibilities for building and experimenting with the discrete event simulation model. (Yes/No)

Develop a conceptual model of the idea, product, service, or process. (Yes/No)

Identify the CTPs, including:

Item (entity or transaction) being processed. (Yes/No)

Activity being performed on the item. (Yes/No)

Resources needed to process the item. (Yes/No)

Connections between the activities being performed on the items. (Yes/No)

Properties (numerical characteristics) of the activities, entities, or resources. (Yes/No)

Control logic (rules) by which items are processed. (Yes/No)

Flowchart the connections between activities of the system by relating the CTPs to the CTQs. (Yes/No)

Compared the flows of the items from the model and actual system. (Yes/No)

Collect the data needed to define the parameters of the simulation model: (Yes/No)

Arrival time distributions. (Yes/No)

Service time distributions. (Yes/No)

Attributes of the items. (Yes/No)

Storage and wait time statistics. (Yes/No)

Resources required by each activity. (Yes/No)

Control logic of the system. (Yes/No)

Develop a computer model for the system. (Yes/No)

Run and validate the simulation model against the real system. (Yes/No)

Experiment to identify the optimal system, best CTPs for the CTQs. (Yes/No)

Run, record, and analyze the experimental data. (Yes/No)

Study the results and select the best high-level design. (Yes/No)

Make recommendations concerning the best design concept by:

Documenting the models assumptions. (Yes/No)

Preparing a report and presentation. (Yes/No)

Avoiding the use of technical jargon. (Yes/No)

Transfer the Model to the Process Owner with Design Scorecards **(Yes/No)**

Conduct an Analyze Phase Tollgate Review **(Yes/No)**

6.11 OUTPUTS FROM THE ANALYZE PHASE

The Analyze Phase has two primary outputs:

- A high-level design (including CTQs and high-level CTPs).
- A set of design scorecards for the best high-level design CTQs and high-level CTPs.

SUMMARY

The Analyze Phase of the DMADV model consists of using creative techniques to develop a set of potential high-level design concepts, using a Pugh Matrix to compare and contrast the alternative design concepts, reducing the set of design concepts based on their potential for risk, optimizing Total Life Cycle Cost of the best design, developing a process model for the best design (perhaps a discrete event simulation, if appropriate), and preparing design scorecards for the best high-level design.

REFERENCES

1. G. Altshuller, *And Suddenly the Inventor Appeared: TRIZ, the Theory of Inventive Problem Solving*, 2nd ed. Translated by Lev Shulyak. (Worcester, MA: Technical Innovation Center, Inc., 1996).

2. E. de Bono, *Teach Your Child How to Think* (New York: Penguin Books, 1992).

3. G. Dieter, *Engineering Design: A Materials and Processing Approach*, 2nd ed. (New York: McGraw-Hill, 1991).

4. E. Domb, J. Miller, E. MacGran, and M. Slocum, "The 39 Features of Altshuller's Contradiction Matrix," *The TRIZ Journal*, July 1997.

5. E. Domb, "Contradictions: Air Bag Applications," *The TRIZ Journal*, July 1997.

6. R. Dovich, *Reliability Statistics* (Milwaukee, WI: ASQ Press, 1990).

7. E. Iakovou, and J.E. Pachon, "Optimization of the Transportation System at a University: A Continuous Improvement Quality Management Methodology," *Quality Engineering*, Vol. 13, No. 3, March 2001, pp.427–435.

8. SigmaFlow Process Analysis and Design, Mapper, Workbench, and Modeler, Version 2 (Plano, TX: www.SigmaFlow.com, 2005).

9. J. Juran, *Quality Control Handbook*, 4th ed. (New York: McGraw-Hill, 1988).

10. P. Kotler, *Marketing Management: Analysis, Planning, and Control*, 9th ed. (Upper Saddle River, NJ: Prentice Hall, 1999).

11. J. Terninko, "40 Inventive Principles with Social Examples," *The TRIZ Journal*, June 2001.

DESIGN PHASE

SECTIONS

LEARNING OBJECTIVES

After reading this chapter, you will know how to:

- Construct a detailed design.
- Create operational definitions for each detailed CTP.

- Validate the measurement systems for each detailed CTP.
- Estimate the capability for each detailed CTP.
- Prepare a control and verification plan.
- Pass a Design Phase tollgate review.

INTRODUCTION

PD team members use the Design Phase of the DMADV model to move from the high-level design they developed in the Analyze Phase to a detailed design. PD team members will use various tools and methods to predict the sigma level of the detailed design. After the Design Phase, PD team members will build and pilot test a prototype of the product, service, or process under study. Additionally, PD team members will develop plans for full-scale production of the product or delivery of the service.

The Design Phase has five steps:

1. Constructing a detailed design (converting CTQs and high-level CTPs into detailed CTPs). CTPs can exist at several levels of detail—for example, a CTQ for a dormitory room may be a private bathroom. Examples of some high-level CTPs that relate to the private bathroom CTQ include: carpeted floor, bathtub and shower, and glass shower stall door. Examples of more detailed CTPs for the bathtub include: full size, white surface, and non-skid surface on the bottom of the tub. Even more detailed CTPs for the non-skid surface on the bottom of the tub include: add-on white adhesive strips or built in non-skid strips.

2. Operationally defining the detailed CTPs.

3. Validating the measurement systems for each detailed CTP.

4. Establishing the baseline capabilities of the detailed CTPs.

5. Preparing a verification plan.

Dormitory Example. As discussed previously, when appropriate, CTQs and high-level CTPs can be more narrowly defined into detailed CTPs. In the dormitory example, it is overkill to attempt to convert the CTQs and high-level CTPs into detailed CTPs. For instance, the inclusion of a queen-size bed (CTQ) cannot easily or reasonably be converted into detailed level design data such that you could measure Defects per Million Opportunities for a queen-size bed (detailed CTP).

7.1 STEPS OF THE DESIGN PHASE

The first step of the Design Phase is constructing a detailed design for the product, service, or process under study. This involves PD team members doing the following sub-steps:

- Developing the elements of the detailed design.
- Determining the details for the best design considering alternative detailed designs, selecting the best alternative detailed design, developing the specifics of the best detailed design, procuring the necessary materials, etc.
- Identifying targets for the detailed CTPs by calculating nominal values and specification limits and identifying control points and measurement systems.

The second step of the Design Phase is creating operational definitions for detailed CTPs.

The third step of the Design Phase is validating the measurement systems that will be needed to audit performance of the detailed CTPs.

The fourth step of the Design Phase is estimating the capability of the selected detailed design to meet the targets established for each CTP. This involves predicting and improving the capability of the detailed design using tools such as capability analysis, FMEA analysis, simulation, or design scorecards; and conducting design reviews to assess risks considering capability and producibility, compliance, hardware, and software. PD team members must ensure that the design is fully integrated into its environment before they finalize the design.

The fifth step of the Design Phase is preparing a control and verification plan. This step requires PD team members to develop a control strategy that considers control charting or performance audits of the detailed CTPs, identifies process owners and stakeholders, and documents the detailed design.

7.2 INPUTS OF THE DESIGN PHASE

The inputs from the Analyze Phase to the Design Phase of the DMADV model are the following:

- A high-level design (including CTQs and high-level CTPs for product or service or processes, facilities, equipment, materials and supplies, information, and people).
- A set of design scorecards for the best high-level design.

7.3 CONSTRUCTING A DETAILED DESIGN

Developing Elements of the Detailed Design

PD team members move from a high-level design to a detailed design by moving from general CTQs to high-level CTPs to detailed CTPs (e.g., dimensions, brand names, etc.).

Identifying the Specific Details for CTPs with QFD

Recall that QFD was discussed in the Measure Phase in Chapter 5, "Measure Phase," as a tool to translate the "Voice of the Customer" needs and wants into CTQs and CTPs. In this chapter, PD team members use QFD to translate CTQs and high-level CTPs into detailed CTPs (see Figure 7.1).

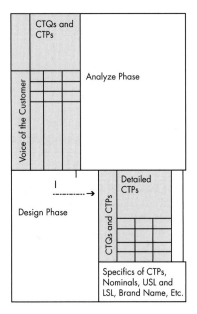

FIGURE 7.1   QFD Matrices

QFD Methodology Flow

Quality Function Deployment for services has two basic matrices: (1) Matrix 1: "Voice of the Customer" by "CTQs and CTPs" matrix; and (2) Matrix 2: "CTQs and CTPs" by "Detailed CTPs."

Matrix 1

The "Voice of the Customer" by "CTQ" matrix is constructed using the steps discussed in detail in Section 5.7.

Matrix 2

The bottom of Figure 7.1 shows the "CTQs and CTPs" by "Detailed CTPs" matrix. The CTQs defined in Matrix 1 become the "rows" that are listed down the left side of Matrix 2 along with priorities (based on the importance ratings from Matrix 1) and target values. Matrix 2 is prepared in the same manner as Matrix 1. Table 7.1 shows an example of a section of a QFD Matrix 2 for the dormitory example.

TABLE 7.1　Partial Dormitory QFD Matrix 2

CTQs and High-Level CTPs	Detailed CTPs							Importance Ranking
	Oven	Refrigerator	Microwave	Large Corner Desk	Executive Desk Chair	Additional Desk Chairs	...	
Kitchenette	9	9	9	0	0	0	...	
Office Area	0	0	0	9	9	9	...	
...	...	...	...	...	...	...	...	
...	...	...	...	...	...	...	...	
...	...	...	...	...	...	...	...	
...	...	...	...	...	...	...	...	
Un-normalized Weights								
Normalized Weights								
Specific Detailed CTPs (Nominals, Specs, Brands, etc.)	Whirlpool Model 123/A	Frigidaire Model C54-X	...	...	...	...	...	

QFD Process

Remember, QFD requires multiple functional disciplines to adequately address all of its components. Additionally, it requires more time upfront in the design function. Consequently, less time is spent downstream because of differences of opinion over design issues or redesign because the product was not on target. It leads to consensus decisions, greater commitment to the development effort, better coordination, and reduced time over the course of the development effort.

7.4 DEVELOP DETAILED CTPS FOR CTQS AND HIGH-LEVEL CTPS

Language of CTQs and CTPs

If a detailed CTP is defined by variables data, then it may have a nominal value and specification limits, such that the detailed CTPs flow-up to meet the requirements of the CTQs and high-level CTPs (nominal values and specification limits); or conversely, the CTQs and CTPs flow-down to realistic detailed CTPs.

Specifications state a boundary, or boundaries, that apply to individual units of a product or service. An individual unit of product or service is considered to conform to a specification if it is on or inside the boundary or boundaries; this is the goal post view of quality. Individual unit specifications are made up of two parts; together they form a third part.

The first part of an individual unit specification is the nominal value. This is the desired value for process performance mandated by the customer's needs. Ideally, if all quality characteristics were at nominal, products and services would perform as expected over their life cycle.

The second part of an individual unit specification is a tolerance. A tolerance is an allowable departure from a nominal value established by design engineers that is deemed nonharmful to the functioning of the product or service over its life cycle. It is important to realize that interdependencies between the CTPs may create situations in which the tolerance limits of one CTP may impact the tolerance limits of another CTP. For example, fire is caused by the interaction between oxygen, fuel, and an ignition source. A negative departure from the optimal (nominal) amount of oxygen required for a fire of a given size, and a departure from the optimal (nominal) amount of fuel required for a fire of a given size, may create a situation in which it is not possible to start a fire.

The specification limits of individual units are the boundaries created by adding and/or subtracting appropriate tolerances from a nominal value. The upper and lower specification limits are specified by:

USL = Nominal + Upper Tolerance

LSL = Nominal – Lower Tolerance

where USL is the upper specification limit and LSL is the lower specification limit; or one-sided specification limits (i.e., either USL or LSL only).

Often the Lower Tolerance and Upper Tolerance are the same, but this is not always the case. Note that the preceding notation allows for the tolerance range below and above the nominal to be different as the nominal is not required to be centered between the specification limits. An example of such a tolerance is the gap between two door panels on an automobile, which would be a lower specification of 0 inches, a nominal of 0.15 inches, and an upper specification of 0.25 inches. Additionally, many cases exist in which there is only an Upper Tolerance or a Lower Tolerance.

Another example of a specification can be seen in a monthly accounting report that must be completed in 7 days (nominal), but no earlier than 4 days (lower specification limit—not all the necessary data will be available) and no later than 10 days (upper specification limit—the due date for the report in the board meeting).

From the earlier discussion of the philosophy of continuous reduction of variation, you saw that the goal of modern management should not be 100-percent conformance to specifications (zero defects), but the never-ending reduction of process variation within specification limits so that all products, services, or processes are as close to nominal as possible. This is the Taguchi Loss Function view of quality. Specified tolerances become increasingly irrelevant as process variation is reduced so that the outputs of the process are well within specification limits.

Flow-Up CTPs

Dimensions are created by the assembly of the steps in a service or component parts of a product. These created (flow-up) dimensions have statistical distributions. For example, if nine services (CTPs) are put together to form a one-stop-shopping service (CTQ), the distribution of the one-stop-shopping service (CTQ) is a newly created dimension. Management must be able to control and reduce the variation of these created dimensions so the final assemblies will perform as desired for the customer over the life cycle of the service or product. Understanding and controlling these flow-up dimensions requires a working knowledge of the statistical rules of created dimensions.

Law of the Addition of Component Dimension Averages

If component steps or parts are assembled so that the individual step or component dimensions are added to one another, the average dimension of the assembly will equal the sum of the individual component average dimensions, assuming the assembly adds no measurable dimension.

Example. If three service steps are put together to create a one-stop-shopping service, the average service time of the one-stop-shopping service equals the sum of the average service times of the individual services:

Average service time for the one-stop-shopping service:

$$X_{assembly} = X_1 + X_2 + X_3,$$

where

X_1 = Average service time of service 1

X_2 = Average service time of service 2

X_3 = Average service time of service 3

For example, consider a service process that consists of the serial delivery of Service 1, Service 2, and Service 3. Service 1 has an average service time of 10 minutes, Service 2 has an average service time of 20 minutes, and Service 3 has an average service time of 30 minutes. Consequently, the average one-stop-shopping service time is the sum of all three averages, or 60 minutes (10 min + 20 min + 30 min):

$$X_{assembly} = X_1 + X_2 + X_3 = 10 \text{ min} + 20 \text{ min} + 30 \text{ min} = 60 \text{ min}$$

The preceding law holds only if the processes generating the steps or parts are independent of each other (i.e., the results of one do not impact the results of the other) and in statistical control (i.e., they exhibit a predictable system of variation).

Independence among components is not always the case. For example, suppose the time it takes to have a meal served at a restaurant is composed of the three steps: Step 1: take the order; Step 2: cook the order; and Step 3: deliver the order. If the first step is done incorrectly, there will be a substantial impact on the second and third steps.

Law of the Sums and Differences of Component Dimension Averages

If the component steps of a service or the component of parts of a product are assembled so that the individual component parts are added and subtracted from one another, the average dimension of the assembly will then equal the algebraic sum or difference of the individual component average dimensions. In the example concerning the automobile door gap dimension between two panels, the gap is determined by the difference in placements and sizes between two door panels. It is possible that the panels will not fit together, making the difference between the panels a negative gap (gap is less than 0), which is a physical impossibility. Consequently, designers may establish lower bounds so that the dimension of the gap has practical meaning.

Example. An example of the law of sums and differences of component dimension averages can be seen in an earring. If an earring post is projected through an ear lobe, the average length of the earring post projection through the ear lobe and the clasp equals the difference between the average length of the post minus the sum of the average widths of the ear lobe and the clasp:

$$X_{pp} = X_p - (X_e + X_c),$$

where

X_{pp} = Average post projection
X_p = Average length of a post
X_e = Average width of an ear lobe
X_c = Average width of a clasp

See Figure 7.2 for a picture of an earring with a post and clasp.

The earring post has an average length of $8/16^{th}$ of an inch. An ear lobe has an average width of $5/16^{th}$ of an inch, and an earring clasp has an average width of $2/16^{th}$ of an inch. Consequently, the average post projection through the ear lobe and clasp is $1/16^{th}$ of an inch:

$$X_{pp} = X_p - (X_e + X_c), = 8/16 - (5/16 + 2/16) = 1/16$$

Again, the preceding law holds only for statistically independent component processes in statistical control.

FIGURE 7.2 Picture of an Earring

Law of the Addition of Component Dimension Standard Deviations

If the component steps of a service or the component parts of a product are assembled at random (for example, so that each component step or part is drawn randomly with no selection criteria), the standard deviation of the assembly will be the square root of the sum of the component variances, regardless of whether the components are added or subtracted from each other. This law applies to assemblies in which the component steps and parts combine linearly and are statistically independent.

$$S_{pp} = \sqrt{S_p^2 + S_e^2 + S_c^2} = \sqrt{(0.007)^2 + (0.010)^2 + (0.003)^2} = 0.01257 \, \text{in.}$$

Example. Consider again the earring post projection problem. Now consider that the standard deviation of the post length, S_p, is 0.007 in., the standard deviation of the ear lobe width, S_e, is 0.010 in., and the standard deviation of the clasp width is 0.003 in. The standard deviation of the bolt projection is:

You must realize that the standard deviation of the bolt projection is not 0.020 inches, the sum of the individual component standard deviations. The square root of the sum of the individual component variances will be no greater than the sum of the individual component standard deviations. In fact, the square root will always be less than the sum of individual component standard deviations as long as 2 or more of the standard deviations are greater than 0. This means that the assembly-to-assembly variation among random assemblies will be less than would be indicated by summing the individual components' unit-to-unit variations. Again, the preceding law holds only for statistically independent component processes in statistical control.

Law of the Average for Created Areas and Volumes for Rectangular Constructions

If an area or volume is created by the assembly of component parts, then the average area or volume of the assembly will equal the product of the individual component average dimensions, assuming the component parts are stable and independent.

Example. Because a refrigerated freight car must be air conditioned, you need to estimate the internal volume of the freight car. The average internal volume of the freight car equals the product of the average length, the average height, and the average width:

$$X_v = (X_l)(X_h)(X_w),$$

where

X_v = Average internal volume of the freight car
X_l = Average length

X_h = Average height
X_w = Average width

The average length is 30 feet, the average height is 10 feet, and the average width is 8 feet. Therefore, the average volume of the freight car is as follows:

$$X_v = (X_l)(X_h)(X_w) = (30 \text{ ft.})(10 \text{ ft.})(8 \text{ ft.}) = 2,400 \text{ cubic feet}$$

Again, the preceding law holds only for statistically independent component processes in statistical control.

Law of the Standard Deviation for Created Areas and Volumes for Rectangular Constructions

If an area or volume is created by the assembly of component steps of a service or the component parts of a product, you calculate the standard deviation of the created area or volume:

$$S_{area} = \sqrt{X_s^2 S_L^2 + X_L^2 S_s^2 + S_L^2 S_s^2}$$

where

X_s = Average length of the short side
X_L = Average length of the long side
S_s = Standard deviation of length of the short side
S_L = Standard deviation of length of the long side

$$S_{volume} = \sqrt{X_h^2 X_w^2 S_L^2 + X_L^2 X_w^2 S_h^2 + X_h^2 X_L^2 S_w^2 + X_h^2 S_L^2 S_s^2 + X_L^2 S_h^2 S_w^2 + X_w^2 S_h^2 S_L^2 + S_L^2 S_h^2 S_w^2}$$

where

X_w = Average width
S_w = Standard deviation of the width

X_h, X_L, S_h, and S_L are defined above.

Example. If the means and standard deviations for the freight car's dimensions are:

X_L = 30 ft. and S_L = 1/4 ft.
X_h = 10 ft. and S_h = 1/8 ft.
X_w = 8 ft. and S_w = 1/8 ft

Then the standard deviation of the freight car's volume is the following:

$$S_{volume} = \sqrt{X_h^2 X_w^2 S_L^2 + X_L^2 X_w^2 S_h^2 + X_h^2 X_L^2 S_w^2 + X_h^2 S_L^2 S_S^2 + X_L^2 S_h^2 S_w^2 + X_w^2 S_h^2 S_L^2 + S_L^2 S_h^2 S_w^2}$$
$$= \sqrt{2,706.63}$$
$$= 50.025 \text{ cubic feet}$$

Again, the preceding law holds only for component processes that are statistically independent and in statistical control.

Flow-Down CTQs

Basic Concept of Flow-Down

Flow-down is the design function in which a CTQ is broken down into high-level CTPs, or high-level CTPs are broken down into detailed CTPs. For example, a "design process" consists of 3 steps: Step 1 is collecting "Voice of the Stakeholder" data for a design, Step 2 is preparing the design, and Step 3 is delivering the design to the client. Ideally, the client wants the design in exactly three weeks (Nominal = 3 weeks), but no later than four weeks (USL = 4 weeks). Hence, the CTQ is defined as the number of weeks to deliver a design to a client, with nominal being 3 weeks and the upper specification being 4 weeks.

The CTQ is defined by the client and must be flowed down to the component steps. Returning to the "design process" example, observe the following flow-down situation:

Start → Step 1 → Step 2 → Step 3 → Stop
(Start) → (Collect VoC) → (Prepare Design) → (Deliver Design) → (Stop)

Cycle time to deliver is defined by the following:

(Step 1) ————————————> (Step 2) ————————————>(Step 3)
(Step 1 Nominal = ?)   (Step 2 Nominal = ?)   (Step 3 Nominal = ?)
(Step 1 USL = ?)   (Step 2 USL = ?)   (Step 3 USL = ?)

At the time of stop, the results for Overall Cycle time are as follows:

(Nominal = 3 wks)
(USL = 4 wks)

The nominal at the stop time of 3 weeks and upper specification limit of 4 weeks is achieved by constructing a transfer function (Overall Cycle Time = Step 1 + Step 2 + Step 3) and flowing down performance to Steps 1, 2, and 3.

Flow-Down Logic. The customer has indicated that they wish to have the design delivered in no more than 4 weeks. If this 3-step process is ongoing and the goal is to always have a design delivered in 3 weeks and no longer than 4 weeks, we will assume that the goal of the process is a mean of 3 weeks, with all customer designs to be delivered no later than 4 weeks. If the goal is to design a process that will meet all customers design delivery requirements with a Six Sigma level of performance, assuming no shift in the process mean, then it implies that the process must have a standard deviation small enough to ensure that no more than 2 times out of a billion designs delivered does it take more than 4 weeks. In other words, if it is known that the process has a mean time to delivery of 3 weeks, then a standard deviation needed is defined as:

$$4 \text{ weeks} = 3 \text{ weeks} + 6 * S_{ST}$$

where S_{ST} = short-term standard deviation of the design delivery process (zero sigma shift in the process mean).

In other words,

$$S_{ST} = 1/6 \text{ week}$$

The short-term standard deviation refers to how well the design delivery process can be managed when it is closely monitored as few changes or problems are expected. Assume a short-term normal distribution with a mean of M and a standard deviation of S_{ST}. The Voice of the Customer has stated an USL = $M + 6S_{ST}$. The short-term distribution and USL are shown in Figure 7.3. In Figure 7.3, the X-axis is marked in increments of $1.5S_{ST}$ from $M - 6S_{ST}$ to $M + 6S_{ST}$.

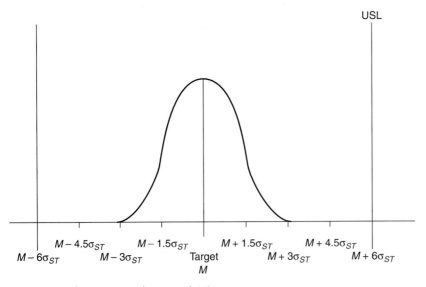

FIGURE 7.3   Short-Term Distribution with USL

Over the long term, when the design delivery process is not as closely monitored as it is in the short term, it is possible that changes or perturbations may occur—for example, one of the designers becomes ill in the middle of the process. These perturbations may result in shifting of the process cycle times, often lengthening the average delivery time for the delivery of a design. The actual amount of the "shift" between the short-term process and the long-term process depends on the level of process stability and control. In practice, it is not unusual for a shift of 1.5 standard deviations to go undetected when control charts are used only to find points outside of the control limits. A shift of 1.5 standard deviations in a process with no change in the underlying process standard deviation will yield 0.066807 points outside of the upper control limits or 1 out of 16 points. If a process shifts more than 1.5 standard deviations, then there is a greater likelihood of observing out of control points, and steps would be taken to eliminate the shift. Recall, Six Sigma performance represents 3.4 defects per million opportunities, assuming a 1.5 standard deviation shift in the process mean. In the design process example, it is the likelihood of observing an overall design delivery cycle time greater than 4 weeks, if the process average shifts 1.5 standard deviations above the average of 3 weeks; that is, a shift up of 0.25 weeks in the overall average cycle time to deliver a design to a customer deviations (0.25 weeks = 1.5 * S_{ST} = 1.5 * 1/6).

Assume that the mean of the short-term distribution shown in Figure 7.3 is shifted from M to $M + 1.5S_{ST}$, with the same standard deviation (S_{ST}) (see Figure 7.4). $M + 4.5S_{ST}$ on the shifted short-term distribution is 66.6% of the distance between the shifted mean ($M + 1.5S_{ST}$) and the USL ($M + 6S_{ST}$).

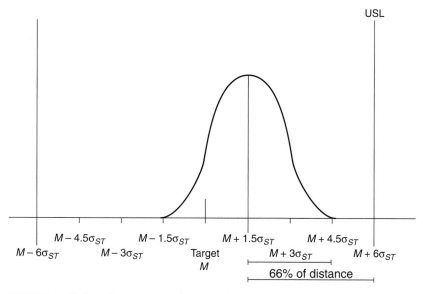

FIGURE 7.4 Shifted Short-Term Distribution with USL

The long-term distribution has a greater variance than the short-term distribution. For example, assume a long-term normal distribution is created by shifting the mean of the original short-term normal distribution up and down by $1.5S_{ST}$ (see Figure 7.5). The mean of the long-term distribution is M (the same as the original short-term distribution), but the standard deviation of the long-term distribution is 1.5 times the standard deviation of the short-term distribution; that is, $S_{LT} = 1.5S_{ST}$. $M + 3S_{LT}$ on the long-term distribution is the same point on the X-axis as $M + 4.5\ S_{ST}$ on the non-shifted short-term distribution.

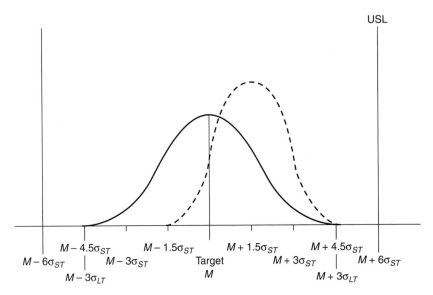

FIGURE 7.5 Long-Term Distribution with USL

$M + 4.5\ S_{ST}$ is 66.6% of the distance between the shifted short-term mean ($M + 1.5\ S_{ST}$) and the USL ($M + 6\ S_{ST}$) on the shifted short-term distribution (see Figure 7.5). $M + 3S_{LT}$ (same as $M + 4.5S_{ST}$ on the shifted short-term distribution) on the long-term distribution is $3S_{LT}$ above M on the long-term distribution.

"*Process Design*" *Example.* Assume the 3-week target is flowed down to the CTPs as follows.

Step 1: Collect VoC data for the design = 1 week.

Step 2: Prepare the design = 1 week.

Step 3: Deliver the design = 1 week.

Because overall delivery time for the design = step 1 + step 2 + step 3, the transfer functions for the flow-down mean and standard deviation are the following:

$$M_{Overall} = f(M_{Step1}, M_{Step2}, M_{Step3}) = M_{Step1} + M_{Step2} + M_{Step3}$$
$$S_{Overall} = \sqrt{Variance_{Step1} + Variance_{Step2} + Variance_{Step3}}$$

Now, assume equal allocation of the variance throughout steps 1, 2, and 3; hence, $Variance_{Step1} = Variance_{Step2} = Variance_{Step3}$. Therefore,

Overall Process *Variance = Variance*$_{Step1}$+ Variance$_{Step2}$ + Variance$_{Step3}$

$$= 3 * Variance_{Step1}$$

$$S_{ST}^2 = (1/6)^2 = 3 * Variance_{Step1}$$

Variance$_{Step1}$ = 1/108 and

$$S_{Step1} = \sqrt{\frac{1}{108}} = 0.096225.$$

Therefore, steps 1, 2, and 3 should be such that each step should have a distribution to completion with an average of 1 week and a standard deviation of 0.096225 weeks (which is approximately 16.17 hours). The overall cycle time design delivery process is a serial process; hence, step1 must be completed before step 2, and step 2 must be completed before step 3. Consequently, Overall Cycle Time for the design delivery process will have a mean of 3 weeks with a standard deviation of 1/6 week (approximately 28.0 hours). To demonstrate this going the other way, using hours instead of fractions of a week as the units of measure:

Variance (Overall Process) = (16.17 hours)^2 + (16.17 hours)^2 + (16.17 hours)^2 = 784 hours.

Standard Deviation Overall Process = $\sqrt{784}$ = 28 hours = 1/6 of a week.

If in this example, the long-term standard deviation is 1.5 times greater than the short term standard deviation (in this example, 24.25 hours), then it can be shown that the long-term standard deviation of the Overall Cycle Time for the Design Delivery process will be 42 hours, which is 1.5 times the short-term standard deviation of 28 hours for the Overall Cycle Time for the Design Delivery process.

As to determining the upper and lower specifications of the distribution of completion times for each step, assume that the distribution of processing times for each step is normally distributed, and we want to keep these individual steps in a state of statistical control with the specifications matching upper and lower control limits for the individual process results for each step. In this way, the specifications of each process step can be set so that we maintain the process within 3 standard deviations of its mean of 1 week. (See the discussion of natural limits later in this chapter.) In this case, you would want each step to be completed with a mean of 1 week, a LSL of (1 week – 3 * 16.17 hours), and a USL of (1 week + 3 * 16.17 hours), which is about 1 week plus or minus 0.289 weeks. A control chart should allow you to catch an increase in variation of 1.5 times the short-term variation, or a process shift of 1.5 standard deviations. In that way, you are likely to guarantee that you maintain the Overall Cycle Time of Design Delivery with a short-term standard deviation of 28 hours and a long-term standard deviation of 42 hours, thus allowing you to perform no worse than a Six Sigma level.

Consequences of Failure to Flow-Down

Three options exist if the detailed designs cannot deliver the detailed CTPs required by the CTQs and high-level CTPs, given the available budget.

The first consequence is that the product, service, or process in question needs to be redesigned to achieve design and/or budgetary targets. A helpful technique for checking to determine if the designed or redesigned detailed CTPs meet the specifications for all CTQs and CTPs is to perform a flow-up capability analysis. Flow-up capability analysis creates the opportunity for designers to determine if flow-down targets and tolerances actually achieve CTQs and higher-level CTPs targets and tolerances. In our previous design delivery process example, we showed a flow-up of individual step standard deviations to the overall process standard deviation in units of hours. The flow-up indicates that our analysis of the flow-down was correct.

The second consequence is that design trade-offs must be made among the detailed CTPs to achieve the design and/or budgetary targets for all CTQs and high-level CTPs. Design trade-offs answer the question: Can flow-down targets and tolerances achieve higher-level targets and tolerances?

For example, suppose PD team members determined that:

$Mean_{Step1}$ = 1.2 weeks; $Mean_{Step2}$ = 1.0 week; and $Mean_{Step3}$ = 0.8 week

S_{Step1} = 0.11 week and S_{Step2} = 0.096225 week and S_{Step3} = 0.06 week

from similar processes. So,

$Variance_{Step1}$ = $(0.11)^2$ = 0.0121; $Variance_{Step2}$ = $(0.096225)^2$ = 0.00925925;

$Variance_{Step3}$ = $(0.06)^2$ = 0.0036.

Now, team members must determine if the detailed CTPs for steps 1, 2, and 3 meet the specifications for the Overall Design Delivery Cycle Time (CTQ). In other words, do steps 1, 2, and 3 flow-up to the requirements of Overall Cycle Time for the Design Delivery process?

You compute the mean for the Overall Cycle Time for the Design Delivery process as follows:

$M_{Overall} = M_{step1} + M_{step2} + M_{step3}$ = 1.2 + 1.0 + 0.8 = 3.0 weeks

This meets the flow-up target (nominal value) for the Overall Cycle Time for the Design Delivery process mean.

You compute the standard deviation for Overall Cycle Time for the Design Delivery process as follows:

$$S_{Overall} = \sqrt{Variance_{Step1} + Variance_{Step2} + Variance_{Step3}}$$
$$= \sqrt{(0.0121 + 0.00925925 + 0.0036)}$$
$$= 0.158$$

This meets the flow-up target short-term standard deviation for the Overall Cycle Time for the Design Delivery process because 0.158 < 0.167 (which is 1/6 week).

To switch things around, suppose PD team members have determined that $S_{Step2} = 0.21$ weeks instead of $S_{Step2} = 0.096225$ weeks ($Variance_{Step2} = 0.0441$). Now, PD team members must determine if the detailed CTPs for steps 1, 2, and 3 meet the Overall Cycle Time for the Design Delivery process specifications.

Again the mean of Overall Cycle Time for the Design Delivery process mean is 3 weeks. This meets the flow-up target (nominal value) for the Overall Cycle Time for the Design Delivery process mean. Now you compute the Overall Cycle Time for the Design Delivery process standard deviation:

$$S_{Overall} = \sqrt{Variance_{Step1} + Variance_{Step2} + Variance_{Step3}}$$
$$= \sqrt{0.0121 + 0.0441 + 0.0036} = 0.2445$$

In this case, the detailed CTP tolerances did not flow up because $0.2445 > 0.167$ (or 1/6 week). Thus, PD team members may have to make process improvements to one of the steps, likely step 2 as it has the largest standard deviation, or have to decide upon trade-offs between flow-down targets and/or tolerances.

The third consequence is that the design is abandoned in favor of other, more promising, uses for the resources that have been earmarked for the design in question.

7.5 Create a Comprehensive Set of Detailed CTPs

For services, CTPs are frequently defined using the second QFD house; that is, high-level design requirements (CTQs and high-level CTPs) by detailed CTPs. Detailed CTPs need to be developed for the following aspects of the product, service, or process being designed by PD team members.

- **Product or Service Detailed CTPs**—These detailed CTPs include all detail necessary to manufacture products or deliver services; for example, descriptions of services with targets and tolerances that consider all stakeholder voices (customer, investor, regulator, legal, etc.).

- **Process Detailed CTPs**—These detailed CTPs include all high-level and detailed flowcharts and/or process maps necessary to manufacture products, deliver services, or provide process outputs.

- **Human System Detailed CTPs**—These detailed CTPs include job descriptions, skill requirements, educational history, experience, hiring policies, training policies, supervisory processes, performance enhancement processes (including extrinsic motivators), and management style.

- **Information System Detailed CTPs**—These detailed CTPs include all hardware, software, and humanware required to manufacture products, deliver services, or provide process outputs.

- **Equipment and Tools Detailed CTPs**—These detailed CTPs include descriptions, instructions and drawings, set-up procedures and specifications, capabilities, and operating conditions.

- **Material and Supply Detailed CTPs**—These detailed CTPs include descriptions, instructions for use, specifications, conditions for use, accounting information (e.g., billing policies), inventory policies, and replenishment processes, to name a few material and supply detailed CTPs required to manufacture products, deliver services, or provide process outputs.

- **Buildings and Grounds Detailed CTPs**—These detailed CTPs include floor plans, and space layout drawings and models.

7.6 OPERATIONALLY DEFINE EACH DETAILED CTP

Recall from the Measure Phase in Chapter 5 that an operational definition promotes understanding between people by putting communicable meaning into words. An operational definition contains three parts: a criterion to be applied to an object or group, a test of the object or group, and a decision as to whether the object or group met the criterion.

7.7 VALIDATE THE MEASUREMENT SYSTEM FOR EACH DETAILED CTP

Recall from the Measure Phase that each CTQ and CTP must have a valid measurement system. A valid measurement system is a prerequisite for valid decision making.

7.8 ESTABLISH BASELINE CAPABILITIES FOR EACH CTQ AND CTP

Background

Baseline data needs to be collected to determine the stability and capability of each detailed CTP. The collection of baseline data requires a data collection plan. The elements of a data collection plan include a data collection repository or form, a sampling plan (sample size, sample frequency), and sampling instructions (who, where, when, and how).

Collect and Analyze Baseline Data for Appropriate Detailed CTPs

Team members collect baseline data for appropriate detailed CTPs. For example, waiting times in a bank are measured by a clock that is accurate to 1 second. A wait time longer than 5 minutes (300 seconds) is deemed unacceptable by customers (Voice of the Customer). A sample of the last five customer wait times every hour (the bank is open eight hours per day) is collected for two weeks (Monday through Friday). Table 7.2 lists the 400 wait times in sequential order (across the rows).

TABLE 7.2 Bank Wait Time Data

81	185	274	232	239	112	148	155	174	166	149	261	172
121	181	114	169	160	183	124	89	23	119	132	172	217
240	190	294	171	200	231	162	218	198	170	207	168	183
132	307	138	246	77	161	221	181	102	154	258	193	23
262	191	223	308	279	198	199	108	238	222	235	229	300
148	185	162	150	192	181	220	256	167	253	153	178	127
95	260	168	166	238	236	121	236	334	90	189	116	258
224	74	302	162	151	224	153	204	67	188	214	251	203
210	120	110	186	108	140	166	175	170	184	117	140	225
140	104	250	176	146	172	112	217	243	226	228	246	124
65	176	118	142	177	188	132	248	162	262	90	155	228
80	180	195	246	75	310	144	125	85	168	264	237	106
226	191	128	83	206	52	217	140	148	20	190	179	105
133	157	226	186	201	211	298	144	133	269	128	157	136
149	123	119	120	283	186	319	155	105	160	151	215	127
111	58	243	52	196	159	160	211	226	214	169	81	188
159	179	136	110	191	230	141	146	187	206	109	142	149
164	255	100	122	32	212	174	163	120	201	184	205	233
249	188	139	129	146	230	127	123	159	352	172	277	254
109	149	139	207	153	250	250	257	124	263	200	147	221
155	167	5	174	231	223	174	196	192	142	215	201	178
129	256	118	129	42	187	67	265	176	240	171	240	187
112	175	255	173	111	225	122	113	238	134	188	147	138
241	173	124	203	155	208	215	164	209	197	320	174	174
267	163	136	146	253	89	188	113	219	100	192	131	133
154	110	201	225	116	69	136	269	178	209	119	217	183
232	166	215	221	259	73	206	199	121	201	163	233	97
78	177	257	201	283	225	193	233	193	190	224	108	157
120	228	180	104	208	143	186	167	203	98	44	162	190
309	162	175	246	218	223	245	140	206	79	118	201	129
84	102	110	77	223	122	171	241	113	112			

Note: The complete data actually includes the hour of the day, the sequence of how the customers within each hour were collected, the day of the week, and the week. By organizing the data in this way, you will know if there are any data values that are missing.

 BANK

Team members analyze the baseline data to answer the following questions:

- Does the baseline data for the detailed CTP exhibit any patterns over time? A run chart [see Reference 1] is used to study raw baseline data over time.
- Is the baseline data for the detailed CTP stable? Does it exhibit any special causes of variation? Control charts [see Reference 1] are used to determine the stability of a process.
- If the detailed CTP is not stable (i.e., it exhibits special causes of variation), PD team members determine the location of the special causes of variation to take appropriate corrective actions to stabilize the detailed CTP. Again, you use a control chart to identify where and when special causes of variation occur. However, you do not use a control chart to identify the causes of special variations. You use tools such as log sheets, brainstorming, and cause and effect diagrams to identify the causes of special variation [see Reference 1].
- If the baseline data for the detailed CTP is stable, then you need to determine the characteristics of its distribution. In other words, what is its spread (variation), shape (distribution), and center (mean, median and mode)? See Reference 1 for a discussion of descriptive statistics.

The answers to these questions for the "Waiting Times in a Bank" baseline data are as follows:

- **Question 1:** Does the baseline data for the "Waiting Times in a Bank" exhibit any patterns over time?

  Figure 7.6 shows a run chart of the wait times for each subgroup of five customers.

  Figure 7.6 reveals individual wait times randomly scattered around a mean wait time of about 175 seconds. The variability of wait times seems to be relatively constant over all of the subgroups and fluctuates roughly between 60 seconds and 350 seconds. Additionally, Figure 7.6 shows a connected plot of points that are the subgroup averages computed from the actual data.

- **Question 2:** Is the baseline data for the "Waiting Times in a Bank" stable? Does it exhibit any special causes of variation? If "Waiting Times in a Bank" are stable, what are their characteristics?

  Figures 7.7 and 7.8 are $\bar{X}$ and R-charts from Minitab and JMP statistical software packages, respectively, of the subgroups of five customer wait times. They show that both the R-chart and the $\bar{X}$ chart are stable. Neither chart exhibits any special causes of variation in the wait time in a bank. This control chart analysis verifies the findings from the run chart in Figure 7.6.

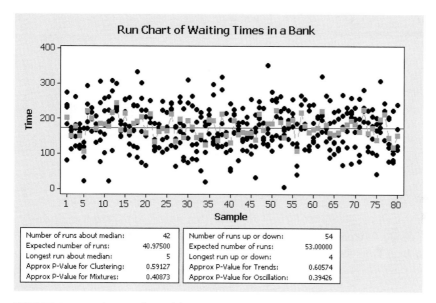

FIGURE 7.6 Minitab Run Chart of the Waiting Times in a Bank

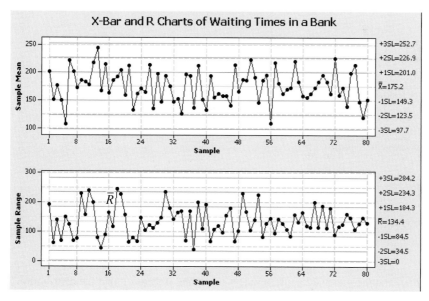

FIGURE 7.7 Minitab $\bar{X}$ and R-Charts of Wait Times in a Bank

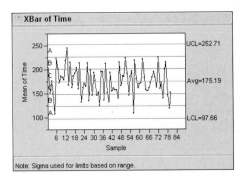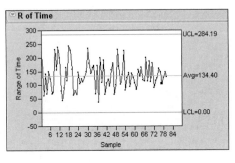

FIGURE 7.8   JMP $\bar{X}$ and R-Charts of Wait Times in a Bank

Figures 7.9 and 7.10 provide a basic statistical analysis [see Reference 1] of the wait times in a bank from the Minitab and JMP statistical software packages, respectively.

```
              Total
Variable      Count     Mean   StDev  Minimum        Q1  Median       Q3  Maximum
Time            400   175.18   59.32     5.00    132.00  174.00   218.00   352.00


Variable      Range
Time         347.00
```

FIGURE 7.9   Minitab Wait Time Statistics for a Bank

Quantiles			Moments	
100.0%	maximum	352.00	Mean	175.185
99.5%		333.93	Std Dev	59.322793
97.5%		299.95	Std Err Mean	2.9661396
90.0%		250.90	upper 95% Mean	181.01621
75.0%	quartile	218.00	lower 95% Mean	169.35379
50.0%	median	174.00	N	400
25.0%	quartile	132.00		
10.0%		104.10		
2.5%		58.18		
0.5%		20.02		
0.0%	minimum	5.00		

FIGURE 7.10   JMP Wait Time Statistics for a Bank

The median and the mean are approximately the same, indicating that the distribution of wait times in a bank is symmetric around the mean of 175 seconds. Further, the standard deviation is approximately 60 seconds. Figures 7.11 and 7.12 are histograms of the wait times from the Minitab and JMP statistical software packages, respectively.

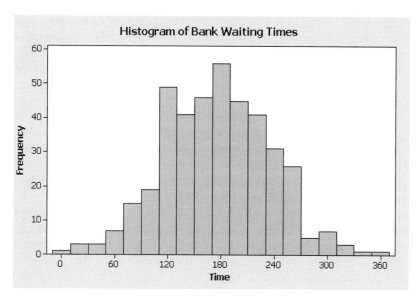

FIGURE 7.11   Minitab Histogram of Wait Times

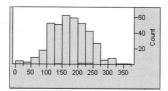

FIGURE 7.12   JMP Histogram of Wait Times

The histogram shows an approximate normal distribution with a mean of 175 seconds with a standard deviation of 60 seconds.

Estimate Process Capability for Appropriate Detailed CTPs

Process capability compares the output of a process ("Voice of the Process") with the customer's specification limits for the outputs ("Voice of the Customer"). A process must be stable (as shown in a control chart) to determine its capability. There are two types of process capability studies: attribute process capability studies and variables process capability studies.

Attribute Process Capability Studies

Attribute process capability studies determine a detailed CTPs capability in terms of fraction defective output or counts of defects for a unit of output. The major tools used in attribute process capability studies are attribute control charts [see Reference 1], and the tools discussed in Chapter 12, "Additional Tools and Methods." The capability of a process being measured by a *p*-chart is $\bar{p}$ (the average fraction defective units generated by the process). The capability of a process being measured by a *c*-chart is $\bar{c}$ (the average number of defects per unit generated by the process for a given area of opportunity). Finally, the capability of a process being measured by a *u*-chart is $\bar{u}$ (the average number of defects per unit generated by the process where the area of opportunity varies from subgroup to subgroup).

Attribute process capability studies typically require an order of magnitude (i.e., 10 or more times) more data than measurement process capability studies, to gain similar confidence from the analysis. In general, an attribute process capability study should contain 20 to 25 samples and each sample should have between 50 and 100 units. Measurement analysis often uses samples of 4 to 6, which is 10% of the size indicated here for attribute data capability studies. This rule is based on experience, as well as statistical theory.

To illustrate an attribute capability study for a detailed CTP, consider the case of a manager of a data entry department who has taken a survey whose results indicated customer dissatisfaction. The manager wants to determine the capability of the data entry operation in her department in terms of the proportion of defective entries produced by day (detailed CTP). She decides to take samples of the first 200 lines of code from each day's output, inspect them for defects, and construct an initial *p*-chart. Table 7.3 shows the raw data, and Figures 7.13 and 7.14 show the initial process control chart from the Minitab and JMP statistical software packages, respectively. The *p*-chart reveals that on days 8 (14 defective lines out of 200 inspected) and 22 (15 defective lines out of 200 inspected), something special likely happened, not attributable to the system, to cause defective lines to be entered. (Recall that out of control points are signals that indicate special causes of variation, but do not prove that is the case.)

TABLE 7.3   *Attribute Process Capability Study on Data Entry Operation*

Day	Number of Entries Inspected	Number of Defective Entries	Fraction of Defective Entries
1	200	6	0.03
2	200	6	0.03
3	200	6	0.03
4	200	5	0.025
5	200	0	0
6	200	0	0
7	200	6	0.03
8	200	14	0.07
9	200	4	0.02
10	200	0	0
11	200	1	0.005
12	200	8	0.04
13	200	2	0.01
14	200	4	0.02
15	200	7	0.035

Day	Number of Entries Inspected	Number of Defective Entries	Fraction of Defective Entries
16	200	1	0.005
17	200	3	0.015
18	200	1	0.005
19	200	4	0.02
20	200	0	0
21	200	4	0.02
22	200	15	0.075
23	200	4	0.02
24	200	1	0.005
Totals	4,800	102	

 DEFECTIVES

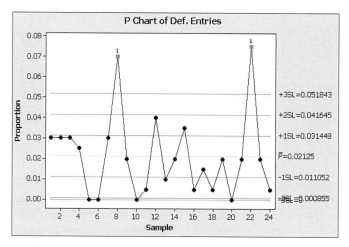

FIGURE 7.13 Minitab p-Chart of Defective Entries

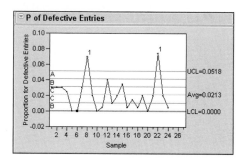

FIGURE 7.14 JMP p-Chart of Defective Entries

The manager calls a meeting of the ten operators to brainstorm for possible special causes of variation on days 8 and 22. Figure 7.15 shows a cause and effect diagram that resulted from the brainstorming session. The ten group members vote that their best guess for the problem on day 8 was a new untrained operator (see cause in Figure 7.15—circled in a cloud) who had been added to the work force. The one day it took the worker to acclimate to the new environment probably caused the unusually high number of errors. The cause of the problem was determined to be management allowing untrained operators to work as they did not consider that training or experience was necessary. To ensure that this special cause will not be repeated, the manager institutes a one-day training program for all appropriate new employees. The ten group members also vote that their best guess for the problem on day 22 was that on the previous evening, the department had run out of paper from the regular vendor, and that it did not expect a new shipment until the morning of day 23. Consequently, the department purchased a one-day supply of paper from a new vendor. The operators found this paper to be of inferior quality. This caused the large number of defective entries. The cause here is that the forecast of the paper requirements was not known and passed on to the current vendor, while the specifications of the paper needed was not passed on to the new vendor. To correct this special cause of variation, the manager revises the firm's relationship with its regular paper vendor and operationally defines acceptable quality for paper.

After eliminating the days for which special causes of variation are found, the manager re-computes the control chart statistics:

Centerline(p) = Average fraction of defective lines = $\bar{p}$

$$\bar{p} = \frac{73}{4,400} = 0.01659 \cong 0.017$$

$$\text{UCL}(p) = 0.044$$

$$\text{LCL}(p) = 0.000$$

Figures 7.16 and 7.17 from Minitab and JMP statistical software packages, respectively, show the revised control chart. The process appears stable. The centerline and control limits were extended out into the future for 25 days. Data from daily samples of 200 lines of code were collected for these 25 days and plotted with respect to the forecasted centerline and control limits. The process was found to be stable. The capability of the process is such that it will produce a mean of 1.7 percent defective lines per day. Further, the percentage defective will rarely surpass 4.4 percent per day.

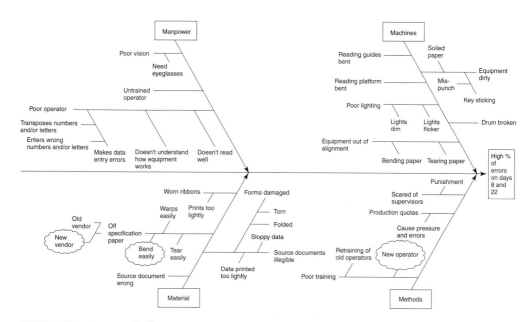

FIGURE 7.15 Cause and Effect Diagram to Determine Special Sources of Variation for All Operators on Days 8 and 22

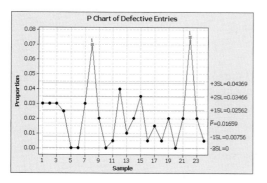

FIGURE 7.16 Minitab Revised *p*-Chart Following Removal of Special Causes

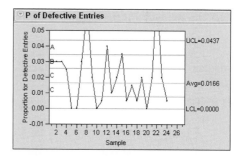

FIGURE 7.17 JMP Revised *p*-Chart Following Removal of Special Causes

Variables Process Capability Studies

Variables process capability studies determine a process's ability to meet specifications for detailed CTPs. The major tools used in variables process capability studies are variables control charts [see Reference 1] and the tools discussed in Chapter 12. Variables control charts are used to stabilize a process so you can determine meaningful upper and lower natural limits.

Natural limits are computed for stable processes by adding and subtracting three times the standard deviation of the process to the process centerline. In general, for any variables control chart, the upper and lower natural limits are:

$$UNL = \bar{\bar{X}} + 3\sigma$$
$$LNL = \bar{\bar{X}} - 3\sigma$$

where σ is computed using either $\bar{R}$ or $\bar{S}$ depending on the subgroup size.

If the variable is stable and normally distributed, then 99.73% of the output of the process will be between the LNL and the UNL.

As a rule, natural limits are equivalent to the control limits on an Individual Value variables control chart. Therefore, for other types of control charts, the natural limits should not be shown.

A statistically valid interpretation of the natural limits requires stability of the process under study. For example, if you select samples of four customer waiting times from a bank every hour, and the process is stable with a process mean subgroup wait time of 42.0 minutes and a mean range of 0.6856 minute or a standard deviation of 0.3333 minute, you can say the following about the process:

The upper natural limit of the process is 43.0 minutes.

The lower natural limit of the process is 41.0 minutes.

Assuming a stable, normal distribution of wait times in the bank, 99.73% of the customer wait times will be between 41.0 and 43.0 minutes. This is what the bank is capable of producing. It is the identity of the process.

Variables process capability studies require far less data than attribute studies. However, a separate variables study may be required for each quality characteristic that can cause a unit to be defective. As a general rule, the time period under study should contain at least 50 samples of between three and six units each.

Example of a Variables Process Capability Study

The student accounts payable process at a major university is comprised of several sub-processes. They are as follows:

1. The student arrives/waits.
2. The clerk pulls the student's record.
3. The clerk takes appropriate action on the student's record and the student leaves.
4. The clerk files the student's record.

One CTQ of the student accounts payable process is the total number of minutes a student and his/her file requires for processing in the student account office.

The total minutes for processing is computed as follows:

Student wait time in line for service (CTP_1) + record-pulling time (CTP_2) + record-process time (CTP_3) + record-filing time (CTP_4)

A sample of four students is drawn each day from the student accounts process. Total time is calculated (sum of wait and processing time) for the first student entering the office at 9:00 A.M., 11:00 A.M., 2:00 P.M., and 4:00 P.M.

$\bar{X}$ and R-charts are used to study the CTQ and CTPs. A dot plot (see Figure 7.18) and $\bar{X}$ and R-charts (see Figures 7.19 and 7.20) from Minitab and JMP statistical software packages of "total time" for 52 weeks show a stable and normal process with a mean of 1,223 seconds (20.4 minutes) and a standard deviation of 285 seconds, or 4.8 minutes.

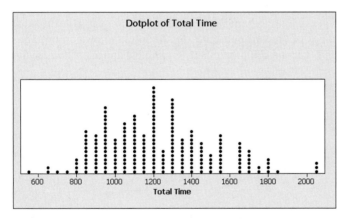

FIGURE 7.18 Minitab Dot Plot of Total Processing Time

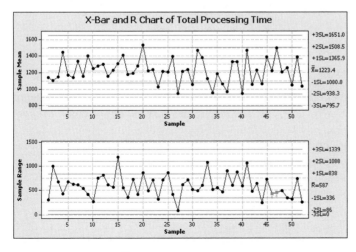

FIGURE 7.19 Minitab $\bar{X}$ and R-Charts of Total Processing Time

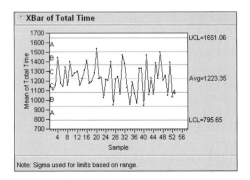

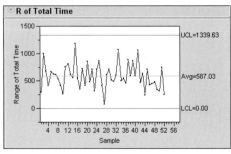

FIGURE 7.20   JMP $\bar{X}$ and R-Charts of Total Processing Time

A dot plot (see Figure 7.21) and $\bar{X}$ and R-charts (see Figures 7.22 and 7.23) from Minitab and JMP statistical software packages of "record pull time" for 52 weeks shows an unstable, bimodal process with a mean of 360.9 seconds (approximately 6 minutes) and a standard deviation of 169 seconds, or 2.8 minutes.

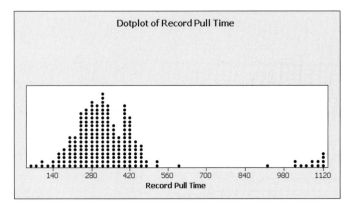

FIGURE 7.21   Minitab Dot Plot of Record Pull Time

Team members analyzed the out of control points on the R-chart (see the bottom panel of Figure 7.22 or the second panel of Figure 7.23) and determined that the out of control (large) ranges were caused by misplaced records that could not be located because they were being processed by another clerk. Brainstorming by team members led to the suggestion that a Post-It® note should be placed in each record's location as it is being processed, indicating who has the record, and that the Post-It® note should be removed after the file is replaced in its location. Consequently, the "Clerk pulls report" sub-process was modified to include this suggestion. Twenty six more weeks of data are collected. Figure 7.24 shows a before (coded 1) and after (coded 2) dot plot of "record pull time." The after data appears to be normally distributed. Figure 7.25 shows a before (coded 1) and after (coded 2) $\bar{X}$ and R-chart from Minitab. The after data shows a stable and normal process with a mean of 296.9 seconds (approximately 5 minutes) and a standard deviation of 99 seconds ($203/d_2=203/2.059=99$ seconds), or 1.65 minutes.

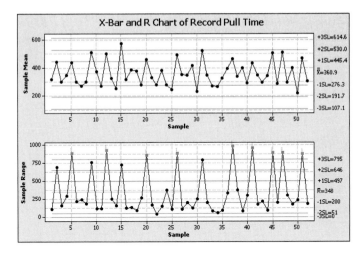

FIGURE 7.22 Minitab $\bar{X}$ and R-Charts of Record Pull Time

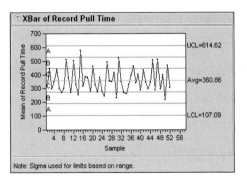
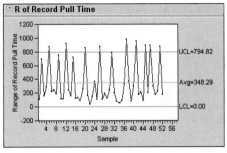

FIGURE 7.23 JMP $\bar{X}$ and R-Charts of Record Pull Time

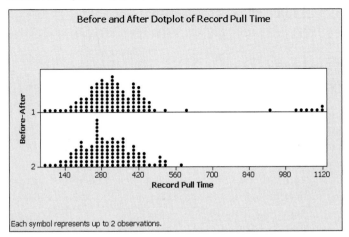

FIGURE 7.24 Minitab Before and After Dot Plot of Record Pull Time

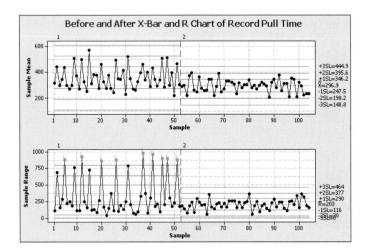

FIGURE 7.25 Minitab Before and After $\bar{X}$ and *R*-Charts of Record Pull Time

A before (coded 1) and after (coded 2) dot plot (see Figure 7.26) and before and after $\bar{X}$ and *R*-charts (see Figure 7.27) from Minitab of the CTQ show a stable and normal process with a lower mean of 1,190.8 seconds and a lower standard deviation of 227 seconds. It seems that the team was successful in stabilizing a chaotic process and creating a slightly improved process.

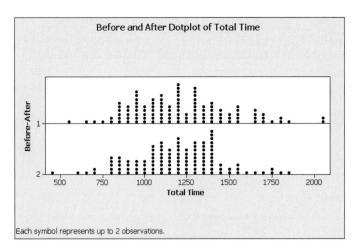

FIGURE 7.26 Minitab Before and After Dot Plot of Total Time

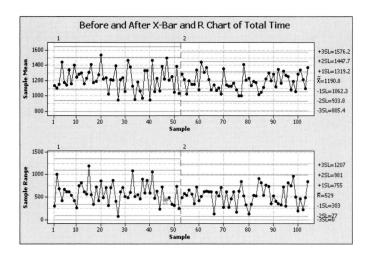

FIGURE 7.27 Minitab Before and After $\bar{X}$ and R-Charts of Total Time

Natural Limits and Specification Limits. Natural limits ("Voice of the Process") and specification limits ("Voice of the Customer") are comparable quantities for stable processes because they are both measured with respect to the individual units of output generated by the process under study. There are four basic relationships between natural limits and specification limits for stable processes. Each relationship is portrayed using a stable normal distribution.

Relationship 1. The process's natural limits are inside the specification limits and the process is centered on nominal. This is illustrated in Figure 7.28(a).

Relationship 2. The process's natural limits are inside the specification limits and the process is not centered on nominal. This is illustrated in Figure 7.28(b).

Relationship 3. The process's natural limits are outside the specification limits and the process is centered on nominal. This is illustrated in Figure 7.28(c).

Relationship 4. The process's natural limits are outside the specification limits and the process is not centered on nominal. This is illustrated in Figure 7.28(d).

In the example concerning wait times in a bank, the upper specification limit for acceptable wait times in a bank is 300 seconds; that is, the USL = 300 seconds. From Table 7.2 and the histogram in Figure 7.11 on page 229, you see that 7 of the 400 wait times are greater than the upper specification limit. Hence, 1.75% of the "wait times in a bank" are out of specification from an empirical perspective.

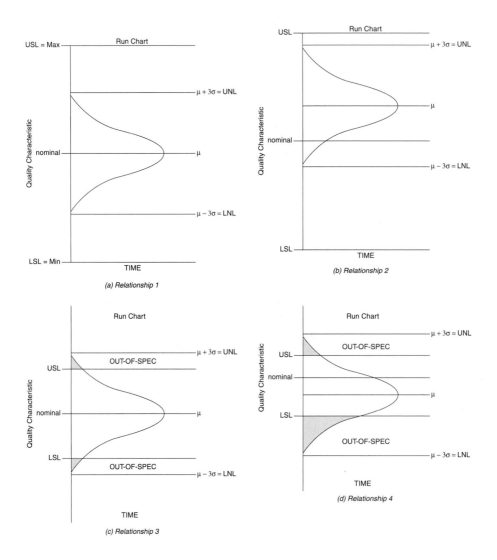

FIGURE 7.28   Relationship Between Natural Limits and Specification Limits

If you assume that the distribution of "wait times in a bank" are stable and normally distributed with a mean of 175 seconds and a standard deviation of approximately 60 seconds, then you can calculate the theoretical proportion of "wait times in a bank" that are over 300 seconds as follows:

$$P(\text{Wait Time} > 300 \text{ seconds}) = 1.0 - P(\text{Wait Time} \le 300 \text{ seconds})$$

$$= 1.0 - P\{Z < \frac{(300 - 175)}{60} = 1.0 - P\{Z < 2.08\} = 1.0 - 0.9812 = 0.0188$$

Hence, 1.88% of all "wait times in a bank" will be more than 300 seconds in duration according to the normal distribution. This translates into about 7.5 of the 400 wait times (0.0188 × 400). In fact, 7 of the wait times were over 300 seconds. The difference is due to the fact that the distribution of "wait times in a bank" is only approximately normally distributed, as it represents only a sample drawn from an ongoing process that is approximately normally distributed. In other words, 1.88% represents the long-term expected percentage of wait times over 300 seconds, while 7 out of the 400 sampled wait times (1.75%) represents the percentage from a sample of 400 that are greater than 300 seconds.

The theoretical DPO (defects per opportunity) for the "waiting times in a bank" baseline data is 0.0188 and the actual DPO is 0.0175. Hence, the theoretical yield from the "wait time in a bank" baseline data is 0.9812 [1.0 − (7.5/400)], while the actual RTY is 0.9825 [1.0 − (7/400)]. The theoretical DPMO is 18,880 (0.0188 × 1,000,000), while the actual DPMO is 17,500 (0.0175 × 1,000,000).

The short-term process sigma for "waiting times in a bank," assuming a 1.5-sigma shift in the process mean over time is approximately 3.6 from a theoretical viewpoint, and 3.5 to 3.6 from an actual viewpoint (see Table 2.3 on page 41). An objective of Six Sigma management is to get long-term process variation that considers both common and special causes of variation to equal short-term process variation, which considers only common causes of variation. (In other words, the goal is to have processes over the long term look the same over any short period of time, which means there is no increase in variation over time and there is no shift in the mean. This is what happens when a process is put into a state of statistical control.) Table 7.4 presents the current and desired conditions, as well as the gap, for the "waiting time in a bank" process. The particular gap between 99.99966% and the actual performance (see Table 7.4) is not shown in the experience of the authors. Rather, the gap is actually equal to the current failure rate as the ideal failure rate is a 0% failure rate. In practice, the ideal failure rate is 0% failure, while 99.99966% represents a "worst case" scenario, assuming the process long-term standard deviation is 1.5 times the short-term standard deviation. If process control is strictly maintained so that there is no shift, then Six Sigma is really 6 standard deviations from the specification, which implies a failure of 1 out of 1 billion, which is close to 0.

TABLE 7.4 *Summary of Waiting Time in a Bank*

CTQ or CTP	Yield			DPMO			Short-Term Process Sigma		
	Current	Desired	Gap	Current	Desired	Gap	Current	Desired	Gap
Wait Times	0.9825	0.9999966	0.0174966	17,500	3.4	17,496.4	3.6–3.7	6.0	2.3–2.4
CTQ2									
...									
...									
CTQ8									

Dormitory Example

In the dormitory example, the CTQs and the high-level CTPs are either present or absent. For example, a television set is either provided or not provided. Hence, it is impossible to have a process capability measure.

7.9 CONDUCT A CAPACITY ANALYSIS

Capacity analysis is a technique used by PD team members to study the resource requirements and statistics (for example, waiting line or queuing statistics and bottleneck statistics) for each detailed CTP in selected configurations of the detailed design. PD team members develop and verify a discrete event simulation model (see Chapter 13, "Discrete Event Simulation Models") of the detailed design to obtain an acceptable replica of the detailed design (detailed CTPs, CTPs, and CTQs). Next, development team members design, conduct, and analyze statistical experiments using the simulation model to identify the settings of the detailed CTPs that optimize the CTPs and CTQs, as well as to estimate the resource requirements for the optimal detailed design.

7.10 PERFORM A FMEA OF THE DETAILED CTPS

As in the Analyze Phase, team members can use a Failure Modes and Effects Analysis (FMEA) to identify, estimate, prioritize, and reduce the risk of failure of the detailed CTPs in the detailed design through the development of actions (process changes on the detailed CTPs) and contingency plans (just-in-case plans based on detailed CTPs).

You use Column 12 in the FMEA chart shown in Table 7.5 to evaluate action plans and contingency plans to potential failure modes (Column 2). Some examples of mistake-proofing methods that you can use in Column 12 of Table 7.5 include, but are not limited to:

1. Use of alarms to bring attention to failure mode conditions; for example, fire alarms and smoke alarms.
2. Use color coding to bring attention to potential failure mode conditions; for example, blue folders for geriatric patients, green folders for pediatric patients, orange folders for diabetic patients, etc.
3. Use hand harnesses to bring attention to a failure mode condition; for example, hand harnesses that pull a worker's hands away from a stamping press before the press can operate.

Once PD team members enter the mistake-proofing actions into Column 12 of Table 7.5, they can complete Columns 13 through 16 of Table 7.5 to determine if the mistake-proofing action taken significantly decreased the RPN to an acceptable level.

TABLE 7.5 Generic FMEA

1	2	3	4	5	6	7	8	9	10	11	12	13	14	15	16
Critical Parameter	Potential Failure Mode	Potential Failure Effect	Severity	Potential Causes	Occurrence	Current Controls	Detection	Before RPN	Recommend Action	Responsibility and Target Date	Action Taken	Severity	Occurrence	Detection	After RPN
Accessible Roof	Fall or Jump	Death	5	Accident	1	None	5	25	Guard Rails	Architect	Guard rails in design	5	1	1	5
			5	Suicide	1	None	5	25	Counseling	DayStar	Early detection program	5	1	1	5
Enforced Quiet Areas	Noise	Inability to study	4	Loud Music/TV	5	None	1	20	Enforced quiet area and hours	Resident master	Enforce quiet area policy	4	1	1	4
		Inability to sleep	4	Loud talking	5	None	1	20							

7.11 CONSTRUCTING DETAILED DESIGN SCORECARDS

In this step of the Design Phase, PD team members create scorecards for the detailed CTPs flowed-down from the CTP and CTQ scorecards in the Measure and Analyze phases. Recall, a design scorecard has two parts: Part A and Part B (see Table 7.6).

Part A presents the Voice of the Customer for each detailed CTP. The detailed CTPs listed in Part A are frequently an output of the second QFD matrix discussed on page 116. The Voice of the Customer for each detailed CTP includes the nominal value, the upper and/or lower specification limit(s), and a flow-down process sigma target.

Part B of the design scorecard presents the simulated statistics for each detailed CTP; that is, the mean, standard deviation, DPU (using the USL and LSL), and the predicted process sigma for the detailed design.

TABLE 7.6   Selected Portions of a Design Scorecard for CTPs

The second QFD matrix is used to identify the CTPs from CTQs.					Capability analysis using discrete event simulation is used to predict the performance of the CTPs in the detailed design.			
Scorecard—Part A (Voice of the CTP)					Scorecard—Part B (Predicted Voice of the CTP)			
CTP	Target (Nominal)	LSL	USL	Sigma Target	Mean	Standard Deviation	DPMO	Predicted Sigma
Time to provide concierge services	Nominal = 0 sec.	LSL = 0 sec.	USL = 120 sec.	4.0	M = 90	S = 10	P(X > USL) = .01350 DPMO = 1,350	4.5

7.12 PERFORMING ACCOUNTING ANALYSIS

Just as there are targets and specifications for product, service, and process characteristics in an overall design, there are budgetary requirements (constraints) for the product, service, or process characteristics. If the cost of developing and delivering a new design exceeds the benefits expected to be gained from implementing the new design, there are four decisions that can be made:

1. Do not implement the new design.
2. Investigate potential tradeoffs in the performance levels of the new design characteristics to decrease costs.
3. Investigate other alternative designs, or become more creative with respect to the characteristics of the current design.
4. Decide to go ahead with the new design for strategic reasons.

Decision 1 is not a good design if the reason you are trying to implement a new design is to overcome issues or problems with your current design. Nonetheless, if it is clear that the cost to implement the design is far too high for the benefits achieved, it is legitimate for leadership to elect to forego the new design.

Decision 2 pursues a new design in phases. The first few phases identify the major tradeoffs required to reduce the cost of the design. The next phases introduce new features or entirely new products, services, and processes that reduce the cost of the new design. You can amortize the cost of implementing a phased design over a longer period of time; that is, the time frame represented by the phases. A phased approach to a new design is sometimes called Multi-Generational Project Planning (MGPP). If the new design is associated with a product, then MGPP can signify Multi-Generational Product Planning.

Decision 3 uses alternative designs identified, but not used, from the Analyze Phase to find less costly designs, or less costly components for a new design. If the overall costs of a new design are high due to so many design elements, perhaps an alternative design can be identified using a Pugh Matrix with fewer design elements. For example, in the dormitory example, a modular design or pre-manufactured framework is utilized to lower the construction cost. Perhaps bundling of appliance costs through single vendors will lower the cost, although the individual appliances may not be "best in class." If the performance does not suffer too much bundling, combining steps or design elements, etc. are potential areas of exploration for alternative designs. Often in products, the cost of implementing the design is closely linked to the cost of manufacturing. Design scorecards are helpful in determining ways to improve the cost side of the implementation or production of the design.

Decision 4 uses the corporate strategy to capture the market—for example, a new design becomes a loss leader for other designs. An example of decision 4 is to design the maternity service of a hospital so it will be a "plus" for pregnant women and their families in a Pugh Matrix sense. The cost to implement such designs is high, which is not recouped from managed care providers, but it may be a "loss leader" service that will influence physician's and patient's hospital selection decisions for other hospital services. If a mother has a great experience with the delivery of her child, she is more likely to choose the same hospital for future services. Moreover, she is likely to choose physicians that are on staff at these hospitals.

Another example for using decision 4 can be seen in a cellular phone provider that subsidizes the cost for new phones to entice current and new customers to purchase additional or new services. Additionally, the cellular provider may work with cellular phone companies to design a new phone that provides services that a Kano analysis shows will be of major interest to customers and that are not available with other cellular providers. Though the cost to develop and sell a new phone may be high, the long-term expectations of an increased market share or increased commitment of current customers may be a positive strategic decision.

The accounting and financial costs of a new design include: (1) operating costs; (2) capital costs; and (3) intellectual property costs. Operating costs include the cost of labor, supplies, maintenance, and support for delivery of the new design. Organizations may vary in their methods for dealing with operating costs depending on their accounting and financial systems. For example, the definition of direct and indirect costs differ across systems. The capital costs associated with the investments so as to enable the design are often considered separately from operating costs. Cash flow is also a consideration. The difference between the revenue and gains from implementing the new design and the operating costs and the depreciation from the capital investments determine the cash flow. Each organization has different systems that will determine what constitutes capital and operating costs along with cash flow. Therefore, you need to consider knowledge of the accounting and financial system employed by the organization when developing new designs. Consequently, many organizations include a finance department representative as a dedicated, or at least, peripheral member of the design team.

7.13 PREPARE A CONTROL AND VERIFICATION PLAN

In this step of the Design Phase, PD team members create a smooth transition between themselves and the Operations and Sales Departments. PD team members develop a control and verification plan to prevent degradation (entropy) of the CTQs, high-level CTPs, and detailed CTPs in the detailed design over time. A format for a control and verification plan for one detailed CTP in the dormitory example is shown in Table 7.7. This table includes:

1. Documentation (for example, a flowchart or schematic) for the detailed design.
2. A list of the CTQs and CTPs.
3. The Voice of the Customer for each CTQ and CTP (nominal, USL, and LSL).
4. A sampling plan to collect data for each CTQ and CTP.
5. A data analysis plan for each CTQ and CTP (for example, a control chart and dot plots).
6. Actions needed to ensure a smooth transition of the detailed design to the Operations and Marketing Departments. Actions are created as a result of the answers to the following questions:

   • Is the design ready for Operations/Production?
   • Is the design ready for Sales?
   • Have all stakeholders bought into the design?
   • Have all CTQs and CTPs been established for the design?
   • Will process owners use the control and verification plan?

Once the preceding control and verification plan is developed, PD team members alert all stakeholders about the detailed design and turn it over to the process owner with appropriate training modules and practice sessions.

Dormitory Example

The control and verification plan does not apply to most of the CTQs and CTPs because the dormitory project is just a concept piece; that is, it has no detailed CTPs. This step also includes a plan to ensure that this new design can be scaled up from the drawing board and can become reality.

TABLE 7.7 Partial Dormitory Control and Verification Plan

Documentation of the Detailed Design (Flowchart or Other Description)	List of CTQs and CTPs	Targets (Nominal Values) for CTQs and CTPs	USL for CTQs and CTPs	LSL for CTQs and CTPs	Sampling Plan for CTQs and CTPs	Data Analysis Plan for CTQs and CTPs	Actions for CTQs and CTPs	
							Short Term	Long Term
Enforced Quiet Areas	Noise level in decibels (dB)	dB < A	USL = B Note: B > A	LSL = 0	Measure dB every 5 minutes	I-MR chart for dB for current day	Install white noise machines in problem rooms	Improve sound insulation in problem rooms

7.14 CONDUCT DESIGN PHASE TOLLGATE REVIEW (CHECK SHEET)

The typical elements of a Design Phase tollgate review are as follows:

Constructed a Comprehensive Set of Detailed CTPs	(Yes/No)
Operationally Defined Each Detailed CTP	(Yes/No)
Validated the Measurement System for Each Detailed CTP	(Yes/No)
Established Baseline Capabilities for Each Detailed CTP	(Yes/No)
Conducted a Capacity Analysis	(Yes/No)
Performed a FMEA of the Detailed CTPs	(Yes/No)
Prepared Detailed Design Scorecards	(Yes/No)
Prepared an Accounting Analysis	(Yes/No)
Delivered a Control and Verification Plan	(Yes/No)
Passed Tollgate Design Phase	(Yes/No)

7.15 OUTPUTS OF THE DESIGN PHASE

The Design Phase has four primary outputs:

- Detailed CTPs including all relevant design scorecards.
- Control and verification plan for the detailed design.
- Transition plan to smoothly transfer the design to the Operations and Sales Departments.
- Master record of the detailed design into the organizational document control system.

These outputs constitute the inputs for the Verify/Validate Phase of the DMADV model.

SUMMARY

The Design Phase of the DMADV model is all about creating a detailed design for the high-level design developed in the Analyze Phase. It involves constructing the design; creating operational definitions for each detailed CTP; validating the measurement systems for detailed CTP; estimating the capability for each detailed CTP; and preparing a control and verification plan. At the end of the Design Phase, there is no doubt about exactly what is being developed; it is a well-defined concept.

REFERENCES

1. H. Gitlow and D. Levine, *Six Sigma for Green Belts and Champions* (Upper Saddle River, NJ: Financial Times-Prentice Hall, 2005).

VERIFY/VALIDATE PHASE

SECTIONS

LEARNING OBJECTIVES

After reading this chapter, you will be able to:

* Build and pilot test a prototype of the desired design.
* Conduct a design review of the detailed design.

- Build and document the full-scale process.
- Transition the full-scale process to the process owner.
- Conduct a Verify/Validate Phase tollgate review.
- Transfer the lessons learned from creating the design to relevant stakeholders of the design.

INTRODUCTION

The Verify/Validate Phase is all about transferring the fully functioning service, product, or process based on the design to the process owner, and diffusing the innovation to all relevant stakeholders of the design throughout the organization's interdependent system of stakeholders. It is the final phase of the DMADV model.

8.1 STEPS OF THE VERIFY/VALIDATE PHASE

The Verify/Validate Phase of the DMADV model has 11 steps, as follows:

1. Build a prototype of the detailed design.
2. Pilot test the prototype of the detailed design.
3. Conduct design reviews using design scorecards.
4. Decide whether or not to scale-up the design to the full-scale process.
5. Build and operate full-scale process.
6. Decide if the full-scale process is meeting business objectives.
7. Build and operate full-scale process.
8. Decide if the full-scale process is meeting business objectives.
9. Conduct Verify/Validate tollgate review (check sheet).
10. Close the DMADV project.
11. Transfer the lessons learned from the project.

8.2 INPUTS TO THE VERIFY/VALIDATE PHASE

The inputs to the Verify/Validate Phase from the Design Phase are the following:

- Detailed CTPs including all relevant design scorecards.
- Control and verification plan for the detailed design.
- Transition plan to smoothly transfer the design to other internal stakeholders (e.g., Marketing, Operations, and Sales Departments).
- Master record of the detailed design into the organizational document control system.

8.3 BUILD A PROTOTYPE OF THE DETAILED DESIGN

Definition of Prototyping

Prototyping is the process of creating mock-up working models of the product, service, or process design under study. Prototypes help people involved with a design to visualize it, see its potential problems and improvements, and speed up decision making and innovation with respect to the design. It is important to realize that prototypes are usually developed and tested under ideal conditions to demonstrate the viability of a design concept. For example, an engineer may hand-build a prototype motor out of carefully selected raw materials, and operate the motor in a "clean room," to validate the design concept.

Traditional Prototyping Methods for Products (Tool and Die)[1]

Tool and die makers are extremely skilled workers usually found in the manufacturing sector. They create tools, dies, and guiding and holding devices that allow machines to generate many of the products you use on a daily basis, from silverware to parts for tractors.

Toolmakers create tools and machines for cutting, shaping, and forming materials. Additionally, they produce jigs and fixtures (devices that hold metal while it is bored, stamped, or drilled) and gauges and other measuring devices. Die makers create metal forms (dies) that are used for shaping metal in stamping and forging operations.

Additionally, they also make metal molds for die casting and for molding materials.

Computers have altered many of the methods employed by tool and die makers. For example, they use computer-aided design (CAD—defined later in this chapter) to develop products and parts by inputting technical specifications into a computer program that electronically

---

[1] Source: Bureau of Labor Statistics, U.S. Department of Labor, Occupational Outlook Handbook, 2004-05 Edition, Tool and Die Makers. http://www.bls.gov/oco/ocos225.htm.

develops drawings. "Numerical tool and process control programmers use computer-aided man- ufacturing (CAM) programs to convert electronic drawings into computer programs that contain instructions for a sequence of cutting tool operations. Once these programs are developed, com- puter numerically controlled (CNC) machines follow the set of instructions contained in the pro- gram to produce the part. Computer-controlled machine tool operators or machinists normally operate CNC machines. However, tool and die makers are trained in both operating CNC machines and writing CNC programs, and they may perform either task. CNC programs are stored electronically for future use, saving time and increasing worker productivity."

"After machining the parts, tool and die makers carefully check the accuracy of the parts using many tools, including coordinate measuring machines (CMM), which use software and sensor arms to compare the dimensions of the part to electronic blueprints. Next, they assemble the different parts into a functioning machine. They file, grind, shim, and adjust the different parts to properly fit them together. Finally, the tool and die makers set up a test run using the tools or dies they have made to make sure that the manufactured parts meet specifications. If problems occur, they compensate by adjusting the tools or dies."

Tool and die methods are not usually utilized in the delivery of most services. The outputs of tool and die methods may help those services focused on repair and maintenance of the pro- posed designs. When a prototype of an automobile engine bay is constructed, it can be studied for ease of maintenance due to the placement of various subsystems. For example, the ease of changing the oil, filter, and other similar service items can be studied. This may already be known from CAD models, though having a mocked up engine bay will allow further scrutiny. There are likely many lessons that can be learned from tool and die methods that could be applied to the delivery of services, but that topic is beyond the scope of this book.

Rapid Prototyping Methods for Products

Definition

Rapid prototyping is a method that creates a physical model of a design using a Computer Aided Design (CAD) model. CAD is defined as any design activity that involves the effective use of the computer to create, modify, or document an engineering design. CAD is most associated with the use of an interactive computer graphics system, referred to as a CAD system.

Benefits of CAD

There are four distinct benefits of using CAD for the design process. First, CAD helps a designer to better conceptualize a product and its components. If a designer has a good concep- tualization of a design, then she or he is better able to synthesize, analyze, and document the design. Second, CAD helps a designer consider a large number and variety of alternative designs. Third, CAD improves the design documentation process. The graphical output of a CAD system frequently results in better documentation of a design due to greater standardization among drawings, fewer drafting errors, and greater legibility of design documentation. Fourth, CAD automatically creates a design database.

Benefits of Rapid Prototyping

Rapid prototyping, using CAD models, can turn a conceptual design into a working physical model in minutes or hours, thereby promoting visualization and concept verification of the design. Rapid prototypes can serve as final products, given suitable materials (e.g., medical orthotics, such as false legs). Additionally, rapid prototyping can be used to produce tools for manufacturing, as an alternative to tool and die methods. An example of a product created using rapid prototyping can be seen in Figure 8.1.

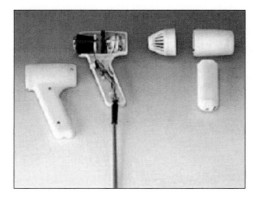

FIGURE 8.1   Product Created through Rapid Prototyping

Rapid Prototyping Methods[2] Useful for Services

Many methods for rapidly prototyping services exist and are used by PD teams. In this section, eight of the more commonly used rapid prototyping methods for services are described and illustrated in the context of the dormitory example. They are: scenarios, videography, role play, tagging the whales, behavioral mapping, consumer journals, storytelling, and intellectual SWOT teams.

Scenarios

PD team members create alternative applications for the design that demonstrate its use under a variety of conditions (scenarios). In the dormitory example, team members brainstormed for possible design modifications that would create acceptable alternative uses for a dormitory room. For example, in one scenario. a student likes to play loud music or listen to TV late at night, while another student wants quiet at those times. Consequently, team members generated the idea of wiring the room for earphone plug-ins for stereos and TVs by beds, desks, and lounge chairs. This creates the possibility of two alternative living scenarios, noisy and quiet, coexisting in the same room.

[2] Adapted from: *Business Week*, May 17, 2004, pp. 86–94.

Scenarios are also useful in the beginning of a design effort when considering a new design concept. For example, the dormitory can be placed closer to certain parts of campus, there can be a mix of fields of study or similar fields of studies by the dorm residents, there can be a mix of age groups versus a more homogeneous range of ages. Scenarios are useful at the Analyze Phase and at the more detailed Design Phase. Perhaps scenarios should be studied throughout the whole process.

Videography

Videography is an alternative to Scenarios. PD team members use videography to create short movies depicting the consumer's experience with a product, service, or process. In the dormitory example, team members shot a video depicting two students living in the same room under the conditions described in the preceding scenario example. After watching the video, team members realized at least one possible alternative design for resolving the conflict: wire the room for ear phone plug-ins by the beds, desks, and lounge chairs. Additionally, videography can help set up design goals at the Analyze Phase.

Role Play

PD team members ask different types of customers (market segments) to role play their use of the design. In the dormitory example, PD team members asked a small sample of undergraduate and graduate students to role play their living habits in their dorm rooms. The team members discovered that undergraduate students use a dormitory room very differently than graduate students. Undergraduates use their rooms for social purposes, such as talking, snacking, and listening to music. On the other hand, graduate students may use their rooms as quiet areas for studying. Of course, there will be overlap in the use of a dormitory between the undergraduate and graduate market segments.

Tagging the Whales

PD team members select a particular user (with permission) and observe his or her habits in using a product, service, or process. In the dormitory example, tagging the whales involves selecting a particular set of students and observing them constantly for a given period of time. This method frequently uncovers behaviors that the students themselves don't know they exhibit. For example, one team member followed a particular student around for several hours and discovered that the student went to his aunt's house to borrow a vacuum cleaner. This led PD team members to generate the idea of having shared vacuum cleaners on each floor in the dormitory that students can check out for use in their rooms.

Behavioral Mapping

PD team members can photograph or video a user's experience with a product, service, or process. Behavioral mapping is a combination of videography and tagging the whales.

Consumer Journal

PD team members ask selected users of the design to record their experiences with the design in a journal. In the dormitory example, PD team members asked a select group of residents in a dormitory to keep a journal of their positive and negative experiences with their dormitory room. Analysis of the journals revealed that the inability to make popcorn or heat up soup was a common problem. This led team members to the idea of a kitchenette, or at least a microwave oven, in each room.

Storytelling

PD team members ask users of the design to tell personal stories of their experiences with the design. PD team members record the stories. Storytelling is an alternative to the consumer journal that places less strain on the respondent.

Intellectual SWOT Teams

PD team members assemble a team of people with extremely diverse theoretical views of life, and consequently, of the design. In the dormitory example, a SWOT team might include a business person, an architect, a sociologist, a student, a historian, an artist, and a physician. This team would brainstorm for possible problems and solutions to the new dormitory design.

General Rules for Rapid Prototyping of Services

PD team members use three general rules when prototyping designs. The first rule is simplicity. Team members should create simple mock-ups of the service design. Frills should be ignored at this stage to prevent hang-ups and delays. The second rule is speed. Team members should create simple mock-ups quickly, again to prevent hang-ups and delays. The third rule is inclusion. Team members create mock-ups whenever they can for products, services, or processes. These three rules promote an environment of "can do" in creating prototypes for designs.

8.4 PILOT TEST THE PROTOTYPE OF THE DETAILED DESIGN

Purpose of a Pilot Test

A *prototype* is used by PD team members to test a design concept under ideal conditions, while a *pilot test* is used to test a design concept under actual conditions of use, perhaps on a small scale or for a limited time period. Pilot tests confirm that the design CTQs and CTPs surpass the design input requirements. You need to remember to calibrate and control all appropriate verification and validation activities.

PD team members ensure that all design functions are transferred, tested, labeled, displayed; outputs are generated and reviewed; and the results are documented by each production or service delivery location. They compare instructions with each manufacturer's and regulator's requirements and the operator manual. Additionally, they perform all verification and validation functions in strict accordance with approved and updated written protocols including the conditions for conducting pilot tests.

Objectives of a Pilot Test

There are five objectives for a pilot test: transferring the design, collecting data, creating buy-in, eliminating risks, and decreasing capital investment.

The first use of a pilot test, transferring the design to production or service delivery locations, concerns ensuring that the design is deployed throughout the stakeholders of the design with minimum unit-to-unit variation in output such that all producers of products and deliverers of services surpass design specifications (as in the Taguchi Loss Function). The design transfer process ensures that a verified and complete set of specifications for all detailed CTPs, high-level CTPs and CTQs:

- Meet design requirements for customer satisfaction.

- Are documented for the training of production, installation, and service personnel.

- Include a quality control plan.

- Include training for appropriate production, installation, and service employees.

Specifications are transferred via electronic and/or paper documentation using a Device Master Record (DMR). A **Device Master Record (DMR)** is a data file that contains all of the routine documentation required to generate products or deliver services in accordance with the specifications and nominal values for all CTQs and CTPs. The final design CTQs and CTPs form the contents of the DMR. A DMR documents the methods and specifications for a product, service, or process. The elements of a specification that are necessary for the appropriate transfer to product production or service delivery locations are:

1. Name of the product or service.
2. Verbal descriptions and intended use(s) for each CTQ including a list of any contradictions between CTQs and any relevant human interface issues, operating condition issues (for example, operating temperature, vibration range, humidity range, acceptable shelf life), and safety issues (for example, personnel training and safeguard devices).
3. Classification of CTQs (for example, regulatory or functional).
4. Specifications and nominal value(s) for CTQs; for example, cycle time (to process a bank loan), weight (of a 4.0 ounce ice cream cone), or color (of hair dye).
5. Quality control process review chart for the design. A quality control process review chart has four columns:

   - Column 1: An integrated flowchart of the production or service delivery process with the stakeholders in the columns and the steps in the rows (see Figure 8.2).
   - Column 2: A list of the key objectives for each step in the process (row in Column 1; see Figure 8.2).
   - Column 3: A list of the key indicators for each key objective in the process (row in Column 1; see Figure 8.2).

- Column 4: A list of the contingency plans in the event of a failure mode for one of the key indicators for each step in the process (row in Column 1; see Figure 8.2).

Integrated Flowchart of the Process			Key Objective	Key Indicator	Contingency Plan
Order Taking	Delivery	After Sale Service			
Start					
Receive Order			Decrease errors in order taking process	% errors in order taking process by month	problem with order hotline number is:
	Provide service		Decrease cycle time to provide service	Mean and standard deviation of service cycle times by day	
Receive call for after sale service			Decrease errors in order taking for after sale service call process	% errors in order taking for after sale service process by month	problem with after sale service order hotline number is:
		Provide after sales service	Decrease cycle time to provide after sale service	Mean and standard deviation of after sale service cycle times by day	
	Stop				

FIGURE 8.2 Quality Control Process Review Documentation

In the dormitory example, the DMR was transferred to the Dean of the School of Business Administration as he is the process owner of the new dormitory. It is then his decision to determine who will receive copies of the DMR.

The second use of a pilot test, collecting data, relates to information (data) on the performance of a design. The most frequently used tools to accomplish data collection are control charts [see Reference 2] and design scorecards (see Chapter 6, "Analyze Phase," and Chapter 7, "Design Phase"). Remember, you can conduct pilot testing at more than one location. For example, if a fast food restaurant chain decides to implement a new process for "greeting hungry customers within 15 seconds of their walking in the front door," it may conduct the pilot test at many franchises simultaneously. Consequently, it is critical that PD team members collect data to determine if each pilot test location is correctly utilizing the design specifications and generating products or services that are predictably produced or delivered with low unit-to-unit variation within specifications. For example, in the fast food restaurant chain example, histograms of the number of seconds to greet patrons walking in the front door are shown in Figure 8.3. The centered distribution in Figure 8.3 shows the greeting time distribution for Franchise A, while the distributions to the right of center and the left of center show the greeting time distributions for Franchisees B and C. Observe that Figure 8.3 clearly shows that Franchise B is having difficulty meeting the USL of 15 seconds.

The third use of a pilot test, creating buy-in, concerns promoting acceptance from process owners such as the Operations, Maintenance, and Sales departments. Two important parts of creating buy-in for a design are trialability and observability. Trialability is the degree to which a design may be experimented with by the appropriate departments. Observability is the extent to which a design is visible to the relevant departments. In the dormitory example, PD team members kept the Dean of the School of Business Administration involved in all phases of the tollgate review process, thereby creating his buy-in to the dormitory design.

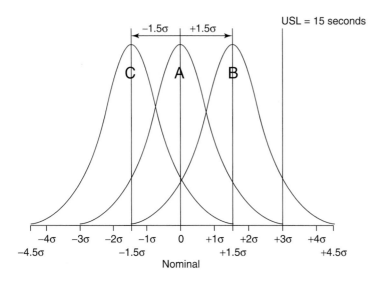

FIGURE 8.3 Greeting Time Distributions in a Restaurant

The fourth use of a pilot test, eliminating risk, concerns identifying and reducing the risks associated with failure modes and error modes. FMEA, risk analysis, and related tools are often used for this purpose (see Chapter 4, "Define Phase"). Contingency planning is part of FMEA and risk analysis. Pilot tests provide the opportunity to determine the effect of contingency plans on a design. In the dormitory example, the Dean of the School of Business Administration participated in, and accepted, all FMEAs with their contingency plans developed by PD team members.

The fifth use of a pilot test, decreasing capital investment, concerns reducing the financial requirements of testing the worthiness of a design in a realistic setting. A pilot test creates the opportunity to study a design for a limited time frame and a given budget. This use of a pilot study was not possible in the dormitory example due to the impracticality of building a dormitory solely for a pilot test. Simulation may be a practical alternative when the cost to pilot is too high. A simulation can discover hidden costs such as the ease of access of fire or other emergency services to the dormitory. It may reveal that access for these emergency services is not optimal, so to avoid costs (e.g., fires, litigation for unsafe conditions, etc.), the dormitory needs to have better accessibility. Also, the intangible costs of inconveniences to dormitory residents due to lack of ease of egress and accessibility to other locations can be considered.

Develop a Plan for Pilot Testing the Prototype

PD team members prepare a plan for a pilot test of the new design. There are two important considerations when developing a pilot test plan for a prototype. First, team members need to understand the effects of the detailed CTPs on each other, and on the CTQs. Second, team members need to get approval for the pilot test from all relevant managers. For example, a pilot test may require that a functioning process be reconfigured for a period of time. Personnel responsible for the output of the affected process may worry about the effect of a potential decrease in output on their design scorecards. Management must deal with these valid concerns before the pilot test. Again, simulation may be the only way to answer this due to the impracticality of building a dormitory solely for a pilot test.

Hold Pilot Release Readiness Review

PD team members conduct a readiness review of the impending pilot test procedure to ensure that there are no surprises, or at least as few surprises as is humanly possible. A readiness review may require team members to "go back to the drawing board" to revise the procedures for the pilot test. This can be frustrating because an inadequate readiness review frequently occurs in the presence of deadlines and tremendous pressure. Again, only a simulation may help with the dormitory design due to the impracticality of building a dormitory solely for a pilot test.

Conduct Pilot Test of the Prototype of the Detailed Design

If the pilot release readiness review is successful, then PD team members conduct and supervise the actual pilot test of the design. Five helpful hints for conducting a successful pilot test of a design are as follows:

1. Involve users of pilot test instructions in the creation of the pilot test instructions so that no crucial steps are omitted from the instructions and the instructions reflect what must actually be accomplished.
2. Create user friendly instructions for conducting a pilot test. Instructions must be: legible, brief as possible (but with all necessary detail), accessible, specify the desired output, not contain any unnecessary steps, appropriate for the educational level of the users, and in the user's language (English, Spanish, etc.).
3. Develop and utilize a standardized method for updating pilot test procedures.
4. Involve suppliers early in the Define Phase of the DMADV model. Of course, if a team is at the Verify Phase and suppliers were not involved in the Design Phase, there is a problem!
5. Make sure that all departments and appropriate stakeholders communicate freely concerning the design.

8.5 CONDUCT DESIGN REVIEWS USING DESIGN SCORECARDS

PD team members, in conjunction with the process owner and champion, conduct a design review for the new design. A design review is a type of management review that is a well-documented, comprehensive, and systematic examination of a design with the following purposes:

- Evaluate the adequacy of the design with respect to each detailed CTPs, high-level CTPs and CTQs stability, distributional shape, variability, and mean. Team members should consider the following types of design requirements: overall performance, component performance (components, accessories, software, labeling and packaging, installation, and service), and safety; compatibility with other systems; ergonomics; and environmental compatibility, documentation, and resources required for production and/or service that should all be represented in the design scorecards.

- Evaluate the capability of the design to meet these requirements with respect to specification limits, nominal values, DPMOs, and Process Sigmas for the detailed CTPs, high-level CTPs, and CTQs.

- Decide if the design is "ready" (perhaps at risk) for full-scale implementation by:

  - Analyzing the gaps between required performance (target, USL, LSL, DPU, DPMO, Process Sigma). Significant gaps lead to potential redesigns.

  - Predicting performance from simulations ($\overline{X}$, standard deviation, DPMO, Process Sigma).

  - Pilot testing performance using simulations ($\overline{X}$, standard deviation, DPMO, Process Sigma).

  - Identifying design problems.

- Assign action responsibilities.

Design reviews are formal meetings that include individuals who know about the technical aspects of the design; for example, R&D, System Designers, Technical Support Services, Delivery, Installation and Service, Quality, Marketing, Purchasing and Contractors, and representatives knowledgeable about the demands of Regulatory Agencies.

Minutes of design review meetings should be taken and distributed to all relevant individuals to clarify the "to do" items for the next meeting and who is responsible for each "to do" item. The design review meeting minutes should include:

- List of attendees (and absences).

- Meeting date and location.

- Agenda items including issues to identify and solve, as well as "to do" items from the last meeting.

- Decisions and/or conclusions reached, including "to do" items for the next meeting; for example, notes and/or drawings. Such documents show that plans were followed and the history of the design.

Meeting minutes and results are made a part of the design history file.

Design review meetings should consider the following issues:

- Has proper installation been provided for all equipment needed to provide the product or deliver the service? This requires design review team members to consider the following issues: design of equipment features; conditions for a particular installation of the design; calibration of the installation within the context of the installation conditions; and preventive maintenance policies and procedures, which include cleaning requirements, human factors, safety features, documentation, spare parts inventory policies, and environmental conditions for installation.

- Have all CTQs, high-level CTPs, and detailed CTPs surpassed their specifications for the production of product or the delivery of services? This requires design team members to consider the following issues: designing experiments to optimize the capability of the process; implementing appropriate operating, process control; and preventive maintenance procedures including cleaning and calibration, as well as training requirements.

- Does the product or service perform as required by customers? This requires design team members to consider the following issues: operability of the actual product or service process parameters and procedures; stability and repeatability of the product or delivery of service process; acceptability of the product or service to customers; and worst-case testing of the product or service under a wide range of conditions.

A checklist of the issues PD team members must consider in a design review includes the following:

- Identification of the process to be validated.
- Identification of products or services to be generated using this process.
- Criteria for a successful design review including the length and duration of the study.
- Identification of the operating conditions of the process; for example, personnel (qualifications, schedules, etc.), shifts, equipment, and necessary utilities.
- Development of a detailed flowchart of the process, including specifications for the products or services and their component parts, specifications for input materials, and environmental factors (internal and external).
- Identifying the objective and subjective process and product/service parameters to be controlled and monitored, and the statistical methods for controlling and monitoring them, including maintenance and repair parameters.
- Defining nonconformance for both objective and subjective process and product/ service parameters.

Again, this step was not possible in the dormitory example due to the dormitory design being a concept piece without detailed CTPs.

8.6 DECIDE WHETHER OR NOT TO SCALE-UP DESIGN

After the design review has been conducted and the design scorecards have been prepared, PD team members, in conjunction with appropriate managers, must make a GO (scale-up the design to full-scale production of products or delivery of services) decision or a NO GO (go back to the appropriate phase of the DMADV model) decision. The NO GO decision takes real courage. Remember that most of the cost associated with a product or service is determined when they are designed. Often, rushed designs create poor products and services that result in high long-term costs.

8.7 BUILD AND OPERATE FULL-SCALE PROCESS

PD team members along with appropriate personnel oversee the construction and operation of the full-scale process that was designed to generate products or services. Appropriate personnel can include: the designated process owner, engineers, architects, sub contractors, vendors, and attorneys. Project management tools, such as Gantt charts or more sophisticated scheduling methods, should be used to monitor the process of turning a design into a functioning physical or process reality.

    With respect to the dormitory example, this section explains the activities that must take place to ensure that the new dormitory design can be scaled up from the drawing board to a physical reality. The floor plans and three-dimensional renderings need to become prototypes for testing, and from there, to become the means for constructing a fully functional residential college building. Taking this design from the computer through construction requires a three-tiered plan.

    The first tier involves designing the building itself and the relationships with the actual designers and architects. There needs to be a concurrent checks-and-balances system between the university, designers, and architects. The first step toward ensuring that the university, architects, and designers understand what they are to contribute to the new construction project is understanding the needs of all the stakeholders, the interdependencies of the major system design elements, and the schedule and budget constraints, along with the performance scorecards that serve as a major means by which the outcomes will be judged. By doing this, the needs and wants of the university and potential residents will be explained. This building is distinct in that it is not a dormitory, apartment, or luxury hotel. Rather, it is a merger of these three concepts. Scenario planning is appropriate here to determine if the merger of the three concepts works well. Additionally, the professionals also need to obtain information related to academic and social areas. The second step is to ensure that the university, architects, and designers have accurately contributed what they have agreed to contribute to the project. This can be accomplished by having a control and verification that includes a process for auditing the design and its assumptions, such as how many cubic feet of air should flow through a room at a given time. This would require a system of experts to sign off on the design. Next, the approved technical specifications would be taken to the stakeholders of the design for approval.

Once the design is completed and independently validated, the second tier of the verification phase can begin. This second tier is related to moving from paper to concrete. The first step in the second tier is the selection of contractors to do the work. The university has a system in place to receive bids from contractors, and choose from these bids. However, this system needs to be reviewed to ensure that the lowest bid does not necessarily win out, but instead that the lowest total cost bid wins out. Each bid should be studied to prevent unplanned and expensive rework. This determination of the lowest total cost contractor will help to prevent unpleasant surprises in time and cost. The second step in the second tier involves the creation of a flexible Gantt chart to provide a schedule for the construction project. The third step in the second tier is an offshoot of the second step, which is the utilization of an expert in material flow to ensure that efficiency is maintained, and that all materials are centrally ordered. One proposal, which will be further developed in the Verify/Validate Phase, is to have a Bill of Lading Check Sheet System, which will track all materials being ordered, and when they are to arrive. This will help to ensure that there are no shortages, and that warehousing space will not become a problem and become an additional hidden cost. Finally, the last step in the second tier is establishing some type of monitoring system to follow the progress of construction and to help prevent hidden costs, such as rework, from creeping into the final cost.

The third tier relates to taking the completed building and transferring it to its new owners. This involves a variety of processes; for example, maintenance processes, occupancy processes, and educational processes. Flowcharts, metrics, and controls need to be drafted for all of these processes. It is worth noting that while this sounds like the shortest section in the verification plan, it is actually the longest and most difficult. This tier includes creating replacement plans for long-term items such as plumbing, as well as short-term items, such as how to regulate students' move-in. Poor planning with these processes could be disastrous later despite the fact that the physical building could be perfect.

8.8 DECIDE IF THE FULL-SCALE PROCESS IS MEETING BUSINESS OBJECTIVES

One of the final tasks of the PD team is to study the dashboard associated with the new design. Are key objectives, as measured by their key indicators, being met in full-scale production of the product or delivery of the service? Recall from Chapter 3, "Macro Model of Six Sigma Management (Dashboards)," that there are four aspects of the design that must be considered when evaluating its contribution to an organization:

- Financial objectives and indicators
- Process objectives and indicators
- Customer objectives and indicators
- Employee objectives and indicators

Financial Objectives

Examples of financial key objectives include management's and stockholder's desire for more profit, market share, dominance and growth, and the desire for less waste, turnover, financial loss, and customer defection.

Process Objectives

Examples of process improvement and innovation key objectives include: (1) management's desire for consistency and uniformity of output; (2) high productivity; (3) products, services, and processes that exceed the needs and wants of current and future stakeholders; (4) products, services, and processes that are easy to create and have a low cost to provide; (5) products and services that surpass technical specifications; (6) products and services that do not incur warranty costs; and (7) products that are easy to distribute throughout the channels of distribution.

Customer Objectives

There are four types of customer satisfaction key objectives: (1) customer's desired outcomes; (2) customer's undesired outcomes; (3) customer's desired product and service attributes; and (4) customer's desired process characteristics. Examples of customer desired key objectives include joy, security, personal time, belonging, and health; examples of customer's undesired outcomes include avoidance or elimination of death, taxes, discomfort, wasted time, and frustration. Examples of customer's desired product and service attribute key objectives include ease-of-use, accessibility, low cost of ownership, durability, and appeal. Examples of customer's desired process characteristic key objectives include timely arrival of product, no waiting time, and ease of acquisition.

Employee Objectives

Examples of employee growth and development key objectives include improving leadership skills, providing training opportunities, providing educational opportunities, and creating the opportunity to work on stimulating special assignments.

8.9 DOCUMENT THE FULL-SCALE PROCESS

International Standards Organization (ISO) established criteria for a system of documenting what you do and doing what you document. It is a critical first step to managing a process. PD team members document a process by answering the following questions.

1. Who is involved at each step of the new process?
2. What should they be doing with respect to standard operating procedures?

3. Why should they follow the standard operating procedures?

4. Where should they be doing the standard operating procedures?

5. When should they be doing the standard operating procedures?

6. How should they be doing the standard operating procedures?

7. How much will it cost to do the standard operating procedures?

8. Is additional training needed to perform the standard operating procedures?

9. How often should the standard operating procedures be monitored?

10. Who will monitor the standard operating procedures?

11. Who will make decisions on the future outputs of the standard operating procedures?

The answers to the preceding questions are formalized in training manuals, training programs for existing and new employees, and, if appropriate, ISO documentation.

ISO 9000 and ISO 14000

The ISO 9000 and ISO 14000 families of standards are among ISO's most widely known and successful standards. ISO 9000 has become an international reference for quality requirements in business-to-business dealings, and ISO 14000 looks set to achieve at least as much, if not more, in helping organizations to meet their environmental challenges.

Generic Table of Contents of an ISO Standard

A generic table of contents for an ISO product or service specification is shown next:

- Applicable documents
  - Internal documents
    - Drawing of product or service
    - Drawing of package
    - Specifications for component parts
  - External documents
    - Regulations
    - Accepted standards
- Product description
  - Features of product or service
  - Variations of product or service features
- Product provisions
  - Functioning of product or service (General, Operating characteristics, Acceptable noise level, Acceptable pollution, etc.)

- Materials specifications
- Workmanship specifications
- Safety requirements
- Dimensions and/or Cycle time (specifications)
- Finish appearance
- Marking
- Manufacture or Delivery
  - Fabrication
  - Painting
  - Assembly
  - Delivery mechanisms
- Shipping
  - Packaging
    - Requirements
    - Tests
  - Marking and Labeling
- Inspection or sampling plan

8.10 TRANSITION FULL-SCALE PROCESS TO OWNERS WITH A CONTROL PLAN

PD team members create a list of questions they must answer to ensure a smooth transition of the new design to the Marketing, Operations, and Sales departments. The list should address the following issues:

- Has the design been successfully pilot tested by PD team members?
- Is the full-scale process up and running?
- Does the full-scale process have a functioning control plan?
- Has the full-scale system been documented?
- Has all training been conducted for process stakeholders?
- Does the full-scale process result in the desired business objectives?
- Will the outputs of the full-scale process satisfy (delight) stakeholders?
- Have process owners bought into the next generation of the Multi-Generational Product Plan?

If the answers to all of the preceding questions are "yes," then the full-scale version of the design is ready to be transferred to its process owners. If the answer(s) to any of the preceding questions is "no" or "I don't know," then the design must be recycled back to the appropriate phase of the DMADV model.

8.11 CONDUCT VERIFY/VALIDATE PHASE TOLLGATE REVIEW (CHECK SHEET)

The typical elements of a Verify/Validate Tollgate Review are as follows:

Build a prototype of the detailed design.	(Yes/No)
Pilot test the prototype of the detailed design.	(Yes/No)
Conduct design reviews using design scorecards.	(Yes/No)
Decide whether or not to scale-up design.	(Yes/No)
Build and operate full-scale process.	(Yes/No)
Decide if full-scale process is meeting business objectives.	(Yes/No)
Document the full-scale process.	(Yes/No)
Transition full-scale process to owners with a control plan.	(Yes/No)
Conduct Verify/Validate Phase tollgate review.	(Yes/No)
Close the DMADV project.	(Yes/No)
Transfer the lessons learned from the project.	(Yes/No)

8.12 CLOSE THE DMADV PROJECT

Several things occur at this point in the Verify/Validate Phase of the DMADV model:

- First, the design has been completely turned over to the appropriate process owner with a control plan.

- Second, the PD team makes a final review of the relevant phase of the MGPP that has been completed and makes appropriate recommendations to the process owner.

- Third, the process owner continuously turns the PDSA cycle to act on improvements discovered by PD team members as an evolution in future phases of the MGPP, but not yet implemented in the design.

- Fourth, the DMADV project team is disbanded and the team members, the process owner, champion, and team leader (black belt or green belt) celebrate their success.

- Fifth, the process owner collects data, via the control plan, on whether the design is achieving its business objectives and generates appropriate accounting documentation on the project's benefits/costs.

8.13 TRANSFER THE LESSONS LEARNED FROM THE PROJECT

Introduction

This section explains the theories and methods for diffusing designs within an organization, between organizations, and to end users of the design.

You might be inclined to assume that all concerned parties would accept constructive innovations, but nothing is further from the truth. For example, in the early days of long sea voyages, scurvy was the leading cause of death among sailors. One hundred of the 160 men sailing with Vasco de Gamma in 1497 died of scurvy. In 1601, the English sea captain James Lancaster discovered that consuming citrus eradicated scurvy. However, not until 1795 did the British Navy routinely stock citrus on all sailing ships, 194 years later. Further, not until 1865 did the British Board of Trade stock citrus in the merchant marine, 264 years later. Why? Who would object? What is the down side to keeping citrus on sailing ships? The point is that innovations do not spread only as a natural consequence of their value. The same rules that apply for diffusing citrus in the British Navy and merchant marine apply to diffusing innovations between and within organizations, and to end users.

Inter (between)-organization diffusion explains how innovations flow from an external source into an organization, group, club, tribe, etc. Intra (within)-organization diffusion explains how innovations spread among the different areas within an organization. Each type of diffusion requires some unique methods.

How to diffuse innovations is not obvious. For example, creating a newsletter or having a meeting for all interested persons is *not* the way to reliably diffuse innovations; other methods are needed. This section presents generic models for both interfirm and intrafirm diffusion of innovations.

Diffusion is "the process by which an innovation is communicated through certain channels over time among the members of a social system." "An innovation is an idea, practice, or object that is perceived as new by an individual or other unit of adoption." "Most potential adopters do not evaluate an innovation on the basis of scientific studies of its consequences; rather, they depend on a subjective evaluation from other individuals like themselves who have previously adopted the innovation." "The heart of the diffusion process consists of the modeling and imitation by potential adopters of their network partners who have previously adopted the innovation" [see Reference 3].

Perceived Attributes of Innovations

Rogers defines five perceived attributes of innovations:

- Relative advantage
- Compatibility
- Complexity
- Trialability
- Observability

Relative Advantage

Relative advantage is the degree to which an innovation is perceived as being better than the idea it supersedes. The dimensions of relative advantage include economic profitability, initial cost, comfort, social prestige, time and effort, and immediacy of the reward.

The concept of a Pugh Matrix to compare current versus innovated designs is worth noting here. The Pugh Matrix makes it more obvious if an innovation is better than the current standard.

Compatibility

Compatibility is the degree to which an innovation is perceived as consistent with the existing values, past experiences, and needs of potential adopters. The name given to an innovation often affects its perceived compatibility, and therefore its adoption rate. The name of an innovation should be meaningful to the target audience. The positioning of an innovation rests on accurately measuring its compatibility with previous ideas.

Complexity

Complexity is the degree to which an innovation is perceived as relatively difficult to understand and to use by the potential adopter.

Trialability

Trialability is the degree to which a potential adopter can experiment with an innovation on a limited basis.

Observability

Observability is the degree to which the results of an innovation are visible to potential adopters.

Adopter Categories

Table 8.1 shows five adopter categories [see Reference 3].

TABLE 8.1 Adopter Categories and Percentages

Adopter Category	% of a System in Each Category
Innovator	2.5
Early adopter (Opinion leader)	13.5
Early majority	34.0
Late majority	34.0
Laggard	16.0

Innovators are venturesome, cosmopolitan, and friendly with a clique of innovators outside of their system. They possess substantial financial resources and understand complex technical knowledge. However, they may not be respected by the members of their system. They are considered to be unreliable by their near peers due to their attraction to new things. Innovators are frequently the gatekeepers of new ideas into their system.

Early adopters are well respected by their peers, have a local network of contacts, are opinion leaders, and are role models for other members of their system. They are the embodiment of successful, discrete use of ideas. Early adopters are the key to diffusing innovations within a system.

Early majority deliberate for some time before adopting new ideas and interact frequently with their peers. They are not opinion leaders.

Late majority require peer pressure to adopt an innovation. They have limited economic resources that require the removal of uncertainty surrounding an innovation.

Laggards are near isolates in their system. They are suspicious of innovation and their reference point is in the past.

Opinion leaders (early adopters) are the key to the diffusion process. Those seeking to diffuse an innovation within a system need to obtain the commitment of the opinion leaders within the system in which diffusion is to take place. Only opinion leaders command the respect and admiration of their peers necessary to diffuse an innovation. However, opinion leadership is a characteristic that can be used up by overzealous diffusers of innovations. If the early majority, late majority, and laggards in a system see an opinion leader as frequently aligning himself or herself with new ideas, the opinion leader begins to look less and less like the embodiment of the successful, discrete use of ideas, and more and more like an innovator.

Innovation-Decision Process

Regardless of an individual's adopter category, he or she must go through the innovation-decision process with respect to an innovation. This process consists of how an individual or other decision-making unit passes from first knowledge of an innovation, to forming an attitude about the innovation, to a decision to adopt or reject the innovation, to implementation of the innovation, and to confirmation of the innovation decision. The innovation-decision process consists of five stages:

- Knowledge stage
- Persuasion stage
- Decision stage
- Implementation stage
- Confirmation stage

The **knowledge stage** occurs when a decision-making unit (individual or group) is exposed to an innovation's existence and gains some understanding of how it functions. Mass media is a particularly effective channel of communication in the knowledge stage.

The **persuasion stage** occurs when a decision-making unit forms a favorable or unfavorable attitude (feeling) toward the innovation. Interpersonal communication is the key to an individual passing through the persuasion stage with positive feelings toward the innovation.

The **decision stage** occurs when an individual or some other decision-making unit engages in the activities that lead to a choice to adopt or reject (or re-invent) the innovation.

The **implementation stage** occurs when a decision-making unit actually uses the innovation.

The **confirmation stage** occurs when a decision-making unit seeks reinforcement of an innovation-decision already made, or reverses a previous decision to adopt or reject the innovation if exposed to conflicting messages about the innovation.

Rate of Adoption

The rate of diffusion of an innovation by the members of a system is called the **rate of adoption**. The rate of adoption is frequently measured by the cumulative percentage of the members of a system that implement the innovation. Figure 8.4 shows a classic adoption curve for an innovation.

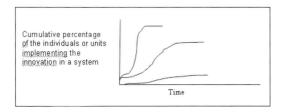

FIGURE 8.4 Adoption Rate for an Innovation

The *S*-curve on the top represents the rapid and successful diffusion of an innovation; for example, the adoption curve for Viagra. The middle *S*-curve represents a slower and moderately successful diffusion of an innovation. The *S*-curve on the bottom represents an unsuccessful diffusion of an innovation.

Demand and Supply Factors

The methods for successfully diffusing an innovation between systems may not be successful for diffusing an innovation within a system. The between system diffusion strategy is based mostly on the demand-based factors of diffusion. The within system diffusion strategy is based on both demand-based and supply-based factors of diffusion.

A demand-based diffusion strategy relies upon identifying and approaching influential early adopters (opinion leaders), and then enhancing their ability to influence others to adopt an innovation. This is clearly a demand-based diffusion strategy because it increases the demand for the innovation.

A supply-based diffusion strategy involves managing the process and conditions under which innovations are made available to potential adopters. The conditions are that all potential adopters have access to a conveniently priced and adequately developed innovation. This is clearly a supply-based strategy because it increases the supply of an innovation.

A demand-based diffusion strategy makes sense as long as the following supply-based factors are in place. First, the innovation remains the same over the diffusion process. This assumption becomes increasingly untenable as the length of the diffusion process increases. Second, the organizational environment is equivalent for all potential adopting units. Third, the price of the innovation is equal for all potential adopters. The second and third assumptions are frequently untrue. The point here is that a demand-based strategy contains some potential difficulties when dealing with an innovation that takes a long time to diffuse in an environment in which potential adopters do not have equal access to the innovation.

Organizational Factors

If an organization has no difficulties with the diffusion of an innovation, it should be able to "specify milestones, budgets, and expectations for the diffusion process" [see Reference 4]. If difficulties do occur with the diffusion of an innovation, the preceding becomes problematic. The most likely causes of diffusion problems within an organization are [see Reference 4]:

- Lack of absorptive capacity of the adopter
- Ambiguity
- An arduous relationship between the diffuser and the adopter

Lack of absorptive capacity is a potential adopter's inability to exploit external sources of knowledge. One strategy to reduce lack of absorptive capacity is to develop the learning capacity of potential adopters of an innovation.

Ambiguity is a potential adopter's inability to comprehend the factors leading to the success and/or failure of an innovation. A strategy to reduce ambiguity is to systematically improve management's understanding of the factors that affect the success and/or failure of the innovation and to improve their ability to communicate these factors to potential adopters.

An arduous relationship exists when a potential adopter's relationship with a diffuser of an innovation is laborious, distant, and lacks any sense of intimacy. A strategy to improve arduous relationships is to foster intimacy between potential adopters and the diffusers of an innovation.

You can contrast the preceding organizational factors with the conventional wisdom that attributes diffusion problems almost exclusively to motivational factors. Motivational factors include: jealousy, lack of incentives, lack of confidence, low priority, lack of buy-in, inclination to reinvent the wheel or to plow the same fields twice, adopter's refusal to do exactly what she/he is told, resistance to change, lack of commitment, turf protection, and, of course, the NIH (not invented here) syndrome.

The organizational factors lead to the conclusion that using only motivational factors to improve diffusion of an innovation is not an effective strategy. Rather, diffusers of the innovation should devote their scarce resources and managerial attention to:

1. Developing the learning capacity of potential adopters of an innovation.

2. Systematically improving management's understanding of the factors that affect the success and or failure of the innovation and improving their ability to communicate these factors to potential adopters.

3. Increasing intimacy between potential adopters and the diffusers of an innovation.

An Alternative Measure for Rate of Adoption

The problem that can occur with Rogers' definition of "rate of adoption" is caused by confusion over when an innovation has been actually adopted by a decision-making unit. Rogers' model for the rate of adoption is appropriate only when the adoption decision is made once for all elements within an adopting system. For example, the decision to support a particular type of computer system is made simultaneously for all units within an organization. However, Rogers' model for rate of adoption is not appropriate when the diffusion of an innovation is gradual. For example, one surgeon in a hospital has adopted an innovation, but the other twenty-nine surgeons choose to wait, each on his or her own adoption schedule. This situation is referred to as *gradual diffusion*. In this case, can you say that the innovation has been diffused to the hospital? Many would answer "no" to this question. Consequently, an alternative definition for the rate of adoption for gradual diffusion [see Reference 1] is the number of decision-making units within a system actually adopting an innovation divided by the total number of decision-making units within the system that could potentially adopt the innovation.

A Demand-Based Diffusion Strategy

Introduction

A demand-based strategy makes sense when the supply-based factors are approximately equal for all potential adopters. Recall, a demand-based strategy focuses diffusion effort on opinion leaders (early majority) to influence other potential adopters and thereby create demand for the innovation. This logic is based on the following supply-based assumptions:

- The innovation remains the same over the diffusion process.

- The organizational environment is equivalent in all adopting units.

- The price of the innovation is equal for all potential adopters.

The demand-based strategy diffusion model consists of three parts:

- Preparing the infrastructure for a diffusion plan.

- Developing a diffusion plan.

- Executing a diffusion plan.

Table 8.2 represents a generic Gantt chart of the model.

TABLE 8.2 Generic Gantt Chart for a Demand-Based Diffusion Plan

Task to be accomplished in the diffusion plan	Responsibility	Time Periods							
Preparing infrastructure for the diffusion plan		**1**	**2**	**3**	**4**	**5**	**6**	**7**	**8**
1. Establish diffusion as part of strategic plan and assign an executive responsibility for the diffusion.	Top Mgt. and Executive	X							
2. Form diffusion team.	Team		X						
3. Define experimental and target systems (segment the market).	Executive and Team			X					
4. Develop indicator for adoption rate.	Team				X				
5. Prepare schedule for diffusion plan.	Team				X				
6. Implement support structure.	Team				X				
Developing a demand-based diffusion strategy									
1. Develop video and brochure.	Team				X				
2. Identify opinion leaders.	Team				X				
3. Prepare motivational plan.	Team					X			
Executing a demand-based diffusion strategy									
1. Call a meeting.	Team						X		
2. Monitor the schedule.	Executive							X	X
3. Execute motivational plan.	Executive							X	X
4. Follow-up on the diffusion plan.	Executive							X	X

Preparing the Infrastructure for a Diffusion Plan

Successful diffusion of an innovation requires a diffusion plan. The infrastructure for a demand-based diffusion plan has six parts. First, the top management of the system in which the innovation is to be diffused must make diffusion a strategic objective and assign an executive accountability for the diffusion. Second, the executive establishes a team to spearhead the diffusion process. Third, the executive identifies the experimental system (if one is required) and the segments of the target system for which the diffusion process is to take place. An experimental system, sometimes called a pilot test, is a component of a larger system (in time or place) in which it is possible to modify and test a diffusion concept to meet the needs and wants of a particular market segment; for example, one hospital in a hospital chain. A target system is a larger system that is considering adopting the diffusion. Fourth, team members must develop an indicator (with a sampling plan) to measure and monitor the adoption rate of the innovation among opinion leaders. Fifth, the team prepares a schedule for the diffusion plan. Sixth, team members develop the support services needed for the diffusion process; for example, telephone, e-mail, and facsimile machines. Additionally, the executive should make sure that the support services do not overwhelm the diffusion team members. The preceding infrastructure is required for successfully diffusing an innovation in an organization.

Developing a Demand-Based Diffusion Plan

Once the structure of the diffusion plan is in place, the executive and team members can develop the actual diffusion plan. The key elements of a diffusion plan are as follows.

Key Element 1. Team members develop a videotape and several brochures about the innovation for the experimental and target systems. The videotape is developed for all selected market segments for the innovation, while a unique brochure is developed for each selected market segment (niche) using the language of that market segment. The videotape is in five parts. Part One presents the leader of the organization naming the innovation. The appropriate highest-ranking executive explains the theory underlying the innovation. The team leader describes the characteristics of the innovation, consisting of the relative advantage of the innovation over ideas that compete with it, compatibility of the innovation with the organization's prevailing culture, complexity of the innovation in comparison with competing ideas, trialability, or the ease with which a potential adopter can conduct trial experiments with the innovation, and observability, or how easy it is for a potential adopter to see the innovation in action. The second part of the videotape shows team members using the innovation in their local setting. The third part of the videotape presents testimonials of other users of the change (if available). The fourth part of the videotape shows team members briefly answering commonly asked questions about the innovation. The questions commonly asked by potential adopters at each stage of the innovation-decision process are as follows:

- The knowledge stage questions are:
    1. Describe the innovation?
    2. How does it work?
    3. Why does it work?

- The persuasion stage questions are:

    1.   Explain the advantages of the innovation?

    2.   What are the disadvantages of the innovation?

  The characteristics of an innovation (relative advantage, etc.) are important in the persuasion stage.

- The decision stage questions are:

    1.   When can I see a demonstration of the innovation?

    2.   Can I use the innovation on a trial basis?

- The implementation stage questions are:

    1.   Where do I obtain the innovation?

    2.   How do I use it?

    3.   What problems will I encounter when I use the innovation?

    4.   How can I solve the above problem(s)?

- The confirmation stage questions are:

    1.   Did I make the correct decision in adopting/rejecting the innovation?

    2.   What are the consequences of adopting/rejecting the innovation?

The fifth part of the videotape shows a process improvement specialist explaining how to use the innovation in each adopting area. The brochure contains all the same information as the videotape, except it is tailored for a particular market segment and contains more detailed information on the commonly asked questions. Tailoring a brochure for a market segment can be accomplished by using the language of the market segment or examples specific to the market segment.

Key element 1 is much like scenario staging that can be done as design concepts are "vetted" for congruency of those who will be living with the design.

Key Element 2. Team members identify opinion leaders in the target systems. Recall, opinion leaders are at the heart of the demand-based diffusion process. Table 8.3 presents four methods for identifying opinion leaders. Each has its advantages and disadvantages [see Reference 3]. The "informants rating method" is suggested for small systems due to its low cost and time expenditure. The "sociometric method" is suggested for large systems due to its ease of administration and adaptability to organizational conditions.

You can use the following steps for identifying opinion leaders, assuming team members have selected the "informant rating method." First, team members select a judgment sample of internal experts who propose names of potential opinion leaders within their organization with respect to the innovation. Second, the internal experts ask themselves: "Who are the opinion leaders in my organization with respect to the innovation?" Third, team members create a list of opinion leaders.

TABLE 8.3 Identifying Opinion Leadership

Measurement Method	Description	Question Asked	Advantages	Limitations
Sociometric method (most popular method)	Ask system members whom they go to for advice and information about a new idea.	Who is your opinion leader?	Easy to administer, adaptable to different settings, highest validity.	Complex and requires a large number of respondents to find an opinion leader. Works best on population, not on sample.
Informant ratings	Subjectively selected key informants designate opinion leaders.	Who are the opinion leaders in this system?	Low cost and time expenditure compared to sociometric method.	Each informant must be thoroughly familiar with the system.
Self-designating method	Ask each respondent to designate himself or herself as an opinion leader.	Are you an opinion leader in this system?	Measures individual's perceptions of his/her opinion leadership, which influences his/her behavior.	Accuracy dependent on respondent's self image.
Observation	Identify and record communication network links as they occur.	None.	High validity.	Obtrusive, works best in a small system, requires much patience.

Key Element 3. Team members prepare a motivational plan to induce opinion leaders to try the innovation. The motivational plan must have the commitment of the top management of the organization. The motivation plan should consider a balance of extrinsic and intrinsic motivators. It should employ extrinsic motivators such as no loss of income guarantees, CEU credits, and confidential training for sensitive egos, etc., and stimulate intrinsic motivation by creating fertile ground for relevant personnel to experience joy in work.

Executing a Demand-Based Diffusion Strategy

The executive in charge and team members execute a demand-based diffusion strategy by:

- Calling a meeting of all opinion leaders and top management.
- Monitoring the schedule for the diffusion plan.
- Executing the motivational plan.
- Following up on the progress of the diffusion plan.

Team members call a meeting of the opinion leaders with the express purpose of introducing and demonstrating the innovation. The agenda for the meeting should include: a description of innovation by team members, the benefits and costs of the innovation by team members, a preview of video of team members using the innovation, a brochure with commonly asked questions about the innovation, an actual demonstration of the innovation by team members, a discussion of the incentives to try the innovation by the CEO, questions and answers by both the CEO and team members, and a sign-up sheet for opinion leaders to try the innovation with the guidance of the diffusion team.

The executive in charge of the demand-based diffusion plan prepares and monitors a schedule of interactive demonstrations for each opinion leader led by team members. Notes are kept on cancellations and reschedules. Team members provide the executive in charge of the diffusion plan a weekly status report. The executive takes action on any delays or problems.

The executive creates an environment conducive to the release of intrinsic motivation on the part of opinion leaders with respect to the innovation. Where deemed appropriate, the executive oversees the awarding of extrinsic motivators to opinion leaders for using the innovation in his or her area.

The executive follows up on the delays and any problems with the diffusion plan. He or she checks in with each opinion leader every week and reviews overall progress toward diffusion of the innovation on a monthly basis.

A Demand- and Supply-Based Diffusion Strategy

Supply Factors

The demand-based model discussed previously does not make sense if the supply-based factors are not equal for all potential adopters. Here, diffusion strategists should consider a model that uses a balance of both demand (opinion leader strategy) and supply-based factors for the diffusion of an innovation, with more emphasis on the supply-based factors [see Reference 3].

The supply factors of intrafirm diffusion focuses on providing a conveniently priced and adequately developed innovation. This was the function of the Define, Measure, Analyze, and Design Phases of the DMADV model.

Organizational Factors

Three organizational factors key to the demand-supply based diffusion strategy are the following:

1. Developing the learning capacity of potential adopters of an innovation.

2. Systematically improving management's understanding of the factors that affect the success and/or failure of the innovation and improving their ability to communicate these factors to potential adopters.

3. Increasing intimacy between potential adopters and the diffusers of an innovation.

You can use the model in Table 8.4 to focus attention on the first of these three organizational factors. The model has three steps:

1. Diffusion team members identify all potential adopters (see Column 1 of Table 8.4).
2. Diffusion team members list all CTPs for product or service (see Columns 2 through *i* of Table 8.4).
3. Diffusion team members rate each potential adopter's learning capacity for each CTP on a scale from (1) to (5) where (1) is very high learning capacity and (5) is very low learning capacity.
4. Diffusion team members focus attention on improving the learning capacity of each potential adopter with respect to the CTPs for which they have high scores (or low learning capacity).

The preceding process could be accomplished subjectively for a simple innovation.

TABLE 8.4   Focusing Attention on Organizational Factors for a Demand- and Supply-Based Diffusion Strategy

Potential Adopters	CTPs		
	Adopter Rating for CTP 1	**Adopter Rating for CTP 2**	**Adopter Rating for CTP *i***
Mr. A	5	2	4
Ms. B.	2	2	5
....		...	

You can use the model in Table 8.5 to focus attention on the second of the organizational factors. The model has four steps:

1. Diffusion team members identify all managers involved in diffusing the innovation within their organization (see Column 1 of Table 8.5).
2. List all of the CTPs for the innovation (see Columns 2 through *i* of Table 8.5).
3. Diffusion team members rank each managers' ability to understand, explain, and communicate information about each CTP on a scale of one (1) to five (5), where 1 is very good ability and 5 is very poor ability.
4. Diffusion team members allocate resources to improve the communication skills of managers for the CTPs for which they have high scores (or very poor ability).

The preceding process could be accomplished subjectively for a simple innovation.

TABLE 8.5   Focusing Attention on Managers with Difficulty Communicating Information About Specific CTPs

	CTPs		
	CTP 1	**CTP 2**	**CTP *i***
List of Managers			
Mr. X	5	2	
Ms. Y	1	5	
Ms. Z	3	1	

You can use the model in Table 8.6 to focus attention on the third of the organizational factors. The model has three steps:

1. List diffusion team members.
2. List potential adopters.
3. Create potential adopter–innovation team member pairings.

Each potential adopter should be assigned to at least one diffusion team member. This process could be accomplished subjectively for a simple innovation.

TABLE 8.6   Assignment of Potential Adopters to Diffusion Team Members

Diffusion Team Members	**Potential Adopters**		
	Adopter 1	**Adopter 2**	**Adopter *i***
Member A	X	X	
Member B			X

You can use Tables 8.4 through 8.6 to create organizational factors that create a positive environment for the supply-demand based diffusion strategy.

Consider the Diffusion of a Design Throughout the Entire DMADV Model

It can be argued that a design concept, at least from a high level, should be "vetted" from very early in the design process at the Define Phase. Moreover, if a new product, service, or process is developed and delivered before users are ready to use it, then it may be considered a waste of effort. The following equation should be considered when planning the diffusion process for a new design:

Effectiveness of the Design = (Quality of the Design) × (Acceptability of the Design).

Consequently, not only should the DMADV model consider the quality of a design, but it should consider the acceptability of a design. This means that scenario planning, videos, trials, etc. of alternative design concepts should be incorporated into a design, as the design unfolds through the DMADV model.

8.14 OUTPUTS OF THE VERIFY/VALIDATE PHASE

The outputs of the Verify/Validate Phase are as follows:

- Transfer of full-scale innovation process to owners.
- Diffusion of the new design throughout the organization and to other appropriate organizations.

SUMMARY

This chapter presents the Verify/Validate Phase of the DMADV model. This phase describes how to: build a prototype of the detailed design developed in the Design Phase, conduct a design review using a design scorecard, decide whether to scale-up the detailed design, build and operate the full-scale process, decide if the full-scale process is meeting business objectives, document the full-scale process, transition the full-scale process to the process owner with a control plan, conduct a tollgate review, close the DMADV project, celebrate the project team's success, and transfer the lessons learned from the project to all appropriate organizations. Additionally, this chapter presents the conclusion of the dormitory case study.

REFERENCES

1. Cool, K., Dierickx, I., and Szulanski, G., "Diffusion of Innovations Within Organizations: Electronic Switching in the Bell System, 1971–1982," *Organization Science*, 8, 5, September/October 1997, pp. 543–559.

2. Gitlow, H. S., and D. M. Levine, *Six Sigma for Green Belts and Champions* (Upper Saddle River, NJ: Financial Times Prentice Hall, 2005).

3. Rogers, E., *Diffusion of Innovations*, 4th ed. (New York: The Free Press, 1995).

4. Szulanski, G., "Exploring Internal Stickiness: Impediments to the Transfer of Best Practices Within the Firm," *Strategic Management Journal*, 1996, 17: pp. 27–43.

Design for Six Sigma Tools and Methods

BASICS OF STATISTICAL STUDIES

SECTIONS

LEARNING OBJECTIVES

After reading this chapter, you will be able to:

* Distinguish between enumerative and analytic studies.
* Understand the importance of operational definitions.
* Use the Minitab 14 and JMP statistical software packages.

9.1 STATISTICS AND DESIGN FOR SIX SIGMA

This chapter begins the third part of this text. Many Design for Six Sigma tools and methods involve *statistics*. What exactly is meant by statistics, and why is statistics such an integral part of Design for Six Sigma management? To understand the importance of statistics for improving quality, you can go back to a famous 1925 quote of Walter Shewhart, widely considered to be the father of quality control:

> "The long-range contribution of statistics depends not so much upon getting a lot of highly trained statisticians into industry as it does in creating a statistically minded generation of physicists, chemists, engineers, and others (managers—inserted by the authors) who will in any way have a hand in developing and directing the production processes of tomorrow."

This quote is consistent with the goal of the next four chapters. The objective of Chapters 9–12 is for you to learn enough so that you will be able to use statistical methods as an integral part of Design for Six Sigma management. Using Minitab 14 and/or JMP statistical software will help you achieve this goal while at the same time minimize your need for formulas and computations. This text assumes that you are familiar with the Six Sigma DMAIC model and those statistical tools used with the DMAIC model, such as charts and tables, descriptive statistics, confidence intervals, hypothesis testing, and statistical process control charts [see Reference 4].

The definition of *statistics*, according to Deming [see Reference 3], is to study and understand variation in processes and populations, interactions among the variables in processes and populations, operational definitions (definitions of process and population variables that promote effective communication between people), and ultimately, to take action to reduce variation in a process or population. Hence, statistics is broadly defined as the study of data to provide a basis for action on a population or process. Statistics is often divided into two branches: descriptive statistics and inferential statistics.

Descriptive statistics focus on the collection, analysis, presentation, and description of a set of data. For example, the United States Census Bureau collects data every 10 years (and has done so since 1790) concerning many characteristics of residents of the United States. Another example of descriptive statistics is the employee benefits used by the employees of an organization in fiscal year 2005. These benefits might include healthcare costs, dental costs, sick leave, and the specific healthcare provider chosen by the employee.

Inferential statistics focus on making decisions about a large set of data, called the **population**, from a subset of the data, called the **sample**. The invention of the computer eased the computational burden of statistical methods and opened up access to these methods to a wide audience. Today, the preferred approach is to use statistical software such as Minitab or JMP (as we will do in this book) to perform the computations involved in using various statistical methods.

9.2 ENUMERATIVE AND ANALYTIC STUDIES

There are two types of statistical studies: enumerative and analytic. The two types of studies have different purposes, so you need to understand the distinction between them.

Enumerative studies are used to draw conclusions about a population fixed in place and time. A common example of an enumerative study is a political poll in which you select a sample of registered voters from a list of all registered voters in a particular geographical area as of June 2005. Based on the results of the sample, statistical inferences are made about the entire voter registration list in the geographical area as of June 2005. Another example of an enumerative study is a study of the average weight of roofing shingles manufactured by a factory in 2005. Based on a sample of shingles selected, inferences can be made about the average weight of the shingles manufactured in 2005. Dynamic questions, such as why the people reside where they do or why the weight of the roofing shingles varies, are not considered in an enumerative study. Each of these examples is time-specific and static; there is no reference to the past or the future.

Analytic studies are used to study the cause-and-effect systems of a process to improve the future functioning of a process. An example of an analytic study related to the roofing shingles previously mentioned is to study why there was variation in the average weight of the roofing shingles manufactured over time and what factors could be causing this variation to improve the future production of shingles. Another example of an analytical study is determining why there is variation in the time it takes to fulfill orders that are received at a web site. Other examples of analytic studies are comparing the output of two paper machines over time to determine whether one is more productive and comparing ways of marketing a financial service to increase market share. All of these examples focus on the future, not on the past or present. You use the information to make dynamic decisions to improve the future functioning of a process.

Distinguishing Enumerative and Analytic Studies

A simple rule for distinguishing between an enumerative study and an analytic study is as follows: If a 100% sample answers the question under investigation, the study is enumerative; if not, the study is analytic.

9.3 TYPES OF VARIABLES

Numerical information collected about a product, service, process, individual, or item is called **data**. Because no two things are exactly alike, data inherently varies. Each characteristic of interest is referred to as a **variable**. Data are classified into two types: attribute data and measurement data.

Attribute data (also referred to as *classification* or *count data*) occurs when a variable is either classified into categories or used to count occurrences of a phenomenon. Attribute data places an item or person into one of two or more categories. For example, gender has only two categories. In other cases, there are many possible categories into which the variable can be classified. For example, there could be many reasons for a defective product or service.

Regardless of the number of categories, the data consists of the number or frequency of items in a particular category, whether it is the number of voters in a sample who prefer a particular candidate in an election or the number of occurrences of each reason for a defective product or service. Count data consists of the number of occurrences of a phenomenon in an item or person. Examples of count data are the number of blemishes in a yard of fabric or the number of cars entering a highway at a certain location during a specific time period.

Measurement data (also referred to as *continuous* or *variables data*) results from a measurement taken on an item or person. Any value can theoretically occur, limited only by the precision of the measuring process. For example, height, weight, temperature, and cycle time are examples of measurement data.

Variables can also be described according to the level of measurement scale. There are four scales of measurement: nominal, ordinal, interval, and ratio. Attribute data classified into categories is **nominal scale** data—for example, conforming versus non-conforming, on versus off, male versus female, and so on. No ranking of the data is implied. Nominal scale data is the weakest form of measurement. An **ordinal scale** is used for data that can be ranked, but cannot be measured—for example, ranking attitudes on a 1 to 5 scale, where 1 = very dissatisfied, 2 = dissatisfied, 3 = neutral, 4 = satisfied, and 5 = very satisfied. Ordinal scale data involves a stronger form of measurement than attribute data. However, differences between categories cannot be measured. Measurement data also can be classified into interval- and ratio-scaled data. In an **interval scale**, differences between measurements are a meaningful amount, but there is no true zero point. In a **ratio scale**, not only are differences between measurements a meaningful amount, but there is a true zero point. Temperature in degrees Fahrenheit or Celsius is interval scaled because the difference between 30 and 32 degrees is the same as the difference between 38 and 40 degrees, but there is no true zero point ($0°$ F is not the same as $0°$ C). Weight and cycle time are ratio-scaled variables that have a true zero point; zero pounds are the same as zero grams. Twenty minutes is twice as long as ten minutes, and ten minutes is twice as long as five minutes.

9.4 OPERATIONAL DEFINITIONS

Operational definitions were discussed in Chapter 5, "Measure Phase." Recall that major problems occur when the measurement definitions for CTQs and CTPs are inconsistent over time or vary from individual to individual. Ambiguous definitions, such as defective, safe, round, and hot, have no meaning that can be communicated unless they are operationally defined.

> An **operational definition** is a definition that provides communicable meaning to the users of the definition.

An example [see Reference 2] that illustrates the importance of operational definitions is reflected in the 2000 U.S. Presidential election and the disputed ballots in the state of Florida. A review of 175,010 Florida ballots that were rejected for either no presidential vote or votes for two or more candidates was conducted with the help of the National Opinion Research Center of the University of Chicago. Nine operational definitions were used to evaluate the ballots to determine whether they should be counted. The nine operational definitions led to different results. Three of the operational definitions (including one pursued by Al Gore) led to margins of victory for George Bush that ranged from 225 to 493 votes. Six of the operational definitions (including one pursued by George Bush) led to margins of victory for Al Gore that ranged from 42 to 171 votes.

SUMMARY

This chapter has provided an introduction to the field of statistics and why statistics is such a vital tool in Six Sigma management.

REFERENCES

1. Berenson, M. L., D. M. Levine, and T. C. Krehbiel, *Basic Business Statistics: Concepts and Applications*, 10th ed. (Upper Saddle River, NJ: Prentice Hall, 2006).

2. Calmes, J. and E. P., Foldessy, "In Election Review, Bush Wins with No Supreme Court Help," *Wall Street Journal*, November 12, 2001, A1, A14.

3. Deming, W. E., *Some Theory of Sampling* (New York: John Wiley, 1950).

4. Gitlow, H. S., and D. M. Levine, *Six Sigma for Green Belts and Champions* (Upper Saddle River, NJ: Financial Times Prentice Hall, 2005).

5. Hahn, G. J. and W. Q. Meeker, "Assumptions for Statistical Inference," *The American Statistician*, 1993, 47, 1–11.

6. JMP Version 6 (Cary, NC: SAS Institute, 2005).

7. Minitab Version 14 (State College, PA: Minitab, 2004).

A P P E N D I X   9.1

INTRODUCTION TO MINITAB VERSION 14

Minitab Overview

Minitab is an example of a statistical package, a set of programs designed to perform statistical analysis to a high degree of numerical accuracy. Minitab initially evolved from efforts at Pennsylvania State University to improve the teaching of statistics and quickly spread to many other colleges and universities. Today, while maintaining its academic base, Minitab has become a commercial product that is used in many large corporations and is widely used by companies involved in Design of Six Sigma.

In Minitab, you create and open **projects** to store all of your data and results. A **session**, or log of activities, a **Project Manager** that summarizes the project contents, and any worksheets or graphs used are the components that form a project. Project components are displayed in separate windows inside the Minitab application window. By default, you will see only the session and one worksheet window when you begin a new project in Minitab. (You can bring any window to the front by selecting the window in the Minitab Windows menu.) You can open and save an entire project or, as is done in this text, open and save worksheets. Minitab's statistical rigor, availability for many different types of computer systems, and commercial acceptance make this program a great tool for using statistics in Six Sigma management.

Using Minitab Worksheets

You enter data in a Minitab worksheet so that each variable is assigned to a column. Minitab worksheets are organized as numbered rows and columns numbered in the form *Cn*, in which C1 is the first column. You enter variable labels in a special unnumbered row that precedes row 1 (see Figure A9.1). Unlike worksheets in program such as Microsoft Excel, currently, Minitab worksheets do not accept formulas and do not automatically recalculate themselves when you change the values of the supporting data.

By default, Minitab names opened worksheets serially in the form of Worksheet1, Worksheet2, and so on. Better names are ones that reflect the content of the worksheets, such as **ORDER** for a worksheet that contains data for the order fulfillment times. To give a sheet a descriptive name, open the Project Manager window, right-click the icon for the worksheet, select **Rename** from the shortcut menu, and type in the new name.

Opening and Saving Worksheets and Other Components

You open worksheets to use data that have been created by you or others at an earlier time. To open a Minitab worksheet, first select **File → Open Worksheet**. In the Open Worksheet dialog box that appears (see Figure A9.2):

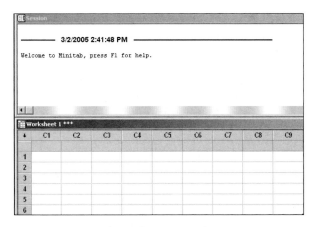

FIGURE A9.1   Minitab Application Window

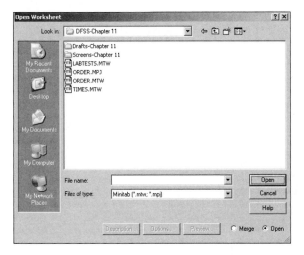

FIGURE A9.2   Minitab Open Worksheet Dialog Box

1. Select the appropriate folder (also known as a directory) from the Look in: drop-down list box.

2. Check, and select, if necessary, the proper Files of type: value from the drop-down list at the bottom of the dialog box. Typically, you will not need to make this selection because the default choice will list all Minitab worksheets and projects. However, to list all Microsoft Excel files, select Excel (*.xls); to list every file in the folder, select All.

3. If necessary, change the display of files in the central files list box by clicking the rightmost (View menu) button on the top row of buttons and selecting the appropriate view from the drop-down list.

4. Select the file to be opened from the files list box. If the file does not appear, verify that steps 1, 2, and 3 were done correctly.

5. Click the **Open** button.

To open a Minitab Project that can include the session, worksheets, and graphs, select Minitab Project in step 2 or select the similar **File ➔ Open Project**. Individual graphs can be opened as well by selecting **File ➔ Open Graph**.

You can save a worksheet individually to ensure its future availability, to protect yourself against a system failure, or to later import it into another project. To save a worksheet, select the worksheet's window, then select **File ➔ Save Current Worksheet As**. In the Save Worksheet As dialog box that appears (see Figure A9.3):

1. Select the appropriate folder from the Save in: drop-down list box.

2. Check and select, if necessary, the proper Save as: type value from the

drop-down list at the bottom of the dialog box. Typically, you will want to accept the default choice, Minitab, but select Minitab Portable to use the data on a different type of computer system or select an earlier version, such as Minitab 13, to use the data in that earlier version.

3. Enter (or edit) the name of the file in the File name: edit box.

4. Optionally, click the Description button, and in the Worksheet Description dialog box (not shown), enter documentary information and click the OK button.

5. Click the **Save** button (in the Save Worksheet As dialog box).

To save a Minitab Project, select the similar **File ➔ Save Project As**. The Save Project As dialog box (not shown) contains an Options button that displays the Save Project–Options dialog box in which you can indicate which project components other than worksheets (session, dialog settings, graphs, and Project Manager content) will be saved.

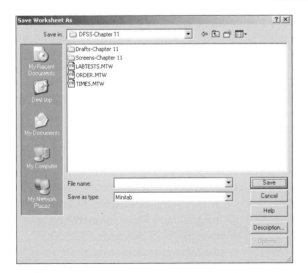

FIGURE A9.3   Minitab Save Worksheet As Dialog Box

You can save individual graphs and the session separately by first selecting their windows, then selecting the similar **File → Save Graph As** or **File → Save Session As**, as appropriate. Minitab graphs can be saved in either a Minitab graph format or any one of several common graphics formats, and Session files can be saved as simple or formatted text files.

You can repeat a save procedure and save a worksheet, project, or other component using a second name as an easy way to create a backup copy that can be used should some problem make your original file unusable.

Printing Worksheets, Graphs, and Sessions

Printing components gives you the means to study and review data and results away from the computer screen. To print a specific worksheet, graph, or session:

1. Select the window of the worksheet, graph, or session to be printed.

2. Select **File → Print** *object,* where *object* is either Worksheet, Graph, or Session Window, depending on the component window you selected.

3. If you are printing a worksheet, select formatting options and add a title in the Data Window Print Options dialog box that appears; then click the **OK** button in that dialog box (see Figure A9.4).

4. In the Print dialog box that appears, select the printer to be used, set the Number of copies to the proper value, and click the **OK** button.

After printing, you should verify the contents of your printout. Most printing problems or failures will trigger the display of an informational dialog box. Click the **OK** button of any such dialog box and correct the problem noted before attempting a second print operation.

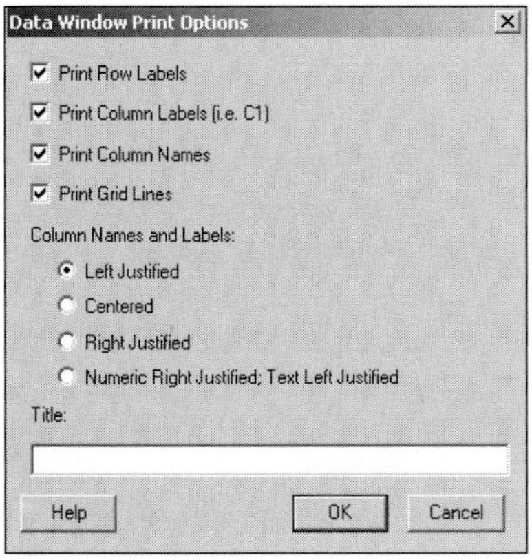

FIGURE A9.4   Minitab Data Window Print Options Dialog Box

A P P E N D I X   9.2

INTRODUCTION TO JMP VERSION 6

JMP Overview

JMP is an example of a statistical package, a set of programs designed to perform statistical analysis to a high degree of numerical accuracy. JMP was developed by the SAS Institute, Inc. JMP's statistical rigor, availability for different types of computer systems, and commercial acceptance make this program a great tool for using statistics in Six Sigma management.

Using JMP Data Tables

You start JMP by double-clicking the JMP application icon. A JMP session begins by displaying a menu bar and a JMP Starter window (see Figure A9.5).

You use a JMP data table to enter data for variables by column. If you are creating a new set of data, select **File ➔ New** or the **New Data Table** button. If you are opening an existing JMP file, select **File ➔ Open** or the **Open Data Table** button.

Opening a file creates a JMP data table. Figure A9.6 illustrates the data table window for a data set labeled **TIMES.JMP**. Each row is identified with a row number and each column has a column label. The blue triangle to the left of the column name in the panel on the left side of the data table window indicates that this variable is continuous (or you can click the blue triangle to get a pop-up menu that also indicates that the variable in the column is continuous). A set of red vertical bars

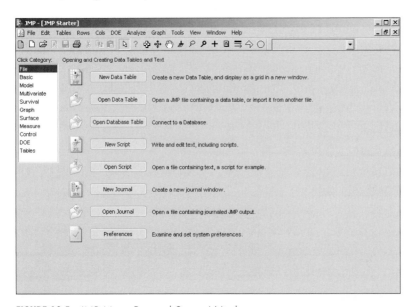

FIGURE A9.5 JMP Menu Bar and Starter Window

indicates a nominal scale variable, while a set of green vertical bars indicates an ordinal scale variable.

	Time
1	39
2	29
3	43
4	52
5	39
6	44
7	40
8	31
9	44
10	35

TIMES

Columns (1/1)
Time

Rows	
All rows	10
Selected	1
Excluded	0
Hidden	0
Labelled	0

FIGURE A9.6   JMP Data Table Window

DESIGN OF EXPERIMENTS

SECTIONS

LEARNING OBJECTIVES

After reading this chapter, you will be able to:

- Understand the basic concepts of experimental design.
- Conduct 2^k factorial designs and interpret the effect of interactions.
- Conduct fractional factorial designs and interpret the effect of interactions.

INTRODUCTION

Design of Experiments (DoE) is a collection of statistical methods for studying the relationships between **independent variables**, the Xs or CTPs, and their interactions (also called *factors, input variables,* or *process variables*) on a **dependent variable**, the

Y (or CTQ). Additionally, you can use design of experiments to minimize the effects of background variables on understanding the relationships between the CTPs or *X*(s) and CTQ or *Y.* A **background variable** (also called *noise variable* or *lurking variable*) is a variable that can potentially affect the dependent variable (*Y* or CTQ) in an experiment, but is not of interest as an independent variable (CTP or *X*).

The concepts of experimental design discussed in this chapter represent an *active* intervention into a process by Six Sigma team members. Process changes are planned and tested by team members, and the data that is collected from those changes is studied to determine the effect of the process change. This type of experiment does more than passively collect data from a functioning process. It actively intervenes in the function of the process to conduct experiments concerning the effects of the *X*s and their interactions on a *Y.*

10.1 DESIGN OF EXPERIMENTS: BACKGROUND AND RATIONALE

The ideas involved in the design of experiments are not new. They were originally developed by R. A. Fisher in England early in the twentieth century [see References 1 and 4]. His original work focused on improving agricultural experimentation. Fisher's contributions to experimental design were based on several fundamental principles. First, Fisher developed an experimental strategy that purposely designed experiments to simultaneously study several factors (*X*s) of interest on a CTQ (*Y*). This approach was considered novel, because it contrasted with the scientific method as practiced in the nineteenth century of varying only one factor at a time. Second, he developed the concept of randomization that allows for the control and measurement of variation resulting from factors (*X*s) not considered in the experiment. Fisher realized that, in conducting an agricultural experiment in the field, not all factors could be foreseen (background variables). Thus, he determined the particular treatment levels received by each plot of land (the individual observations) by a method of random assignment. Any differences between different plots that received the same treatment could be considered to be due to random variation or experimental error.

The methods of experimental design have been used not only in agricultural experimentation, but also in industrial applications [see Reference 1]. They form a critical component of the statistical methods used in Six Sigma management, particularly in the Analyze and Design Phases of the DMADV model.

10.2 TWO-FACTOR FACTORIAL DESIGNS

This section begins the study of experimental designs in which more than one factor (X) is examined simultaneously. These experimental designs are called **factorial designs** because they simultaneously evaluate the effects of two or more factors (Xs) on a CTQ (Y). This section discusses the simplest factorial design, the two-factor design. In addition, although you can include any number of levels of a factor in a design, for pedagogical simplicity, only the special circumstance in which there are two levels (or treatments) for each factor of interest (CTP or X) will be considered in this book. Designs that contain more than two levels of a factor are logical extensions of the two-level case. In addition, this text only considers situations in which there are equal numbers of **replicates** (that is, the sample size) for each combination of the levels of the factors (Xs).

Owing to the complexity of the calculations involved, particularly as the number of levels of each factor increases and the number of *replications* in each cell increases, statistical software such as Minitab and JMP is used both to design experiments and to analyze data collected from them.

In the one-way completely randomized design model [see References 6, 7, 9, and 12], the sum of squares total (SST) is subdivided into sum of squares among groups (SSA) and sum of squares within groups (SSW). For the two-factor factorial design model with equal replication in each cell, the **sum of squares total** (SST) is subdivided into **sum of squares due to factor A or X_A (SSA)**, **sum of squares due to factor B or X_B (SSB)**, **sum of squares due to the interacting effect of A and B ($SSAB$)**, and **sum of squares due to random error** (SSE). This partitioning of the SST is displayed in Figure 10.1.

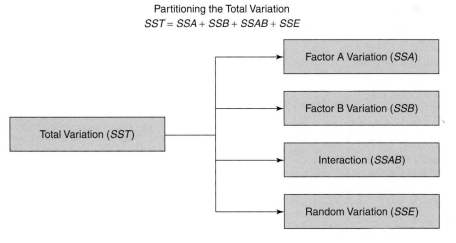

Partitioning the Total Variation
$$SST = SSA + SSB + SSAB + SSE$$

FIGURE 10.1 Partitioning the Total Variation in a Two-Factor Factorial Design Model

The SST represents the total variation among all the values around the grand mean of the CTQ. The SSA represents the differences among the various mean levels of factor A and the grand mean of the CTQ. The SSB represents the differences among the various mean levels of factor B and the grand mean of the CTQ. The *SSAB* represents the effect of the combinations of factor A and factor B on the CTQ. The *SSE* represents the differences among the individual values of the CTQ within each cell (combinations of one level of X_A and one level of X_B) and the corresponding cell mean. If each sum of squares is divided by its associated degrees of freedom, you have the four variances or mean square terms (*MSA*, *MSB*, *MSAB*, and *MSE*) needed for analysis of variance (ANOVA).

If the levels of factor A and factor B have been *specifically selected* for analysis (rather than being *randomly selected* from a population of possible levels[1]), there are three tests of hypotheses in the two-way ANOVA:

1. **Test of no difference due to factor A** (mean level of the CTQ is not affected by factor A):

    H_0: All levels of factor A have the same mean value of the CTQ

    against the alternative.

    H_1: Not all levels of factor A have the same mean value of the CTQ.

    This test of hypothesis consists of an F test of *MSA* divided by *MSE*.

2. **Test of no difference due to factor B** (mean level of the CTQ is not affected by factor B):

    H_0: All levels of factor B have the same mean value of the CTQ

    against the alternative.

    H_1: Not all levels of factor B have the same mean value of the CTQ.

    This test of hypothesis consists of an F test of *MSB* divided by *MSE*.

3. **Test of no interaction of factors A and B**:

    H_0: The interaction between factors A and B on the CTQ does not affect the mean level of the CTQ

    against the alternative.

    H_1: There is an interacting effect between factors A and B on the CTQ.

    This test of hypothesis consists of an F test of *MSAB* divided by *MSE*.

The entire set of steps is summarized in the ANOVA table of Table 10.1.

To illustrate the two-way Analysis of Variance, a hotel wanted to develop a new system for delivering room service breakfasts. In the current system, an order form is left on the bed in each room. If the customer wishes to receive a room service breakfast, he or she places the order form on the doorknob before 11 P.M. The current system includes a delivery time that provides a 15-minute interval for desired delivery time (6:30–6:45 A.M., 6:45–7:00 A.M., and so on). The new system is designed to allow the customer to request a specific delivery time. The hotel wants to measure the difference between the actual delivery time and the requested delivery time of room service orders for breakfast. (A negative time means that the order was delivered before the requested time. A positive time means that the order was delivered after the requested time.) The factors included were the menu choice (X_1) [American or Continental] and the desired time period in which the order was to be delivered (X_2) [Early Time Period (6:30–8:00 A.M.) or Late Time Period (8:00–9:30 A.M.)]. Ten orders for each combination of menu choice and desired time period were studied on a particular day. Table 10.2 displays the results.

---

[1] A discussion of random effects models is beyond the scope of this book [see References 7, 9, and 12].

TABLE 10.1   ANOVA Table for the Two-Factor Model with Replication

Source	Degrees of Freedom	Sum of Squares	Mean Square (Variance)	F
A	$r-1$	SSA	$MSA = \dfrac{SSA}{r-1}$	$F = \dfrac{MSA}{MSE}$
B	$c-1$	SSB	$MSB = \dfrac{SSB}{c-1}$	$F = \dfrac{MSB}{MSE}$
AB	$(r-1)(c-1)$	SSAB	$MSAB = \dfrac{SSAB}{(r-1)(c-1)}$	$F = \dfrac{MSAB}{MSE}$
Error	$rc(n'-1)$	SSE	$MSE = \dfrac{SSE}{rc(n'-1)}$	
Total	$n-1$	SST		

where
r = number of levels of factor A
c = number of levels of factor B
n' = number of values (replications) for each cell, assuming that each cell has an equal number of replications
n = total number of observations in the experiment

TABLE 10.2   Difference Between the Actual Delivery Time and the Requested Delivery Time of Room Service Orders (in Minutes) for Breakfast Based on Menu Choice and Desired Time Period

Delivery Time Difference (minutes)	Desired Time	
	X_2 = Early Time Period	X_2 = Late Time Period
X_1 = Continental	1.2	-2.5
	2.1	3.0
	3.3	-0.2
	4.4	1.2
	3.4	1.2
	5.3	0.7
	2.2	-1.3
	1.0	0.2
	5.4	-0.5
	1.4	3.8
X_1 = American	4.4	6.0
	1.1	2.3

(continued)

TABLE 10.2 Difference Between the Actual Delivery Time and the Requested Delivery Time of Room Service Orders (in Minutes) for Breakfast Based on Menu Choice and Desired Time Period (Continued)

Delivery Time Difference (minutes)	Desired Time	
	X_2 = Early Time Period	X_2 = Late Time Period
	4.8	4.2
	7.1	3.8
	6.7	5.5
	5.6	1.8
	9.5	5.1
	4.1	4.2
	7.9	4.9
	9.4	4.0

BREAKFAST

The design used in this example is called a 2 × 2 design with ten replications. The first number refers to the number of levels for the first factor, and the second number refers to the number of levels for the second factor. This design is also referred to as a 2^2 design, where the exponent indicates that there are two factors each with two treatment levels. Figure 10.2 represents Minitab output for these data. Figure 10.3 illustrates JMP output.

```
Source        DF      SS       MS      F     P
Menu Choice    1  112.560  112.560  30.44 0.000
Desired Time   1   46.010   46.010  12.44 0.001
Interaction    1    0.702    0.702   0.19 0.666
Error         36  133.105    3.697
Total         39  292.378

S = 1.923   R-Sq = 54.47%   R-Sq(adj) = 50.68%


                        Individual 95% CIs For Mean Based on
                        Pooled StDev
Menu Choice   Mean   ----+---------+---------+---------+-----
American      5.120                             (-----*-----)
Continental   1.765  (-----*-----)
                     ----+---------+---------+---------+-----
                      1.5       3.0       4.5       6.0


                        Individual 95% CIs For Mean Based on
Desired                 Pooled StDev
Time          Mean   -----+---------+---------+---------+----
Early         4.515                      (--------*--------)
Late          2.370  (--------*-------)
```

FIGURE 10.2 Minitab Output for the Breakfast Delivery Data

Response Delivery Time Difference

Whole Model

Actual by Predicted Plot

Summary of Fit

RSquare	0.54475
RSquare Adj	0.506812
Root Mean Square Error	1.922852
Mean of Response	3.4425
Observations (or Sum Wgts)	40

Analysis of Variance

Source	DF	Sum of Squares	Mean Square	F Ratio
Model	3	159.27275	53.0909	14.3591
Error	36	133.10500	3.6974	Prob > F
C. Total	39	292.37775		<.0001

Parameter Estimates

Term	Estimate	Std Error	t Ratio	Prob>|t|
Intercept	3.4425	0.30403	11.32	<.0001
Menu Choice[American]	1.6775	0.30403	5.52	<.0001
Desired Time[Early]	1.0725	0.30403	3.53	0.0012
Menu Choice[American]*Desired Time[Early]	-0.1325	0.30403	-0.44	0.6656

Effect Tests

Source	Nparm	DF	Sum of Squares	F Ratio	Prob > F
Menu Choice	1	1	112.56025	30.4434	<.0001
Desired Time	1	1	46.01025	12.4441	0.0012
Menu Choice*Desired Time	1	1	0.70225	0.1899	0.6656

Least Squares Means Table

Level	Least Sq Mean	Std Error
American,Early	6.0600000	0.60805930
American,Late	4.1800000	0.60805930
Continental,Early	2.9700000	0.60805930
Continental,Late	0.5600000	0.60805930

Menu Choice

Least Squares Means Table

Level	Least Sq Mean	Std Error	Mean
American	5.1200000	0.42996285	5.12000
Continental	1.7650000	0.42996285	1.76500

Desired Time

Least Squares Means Table

Level	Least Sq Mean	Std Error	Mean
Early	4.5150000	0.42996285	4.51500
Late	2.3700000	0.42996285	2.37000

FIGURE 10.3 JMP Output for the Breakfast Delivery Data

From Figure 10.2 or 10.3, the tests of hypotheses are as follows (at the $\alpha = 0.05$ level of significance):

1. **Test for interaction:** Because the F statistic for the interaction effect = 0.19 and the p-value is $0.666 > 0.05$, you do not reject the null hypothesis. There is insufficient evidence of any interaction between menu choice and desired time period.

2. **Test for menu choice:** Because the F statistic for the menu choice = 30.44 and the p-value is $0.000 < 0.05$, you reject the null hypothesis. There is evidence of an effect of menu choice on the difference between actual delivery time and requested delivery time. The difference between actual delivery time and requested delivery time is higher for an American breakfast than for a Continental breakfast.

3. **Test for desired delivery time:** Because the F statistic for the desired delivery time = 12.44 and the p-value is $0.001 < 0.05$, you reject the null hypothesis. There is evidence of an effect of desired delivery time on the difference between actual delivery time and requested delivery time. The difference between actual delivery time and requested delivery time is higher for breakfast delivered earlier in the morning than later in the morning.

Table 10.3 summarizes the means for each combination of menu choice and desired delivery time.

TABLE 10.3   Mean Difference of Actual Delivery Time and the Requested Delivery Time (in Minutes) of Room Service Orders for Breakfast Based on Menu Choice and Desired Time Period

	Desired Time		
Delivery Time Difference	**Early**	**Late**	**Row Mean**
Continental	2.970	0.56	1.7650
American	6.060	4.18	5.1200
Column Mean	4.515	2.37	3.4425

From Table 10.3, you can reach several conclusions. In terms of the individual factors (called the main effects, Xs or CTPs), there is a difference in the mean delivery time difference (CTQ) between the Continental and American menu choices, or X_1 (1.765 versus 5.12 minutes). The size of the effect for menu choice is $5.12 - 1.765 = 3.355$ minutes. There is also a difference in the mean delivery time difference (CTQ) between the early and late levels of desired delivery times, or X_2. The early level of desired delivery time has a mean delivery time difference of 4.515 minutes, and the late level of desired delivery time has a mean delivery time difference of 2.37 minutes. Thus, the effect due to desired delivery time is $4.515 - 2.37 = 2.145$ minutes. Figure 10.4 provides plots for these two main effects using Minitab. Figure 10.5 provides JMP output.

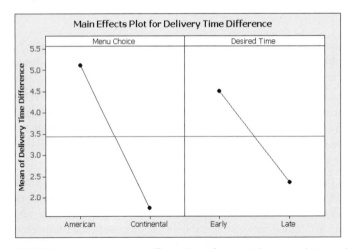

FIGURE 10.4   Minitab Main Effects Plots of Menu Choice and Desired Delivery Time

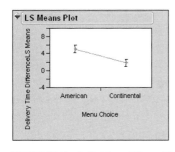
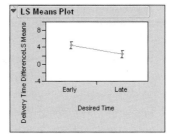

FIGURE 10.5 JMP Main Effects Plots

Now that the main effects of menu choice and desired delivery time have been studied, the question remains as to what is meant by interaction between factors. To understand the meaning of **interaction**, first consider what is meant by the absence of interaction.

> If there is no interaction between two factors (A and B), then any difference in the dependent variable (CTQ) between the two levels of factor A (X_A) would be the same at each level of factor B (X_B).

In terms of the factors in this example, if there was no interaction between menu choice and desired delivery time, any difference in the delivery time difference between Continental and American breakfasts would be the same for early delivery times as for late delivery times. From Table 10.3, you see that for a Continental breakfast, the difference in delivery time difference between early and late delivery times is 2.41 minutes, and for an American breakfast, the difference in delivery time difference between early and late delivery times is 1.88 minutes.

You can present the interaction between two factors in an interaction plot. If there is no interaction between the factors, the lines for the two levels will be approximately parallel. Figure 10.6 is a Minitab interaction plot for these data. Figure 10.7 is a JMP interaction plot.

In the Minitab interaction plot displayed in Figure 10.6, you can use either the bottom-left or the top-right panels of this plot, depending on whether you want to focus on menu choice or desired delivery time. Referring to the upper-right panel, the levels on the horizontal axis represent the desired delivery time levels for each menu choice. Referring to the lower-left panel, the levels on the horizontal axis represent the menu choices for each desired delivery time. An examination of either panel shows that the lines are roughly parallel, indicating very little interaction between the menu choice and desired delivery time factors.

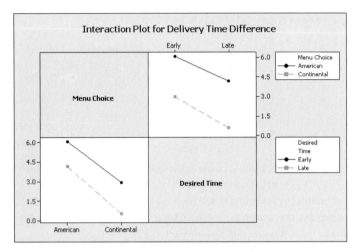

FIGURE 10.6 Minitab Interaction Plots for the Breakfast Delivery Example

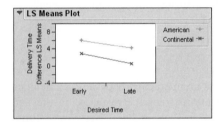

FIGURE 10.7 JMP Interaction Plots for the Breakfast Delivery Example

To study an example that has an interaction, suppose the results for the breakfast study of Table 10.2 were as in Table 10.4.

TABLE 10.4 Difference Between the Actual Delivery Time and the Requested Delivery Time of Room Service Orders (in Minutes) for Breakfast Based on Menu Choice and Desired Time Period

Delivery Time Difference (minutes)	Desired Time	
	X_2 = Early	X_2 = Late
X_1 = Continental	1.2	-0.5
	2.1	5.0
	3.3	1.8
	4.4	3.2
	3.4	3.2

Delivery Time Difference (minutes)	Desired Time	
	X_2 = Early	X_2 = Late
	5.3	2.7
	2.2	0.7
	1.0	2.2
	5.4	1.5
	1.4	5.8
X_1 = American	4.4	6.0
	1.1	2.3
	4.8	4.2
	7.1	3.8
	6.7	5.5
	5.6	1.8
	9.5	5.1
	4.1	4.2
	7.9	4.9
	9.4	4.0

BREAKFAST2

Figures 10.8 and 10.9 present the Minitab and JMP interaction plots for these data. Table 10.5 summarizes the means for each combination of menu choice and desired delivery time.

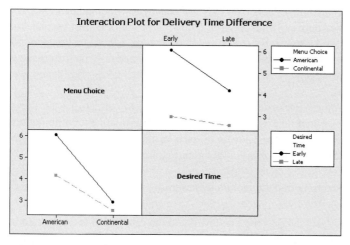

FIGURE 10.8 Minitab Interaction Plots for the Revised Breakfast Delivery Example

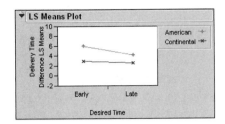

FIGURE 10.9   JMP Interaction Plots for the Revised Breakfast Delivery Example

TABLE 10.5   Mean Difference of Actual Delivery Time and the Requested Delivery Time of Room
Service Orders (in Minutes) for Breakfast Based on Menu Choice and Desired Time Period

Delivery Time Difference	Desired Time		Row Mean
	Early	**Late**	**Row Mean**
Continental	2.970	2.56	2.7650
American	6.060	4.18	5.1200
Column Mean	4.515	3.37	3.9425

From Table 10.5 and Figures 10.8 and 10.9, observe that the difference in the actual and
desired delivery time for an American breakfast is much greater at the earlier time than the later
time. The difference in the actual and desired delivery time for a Continental breakfast is slightly
higher for the early time than for the late time. The possible existence of an interaction effect
complicates the interpretation of the main effects. You may not be able to conclude that there is a
difference in the actual and desired delivery time between the two types of breakfast because the
difference may not be the same for the two desired delivery time periods. Likewise, you may not
be able to conclude that there is a difference between the time periods because the difference is
not the same for the two types of breakfasts. In sum, the interaction effect takes precedence over
any interpretation of main effects.

Notation for Interaction Effects. Determining the magnitude of the effect of each factor
and interaction becomes complex when many factors are involved. The treatment combinations
(the simultaneous combinations of the different levels of each of the *X*s or factors) are represented using a special notation. The steps involved in this notation are as follows.

1. A shorthand notation is used to define the factors by assigning a letter, such as *A*, *B*, or *C*,
    to each factor.
2. One level of each factor is designated as the low level, and the other level is designated as
    the high level. The high and low levels are defined by the nature of the factor (e.g., high
    speed versus low speed). In cases where levels are not defined by the factor being studied,
    it is common practice to set the current operating level as the low level.

3. A table is developed in which the columns represent the factors and their interactions, and the rows represent the different combinations, called **treatment combinations**, created by setting the factors at their different levels. Treatment combinations are defined only by the high levels of the factors. For example, in a two-factor design, if only the high level of factor *A* is present, the treatment combination is specified as *a*. If only the high level of factor *B* is present, the treatment combination is specified as *b*. If the high levels of factors *A* and *B* are present, the treatment combination is specified as *ab*. The treatment combination that contains the low level of all the factors is specified as (1).

4. Each factor is listed in a column. For each factor, a minus (–) sign is included in the row if the low level is present and a plus (+) sign is included if the high level of the factor is present. The sign for an interaction effect is the product of the signs that define the interaction. Thus, the sign for the *AB* interaction is the product of the signs in the particular row for factors *A* and *B* (for example, if the row has a plus sign for *A* and a plus sign for *B* or a minus sign for *A* and a minus sign for *B*, the interaction *AB* sign is a plus. If the row has a plus sign for *A* and a minus sign for *B* or a minus sign for *A* and a plus sign for *B*, the interaction *AB* sign is a minus).

The treatment combinations for the data in Table 10.3 on page 304, using the special notation, are displayed in Table 10.6.

TABLE 10.6 Computing the Mean Effects for Factors *A*, *B*, and *AB* in the 2^2 Design for the Breakfast Delivery Data

Treatment combination	Notation	Mean Response	Breakfast Type A	Time period B	AB
Continental, early	(1)	2.97	–	–	+
American, early	a	6.06	+	–	–
Continental, late	b	0.56	–	+	–
American, late	ab	4.18	+	+	+

Computing the Estimated Effects (optional)

You compute the mean effect for each factor or interaction by multiplying the mean response for the row by the sign in the column and summing these products over all the rows. You divide this sum by the number of plus signs used in computing the effect.

For a two-factor design, the mean effects for factor *A*, factor *B*, and the interaction of *A* and *B* are as follows:

$$A = \frac{1}{2}\left(a + ab - b - (1)\right) \tag{10.1a}$$

$$B = \frac{1}{2}\left(b + ab - a - (1)\right)$$
(10.1b)

$$AB = \frac{1}{2}\left(ab - a - b + (1)\right)$$
(10.1c)

From Equations (10.1a–10.1c) and Table 10.6,

$$A = \frac{1}{2}\left(6.06 + 4.18 - 0.56 - 2.97\right)$$

$$= \frac{6.71}{2}$$

$$= 3.355$$

Thus, the mean difference in the actual and desired delivery time for an American breakfast is 3.355 minutes greater than the mean for a Continental breakfast, a conclusion previously stated on page 304.

$$B = \frac{1}{2}\left(0.56 + 4.18 - 6.06 - 2.97\right)$$

$$= -\frac{4.29}{2}$$

$$= -2.145$$

Thus, the difference in the actual and desired delivery time is 2.145 minutes less for late times than for early times.

$$AB = \frac{1}{2}\left(4.18 - 6.06 - 0.56 + 2.97\right)$$

$$= \frac{0.53}{2}$$

$$= 0.265$$

The interaction means that the mean effect of combining the high level of breakfast type and desired time is 0.265 minutes greater than the mean difference between desired times for the breakfast types. This occurs because the mean difference in the actual and desired delivery time is 3.62 minutes greater for an American breakfast at a late time than for a Continental breakfast at a late time (4.18 as compared to 0.56), while the mean difference in the actual and desired delivery time for an American breakfast as compared to a Continental breakfast is $5.12 - 1.765 = 3.355$ minutes. The difference between 3.62 minutes and 3.355 minutes is the interaction effect of 0.265 minutes.

10.3 2^k FACTORIAL DESIGNS

The two-factor factorial design is the most elementary of all factorial designs. In this section, the concepts developed for the two-factor 2^2 design in Section 10.2 are extended to the more general factorial design that has three or more factors. With this design, there are 2^k treatment combinations, where k = the number of factors (CTPs or Xs)—for example, $2^3 = 2 \times 2 \times 2 = 8$ treatment combinations. Table 10.7 extends the format of Table 10.6 to the 2^3 design in standard order. **Standard order** is an arrangement for listing trials in which the first factor alternates between – and +, the second factor alternates between –,– and +,+, the third factor alternates between –,–,–,– and +,+,+,+, and so on.

TABLE 10.7 Computing Effects for Factors A, B, C, and Interactions AB, AC, BC, and ABC in the 2^3 Design in Standard Order

				Effects			
Notation	***A***	***B***	***C***	***AB***	***AC***	***BC***	***ABC***
(1)	–	–	–	+	+	+	–
a	+	–	–	–	–	+	+
b	–	+	–	–	+	–	+
ab	+	+	–	+	–	–	–
c	–	–	+	+	–	–	+
ac	+	–	+	–	+	–	–
bc	–	+	+	–	–	+	–
abc	+	+	+	+	+	+	+

To illustrate the 2^3 design, suppose that the hotel also wanted to study the process of delivering room service meals at dinner time. Three factors were to be considered in studying the delivery time. They were:

1. Complexity of the meal: low versus high.
2. Elevator used for delivering the meal: service versus main.
3. Order volume in the kitchen at the time of the order: low versus high.

Each treatment combination consists of five replications. The results from this experiment are presented in Table 10.8.

TABLE 10.8 Results for a 2^3 Design Involving the Delivery Time (CTQ) Based on Complexity of the Meal (X_A), Elevator Used (X_B), and Order Volume in the Kitchen (X_C) Treatment Combinations

Complexity	Elevator	Order Volume	Notation	Delivery Time
Low	Service	Low	1	31.4, 31.6, 28.6, 36.3, 30.6
High	Service	Low	a	42.7, 30.6, 38.5, 28.2, 41.4
Low	Main	Low	b	41.5, 33.5, 39.0, 31.1, 39.1
High	Main	Low	ab	35.1, 32.0, 36.9, 39.9, 36.0
Low	Service	High	c	44.1, 35.5, 40.5, 34.8, 42.4
High	Service	High	ac	50.4, 49.3, 45.1, 44.0, 51.3
Low	Main	High	bc	43.4, 45.0, 28.1, 33.4, 45.0
High	Main	High	abc	45.2, 52.1, 49.5, 47.3, 47.3

 DINNER

Figure 10.10 presents the eight treatment combinations (and their mean responses) in the form of a cube.

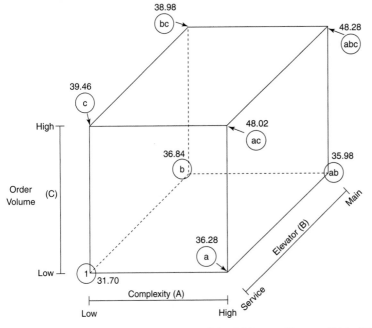

FIGURE 10.10 Geometric Representation of the 2^3 Design (Source: Table 10.8)

Figure 10.11 represents Minitab ANOVA output of the estimated effects of meal complexity, elevator, and order volume on the delivery time of room service dinners. Figure 10.12 is JMP output. The coefficients shown in the JMP output are half the value of the effects.

```
Estimated Effects and Coefficients for Delivery Time (coded units)

Term                             Effect     Coef  SE Coef      T     P
Constant                                  39.4425   0.7346  53.69  0.000
Complexity                       5.3950   2.6975   0.7346   3.67  0.001
Elevator                         1.1550   0.5775   0.7346   0.79  0.438
Order Volume                     8.4850   4.2425   0.7346   5.77  0.000
Complexity*Elevator             -1.1750  -0.5875   0.7346  -0.80  0.430
Complexity*Order Volume          3.5350   1.7675   0.7346   2.41  0.022
Elevator*Order Volume           -1.2650  -0.6325   0.7346  -0.86  0.396
Complexity*Elevator*Order Volume 1.5450   0.7725   0.7346   1.05  0.301


S = 4.64632   R-Sq = 63.52%   R-Sq(adj) = 55.54%


Analysis of Variance for Delivery Time (coded units)

Source              DF   Seq SS   Adj SS  Adj MS      F      P
Main Effects         3  1024.35  1024.35  341.45  15.82  0.000
2-Way Interactions   3   154.77   154.77   51.59   2.39  0.087
3-Way Interactions   1    23.87    23.87   23.87   1.11  0.301
Residual Error      32   690.82   690.82   21.59
  Pure Error        32   690.82   690.82   21.59
Total               39  1893.82
```

FIGURE 10.11   Minitab ANOVA Output of Meal Complexity, Elevator, and Order Volume on the Delivery Time of Room Service Dinners

Term	Estimate	Std Error	t Ratio	Prob>|t|
Intercept	39.4425	0.734647	53.69	<.0001*
Complexity[Low]	-2.6975	0.734647	-3.67	0.0009*
Elevator[Main]	0.5775	0.734647	0.79	0.4376
Complexity[Low]*Elevator[Main]	0.5875	0.734647	0.80	0.4298
Order Volume[Low]	-4.2425	0.734647	-5.77	<.0001*
Complexity[Low]*Order Volume[Low]	1.7675	0.734647	2.41	0.0221*
Elevator[Main]*Order Volume[Low]	0.6325	0.734647	0.86	0.3957
Complexity[Low]*Elevator[Main]*Order Volume[Low]	0.7725	0.734647	1.05	0.3009

Source	Nparm	DF	Sum of Squares	F Ratio	Prob > F
Complexity	1	1	291.06025	13.4823	0.0009*
Elevator	1	1	13.34025	0.6179	0.4376
Complexity*Elevator	1	1	13.80625	0.6395	0.4298
Order Volume	1	1	719.95225	33.3493	<.0001*
Complexity*Order Volume	1	1	124.96225	5.7884	0.0221*
Elevator*Order Volume	1	1	16.00225	0.7412	0.3957
Complexity*Elevator*Order Volume	1	1	23.87025	1.1057	0.3009

FIGURE 10.12   JMP ANOVA Output of Meal Complexity, Elevator, and Order Volume on the Delivery Time of Room Service Dinners

Figures 10.13 and 10.14 display the main effects plot for these data, and Figures 10.15 and 10.16 present the interaction plots.

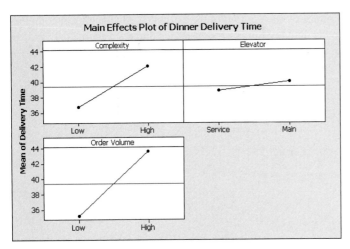

FIGURE 10.13   Minitab Main Effects Plots for the Delivery Time of Room Service Dinners in the 2^3 Experiment

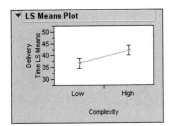 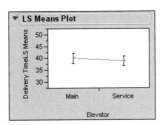 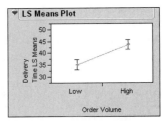

FIGURE 10.14   JMP Main Effects Plots for the Delivery Time of Room Service Dinners in the 2^3 Experiment

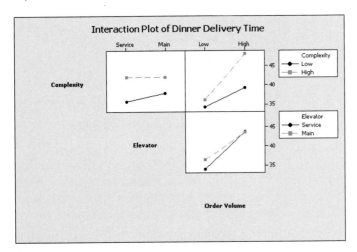

FIGURE 10.15   Minitab Interaction Plots for the Delivery Time of Room Service Dinners in the 2^3 Experiment

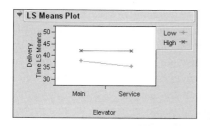
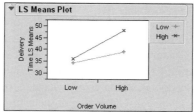

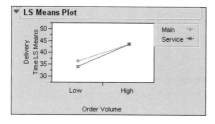

FIGURE 10.16   JMP Interaction Plots for the Delivery Time of Room Service Dinners in the 2^3 Experiment

From the ANOVA results of Figures 10.11 and 10.12, the main effects plot illustrated in Figures 10.13 and 10.14, and the interaction plots in Figures 10.15 and 10.16, you can conclude that:

1. The mean delivery time is significantly higher (p-value = 0.001) for meals that are highly complex to prepare than for meals that have a low complexity in their preparation. The highly complex meals have a mean delivery time of 5.395 minutes more than low complex meals.

2. There is insufficient evidence of a statistically significant difference in the mean delivery time based on the elevator used to deliver the meals. The mean delivery time for meals delivered using the main elevator is 1.155 minutes higher than for meals delivered using the service elevator.

3. The mean delivery time is significantly higher (p-value = 0.000) when the order volume in the kitchen is high than when the order volume in the kitchen is low. The mean delivery time is 8.485 minutes more when the order volume in the kitchen is high than when the order volume in the kitchen is low.

4. Only the interaction between meal complexity and order volume is statistically significant (p-value = 0.022). The effects of A (Meal Complexity) and C (Order Volume) are interacting due to the large effect caused by the presence of the high level of meal complexity and the high level of order volume. The interpretation of this interacting effect is that the mean difference in the delivery time for highly complex meals as compared with meals of low complexity is 3.535 minutes more when there is high order volume than for the mean of low and high order volume.

In many instances, you may not be able to or it may be prohibitively expensive to take more than one replication for each treatment combination. When this is the case, you are unable to compute a separate measure of the error variance and, therefore, not able to conduct an ANOVA of the effects and interactions. However, you can carry out a preliminary screening step using a **half-normal plot** [see Reference 5] to screen out interactions that do not appear to have any effect and combine them into an error variance. This half-normal plot is a type of normal probability plot in which the absolute value of the estimated effects is plotted on normal probability paper in rank order. Figures 10.17 and 10.18 show the estimated effects and their associated cumulative probabilities for the dinner delivery time example in the normal and half-normal probability plot.

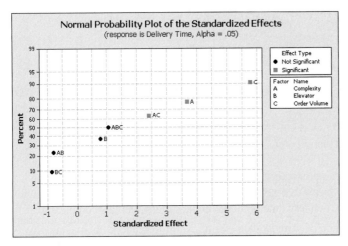

FIGURE 10.17   Minitab Normal Probability Plot for the 2^3 Design for the Dinner Delivery Time Example

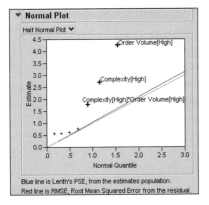

FIGURE 10.18   JMP Half-Normal Probability Plot for the 2^3 Design for the Dinner Delivery Time Example

When there is only one replication per treatment combination, you use the normal probability plot to determine which factors and interaction effects are not important (and thus, not different from zero) [see Reference 10]. In the normal probability plot, any factors or interactions whose observed effects are due to chance are expected to be randomly distributed around zero, with some being slightly below zero and others being slightly above zero. (In the half-normal plot, negative values have been converted to positive values.) These effects will tend to fall along a straight line. The effects that may be important have mean values different from zero and are located a substantial distance away from the hypothetical vertical line that represents no effect.

From Figures 10.17 and 10.18, observe that the most important effects are *A*, *C*, and *AC*. These results are consistent with those seen in the ANOVA, main effects plot, and the interaction plot of Figures 10.11–10.16.

Table 10.9 reorganizes the results of Table 10.8 to focus on factors *A* and *C*.

TABLE 10.9   *Mean Delivery Time (in Minutes) by Complexity of Meal and Order Volume*

	Order Volume	
Meal Complexity	**Low**	**High**
Low	34.27	39.22
High	36.13	48.15

From Table 10.9, the mean delivery time for high meal complexity is 1.86 minutes higher than for low meal complexity when there is low order volume, but is 8.93 minutes higher for high meal complexity than for low meal complexity when there is high order volume. The difference of $8.93 - 1.86 = 7.07$, divided by 2 (to account for the two levels of factor *C*), represents the interaction effect of 3.535 for factors *A* (meal complexity) and *C* (order volume).

Computing the Estimated Effects and Interaction Effects (optional)

For each of the main effects, the estimated effect consists of the mean at the high level of the factor minus the mean at the low level of the factor. Thus, for factors *A*, *B*, and *C*,

$$A = \frac{1}{4}\left[a + ab + ac + abc - (1) - b - c - bc\right] \tag{10.2a}$$

$$B = \frac{1}{4}\left[b + ab + bc + abc - (1) - a - c - ac\right] \tag{10.2b}$$

$$C = \frac{1}{4}\left[c + ac + bc + abc - (1) - a - b - ab\right] \tag{10.2c}$$

The two-way interactions are measured as one-half the difference in the average of one effect at the two levels of the other effect. Thus, for the interactions *AB*, *AC*, and *BC*,

$$AB = \frac{1}{4}\left[abc - bc + ab - b - ac + c - a + (1)\right] \tag{10.3a}$$

$$AC = \frac{1}{4}\left[(1) - a + b - ab - c + ac - bc + abc\right] \tag{10.3b}$$

$$BC = \frac{1}{4}\left[(1) + a - b - ab - c - ac + bc + abc\right] \tag{10.3c}$$

The ABC interaction is defined as the average difference in the AB interaction for the two levels of factor C. Thus,

$$ABC = \frac{1}{4}\left[abc - bc - ac + c - ab + b + a - (1)\right] \tag{10.4}$$

Table 10.10 represents the format needed to compute the effects for the delivery time example.

TABLE 10.10 Computing Effects for Factors A, B, and C and Interactions AB, AC, BC, and ABC in the 2^3 Design

Mean Notation	Delivery Time	A	B	C	Effect AB	AC	BC	ABC
(1)	31.70	−	−	−	+	+	+	−
a	36.28	+	−	−	−	−	+	+
b	36.84	−	+	−	−	+	−	+
ab	35.98	+	+	−	+	−	−	−
c	39.46	−	−	+	+	−	−	+
ac	48.02	+	−	+	−	+	−	−
bc	38.98	−	+	+	−	−	+	−
abc	48.28	+	+	+	+	+	+	+

From Table 10.10 and Equations (10.2), (10.3), and (10.4):

$$A = \frac{-31.70 + 36.28 - 36.84 + 35.98 - 39.46 + 48.02 - 38.98 + 48.28}{4}$$

$$= \frac{21.58}{4}$$

$$= 5.395$$

$$B = \frac{-31.70 - 36.28 + 36.84 + 35.98 - 39.46 - 48.02 + 38.98 + 48.28}{4}$$

$$= \frac{4.62}{4}$$

$$= 1.155$$

$$C = \frac{-31.70 - 36.28 - 36.84 - 35.98 + 39.46 + 48.02 + 38.98 + 48.28}{4}$$

$$= \frac{33.94}{4}$$

$$= 8.485$$

$$AB = \frac{+31.70 - 36.28 - 36.84 + 35.98 + 39.46 - 48.02 - 38.98 + 48.28}{4}$$

$$= \frac{-4.7}{4}$$

$$= -1.175$$

$$AC = \frac{+31.70 - 36.28 + 36.84 - 35.98 - 39.46 + 48.02 - 38.98 + 48.28}{4}$$

$$= \frac{14.14}{4}$$

$$= 3.535$$

$$BC = \frac{+31.70 + 36.28 - 36.84 - 35.98 - 39.46 - 48.02 + 38.98 + 48.28}{4}$$

$$= \frac{-5.06}{4}$$

$$= -1.265$$

$$ABC = \frac{-31.70 + 36.28 + 36.84 - 35.98 + 39.46 - 48.02 - 38.98 + 48.28}{4}$$

$$= \frac{6.18}{4}$$

$$= 1.545$$

To study a factorial design that has more than three factors (Xs), consider an experiment involving a cake mix. Each year, millions of cake mixes are sold by food processing companies. A cake mix consists of a packet containing flour, shortening, and egg powder that will (it is hoped) provide a good-tasting cake. One difficulty in determining the amount of these ingredients to include in the packet to maximize the tastiness of the cake relates to the fact that consumers might not precisely follow the recommended oven temperature and baking time. An experiment is conducted in which each factor is tested at a higher level than called for in the instructions and at a lower level than called for in the instructions. The goal of the experiment is to determine which factors have an effect on the taste rating of the cake and the levels of the factors that will provide the cake with the highest taste rating. Five factors were to be considered: flour, shortening, egg powder, oven temperature, and baking time. Only one observation for each of the $2^5 = 32$ treatment combinations was collected. Table 10.11 presents the taste rating for each treatment combination obtained from a taste-testing expert.

TABLE 10.11   Taste Rating for Cake Mix Combinations

Treatment combination	Flour (A)	Shortening (B)	Egg Powder (C)	Oven Temp (D)	Bake Time (E)	Rating Score (Y)
(1)	−	−	−	−	−	1.1
a	+	−	−	−	−	3.8
b	−	+	−	−	−	3.7
ab	+	+	−	−	−	4.5
c	−	−	+	−	−	4.2
ac	+	−	+	−	−	5.2
bc	−	+	+	−	−	3.1
abc	+	+	+	−	−	3.9
d	−	−	−	+	−	5.7
ad	+	−	−	+	−	4.9
bd	−	+	−	+	−	5.1
abd	+	+	−	+	−	6.4
cd	−	−	+	+	−	6.8
acd	+	−	+	+	−	6.0
bcd	−	+	+	+	−	6.3
abcd	+	+	+	+	−	5.5
e	−	−	−	−	+	6.4
ae	+	−	−	−	+	4.3
be	−	+	−	−	+	6.7
abe	+	+	−	−	+	5.8
ce	−	−	+	−	+	6.5
ace	+	−	+	−	+	5.9
bce	−	+	+	−	+	6.4
abce	+	+	+	−	+	5.0
de	−	−	−	+	+	1.3
ade	+	−	−	+	+	2.1
bde	−	+	−	+	+	2.9
abde	+	+	−	+	+	5.2
cde	−	−	+	+	+	3.5
acde	+	−	+	+	+	5.7
bcde	−	+	+	+	+	3.0
abcde	+	+	+	+	+	5.4

 CAKE

Figure 10.19 presents the Minitab output of the estimated effects for the cake mix design. Figure 10.20 illustrates JMP output of the coefficients, which are half the value of the effects.

```
Estimated Effects and Coefficients for Rating (coded units)

Term                                   Effect     Coef
Constant                                         4.759
Flour                                   0.431    0.216
Shortening                              0.344    0.172
Egg Powder                              0.781    0.391
ovenTemp                               -0.044   -0.022
BakeTime                               -0.006   -0.003
Flour*Shortening                        0.131    0.066
Flour*Egg Powder                       -0.081   -0.041
Flour*ovenTemp                          0.394    0.197
Flour*BakeTime                         -0.094   -0.047
Shortening*Egg Powder                  -0.994   -0.497
Shortening*ovenTemp                     0.131    0.066
Shortening*BakeTime                     0.244    0.122
Egg Powder*ovenTemp                     0.294    0.147
Egg Powder*BakeTime                     0.056    0.028
ovenTemp*BakeTime                      -2.194   -1.097
Flour*Shortening*Egg Powder            -0.231   -0.116
Flour*Shortening*ovenTemp               0.344    0.172
Flour*Egg Powder*ovenTemp               0.006    0.003
Flour*Shortening*BakeTime               0.131    0.066
Flour*Egg Powder*BakeTime               0.394    0.197
Flour*ovenTemp*BakeTime                 1.194    0.597
Shortening*Egg Powder*ovenTemp          0.069    0.034
Shortening*Egg Powder*BakeTime         -0.044   -0.022
Shortening*ovenTemp*BakeTime            0.256    0.128
Egg Powder*ovenTemp*BakeTime            0.394    0.197
Flour*Shortening*Egg Powder*ovenTemp   -0.194   -0.097
Flour*Shortening*Egg Powder*BakeTime   -0.181   -0.091
Flour*Shortening*ovenTemp*BakeTime     -0.181   -0.091
Flour*Egg Powder*ovenTemp*BakeTime      0.056    0.028
Shortening*Egg Powder*ovenTemp*        -0.406   -0.203
  BakeTime
Flour*Shortening*Egg Powder*            0.281    0.141
  ovenTemp*BakeTime
```

FIGURE 10.19 Minitab Estimated Effects for the Cake Mix Example

Response Rating

Parameter Estimates

Term	Estimate	Std Error	t Ratio	Prob>|t|
Intercept	4.759375	.	.	.
Flour[low]	-0.215625	.	.	.
Shortening[low]	-0.171875	.	.	.
Flour[low]*Shortening[low]	0.065625	.	.	.
Egg Powder[low]	-0.390625	.	.	.
Flour[low]*Egg Powder[low]	-0.040625	.	.	.
Shortening[low]*Egg Powder[low]	-0.496875	.	.	.
Flour[low]*Shortening[low]*Egg Powder[low]	0.115625	.	.	.
ovenTemp[low]	0.021875	.	.	.
Flour[low]*ovenTemp[low]	0.196875	.	.	.
Shortening[low]*ovenTemp[low]	0.065625	.	.	.
Flour[low]*Shortening[low]*ovenTemp[low]	-0.171875	.	.	.
Egg Powder[low]*ovenTemp[low]	0.146875	.	.	.
Flour[low]*Egg Powder[low]*ovenTemp[low]	-0.003125	.	.	.
Shortening[low]*Egg Powder[low]*ovenTemp[low]	-0.034375	.	.	.
Flour[low]*Shortening[low]*Egg Powder[low]*ovenTemp[low]	-0.096875	.	.	.
BakeTime[low]	0.003125	.	.	.
Flour[low]*BakeTime[low]	-0.046875	.	.	.
Shortening[low]*BakeTime[low]	0.121875	.	.	.
Flour[low]*Shortening[low]*BakeTime[low]	-0.065625	.	.	.
Egg Powder[low]*BakeTime[low]	0.028125	.	.	.
Flour[low]*Egg Powder[low]*BakeTime[low]	-0.196875	.	.	.
Shortening[low]*Egg Powder[low]*BakeTime[low]	0.021875	.	.	.
Flour[low]*Shortening[low]*Egg Powder[low]*BakeTime[low]	-0.090625	.	.	.
ovenTemp[low]*BakeTime[low]	-1.096875	.	.	.
Flour[low]*ovenTemp[low]*BakeTime[low]	-0.596875	.	.	.
Shortening[low]*ovenTemp[low]*BakeTime[low]	-0.128125	.	.	.
Flour[low]*Shortening[low]*ovenTemp[low]*BakeTime[low]	-0.090625	.	.	.
Egg Powder[low]*ovenTemp[low]*BakeTime[low]	-0.196875	.	.	.
Flour[low]*Egg Powder[low]*ovenTemp[low]*BakeTime[low]	0.028125	.	.	.
Shortening[low]*Egg Powder[low]*ovenTemp[low]*BakeTime[low]	-0.203125	.	.	.
Flour[low]*Shortening[low]*Egg Powder[low]*ovenTemp[low]*BakeTime[low]	-0.140625	.	.	.

FIGURE 10.20 JMP Estimated Coefficients for the Cake Mix Example

Figures 10.21 and 10.22 are a Minitab normal probability plot and a JMP half-normal plot of the estimated effects for the cake mix design.

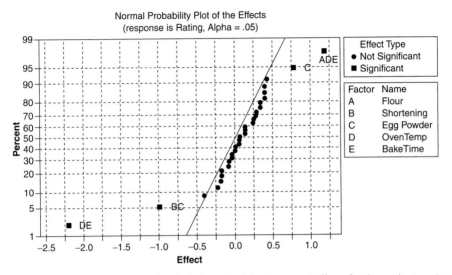

FIGURE 10.21   Minitab Normal Probability Plot of the Estimated Effects for the Cake Mix Design

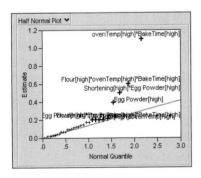

FIGURE 10.22   JMP Half-Normal Probability Plot of the Estimated Effects for the Cake Mix Design

From Figure 10.21 or 10.22, you see that only effects *C*, *BC*, *DE*, and *ADE* plot far away from a straight line that is approximately zero on the *X* axis. Minitab indicates that these terms are statistically significant, according to criteria developed by Lenth [see Reference 10]. From Figure 10.21 or 10.22, factor *C* (Egg Powder), the *BC* (Shortening–Egg Powder) interaction, the *DE* (Oven Temperature–Bake Time) interaction, and the *ADE* (Flour–Oven Temperature–Bake Time) interaction are far from a hypothetical vertical line at zero. Thus, you can consider all third-order interactions (except *ADE*), all fourth-order interactions, and the single fifth-order interaction (*ABCDE*) as consisting only of random error. You can eliminate these effects from the ANOVA model and combine them into an estimate of the error variance. The ANOVA model computed by Minitab with these effects combined into an error variance is displayed in Figure 10.23. The model computed by JMP is displayed in Figure 10.24.

```
Term                      Effect    Coef  SE Coef      T      P
Constant                          4.759   0.1240  38.40  0.000
Flour                      0.431   0.216   0.1240   1.74  0.102
Shortening                 0.344   0.172   0.1240   1.39  0.186
Egg Powder                 0.781   0.391   0.1240   3.15  0.007
ovenTemp                  -0.044  -0.022   0.1240  -0.18  0.862
BakeTime                  -0.006  -0.003   0.1240  -0.03  0.980
Flour*Shortening           0.131   0.066   0.1240   0.53  0.604
Flour*Egg Powder          -0.081  -0.041   0.1240  -0.33  0.748
Flour*ovenTemp             0.394   0.197   0.1240   1.59  0.133
Flour*BakeTime            -0.094  -0.047   0.1240  -0.38  0.711
Shortening*Egg Powder     -0.994  -0.497   0.1240  -4.01  0.001
Shortening*ovenTemp        0.131   0.066   0.1240   0.53  0.604
Shortening*BakeTime        0.244   0.122   0.1240   0.98  0.341
Egg Powder*ovenTemp        0.294   0.147   0.1240   1.18  0.254
Egg Powder*BakeTime        0.056   0.028   0.1240   0.23  0.824
ovenTemp*BakeTime         -2.194  -1.097   0.1240  -8.85  0.000
Flour*ovenTemp*BakeTime    1.194   0.597   0.1240   4.82  0.000
Analysis of Variance for Rating (coded units)

Source               DF  Seq SS  Adj SS   Adj MS      F      P
Main Effects          5   7.332   7.332   1.4663   2.98  0.046
2-Way Interactions   10  49.231  49.231   4.9231  10.01  0.000
3-Way Interactions    1  11.400  11.400  11.4003  23.19  0.000
Residual Error       15   7.375   7.375   0.4916
```

FIGURE 10.23 Minitab ANOVA Model for the Cake Mix Example

▼ ⊙ **Response Rating**

  ▶ **Actual by Predicted Plot**

  ▶ **Summary of Fit**

  ▼ **Analysis of Variance**

Source	DF	Sum of Squares	Mean Square	F Ratio
Model	16	67.962500	4.24766	8.6397
Error	15	7.374688	0.49165	Prob > F
C. Total	31	75.337188		<.0001*

  ▼ **Parameter Estimates**

Term	Estimate	Std Error	t Ratio	Prob>|t|
Intercept	4.759375	0.123951	38.40	<.0001*
Flour[low]	-0.215625	0.123951	-1.74	0.1024
Shortening[low]	-0.171875	0.123951	-1.39	0.1858
Egg Powder[low]	-0.390625	0.123951	-3.15	0.0066*
ovenTemp[low]	0.021875	0.123951	0.18	0.8623
BakeTime[low]	0.003125	0.123951	0.03	0.9802
Flour[low]*Shortening[low]	0.065625	0.123951	0.53	0.6042
Flour[low]*Egg Powder[low]	-0.040625	0.123951	-0.33	0.7476
Flour[low]*ovenTemp[low]	0.196875	0.123951	1.59	0.1331
Flour[low]*BakeTime[low]	-0.046875	0.123951	-0.38	0.7106
Shortening[low]*Egg Powder[low]	-0.496875	0.123951	-4.01	0.0011*
Shortening[low]*ovenTemp[low]	0.065625	0.123951	0.53	0.6042
Shortening[low]*BakeTime[low]	0.121875	0.123951	0.98	0.3411
Egg Powder[low]*ovenTemp[low]	0.146875	0.123951	1.18	0.2545
Egg Powder[low]*BakeTime[low]	0.028125	0.123951	0.23	0.8236
ovenTemp[low]*BakeTime[low]	-1.096875	0.123951	-8.85	<.0001*
Flour[low]*ovenTemp[low]*BakeTime[low]	-0.596875	0.123951	-4.82	0.0002*

FIGURE 10.24 JMP ANOVA Model for the Cake Mix Example

From Figure 10.23 or 10.24, using the 0.05 level of significance, you see that factor C (Egg Powder) with a p-value of 0.007, the BC (Shortening–Egg Powder) interaction (p-value = 0.001), the DE (Oven Temperature–Bake Time) interaction (p-value = 0.000), and the ADE (Flour–Oven Temperature–Bake Time) interaction (p-value = 0.000) are all highly significant. The significance of these interactions complicates any interpretation of the main effects. Although egg powder significantly affects taste rating (with high amount providing a better rating than low amount), the significance of the Shortening–Egg Powder interaction means that the difference in egg powder is not the same for the two levels of shortening. Because neither effect *D* nor *E* was significant, the significance of the *DE* (Oven Temperature–Bake Time) interaction indicates a crossing effect (see Figures 10.27 and 10.28). This occurs because the rating is high for low oven temperature and high baking time and for high oven temperature and low baking time. The significance of the *ADE* (Flour–Oven Temperature–Bake Time) interaction means that the interaction of oven temperature and baking time is not the same for low and high amounts of flour.

Figure 10.25 and 10.26 present main effects plots, and Figures 10.27 and 10.28 are interaction plots for the cake mix design.

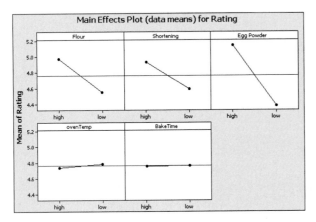

FIGURE 10.25 Minitab Main Effects Plots for the Cake Mix Design

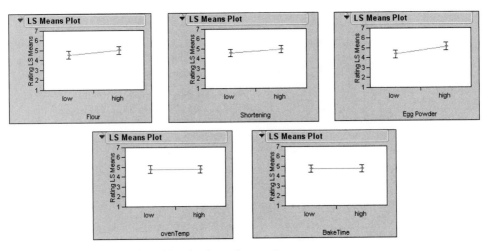

FIGURE 10.26 JMP Main Effects Plots for the Cake Mix Design

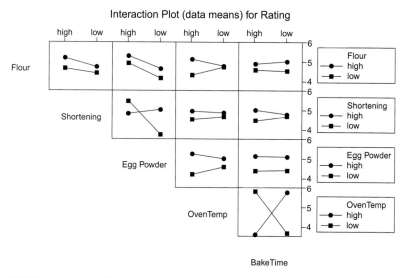

FIGURE 10.27 Minitab Interaction Plots for the Cake Mix Design

To further your understanding of these results, you can examine the interaction plots in Figures 10.27 and 10.28 along with Tables 10.12–10.15, which provide the mean values for combinations of shortening and egg powder, oven temperature and baking temperature, and oven temperature and baking time for each level of flour.

TABLE 10.12 Mean Rating for Each Level of Shortening and Egg Powder

	Egg Powder	
Shortening	**Low**	**High**
Low	3.7000	5.475
High	5.0375	4.825

TABLE 10.13 Mean Rating for Each Level of Oven Temperature and Baking Time

	Baking Time	
Oven Temperature	**Low**	**High**
Low	3.6875	5.8750
High	5.8375	3.6375

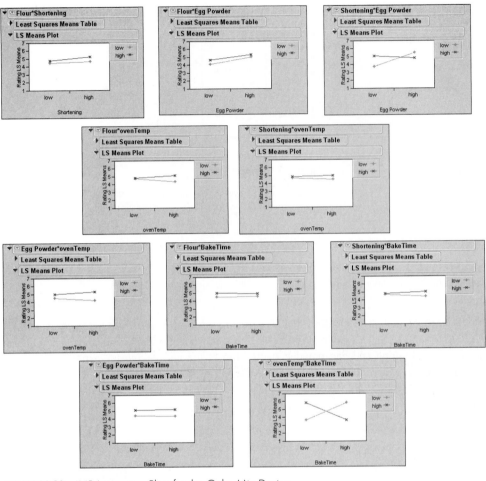

FIGURE 10.28 JMP Interaction Plots for the Cake Mix Design

TABLE 10.14 Mean Rating for Each Level of Oven Temperature and Baking Time for the Low Level of Flour

Oven Temperature	Baking Time	
	Low	**High**
Low	3.025	6.500
High	5.975	2.675

TABLE 10.15 Mean Rating for Each Level of Oven Temperature and Baking Time for the High Level of Flour

	Baking Time	
Oven Temperature	**Low**	**High**
Low	4.35	5.25
High	5.70	4.60

From Figures 10.27 and 10.28 and Table 10.12, you see that for low levels of shortening, the mean rating is much better for the high level of egg powder (5.475) than for the low level of egg powder (3.70). For a high level of shortening, the results are quite different. The rating is slightly better for low egg powder (5.0375) than for high egg powder (4.825).

Turning to the interaction of oven temperature and baking time, from Figures 10.27 and 10.28 and Table 10.13, you see that the mean rating is best for low oven temperature and high baking time (5.875) or high oven temperature and low baking time (5.8375). The rating is worse when there is both low oven temperature and low baking time (3.6875) or high oven temperature and high baking time (3.6375). However, the interaction of oven temperature and baking time is different for each of the two levels of flour. From Tables 10.14 and 10.15, the interaction seen in Table 10.13 is much more pronounced for the low level of flour than for the high level of flour.

Thus, how can you choose the level of flour, shortening, and egg powder that will result in the highest rating? Based on these results, you probably should choose high flour, low shortening, and high egg powder. The rationale for this is as follows:

1. Based on Tables 10.14 and 10.15, using a high level of flour will improve the rating and reduce the effect of oven temperature and baking time.

2. Based on Table 10.12, using a low level of shortening and a high level of egg powder provides the best rating.

3. In addition, the consumer should be warned not to use oven temperature and baking time that are both too low or both too high.

10.4 FRACTIONAL FACTORIAL DESIGNS

When you are considering four or more factors (Xs), simultaneously running all possible treatment combinations often becomes costly or impossible. For example, 4 factors each with 2 levels involve 16 treatment combinations; 5 factors each with 2 levels involve 32 treatment combinations; and 7 factors each with 2 levels involve 128 treatment combinations. Thus, as the number of factors in an experiment increases, Six Sigma team members need to have a rational way of choosing a subset of the treatment combinations so that they can conduct a cost-effective experiment with meaningful results. One way to do this is through the use of a fractional factorial design.

In a **fractional factorial design**, you use only a subset of all possible treatment combinations. However, as a consequence of reducing experimental size, you will not be able to independently estimate all the effects. In other words, there is a loss of information. If you design the experiment appropriately, higher-order interactions often can be confounded with lower-order terms. You assume that the higher-order interaction effects are negligible, so what remains are relatively good estimates of the lower-order interactions. If you reduce the experimental size too much, lower-order interactions, such as two-factor interactions, may become confounded with main effects or other two-factor interactions. It is advantageous to use fractional designs that allow good estimates of main effects and two-factor interactions. One approach is to choose the treatment combinations so that each main effect can be independently estimated without being confused or confounded with any estimate of the two-factor interactions. When a main effect or an interaction is **confounded**, its effect cannot be isolated from the main effect of some other factor or interaction.

Designs in which main effects are confounded with two-way interactions (such as *A* being confounded with *BC*) are called **Resolution III designs**. In other words, confounding main effects (one factor) with two-way interactions (two factors) yields Resolution III designs (one factor + two-way interaction = Resolution III design).

In **Resolution IV designs**, a two-way interaction, such as *AB*, is confounded with another two-way interaction, such as *CD* (two-way interaction + two-way interaction = Resolution IV design), or a main effect such as *A* is confounded with a three-way interaction, such as *BCD* (one factor + three-way interaction = Resolution IV design).

In **Resolution V designs**, main effects and two-way interactions are confounded with three-way or higher-order interactions (such as *ABC* or *ABCD*). In other words, confounding main effects (one factor) with four-way interactions (four factors) yields Resolution V designs (one factor + four-way interaction = Resolution V design). Also, confounding two-way interactions (two factors) with three-way interactions (three factors) yields Resolution V designs (two-way interaction + three-way interaction = Resolution V design).

Choosing the Treatment Combinations

To choose a subset of the treatment combinations, you can begin with a 2^4 design. Table 10.16 presents the 16 possible treatment combinations for this full factorial design, along with the pattern of pluses and minuses for the main effects (the columns headed by *A*, *B*, *C*, and *D*) and the *ABCD* interaction.

TABLE 10.16   Treatment Combinations for the 2^4 Design in Standard Order

Notation	A	B	C	D	ABCD
(1)	–	–	–	–	+
a	+	–	–	–	–
b	–	+	–	–	–
ab	+	+	–	–	+
c	–	–	+	–	–

Notation	A	B	C	D	ABCD
ac	+	−	+	−	+
bc	−	+	+	−	+
abc	+	+	+	−	−
d	−	−	−	+	−
ad	+	−	−	+	+
bd	−	+	−	+	+
abd	+	+	−	+	−
cd	−	−	+	+	+
acd	+	−	+	+	−
bcd	−	+	+	+	−
abcd	+	+	+	+	+

In a fractional factorial design with four factors in which half the treatment combinations are chosen, only eight treatment combinations are available from the possible 16 combinations. With only eight treatment combinations, you cannot estimate as many effects as compared with the full factorial 2^4 design, in which there are 16 combinations. If you are willing to assume that the four-way interaction, *ABCD*, is not significant, the fraction or subset of eight treatment combinations (called a *half-replicate*) out of the possible 16 could be selected, so that either:

1. The eight treatment combinations all have a plus sign in the column headed by *ABCD*.
2. The eight treatment combinations all have a minus sign in the column headed by *ABCD*.

If you use such a design, the *ABCD* interaction is the **defining contrast**, from which the factors and interactions that are confounded with each other can be determined. With *ABCD* as the defining contrast, factor *A* is confounded with interaction *BCD* because *A* and *ABCD* differ only by *BCD*. *BCD* is also called an **alias** of *A*, because the effects of *BCD* and *A* cannot be separated in this fractional factorial design. Thus, the *A* main effect is equivalent to the *BCD* interaction. If you are willing to assume that the *BCD* interaction is negligible, when you evaluate the mean main effect of *A*, you state that this is the effect of factor *A* (even though it could have been the effect of the *BCD* interaction). If the half-replicate chosen has a plus sign in column *ABCD*, then *A* is confounded with *BCD*. If the half-replicate chosen has a minus sign in column *ABCD*, then *A* is confounded with *−BCD*. In a similar manner, *B* is confounded with *ACD*; *C* is confounded with *ABD*; *D* is confounded with *ABC*; *AB* is confounded with *CD*; *AC* is confounded with *BD*, and *AD* is confounded with *BC*. Thus, this design is a Resolution IV design.

From this pattern of confounded effects, observe that in this design (which is called a 2^{4-1} fractional factorial design), the two-factor interaction terms are confounded with each other. Thus, you cannot separate *AB* and *CD*, *AC* and *BD*, and *AD* and *BC*. If any of these interaction terms are found to be important, you will not be able to know whether the effect is due to one term or the other.

As a first example of a fractional factorial design, a 2^{4-1} design in which eight treatments have been chosen from the total of 16 possible combinations and the defining contrast is *ABCD* is considered. In addition to the experimental design used in Section 10.3 on page 311, the hotel decided to conduct an experiment in its restaurant kitchen to measure the preparation time for various meals. The four factors studied were whether there was a dessert (no or yes), the number of side dishes (less than two or two or more), whether the side dishes included a potato (no or yes), and the type of entrée (fish or meat). The restaurant was only able to conduct this experiment with eight meals at a particular time. A half-replicate of a full factorial design was used. Table 10.17 shows the full factorial design.

TABLE 10.17   Sixteen Treatment Combinations in a 2^4 Experiment in Standard Order

Notation	Mean Preparation Time (Y)	A	B	C	D	Defining Contrast ABCD
(1)		−	−	−	−	+
a		+	−	−	−	−
b		−	+	−	−	−
ab		+	+	−	−	+
c		−	−	+	−	−
ac		+	−	+	−	+
bc		−	+	+	−	+
abc		+	+	+	−	−
d		−	−	−	+	−
ad		+	−	−	+	+
bd		−	+	−	+	+
abd		+	+	−	+	−
cd		−	−	+	+	+
acd		+	−	+	+	−
bcd		−	+	+	+	−
abcd		+	+	+	+	+

The half-replicate (using only the plus signs from the *ABCD* column) from the defining contrast (*ABCD*) is shown in Table 10.18.

TABLE 10.18 Preparation Time for Eight Treatment Combinations in the 2^{4-1} Experiment in Standard Order

Notation	Preparation Time	A	B	C	D	AB+ CD	AC+ BD	AD+ BC
(1)	17.7	−	−	−	−	+	+	+
ab	24.0	+	+	−	−	+	−	−
ac	21.7	+	−	+	−	−	+	−
bc	22.8	−	+	+	−	−	−	+
ad	27.2	+	−	−	+	−	−	+
bd	28.3	−	+	−	+	−	+	−
cd	30.4	−	−	+	+	+	−	−
abcd	36.5	+	+	+	+	+	+	+

 PREPARATION

In this design, the two-way interactions are confounded with each other; specifically, *AB* with *CD*, *AC* with *BD*, and *AD* with *BC*. This is a Resolution IV design.

Using the results presented in Table 10.18, for this 2^{4-1} design, you can evaluate $2^{4-1} - 1 = 7$ effects (*A*, *B*, *C*, *D*, *AB*, *AC*, and *AD*), as long as you realize that *A* is confounded with *BCD*, *B* is confounded with *ACD*, *C* is confounded with *ABD*, *D* is confounded with *ABC*, *AB* is confounded with *CD*, *AC* is confounded with *BD*, and *AD* is confounded with *BC*. Figure 10.29 provides the mean effects for these factors computed by Minitab. Figure 10.30 includes the coefficients (half the effects) computed by JMP.

```
Estimated Effects and Coefficients for Preparation Time (coded units)

Term                   Effect    Coef
Constant                       26.0750
Dessert                2.5500   1.2750
Side Dishes            3.6500   1.8250
Potato                 3.5500   1.7750
Entree                 9.0500   4.5250
Dessert*Side Dishes    2.1500   1.0750
Dessert*Potato        -0.0500  -0.0250
Dessert*Entree        -0.0500  -0.0250
```

FIGURE 10.29 Minitab Estimated Effects for the Meal Preparation Fractional Factorial Design

Response Preparation Time				
► Summary of Fit				
► Analysis of Variance				
▼ Parameter Estimates				
Term	Estimate	Std Error	t Ratio	Prob>|t|
Intercept	26.075	.	.	.
Dessert[No]	-1.275	.	.	.
Side Dishes[Less than two]	-1.825	.	.	.
Potato[No]	-1.775	.	.	.
Entree[Fish]	-4.525	.	.	.
Dessert[No]*Side Dishes[Less than two]	1.075	.	.	.
Dessert[No]*Potato[No]	-0.025	.	.	.
Dessert[No]*Entree[Fish]	-0.025	.	.	.

FIGURE 10.30 JMP Estimated Coefficients for the Meal Preparation Fractional Factorial Design

These mean effects are depicted in Figures 10.31 and 10.32 in a normal probability plot and a half-normal plot.

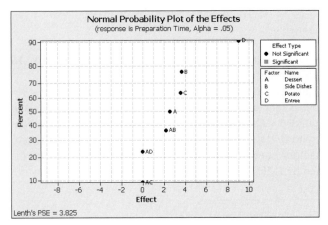

FIGURE 10.31 Minitab Normal Probability Plot for the 2^{4-1} Design for the Meal Preparation Experiment

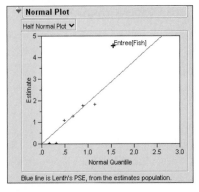

FIGURE 10.32 JMP Half-Normal Probability Plot for the 2^{4-1} Design for the Meal Preparation Experiment

Figures 10.33 and 10.34 are main effects plots, and Figures 10.35 and 10.36 are interaction plots.

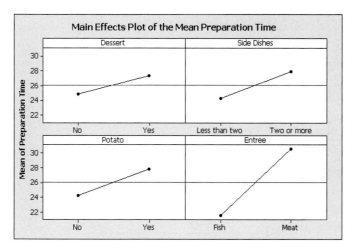

FIGURE 10.33 Minitab Main Effects Plots for the 2^{4-1} Design for the Meal Preparation Experiment

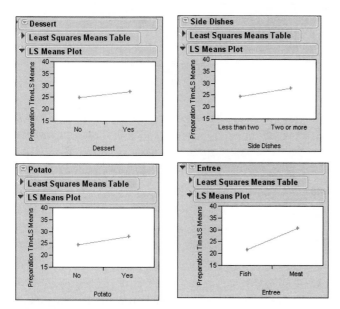

FIGURE 10.34 JMP Main Effects Plots for the 2^{4-1} Design for the Meal Preparation Experiment

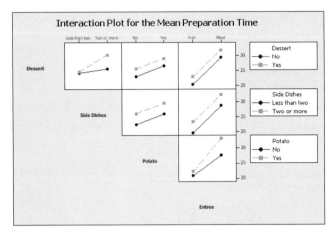

FIGURE 10.35   Minitab Interaction Plots for the 2^{4-1} Design for the Meal Preparation Experiment

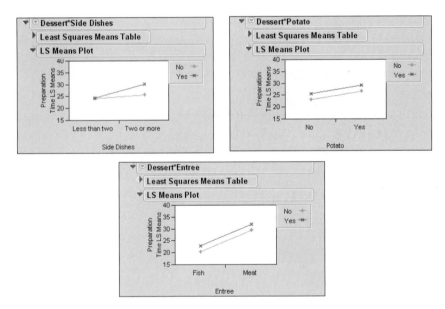

FIGURE 10.36   JMP Interaction Plots for the 2^{4-1} Design for the Meal Preparation Experiment

From Figure 10.31 or 10.32, you see that factor D appears to plot away from a straight line that is approximately zero on the X axis. From Figure 10.33 or 10.34, you can see that that the mean preparation time is higher for meat than for fish entrées. From Figure 10.35 or 10.36, only the interaction of dessert and number of side dishes might be important.

After considering the results of this experiment, management of the hotel decided to conduct another experiment to study the preparation time of meals that involved five factors (Xs). These factors were (A), the type of entrée (fish or meat); (B), the type of beverage (cold versus warm); (C), the order volume in the kitchen at the time of the order (low versus high); (D), whether there was a dessert (no or yes); and (E), the complexity of the meal (low versus high). Because the restaurant was only able to study 16 different treatment combinations, a 2^{5-1} design, a half-replicate of a 2^5 design, was used. The standard order matrix for a full factorial 2^5 design is shown in Table 10.19.

TABLE 10.19 Standard Order Design Matrix for a Full Factorial 2^5 Experiment

Notation	Response Variable (Y)	A	B	C	D	E	ABCDE
(1)		−	−	−	−	−	−
a		+	−	−	−	−	+
b		−	+	−	−	−	+
ab		+	+	−	−	−	−
c		−	−	+	−	−	+
ac		+	−	+	−	−	−
bc		−	+	+	−	−	−
abc		+	+	+	−	−	+
d		−	−	−	+	−	+
ad		+	−	−	+	−	−
bd		−	+	−	+	−	−
abd		+	+	−	+	−	+
cd		−	−	+	+	−	−
acd		+	−	+	+	−	+
bcd		−	+	+	+	−	+
abcd		+	+	+	+	−	−
e		−	−	−	−	+	+
ae		+	−	−	−	+	−
be		−	+	−	−	+	−
abe		+	+	−	−	+	+
ce		−	−	+	−	+	−
ace		+	−	+	−	+	+
bce		−	+	+	−	+	+
abce		+	+	+	−	+	−
de		−	−	−	+	+	−
ade		+	−	−	+	+	+
bde		−	+	−	+	+	+
abde		+	+	−	+	+	−
cde		−	−	+	+	+	+
acde		+	−	+	+	+	−
bcde		−	+	+	+	+	−
abcde		+	+	+	+	+	+

Table 10.20 presents the results of the half-replicate experiment (using the minus signs in the *ABCDE* column).

TABLE 10.20   Data for the Meal Preparation Study Involving Five Factors

Treatment Combination	Preparation Time	Treatment Combination	Preparation Time
(1)	10.3	ae	27.9
ab	26.4	be	18.5
ac	32.8	ce	30.9
bc	26.8	abce	43.1
ad	24.6	de	20.9
bd	16.8	abde	29.7
cd	27.6	acde	44.6
abcd	33.8	bcde	38.0

 **PREPARATION2**

The subset or fraction of 16 treatment combinations used in Table 10.20 is based on the five-factor interaction *ABCDE* as the defining contrast. This produces a Resolution V design in which you can estimate all main effects and two-factor interactions independently of each other. Each main effect is confounded with a four-factor interaction, and each two-factor interaction is confounded with a three-factor interaction. For this design, Table 10.21 summarizes the set of confounded effects.

TABLE 10.21   Confounded Effects for the 2^{5-1} Design with ABCDE as the Defining Contrast

Effect	Confounded with	Effect	Confounded with
A	BCDE	AE	BCD
B	ACDE	BC	ADE
C	ABDE	BD	ACE
D	ABCE	BE	ACD
E	ABCD	CD	ABE
AB	CDE	CE	ABD
AC	BDE	DE	ABC
AD	BCE		

Figure 10.37 provides the mean effects for these factors computed by Minitab. Figure 10.38 includes the coefficients (half the effects) computed by JMP.

```
Estimated Effects and Coefficients for Preparation Time (coded units)

Term                        Effect      Coef
Constant                                28.2938
Entree                      9.1375      4.5688
Beverage                    1.6875      0.8438
Order Volume               12.8125      6.4063
Dessert                     2.4125      1.2063
Complexity                  6.8125      3.4063
Entree*Beverage            -0.9125     -0.4563
Entree*Order Volume        -1.3875     -0.6937
Entree*Dessert             -1.7875     -0.8938
Entree*Complexity           0.1125      0.0563
Beverage*Order Volume      -0.2375     -0.1187
Beverage*Dessert           -1.5375     -0.7688
Beverage*Complexity        -0.4375     -0.2187
Order Volume*Dessert        0.1875      0.0938
Order Volume*Complexity     2.0875      1.0437
Dessert*Complexity          0.7875      0.3938
```

FIGURE 10.37 Estimated Effects from Minitab for the Five-Factor Meal Preparation Fractional Factorial Design

```
Response Preparation Time
  Summary of Fit
  Parameter Estimates
Term                                      Estimate   Std Error   t Ratio   Prob>|t|
Intercept                                 28.29375
Entree[Fish]                              -4.56875
Beverage[Cold]                            -0.84375
Order Volume[Low]                         -6.40625
Dessert[No]                               -1.20625
Complexity[Low]                           -3.40625
Entree[Fish]*Beverage[Cold]               -0.45625
Entree[Fish]*Order Volume[Low]            -0.69375
Entree[Fish]*Dessert[No]                  -0.89375
Entree[Fish]*Complexity[Low]               0.05625
Beverage[Cold]*Order Volume[Low]          -0.11875
Beverage[Cold]*Dessert[No]                -0.76875
Beverage[Cold]*Complexity[Low]            -0.21875
Order Volume[Low]*Dessert[No]              0.09375
Order Volume[Low]*Complexity[Low]          1.04375
Dessert[No]*Complexity[Low]                0.39375
```

FIGURE 10.38 Estimated Coefficients from JMP for the Five-Factor Meal Preparation Fractional Factorial Design

Figures 10.39 and 10.40 are a Minitab normal probability plot and a JMP half-normal plot for the meal preparation experiment.

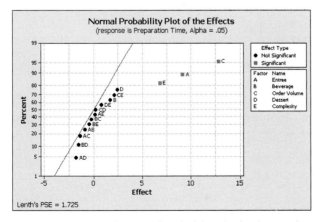

FIGURE 10.39 Minitab Normal Probability Plot for the Meal Preparation Experiment

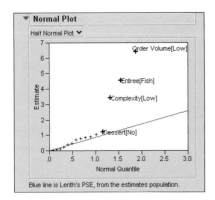

FIGURE 10.40   JMP Half-Normal Probability Plot for the Meal Preparation Experiment

From Figures 10.39 or 10.40, you see that factors *A*, *C*, and *E* plot far away from the straight line that is approximately zero on the *X* axis. Minitab indicates that these terms are statistically significant, according to criteria developed by Lenth [see Reference 10]. Thus, you can consider all interactions as consisting only of random error. You can eliminate these interaction effects from the ANOVA model and combine them to estimate an error variance. Figures 10.41 and 10.42 represent The ANOVA model with these interaction effects combined into an error variance.

```
Estimated Effects and Coefficients for Preparation Time (coded units)

Term           Effect     Coef  SE Coef     T       P
Constant               28.2938   0.5829  48.54  0.000
Entree         9.1375    4.5688   0.5829   7.84  0.000
Beverage       1.6875    0.8438   0.5829   1.45  0.178
Order Volume  12.8125    6.4063   0.5829  10.99  0.000
Dessert        2.4125    1.2062   0.5829   2.07  0.065
Complexity     6.8125    3.4063   0.5829   5.84  0.000


S = 2.33155   R-Sq = 95.70%   R-Sq(adj) = 93.56%


Analysis of Variance for Preparation Time (coded units)

Source          DF   Seq SS    Adj SS   Adj MS      F      P
Main Effects     5  1210.93   1210.93  242.186  44.55  0.000
Residual Error  10    54.36     54.36    5.436
Total           15  1265.29
```

FIGURE 10.41   ANOVA Model from Minitab for the Meal Preparation Experiment

From Figures 10.41 or 10.42, you see that the main effects of entrée, order volume, and complexity of the meal are highly significantly with *p*-values of 0.000.

Response Preparation Time

▸ **Actual by Predicted Plot**

▸ **Summary of Fit**

▾ **Analysis of Variance**

Source	DF	Sum of Squares	Mean Square	F Ratio
Model	5	1210.9281	242.186	44.5512
Error	10	54.3612	5.436	Prob > F
C. Total	15	1265.2894		<.0001*

▾ **Parameter Estimates**

Term	Estimate	Std Error	t Ratio	Prob>|t|
Intercept	28.29375	0.582887	48.54	<.0001*
Entree[Fish]	-4.56875	0.582887	-7.84	<.0001*
Beverage[Cold]	-0.84375	0.582887	-1.45	0.1784
Order Volume[Low]	-6.40625	0.582887	-10.99	<.0001*
Dessert[No]	-1.20625	0.582887	-2.07	0.0653
Complexity[Low]	-3.40625	0.582887	-5.84	0.0002*

▾ **Effect Tests**

Source	Nparm	DF	Sum of Squares	F Ratio	Prob > F
Entree	1	1	333.97562	61.4363	<.0001*
Beverage	1	1	11.39063	2.0954	0.1784
Order Volume	1	1	656.64063	120.7920	<.0001*
Dessert	1	1	23.28063	4.2826	0.0653
Complexity	1	1	185.64062	34.1494	0.0002*

FIGURE 10.42 ANOVA Model from JMP for the Meal Preparation Experiment

Figures 10.43 and 10.44 are main effects plots, and Figures 10.45 and 10.46 are interaction plots.

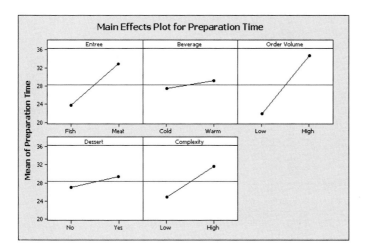

FIGURE 10.43 Minitab Main Effects Plots for the Meal Preparation Experiment

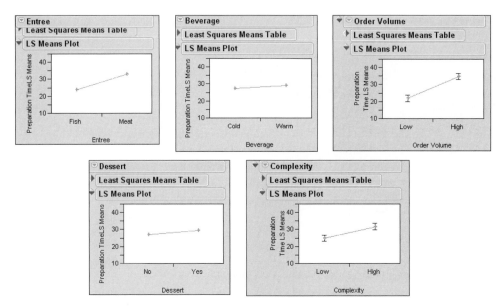

FIGURE 10.44   JMP Main Effects Plots for the Meal Preparation Experiment

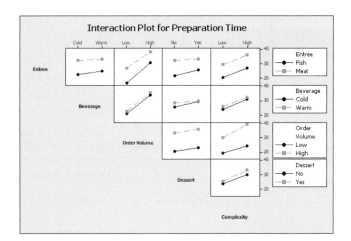

FIGURE 10.45   Minitab Interaction Plots for the Meal Preparation Experiment

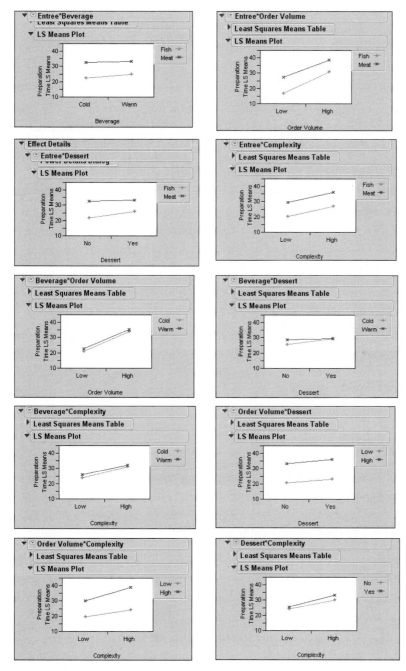

FIGURE 10.46 JMP Interaction Plots for the Meal Preparation Experiment

From Figures 10.41 and 10.42, you see that the mean preparation time is higher by 9.1375 minutes for meat entrées as compared to fish entrées, is higher by 1.6875 minutes for warm beverages than for cold beverages, is higher by 12.8125 minutes when there is high order volume, is higher by 2.4125 minutes when there is a dessert ordered, and is higher by 6.8125 minutes when the meal is highly complex. Consistent with the results of Figure 10.39 or 10.40 on page 337-338, none of the interactions appear to be important.

In this section, two fractional factorial designs that you can use when it is not feasible to evaluate all possible treatment combinations have been discussed. These two designs are only a small subset of the many fractional factorial designs that you can use. The 2^{4-1} and 2^{5-1} designs are examples of designs that involve the selection of a half-replicate (8 out of 16 or 16 out of 32 treatment combinations) of a full factorial design. Other designs you can consider involve a quarter-replicate (such as 2^{5-2} and 2^{6-2} designs) or even smaller replicates in which only main effects can be estimated (for instance, a 2^{15-11} design). For further information, see References 7, 9, and 12.

SUMMARY

In this chapter, the basic aspects of design of experiments have been developed. You have seen how the factorial design, by allowing for the measurement of the size of interaction effects, offers a substantial benefit as compared with the one-factor design. Although several designs were discussed, you should be aware that the topics covered in this book have barely "scratched the surface" of the subject of the design of experiments. For further information, see References 7, 9, and 12.

REFERENCES

1. Bisgaard, S., "Industrial Use of Statistically Designed Experiments: Case Study References and Some Historical Anecdotes," *Quality Engineering*, 4, 1992, pp. 547–562.

2. Box, G. E. P., "Do Interactions Matter?" *Quality Engineering*, 2, 1990, pp. 365–369.

3. Box, G. E. P., "What Can You Find out from Eight Experimental Runs," *Quality Engineering*, 4, 1992, pp. 619–627.

4. Box, J. F., "R. A. Fisher and the Design of Experiments," *American Statistician*, 34, 1980, pp. 1–10.

5. Daniel, C., "Use of Half-Normal Plots in Interpreting Factorial Two-Level Experiments," *Technometrics*, 1, 1959, pp. 311–341.

6. Gitlow, H. S., and D. M. Levine, *Six Sigma for Green Belts and Champions* (Upper Saddle River, NJ: Financial Times Prentice Hall, 2005).

7. Hicks, C. R., and K. V. Turner, *Fundamental Concepts in the Design of Experiments*, 5th Ed. (New York: Oxford University Press, 1999).

8. *JMP Version 6* (Cary, NC: SAS Institute, 2005).

9. Kutner, M. H., C. Nachtsheim, J. Neter, and W. Li, *Applied Linear Statistical Models*, 5th ed. (New York: McGraw-Hill-Irwin, 2005).

10. Lenth, R. V., "Quick and Easy Analysis of Unreplicated Factorials," *Technometrics*, 31, 1989, pp. 469–473.

11. *Minitab for Windows Version 14* (State College, PA: Minitab, 2004).

12. Montgomery, D. C., *Design and Analysis of Experiments*, 6th ed. (New York: John Wiley, 2005).

A P P E N D I X   10.1

Using Minitab for the Design

of Experiments

Two-Way ANOVA

To generate a two-way ANOVA, open the **BREAKFAST.MTW** worksheet. Select **Stat → ANOVA → Two-Way**, and then do the following:

1. In the Two-Way Analysis of Variance dialog box (see Figure A10.1), enter **C1** or **Delivery Time Difference** in the Response: edit box.

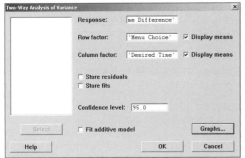

FIGURE A10.1 Minitab Two-Way Analysis of Variance Dialog Box

2. In the Row Factor: edit box, enter **C2** or **Menu Choice**. Select the **Display means** check box.

3. In the Column Factor: edit box, enter **C3** or **Desired Time**. Select the **Display means** check box.

4. Click the **OK** button.

Main Effects Plot

To generate a main effects plot using Minitab, open the **BREAKFAST.MTW** worksheet. Select **Stat → ANOVA → Main Effects Plot**, and then do the following:

1. In the Main Effects Plot dialog box (see Figure A10.2), enter **C1** or **Delivery Time Difference** in the Responses: edit box.

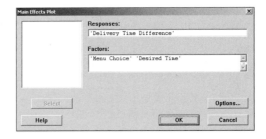

FIGURE A 10.2 Minitab Main Effects Plot Dialog Box

2. In the Factors: edit box, enter **C2** or **Menu Choice** and **C3** or **Desired Time**.

3. Click the **OK** button.

Interaction Plot

To generate an interaction plot using Minitab, open the **BREAKFAST.MTW** worksheet. Select **Stat → ANOVA → Interactions Plot**, and then do the following:

1. In the Interactions Plot dialog box (see Figure A10.3), enter **C1** or **Delivery Time Difference** in the Responses: edit box.

FIGURE A10.4 Minitab Dialog Box to Create a Design

2. In the Define Custom Factorial Design dialog box (see Figure A10.5), enter **C1** or **Flour**, **C2** or **Shortening**, **C3** or **Egg Powder**, **C4** or **ovenTemp**, or **C5** or **BakeTime** in the Factors: edit box. Select the **2-level factorial** option button. Click the **Low/High** button.

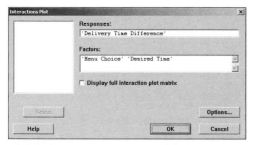

FIGURE A 10.3 Minitab Interactions Plot Dialog Box

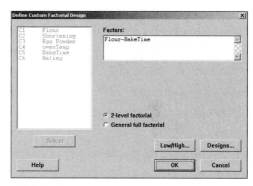

FIGURE A10.5 Minitab Define Custom Factorial Design Dialog Box

2. In the Factors: edit box, enter **C2** or **Menu Choice** and **C3** or **Desired Time**.

3. Click the **OK** button.

Factorial Design

To compute the estimated effects and ANOVA in a factorial design along with a normal probability plot of the effects, open the **CAKE.MTW** worksheet. Select **Stat → DOE → Factorial → Analyze Factorial Design**, and then do the following:

1. Click **Yes** in the Minitab dialog box (see Figure A10.4) that appears because Minitab has not yet created a design.

3. Enter the low and high values for each factor in the Design Custom Factorial Design—Low/High dialog box (see Figure A10.6). Click the **OK** button to return to the Design Custom Factorial Design dialog box. Click the **OK** button.

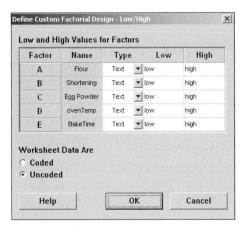

FIGURE A10.6   Minitab Define Custom Factorial Design—Low/High Dialog Box

4.   In the Analyze Factorial Design dialog box (see Figure A10.7), enter **C6** or **Rating** in the Responses: edit box.

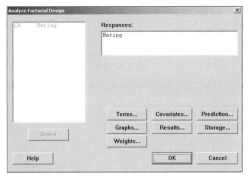

FIGURE A10.7   Minitab Analyze Factorial Design Dialog Box

5.   Click the **Terms** button. In the Analyze Factorial Design—Terms dialog box (see Figure A10.8), because this is a full factorial design, enter **5** in the Include terms in the model up through order: drop-down list box. (Use arrow keys to add terms and delete terms if desired.) Click the **OK** button.

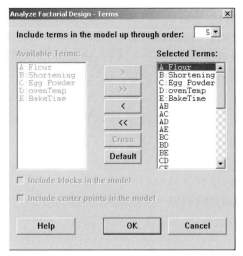

FIGURE A10.8   Minitab Analyze Factorial Design—Terms Dialog Box

6.   In the Analyze Factorial Design dialog box (Figure A10.7), click the **Graphs** button. In the Analyze Factorial Design—Graphs dialog box (see Figure A10.9), under Effects Plots, select the **Normal** check box to generate a normal probability plot for the effects. (Select Pareto to generate a Pareto diagram of the effects.) Click the **OK** button.

7.   In the Analyze Factorial Design dialog box (Figure A10.7), click the **OK** button.

8.   To label all the effects on the normal probability plot, right-click on the normal probability plot and select **Graph Options**. Select the **Label all effects** option button.

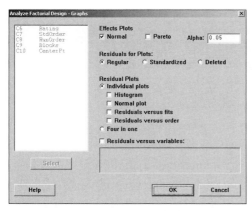

FIGURE A10.9 Minitab Analyze Factorial Design—Graphs Dialog Box

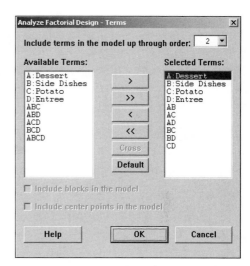

FIGURE A10.10 Minitab Analyze Factorial Design—Terms Dialog Box

Fractional Factorial Design

Follow the steps shown for the factorial design, except for step 5. In the Analyze Factorial Design—Terms dialog box, enter the value in the edit box that indicates the highest interactions included in the model. For example, in the 2^{4-1} fractional factorial design used for the meal preparation example, open the **PREPARATION.MTW** worksheet. In the Analyze Factorial Design—Terms dialog box (Figure A10.10), enter **2** in the Include terms in the model up through order: edit box because only the *AB*, *AC*, *AD*, *BC*, *BD*, and *CD* interactions are to be included.

Appendix 10.2

Using JMP for the Design of Experiments

You select **Analyze → Fit Model** on the menu bar to generate a two-way ANOVA, a factorial design, or a fractional factorial design.

Two-Way ANOVA

To generate a two-way ANOVA, open the **BREAKFAST.JMP** data table. Select **Analyze → Fit Model**. Then, do the following:

1. In the Model Specification dialog box (see Figure A10.11), select **Delivery Time Difference** and click the **Y** button.

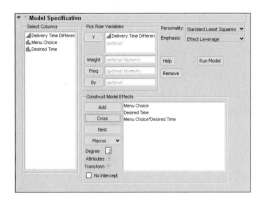

FIGURE A10.11   JMP Fit Model Dialog Box for the Two-Way ANOVA

2. Select **Menu Choice** and click the **Add** button. Select **Desired Time** and click the **Add** button.

3. Select **Menu Choice** and **Desired Time** and click the **Cross** button.

   (Note: Instead of steps 2 and 3, you could select **Menu Choice** and **Desired Time** and select **Full Factorial** in the Macros pop-up menu.)

4. In the Personality drop-down list box, select **Standard Least Squares**.

5. Click the **Run Model** button.

6. To generate a Main Effects Plot, click on the red triangle next to the main effect of interest and select **LS Means Plot**. For example, to generate a Main Effects Plot for Menu Choice, click the red triangle next to **Menu Choice** and select **LSMeans Plot** (see Figure A10.12).

7. To generate an interaction plot, click on the red triangle next to **Menu Choice *Desired Time** and select **LSMeans Plot** (see Figure A10.12).

FIGURE A10.12   Generating a JMP Main Effects or Interaction Plot

Factorial Design

To generate a factorial design, open the **DINNER.JMP** data table. Select **Analyze ➔ Fit Model**. Then, do the following:

1. In the Model Specification dialog box (see Figure A10.11), select **Delivery Time** and click the **Y** button.

2. Select **Complexity**, **Elevator**, and **Order Volume**. In the Macros pop-up menu, select **Full Factorial**.

3. In the Personality drop-down list box, select **Standard Least Squares**.

4. Click the **Run Model** button.

5. To generate a Main Effects Plot, click Effect Details and click the red triangle next to the main effect of interest and select **LS Means Plot**. For example, to generate a Main Effects Plot for Complexity, click the red triangle next to **Complexity** and select **LSMeans Plot**. To generate an interaction plot, click the red triangle next to **Complexity *Order Volume** and select **LSMeans Plot**.

6. To generate a normal probability plot, click the arrow next to the response variable of interest and select **Effect Screening ➔ Normal Plot** (see Figure A10.13). To change the normal probability plot into a half-normal plot in which all the estimates are positive, click the arrow next to **Normal Plot** just above the normal probability plot, and select **Half Normal Plot**.

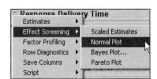

FIGURE A10.13   Generating a JMP Normal Probability Plot

Fractional Factorial Design

Follow all steps shown for the factorial design except for step 2. Open the **PREPARATION.JMP** data table. Select **Analyze ➔ Fit Model**. Then, do the following:

1. In the Fit Model dialog box (see Figure A10.11), select **Preparation Time** and click the **Y** button.

2. Select **Dessert**, **Side Dishes, Potato**, and **Entree**. In the Macros pop-up menu, select **Factorial to degree**. Enter **2** in the Degree edit box. Because this is a fractional factorial design with confounded two-factor interactions, select **Side Dishes*Potato**, **Side Dishes * Entree**, and **Potato *Entrée**, and click the **Remove** button.

3. In the Personality drop-down list box, select **Standard Least Squares**.

4. Click the **Run Model** button.

5. To generate a Main Effects Plot, click **Effects Details**, then click the red triangle next to the main effect of interest and select **LSMeans Plot**. For example, to generate a Main Effects Plot for Dessert, click the red triangle next to **Dessert** and select **LSMeans Plot**. To generate an interaction plot, click the red triangle next to **Dessert * Side Dishes** and select **LSMeans Plot**.

6. To generate a normal probability plot, click the arrow next to the response variable of interest and select **Effect Screening ➔ Normal Plot** (see Figure A10.13). To change the normal probability plot into a half-normal plot in which the estimates are positive, select **Normal Plot** right above the normal probability plot, and select **Half-Normal**.

MULTIPLE REGRESSION

SECTIONS

LEARNING OBJECTIVES

After reading this chapter, you will be able to:

- Develop a multiple regression model.
- Interpret the regression coefficients in a multiple regression model.
- Determine which independent variables to include in the regression model.
- Use categorical (nominal scaled) independent variables in a regression model.
- Build a multiple regression model.
- Predict a categorical dependent variable using logistic regression.

INTRODUCTION

This chapter introduces you to **multiple regression models** that use two or more independent variables (*X*s) to predict the value of a dependent variable (*Y*).

11.1 REVIEW OF SIMPLE LINEAR REGRESSION

Introduction

This section discusses **simple linear regression** in which a *single measurement type* (numerical) independent variable (CTP or *X*) is used to predict the measurement type (numerical) dependent variable *Y* or CTQ. The remainder of the chapter discusses *multiple regression models* that use several independent variables to predict a dependent variable *Y*.

In regression analysis, you use the **scatter plot** to plot the relationship between an *X* variable on the horizontal axis and a *Y* variable on the vertical axis. The nature of the relationship between two variables can take many forms, ranging from simple to extremely complicated mathematical functions—for example, from a simple linear relationship to a complex curvilinear or exponential relationship. Scatter plots only informally help you identify the relationship between the dependent *Y* and the independent *X* variable in a simple regression model. To specify the numeric relationship between the variables, you need to develop an equation that best represents the relationship.

Determining the Simple Linear Regression Equation

Once you determine that a straight-line relationship exists between a dependent variable *Y* and the independent variable *X*, you need to determine which straight line to use to represent the relationship. Two values define any straight line: the *Y* intercept and the slope. The **Y intercept** is the value of *Y* when $X = 0$, represented by the symbol b_0. The **slope** is the change in *Y* per unit change in *X* represented by the symbol b_1. A positive slope means *Y* increases as *X* increases. A negative slope means *Y* decreases as *X* increases.

You use the *Y* intercept and the slope to develop the prediction for the dependent variable *Y*.

$$\text{Predicted } Y = Y \text{ intercept} + (\text{slope} \times X \text{ value}) \tag{11.1a}$$

or

$$\text{Predicted } Y = b_0 + b_1 X \tag{11.1b}$$

The Y intercept (b_0) and the slope (b_1) are known as the **regression coefficients**. Multiplying a specific X value by the slope and then adding the Y intercept generates the predicted Y value. The equation $Y = b_0 + b_1X$ is used to express this relationship for the regression line from the smallest to the largest values of the independent variable (X). It is dangerous to extend the regression line beyond the range of the independent variable because the nature of the relationship between X and Y may change—for example, from linear to curvilinear.

The most common method for finding the Y intercept and the slope is the **least-squares method**. This method minimizes the sum of the squared differences between the actual values of the dependent variable (Y) and the predicted values of the dependent variable.

For plotted sets of X and Y values, there are many possible straight lines, each with their own values of b_0 and b_1, that might seem to fit the data. The least-squares method finds the values for the Y intercept and the slope that makes the sum of the squared differences between the actual values of the dependent variable Y and the predicted values of Y as small as possible.

Calculating the Y intercept and the slope using the least-squares method is tedious and can be subject to rounding errors if you use a simple four-function calculator. You will get more accurate results much faster if you use regression software available in Minitab or JMP to perform the calculations.

You can use a regression model for predicting values of a dependent variable (Y) from an independent variable (X) only within the **relevant range** (domain) of the independent variable. Again, this range is all values from the smallest to the largest X used to develop the regression model. You should not extrapolate beyond the range of X values.

Measures of Variation

Once a regression model has been fit to a set of data, three measures of variation determine how much of the variation in the dependent variable Y can be explained by variation in the independent variable X. The first measure, the **total sum of squares (SST)**, is a measure of variation of the Y values around their mean, $\overline{Y}$. In a regression analysis, the total variation or total sum of squares is subdivided into **explained variation or regression sum of squares (SSR)**, that which is due to the relationship between X and Y, and **unexplained variation or error sum of squares (SSE)**, that which is due to factors other than the relationship between X and Y.

Total sum of squares = regression sum of squares + error sum of squares $\qquad$ (11.2)

The total sum of squares (SST) is the measure of variation of the Y_i values around their mean. The total sum of squares (SST) is equal to the sum of the squared differences between each observed Y value and the mean value of Y:

SST = sum (observed Y value – mean Y value)^2 $\qquad$ (11.3)

The regression sum of squares (SSR) is the variation that is due to the relationship between X and Y. The regression sum of squares (SSR) is equal to the sum of the squared differences between the Y that is predicted from the regression equation and the mean value of Y:

SSR = sum (predicted Y value - mean Y value)^2 $\qquad$ (11.4)

The error sum of squares (*SSE*) is the variation that is due to factors other than the relationship between *X* and *Y*. The error sum of squares (*SSE*) is equal to the sum of the squared differences between each observed *Y* value and the predicted value of *Y*:

$$SSE = \text{sum (observed } Y \text{ value} - \text{predicted } Y \text{ value})^2 \tag{11.5}$$

The Coefficient of Determination

By themselves, *SSR*, *SSE*, and *SST* provide little that can be directly interpreted. The **coefficient of determination** (r^2) is the ratio of the regression sum of squares (*SSR*) to the total sum of squares (*SST*). It measures the proportion of variation in *Y* that is explained by the independent variable (*X)* in the regression model. The ratio is expressed as the following:

$$r^2 = \frac{\text{regression sum of squares}}{\text{total sum of squares}} = \frac{SSR}{SST} \tag{11.6}$$

The Coefficient of Correlation

The **coefficient of correlation** is the measure of the strength of the linear relationship between two variables, represented by the symbol *r*. The values of this coefficient vary from -1, which indicates perfect negative correlation, to +1, which indicates perfect positive correlation. In simple linear regression, the sign of the correlation coefficient *r* is the same as the sign of the slope. If the slope is positive, *r* is positive. If the slope is negative, *r* is negative. In simple linear regression, the coefficient of correlation (*r*) is the square root of the coefficient of determination r^2.

In general, you must remember that just because two variables are strongly correlated, you cannot always conclude that there is a cause-and-effect relationship between the variables. Three factors are required to demonstrate a cause-and-effect relationship: (1) statistically significant correlation; (2) absence of other causal factors (*X*s); and (3) sequence of events. An example of a sequence of events is that $X_1 = 1$ always precedes $X_2 = 1$.

Standard Error of the Estimate

The **standard error of the estimate** is the standard deviation around the fitted line of regression that measures the variability of the actual *Y* values from the predicted *Y*, represented by the symbol S_{YX}. Although the least-squares method results in the line that fits the data with the minimum amount of variation, unless the coefficient of determination $r^2 = 1.0$, the regression equation is not a perfect predictor.

Assumptions

The assumptions necessary for regression are similar to those of the analysis of variance because both topics fall under the general heading of *linear models* [see Reference 4].

The four **assumptions of regression** (known by the acronym LINE) are as follows:

- **L**inearity between Y and X.
- **I**ndependence of errors between the actual and predicted values of Y.
- **N**ormality of the distribution of error terms (differences between the actual and predicted values of Y).
- **E**qual variance (also called *homoscedasticity*) for the distribution of Y for each level of the independent variable (X).

The first assumption, **linearity**, states that the relationship between Y and X is linear. The second assumption, **independence of errors**, requires that the errors around the regression line are independent from one another. This assumption is particularly important when data are collected over a period of time. In such situations, the errors for a specific time period are often correlated with those of the previous time period [see References 1 and 4]. The third assumption, **normality**, requires that the errors are normally distributed at each value of X. Regression analysis is fairly robust against departures from the normality assumption. As long as the distribution of the errors at each level of X is not extremely different from a normal distribution, inferences about the Y intercept and the slope are not seriously affected. The fourth assumption, **equal variance** or **homoscedasticity**, requires that the variance of the errors are constant for all values of X. In other words, the variability of Y values will be the same when X is a low value as when X is a high value. The equal variance assumption is important for using the least-squares method of determining the regression coefficients. If there are serious departures from this assumption, you can use either data transformations or weighted least-squares methods [see Reference 4].

Residual Analysis

The graphical method **residual analysis** allows you to evaluate whether the regression model that has been fitted to the data is an appropriate model *and* determine whether there are violations of the assumptions of the regression model. The **residual** is the difference between the observed and predicted values of the dependent variable for a given value of X.

$$\text{Residual} = (\text{Observed value of } Y) - (\text{Predicted value of } Y) \tag{11.7}$$

To evaluate linearity, you plot the residuals on the vertical axis against the corresponding X values of the independent variable on the horizontal axis. If the fitted model is appropriate for the data, there will be no apparent pattern in this plot; that is, there will only be random variation of the residuals around the average value of Y over all values of X. However, if the fitted model is not appropriate, there will be a clear relationship between the X values and the residuals.

You can evaluate the assumption of independence of the errors by plotting the residuals in the order or sequence in which the observed data were collected. Data collected over periods of time sometimes exhibit an *autocorrelation* effect among successive observations. In these instances, there is a relationship between consecutive residuals. If this relationship exists (which violates the assumption of independence), it will be apparent in the plot of the residuals versus the time in which the data were collected. You can also test for autocorrelation using the Durbin-Watson statistic [see References 1 and 4].

To evaluate the assumption of normality of the variation around the line of regression, you plot the residuals in a histogram, box-and-whisker plot, or a normal probability plot [see Reference 1]. To evaluate the equal variance assumption, you use the same plot that you used to evaluate the aptness of the fitted model.

Inferences About the Slope

After using residual analysis to show that the assumptions of a least-squares regression model have not been seriously violated and that the straight-line model is appropriate, you can make inferences about the linear relationship between the dependent and independent variables in a population based on your sample results.

You can determine the existence of a significant relationship between the X and Y variables by testing whether β_1 (the population slope) is equal to 0. If you reject this hypothesis based on a random sample, you conclude that there is evidence of a linear relationship between Y and X. The null and alternative hypotheses are:

H_0: $\beta_1 = 0$ (There is no linear relationship.)

H_1: $\beta_1 \neq 0$ (There is a linear relationship.)

The test statistic follows the t distribution with the degrees of freedom equal to the sample size minus 2 [see Reference 1]. The test statistic is equal to the sample slope divided by the standard error of the slope:

$$t = \frac{\text{sample slope}}{\text{standard error of the slope}} \qquad (11.8)$$

You can also use an F test to determine whether the slope in simple linear regression is statistically significant. In testing for the significance of the slope, the F test is the ratio of the variance that is due to the regression (MSR) divided by the error variance (MSE). Table 11.1 is the Analysis of Variance summary table.

11.2 DEVELOPING THE MULTIPLE REGRESSION MODEL

You can use multiple regression analysis to assist a moving company owner to develop a more accurate method of predicting the labor hours needed for a moving job by using the volume of goods (in cubic feet) that is being moved and the number of pieces of large furniture (such as beds, couches, china closets, and dressers) that need to be moved. The manager has collected the following data (shown in Table 11.2) for a random sample of 36 moves for 2005 and has eliminated the travel time portion of the time needed for the move.

TABLE 11.1 ANOVA table for Testing the Significance of a Regression Coefficient

Source	df	Sum of Squares	Mean Square (Variance)	F
Regression	k	SSR	$MSR = \dfrac{SSR}{k}$	$F = \dfrac{MSR}{MSE}$
Error	$n - k - 1$	SSE	$MSE = \dfrac{SSE}{n-k-1}$	
Total	$n - 1$	SST		

where

n = sample size

k = number of independent variables

TABLE 11.2 Labor Hours, Cubic Feet, and Number of Pieces of Large Furniture

Hours	Feet	Large	Hours	Feet	Large
24.00	545	3	25.00	557	2
13.50	400	2	45.00	1,028	5
26.25	562	2	29.00	793	4
25.00	540	2	21.00	523	3
9.00	220	1	22.00	564	3
20.00	344	3	16.50	312	2
22.00	569	2	37.00	757	3
11.25	340	1	32.00	600	3
50.00	900	6	34.00	796	3
12.00	285	1	25.00	577	3
38.75	865	4	31.00	500	4
40.00	831	4	24.00	695	3
19.50	344	3	40.00	1,054	4
18.00	360	2	27.00	486	3
28.00	750	3	18.00	442	2
27.00	650	2	62.50	1,249	5
21.00	415	2	53.75	995	6
15.00	275	2	79.50	1,397	7

 MOVING

With two independent variables and a dependent variable, the data are in three dimensions. Figure 11.1 illustrates a three-dimensional graph constructed by Minitab.

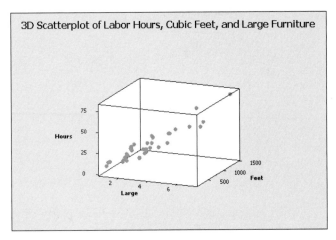

FIGURE 11.1 Minitab 3D Graph of Labor Hours, Cubic Feet, and Number of Pieces of Large Furniture

Interpreting the Regression Coefficients

When there are several independent variables, you can extend the simple linear regression model of Equation (11.1) on page 352 by assuming a straight-line or linear relationship between each independent variable and the dependent variable. For example, with two independent variables, the multiple regression model is:

$$\text{Predicted } Y = Y \text{ intercept} + (\text{slope of } X_1 \times X_1 \text{ value}) + (\text{slope of } X_2 \times X_2 \text{ value}) \qquad (11.9a)$$

or

$$\text{Predicted } Y = b_0 + b_1 X_1 + b_2 X_2 \qquad (11.9b)$$

In the simple regression model, the slope represents the change in the mean of Y per unit change in X and does not take into account any other variables besides the single independent variable included in the model. In the multiple regression model with two independent variables, the slope of Y with X_1 represents the change in the mean of Y per unit change in X_1, taking into account the effect of X_2. This slope is called a **net regression coefficient**. (Some statisticians refer to net regression coefficients as *partial regression coefficients*.)

As in simple linear regression, you use the least-squares method and software such as Minitab or JMP to compute the regression coefficients. Figure 11.2 presents Minitab output for the moving company data, and Figure 11.3 illustrates JMP output.

```
The regression equation is
Hours = - 3.92 + 0.0319 Feet + 4.22 Large

Predictor        Coef   SE Coef       T      P
Constant       -3.915     1.674   -2.34  0.026
Feet         0.031924  0.004604    6.93  0.000
Large          4.2228    0.9142    4.62  0.000

S = 3.98000   R-Sq = 93.3%   R-Sq(adj) = 92.9%

Analysis of Variance
Source          DF      SS      MS       F      P
Regression       2  7248.7  3624.4  228.80  0.000
Residual Error  33   522.7    15.8
Total           35  7771.4

Predicted Values for New Observations
New
Obs     Fit  SE Fit          95% CI              95% PI
  1  24.715   0.852  (22.981, 26.450)  (16.434, 32.996)

Values of Predictors for New Observations
New
Obs  Feet  Large
  1   500   3.00
```

FIGURE 11.2 Partial Minitab Output for the Moving Company Data

Response Hours

Whole Model

Summary of Fit

RSquare	0.932737
RSquare Adj	0.92866
Root Mean Square Error	3.979995
Mean of Response	28.95833
Observations (or Sum Wgts)	36

Analysis of Variance

Source	DF	Sum of Squares	Mean Square	F Ratio
Model	2	7248.7056	3624.35	228.8049
Error	33	522.7319	15.84	Prob > F
C. Total	35	7771.4375		<.0001

Lack Of Fit

Parameter Estimates

Term	Estimate	Std Error	t Ratio	Prob>|t|
Intercept	-3.915221	1.67379	-2.34	0.0255
Feet	0.0319243	0.004604	6.93	<.0001
Large	4.2228339	0.91419	4.62	<.0001

Effect Tests

Source	Nparm	DF	Sum of Squares	F Ratio	Prob > F
Feet	1	1	761.58318	48.0787	<.0001
Large	1	1	337.98673	21.3371	<.0001

FIGURE 11.3 Partial JMP Output for the Moving Company Data

The results show the slope of Y with X_1 (b_1= 0.0319), the slope of Y with X_2 (b_2 = 4.2228), and the Y intercept b_0 = -3.915. Thus, the multiple regression equation is:

Predicted value of labor hours = -3.915 + (0.0319 × cubic feet moved) + (4.2228 × large furniture)

The slope b_1 was computed as +0.0319. This means that for each increase of 1 unit in X_1, the mean value of Y is estimated to increase by 0.0319 units, holding constant the effect of X_2. In other words, holding constant the number of pieces of large furniture, for each increase of 1 cubic foot in the amount to be moved, the fitted model predicts that the expected labor hours are estimated to increase by 0.0319 hours. The slope b_2 was computed as +4.2228. This means that for each increase of 1 unit in X_2, the mean value of Y is estimated to increase by 4.2228 units, holding constant the effect of X_1. In other words, holding constant the amount to be moved, for each additional piece of large furniture, the fitted model predicts that the expected labor hours are estimated to increase by 4.2228 hours. The Y intercept b_0 was computed to be -3.915. The Y intercept represents the mean value of Y when X equals 0. Because the cubic feet moved cannot be less than 0, the Y intercept has no practical interpretation. Recall that a regression model is only valid within the ranges (domains) of the independent variables.

As stated earlier, regression coefficients in multiple regression are called *net regression coefficients* and measure the mean change in Y per unit change in a particular X, *holding constant the effect of the other X variables*. For example, in the moving company study, for a move with a given number of pieces of large furniture, the mean labor hours are estimated to increase by 0.0319 hours for each 1 cubic foot increase in the amount to be moved. Another way to interpret this "net effect" is to think of two moves with an equal number of pieces of large furniture. If the first move consists of 1 cubic foot more than the other move, the "net effect" of this difference is that the first move is predicted to take 0.0319 more labor hours than the other move. To interpret the net effect of the number of pieces of large furniture, you can consider two moves that have the same cubic footage. If the first move has one additional piece of large furniture, the net effect of this difference is that the first move is predicted to take 4.2228 more labor hours than the other move.

Predicting the Dependent Variable Y

As in simple linear regression, you can use the multiple regression equation to predict values of the dependent variable. For example, the predicted labor hours for a move with 500 cubic feet with three large pieces of furniture to be moved is as follows:

Predicted $Y = Y$ intercept + (slope of $X_1 \times X_1$ value) + (slope of $X_2 \times X_2$ value)

$= -3.915 + (0.0319 \times 500) + (4.2228 \times 3) = 24.715$

You predict that the mean labor hours for a move with 500 cubic feet and three large pieces of furniture to be moved are 24.715 hours.

As was the case in simple linear regression, after you have predicted Y and done a residual analysis (see Section 11.4), you can construct a confidence interval estimate of the mean response and a prediction interval for an individual response [see Reference 1]. Figure 11.2 on page 359 presents confidence and prediction intervals computed using Minitab for predicting the labor hours. The 95% confidence interval estimate of the mean labor hours with 500 cubic feet and three large pieces of furniture to be moved is between 22.981 and 26.45 hours. The prediction interval for an individual move is between 16.434 and 32.996 hours.

11.3 COEFFICIENT OF MULTIPLE DETERMINATION AND THE OVERALL F TEST

Coefficients of Multiple Determination

In simple linear regression, you computed the coefficient of determination (r^2) that measures the variation in Y that is explained by the independent variable X in the simple linear regression model. In multiple regression, the coefficient of multiple determination represents the proportion of the variation in Y that is explained by the selected set of independent variables. In the moving company example, from Figure 11.2 or 11.3 on page 359, $SSR = 7,248.7$, and $SST = 7,771.4$. Thus,

$$r^2 = \frac{\text{regression sum of squares}}{\text{total sum of squares}} = \frac{SSR}{SST}$$

$$= \frac{7,248.7}{7,771.4}$$

$$= 0.933$$

The coefficient of multiple determination, ($r^2 = 0.933$) indicates that 93.3% of the variation in labor hours is explained by the variation in the cubic footage and the variation in the number of pieces of large furniture to be moved.

Test for the Significance of the Overall Multiple Regression Model

The **overall F test** is used to test for the significance of the overall multiple regression model. You use this test to determine whether there is a significant relationship between the dependent variable and the entire set of independent variables. Because there is more than one independent variable, you have the following null and alternative hypotheses:

H_0: No linear relationship between the dependent variable and the independent variables ($\beta_1 = \beta_2 = \beta_3 = \cdots = \beta_k = 0$, where k = the number of independent variables).

H_1: Linear relationship between the dependent variable and at least one of the independent variables (at least one $\beta_i \neq 0$).

Table 11.3 presents the ANOVA summary table.

TABLE 11.3　ANOVA Summary Table for the Overall F Test

Source	Degrees of Freedom	Sum of Squares	Mean Square (Variance)	F
Regression	k	SSR	$MSR = \dfrac{SSR}{k}$	$F = \dfrac{MSR}{MSE}$
Error	$n - k - 1$	SSE	$MSE = \dfrac{SSE}{n - k - 1}$	
Total	$n - 1$	SST		

where

n = sample size

k = number of independent variables

From Figure 11.2 or 11.3 on page 359, the F statistic given in the ANOVA summary table is 228.80 and the p-value = 0.000. Because the p-value = 0.000 < 0.05, you reject H_0 and conclude that at least one of the independent variables (cubic footage and/or the number of pieces of large furniture moved) is related to labor hours.

11.4 RESIDUAL ANALYSIS FOR THE MULTIPLE REGRESSION MODEL

In simple linear regression, you used residual analysis to evaluate the appropriateness of using the simple linear regression model for a set of data. For the multiple regression model with two independent variables, you need to construct and analyze the following residual plots:

1. Residuals versus the predicted value of Y.
2. Residuals versus the first independent variable X_1.
3. Residuals versus the second independent variable X_2.
4. Residuals versus time (if the data has been collected in time order).

The first residual plot examines the pattern of residuals versus the predicted values of Y. If the residuals show a pattern for different predicted values of Y, there is evidence of a possible curvilinear effect in at least one independent variable, a possible violation to the assumption of equal variance, and/or the need to transform the Y variable. The second and third residual plots involve the independent variables. Patterns in the plot of the residuals versus an independent variable may indicate the existence of a curvilinear effect and, therefore, indicate the need to add a curvilinear independent variable to the multiple regression model [see References 1 and 4]. The fourth type of plot is used to investigate patterns in the residuals to validate the independence assumption when the data are collected in time order.

Figures 11.4 and 11.5 are the Minitab and JMP residual plots for the moving company example. In Figure 11.4 or 11.5, there is very little or no pattern in the relationship between the residuals and the cubic feet moved (X_1), the number of pieces of large furniture moved (X_2), or the predicted value of Y. Thus, you can conclude that the multiple regression model is appropriate for predicting labor hours.

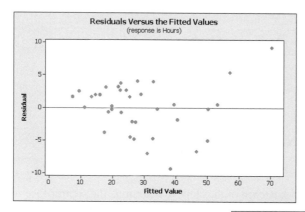

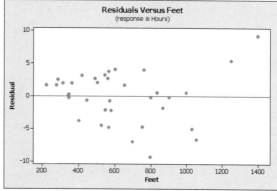

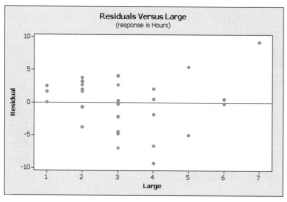

FIGURE 11.4 Minitab Residual Plots for the Moving Company Model: Residuals Versus Predicted Y; Residuals Versus Cubic Feet Moved; Residuals Versus the Number of Pieces of Large Furniture Moved

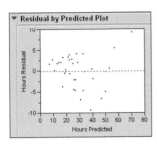 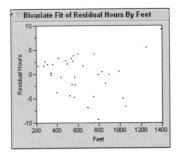 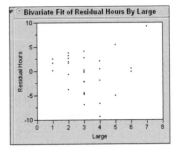

FIGURE 11.5 JMP Residual Plots for the Moving Company Model: Residuals Versus Predicted Y; Residuals Versus Cubic Feet Moved; Residuals Versus the Number of Pieces of Large Furniture Moved

11.5 INFERENCES CONCERNING THE POPULATION REGRESSION COEFFICIENTS

In simple linear regression, you tested the existence of the slope to determine the significance of the relationship between X and Y. In this section, this is extended to the multiple regression model.

Tests of Hypothesis

In a simple linear regression model, to test a hypothesis concerning the population slope, you used the t test:

$$t = \frac{\text{sample slope}}{\text{standard error of the slope}} = \frac{b_1 - 0}{S_{b_1}}$$

To test the significance of the cubic feet moved (X_1) or the number of pieces of large furniture moved (X_2), you refer to Figure 11.2 or 11.3 on page 359. The null hypothesis for each independent variable is that there is no linear relationship between labor hours and the independent variable holding constant the effect of the other independent variables. The alternative hypothesis is that there is a linear relationship between labor hours and the independent variable holding constant the effect of the other independent variables.

For the cubic feet moved, the t statistic is 6.93 and the p-value is 0.000. Because the p-value is $0.000 < 0.05$, you reject the null hypothesis and conclude that there is a linear relationship between labor hours and the cubic feet moved (X_1). For the number of pieces of large furniture moved, the t statistic is 4.62 and the p-value is 0.000. Because the p-value is $0.000 < 0.05$, you reject the null hypothesis and conclude that there is a linear relationship between labor hours and the number of pieces of large furniture moved (X_2).

The *t* test of significance for a particular regression coefficient is actually a test for the significance of adding a particular variable into a regression model given that the other variable is included. Because each of the two independent variables is significant, both should be included in the regression model. Therefore, the *t* test for the regression coefficient is equivalent to testing for the contribution of each independent variable.

Confidence Interval Estimation

You can construct confidence interval estimates of the population slope in multiple regression analysis by multiplying the *t* statistic by the standard error of the slope and then adding and subtracting this product to the sample slope.

Confidence interval of slope = Sample slope ± *t* statistic × (standard error of the slope)

For the moving company data, using the Minitab and JMP regression results in Figures 11.2 and 11.3 on page 359, you calculate the lower and upper limits of the 95% confidence interval estimate for the slope of cubic footage and labor hours as follows.
There are 36 – 2 – 1 = 33 degrees of freedom; hence, the *t* statistic is 2.0345. Thus,

Confidence interval of slope = Sample slope ± *t* statistic (standard error of the slope)
= 0.0319 ± (2.0345)(0.0046)
= 0.0319 ± 0.0094 = 0.0225 to 0.0413

With 95% confidence, the lower limit is 0.0225 hours and the upper limit is 0.0413 hours. The confidence interval indicates that for each increase of 1 cubic foot moved, mean labor hours are estimated to increase by at least 0.0225 hours but less than 0.0413 hours, holding constant the number of pieces of large furniture moved.
To calculate the confidence interval estimate of the slope of the number of pieces of large furniture moved and labor hours, you have:

Sample slope ± *t* statistic (standard error of the slope)
4.2228 ± (2.0345)(0.9142)
4.2228 ± 1.8599 = 2.3629 to 6.0827

With 95% confidence, the lower limit is 2.3629 hours and the upper limit is 6.0827 hours. The confidence interval indicates that for each increase of one piece of large furniture moved, mean labor hours are estimated to increase by at least 2.3629 hours but less than 6.0827 hours, holding constant the cubic footage moved.

11.6 USING DUMMY VARIABLES AND INTERACTION TERMS IN REGRESSION MODELS

The multiple regression models discussed in Sections 11.2–11.5 assumed that each X variable is a measurement type variable. However, in some situations, you might want to include categorical variables as independent variables in the regression model. The use of dummy variables allows you to include categorical independent variables as part of the regression model. If a given categorical independent variable has two categories, then you need only one dummy variable to represent the two categories. A particular dummy variable, say X_3, is defined as follows:

$X_3 = 0$ if the value is in category 1

$X_3 = 1$ if the value is in category 2

To illustrate the application of dummy variables in regression, consider the moving company example in which you are predicting labor hours based on the cubic feet moved and whether the apartment building had an elevator. To include the categorical variable concerning the presence of an elevator, you define the dummy variable as follows:

$X_3 = 0$ if the apartment building does not have an elevator

$X_3 = 1$ if the apartment building has an elevator

Table 11.4 lists the labor hours, cubic feet to be moved, and presence of an elevator in the apartment building. In the 4th and 8th columns of Table 11.4, you can see how the categorical data are converted to numerical values.

TABLE 11.4   Labor Hours, Cubic Feet to be Moved, and Presence of an Elevator

Hours (Y)	Feet (X_1)	Elevator (X_2)	Elevator (Coded) (X_3)	Hours (Y)	Feet (X_1)	Elevator (X_2)	Elevator (Coded) (X_3)
24.00	545	Yes	1	25.00	557	Yes	1
13.50	400	Yes	1	45.00	1,028	Yes	1
26.25	562	No	0	29.00	793	Yes	1
25.00	540	No	0	21.00	523	Yes	1
9.00	220	Yes	1	22.00	564	Yes	1
20.00	344	Yes	1	16.50	312	Yes	1
22.00	569	Yes	1	37.00	757	No	0
11.25	340	Yes	1	32.00	600	No	0

Hours (Y)	Feet (X₁)	Eleva- tor (X₂)	Elevator (Coded) (X₃)	Hours (Y)	Feet (X₁)	Eleva- tor (X₂)	Elevator (Coded) (X₃)
11.25	340	Yes	1	32.00	600	No	0
50.00	900	Yes	1	34.00	796	Yes	1
12.00	285	Yes	1	25.00	577	Yes	1
38.75	865	Yes	1	31.00	500	Yes	1
40.00	831	Yes	1	24.00	695	Yes	1
19.50	344	Yes	1	40.00	1,054	Yes	1
18.00	360	Yes	1	27.00	486	Yes	1
28.00	750	Yes	1	18.00	442	Yes	1
27.00	650	Yes	1	62.50	1,249	No	0
21.00	415	No	0	53.75	995	Yes	1
15.00	275	Yes	1	79.50	1,397	No	0

⬢ MOVING

Assuming that the slope of labor hours with the cubic feet moved is the same for apartments that have and do not have an elevator, the multiple regression model is the following:

Predicted labor hours = Y intercept + [slope with cubic feet × cubic feet value]
+ [slope with presence of elevator × coded elevator value]

Figures 11.6 and 11.7 provide Minitab and JMP output for this model.

```
The regression equation is
Hours = 2.45 + 0.0482 Feet - 4.53 ElevatorD


Predictor     Coef    SE Coef     T      P
Constant     2.451     2.984    0.82   0.417
Feet       0.048205  0.003010  16.01   0.000
ElevatorD   -4.528     2.104   -2.15   0.039


S = 4.78249   R-Sq = 90.3%   R-Sq(adj) = 89.7%


Analysis of Variance

Source          DF      SS      MS      F      P
Regression       2   7016.7  3508.3  153.39  0.000
Residual Error  33    754.8    22.9
Total           35   7771.4
```

FIGURE 11.6 Minitab Output for the Moving Company Dummy Variable Model

Response Hours

▼ **Whole Model**

▶ **Actual by Predicted Plot**

▼ **Summary of Fit**

RSquare	0.902877
RSquare Adj	0.896991
Root Mean Square Error	4.782487
Mean of Response	28.95833
Observations (or Sum Wgts)	36

▼ **Analysis of Variance**

Source	DF	Sum of Squares	Mean Square	F Ratio
Model	2	7016.6556	3508.33	153.3884
Error	33	754.7819	22.87	Prob > F
C. Total	35	7771.4375		<.0001

▶ **Lack Of Fit**

▼ **Parameter Estimates**

Term	Estimate	Std Error	t Ratio	Prob>|t|
Intercept	2.451221	2.98352	0.82	0.4172
Feet	0.048205	0.00301	16.01	<.0001
ElevatorD	-4.528274	2.104084	-2.15	0.0388

FIGURE 11.7 JMP Output for the Moving Company Dummy Variable Model

From Figure 11.6 or 11.7, the regression equation is:

Predicted labor hours = 2.451 + (0.0482 × cubic feet value) –
(4.528 × coded elevator value)

For moves in buildings without an elevator, you substitute 0 as the coded elevator value into the regression equation

Predicted labor hours = 2.451 + (0.0482 × cubic feet value) – [4.528 × (0)]
Predicted labor hours = 2.451 + (0.0482 × cubic feet value)

For moves in buildings with an elevator, you substitute 1 as the coded elevator value into the regression equation:

Predicted labor hours = 2.451 + (0.0482 × cubic feet value) – [4.528 × (1)]
Predicted labor hours = 2.451 + (0.0482 × cubic feet value) – 4.528
Predicted labor hours = -2.077 + (0.0482 × cubic feet value)

In this model, you interpret the regression coefficients as follows:

1. Holding constant whether or not the move occurs in an apartment building with an elevator, for each increase of 1.0 cubic feet in the amount moved, the mean labor hours are estimated to increase by 0.0482 hours.

2. Holding constant the number of cubic feet moved, the presence of an elevator in the apartment building where the move takes place decreases the mean estimated labor hours by 4.528 hours.

In Figure 11.6 or 11.7, the t statistic for the slope of cubic feet with labor hours is 16.01 and the p-value is approximately 0.000. The t statistic for presence of an elevator is -2.15 and the p-value is 0.039. Thus, each of the two variables makes a significant contribution to the model at a level of significance of 0.05. In addition, the coefficient of multiple determination indicates that 90.3% of the variation in labor hours is explained by variation in the cubic feet and whether or not the apartment building has an elevator.

In the regression models discussed so far, the *effect* an independent variable has on the dependent variable was assumed to be statistically independent of the other independent variables in the model. An **interaction** occurs if the *effect* of an independent variable on the dependent variable is related to the *value* of a second independent variable.

To model an interaction effect in a regression model, you use an **interaction term** (sometimes referred to as a **cross-product term**). To illustrate the concept of interaction and use of an interaction term, return to the moving company example. In the regression model of Figures 11.6 and 11.7, you assumed that the effect that cubic feet has on the labor hours is independent of whether or not the apartment building has an elevator. In other words, you assumed that the slope of labor hours with cubic feet is the same for moves from apartment buildings with an elevator as it is for apartment buildings without an elevator. If these two slopes are different, an interaction between cubic feet and elevator exists.

To evaluate a hypothesis of equal slopes of a dependent Y variable with the independent variable X, you first define an interaction term that consists of the product of the independent variable X_1 and the dummy variable X_2. You then test whether this interaction variable makes a significant contribution to a regression model that contains the other X variables. If the interaction is significant, you cannot use the original model for prediction. For the data of Table 11.4 on page 366, you define the new variable as the product of cubic feet and the elevator dummy variable.

Figure 11.8 illustrates Minitab output for this regression model, which includes the cubic feet X_1, the presence of an elevator X_2, and the interaction of cubic feet X_1, and the presence of an elevator X_2 (which is defined as X_3). Figure 11.9 displays JMP output.

```
The regression equation is
Hours = - 4.73 + 0.0573 Feet + 5.46 ElevatorD - 0.0139 Feet*ElevatorD


Predictor           Coef   SE Coef       T      P
Constant          -4.726     4.153   -1.14  0.264
Feet            0.057306  0.004808   11.92  0.000
ElevatorD          5.461     4.705    1.16  0.254
Feet*ElevatorD -0.013899  0.005941   -2.34  0.026


S = 4.48799   R-Sq = 91.7%   R-Sq(adj) = 90.9%


Analysis of Variance

Source          DF      SS      MS       F      P
Regression       3  7126.9  2375.6  117.94  0.000
Residual Error  32   644.5    20.1
Total           35  7771.4
```

FIGURE 11.8 Minitab Output for a Regression Model that Includes Cubic Feet, Presence of an Elevator, and Interaction of Cubic Feet and an Elevator

Response Hours

Whole Model

Actual by Predicted Plot

Summary of Fit

RSquare	0.917062
RSquare Adj	0.909287
Root Mean Square Error	4.487986
Mean of Response	28.95833
Observations (or Sum Wgts)	36

Analysis of Variance

Source	DF	Sum of Squares	Mean Square	F Ratio
Model	3	7126.8929	2375.63	117.9440
Error	32	644.5446	20.14	Prob > F
C. Total	35	7771.4375		<.0001*

Lack Of Fit

Parameter Estimates

Term	Estimate	Std Error	t Ratio	Prob>|t|
Intercept	-4.725958	4.153417	-1.14	0.2636
Feet	0.0573065	0.004808	11.92	<.0001*
ElevatorD	5.4613838	4.704514	1.16	0.2543
Feet*ElevatorD	-0.013899	0.005941	-2.34	0.0257*

FIGURE 11.9 JMP Output for a Regression Model that Includes Cubic Feet, Presence of an Elevator, and Interaction of Cubic Feet and an Elevator

To test for the existence of an interaction, you use the null hypothesis that there is no interaction between cubic feet and an elevator versus the alternative hypothesis that there is an interaction between cubic feet and an elevator. In Figure 11.8 or 11.9, the t statistic for the interaction of cubic feet and an elevator is -2.34. Because the p-value = 0.026 < 0.05, you reject the null hypothesis. Therefore, the interaction term make a significant contribution to the model given that cubic feet and presence of an elevator are already included. Therefore, you need to use a regression model that includes cubic feet, presence of an elevator, and the interaction of cubic feet and presence of an elevator.

From Figure 11.8 or 11.9, this regression model is as follows:

Predicted labor hours = -4.726 + (0.0573 × cubic feet value) +
(5.461 × coded elevator value) – (0.0139 × cubic feet value × coded elevator value)

11.7 COLLINEARITY

One important problem in the application of multiple regression analysis involves the possible collinearity of the independent variables. This condition refers to situations in which one or more of the independent variables are highly correlated with each other. In such situations, the different variables do not provide new information, and it is difficult to separate the effect of such variables on the dependent variable. When collinearity exists, the values of the regression coefficients for the correlated variables may fluctuate drastically, depending on which independent variables are included in the model.

One method of measuring collinearity is the **variance inflationary factor (*VIF*)** for each independent variable. The *VIF* is directly related to the coefficient of determination between a particular independent variable and all the other independent variables. When a particular independent variable has a small coefficient of determination with the other independent variables, its *VIF* will be small (below 5). When a particular independent variable has a large coefficient of determination with the other independent variables, its *VIF* will be large (above 5). You compute *VIF* as follows.

$$VIF = \frac{1}{1 - R^2} \tag{11.10}$$

where R^2 is the coefficient of multiple determination of an independent variable with all other independent variables.

If there are only two independent variables, R_1^2 is the coefficient of determination between X_1 and X_2. It is identical to R_2^2, which is the coefficient of determination between X_2 and X_1. If, for example, there are three independent variables, then R_1^2 is the coefficient of multiple determination of X_1 with X_2 and X_3; R_2^2 is the coefficient of multiple determination of X_2 with X_1 and X_3; and R_3^2 is the coefficient of multiple determination of X_3 with X_1 and X_2.

If a set of independent variables is uncorrelated, each *VIF* is equal to 1. If the set is highly intercorrelated, then a *VIF* might even exceed 10. Many statisticians [see Reference 7] have suggested that you use alternatives to least-squares regression if the maximum *VIF* is greater than 5.

You need to proceed with extreme caution when using a multiple regression model that has one or more large *VIF* values. You can use the model to predict values of the dependent variable *only* in the case where the values of the independent variables used in the prediction are consistent with the values observed in the data set. However, you cannot extrapolate to values of the independent variables not observed in the sample data, and since the independent variables contain overlapping information, you should always avoid interpreting the coefficient estimates (i.e., there is no way to accurately estimate the individual effects of the independent variables). One solution to the problem is to delete the variable with the largest *VIF* value. The reduced model (i.e., the model with the independent variable with the largest *VIF* value deleted) is often free of collinearity problems. If you determine that all the independent variables are needed in the model, you can use methods discussed in References 4, 5, and 7.

In the moving company data of Section 11.2, the correlation between the two independent variables, cubic feet and number of pieces of large furniture, is 0.854. Therefore, because there are only two independent variables in the model, using Equation (11.10):

$$VIF_1 = VIF_2 = \frac{1}{1 - (0.854)^2}$$
$$= 3.69$$

Thus, you can conclude that there is some collinearity for the moving company data. However, since the *VIF* is below 5, you can include both independent variables in the regression model.

11.8 Model Building

In this section, you will learn a structured approach to building the most appropriate regression model.

For example, the director of operations for a television station needs to look for ways to reduce labor expenses. Currently, the unionized graphic artists at the station receive hourly pay for a significant number of hours in which they are idle. These hours are called *standby hours*. You have collected data concerning standby hours and four factors that you suspect are related to the excessive number of standby hours the station is currently experiencing: the total number of staff present, remote hours, Dubner hours, and total labor hours. You plan to build a multiple regression model to help determine which factors most heavily affect standby hours. You believe that an appropriate model will help you to predict the number of future standby hours, identify the root causes for excessive amounts of standby hours, and allow you to reduce the total number of future standby hours. How do you build the model with the most appropriate mix of independent variables? Table 11.5 presents the data.

TABLE 11.5 Predicting Standby Hours Based on Total Staff Present, Remote Hours, Dubner Hours, and Total Labor Hours

Week	Standby Hours	Total Staff Present	Remote Hours	Dubner Hours	Total Labor Hours
1	245	338	414	323	2,001
2	177	333	598	340	2,030
3	271	358	656	340	2,226
4	211	372	631	352	2,154
5	196	339	528	380	2,078
6	135	289	409	339	2,080
7	195	334	382	331	2,073
8	118	293	399	311	1,758
9	116	325	343	328	1,624
10	147	311	338	353	1,889
11	154	304	353	518	1,988
12	146	312	289	440	2,049
13	115	283	388	276	1,796
14	161	307	402	207	1,720
15	274	322	151	287	2,056
16	245	335	228	290	1,890
17	201	350	271	355	2,187
18	183	339	440	300	2,032
19	237	327	475	284	1,856
20	175	328	347	337	2,068
21	152	319	449	279	1,813
22	188	325	336	244	1,808

Week	Standby Hours	Total Staff Present	Remote Hours	Dubner Hours	Total Labor Hours
23	188	322	267	253	1,834
24	197	317	235	272	1,973
25	261	315	164	223	1,839
26	232	331	270	272	1,935

 STANDBY

Before you develop a model to predict standby hours, you need to consider the principle of parsimony. **Parsimony** means that you want to develop a regression model that includes the fewest number of independent variables that permit an adequate interpretation of the dependent variable. Regression models with fewer independent variables are easier to interpret, particularly because they are less likely affected by collinearity problems (described in Section 11.7).

The selection of an appropriate model when many independent variables are under consideration involves complexities that are not present with a model with only two independent variables. The evaluation of all possible regression models is more computationally complex, and although you can quantitatively evaluate competing models, there may not be a *uniquely best* model but rather several *equally appropriate* models.

To begin analyzing the standby hours data, the *VIF* [see Equation (11.10) on page 371] is computed to measure the amount of collinearity among the independent variables. Figure 11.10 shows Minitab output of the *VIF* values along with the regression equation. Observe that all the *VIF* values are relatively small, ranging from a high of 2.0 for the total labor hours to a low of 1.2 for remote hours. Thus, on the basis of the criteria developed by Snee that all *VIF* values should be less than 5.0 [see Reference 7], there is little evidence of collinearity among the set of independent variables.

```
The regression equation is
Standby = - 331 + 1.25 Staff - 0.118 Remote - 0.297 Dubner + 0.131 Labor


Predictor    Coef  SE Coef     T      P   VIF
Constant   -330.8    110.9  -2.98  0.007
Staff      1.2456   0.4121   3.02  0.006  1.7
Remote    -0.11842  0.05432  -2.18  0.041  1.2
Dubner    -0.2971   0.1179   -2.52  0.020  1.5
Labor      0.13053  0.05932   2.20  0.039  2.0


S = 31.8350   R-Sq = 62.3%   R-Sq(adj) = 55.1%


Analysis of Variance

Source          DF    SS    MS     F      P
Regression       4  35182  8795  8.68  0.000
Residual Error  21  21283  1013
Total           25  56465
```

FIGURE 11.10   Minitab Regression Model to Predict Standby Hours Based on Four Independent Variables

The Stepwise Regression Approach to Model Building

You continue your analysis of the standby hours data by attempting to determine the sub-set of all independent variables that yield an adequate and appropriate model. The first approach described here is **stepwise regression**, which attempts to find the "best" regression model without examining all possible models.

In Section 11.5, you used the t test or F test to determine whether a particular slope made a significant contribution to a multiple regression model. Stepwise regression extends these tests to a model with any number of independent variables. An important feature of this stepwise approach is that an independent variable that has entered into the model at an early stage may subsequently be removed after other independent variables are considered. Thus, in stepwise regression, variables are either added to or deleted from the regression model at each step of the model-building process. The stepwise procedure terminates with the selection of a best-fitting model when no additional variables can be added to or deleted from the last model evaluated.

Figure 11.11 represents Minitab stepwise regression output for the standby hours data, while Figure 11.12 illustrates JMP output. For this example, a significance level of 0.05 is used to enter a variable into the model or to delete a variable from the model. The first variable entered into the model is total staff, the variable that correlates most highly with the dependent variable standby hours. Because the p-value of 0.001 is less than 0.05, total staff is included in the regres-sion model.

```
 Alpha-to-Enter: 0.05  Alpha-to-Remove: 0.05


Response is Standby on 4 predictors, with N = 26


Step              1       2
Constant      -272.4  -330.7

Staff           1.42    1.76
T-Value         3.72    4.66
P-Value        0.001   0.000

Remote                 -0.139
T-Value                 -2.36
P-Value                 0.027

S               38.6    35.4
R-Sq           36.60   48.99
R-Sq(adj)      33.96   44.56
Mallows C-p     13.3     8.4
```

FIGURE 11.11   Minitab Stepwise Regression Output for the Standby Hours Data

The next step involves selecting a second variable for the model. The second variable cho-sen is one that makes the largest contribution to the model, given that the first independent vari-able has been selected. For this model, the second variable is remote hours. Because the p-value of 0.027 for remote hours is less than 0.05, remote hours is included in the regression model.

After remote hours is entered into the model, the stepwise procedure determines whether total staff is still an important contributing variable or whether it can be eliminated from the model. Because the p-value of 0.0001 for total staff is less than 0.05, total staff remains in the regression model.

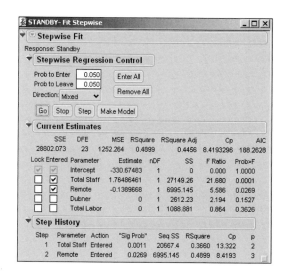

FIGURE 11.12 JMP Stepwise Regression Output for the Standby Hours Data

The next step involves selecting a third independent variable for the model. Because none of the other variables meets the 0.05 criterion for entry into the model, the stepwise procedure terminates with a model that includes total staff present and the number of remote hours.

This stepwise regression approach to model building was originally developed more than four decades ago, in an era in which regression analysis on mainframe computers involved the costly use of large amounts of processing time. Under such conditions, stepwise regression became widely used, although it provides a limited evaluation of alternative models. With today's extremely fast personal computers, the evaluation of many different regression models is completed quickly at a very small cost. Thus, a more general way of evaluating alternative regression models, in this era of fast computers, is the best subsets approach discussed next. Stepwise regression is not obsolete, however. Today, many businesses use stepwise regression as part of a new research technique called **data mining**, where huge data sets are explored to discover significant statistical relationships among a large number of variables. These data sets are so large that the best-subsets approach is impractical.

The Best-Subsets Approach to Model Building

The **best-subsets approach** evaluates either all possible regression models for a given set of independent variables or the best subsets of models for a given number of independent variables. Figure 11.13 presents Minitab output of all possible regression models for the standby hours data, while Figure 11.14 illustrates JMP output.

A criterion often used in model building is the adjusted r^2, which adjusts the r^2 of each model to account for the number of variables in the model, as well as for the sample size. Because model building requires you to compare models with different numbers of independent variables, the adjusted r^2 is more appropriate than r^2.

```
Response is Standby

                                        R D
                                        S e u L
                                        t m b a
                                        a o n b
                             Mallows     f t e o
Vars  R-Sq  R-Sq(adj)        C-p      S  f e r r
  1   36.6     34.0         13.3  38.621  X
  1   17.1     13.7         24.2  44.162        X
  1    6.0      2.1         30.4  47.035     X
  2   49.0     44.6          8.4  35.387  X X
  2   45.0     40.2         10.6  36.749  X   X
  2   42.9     37.9         11.8  37.447      X X
  3   53.8     47.5          7.8  34.443  X   X X
  3   53.6     47.3          7.8  34.503  X X X
  3   50.9     44.2          9.3  35.492  X X   X
  4   62.3     55.1          5.0  31.835  X X X X
```

FIGURE 11.13   Minitab Best-Subsets Regression Output for the Standby Hours Data

Model	Number	RSquare	RMSE
Stepwise Fit			
All Possible Models			
Total Staff,Remote,Dubner,Total Labor	4	0.6231	31.8350
Total Staff,Dubner,Total Labor	3	0.5378	34.4426
Total Staff,Remote,Dubner	3	0.5362	34.5029
Total Staff,Remote,Total Labor	3	0.5092	35.4921
Remote,Dubner,Total Labor	3	0.4591	37.2608
Total Staff,Remote	2	0.4899	35.3873
Total Staff,Dubner	2	0.4499	36.7490
Dubner,Total Labor	2	0.4288	37.4466
Total Staff,Total Labor	2	0.3754	39.1579
Remote,Total Labor	2	0.2238	43.6540
Remote,Dubner	2	0.0612	48.0087
Total Staff	1	0.3660	38.6206
Total Labor	1	0.1710	44.1619
Dubner	1	0.0597	47.0345
Remote	1	0.0091	48.2836

FIGURE 11.14   JMP All Possible Regression Models Output for the Standby Hours Data

Referring to Figure 11.13, you see that the adjusted r^2 reaches a maximum value of 55.1 when all four independent variables plus the intercept term (for a total of five estimated regression coefficients) are included in the model. Observe that Figure 11.14 provides only the r^2 value for each model, but highlights the model with the highest r^2 for a given number of independent variables. You can then use the stepwise features of JMP to compute the adjusted r^2 for any model along with the C_p statistic, which will be discussed next.

A second criterion often used in the evaluation of competing models is the C_p statistic developed by Mallows [see Reference 4]. The C_p statistic[1] measures the differences between a fitted regression model and a *true* model, along with random error.

When a regression model with k independent variables contains only random differences from a *true* model, the mean value of C_p is the number of regression coefficients including the Y intercept in the model. Thus, in evaluating many alternative regression models, the goal is to find models whose C_p is close to or less than the number of regression coefficients including the Y intercept in the model.

In Figure 11.13 above, you see that only the model with all four independent variables considered contains a C_p value close to or below the number of regression coefficients including the

---

[1] The C_p presented in this section is entirely different from the C_p statistic that measures the capability of a process.

Y intercept in the model. Therefore, you should choose this model. Although it was not the case here, the C_p statistic often provides several alternative models for you to evaluate in greater depth using other criteria such as parsimony, interpretability, and departure from model assumptions (as evaluated by residual analysis). The model selected using stepwise regression has a C_p value of 8.4, which is substantially above the suggested criterion of the number of regression coefficients including the Y intercept in the model (equals 3 for that model).

When you have finished selecting the independent variables to include in the model, you should perform a residual analysis to evaluate the aptness of the selected model. Figure 11.15 presents Minitab residual analysis output.

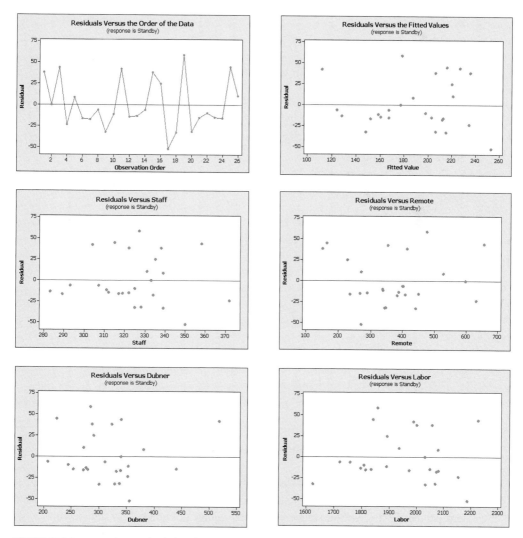

FIGURE 11.15 Minitab Residual Plots for the Standby Hours Data

You see that the plots of the residuals versus the total staff, the remote hours, the Dubner hours, and the total labor hours all reveal no apparent pattern. In addition, a histogram of the residuals (not shown here) indicates only moderate departure from normality.

Thus, from Figure 11.10 on page 373, the regression equation is:

Predicted standby hours = -330.83 + [1.2456 × total staff hours] – [0.1184 × total remote hours] – [0.2971 × Dubner hours] + [0.1305 × total labor hours]

The C_p Statistic (Optional)

$$C_p = \frac{(1 - R_k^2)(n - T)}{1 - R_T^2} - [n - 2(k+1)] \tag{11.11}$$

where

  k = number of independent variables included in a regression model

  T = total number of regression coefficients (including the intercept) to be estimated

     in the full regression model

  R_k^2 = coefficient of multiple determination for a regression model that

     has k independent variables

  R_T^2 = coefficient of multiple determination for a full regression model

     that contains all T estimated regression coefficients

Using Equation (11.11) to compute C_p for the model containing total staff present and remote hours,

  $n = 26$ $k = 2$ $T = 4 + 1 = 5$ $R_k^2 = 0.490$ $R_T^2 = 0.623$

so that

$$C_p = \frac{(1 - 0.49)(26 - 5)}{1 - 0.623} - [26 - 2(2 + 1)]$$
$$= 8.42$$

To summarize, you should follow these steps when building a regression model:

1. Compile a list of all potential independent variables.

2. Fit a regression model that includes all the independent variables under consideration and determine the *VIF* for each independent variable. Three possible results can occur:

    a. None of the independent variables have a *VIF* > 5; proceed to step 3.

   b. One of the independent variables has a *VIF* > 5; eliminate that independent variable and proceed to step 3.

   c. More than one of the independent variables has a *VIF* > 5; eliminate the independent variable that has the highest *VIF*, and repeat step 2.

3. Perform a best-subsets or all-subsets regression with the remaining independent variables and determine the C_p statistic and/or the adjusted r^2 for each model

4. List all models that have C_p close to or less than $(k + 1)$ and/or a high adjusted r^2.

5. From those models listed in step 5, choose a best model.

6. Perform a complete analysis of the model chosen, including a residual analysis.

7. Depending on the results of the residual analysis, add curvilinear terms, transform variables and reanalyze the data.

8. Use the selected model for prediction and inference.

Figure 11.16 represents a road map for these steps in model building.

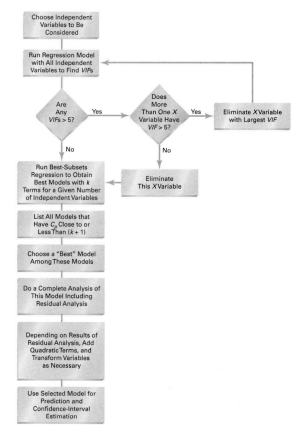

FIGURE 11.16 Road Map for Model Building

Model Validation

The final step in the model building process is to validate the regression model. This step involves checking the model against data that was not part of the analyzed sample. Several ways of validating a regression model are as follows:

1. Collect new data and compare the results.
2. Compare the results of the regression model to theoretical expectations or previous results.
3. If the data set is large, split the data into two parts: the main sample and a hold-out sample. You use the main sample to develop your regression model and the hold-out sample to validate the regression model. The hold-out sample provides an opportunity to test the validity of the regression model on a data set other than the data set (the main sample) used to develop the regression model.

Perhaps the best way of validating a regression model is by collecting new data. If the results with new data are consistent to the fitted regression model, you have strong reason to believe that the fitted regression model is applicable in a wide set of circumstances.

If it is not possible to collect new data, you can compare your regression coefficients and predictions to theoretical expectations or other empirical results.

11.9 LOGISTIC REGRESSION

The discussion of the simple linear regression model in Section 11.1 and the multiple regression models in Sections 11.2–11.8 only considered measurement type dependent variables. However, sometimes, the dependent variable is a categorical variable that takes on one of only two possible values. For example, a customer is satisfied or a customer is not satisfied. The use of simple or multiple least-squares regression for a two-category response variable (CTQ or Y) often violates the normality assumption and can lead to impossible values of the CTQ (Y).

An alternative approach, **logistic regression**, originally applied in the health sciences [see Reference 2], enables you to use regression models to predict the probability of a particular categorical binary response for a given set of independent variables (CTPs or Xs). This logistic regression model is based on the **odds ratio**, which represents the probability of a success compared with the probability of failure:

$$\text{Odds ratio} = \frac{\text{probability of success}}{1 - \text{probability of success}} \tag{11.12}$$

Using Equation (11.12), if the probability of success for an event is 0.50, the odds ratio is as follows:

$$\text{Odds ratio} = \frac{0.50}{1 - 0.50} = 1.0, \text{ or } 1 \text{ to } 1$$

If the probability of success for an event is 0.75, the odds ratio is as follows:

$$\text{Odds ratio} = \frac{0.75}{1-0.75} = 3.0, \text{ or } 3 \text{ to } 1$$

The logistic regression model is based on the natural logarithm (LN) of this odds ratio. The logistic regression model for two independent variables is the following:

LN(estimated odds ratio) = Y intercept + (slope of $X_1 \times X_1$ value) + (slope of $X_2 \times X_2$ value) (11.13a)

or

LN(estimated odds ratio) = $b_0 + b_1 X_1 + b_2 X_2$ (11.13b)

A mathematical method called *maximum likelihood estimation* is usually used to develop a regression equation to predict the natural logarithm of this odds ratio. Once you have determined the logistic regression equation, you compute the estimated odds ratio.

Estimated odds ratio = $e^{\text{LN(estimated odds ratio)}}$ (11.14)

where e is the mathematical constant 2.718282.

Once you have computed the estimated odds ratio, you find the estimated probability of success:

$$\text{Estimated probability of success} = \frac{\text{estimated odds ratio}}{1+\text{estimated odds ratio}}$$ (11.15)

Logarithms (Optional)

The logarithm of a number is the power that the base number needs to be raised to in order to equal the number of interest. For example:

$10 \times 10 = 10^2 = 100$

The number 10 raised to the second power (squared) equals 100. Base 10 logarithms are called *common logarithms* (and use the symbol LOG). Because 100 is equal to 10 raised to the second power, the logarithm of 100 is 2. Using another example, the logarithm of 80 is approximately 1.903. (You can use a scientific calculator to compute this.) This means that 10 raised to the 1.903 power equals 80.

Natural logarithms (which use the symbol LN) have a base that is the mathematical constant e, approximately equal to 2.718282. The natural logarithm of 100 is approximately equal to 4.6052. This means that e ($e = 2.718282$) raised to the 4.6052 power equals 100.

To illustrate the logistic regression model, recall from Chapter 10, "Design of Experiments," that a hotel that served many business customers had instituted a new process of delivering breakfast via room service. When customers finished breakfast, they were asked to indicate whether they were satisfied with the delivery process. Table 11.6 summarizes the results from a random sample of 30 customers, along with the delivery time difference and whether the customer had previously stayed at the hotel.

TABLE 11.6 Customer Satisfaction, Delivery Time Difference, and Previous Stay at Hotel

Satisfaction	Delivery Time Difference	Previous
No	6.1	No
Yes	4.5	Yes
Yes	0.8	No
Yes	1.3	Yes
Yes	3.6	Yes
Yes	2.7	Yes
No	5.9	No
Yes	4.5	Yes
No	4.8	Yes
Yes	2.1	No
Yes	4.1	Yes
No	5.6	Yes
Yes	3.8	Yes
Yes	2.3	No
No	3.2	No
Yes	3.6	Yes
No	6.0	No
Yes	4.4	Yes
Yes	0.9	No
Yes	1.2	Yes
No	3.8	No
Yes	3.5	Yes
No	4.0	Yes
Yes	4.3	Yes
No	4.9	Yes
Yes	2.3	No
Yes	3.8	Yes
No	5.9	Yes
Yes	3.7	Yes
Yes	2.5	No

 SATISFACTION

Figures 11.17 and 11.18 represent Minitab and JMP output for the logistic regression model. There are two independent variables, X_1 (delivery time difference) and X_2 (previous stay at hotel).

```
Logistic Regression Table
                                                                     95%
                                                                      CI
Predictor                     Coef  SE Coef      Z      P  Odds Ratio  Lower
Constant                   14.7567  6.56055   2.25  0.024
Delivery Time Difference  -5.05457  2.27853  -2.22  0.027        0.01   0.00
Previous
 1                         8.43943  4.29026   1.97  0.049     4625.91   1.03

Predictor                      Upper
Constant
Delivery Time Difference        0.56
Previous
 1                       20755983.77

Log-Likelihood = -5.629
Test that all slopes are zero: G = 26.933, DF = 2, P-Value = 0.000


Goodness-of-Fit Tests

Method           Chi-Square  DF      P
Pearson             22.7232  23  0.477
Deviance            11.2581  23  0.980
Hosmer-Lemeshow      8.9074   8  0.350
```

FIGURE 11.17 Minitab Logistic Regression Output for the Hotel Satisfaction Data

Nominal Logistic Fit for Satisfaction

Iteration History

Whole Model Test

Model	-LogLikelihood	DF	ChiSquare	Prob>ChiSq
Difference	13.466395	2	26.93279	<.0001*
Full	5.629030			
Reduced	19.095425			

RSquare (U)	0.7052
Observations (or Sum Wgts)	30

Converged by Gradient

Lack Of Fit

Source	DF	-LogLikelihood	ChiSquare
Lack Of Fit	23	5.6290301	11.25806
Saturated	25	0.0000000	Prob>ChiSq
Fitted	2	5.6290301	0.9804

Parameter Estimates

Term	Estimate	Std Error	ChiSquare	Prob>ChiSq
Intercept	-14.756524	6.5604911	5.06	0.0245*
Delivery Time Difference	5.05451072	2.2785101	4.92	0.0265*
Previous	-8.439329	4.2902227	3.87	0.0492*

For log odds of 0/1

Effect Likelihood Ratio Tests

Source	Nparm	DF	L-R ChiSquare	Prob>ChiSq
Delivery Time Difference	1	1	25.8008399	<.0001*
Previous	1	1	10.159666	0.0014*

FIGURE 11.18 JMP Logistic Regression Output for the Hotel Satisfaction Data

(Because the first value for satisfaction is not satisfied (0), JMP is predicting the probability of not being satisfied while Minitab is predicting the probability of being satisfied. Thus, the signs of the regression coefficients are the opposite of those shown by Minitab.)

From Figure 11.17, the regression model is stated as:

$$LN \text{ (estimated odds ratio)} = 14.7567 - 5.05457X_1 + 8.43943X_2$$

The regression coefficients are interpreted as follows:

1. The regression constant is 14.7567. Thus, for a customer who did not have any delivery time difference and who did not stay at the hotel previously, the estimated natural logarithm of the odds ratio of being satisfied with the delivery service is 14.7567.

2. The regression coefficient for delivery time difference is -5.05457. Therefore, holding constant the effect of whether the customer had previously stayed at the hotel, for each increase of one minute in the delivery time difference, the estimated natural logarithm of the odds ratio of being satisfied with the delivery service decreases by 5.05457. Therefore, the longer the delivery time difference, the less likely the customer is to be satisfied with the delivery service.

3. The regression coefficient for previous stay at the hotel is 8.43943. Holding constant the delivery time difference, the estimated natural logarithm of the odds ratio of being satisfied with the delivery service increases by 8.43943 for customers who have previously stayed at the hotel compared with customers who have not previously stayed at the hotel. Therefore, customers who have previously stayed at the hotel are more likely to be satisfied with the delivery service.

As was the case with least-squares regression models, a main purpose of performing logistic regression analysis is to provide predictions of a dependent variable. For example, consider a customer who had a delivery time difference of 4 minutes and previously stayed at the hotel. What is the probability this customer will be satisfied with the delivery service? Using delivery time difference = 4 minutes and previous stay = Yes ($X_2 = 1$) from Figure 11.17, you have:

$$LN(\text{estimated odds ratio}) = 14.7567 - (5.05457 \times 4) + (8.43943 \times 1) = 2.97785$$

Using Equation (11.14) on page 381:

$$\text{estimated odds ratio} = e^{2.97785} = 19.6455$$

Therefore, the odds are 19.6455 to 1 that a customer who had a delivery time difference of 4 minutes and previously stayed at the hotel will be satisfied with the delivery service. Using Equation (11.15) on page 381, this odds ratio can be converted to a probability:

Thus, the estimated probability is 0.9516 that a customer who had a delivery time difference of 4 minutes and previously stayed at the hotel will be satisfied with the delivery service. In other words, 95.16% of such individuals are expected to be satisfied with the delivery service.

Now that you have used the logistic regression model for prediction, you can consider whether the model is a good-fitting model and whether each of the independent variables included in the model makes a significant contribution to the model. The **deviance statistic** is frequently used to determine whether or not the current model provides a good fit to the data. This statistic measures the fit of the current model compared with a model that has as many parameters as there are data points (what is called a *saturated* model). The null and alternative hypotheses are:

H_0: The model is a good-fitting model.

H_1: The model is not a good-fitting model.

When using the deviance (or lack of fit) statistic for logistic regression, the null hypothesis represents a good-fitting model, which is the opposite of the null hypothesis when using the F test for the multiple regression model (see Section 11.2). From Figure 11.17 or 11.18 on page 383, the deviance (or lack of fit) = 11.2581 and the p-value = 0.980 > 0.05. Thus, you do not reject H_0, and you conclude that the model is a good-fitting one.

Now that you have concluded that the model is a good-fitting one, you need to evaluate whether each of the independent variables makes a significant contribution to the model in the presence of the others. As was the case with multiple regression in Section 11.5, the test statistic is based on the ratio of the regression coefficient to the standard error of the regression coefficient. In logistic regression, this ratio is defined by the **Wald statistic**, which approximately follows the normal distribution. In Figure 11.17, the Wald statistic $Z = -2.22$ for delivery time difference and 1.97 for previous stay at the hotel. In Figure 11.18, the square of the Wald statistic, labeled as Chisquare, is provided (for these data, $(-2.22)^2 = 4.92$ and $(1.97)^2 = 3.87$). Because $-2.22 < 1.96$ and $1.97 > 1.96$ and the p-values are 0.027 and 0.049, you can conclude that each of the two explanatory variables makes a contribution to the model in the presence of the other. Therefore, you should include both independent variables in the model.

SUMMARY

In this chapter, you learned how to use several independent variables to predict a dependent variable (CTQ). You used independent and dependent variables that were either measurement type or categorical and also applied both stepwise and all possible regression approaches.

REFERENCES

1. Berenson, M. L., D. M. Levine, and T. C. Krehbiel, *Basic Business Statistics: Concepts and Applications*, 10th ed. (Upper Saddle River, NJ: Prentice Hall, 2006).

2. Hosmer, D. W., and S. Lemeshow, *Applied Logistic Regression*, 2nd ed. (New York: Wiley, 2001).

3. *JMP Version 6* (Cary, NC: SAS Institute, 2005).

4. Kutner, M. H., C. Nachtsheim, J. Neter, and W. Li, *Applied Linear Statistical Models*, 5th ed. (New York: McGraw-Hill-Irwin, 2005).

5. Marquardt, D. W., "You should standardize the predictor variables in your regression models," discussion of "A critique of some ridge regression methods," by G. Smith and F. Campbell, *Journal of the American Statistical Association*, 75 (1980): 87–91.

6. *Minitab for Windows Version 14* (State College, PA: Minitab Inc., 2004).

7. Snee, R. D., "Some aspects of nonorthogonal data analysis, part I. Developing prediction equations," *Journal of Quality Technology*, 5 (1973): 67–79.

APPENDIX 11.1

USING MINITAB FOR MULTIPLE REGRESSION

Generating a Multiple Regression Equation

To carry out a multiple regression analysis for the moving company data, open the **MOVING.MTW** worksheet and select **Stat→ Regression→ Regression**.

1. Enter **C1** or **Hours** in the Response: edit box and **C2** or **Feet** and **C3** or **Large** in the Predictors: edit box. Click the **Graphs** button.

2. In the Regression—Graphs dialog box, in the Residuals for Plots: edit box, select the **Regular** option button. For Residual Plots, select the **Histogram of residuals** and the **Residuals versus fits** check boxes. In the Residuals versus the variables: edit box, select **C2** or **Feet** and **C3** or **Large**. Click the **OK** button to return to the Regression dialog box.

3. Click the **Results** option button. In the Regression Results dialog box, click the **In addition, the full table of fits and residuals** option button. Click the **OK** button to return to the Regression dialog box.

4. Click the **Options** button. Select the **Variance inflation factors** check box. In the Prediction interval for new observations: edit box, enter the desired values for Feet and Large. Enter **95** in the Confidence level: edit box. Click the **OK** button to return to the Regression dialog box. Click the **OK** button.

Using Minitab for a Three-Dimensional Plot

You can use Minitab to construct a three-dimensional plot when there are two independent variables in the regression model. To illustrate the three-dimensional plot with the moving company data, open the **MOVING.MTW** worksheet. Select **Graph → 3D Scatterplot**.

1. In the 3D Scatterplots dialog box, select the **Simple** button.

2. In the 3D Scatterplot—Simple dialog box (see Figure A11.1), enter **C1** or **Hours** in the Z variable edit box, **C2** or **Feet** in the Y variable edit box, and **C3** or **Large** in the X variable edit box. Click the **OK** button.

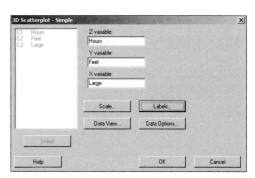

FIGURE A11.1 Minitab 3D Scatterplot—Simple Dialog Box

Using Minitab for Dummy Variables and Interactions

In order to perform regression analysis with dummy variables, the categories of the dummy variable are coded as 0 and 1. If the dummy variable has not already been coded as a 0–1 variable, Minitab can recode the variable. To illustrate this with the moving company data, open the **MOVING.MTW** worksheet. In this worksheet, the elevator variable in column C4 has been entered as Yes and No. To recode this variable using Minitab, select **Calc → Make Indicator Variables**. In the Indicator variables for: edit box, enter **Elevator** or **C4**. In the Store results in: edit box, enter **C5 C6**, because you need to specify a column for each possible definition of the dummy variable even though only one column (C6) will be used in the regression analysis. Click the **OK** button. Observe that No is coded as 1 in C5, and Yes is coded as 1 in C6. Label C6 as **ElevatorD**.

To define an interaction term that is the product of cubic feet and the dummy variable elevator, select **Calc → Calculator**. In the Store result in variable: edit box, enter **C7**. In the Expression: edit box, enter **Feet * ElevatorD** or **C2 * C6**. Click the **OK** button. C7 now contains a new *X* variable that is the product of C2 and C6. Label C7 as **Feet * ElevatorD**.

Using Minitab for Stepwise Regression and Best-Subsets Regression

You can use Minitab for model building with either stepwise regression or best-subsets regression. To illustrate model building with the standby hours data, open the **STANDBY.MTW** worksheet. To perform stepwise regression, select **Stat → Regression → Stepwise**.

1. In the Stepwise Regression dialog box (see Figure A11.2) in the Response: edit box, enter **STANDBY** or **C1**.

2. In the Predictors: edit box, enter **Staff** or **C2**, **Remote** or **C3**, **Dubner** or **C4**, and **Labor** or **C5**. Click the **Methods** button.

3. In the Stepwise—Methods dialog box (see Figure A11.3), select the **Stepwise** option button. Enter **0.05** in the Alpha to enter: edit box and **0.05** in the Alpha to remove edit box. Enter **4** in the *F* to enter: edit box and **4** in the *F* to remove: edit box. Click the **OK** button to return to the Stepwise Regression dialog box. Click the **OK** button.

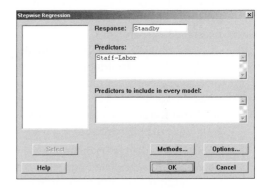

FIGURE A11.2 Minitab Stepwise Regression Dialog Box

To perform a best-subsets regression, select **Stat → Regression → Best Subsets**.

1. In the Best Subsets Regression dialog box (see Figure A11.4), in the Response: edit box, enter **Standby** or **C1**.

2. In the Free Predictors: edit box, enter **Staff** or **C2**, **Remote** or **C3**, **Dubner** or **C4**, and **Labor** or **C5**. Click the **Options** button. Enter **3** in the Models of each size to print edit box. Click the **OK** button to return to the Best Subsets Regression dialog box. Click the **OK** button.

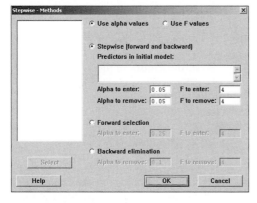

FIGURE A11.3 Minitab Stepwise—Methods Dialog Box

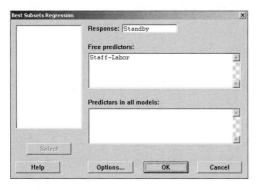

FIGURE A11.4 Minitab Best Subsets Regression Dialog Box

Using Minitab for Logistic Regression

To illustrate the use of Minitab for logistic regression with the room service delivery satisfaction example, open the **SATISFACTION. MTW** worksheet. To perform a logistic regression, select **Stat → Regression → Binary Logistic Regression**.

In the Binary Logistic Regression dialog box (see Figure A11.5), in the Response: edit box, enter **C1** or **Satisfaction**. In the Model: edit box, enter **C2** or **Delivery Time Difference** and **C3** or **Previous**. In the Factors: edit box, enter **C3** or **Previous** because it is a categorical variable. Click the **OK** button.

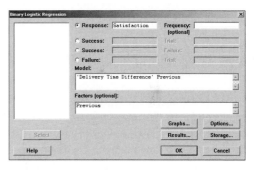

FIGURE A11.5 Minitab Binary Logistic Regression Dialog Box

Appendix 11.2

USING JMP FOR MULTIPLE REGRESSION

Generating a Multiple Regression Equation

To carry out a multiple regression analysis for the moving company data, open the **MOVING.JMP** data table and select **Analyze → Fit Model**.

1. Select **Hours** and click the **Y** button.

2. Select **Feet** and **Large** and click the **Add** button. Click the **Run Model** button.

3. To generate residual plots for each independent variable, click the red triangle to the left of Response Hours. Select **Save Columns →
Residuals** (see Figure A11.6).

FIGURE A11.6   Using JMP to Save Residuals

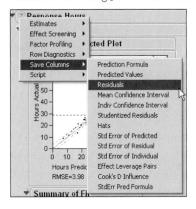

4. Select **Analyze → Fit Y by X**. Enter **Residual Hours** in the **Y**, **Response** box. Enter **Feet** in the **X**, **Factor** edit box. Click the **OK** button.

5. Select **Analyze → Fit Y by X**. Enter **Residual Hours** in the **Y**, **Response** box. Enter **Large** in the **X, Factor** edit box. Click the **OK** button.

Using JMP for Dummy Variables

To create a dummy variable for presence of an elevator coded as a 0–1 variable for the moving company data, open the **MOVING.JMP** data table. Select **Cols →
New Column**. Then select **Column Properties → Formula → Conditional → If** and do the following (see Figure A11.7):

1. Enter **Elevator == "Yes"** in the expression area.

2. Enter **1** as the clause in the then area.

3. Enter **0** as the clause in the else area.

4. Click the **OK** button.

5. Select **Continuous** in the Data Type option box. If you do not code Elevator as a continuous variable, JMP uses a -1, 0, +1 coding scheme instead of a 0 and 1 coding scheme [see Reference 3]. With this coding scheme, the regression coefficients are interpreted

as how much the response for each level differs from the average across all levels. Provide a name for the variable in the Column Name edit box. Click the **OK** button.

6. Select **Analyze → Fit Model**.

7. Select **Hours** and click the **Y** button.

8. Select **Feet** and **ElevatorD** (or the name of the variable you just created) and click the **Add** button. Click the **Run Model** button.

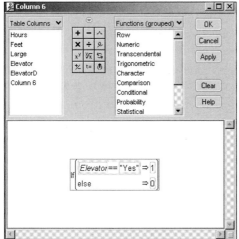

FIGURE A11.7 Using JMP to Create a Dummy Variable

To generate residual plots for each independent variable, click the red triangle to the left of Response Hours. Select **Save Columns → Residuals**.

1. Select **Analyze → Fit Y by X**. Enter **Residual Hours** in the **Y**, **Response** box. Enter **Feet** in the **X**, **Factor** edit box. Click the **OK** button.

2. Select **Analyze → Fit Y by X**. Enter **Residual Hours** in the **Y**, **Response** box. Enter **ElevatorD** in the **X**, **Factor** edit box. Click the **OK** button.

Using JMP for Interactions

To generate a regression model with an interaction term, open the **MOVING.JMP** data table. Select **Cols → New Column → Column Properties → Formula** and do the following:

1. Enter **Feet* ElevatorD** in the expression area. Click the **OK** button.

2. Enter **Feet* ElevatorD** in the Column Name edit box. Click the **OK** button.

3. Select **Analyze → Fit Model**.

4. Select **Hours** and click the **Y** button.

5. Select **Feet, ElevatorD,** and **Feet* ElevatorD** and click the **Add** button.

6. Click the **Run Model** button.

Using JMP for Stepwise Regression and All Possible Regressions

You can use JMP for model building with either stepwise regression or all possible regressions. To illustrate model building with the standby hours data, open the **STANDBY.JMP** worksheet. Select **Analyze → Fit Model**.

1. Select **Standby** and click the **Y** button.

2. Select **Total Staff**, **Remote**, **Dubner**, and **Labor Hours** and click the **Add** button.

3. In the Personality: edit box, select **Stepwise**. Select **Run Model**.

4. In the Stepwise Regression Control area (see Figure A11.8), enter **0.05** in the Prob to Enter: edit box. Enter **0.05** in the Prob to Leave: edit box. Select **Mixed** in the Direction drop-down list box. Click the **Go** button.

FIGURE A11.8   JMP Stepwise Fit Dialog Box

5. To generate all possible regression
    models, click the red triangle to the left
    of Stepwise Fit. Select **All Possible
    Models** in the **Direction** drop-down
    list box. Click the **Go** button.

Using JMP for Logistic Regression

To illustrate the use of JMP for logistic
regression with the room service delivery satisfaction example, open the **SATISFACTION.
JMP** worksheet.

1. Highlight the **Satisfaction** column.
    Select **Cols → Col Info**. Select
    Nominal in the Modeling Type
    options box. Click the **OK** button. Do
    the same for the **Previous** column.
2. To perform a logistic regression, select
    Analyze → Fit Model.
3. Select **Satisfaction** and click the **Y**
    button.
4. Select **Delivery Time Difference** and
    Previous and click the **Add** button.
    Click the **Run Model** button.

The regression coefficients computed by
JMP are not the same as those computed by
Minitab. This occurs because JMP uses a -1, 0,
+1 coding scheme instead of a 0 and 1 coding
scheme [see Reference 3]. With this coding
scheme, the regression coefficients are interpreted as how much the response for each level
differs from the average across all levels.

ADDITIONAL TOOLS AND METHODS

SECTIONS

LEARNING OBJECTIVES

After reading this chapter, you will be able to:

- Use diagnostic tools for stabilizing, improving, and innovating a process.
- Brainstorm for ideas about a process, product, service, or design.
- Identify the structure for a set of ideas generated in a brainstorming session using an affinity diagram.
- Understand the relationships between the CTQ(s) and CTPs (Xs) using a cause-and-effect diagram.
- Use check sheets to collect data.
- Use stratification to identify the root cause(s) of variation in a CTQ or a CTP (X).
- Schedule a project using a Gantt chart.

INTRODUCTION

In addition to the quantitative tools discussed in Chapter 10, "Design of Experiments" and Chapter 11, "Multiple Regression," this chapter presents additional diagnostic techniques and tools. The techniques and tools are brainstorming, affinity diagrams, cause-and-effect diagrams, check sheets, stratification, and Gantt charts.

12.1 BRAINSTORMING

Brainstorming is a technique used to elicit a large number of ideas from a group using their collective thinking power. It normally takes place in a structured session involving between 3 and 12 people, with 5 or 6 people being the optimal group size. The group should include a variety of people, not all of whom should be technical experts in the particular area under study.

The group facilitator (green belt or black belt) keeps the group members focused, prevents distractions, keeps ideas flowing, and records the outputs (or makes sure that the group members record their own outputs). The brainstorming session should be a closed-door meeting to prevent distractions. Seating should be arranged in a U-shape or circle to promote the flow of ideas among group members.

Procedure

The following steps are recommended *prior to* a brainstorming session:

1. Clearly define the subject of the brainstorming session. This is important. You do not want to have any arguments over the purpose of the brainstorming session at the beginning of the first meeting.
2. Conduct library and internet research on the topic. You do not want the participants in the brainstorming session to reinvent the wheel.
3. Prepare a list of the ideas identified in step 2 and provide a copy to each of the participants before the session.
4. Identify all members of the brainstorming group and select the facilitator (green belt or black belt).
5. Invite all participants to the brainstorming session and remind them to study the list of ideas provided to them on the topic.

The following steps are recommended *at* a brainstorming session:

1. The facilitator posts the topic so that it can be clearly seen by all team members.
2. Each team member prepares a list of ideas about the topic on a piece of paper, or on 3×5 cards with one idea per card. This should take no longer than 10 to 15 minutes. Remind the group members to add to the list of ideas provided to them prior to the brainstorming session.
3. In a circular fashion, each team member reads one idea at a time from his/her list of ideas. As ideas are read, the facilitator records and displays each idea on a flip chart, or alternatively, each team member places his or her 3×5 card in one pile in the middle of the team members. Team members ignore any structure that might exist among the 3×5 cards. Group members continue reading in this circular fashion until all the ideas on everyone's list are read.
4. If a member's next idea is a duplicate of a previously stated idea, then that member goes on to the next idea on his or her list.
5. After each idea is read by a group member, the leader requests all other group members to think of new ideas. Hearing others' ideas may result in new ideas. This is called **piggybacking**. Piggybacking is a very important part of brainstorming. Without piggybacking, team members could just mail in their brainstormed ideas. Piggybacking is where the synergistic and creative magic of brainstorming occurs. The leader continues asking each group member, in turn, for new ideas, until no one can think of any more.
6. Members are free to pass on each go-around but should be encouraged to add something.
7. If the group reaches an impasse, the leader can ask for everyone's "wildest idea." A wild idea can stimulate a valid one from someone else.
8. Brainstorming continues until all team members "pass."

Rules

The following rules should be observed by the participants to ensure that participation is not inhibited:

1. Do not criticize anyone's ideas, by word or gesture.
2. Do not discuss any ideas during the session, except for clarification.
3. Do not hesitate to suggest an idea because it sounds "silly." Many times, such an idea can lead to a "great" idea.
4. Do not allow any group member to present more than one idea at a time.
5. Do not allow the group to be dominated by one or two people.
6. Do not let brainstorming become a gripe session.

Example

A brainstorming session was conducted at a private university during 2003 to identify crises. Internet and library searches were performed prior to the brainstorming session. The purpose of the searches was to identify crises at other universities. The results of these searches were input into the brainstorming session.

The members of the brainstorming session were top-level administrators from selected divisions within the university. All members were viewed by senior management as being capable of identifying current crises and potential threats to the university. A list of 174 crises was the outcome of that brainstorming session. Table 12.1 shows a partial listing (74 of the 174) of the crises.

TABLE 12.1 Partial Brainstormed List of Crises Facing a Private University

1.	Local funding drying up.
2.	Federal funding drying up.
3.	State funding drying up.
4.	Grant dollars as a percentage of applications declining.
5.	Competition for research awards increasing.
6.	No mandatory retirement age.
7.	Some faculty unable to get grants.
8.	Insufficient teaching load to cover all courses offered.
9.	Focus on teaching, as opposed to learning.
10.	Business universities adding competition.
11.	Students focusing on "getting a job," not education for self improvement.
12.	K–12 not doing its job.
13.	U.S. population becoming more diversified.
14.	Drop in number of high school graduates.
15.	Majority of high school students less able to afford university education.
16.	Low faculty productivity.
17.	Some universities have lowered entrance qualifications.
18.	We are *not* focusing on the nontraditional students.
19.	Our schedule is set for the convenience of faculty and traditional students.
20.	Faculty are not student focused.
21.	We need to focus on K–80 education.
22.	We must use our resources more effectively.
23.	Security costs are much higher.
24.	Security is vital to our image.
25.	The Internet communicates image issues fast and world-wide.
26.	More money earmarked for federal regulations.
27.	Insurance rates have increased substantially.
28.	Need to beef up the use of technology.
29.	Need to use more interactive instruction.
30.	Need to educate staff and faculty that "Education is a business."
31.	Use carrots to drive change—not the stick.

32.   Need to solicit ideas for change from the staff.

33.   We need to change our culture here.

34.   We do not work well together.

35.   We do not communicate amongst ourselves.

36.   We do not have the freedom to change gradually.

37.   We need to create or plan a crisis to get people moving.

38.   We can no longer afford to be all things to all people.

39.   We are good at finding crises, but not good at solving them.

40.   Academia has difficulty defining its stakeholders.

41.   It is easier to do something and apologize than to ask permission.

42.   University is a culture of asking permission.

43.   Some colleges within the university have "passé" curriculum.

44.   Change is talked about, but not financially supported.

45.   We allocate resources in ways that do not reward innovation.

46.   Funding is not based on strategic planning.

47.   Getting information technology is a crisis.

48.   Getting information technology used is a crisis.

49.   Difficult to change the culture and attitudes of people so they will use technology.

50.   We need better classrooms for our students.

51.   We need better dorm rooms for our students.

52.   Our dorm rooms need to be built with the future in mind.

53.   Professors view themselves as independent contractors, not as employees.

54.   Need to build trust with faculty.

55.   Security for access to scholarly communications is an issue.

56.   The Internet is changing the definition of publishing.

57.   Issues of "ownership" of information and charging for access need to be addressed.

58.   How scholars communicate is changing.

59.   Technology is changing the need for libraries in current format.

60.   We have a crisis in our social contract with society.

61.   People do not trust institutions anymore.

62.   Concerns about research ethics.

63.   People are "bitter" about their "contract" with the university.

64.   Some organizations and people are more "loyal" than others.

65.   We do not communicate the "depth" we have.

66.   We do not share or use the capability of one part of the university with other parts of the university.

67.   We need more entrepreneurial managers.

68.   Need to shift from "industrial age" to "information age" model.

69.   People need different skills at different times—JIT (just in time) training.

70.   Old attitude: "If we sit here, people will come to us."

71.   We need more endowment.

72.   We need more dollars to use to change things.

73.   University needs to be more aggressive and open to dollar-generating innovations.

74.   Poor relationship between our image and what we offer.

Sometimes, ideas that are generated in a brainstorming session are inappropriate, or not polite, or "politically incorrect." Consequently, people may not verbalize them due to fear of criticism or fear of offending someone. This is a weakness of brainstorming. Nevertheless, a very offensive idea could possibly stimulate someone to think of a fantastic idea.

12.2 AFFINITY DIAGRAM

An **affinity diagram** is used to organize verbal and pictorial data consisting of facts, opinions, intuition, and experience into natural clusters that bring out the latent structure of the problem under study. Frequently, the input into an affinity diagram is the output of a brainstorming session.

Construction

Constructing an affinity diagram begins with identifying a problem. Team composition usually consists of the same people and facilitator who participated in the brainstorming session about the problem under study.

A team should take the following steps to construct an affinity diagram:

1. The team leader transfers all the ideas generated from a brainstorming session to 3×5 cards, recording one idea per card, or collects each team member's 3×5 cards.

2. The team leader spreads all the 3×5 cards on a large surface (table) in no particular order, but all cards face the same direction.

3. *In silence*, all group members simultaneously move the 3×5 cards into clusters so the 3×5 cards in a cluster seem to be related; that is, they have an unspoken affinity (underlying theme) for each other. One team member may move a card to one cluster, and another team member may move the card back to its former cluster; this may go on for a time, but the card will eventually find a home cluster. Clustering is finished once group members stop moving cards. If clustering continues for too long, too few piles may remain, thereby hiding the latent structure of the problem. Cards that do not fit into any cluster should be placed in a miscellaneous cluster.

4. After team members agree that the clusters are complete (usually 3 to 15 clusters emerge), they study the cards in each cluster and prepare a header card that states the underlying theme for each cluster. The header card should contain a short sentence stating the theme represented by the cards in the cluster. For example, the header card should not say, "infrastructure." Rather, it should say: "Improve the buildings and grounds of the company." The team leader prepares the header cards.

5. The team leader transfers the information from the header cards and 3 × 5 cards onto a flip chart, or "butcher paper" (usually rolled paper 36 inches in width), and draws a circle around each cluster. The transfer of information involves either rewriting the header cards and ideas from the clusters onto the flip chart or taping the header cards and 3 × 5 cards from each cluster onto the flip chart. Related clusters are joined with connecting lines. Team members then discuss each cluster's relationship to the problem under study and make any necessary changes to the affinity diagram.

6. The underlying structure of the problem, usually typified by the names of the header cards, is used to understand the product, service, or process problem under study.

Example

A subset of the affinity diagram developed from the 174 brainstormed crises facing a private university (see Table 12.1) is shown in Table 12.2.

TABLE 12.2 Affinity Diagram of Crises Facing a Private University

---

INADEQUATE EDUCATIONAL SYSTEM

Poor productivity.
Insufficient teaching load to cover all courses offered.
Low faculty productivity.
Our schedule is set for the convenience of faculty and traditional students.
No mandatory retirement age.
Some faculty unable to get grants.
Ineffective educational philosophy.
Focus on teaching, as opposed to learning.
Faculty are not student focused.
Need to educate staff and faculty that "Education is a business."
Use carrots to drive change—not the stick.
Need to solicit ideas for change from the staff.
Some colleges within the university have "passé" curriculum.

DYSFUNCTIONAL CULTURE

We need to change our culture here.
We do not work well together.
We do not communicate amongst ourselves.
We do not have the freedom to change gradually.
We are good at finding crises, but not good at solving them.
It is easier to do something and apologize than to ask permission.

(continued)

TABLE 12.2   Affinity Diagram of Crises Facing a Private University (Continued)

University is a culture of asking permission.

Change is talked about, but not financially supported.

We allocate resources in ways that do not reward innovation.

Funding is not based on strategic planning.

Difficult to change the culture and attitudes of people so they will use technology.

Professors view themselves as independent contractors, not as employees.

Need to build trust with faculty.

We have a crisis in our social contract with society.

We do not communicate the "depth" we have.

We do not share the capability between parts of the university.

We need more entrepreneurial managers.

People need different skills at different times.

INEFFECTIVE INTERNAL SYSTEMS TO SUPPORT THE FUTURE

Insufficient technology.

Keep up with technology.

The Internet communicates image issues fast and world-wide.

Need to beef up the use of technology.

Security for access to scholarly communications is an issue.

The Internet is changing the definition of publishing.

Issues of "ownership" of information and charging for access need to be addressed.

How scholars communicate is changing.

Technology is changing the need for libraries in current format.

Need to shift from "industrial age" to "information age" model.

Insufficient infrastructure.

Keep up with infrastructure.

We must use our resources more effectively.

We need better classrooms for our students.

We need better dorm rooms for our students.

Our dorm rooms need to be built with the future in mind.

Getting information technology is a crisis.

Getting information technology used is a crisis.

UNCLEAR UNDERSTANDING OF IDENTITY

We need to focus on K–80 education.

We are *not* focusing on the nontraditional students.

Need to use more interactive instruction.

We need to get people moving.

We can no longer afford to be all things to all people.

Academia has difficulty defining its stakeholders.

Poor relationship between our image and what we offer.

INCREASINGLY HOSTILE EXTERNAL ENVIRONMENT

Safety on campus.

Security is an increasing problem.

Security costs are much higher.

Security is vital to our image.

Competitive environment.

Business universities adding competition.

Some universities have lowered entrance qualifications.

Old attitude: "If we sit here, people will come to us."

K-12 not doing its job.

Changing stakeholders.

Students focusing on "getting a job," not education for self improvement.

U.S. population is becoming more diversified.

Drop in number of high school graduates.

Majority of high school students less able to afford university education.

People do not trust institutions anymore.

People are "bitter" about their "contract" with the university.

Some organizations and people are more "loyal" than others.

Concerns about research ethics.

DECREASING RESOURCE BASE

Need dollars to change things.

Need to be more aggressive and open to dollar-generating innovations.

Local funding drying up.

Federal funding drying up.

State funding drying up.

Grant dollars as a percentage of applications declining.

Competition for research awards increasing.

More money earmarked for federal regulations.

Insurance rates have increased substantially.

We need more endowment.

The six major themes (crises) in the diagram, and their sub-themes (crises), have been organized and reworded to enhance clarity and communicability to stakeholders of the university. As you can see from Table 12.2, the underlying themes are: (1) inadequate educational system; (2) dysfunctional culture; (3) ineffective internal systems to support the future; (4) unclear understanding of identity; (5) increasingly hostile external environment; and (6) decreasing resource base.

12.3 CAUSE-AND-EFFECT DIAGRAM AND MATRIX

A **cause-and-effect (C&E) diagram** is a tool used to organize the possible factors (CTPs or *X*s) that could negatively impact the stability, center, spread, and shape of a CTQ. Cause-and-effect diagrams were discussed briefly in Chapter 5, "Measure Phase." The data analyzed by a cause-and-effect diagram usually comes from a brainstorming session. Cause-and-effect diagrams are also known as *Ishikawa diagrams* or *fishbone diagrams*. Figure 12.1 shows an example of a cause-and-effect diagram for errors in producing printed airline tickets (CTQ) with major causes and subcauses (*X*s).

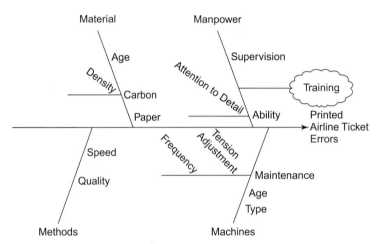

FIGURE 12.1   Cause-and-Effect Diagram for Printed Airline Ticket Errors

Construction

The following steps are recommended for constructing a cause-and-effect diagram:

1. The team leader (green belt or black belt) posts the problem (called an *effect*) for a cause-and-effect diagram in a visible location.

2. Team members are frequently the same individuals who participated in the brainstorming session about the problem (or effect) under study.

3. Team members identify the major causes of the effect under study using a list of universal major causes: machines, methods, material, and manpower.

4. Team members brainstorm for subcauses of each universal cause and prepare one 3 × 5 card for each subcause, or the group uses the 3 × 5 cards from a brainstorming session. Next, they classify each 3 × 5 card into one or more of the universal major causes. Team members are careful to use only 3 × 5 cards that contain potential subcauses of the problem

under study, not solutions. Team members keep subdividing causes into subcauses and sub-subcauses. This procedure creates sub-clusters and sub-sub-clusters of potential causes for each major universal cause.

5. Next, team members brainstorm to fill-in the "holes" in the cause-and-effect diagram.

6. Finally, team members circle the most likely subcause(s). For example, training is circled in a cloud in Figure 12.1.

Constructing a Cause-and-Effect Diagram Using an Affinity Diagram

A particularly effective technique for constructing a cause-and-effect diagram is to combine an affinity diagram and a cause-and-effect diagram. This simply involves substituting the header cards from an affinity diagram for the major universal causes on a cause-and-effect diagram. An example of a cause-and-effect diagram constructed using an affinity diagram to understand the crises facing a university can be seen in Figure 12.2.

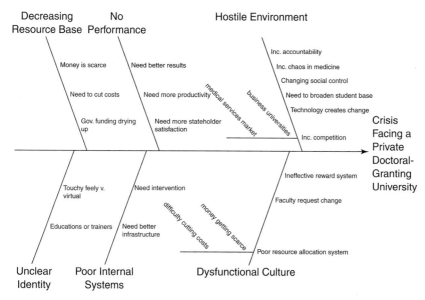

FIGURE 12.2 Cause-and-Effect Diagram of Crisis Facing a Private University

A **cause-and-effect (C&E) matrix** is a tool used to organize the possible causes of problems (CTPs or Xs) for several CTQs simultaneously, and to assist team members in the identification of the most probable causes (CTPs or Xs) for each CTQ. A cause-and-effect matrix is a multivariate cause-and-effect diagram. Cause-and-effect matrices were discussed in detail in Chapter 5.

12.4 CHECK SHEETS

Check sheets are used in Six Sigma projects to collect data on CTPs (*X*s) and CTQs in a format that permits efficient and easy analysis by team members. Three types of check sheets will be discussed: attribute check sheets, measurement check sheets, and defect location check sheets.

Attribute Check Sheet

An **attribute check sheet** is used to gather data about defects in a process. The logical way to collect data about a defect is to determine the number and percentage of defects generated by each cause. Table 12.3 shows an attribute check sheet for the causes of defective responses to telephone calls in a call center.

TABLE 12.3 Attribute Check Sheet of Defects in a Call Center

Type of Defects	Frequency	Percentage
Improper use of English language	2	2.9
Grammatical errors in speech	6	8.6
Inappropriate use of words	3	4.3
Rude response	3	4.3
Didn't know answer to question	25	35.7
Call took too much time	30	42.9
Not available	1	1.4
TOTAL	70	100.1*

* rounding error

This check sheet was created by tallying each type of call defect during four two-hour time periods for one week. It shows the types of defects and how many of each type occurred during the week. Keeping track of these data provides management with information on which to base improvement actions. Assuming that the call center process is stable with respect to defective calls, the process owner's next step is to construct a bar chart called a Pareto diagram [see Reference 1] of the reasons why "call took too much time" and the operator "didn't know the answer to a question." A good place to start studying the "call took too much time" problem is to create a log sheet for a randomly selected sample of calls per day. This may bring to light the biggest contributing factors of long calls. A good place to start studying the "didn't know the answer to the question" problem is to create a log sheet of the questions being asked for a randomly selected sample of calls per day. This may shed light on the questions for which operators most frequently did not know the answer. It makes sense that the same sample of calls per day are used to study the preceding two problems. It would not be surprising if one of the major reasons for "calls took too long" is that the operator "didn't know the answer to a question."

Measurement Check Sheet

Gathering data about a product, service, or process also involves collecting information about measurements, such as cycle time, temperature, size, length, weight, and diameter. These data are best represented on a frequency distribution on a measurement check sheet. Table 12.4 is a measurement check sheet showing the frequency distribution of the cycle times to answer 508 customer's questions that came into a call center between 8:00 A.M. and 5:00 P.M. on January 16, 2005.

TABLE 12.4 Measurement Check Sheet of Cycle Times into a Call Center on January 16, 2005

Cycle Time (in Minutes)	Tally	Frequency
5 < 10 minutes	11111 11111 11111 11111 11111 11111 11111 1	36
10 < 15 minutes	...	178
15 < 20 minutes	...	233
20 < 25 minutes	...	53
25 < 30 minutes	...	8
Total		508

This type of check sheet is a simple way to examine the distribution of a CTQ or CTP (*X*) and its relationship to specification limits (the boundaries of what is considered an acceptable cycle time). The number and percentage of items outside the specification limit is easy to identify so that appropriate action can be taken to reduce the number of defective calls. For example, if a survey of customers revealed that a call that takes 20 minutes or more to answer is unacceptable (upper specification limit > 20), then we see that 12 percent (61/508) of the cycle times for calls are out of specification.

Defect Location Check Sheet

Another way to gather information about defects in a product or design is to use a defect location check sheet. A *defect location check sheet* is a picture of a product or design (or a portion of it) on which an inspector indicates the location and nature of a defect. The inspector is sometimes the person actually doing the work. Figure 12.3 shows a defect location check sheet for collecting data regarding defects on a cube. It shows the location of a defect on the front panel of a cube. The location is marked with an "X." Suppose that an analysis of multiple check sheets reveals that many "Xs" are in the upper-left corner of the cube. If this is so, then further analysis might shed light on the type of defect in the upper-left corner. In turn, this might lead employees to identify the root cause of the defects. This, of course, leads to improvements in the cube production process.

FIGURE 12.3   Defect Location Check Sheet for a Cube

12.5 STRATIFICATION

Stratification is a procedure used to describe the systematic subdivision of a data set. It can be used to break down a problem to discover its root causes and set into motion appropriate corrective actions. Stratification is important to the proper functioning of the DMADV model. Stratification is illustrated in this section using several of the basic tools described earlier in this book.

Stratification and Pareto Diagrams

Figure 12.4 shows 110 observations classified into categories such as A, B, C, etc. By breaking each category into sub-categories (for example, stratifying the 50 items in A into A_1 through A_6 and the 40 items in B into B_1 through B_4), you can focus on the root causes of a problem to establish a corrective action.

In general, when all categories in a Pareto diagram for a CTQ are approximately the same size, as in Figure 12.5(a), stratifying on another CTP or X should be done until a Pareto diagram like the one in Figure 12.5(b) is found. Figure 12.5(a) is called an old mountain stratification (the mountain is worn flat) because no category or categories emerge as the significant few on which to take improvement action. Figure 12.5(b) is called a new mountain stratification (the mountain is young and has high peaks) because one or two categories emerge as the obvious starting point for improvement action. It is critical that anyone using a Pareto diagram continue to stratify a CTQ by different CTPs or Xs until a new mountain Pareto diagram emerges from the analysis. This may require the development of a hypothesis on which CTPs or Xs should be used for stratification in the Pareto diagram (see the DMADV model). Without a new mountain Pareto diagram, there is the absence of a significant few categories, and hence, no prioritization.

For example, a factory kept records on a quarterly basis concerning OSHA (Occupational Safety and Health Administration) reportable accidents over a 5-year period. There were 3,000 accidents in total. The safety director constructed a c-chart [see References 1 and 2] of the data that indicated that the number of accidents per month were a stable and predictable process. Further, he created Pareto diagrams that revealed old mountain structure for accidents broken out by location of accident in the mill, age of person injured, and time of day of the accident, as well as several other characteristics. The safety director conducted some research through the trade association literature and discovered that the "body part injured" and "type of injury" are the two most likely characteristics with which to stratify the accident data. Subsequently, he prepared a Pareto diagram that used body part *and* type of injury as the stratifying characteristic. The analysis revealed that 60% of all accidents ($N = 3,000$) were due to "strains and sprains to the back." "Strains and sprains to the back" was the most significant type of accident in this example. Further stratification of the 1,800 "strains and sprains to the back" accidents by "the method used to lift during the accident" (an X discovered in a review of the safety literature) directed the safety director to require a training program on proper lifting techniques, as opposed to giving everyone a back brace, changing the rules on what can be lifted, etc.

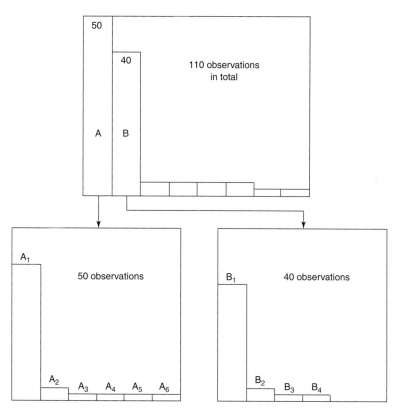

FIGURE 12.4 Pareto Diagrams with Stratification

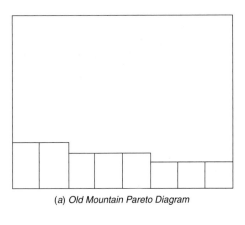

(a) Old Mountain Pareto Diagram

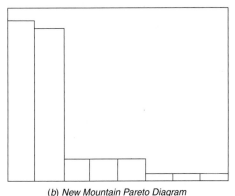

(b) New Mountain Pareto Diagram

FIGURE 12.5 Types of Pareto Diagrams

Stratification and Cause-and-Effect (C&E) Diagrams

Figure 12.6 shows how stratification is used to identify root causes (CTPs or *X*s) that impact CTQs using cause-and-effect diagrams. You see that a second-tier cause-and-effect diagram can be constructed to study in depth any cause (CTP or *X*) shown on a first-tier cause-and-effect diagram, and so on. Stratification continues until the root causes of problems in a CTQ are identified, making possible improvement action(s).

Stratification with Pareto Diagrams and Cause-and-Effect Diagrams

A Pareto diagram is shown in Figure 12.7(a). A cause-and-effect diagram focusing exclusively on one of the bars in the Pareto diagram in Figure 12.7(a) is shown in Figure 12.7(b). This is the correct way to stratify a Pareto diagram to study the root causes of a problem in depth. A cause-and-effect diagram focusing on all the bars in the Pareto diagram in Figure 12.7(a) is shown in Figure 12.7(c). This is the incorrect way to stratify a Pareto diagram to study a problem's root cause(s) in depth. A cause-and-effect diagram should be used to stratify one bar at a time from a Pareto diagram to get an in-depth understanding of the corresponding cause (bar) before any other cause (bar) is studied. This is like peeling an onion to get at its heart.

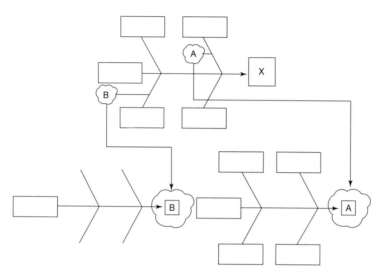

FIGURE 12.6 Stratification and Cause-and-Effect Diagrams

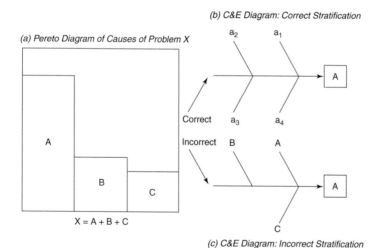

FIGURE 12.7 Stratification with Pareto Diagrams and Cause-and-Effect Diagrams

Stratification with Control Charts, Pareto Diagrams, and Cause-and-Effect Diagrams

A Pareto diagram can be used to identify common causes of variation from a stable process (see Figure 12.8). These common causes of variation can be stratified through Pareto diagrams or cause-and-effect diagrams to determine root causes of problems to identify appropriate improvement actions.

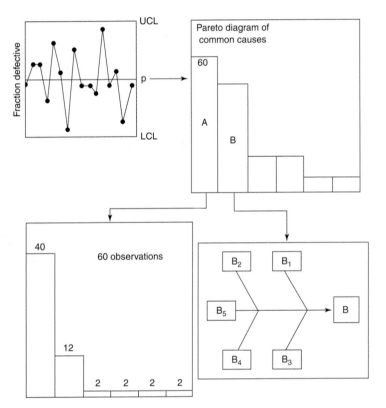

FIGURE 12.8 Stratification with Control Charts, Pareto Diagrams, and Cause-and-Effect Diagrams

Other Combinations of Tools for Stratification

The tools and techniques in this book can be used in combination to identify a problem's (CTQ's) root causes (CTPs or Xs). Once you have determined the root cause(s), you can develop appropriate improvement actions.

12.6 GANTT CHART

A **Gantt chart** is a simple scheduling tool that plots tasks and sub-tasks against time for a Six Sigma project. Once a list of tasks and sub-tasks has been created for a Six Sigma project, then responsibilities can be assigned for each task. Next, team members identify start and stop dates for each task and sub-task. Any comments relevant to a task or sub-task are indicated on the Gantt chart. A generic Gantt chart is shown in Table 12.5. A Gantt chart is useful to identify tasks that can be accomplished in parallel, tasks that cannot start or stop until another task has started or stopped, and time periods that have too many or too few tasks.

TABLE 12.5 Generic Gantt Chart

TASKS	Respon-sibility	TIMELINE (Month)																		COM-MENTS
		J	F	M	A	M	J	J	A	S	O	N	D	J	F	M	A	M	J	
Task 1																				
Sub-Task 1a																				
Sub-Task 1b																				
Task 2																				
Task 3																				
Sub-Task 3a																				
Sub-Task 3b																				
Sub-Task 3c																				

Construction

Each task or sub-task is listed on the vertical axis, as are the person(s) or area(s) responsible for its completion. The horizontal axis is time. It shows the anticipated and actual duration of each task by a bar of the appropriate length. The left end of the bar indicates the earliest start time and the right end of the bar indicates the latest stop time for the task. For example, Table 12.6 shows that activity C cannot start before the end of time period 5 because activity B must be completed before activity C can begin. As each activity is completed, the appropriate bar is shaded.

TABLE 12.6   Example of a Gantt Chart

TASKS	Responsibility	TIMELINE																		
		1	2	3	4	5	6	7	8	9	10	11	12	13	14	15	16	17	18	19
A	HG	■	■	■																	
B	HG		■	■	■																
C	DL						■														
D	DL							■	■	■	■										
E	EP									■	■	■	■	■							
F	EP							■	■			■									
G	EP											■	■	■	■						
H	EP															■	■				
I	HG				■	■	■	■	■	■	■	■	■	■	■	■	■	■	■	■	■

SUMMARY

This chapter presented diagnostic techniques and tools that can be used to help resolve special causes of variation and remove common causes of variation from a process. The techniques discussed in this chapter are brainstorming, affinity diagrams, cause-and-effect diagrams, check sheets, stratification, and Gantt charts.

Brainstorming is a way to elicit a large number of ideas from a group of people in a short period of time. Members of the group use their collective thinking power to generate ideas and unrestrained thoughts.

An affinity diagram is used to organize and consolidate an extensive and unorganized amount of verbal, pictorial, and/or audio data concerning a problem. The data usually consists of facts, opinions, intuition, and experience. Frequently, the input into an affinity diagram is the output of a brainstorming session.

A cause-and-effect (C&E) diagram is a tool used to organize the possible causes of a problem, select the most probable cause, and verify the cause-and-effect relationship between the most probable cause (X) and the problem (effect or CTQ) under study, in order to direct appropriate action to resolving the problem (effect or CTQ) under study. The data analyzed by a cause-and-effect diagram usually comes from a brainstorming session.

Check sheets are used for collecting or gathering data for CTQs, Xs, and CTPs in a logical format. The data collected can be used to construct a control chart, a Pareto diagram, or a histogram.

Stratification is a procedure used to describe the systematic subdivision of CTQ data by Xs or CTPs to obtain a detailed understanding of the CTQs cause-and-effect system. Stratification can be used to break down a CTQ to discover its root causes (Xs or CTPs) and set into motion appropriate corrective actions, called countermeasures.

A Gantt chart is a scheduling tool for relatively small projects. It is a bar chart that plots tasks and sub-tasks against time. Once a list of tasks and sub-tasks has been created for a project, then responsibilities can be assigned and beginning and finishing dates can be scheduled for each task and sub-task.

Individually, the preceding tools and techniques are powerful aids for improvement of a process. However, they take on their true strength when they are used as an integrated system of tools and techniques for diagnosing a process.

REFERENCES

1. Gitlow, H. S., and D. M. Levine, *Six Sigma for Green Belts and Champions* (Upper Saddle River, NJ: Financial Times Prentice Hall, 2005).

2. Gitlow, H., A. Oppenheim, R. Oppenheim, and D. Levine, *Quality Management: Tools and Methods for Improvement* (New York: McGraw-Hill-Irwin, Inc., 3rd ed., 2005).

APPENDIX 12.1

USING MINITAB FOR THE CAUSE-
AND-EFFECT DIAGRAM

To illustrate how to generate a cause-and-effect diagram, refer to the data of Figure 12.1 on page 402 concerning printed airline ticket errors. Open the **FIGURE12-1.MTW** worksheet. The entries on each branch and subbranch of the cause-and-effect diagram have been entered in columns C1–C7, respectively (see Figure A12.1). Select **Stat → Quality Tools → Cause-and-Effect**.

↓	C1-T	C2-T	C3-T	C4-T	C5-T	C6-T	C7-T
	C1-T	C2-T	C3-T	C4-T	C5-T	C6-T	C7-T
1	Age	Density	Quality	Supervision	Atention to Detail	Type	Frequency
2	Carbon		Speed	Ability		Age	Tension Adjustment
3	Paper					Maintenance	
4							

FIGURE A12.1   Minitab Worksheet Showing Cause and Subcause Entries

1. In the Cause-and-Effect Diagram dialog box (see Figure A12.2), in the Causes column, enter **C4** in the Manpower row, **C6** in the Machines row, **C1** in the Material row, and **C3** in the Methods row.

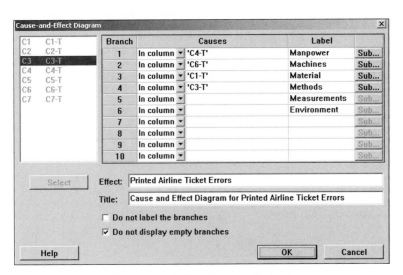

FIGURE A12.2   Minitab Cause-and-Effect Diagram Dialog Box

2. Click the **Sub** button in the Manpower row. In the Cause-and-Effect Diagram—Sub-Branches dialog box (see Figure A12.3), enter **C5** in the Ability row of the Causes column. Click the **OK** button to return to the Cause-and-Effect Diagram dialog box.

3. Click the **Sub** button in the Machines row. In the Cause-and-Effect Diagram—Sub-Branches dialog box, enter **C7** in the Maintenance row of the

Causes column. Click the **OK** button to return to the Cause-and-Effect Diagram dialog box.

4. Click the **Sub** button in the Material row. In the Cause-and-Effect Diagram—Sub-Branches dialog box, enter **C2** in the Carbon row of the Causes column. Click the **OK** button to return to the Cause-and-Effect Diagram dialog box.

5. Click the **OK** button.

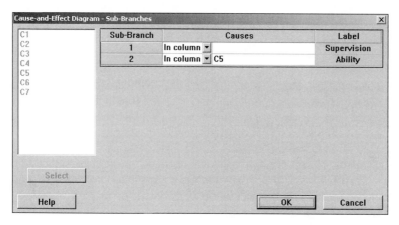

FIGURE A12.3 Minitab Cause-and-Effect Diagram—Sub-Branches Dialog Box for the Manpower Row

Appendix 12.2

Using JMP for the Cause-and-Effect Diagram

To illustrate how to generate a cause-and-effect diagram, refer to the data of Figure 12.1 on page 402 concerning printed airline ticket errors. Open the **FIGURE12-1.JMP** data table. Observe that there are two variables, labeled as Parent and Child (see Figure A12.4). The Parent (Effect) for the cause-and-effect diagram, printed airline ticket errors, has the four Children (Causes) of Material, Manpower, Methods, and Machines (rows 1–4). These correspond to the causes shown in Figure 12.1. Within each cause, subcauses are Children while the cause is the Parent. For example, under Material, the subcauses of Age, Carbon, and Paper are Children of the Parent Material. These are shown in rows 5–7.

Select **Graph → Diagram**. In the Report:Diagram—Ishikawa Cause and Effect Diagram dialog box (see Figure A12.5), enter **Child** in the Y, Child edit box and **Parent** in the X, Parent edit box. Click the **OK** button.

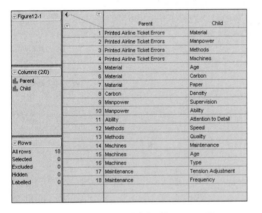

FIGURE A12.4 JMP Data Table Showing Cause and Subcause Entries

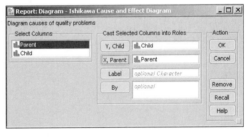

FIGURE A12.5 JMP Report:Diagram—Ishikawa Cause and Effect Diagram Dialog Box

DISCRETE EVENT SIMULATION MODELS[1]

SECTIONS

LEARNING OBJECTIVES

After reading this chapter, you will be able to:

* Define simulation and understand its applications in various industries and settings.
* Understand the advantages, precautions, and pitfalls of simulation modeling.
* Be familiar with simulation terminology.
* Understand how a simulation model works.
* Use experimental designs to optimize a real system using a simulation model.

---

[1] The initial version of Chapter 13 was contributed by Ajay Jain, Ph.D.:
SigmaFlow: Process Analysis and Design
5068 West Plano Parkway
Plano, TX 75093
(972)447-8340
www.SigmaFlow.com

INTRODUCTION

Simulation is a disciplined process of building a model of a system or design, and performing experiments with this model, to analyze and understand the behavior of selected characteristics of the system or design (CTQs), and to evaluate operational strategies (CTPs or Xs) to manage the system or design. In the last decade, a number of off-the-shelf simulation software products (for example, SigmaFlow) have significantly reduced the programming effort of building a simulation model. Now, users can allocate more time studying "what-if" scenarios. This chapter introduces the basic concepts behind discrete event simulation. The term "system" as used in this chapter includes existing processes, products, services, and designs, as well as proposed processes, products, services, and designs.

13.1 WHAT IS SIMULATION?

Simulation provides a model of a system that considers all of the resources and constraints, and their interactions over time, of the system being modeled. It is a tool that creates the opportunity to ask "what-if" questions concerning the performance of alternative constructions of a system. Testing alternatives through experimentation is a logical approach for reducing the uncertainty associated with alternative constructions of a system. The experience gained from experimentation can help you avoid unnecessary and costly ventures. Simulation itself does not solve problems, but it does clearly identify problems and quantitatively evaluate alternative solutions. With simulation, you can quickly try out your ideas at a fraction of the cost of trying them on the real system. Examples of simulation models include: day-to-day operation of a bank, operation of an assembly line, or the staff assignments of a hospital or call center.

13.2 APPLICATIONS OF SIMULATION

There are a number of potential areas for application of simulation. The range of application areas is extremely large and there are numerous examples of the use of simulation in service industries, manufacturing (batch and process), and office environments. Examples of actual simulation studies performed in several of these industries can be found at www.pmcorp.com and www.simulation-modeling.com. Visit these web sites to view several simulation models in operation across a broad range of both service and manufacturing industries.

One area where simulation is commonly used is in systems design, particularly those that involve a high capital investment. In designing a new system, experiments can be performed using a simulation model that would otherwise be impossible to carry out on the actual system because it is not yet implemented. Simulation can significantly reduce the time required to debug and fine-tune a proposed system or design. For example, you can use simulation to test the performance of a new clinic to ascertain the possible output, the level of utilization of nurses/doctors, and any potential problems. Further investigations can be carried out to determine an effective and efficient way to schedule patients, rooms, doctors, and nurses while maximizing the clinic's throughput.

Simulation is being used in a variety of manufacturing and service industries. A list of some of the industries that are currently benefiting from the use of simulation is given in Table 13.1. Table 13.2 lists the application areas and the purpose of using the simulation tool.

TABLE 13.1 Manufacturing and Service Industries Using Simulation Methods

Manufacturing Industries	Service Industries
• Appliance	• Public Services
• Automotive	• Learning Institutions
• Aerospace	• Restaurants
• Electronics	• Banking
• Heavy Equipment	• Healthcare
• Glass and Ceramics	• Government
• Textile	• Disaster Planning
• Food and Beverage	• Waste Management
• Foundries	• Transportation
• Petrochemical (Oil and Gas)	• Distribution
• Furniture	• Aerospace-Military
• Semiconductor	• Hotel Management
	• Amusement Parks

TABLE 13.2 Simulation Application Areas

Application Areas	Used For
• Six Sigma Management	• Elimination of Variation and Waste
• Business Process Management	• Understanding the Dynamics of Wait Time
• People/Transport Flow	• Measuring the Effects of Variances
• Supply Chain Management	• Predicting Wait Time Accurately
• Call Center	• Financial Significance
• Plant/Facility Layout	• Production/Customer Scheduling

(continued)

TABLE 13.2   Simulation Application Areas (Continued)

Application Areas	Used For
• Plant Productivity Improvement • Maintenance Planning • Packaging • Material Handling • Bank Operations, Transaction Processes, Loan Management	• Resource Planning • Work Prioritization • Inventory Management • Quality Management • Task Assignment • Throughput Analysis • Capacity Analysis • Technology Selection: Manual vs. Automated

13.3 WHY USE SIMULATION MODELING?

Not all problems that can be solved with the aid of simulation should be solved using simulation. If the objective is to understand work-flow sequence, then a simple flow diagram will suffice. For simple problems like finding the effective capacity of an operation, or the cumulative scrap rate of a system, simple mathematical calculations can be used.

The following are some of the situations in which simulation can be considered an appropriate tool:

- Simulation is an appropriate tool if developing a mathematical model for a new/existing system is too complex. By building/testing a simulation model of such systems, users can predict the outcomes for possible courses of action without making a large investment in the experiments.

- Simulation is an appropriate tool if the system being studied has interdependent random variables. Random events are an uncontrollable part of life and simulation can help predict the consequences of random events and their likelihood of occurrence.

- Simulation is an appropriate tool if the system dynamics are extremely complex. Complexity is determined by the interdependencies of people, equipment, methods, material and policies, and variability in the system.

- Simulation is an appropriate tool to observe system behavior over time. For example, what is the impact when something occurs in relation to other incidents? How do we see the effect of arriving patients into the emergency room over a period of time? What if a patient arrives in the emergency room when there is no doctor?

13.4 ADVANTAGES OF SIMULATION

Simulation provides Six Sigma team members with the following advantages:

1. Understanding the cause and effect relationships in a system.
2. Identifying bottlenecks, constraints, and barriers in a system.
3. Reducing the cost of experimentation on a system. With simulation, users can build a model to evaluate proposed designs, specifications, and changes without having to commit resources to build the actual system. Users can also evaluate various alternatives such as effects of policies, procedures, and new techniques without having to disrupt the actual system—which may or may not exist yet.
4. Predicting future outcomes of a system. For example, what happens if five new people are hired over the next few months? Or, what happens to total patient waiting time if the scheduled service times for a physician are switched from the morning hours to the afternoon hours?
5. Providing repeatability to study a system by running the simulation model multiple times.
6. Allowing time compression and expansion in which to study a system. Users can control the speed of the simulation; in other words, a simulation can be run over a few seconds or over a few weeks. By controlling the speed of a simulation, team members can analyze what happens over weeks within minutes or spend hours on understanding what happens in seconds.

Simulation is intuitively simple and elegant. PC-based simulation software provides menu-driven options that make it easy to use and enter data. This software facilitates communication, builds consensus, and prepares for change. Further, it is an effective and exciting training tool for team members because it fosters learning about the assumptions underlying a system.

13.5 PRECAUTIONS WHEN USING SIMULATION

Once Six Sigma team members decide that simulation is the appropriate tool to be used to study a system or design, they should take the following precautions. These precautions are as follows:

- Simulation modeling requires some basic knowledge of computer skills and subject matter expertise.
- Simulation modeling creates a model that is as simple as possible, while capturing all the necessary detail to mimic the system under study.
- Simulation modeling generates results (outputs) that are only as good as the inputs (this is known as Garbage in–Garbage out, or GIGO).

- Simulation modeling may create an inappropriate degree of confidence in the simulation results.
- Simulation modeling of a new system may create outputs that are impossible to verify. In such cases, Six Sigma team members have to rely on the expertise of experienced employees and experts.
- Simulation modeling requires adequate project time, qualified personnel, and resources.

13.6 PITFALLS OF SIMULATION MODELS

Some of the potential pitfalls of simulation modeling are listed next:

- Fuzzy simulation objective, project definition, and unreasonable expectations.
- Too much complexity.
- Underestimation of resources.
- Inclusion of variables that have little or no impact on system behavior.
- Inadequate stakeholder involvement, review, and feedback.
- Wrong mix of team skills.
- Communication problems among the stakeholders of the simulation model.
- Not validating the output.
- Insufficient training using simulation methods.
- Making conclusions from a single model replication.
- Making conclusions from animations rather than statistical reports; i.e., users looking at the screen to view how the simulation runs and not spending time studying the actual data generated in reports.
- Little or no interaction between model builder, management, and operational personnel.

13.7 SIMULATION TERMINOLOGY

This section outlines some terminology frequently used when discussing simulation methods.

Definition of a System

A **system** is a collection of interacting components that transforms inputs into outputs toward a common aim, called a *mission statement*. It is the job of management to optimize the entire system toward its aim. This may require the sub-optimization of selected components of the system; for example, a particular department in an organization may have to give up resources to another department in the short run to maximize profit for the overall organization.

Systems exist in all facets of organizations, and an understanding of them is crucial. Many people mistakenly think only of production systems. However, administration, sales, service, human resources, training, maintenance, paper flows, interdepartmental communication, and vendor relations are all systems. Importantly, relationships between people are systems. Most systems can be studied, documented, defined, improved, and innovated.

System Performance Measures

It is important to have performance measures to assess the effectiveness of the system being simulated. Some common performance measures used to assess the effectiveness of a system are as follows:

- *Machine utilization*: The percentage of time a piece of equipment is in productive use.
- *Personnel utilization*: The percentage of time that personnel are engaged in productive activities.
- *Cycle time in the system*: The length of time entities (products, customers) spend in a system from start to finish.
- *Waiting/queuing time*: The length of time entities spend waiting for service.
- *Quality*: The percentage of conforming outputs produced by a system using the goal post view of quality, also called "process sigma with a zero shift in the mean."
- *Cost*: The operating costs of a system.
- *Revenue*: The revenue generated by a system.
- *Throughput*: The number of entities produced by the system.

Discrete Event Simulation Versus Continuous Simulation

A **discrete event** is an instantaneous action that occurs at a unique point in time. A customer arriving at the bank, a car arriving at a service station, a part arriving at a delivery dock, and a machine finishing a cycle are examples of discrete events. The occurrences of these events can cause system states (CTQs) to change [CTQ = f(Event)]. Events usually take place at irregular intervals of time. Simulation time periods are advanced by the time required by individual events. Most manufacturing and service systems are discrete event systems.

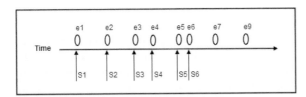

FIGURE 13.1 Discrete Event

In Figure 13.1, Event e1, e2, etc. are occurring at different points in time with no set pattern; i.e., the time between two consecutive events is not constant. Because state changes are event driven, these events cause the system state to change; for example, S1 occurs with e1, S2 with e2, and so on. For this type of simulation, time periods (actually a clock) are moved ahead according to the events—not according to constant time flow.

A **continuous event** is an action without pause. The cholesterol level of a patient, the flow of oil into a tanker, and the volume of a soda tank in a restaurant are examples of continuous events. Continuous events involve a time rate of change (Δt), and they continue uninterrupted with respect to time in relatively continuous and regular fashion [CTQ = f(time)].

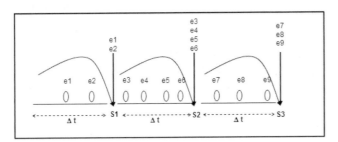

FIGURE 13.2 Continuous Event

In Figure 13.2, simulation (S1, S2, etc.) is timed regularly in equal periods Δt. Events occur in a regular and equally spaced manner and are assumed to take place at the end of a period. For example, events 1 and 2 are assumed to occur at S1, and events e3 through e6 are assumed to occur at S2, exactly after Δt time units.

System state is all of the variables that contain the information necessary to describe a system at any point of time. The state of the system does not refer to whether the system as a whole is busy, down or idle. The state of a system is actually described by the values of all the individual state variables in the system. A state variable might be the number of entities in a particular queue or the status (busy, idle, down) of a particular resource [see Reference 3].

Stochastic Versus Deterministic Simulation

Simulation is very powerful when it comes to modeling randomness in the system. Randomness is inherently present in most systems. Table 13.3 lists some of the variables that exhibit random behavior.

TABLE 13.3   Examples of Random Variables

Random Variable	Examples
Time	Processing time, changeover or setup time, transfer time, repair time, inter-arrival time, time between equipment failure, personnel time on equipment, sick time.
Decision Percentages	% conforming output between time periods "*t*" and "*t* + 1."
Quantities	Arrival batch size, manufacturing batch or lot size, start-up inventory.
Attributes or Labels	Part type, customer type, part size.

A **stochastic model** contains one or more variables that are random in nature. The variable does not have a specific value, but rather a range of values most often derived from a distribution. In such cases, distributions are used to introduce variability into the model and become the source of values. Thus, a stochastic process is composed of a sequence of randomly determined values from a sequence of distributions. The time between any two customer arrivals at a bank is an example of a stochastic variable.

A **deterministic model** is a model that does not contain randomness; i.e., there are no input variables that are random. A spreadsheet analysis could be considered a deterministic model because nothing is uncertain about the parameters. The simulation model can be the same with different types of inputs (random variable or fixed). The difference lies in the results produced by running a model. Running a deterministic model will always generate the same result, whereas results from a stochastic model can differ because of the variability in the inputs. This is the reason why several runs have to be made when using a stochastic model to estimate the expected performance of the system, given a particular configuration of the state variables (Xs).

Static Versus Dynamic Models

A **static model** is a model that is not influenced by time and defines the system mathematically using a set of numerical equations. The input variables used in the equations are averages; consequently, the state of a static model is constant over time. In other words, this type of model does not use a simulation clock—for example, the probability of the outcome of a flip of a fair coin is $P(\text{Head}) = 0.50$. This outcome is not affected by time.

A **dynamic model** is a model that is influenced by time and defines the system using a set of numerical equations. Dynamic models differ from static models because they are event driven. The occurrence of an event can change the values of the variables used in a computation. System behavior and performance are derived by averaging the responses observed over the occurrences of a large quantity of events. The state of the model changes over time using a simulation clock. Many service and manufacturing systems can be represented using a dynamic model—for example, schedule changes, equipment failure, WIP levels, equipment utilizations, customer arrival rates, test times, wait times, defects, and engineering changes are all systems that can be represented using dynamic models.

Steady-State Simulations Versus Terminating Simulations

A **steady-state** simulation is a simulation in which the state of the system is independent of its start-up conditions. A modeler can stop a steady-state simulation any time after steady-state has been achieved without affecting the output of the simulation.

A **terminating** simulation is a simulation that runs for a predetermined length of time or until a specific event occurs. For example, a terminating simulation can be stopped after a certain number of jobs are completed or after the end of a shift. The results of a terminating simulation are based on its output values at the time the simulation was stopped. It is important to realize that the results of terminating simulations are usually dependent upon the initial values and quantities used when starting the model. For this reason, it is important that the start-up conditions in terminating simulation models accurately reflect the start-up circumstances in their real-world counterpart systems.

The decision to employ a steady-state or terminating simulation is made during the preliminary planning stages of a simulation project. The choice is dependent upon the type of system being modeled. A facility that produces electricity 24 hours per day would likely be analyzed with a steady-state simulation. On the other hand, a terminating simulation would be used in most service systems such as call centers, banks, and restaurants that may never reach a steady state. All waiting lines or queues are emptied at the end of the day, such that the system begins the new day with zero items (calls, customers) waiting in the queue.

Warm-Up Period

A warm-up, or start-up, period is the time frame needed for a system to reach "steady-state" (see Figure 13.3). The warm-up period is generally ignored in steady-state simulations and is only used for investigating the effects of transient conditions, such as starting up a new factory or performing changes within an existing facility. The steady-state period of the simulation must be studied to ensure that no long-term trends exist, such as continual build-up of inventory in the system, that suggest the model (hence the real system) will be unstable and unworkable.

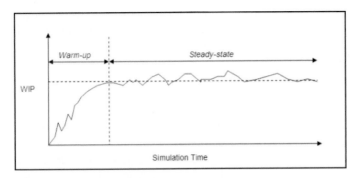

FIGURE 13.3 Warm-Up and Steady-State Periods

A warm-up period is commonly used in manufacturing systems to fill up the system with initial inventory before collecting data. On the other hand, a warm-up period is not commonly used in service systems or terminating simulations because the initial number of customers waiting is zero at the beginning of the simulation period.

Model Verification and Validation

Model verification is the process of determining if a simulation model works as intended by the user. It also affirms if all input data has been correctly incorporated into the model. Consider a simple system consisting of a machine that has a processing time with a stable normal distribution with a mean of 15 minutes and standard deviation of 3 minutes. The cycle time in the model for that machine is verified if the simulation model produces cycle times representative of the specified normal distribution.

The verification effort is usually less time-consuming with simulation software packages that have animation features. Animation, such as people icons moving through the system, is a good tool for confirming system flows and element functions of a model. Some of the useful model verification techniques are as follows:

1. Check the model with known results or against other models.
2. Have the model checked by a qualified independent party.
3. Verify that all important elements have been included in the model.
4. Simulate the system with deterministic values which can be easily verified.

Model validation implies that the results generated by a simulation model correspond to the results generated by the real system. Verification alone does not assure that the model is valid. The model may be logically correct, but may not represent reality. How does one know if the output generated by the simulation model conforms to reality? This can only be possible when model logic, interrelationship between different model elements, input data used, and assumptions made are accurately represented in the model in the way in which the real system operates. Model builders rely on system experts to establish the validity of the results for a new system; that is, a system that does not yet exist.

Additionally, the animation feature of a simulation software package can help establish the validity of a simulation model. Although animation makes it easier to validate a simulation model, decisions concerning the validity of a simulation model should be based on a statistical analysis of the generated results. Some validation techniques are as follows:

1. Compare simulated results with actual results (for existing systems).
2. Use experts to validate simulated results for systems that do not yet exist.
3. Use multifunctional teams to review inputs and outputs of the model.
4. Use sensitivity analysis to study the conditions of parameters under different conditions.

Random Numbers, Seeds, and Streams

Random numbers are numbers that follow no particular pattern. Random numbers with values between zero and one (i.e., decimal random numbers) play a major role in extracting values from probability distributions, and thus, in establishing stochastic behavior in simulation models. A **random number stream** is a sequence of random numbers where each succeeding number is calculated from its predecessor. The initial number is referred to as the **random number seed** and the formula that generates these independent numbers (between 0 and 1) is called a **random number generator**.

Stochastic simulation models frequently use **random variables** to select times and quantities that vary from occurrence to occurrence. First, a random number seed is used to generate a random number stream using a random number generator. Next, these random numbers are used in probability distributions to define the likelihood of the occurrence of a random variable such as inter-arrival time, service time, or time between failures. Values drawn from a probability distribution are called random variables [see Reference 5].

Model Run and Independent Model Replication

A different random number stream is generated whenever the random seed is changed in the random number generator. A single **model run** involves running a simulation with a unique random number stream. An independent **model replication** involves running a given simulation model with a different random number stream (each run uses a different random number seed). Model replications are called **trials**.

Basing decisions solely on the output from a single model run is risky. It is vital to recognize that the results from a single model run of a stochastic simulation are stochastic. Multiple model replications are required when analyzing results from stochastic simulations. The effect of variability can be captured by running multiple simulation trials. Based on the results from multiple trials, it is possible to analyze the output data and make accurate model-based recommendations for the actual system. Many simulation packages allow users to define the number of replications and provide results for individual runs, as well as 95% and 99% confidence limits.

Common Distributions Used in Simulation

Probability distributions are used to introduce variability into a stochastic model and become the source for values. Stochastic simulation models utilize probability distributions to represent a multitude of randomly occurring events. Common examples that use probability distributions include inter-arrival time, processing times, repair times, occurrence of defects, time between failures on a piece of equipment, and so on.

Several standard probability distributions are frequently used with stochastic simulations. Some of these distributions are discussed in Reference 1. Details of other probability distributions commonly used in simulation can be found in simulation textbooks [see Reference 5].

It is important to use probability distributions that are representative of the stochastic processes they are imitating. Many simulation packages contain features that will automatically find standard probability distributions, which are representative of empirical data. There are also other software packages, such as ExpertFit, BestFit, and StatFit, that you can use to identify the distribution that fits the empirical data.

13.8 How Discrete Event Simulation Works

Basics

Simulation software packages consist of several elements (see Figure 13.4). Each element is described next:

1. *Tangible model elements*: Tangible elements are physical elements found in the real world; e.g., machines, people, or equipment. They may be temporary (e.g., parts or customers that pass through the system) or permanent (e.g., machines or equipment that define the system).

2. *Logical elements*: Logical elements are flow elements that link different tangible elements together to create a functional representation of a real system; for example, machine *A* processes part *X* according to a stable normal distribution with a mean of 5 minutes and a standard deviation of 1 minute. The logical relationships are a key part of a simulation model because they define the behavior of the system. Each logical statement (e.g., "start machine *A* if part *X* is waiting in the queue") is simple, but the quantity and variety of logical statements that are dispersed throughout the model create a very complex system.

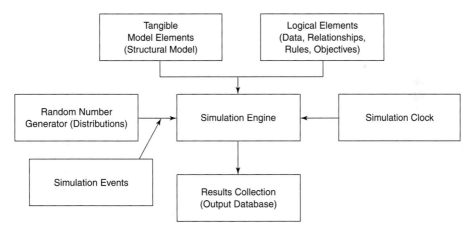

FIGURE 13.4 Structure of a Simulation System

3. *Simulation engine*: A simulation engine controls the logical relationships between various elements. It is central to providing the dynamic, time-based behavior of the model. A simulation engine converts all activities to events, orders them chronologically, and manages their interactions. Events are processed one at a time until the simulation ends. A simulation engine processes the first event by executing the model logic appropriate for it. Any new events that occur as a result of processing the first event are inserted onto the list of events at the appropriate location in the model. It is possible that more than one event may reference the same model logic. This means that the same model logic is used many times during the life of the simulation run.

4. *Random number generator*: A random number generator is used to model randomness in a simulation model. For example, the age of patients walking into a clinic will rarely be fixed; rather, they will vary according to a probability distribution.

5. *Results collection*: Results collection and analysis provides a vehicle for meaningful analysis of a new or existing actual system or design.

6. *Simulation clock*: A simulation clock is used in all simulation software to keep track of the time. The simulation engine works in conjunction with the simulation clock to model the dynamic behavior of an actual system. The simulation engine manages the progress of time and "steps" the simulation model into the future, executing the relevant logical relationships along the way, using the simulation clock.

7. *Simulation events*: Simulation events might include the arrival of a customer at a service desk, the failure of equipment, the completion of a task, or the end of a shift. There are two types of simulation events [see Reference 3].

   • *Scheduled events* are simulation events typically determined by randomly sampling from an input probability distribution that describes the activity time, or time between occurrences, for each particular type of event. Events are usually scheduled at the moment they can be predicted. For example, as soon as an activity begins that takes a specified amount of time, a completion event can be scheduled. These events occur at scheduled times (for example, a task completion or machine failure). For example, suppose a banking process has customers who arrive every 5 minutes, wait in a queue, get serviced for exactly 10 minutes, and then exit the bank. (These inter-arrival and service times are likely to follow a certain distribution where the time values are randomly chosen from the values selected from a probability distribution.) Now, assume that the first customer arrives at time 0. Knowing this, you can schedule the next customer arrival time (second customer will arrive at time 5, third at 10, and so on…). This is an example of a scheduled event. Similarly, at the service desk, as soon as you know when the service starts, you can schedule the service completion event knowing that the service will take 10 minutes to complete. This is another example of a scheduled event. The activity arrival and completion events are examples of scheduled events because as soon as the activity starts, knowing the arrival time and process time of a customer, you can predict the arrival time of the next customer and completion time of the current customer.

   • *Conditional events* are simulation events that occur only when one or more conditions have been satisfied, or events have occurred (for example, the departure of a customer from a waiting line when a service agent becomes available or the shipment of an order when all of the line items have been pulled and consolidated). Using the same example as mentioned previously, all arriving customers wait in the queue if the service station is busy. The customers can leave the queue only when the service station becomes available; i.e., the status of service agent becomes idle from busy. This is an example of a conditional simulation event.

Simulation events may be triggered by a condition, an elapsed time, or some other changing condition (see Figure 13.5). Simulation works by arranging the initially scheduled events chronologically into a list of scheduled events. You then update the clock to the first event in the list and the logic associated with that event gets processed. The processing of an event, whether it is a scheduled event or a conditional event, consists of updating the affected variables in the system, collecting statistics associated with the event, and if animation is included, updating the screen picture. Any consequent, scheduled events are placed into the scheduled events list. Likewise, there may be consequent conditional events resulting from the processing of the event that are put into appropriate waiting lists.

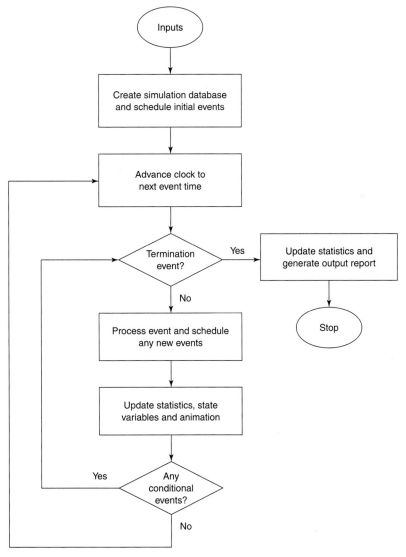

FIGURE 13.5 Logic Diagram of Discrete-Event Simulation

After a scheduled event is processed, any conditional event whose condition is now satisfied also gets processed. When no more conditional events are able to be processed, the clock advances to the next scheduled event time. When an end of a simulation event (which might have been defined as either a scheduled or conditional event) occurs, the simulation terminates and statistical reports are generated. The updating of the clock to the next imminent event, the processing of logic and state changes associated with each event, and the collection of statistical data constitute the essence of discrete-event simulation.

Model Building

Model building is considered an art and a science. Developing expertise as a simulation modeler requires an understanding of system dynamics, knowing how to capture these dynamics, and knowing one or more simulation languages. Simulation model builders set up an initial model, define the logical relationship between its activities, and analyze the results.

Flowcharts. A simulation model requires a flowchart to visualize the system under study. A **flowchart** is a computer representation of a system as defined by the software used to develop the model. A simulation consists of drawing a process with *objects* (things like queues and processes) on the screen with a default structure (routing) between them and *work items* that flow through the process. While building the model, there are many things that need to be considered to provide an accurate abstraction of the system being modeled.

Entities. Entities are the subject of the simulation model and are the *things* that flow through the process, wait in queues, are stored in storages, and are generally worked on. Examples include parts/products, customer calls, customers, transactions, documents, etc. Just as in real life, entities can assume different identities at different times. For example, different entities may get assembled into a single entity (assembling four *tires* and a *chassis* to get one entity "*car*"), or may get split into multiple entities (a single purchase order getting split into three different copies) or grouped together so that they can be processed at once (batch of cookies going into an oven where each entity still maintains its own unique identity).

Entities in a system may be of different types and can have different characteristics such as type, color, ID, and due date. These are defined through features called **attributes** (also known as *labels* or *parameters*). Attributes are very powerful and if understood and used correctly, they can reduce the model size tremendously. You can use attributes to make dynamic decisions based on some characteristic of an entity. Attributes are like variables, and each individual entity can have different values for each of its attributes. You can change values of these attributes during the simulation as they get processed at different process steps. For example, an attribute called *color* can have a value of "white" before going to the painting station (process step), which can be modified to "red" as it comes out of the painting station.

The attributes of an entity can be explained with the help of a simple example. You can think of an attribute as a label on a pair of jeans that includes information about waist size, inseam length, and style. The attributes of the jeans are on a label that goes wherever the jeans go. Anyone can find out the attributes of a particular pair of jeans by looking at the label on the jeans.

Activities and Their Logical Relationships. In addition to flowcharting and modeling entities, the logical relationships (for example, routing decisions, who works on what, priorities, personnel assignments, and shift assignment) between activities need to be defined to run a simulation model. Modeling activities are the basic objects commonly used to define the various steps of a system or design:

- *Work start (entity generator)*: Work start in simulation is not a physical resource but rather a logical resource. It is used to generate the arrival of entities into a system. It can be used to capture the randomness inherent in the arrivals of most entities. Defining the inter-arrival time distribution for an entity is key to any simulation. Inter-arrival means defining the time units *between* the arrivals of any two entities. Most simulation packages use inter-arrival times as opposed to arrival rates, which are the opposite of inter-arrival times. Different types of arrivals can be modeled—for example, time based (appointment based), random (customer support calls), or time dependent (slow hour versus rush hour traffic). Some of the common examples of arrivals include customers arriving at a service center, production orders arriving at a factory, customers arriving at a bank, patients arriving at a hospital, calls arriving at a call center, and patents waiting to be processed by a United States patent office.

- *Storage/queue/waiting area/buffers*: Storage objects are used anytime an entity might have to wait for processing to absorb the variation in the system. Storages are the places where entities get routed to for processing, waiting, or decision making and generally have a holding capacity. When there are multiple entities in storage, many rules can be applied to the order in which they are processed by activities. These include first-in-first-out, last-in-last-out, priority assignment, longest queue, shortest queue, and the age of an entity. Process steps with processing times greater than zero are usually preceded by a storage facility. Examples of situations in which a storage objects are needed include: products awaiting shipment, raw material waiting to be used, people waiting to board an airplane, and people standing in line at a bank/ticket counter. Frequently, modelers neglect to use storage objects.

- *Processes*: A process is anything that performs work on an entity. For modeling purposes, the exact nature of the process (machining, greeting customers, making decisions, transporting, inspection, etc.) is irrelevant. Depending on the task being performed on an entity, a process can also be used to split, combine, group, or ungroup entities. Modelers can use probability distributions to capture randomness or variability that exists in processing times. Other parameters that can be defined for processes include availability, shifts/schedules, maintenance, breakdowns, and downtimes. Time between failures and time to repair should be represented by probability distributions that are representative of the variability of times that is likely to occur. There are three main phases related to a process step:

  - The "before work starts" phase includes setting up machines, grouping similar entities so that they can be processed together, and selecting entities for assembly. A setup might be a tool change in a manufacturing system or cleaning a table before setting the table for another customer in a restaurant. The amount of setup time may be dependent on the current entity to be processed and also on the preceding type of entity.

- The "while work is under way" phase is actually performing the work; for example, processing a document, providing physical therapy, or painting a picture. If desired, the attributes of an entity can be changed after processing.

- The "after work finishes" phase involves making decisions about entities after they are processed. For example, should the entity be split or ungrouped, or where should the entity be sent (routing decision).

- Process steps are normally referred to as primary resources. Secondary resources can be added to process steps if they are required to complete the task. An example of a secondary resource is a surgical team (nurses and doctors) operating on a patient (entity) in an operating room (primary resource). Secondary resources do not have to be available all the time, for example, they can be available in shifts. Primary resources can utilize a variable number of secondary resources, for example, they can work faster given more resources.

- *Work finished (results collector)*: "Work Finished" is a simulation step that is used primarily to record simulation results such as throughput and cycle time. Entities are created at "Work Start" and stay in the system until they reach "Work Finished."

- *Simulation clock*: The simulation clock controls the timing aspect of the simulation. For example, you can use the clock to define the length of the warm-up period and simulation period.

Arrivals of Entities. Entities arriving into a system are usually defined by entity type, arrival quantity, arrival frequency, and arrival pattern. The arrival of entities into systems or designs can follow any one of the following arrival patterns.

1. *Random arrivals*: Random arrivals are entities that arrive into a system, or step in a system, such that the arrival of one entity does not depend on the arrival of another entity.

2. *Scheduled arrivals*: Scheduled arrivals occur when entities arrive independently of one another according to a predefined schedule. These arrivals may occur in quantities greater than one and at an exact or probabilistic time. If the arrival time is probabilistic, the model needs to define the mean time, the variability around the mean time, and the shape of the distribution of arrival times, so as to allow for the arrival of early or late entities. Examples of scheduled arrivals include:

   a. A phone company scheduling the arrival time of a technician for a service call.
   b. A nurse scheduling the arrival time of a patient for a doctor's appointment.
   c. A marketer planning the schedule for the release of a new service.
   d. An engineer scheduling the release of a new design.

3. *Time-dependent arrivals (arrivals within a period)*: Time-dependent arrivals are modeled using different probability distributions at different times of the day. These types of arrivals frequently start out slow at the beginning of a cycle, reach a peak part way through the cycle, and then taper off toward the end of the cycle. Some examples of time-dependent arrivals are as follows:

a. Customer arriving at a restaurant (lunch and dinner times are busy hours).

b. Phone calls arriving at a call center for customer service (8:00 A.M.–9:00 A.M. and 12:00 P.M.–1:00 P.M. are busy hours).

c. Vehicles entering a highway (morning and evening are rush hours).

Modeling Distributions. Probability distributions can be used to model an existing system if Six Sigma team members collect data and use a curve-fitting application to identify an appropriate probability distribution. If a system does not yet exist or there is no data available, Six Sigma team members can use Table 13.4 as a guideline to select the appropriate probability distribution for a simulation model.

TABLE 13.4 List of Selected Probability Distributions Useful for Simulation Modeling

Distributions	Tasks	Parameter 1	Parameter 2	Parameter 3
Normal Distribution [Reference 1]	• Time to perform a task (processing, servicing). • Measure various types of errors.	Mean	Standard Deviation	
Lognormal Distribution [Reference 6]	• Commonly used to define manual activities such as assembly, inspection, or repair. • Time between failures.			
Triangular Distribution [Reference 5]	• Limited empirical data is available. • Situations where only three pieces of information are known about a task (min, most likely, max).	Lower Bound	Mode	Upper Bound
Gamma Distribution [Reference 5]	• Time needed to complete a task/group of tasks. • Manual tasks such as service times or repair times.			

(continued)

TABLE 13.4 List of Selected Probability Distributions Useful for Simulation Modeling (Continued)

Distributions	Tasks	Parameter 1	Parameter 2	Parameter 3
Uniform Distribution [Reference 6]	• Minimal information available on time. • Only minimum and maximum are known.	Lower Bound	Upper Bound	
Weibull Distribution [Reference 6]	• Time to failure on a piece of equipment. • Average life of an electronic component. • Time until failure due to items that wear (bearings, tooling).			
Beta Distribution [Reference 5]	• Proportion of defective items found in a given lot size. • Time to complete an activity when very little or no information is available about the duration of the activity.			
Poisson Distribution [Reference 1]	• Number of defects per item. • Number of times a resource is interrupted each hour.	Mean		
Binomial Distribution [Reference 1]	• Number of successes in n trials.	Number of trials	Probability of success	
Exponential Distribution [Reference 6]	• Random arrivals.	Mean		
Fixed Distribution	• No variation (constant value).	Fixed value (Mean)		

Performing Experiments

Once a simulation model has been built, the next step is to design and perform a series of experiments using the model to see how to improve the actual system under study. Experiments are usually conducted to:

- Find the value of a CTP or *X*, or a combination of CTPs or *X*s, that optimizes a CTQ, and/or
- Compare different design rules, management strategies, system configurations, and/or
- Determine the sensitivity of the system (expected change in performance) to changes in one or more CTPs or *X*s.

When optimizing a system, a modeler identifies the parameters of the CTPs or *X*s and their levels. Experiments are conducted by manipulating the levels of the CTPs or *X*s and determining the effects of these manipulations on the *Y* or CTQ. There are several decisions that need to be made before experimentation can begin, as follows:

- Determine if the objective of the model is to study the steady-state condition. If so, determine the warm-up period.
- Decide if the process is a terminating or a nonterminating system.
- Determine the number of runs for the model (single or multiple runs) and the number of replications for each system configuration.
- Determine the total length and the initial starting conditions for each simulation run.
- Decide on the type of probability distributions to use for each of the *X*s (process times, batch sizes, inter-arrival times, etc.).
- Set the simulation clock to define the length of each simulation run.
- Establish appropriate calendar working days and shift patterns for each simulation run.
- Decide what data to collect and choose appropriate data-capturing mechanisms.
- Examine, validate, and change (if necessary) the default parameters of the simulation package being used to model the system under study.
- Collect data from each simulation run for analysis of the CTQ.

Output Analysis

Modern simulation software packages generate large amounts of valuable data that can be analyzed to interpret the effects of the CTPs or *X*s, and their interactions, on the CTQ. Simulation output is summarized in reports that include: (a) "Snapshot Results" at any point in time; (b) "Results Summary" from a single run; (c) "Results Summary for multiple runs" (Trials); and (d) "Compare Report" for multiple scenario comparisons.

There are two common methods used for output analysis. A simple method is to explore the model visually with subject matter experts. This provides an opportunity to gain an understanding of how the different parts of the model interact with each other and how the performance measures can be affected. This is done by running the model and watching the entities move around on the computer monitor. With numbers and colors changing on the screen, you can see where bottlenecks are building up. By changing the modeling parameters and watching the effects of these changes, you can gain a knowledge and understanding of the way the system behaves. You can then perform statistical analyses on the output to obtain insights into the process under study.

As discussed earlier, stochastic simulation is based on models which use random numbers. In such models, random numbers, random number streams, and random number seeds play an important role when running simulations and analyzing their results. In stochastic models, the distribution of the CTQ generated is dependent on the random numbers that are used to create the distributions of the Xs. Thus, the outputs generated from stochastic inputs are stochastic. This means that different random number seeds (and hence, different random numbers) will generate different output results. This problem is further complicated by the fact that there could be many different random input variables (each using its own random number seed) that interact with each other during a simulation run. Clearly, running a simulation once is inadequate to get any kind of precise estimate of the expected behavior of the system; it is a sample of size one. Multiple and independent model replications are always required with stochastic simulations and the statistical analysis of the output generated by them is a critical prerequisite for making valid conclusions.

13.9 SIMULATION PROJECT MANAGEMENT

There are no strict rules on how to perform a simulation study; however, this section covers the basic steps that are recommended as a guideline. When doing a simulation study, there are several major checkpoints appropriate for formal reviews. Figure 13.6 shows the major checkpoints (diamonds) that occur after "data definition," "model definition," and "experimentation."

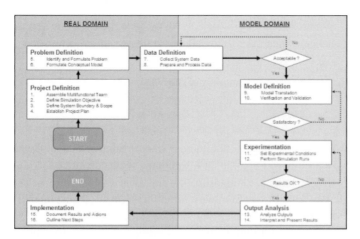

FIGURE 13.6 Steps in a Simulation Study

Project Definition

Define the Objectives of the Simulation. It is important that the objective(s) of a simulation are clear because the objective(s) determine all successive steps in a simulation study. In addition, budget and timelines also need to be discussed as well. Some common objectives for simulations include the following [see Reference 3]:

- *Performance analysis*: How well does the system perform under a given set of parameters (utilization, throughput, waiting times)?

- *Feasibility study*: Is a system capable of meeting customer requirements (throughput, waiting times, etc.); if not, what changes (added resources, improved methods) are recommended for meeting these requirements?

- *Capacity analysis*: What is the maximum processing or production capacity of a system?

- *Comparison study*: How does one system configuration compare with another system configuration?

- *Sensitivity analysis*: Which CTPs or Xs are the most influential on overall system performance?

- *Optimization*: What combination of feasible values for the CTPs or Xs optimizes the CTQs?

- *Decision/response analysis*: What are the relationships between the values of the CTPs or Xs and the values of the CTQ?

- *Constraint analysis*: Where are the constraints or bottlenecks in the system?

- *Communication*: What is the most effective way to depict the dynamic behavior of the system?

Define the Boundaries, Scope, and Assumptions of the System. Defining the boundaries and scope of the system to be simulated is as important as defining its objective(s). Modelers risk putting too much detail into a model if the boundaries and scope are not well defined. For example, do you need to include every detail of every process within each department, or is it appropriate to simply model the output of each department and how they interact with each other? The more steps you have in the model, the more data you have to collect for the model. It is important to simulate only the critical CTPs or Xs in a system and ignore all the others.

Assumptions are a common and required aspect in almost any type of analysis. Sometimes assumptions are made about the data when the data is not readily available. For example, when setting up a new clinic, patient arrival rate may not be known. It is better to start with many assumptions, and reduce them to an appropriate level. An assumption is good until it is discovered that it significantly impacts simulation results. When this occurs, it becomes necessary to reevaluate that assumption. All assumptions must be documented and agreed upon at the onset of a simulation.

Establish Project Plan. A project plan must be created and maintained for a simulation to manage costs, resources, and project scope. Though simulation is cheaper than experimentation with a real system, it is still labor intensive, expensive, and may fail to deliver desired results. It is important that you make realistic projections of the time requirements for modeling, gathering data, experimenting, documenting, and presenting simulation runs.

Problem Definition

Identify and Formulate the Problem. The first and most fundamental step in any problem-solving process is defining the problem. It is very difficult to solve a problem when there are uncertainties regarding the definition of the problem. The problem statement should be clearly defined and known to all members of the project team. It includes system boundaries to be included in the model and must state underlying assumptions.

Formulate the Conceptual Model. Formulating a conceptual model involves making decisions regarding how a system should be represented in terms of the capabilities and elements provided with a simulation package. It involves selecting a proper model by making the following decisions about the model:

1. Functional or structural: A functional model is one in which the model can be defined using an existing mathematical function such as $Y = f(X_1, X_2, X_3)$. A structural model is a model with logical linkages between the different components of the model; for example, flow diagrams.
2. Deterministic or random model.
3. Static or time-dependent (dynamic) model. If the model is dynamic, then is it a continuous flow or discrete event simulation model?

The overall strategy should focus on finding a model concept that minimizes the simulation effort, while ensuring that all objectives of the study are met.

Data Definition

Collect System Data. Data collection is probably the most time-consuming step of creating a simulation model. Data collection complexity increases with the level of detail used in the model. The following guidelines are recommended when collecting data for a simulation model:

a. **Identify data requirements:** Six Sigma team members define the scope of the data to be collected by considering the following factors:
   - Scope of the model—For example, if scope only includes modeling the teller services in a bank, then do not collect data for loan or investment services.
   - Level of detail—For example, if modeling on a department level, then do not collect data for each individual activity level.
   - Relevant factors (CTPs or Xs)—For example, if down times and move times are not relevant, you should ignore them.

- • Output variables (CTQs)—For example, CTQs might include maximum wait time for service, or percentage of wait times for service that are greater than 15 minutes.

b. **Systematize data collection:** Six Sigma team members utilize a systematic method for collecting data. First, they gather general information and then progressively collect additional information, as needed. This consists of a flow diagram that is verified with process experts. Verification of the flow diagram increases buy-in of all the stakeholders of the system being modeled. Second, team members collect data for service schedules, arrival times, service times, and wait times. For example, suppose customers arrive at a bank for service from one of two tellers. Table 13.5 shows one format for a questionnaire that could be used to collect data on the process.

TABLE 13.5　Data Collection Questionnaire for a Bank

Process Step	Distribution					Minimum	Mean	Maximum	Standard Deviation
	Exponential	Poisson	Normal	Triangular	Other				
Start.									
Customers arrive at bank.	X						6/minutes between arrivals		
Customers wait for service from a teller in a single waiting line.				X		0 minutes	8 minutes (Mode)	30 minutes	
Teller A services the customer.				X		0 minutes	2.5 minutes (Mode)	10 minutes	
Teller B services the customer.			X				12 minutes		1.5 minutes
Customer exits the bank.									
Stop.									

c. **Use appropriate sources**: Six Sigma team members can use data that already exists from historical records; for example, if tellers clock in and clock out of a work location. In manufacturing systems, process plans, flow charts, estimated times based on time studies, predetermined time standards, historical data, equipment specifications, vendor claims, personal interviews, or one's own best guess are common sources of data. Similarly, for service systems, log books, time studies, or estimates are common sources of data.

Prepare and Process Data. Modelers should check all data for arithmetic or data entry errors. If appropriate, modelers perform a Gage R&R study (see Section 5.7) on the data. At a minimum, Six Sigma team members do the following:

a. **Prepare a list of assumptions:** Assumptions are generally made when no data or incomplete data are available. For example, you may decide to use mean processing time for an activity when variability in the processing time is unknown. Examples of assumptions include: data are measured in minutes (not hours), transportation times are assumed to be part of processing time, resources are assumed to be available for 24 hours because they do not have an impact on how the model behaves; only high-priority customers are being simulated, daily arrival patterns are not modeled, and so on. Six Sigma team members document all the assumptions used in creating a simulation model before getting too far into the simulation study.

b. **Convert data into a useful form:** Six Sigma team members reformat and prepare data in a form that can be used in a simulation model. For example, you may have a large amount of raw data that you need to convert to a probability distribution, or team members may have to convert two calendar days relevant to an event (start and stop time) into cycle time data .Most simulation packages have calendar and shift functions for this purpose.

Model Definition

An initial simulation model is developed as soon as enough information is available to Six Sigma team members. Waiting until all the information is completely available may unnecessarily delay the model building exercise. Sometimes, initial model definition helps in the identification of missing information and leads to questions about the model, objectives, and scope.

Model Translation. Model translation is the process of mimicking a real-world system with an abstract conceptual model. It includes defining boundaries, time spans, inputs, outputs, and logical relationships (see Figure 13.7). A common mistake often made by an inexperienced modeler is attempting to fully and exactly replicate reality in a model. This is neither possible nor desirable. You should start with a simple model and increase its complexity as needed.

Models can be translated using mathematical formulas, computer languages, spreadsheets, and specialized simulation packages such as SigmaFlow [see Reference 4]. Simulation packages simplify the modeling process by providing input data definition screens, automatically running the model, and generating all the required output reports.

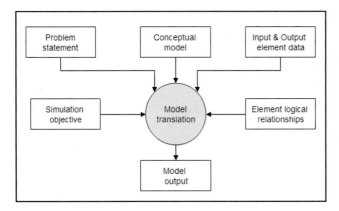

FIGURE 13.7 Model Translation

Verification and Validation. Six Sigma team members check the simulation model for consistency; that is, does the model behave like the real system? Checks are important to establish the credibility of the simulation model. In simulation language, these checks are called model verification and model validation:

- **Model Verification** refers to the accuracy of transforming a real system into a simulation model; in other words, building the *model right*.

- **Model Validation** refers to the degree to which the simulation model behaves with satisfactory accuracy with respect to the real system; in other words, building the *right model*.

Experimentation

Experiments are performed to find the value of a CTP or *X* that optimizes a CTQ, to compare alternative system configuration, or to perform sensitivity analyses on a particular system configuration.

Set Experimental Conditions. Six Sigma team members carefully plan simulation experiments to generate results with minimal expenditures of labor and time. Decisions that must be made prior to running experiments with a simulation model include: length of the warm up period, length of the simulation run, number of runs for a given configuration of the levels of the CTPs or *X*s, output parameters, probability distributions used to model arrival and service times, and decision percentages. Decision percentages are the percentage of entities flowing into a given section of a flowchart. For example, 25% of all patients arriving at a clinic are geriatric and go to clinic A, while 75% of patients are nongeriatric adults and go to clinic B.

Perform Simulation Runs. Experiments are conducted by varying the levels of the CTPs or *X*s and then measuring their effect on the CTQ.

Output Analysis

Results from a simulation study are a sample from an infinite population of possible results because different random numbers generate different results. When presenting results, modelers use graphical tools and animation, while keeping the results as short as necessary for Six Sigma team members to make an informed decision.

Implementation

Documents Results and Actions. Six Sigma team members document a simulation model by listing and describing assumptions, inputs, communications, consequences (results) of a simulation in the real system, and consequences (results) of alternative system configurations. Documentation is a key for verification and validation of a simulation model. It can provide a platform for asking "what-if" questions.

Outline Next Steps. Simulation provides Six Sigma team members an opportunity to find what works, what does not work, and how to improve a system or design; for example:

- Proceed with recommendations.
- Collect more data and do more simulations.
- Perform sensitivity analysis studies.

13.10 OPTIMIZING A PROCESS USING DESIGN OF EXPERIMENTS FROM SIMULATIONS

Introduction

Recall from Chapter 10, **design of experiments** is a set of statistical procedures used to analyze and compare alternative configurations of a system. Simulation is a tool for providing quantitative measures on any number of alternative configurations of a system. It is not an optimization tool that automatically runs all possible scenarios and then delivers the best system configuration. However, modelers can use design of experiments to intelligently set up and run experiments to determine the best system configuration of the CTPs and Xs to optimize a CTQ.

Setting up an experiment includes defining objectives, alternatives, stochastic drivers (random number seed and streams), and CTPs or Xs and their levels (same as inputs) for a simulation study. The responses (outputs) are dependent on which CTPs or Xs are included, and their levels. Experiments involving stochastic CTPs or Xs can be controlled such that each alternative setting of the levels of the CTPs or Xs is subjected to the same randomness by using the same random number streams.

Setting Up a 2^k Full Factorial Experiment

Recall, a full factorial experiment (see Section 10.3) is a method to statistically analyze the effects of k factors (CTPs or Xs) on a CTQ. For a 2^k full factorial design, factor levels are assigned two values: a high level (+ sign) and a low level (– sign). The responses (CTQs) are observed for all possible combinations of factors (CTPs or Xs) and their factor levels.

Table 13.6 shows the factors and factor level used to create a designed experiment for three factors ($k = 3$). This table can be used to create a design matrix (see Table 13.7) that shows the interaction of various factors on the response variable. Each design point requires multiple simulation runs, and the responses calculated for each design point should be statistically analyzed to determine the effects of these factors on selected performance criteria. The effort required to produce the necessary response data increases significantly as the number of factors increases.

TABLE 13.6 Factor and Factor Levels for 2^3 Designed Experiment

Factor (X)	Factor Description	Low Level (–)	High Level (+)
X_1	Number of service people (People)	5	6
X_2	Customer selection strategy (Strategy)	FIFO	By Priority
X_3	Inter-arrival time (Time)	Fixed (6)	Exponential (6)

TABLE 13.7 Design Matrix for 2^3 Factorial Designed Experiments

Run	X_1: People	X_2: Strategy	X_3: Time
1	-	-	-
2	+	-	-
3	-	+	-
4	+	+	-
5	-	-	+
6	+	-	+
7	-	+	+
8	+	+	+

The design matrix tells us the values of the factors that will be used in the model runs for each trial (design point). For example, the trial for run 6 includes 6 service people (X_1), FIFO selection strategy (X_2), and an inter-arrival time of 6 minutes that is exponentially distributed (X_3).

Analyzing 2^k Full Factorial Experiments

Once the experiments has been completed, the results produced should be statistically analyzed to understand the main effects of each CTP or X on the CTQ, as well as the interactive effects between the CTPs or Xs on the CTQ.

You can use Table13.6 and the design matrix of Table 13.7 to set up the experiments in which three factors (people, strategy, and time) are used to analyze customer service time.

The last two columns of Table 13.8 display the cycle time and throughput observed after performing one replication for each run, that is, $n = 1$ for each of 8 runs (trials). Common random number streams are used with each model replication for each run.

TABLE 13.8   Design Matrix and Simulation Results for 2^3 Factorial Designed Experiments

Run	X_1: People	X_2: Strategy	X_3: Time	CTQ_1: Cycle Time	CTQ_2: Throughput
1	-	-	-	$R_1 = 317$	$R_1 = 294$
2	+	-	-	$R_2 = 149$	$R_2 = 355$
3	-	+	-	$R_3 = 278$	$R_3 = 294$
4	+	+	-	$R_4 = 144$	$R_4 = 355$
5	-	-	+	$R_5 = 256$	$R_5 = 291$
6	+	-	+	$R_6 = 128$	$R_6 = 343$
7	-	+	+	$R_7 = 216$	$R_7 = 291$
8	+	+	+	$R_8 = 121$	$R_8 = 343$

SERVICETIME

Figure 13.8 shows a cube plot of the cycle time data showing the shortest cycle time is six "people"–"By PRIORITY"–"Exponential" with a response of 121 minutes. Figure 13.9 shows that there are no strong two-way interactions between the Xs. Figure 13.10 shows the main effects for each X. It shows that "number of people = 6" has the largest impact on cycle time. "Time = exponential" has the next largest impact on cycle time, and "strategy = By PRIORITY" has the smallest impact of cycle time. Consequently, all three plots agree that the optimal configuration is six "people"–"By PRIORITY"–"Exponential" with a response of 121 minutes.

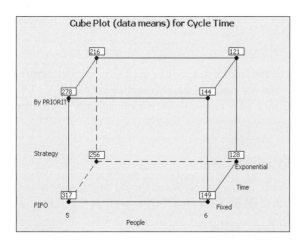

FIGURE 13.8   Minitab Cube Plot (Data Means) for Cycle Time

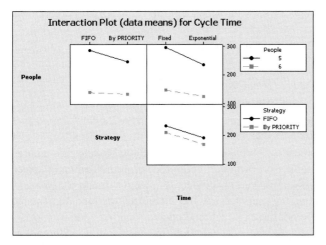

FIGURE 13.9 Minitab Interaction Plot (Data Means) for Cycle Time

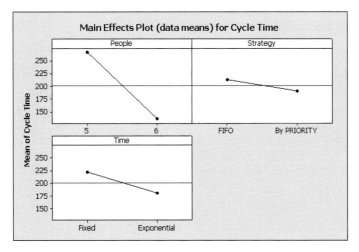

FIGURE 13.10 Minitab Main Effects Plot (Data Means) for Cycle Time

13.11 SERVICE INDUSTRY APPLICATION USING THE SIGMAFLOW SOFTWARE PACKAGE

Introduction

SigmaFlow (www.SigmaFlow.com) is one of many simulation software packages that are currently available. This section demonstrates SigmaFlow for a service industry application. A SigmaFlow CD is located inside the back cover of this book. Once you activate SigmaFlow, you will be able to use it for 30 days. Information is available about purchasing SigmaFlow at www.SigmaFlow.com.

This section demonstrates SigmaFlow Modeler, which is designed assuming the following:

1. Users want an initial model to quickly start to study the structure of a system.
2. Users want to expand a model as additional data becomes available.
3. Users want easy to obtain, but rigorous, performance results from the model.

One of the main impacts of the preceding premises is that SigmaFlow Modeler is not based on programming skill or statistical data, but on flowcharting a process on the computer screen and filling in necessary numeric data. Data for various objects is entered through a data panel (always visible), which makes it intuitive for users to view the data as it is defined and entered into the simulation model. Modelers do not have to click and open a separate window for data entry and review, which can be frustrating at times. In addition, modelers can use SigmaFlow Modeler for traditional number-crunching simulations. As simulations are run, they provide several built-in statistical outputs. Built-in reports include single run summaries, multiple run summaries with confidence interval calculations, alternative comparison reports, individual run reports from a trial run, and time-based graphs.

A Service Industry Application

SigmaFlow Modeler is illustrated using a simple banking example in which customers arrive for service by a teller before exiting the bank. Figure 13.11 shows the customer flow diagram.

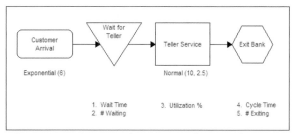

FIGURE 13.11   Customer Flow Diagram for a Bank

Customers arrive at a bank with an inter-arrival time that is exponentially distributed with an average time between arrivals of six minutes. As customers arrive, they are placed in a queue with unlimited capacity. The teller has a capacity of serving one customer at a time. If the teller is available, a customer is taken from the queue and serviced. If the teller is unavailable, the next customer waits in the queue for service. The service time at the teller is normally distributed with a mean of 10 minutes and standard deviation of 2.5 minutes. The customer exits the bank after service from the teller.

SigmaFlow Modeler has specific objects with built-in characteristics (see Table 13.9). For example, a modeler can define the inter-arrival times for "Customers Arrive at Bank" using a "Work Start" object. Similarly, a modeler can define the "Customer Waits for Teller" using a "Storage" object. To learn more about the characteristics of SigmaFlow objects, you can review the SigmaFlow Reference Manual [see Reference 4].

TABLE 13.9 SigmaFlow Objects

Activities	SigmaFlow Objects
Customers Arrive at Bank	Work Start
Customer Waits for Teller	Storage
Teller Services Customer	Process
Customer Exits Bank	Work Finished

Assumptions

Assumptions must be made whenever information is unavailable to construct a simulation model. The bank simulation utilized the following assumptions:

1. No customers are in the queue and the teller is idle at the beginning of the simulation.
2. There is no warm-up period involved in the simulation.
3. Teller service is always equipped with a teller in the simulation.
4. Move times between objects are negligible and not considered in the simulation.
5. Customers are pulled from the queue for servicing by a teller on a FIFO basis.
6. No shifts, breaks, and lunch hours are considered in the simulation.

Performance Measures

Simulation models automatically keep statistics on the CTPs or Xs and CTQs shown in Table 13.10. Column 1 shows the CTPs or Xs, and column 2 shows the objects where various statistics are collected on the CTQ(s).

TABLE 13.10 Simulation Statistics

Performance Measures (CTPs or Xs)	Simulation Objects
Customer Wait Times in Queue for Service by Teller	Storage (Wait for Teller)
Number of Customers Waiting for Service by Teller	Storage (Wait for Teller)
Teller Utilization (%)	Process (Teller Service)
Customer Cycle Time	Work Finished (Exit Bank)
Customer Throughput	Work Finished (Exit Bank)

Building the Model

Figure 13.12 shows the initial screen of SigmaFlow Modeler. You click on "Process Map" to activate the main drawing area where you can begin to enter the flowchart of the process under study using SigmaFlow's basic drawing tools.

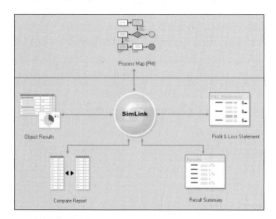

FIGURE 13.12   SigmaFlow Modeler Initial Launch Screen

Clicking once on the "Process Map (PM)" icon in the launch screen takes you to the main drawing screen shown in Figure 13.13. The process map of the system to be simulated is captured on the main drawing area. You can draw the process map using the standard shapes available in the objects toolbar on the left of the main drawing screen. Data definitions for the objects in the main drawing area are captured through the "Object Properties" panel to the right of the main drawing area, as shown in Figure 13.13. Each activity has its own data panel and is activated as you click on the object. For example, Figure 13.13 shows the data panel for the "Customer Arrival" object.

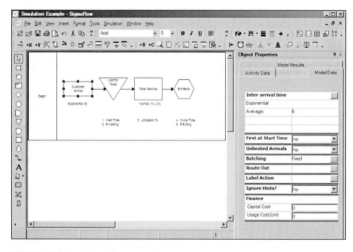

FIGURE 13.13   Main Drawing Screen

Defining the Data for Individual Objects

You start to capture the data associated with the individual objects of the process being simulated once the process map has been entered into the main drawing area. Simulation data is captured for each object in the "Model Data" tab of Object Properties window. One salient feature of SigmaFlow Modeler is that all objects come with some default data. This is provided for first-time users who just want to build and run a model with default data to see how animation works and what kind of data gets collected.

The bank simulation requires the following data:

1. *Inter-arrival time*: The inter-arrival time of customers to the bank is assumed to be exponentially distributed with an average of 6.0 minutes. Inter-arrival time is always defined for the "Work Start" object in SigmaFlow by following these steps:

   a. Click on the **Customer Arrival** flowchart symbol in the main drawing area of Figure 13.13. Select the **Model Data** tab of the Object Properties window shown in Figure 13.14 Panel A.

   b. Click on the button at the right side of the Inter-arrival time row.

   c. In the Inter-arrival times dialog box (see Figure 13.14 Panel B), select **Exponential** from the Distribution drop-down list box. Enter **6** in the Average edit box.

   d. Click **OK** to accept the change. These entries will be displayed in the Object Properties window.

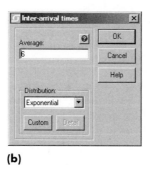

(b)

(a)

FIGURE 13.14 Object Properties

2. *Teller service time*: The service time for customers by a teller is normally distributed with mean of 10.0 minutes and standard deviation of 2.5 minutes. Service time statistics are defined at the process step where this activity takes place.

a. Click on **Teller Service** in the main drawing area of Figure 13.13. Select the **Model Data** tab of the Object Properties window shown in Figure 13.15 Panel A.

b. Click on the button on the right side of the Operation time row..

c. In the Operation Time dialog box (see Figure 13.15 Panel B), select **Normal** from the Distribution drop-down list box. Enter **10** in the Mean edit box and **2.5** in the Standard Deviation edit box.

d. Click **OK** to accept the change. These entries will be displayed in the Object Properties window.

(b)

(a)

FIGURE 13.15   Object Properties for Teller Service Time

You can ignore the other data fields for the preceding objects, as well as other objects, because they will not have an impact on the simulation results.

Setting the Simulation Clock

The Simulation Clock changes and modifies the Clock Properties, establishes the warm-up period, and defines the simulation period. Figure 13.16 shows the Simulation Clock for the bank example. There is no warm-up period, and the length of the simulation run is 480 minutes in the bank example. Follow these steps to set the clock properties for the bank example:

a   Open the Clock Properties window from **Simulation → Modeler Settings → Clock → Clock Properties** menu.

b. Click on the Results Collection Period button. Enter **480** in the edit box. Click **OK**. The simulation will run for 480 minutes and then stop.

c. Leave all settings as shown in Figure 13.16.

d. Click **OK** to accept the Clock properties.

FIGURE 13.16 Simulation Clock

Running the Model

You can run a simulation once you have defined all the object data and run time. To do so, select: **Simulation → Modeler Settings → Clock → Run Menu option.**

At this point, the simulation will start running and you will notice the animation (object color change) on the screen, as well as the time change on the clock toolbar, which gives you the status of the simulation over time. Each process step changes colors over the course of a simulation run: green indicates that the process is "working," red indicates the process is "waiting," orange indicates that the process is "blocked," and the number of units in each process activity is displayed on top of each node.

Collecting Results

After the simulation is finished, you can view the results of individual objects through the "Model Results" tab of that object, as shown in Figure 13.17. You can also selectively add other results to the "Results Summary." The Results Summary provides the following statistics:

1. *Storage (Wait for Teller) Object*: Results are generated for each storage object. The results can be moved selectively to the Results Summary report. Figure 13.17 shows the steps used to add average wait time and average number of customers waiting in the queue to the "Results Summary":

a. Click on **Wait for Teller** in the main drawing area of Figure 13.13. Select the **Model Results** tab in the Object Properties dialog box shown in Figure 13.17. All the results for this object are displayed in the panel.

b. Check the boxes for the results to be added to the Results Summary. Statistics for all of the checked boxes will appear in the Results Summary.

FIGURE 13.17　Object Properties—Counts

The storage results indicate that there were 16 customers still in the queue when the simulation was stopped after 480 minutes. Because it started from an empty state, the minimum number of customers in the queue was zero. The maximum number of customers in the queue during the simulation was 16. Sixty-six customers entered the queue and 16 were still waiting for service at the end of the simulation. The average customer waiting time in the queue was 42.40 minutes. The minimum wait time was 0.00 minutes and the maximum wait time was 116.32 minutes.

2. *Process (Teller Service)*:

a. Click on **Teller Service** in the main drawing area of Figure 13.13. Select the **Model Results** tab in the Object Properties dialog box shown in Figure 13.18. All the results for this object are displayed in the panel.

b. Check the boxes for the results to be added to the "Results Summary;" for example, Percent of Time—Working (for utilization %).

3. *Work Finished (Exit Bank)*:

a. Click on **Exit Bank** in the main drawing area of Figure 13.13. Select the **Model Results** tab of the Object Properties dialog box shown in Figure 13.19. All the results for this object are displayed in the panel.

b. Check the boxes for the results to be added to the Results Summary; for example, Work Completed (for customer throughput) and Time in System—Average (for customer cycle time).

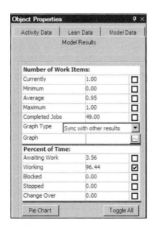

FIGURE 13.18   Object Properties—Time

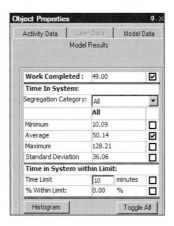

FIGURE 13.19   Object Properties—Work Finished

This results shows that 49 customers were serviced during the selected time period. The average time in the bank was 50.14 minutes, the minimum time was 10.09 minutes, the maximum was 128.21 minutes, and the standard deviation of the time was 36.06 minutes. Also, 0% of customers were serviced within the USL = 10 minutes.

Results Summary

SigmaFlow Modeler automatically builds a result summary based on the boxes selected from the Individual Model Results tab (see Figure 13.20). The Results Summary report can be launched from **Simulation → Simulation Results → Results Summary**.

#	Act #	Department Name	Activity Name	Result Type	Value
1	3	Dept1	Wait for Teller	Average queue size	6.00
2	3	Dept1	Wait for Teller	Average Queuing Time	42.40
3	4	Dept1	Teller Service	Working %	96.44
4	5	Dept1	Exit Bank	Number Completed	49.00
5	5	Dept1	Exit Bank	Average Time in System	50.14

FIGURE 13.20 Results Summary

Observations

Even though this is a simple example of a simple simulation run, it provides an excellent illustration of basic simulation issues that need to be addressed when conducting a simulation study. Imagine a system with dozens of additional processes with many more factors influencing behavior such as downtimes, shifts, resource contention, and priorities. You can see how using simulation software can make simulation a practical analysis tool. Packages such as SigmaFlow can track the many relationships and update the numerous statistics that are present in most simulations. Equally important, these packages are not prone to error and can perform millions of instructions per second with tremendous accuracy.

SUMMARY

This chapter introduced and defined simulation modeling. Further, it presented several applications of simulation, the advantages of simulation, and precautions and pitfalls of simulation modeling. It presented simulation terminology, how a simulation model works, and how to use experimental design to identify the levels of the CTPs and Xs that optimize a CTQ. The chapter ends with the application of SigmaFlow, a simulation software package, to a banking operation.

REFERENCES

1. Gitlow, H. S., and D. M. Levine, *Six Sigma for Green Belts and Champions* (Upper Saddle River, NJ: Financial Times Prentice Hall, 2005).

2. Gogg, T. J., and J. R. A. Mott, *Improve Quality & Productivity With Simulation*, 3rd ed. (Palos Verde, CA: JMI Consulting Group, 1996).

3. Harrell, C. R., and K. Tumay, *Simulation Made Easy—A Manager's Guide* (Norcross, GA: Industrial Engineering and Management Press, Institute of Industrial Engineers, 1995).

4. Jain, A. K., *SigmaFlow Reference Manual* (Dallas, TX: SigmaFlow, 2004).

5. Law, A. M., and W. D. Kelton, *Simulation Modeling and Analysis, Second Edition* (New York: McGraw-Hill, Inc., 1991).

6. Levine, D. M., P. P. Ramsey, and R. Smidt, *Applied Statistics for Engineers and Scientists Using Microsoft Excel and Minitab* (Upper Saddle River, NJ: Prentice Hall, 2001).

ARTICULATING THE VOICE OF THE STAKEHOLDER

SECTIONS

LEARNING OBJECTIVES

After reading this chapter, you will be able to:

- Segment each stakeholder group for an organization; for example, customer segments, employee segments, investor segments, supplier segments, and regulator segments.
- Conduct a Kano survey within each stakeholder segment to identify the Attractive, One-Way, and Must-Be CTQs and CTPs.

INTRODUCTION

The purpose of this chapter is to provide the theory and methods necessary for product development team members to understand the various "voices of stakeholders." These voices include the following:

- Voice of the Customer.
- Voice of the Employee.

- Voice of the Investor.
- Voice of the Supplier.
- Voice of the Community.
- Voice of the Environment.
- Voice of the Buildings and Grounds (the Facilities Administration Department).

Additionally, this chapter explains how to convert raw "Voice of the Stakeholder" data into cognitive images (CTQs and CTPs).

14.1 MARKET SEGMENTATION

Definition

Recall from Chapter 5, "Measure Phase," that **market segmentation** is the process of dividing a market into homogeneous subsets of customers such that the customers in any subset will respond similarly to a marketing mix established for them and differently from customers in another subset. A marketing mix is a combination of product, service, or process features; a price structure; a place (distribution) strategy; and a promotional strategy.

Segmentation Criteria

There are four criteria that team members can use to measure the success of a market segmentation plan [see Reference 11]. First, **sustainability** is the degree to which a segment is large enough and/or profitable enough to be considered for attention with a unique marketing mix. Second, **accessibility** is the degree to which a firm can effectively communicate with the members of a market segment. Third, **measurability** is the degree to which information exists (or is obtainable) on a particular market segment. Fourth, **responsiveness** is the degree to which a selected target market responds to a marketing mix. The ideal market segment is: sustainable (large and/or profitable), easy and inexpensive to communicate with, easy and inexpensive to measure the effect(s) of a marketing mix, and responds well to a marketing mix.

Segmentation Variables

There are three types of market segments. Each segment is defined by its own set of segmentation variables. The three types of market segments are consumer, business, and indirect.

Consumer Market Segments

Consumer market segments are defined by one or more of the following segmentation variables: family life cycle, psychographic, geographic, demographic, and/or buyer behavior.

Family life cycle is a segmentation variable that is a function of the age, marital status, and age of the children of the members of a market segment. The categories of this variable are as follows:

- Young-Single
- Young-Married-No Children
- Young-Married-Youngest Child Under Six
- Young-Married-Youngest Child Six or Over
- Older-Married-With Children
- Older-Married-No Children Under 18
- Older-Single
- Other (e.g., Young-Single-Children)

Market researchers have found this categorization of the members of a market segment to be of great value in segmenting the behavior of the entire market with respect to its response to a marketing mix.

Psychographics include a set of segmentation variables that are used to categorize the personality of the members of a market. Table 14.1 shows the personality traits and their respective classifications.

TABLE 14.1 Psychographic Segmentation Variables

Personality Traits	Classifications
Compulsiveness	Compulsive; Noncompulsive
Gregariousness	Extrovert; Introvert
Autonomy	Dependent; Independent
Conservatism	Conservative; Liberal; Radical
Authoritarianism	Authoritarian; Democratic
Leadership	Leader; Follower
Ambitiousness	High Achiever; Low Achiever

Again, market researchers have found these personality variables to be of great value in segmenting the behavior of an entire market with respect to its response to a marketing mix. For example, the compulsiveness variable may be very useful in helping to sell anti-bacterial soap by identifying individuals with compulsive cleaning habits.

Geographic variables include a set of segmentation variables that are used to categorize the members of a market by where they live and/or work. Table 14.2 shows the geographic areas in the United States and their respective classifications.

TABLE 14.2   Geographic Segmentation Variables for the United States

Population Characteristics	Classifications
Region	Pacific; Mountain; West North Central; West South Central; East North Central; East South Central; South Atlantic; Middle Atlantic; New England
City or SMSA Size	Under 5,000
	5,000–19,999
	20,000–49,999
	50,000–99,999
	100,000–249,999
	250,000–499,999
	500,000–999,999
	1,000,000–3,999,999
	4,000,000 or over
Density	Urban; Suburban; Rural
Climate	Northern; Southern

Once again, market researchers have found geographic variables to be of great value in segmenting the behavior of an entire market with respect to its response to a marketing mix. For example, the density variable may be very useful in helping to determine the optimal size for a box of breakfast cereal by understanding the different shelf sizes in the homes of families in urban versus rural areas.

Demographic variables include a set of segmentation variables that are used to categorize the population characteristics of the members of a market. Table 14.3 shows the population characteristics and their respective classifications.

TABLE 14.3   Demographic Segmentation Variables

Age	Under 6; 6–11; 12–17; 18–34; 35–49; 50–64; 65+
Sex	Male; Female
Family Size	1–2; 3–5; 6+
Income	Under $10,000
	$10,000 to less than $25,000
	$25,000 to less than $50,000
	$50,000 to less than $100,000
	Over $100,000

Occupation	Professional and Technical
	Managers, Officials, and Proprietors
	Etc.
Education	Grade school or less
	Some high school
	Graduated high school
	Some college
	Graduated college
Religion	Catholic
	Protestant
	Jewish
	Other
Race	White; African-American; Asian
Nationality	American; British; French; German; and so on
Social Class	Lower-lower
Note: Social class has several	Upper-lower
definitions; for example, there are the	Lower-middle
Hollingshead, Warner, and Coleman	Middle-middle
definitions (see http://www.siue.edu/	Upper-middle
~rgiacob/475Socialclass.ppt#5).	Lower-upper
	Upper-upper

Market researchers have found demographic variables to be of great value in segmenting the behavior of an entire market with respect to its response to a marketing mix. For example, the religion variable may be very useful in helping to know what food products can be sold to the members of a given religion by understanding their dietary laws. Some Jews eat only kosher food, some Catholics do not eat meat on Fridays, and some Hindus are vegetarian.

Buyer behavior variables include a set of segmentation variables that are used to categorize the buying behavior of the members of a market. Table 14.4 shows the buyer behavior variables and their respective classifications.

TABLE 14.4 Buyer Behavior Variables

Buyer Behavior Variables	Classifications
Usage Rate	Nonuser; Light User; Medium User; Heavy User
Readiness Stage	Unaware; Aware; Interested; Intending to Try; Tried; Regular Buyer
Benefits Sought	Economy; Status; Dependability
End Use	(Varies with product, service, or process)
Brand Loyalty	None; Light; Strong
Factor Sensitivity	Quality; Service; Price; Delivery

Finally, market researchers have found that buyer behavior variables are of great value in segmenting the behavior of an entire market with respect to its response to a given marketing mix. For example, brand loyalty can be very useful in determining the content of a television commercial. "I'd walk a mile for a Camel" was a slogan utilized to sell cigarettes to extreme brand loyalty Camel smokers. "Buy one, get one free" is a technique used to promote the initial purchase of a product.

Business Market Segments

Business market segments can be defined using macro-segmentation or micro-segmentation variables. Macro-segmentation variables are used to define the demographics of organizations. First, geographic location is a variable used to segment the business market by area of the world; for example, Asia or North America, or New York City, New York or Lexington, Kentucky. Second, product use is a variable used to segment the business market according to their usage of a product. For example, a rubber-backed walk-off mat can be used to wipe snow off a customer's feet before entering a store or can be used to wipe grease off a maintenance worker's feet before entering the cafeteria. Third, type of organization is a variable used to segment the business market by different types of organizations. For example, a paper mill may need a heavier grade paper towel for washing hands than an insurance company. Finally, customer size is a segmentation variable useful in segmenting the business market by the number of customers or the volume of sales. For example, a company with one million employees may demand special invoicing requirements, while a company with 10 employees may accept the standard invoice.

Micro-segmentation variables are used to define the purchasing behavior of organizations. First, organizations can be segmented on key purchasing criteria variables such as pre-certified vendor program (Yes or No) or minority vendor program (Yes or No). Second, organizations can be segmented on personal characteristics of purchasing agent variables such as: purchasing agents trained in Six Sigma management (Yes or No), or purchasing agent certified by a national purchasing association (Yes or No). Third, organizations can be segmented on purchasing strategy variables such as electronic versus paper purchasing system, sole source versus multiple source purchasing policy, and competitive bidding on price assuming equal quality versus competitive bidding on quality and price. Finally, organizations can be segmented on importance of purchase variables such as size of purchase order (under $1,000 versus $1,000 or more), or strategic purchase (web page) versus routine purchase (paper supplies).

Indirect Market Segments

Indirect market segments are defined using internal or external segmentation variables. Internal indirect market segmentation variables and their classifications are as follows:

- Position on the organizational chart (top management, middle management, supervisor, employee)
- Division
- Department

For example, a top-level manager and a supervisor may purchase different types of rugs for their offices.

External indirect market segmentation variables and their classifications are as follows:

- Environment (endangered species living in area (Yes/No), world historical site (Yes/No), inner city versus farm country, politically unstable versus politically stable, etc.)
- Community (small versus large, diverse versus homogeneous, etc.)
- Suppliers (supplies versus equipment, etc.)
- Investors (institutional versus individual, etc.)
- Regulators (federal, state, or local, etc.)
- Union (local office versus national office, etc.)
- Legal system (U.S. legal system versus Canadian legal system)

For example, members of diverse and homogeneous communities may purchase different types of "Seasons Greetings" cards to send than members of heterogeneous communities.

Market Segmentation Strategies

Three common market segmentation strategies are: undifferentiated, differentiated, and concentrated. **Undifferentiated market segmentation** is a strategy in which all market segments receive the same marketing mix. This strategy is used if a firm wants to go after the entire market; the same marketing mix is equally effective in all market segments; or when a limited marketing budget prevents multiple marketing mixes.

Differentiated market segmentation is a strategy in which each market segment receives its own unique marketing mix. A marketing mix is unique if at least one of its components (product, price, promotion, or place) is different from the marketing mix for any other segment. This strategy is used if a firm wants to go after all market segments to maximize sales and if a unique marketing mix is needed for each market segment. This is potentially an expensive strategy.

Concentrated market segmentation is a strategy in which only selected market segments receive a unique marketing strategy to maximize sales within those market segments (for example, large and profitable segments). All segments not selected for a unique market mix receive the limited benefit of the market mix from one of the selected market segments.

The market segmentation strategy utilized in a marketing program depends on several factors. First, company resources play an enormous role in determining which marketing strategy is appropriate for a market. Bigger budgets allow for a differentiated strategy, while smaller budgets allow only for an undifferentiated strategy. Second, product or service homogeneity is a significant factor when selecting a marketing strategy. Do the products or services being marketed lend themselves to differentiation via multiple market mixes for different market segments? Third, market homogeneity is also a significant factor when selecting a market strategy. Will the customers in different market segments respond to unique marketing mixes enough to justify the cost of the multiple marketing mixes? Fourth, the stage in the life cycle of a product or service can play a big role in determining which market segmentation strategy is appropriate for a market. For example, an undifferentiated market segmentation strategy may be reasonable for a product in the introductory stage of its life cycle, while a concentrated strategy may be appropriate for the same product in the maturity stage of its life cycle. Fifth, the competition's market strategies are an enormous factor in selecting a market segmentation strategy. If your competition is using a differentiated market segmentation strategy, it might be unwise for your organization to use an undifferentiated strategy.

Market Profile Analysis

Team members need to prioritize the segments within a market for the concentrated marketing strategy to efficiently and effectively utilize the marketing budget. Markets can be prioritized using the taxonomies shown in Table 14.5.

TABLE 14.5 Market Prioritization Variables

Market Characteristic	Measures	Desirable State of Characteristic
Growth potential	Size of market	Large
	Position in market's life cycle (introduction, growth, maturation, decline)	Introduction or growth
Order of entry	Order of entry of competitors into segment	Early entrant into market
	Product and marketing advantage	Significant
Economies of scale	Costs decrease as cumulative sales volume increases	Yes
Competitive attractiveness	Potential share of market segment	Large
	Intensity of rivalry in segment	Low
Investment	Investment in dollars, technology and talent	Small
Reward	Profit	Large
	ROI	Quick
Risk	Stability	Yes
	Probability of losses	Small

A market profile analysis is a subjective weighting of a particular market segment's score on each of the preceding seven market prioritization variables. Recall, the concentrated market segmentation strategy creates unique marketing mixes only for selected market segments (for example, large and profitable segments). Also, recall that the differentiated and undifferentiated segmentation strategies both pursue all the segments in a market.

Market Segmentation Methods

Two methods for segmenting a market are presented in this section: SIPOC analysis and statistical analysis.

SIPOC Analysis. A **SIPOC analysis** is a simple tool for identifying the **S**uppliers and their **I**nputs into a process, the high-level steps of a **P**rocess, the **O**utputs of the process, and the **C**ustomer (market) segments interested in the outputs. Table 14.6 shows the format of a SIPOC analysis.

TABLE 14.6 Format for a Generic SIPOC Analysis

Suppliers		Inputs (*Xs*)		Process (*Xs*)		Outputs (CTQs)		Customer (Market) Segments
	>		>		>		>	

Team members identify relevant suppliers by asking the following questions:

- Where does information and material come from?
- Who are the suppliers?

Team members identify relevant inputs by asking the following questions:

- What do your suppliers provide?
- What effect do the inputs or supplies (*Xs*) have on the process?
- What effect do the inputs or supplies (*Xs*) have on the CTQs?

Team members create a high-level flowchart of the process, taking particular care to identify the beginning and ending points of the process. A **flowchart** is a pictorial summary of the flows and decisions that comprise a process.

Team members identify relevant outputs by asking the following questions:

- What products or services does this process make?
- What are the CTQs that are critical to the customer's perception of quality?

Team members identify the customer (market) segments for the outputs by asking the following questions:

- Who are the customers or market segments of these outputs?
- Have you identified the CTQs for each market segment?

Dormitory Example. Table 14.7 shows a SIPOC analysis of the dormitory project.

TABLE 14.7   Partial SIPOC Analysis for the Dormitory Project

Suppliers	Inputs (Xs)	Process (Xs)	Outputs (CTQs)	Customers (Market Segments)
Architects	Drawing and blueprints	Flowchart of the processes for building new on-campus housing (not shown here)	Dormitory building	Executives in residence
Coral Gables	Permits		Dormitory rooms	M.B.A. students
Contractors	Construction		Public areas	Undergrad business students
Sub-Contractors	Construction		Entertainment areas	Dean of the School of Business
Vendors	Materials and supplies			Campus police for security and safety
				Facilities administration for maintenance, power, water, gas, etc.
				Facilities administration for grounds

Statistical Analysis. You can use statistical analysis to simultaneously study multiple market segmentation variables to identify clusters of customers who will respond similarly to a unique marketing mix. **Cluster analysis** [see Reference 6] is a statistical method that seeks to form groups of customers (market segments) that are homogeneous within a group and heterogeneous between groups with respect to one or more market segmentation variables. The functional form of a cluster analysis is as follows:

$$Y = f(X_{1j}, X_{2j}, X_{3j}, ..., X_{mj})$$

where

Y = Market segment

X_{1j} = Demographic variables

X_{2j} = Psychographic variables

X_{3j} = Buyer-behavior variables

X_{mj} = Other variables

Dormitory Example. Recall from Chapter 5 that the Dean of the School of Business Administration identified three distinct market segments for the new Business School housing construction. These market segments are executives in residence, regular MBA students, and undergraduate business students.

Executives in Residence. The dormitory will have two floors dedicated to executives in residence. The Dean of the School of Business made this decision before the beginning of the project. Executives in residence are individuals who come to campus for one or two weeks to attend a concentrated class. They are a market segment that requires the amenities of a five-star hotel. Therefore, the marketing research effort for this segment focused on studying five-star hotels.

Regular MBA Students. It is proposed that the dormitory have two floors dedicated to regular Master of Business Administration (MBA) students. This is a diverse group. There is a lower age bound around 22 years and an upper age bound around 45 to 50 years. Many of the older students are also married with children. Currently, no regular MBA students live on campus, as no housing options are provided for them. However, over half of the regular MBA students are from outside the state of Florida, so they require local housing to attend classes. This segment presents a financially diverse group with some need-based financial aid, some merit-based scholarships, some receiving funding from their employer, and others paying out of pocket.

Undergraduate Business Students. The undergraduate business students are more homogenous with respect to their age and marital status. According to USNews.com, the average age of full-time undergraduates is 20 years with only 8 percent being above the age of 25, and most of these students are single. Over half the undergraduates are from outside the state of Florida, so they also require local housing. Current options on campus for the undergraduate students include standard double rooms, suite-style double rooms, single rooms, and apartments. Five floors will be dedicated to undergraduate students. The Director of Residence Halls stated, "I have never had a student presented with the opportunity to live in a premium room be unable to find the money to pay for the room."

14.2 KANO SURVEYS

Introduction

Kano surveys embrace a set of market research tools used for three purposes: (1) to improve existing products, services, or processes or to create less-expensive versions of existing products, services, or processes (called Level A surveys); (2) to create major new features for existing products, services, or processes (called Level B surveys); and (3) to invent and innovate an entirely new product, service, or process (called Level C surveys).

Level A Survey—Improved or Less Expensive Designs

Level A surveys are used to improve existing products, services, or processes or to create less-expensive versions of existing products, services, or processes. Level A studies are well documented and understood in the Six Sigma literature [see Reference 5]. Consequently, they will only be briefly discussed in this book.

Level A surveys gather Voice of the Customer data from the market segments selected for study by team members. Voice of the Customer data are either reactive or proactive. Reactive data reaches an organization as a direct result of doing business. Some examples of reactive data are: complaints, compliments, product returns or credits, product/service sales preferences, contract cancellations, market share, customer defections/acquisitions, customer referrals, closure rates of sales calls, web page hits, problem or services hot line calls, technical support calls, accounts receivables where customers refuse to pay as they do not believe the service/product was as expected, and sales data. Proactive data arrives only if an organization collects it through positive action, such as data gathered through interviews, focus groups, surveys, comment cards, sales calls, market research, customer observations, benchmarking, or dashboards. Six Sigma team members use Level A studies to collect and analyze Voice of the Customer data to develop critical to quality characteristics (CTQs). Two examples of the use of Level A studies are waiting times in a hospital and weights for chocolate bars.

Level B Survey—Major New Features of Existing Designs

Level B surveys are used to create major new features for existing products, services, or processes. Table 14.8 shows the four stages and nine steps in a Level B study.

TABLE 14.8 Stages and Steps of a Level B Study

STAGES	STEPS WITHIN STAGES
STAGE ONE Collect Voice of the Lead User (VoU) and Voice of the Customer (VoC) Data	
	Step 1—Select an innovation as the subject of a DFSS project and segment the market for it.
	Step 2—Identify lead users and heavy users in each market segment.
	Step 3—Collect "VoU" and "VoC" data concerning circumstantial issues from each market segment.

STAGES	STEPS WITHIN STAGES
STAGE TWO Analyze VoU and VoC Data	
	Step 4—Classify "VoU" and "VoC" data as circumstantial or product-related data in each market segment.
	Step 5—Determine the critical circumstantial issues to regular users in each market segment.
STAGE THREE Develop New Features	
	Step 6—Determine the focus point for each circumstantial issue in each market segment.
	Step 7—Develop cognitive images (CTQs) for each focus point in each market segment.
STAGE FOUR Evolve Strategies for New Features	
	Step 8—Classify cognitive images (CTQs) by Kano category and cost distribution in each market segment.
	Step 9—Develop strategic themes for each cognitive image (CTQs) for selected market segments.

STAGE ONE: Collect "Voice of the User" (VoU) and "Voice of the Customer" (VoC) Data

STAGE ONE—Step 1: Select an Innovation as the Subject of a DFSS Project and Segment the Market for It

The parking system at the Coral Gables campus of the University of Miami is the subject of this case study. The parking system was selected because of the extraordinarily negative views expressed by a sample of the stakeholders of the university parking system.

A graduate student sampled 50 parkers in the Ring Parking Lot every hour between noon and 2:30 P.M. on April 29, 10:30 A.M. and 2:00 P.M. on April 30, noon and 2:30 P.M. on May 1, and 10:30 A.M. to 2:30 P.M. on May 2. These times were selected due to peak parking demand patterns. The week of April 29 was deemed a typical week for parking by the members of the team. The 50 parkers selected each hour were the first people encountered by the interviewer in each corner and center of the lot.

Each parker was asked the following question:

"I feel _____ about the parking conditions in this particular lot."

1. Extremely Satisfied

2. Satisfied

3. Neutral

4. Dissatisfied

5. Extremely Dissatisfied

6. "It Sucks"

Category 6 was added by the interviewer because a large number of respondents expressed greater dissatisfaction than "Extremely Dissatisfied" with the phrase "It Sucks."

A preliminary *p*-chart of the percentage of students that opted for the "It Sucks" category showed a process in statistical control around an average percentage of 37%. Further, another preliminary *p*-chart of the percentage of students that opted for the "Very Dissatisfied" or "It Sucks" categories showed a process in statistical control around an average of 99%. This indicates a uniform and overwhelming negative attitude toward the parking process in the Ring Lot. The team generalized this attitude to all parkers on the Coral Gables campus through expertise in parking systems.

The market segments examined were commuter students, residential students, faculty, administration, staff, and others. Team members were the director of parking, five employees from the Parking Department, a faculty member, and three graduate students.

STAGE ONE—Step 2: Identify Lead Users and Heavy Users in Each Market Segment

Lead users are consumers of a product, service, or process who are months or years ahead of regular users in their use of the item and will benefit greatly by an innovation. For example, a lead user of a hair dryer may attach a portable battery pack and use it as a body warmer at football games played in cold weather. Lead users are useful for identifying the unknown needs and wants of regular users necessary for creating innovative new features of existing products, services, or processes. Heavy users are useful for identifying the needs and wants of regular users necessary for improving existing products, services, or processes

Identification of Lead User and Heavy User Indicators. Team members ask appropriate people (e.g., managers in companies) to help identify experts with the product under study by asking the following questions:

- "Whom do you regard as the person most expert in the use of this product, service, or process?"

- "Whom do you turn to when facing difficulties with this product, service, or process?"

Once the external and internal expert(s) have been identified, team members ask the following questions:

1. What environment, images, emotions, needs, and wants come to mind when you think of lead users of this product, service, or process? Heavy users?
2. For what purpose do lead users use this product, service, or process? Heavy users?
3. How do lead users use this product, service, or process? Heavy users?
4. Who do you regard as the person who exhibits the most ingenuity with the product, service, or process? How do they exhibit ingenuity?
5. What are the characteristics of a lead user? Of a heavy user?

Next, the experts are asked how lead and heavy users would benefit from resolving the problems that exist with the current product or service.

Finally, the team members construct a "Lead User and Heavy User Characteristics by Market Segment" matrix (see Table 14.9). The rows of Table 14.9 list the identifying factors of lead and heavy users. The columns list the market segments for regular users. The cells contain contact information for one or more lead or heavy users.

TABLE 14.9 Section of the "Lead User and Heavy User Characteristics by Market Segment" Matrix

Lead User or Heavy User Classification	Faculty	Staff	Administrators	Commuter Students	Residential Students	Visitors, Volunteers, Others
People in fraudulent parking permit ring.						
People who know parking rules and use knowledge to beat system.						
People who buy a visitor pass and punch the date with a pencil making sure they don't remove the paper flap with the punched date. They reuse the permit by pasting the paper flap back into place.						
People who buy a one- or two-day pass per week, which is cheaper than buying a yearly permit.						

(continued)

TABLE 14.9   Section of the "Lead User and Heavy User Characteristics by Market Segment" Matrix (Continued)

Lead User or Heavy User Classification	Faculty	Staff	Administrators	Commuter Students	Residential Students	Visitors, Volunteers, Others
People who jam meters with soda caps or gum to prevent the red flag from being visible.						
Students who pay home owners to park in their driveway near campus.						
Students who continually appeal tickets, knowing a reversal is likely.						
People who buy two-part stickers for convertibles and use the two parts on two cars.						
People who use magnetic Pizza Hut signs to park in service spots.						
People who will only speak to a high-level manager.						
People who haven't gotten a ticket in five years.						

Identification of Lead Users and Heavy Users. There are two approaches for identifying lead users and heavy users. In the first approach, team members ask experts to insert names and addresses of lead users and heavy users in a "Lead User and Heavy User Characteristics by Market Segment" matrix. In the second approach, for each market segment, team members develop a questionnaire based on "lead user" and "heavy user" characteristics. The questionnaire should be distributed to a large sample of regular users. Analysis of the questionnaire data involves doing a cluster analysis to identify lead users and heavy users.

STAGE ONE—Step 3: Collect "VoU" and "VoC" Data Concerning Circumstantial Issues from Each Market Segment

Circumstantial data provides insight into the context in which a product, service, or process is used by a lead user. For example, a woman says: "I am very cold." Picture the scene in your mind. The circumstantial data surrounding the statement is that she is in a hospital bed. Does the circumstantial data change your view of the scene? If it does, then you understand the value of circumstantial data. Circumstantial data should always be kept in the language of the customer to maintain its integrity.

Team members gather "Voice of the User" and "Voice of the Customer" data by asking the following questions:

1. What emotions come to mind when you think about the product, service, or process?
2. What needs and wants come to mind when you think about the product, service, or process?
3. What complaints or problems would you like to mention about the product, service, or process?

Parking Example. Team members gathered "Voice of the User" circumstantial data from a judgment sample of lead users and "Voice of the Customer" data from a judgment sample of heavy users. Three questions used to collect data from lead and heavy users of the parking system at the University of Miami are the following:

1. What emotions come to mind when you think about parking on campus?
2. What needs and wants come to mind when you think about parking on campus?
3. What complaints or problems would you like to mention about parking on campus?

STAGE TWO: Analyze "Voice of the User" and "Voice of the Customer" Data

STAGE TWO—Step 4: Classify "Voice of the User" (VoU) and "Voice of the Customer" (VoC) Data as Circumstantial or Product-Related Data for Each Market Segment

Recall the definition of circumstantial data from Step 3. As team members collect circumstantial data, they also accidentally collect product-related data. Product-related data identifies the current expectations and perceptions of lead users and heavy users.

This step involves classifying the collected data into product-related data that is useful for Level A studies and circumstantial data that is useful for Level B and Level C (to be discussed later in this chapter) studies.

Classifying data as product-related or circumstantial takes practice. Table 14.10 shows a matrix that you can use to help classify data by market segment.

TABLE 14.10 Classification Matrix by Market Segment

Selected Market Segment(s)	Raw "Voice of the User" and "Voice of the Customer" Data (in the Language of Respondent)	Data Classification (Product or Circumstantial)
Segment A		
High-priority customer A1	Comment A11	P
	Comment A12	P
	Comment A13	C
Lead User A2	Comment A21	C
	Comment A22	P
Segment B		
Lead User B1	Comment B11	C
High-priority customer B2	Comment B21	C
	Comment B22	P
Lead User B3	Comment B31	C
	Comment B32	C
Segment C		
High-priority customer C1	Comment C11	C
	Comment C12	P
	Comment C13	P

Parking Example. Team members gathered data from lead users and heavy users in Step 3. Some of the data from an interview with one of the lead users separated into product-related and circumstantial data is shown next.

Product-Related Data

[Puts sign on windshield: "Engine won't start."] [Stop people from backing out of parking spaces.] [Add additional spaces.] [Create one-way lanes, not two-way lanes, in parking lots.] [Stop dangerous driving via patrols.]

Circumstantial Data

[I am so annoyed and pissed off at being forced to drive like a manic.] [I get anxious when I realize I have to come to the university and find a parking spot.] [Annoyance.] [Crowded.] [Dangerous]. [People back up without looking. I beep my horn, but they don't hear me.] [Racing to get to a spot before someone else.] [Why aren't there more accidents?] [I always try for a legal spot first.] [Parking garage was full when I went to use it. I never went back to it.] [The flow of traffic is crazy and scary.]

STAGE TWO—Step 5: Determine the Critical Circumstantial Issues to Regular Users in Each Market Segment

Step 5 creates a survey that is given to a large sample of regular users to identify which circumstantial issues are critical to them. This is done when a large amount of circumstantial data results from Steps 3 and 4.

Parking Example. Step 5 was not used in the parking system study.

STAGE THREE: Develop New Features

STAGE THREE—Step 6: Determine the Focus Point for Each Circumstantial Issue in Each Market Segment

Focus points are the underlying needs and wants (themes) upon which circumstantial issues are based. They are identified by team members using affinity diagrams, technical investigations, and lateral thinking. Affinity diagrams are discussed in Section 12.2 on pages 398-401. Technical investigations and lateral thinking are discussed next.

Parking Example. Team members created an affinity diagram using the raw circumstantial data. Part of the affinity diagram is shown next:

Parking Creates Feelings of Stress

Anger over time to find a parking space.

Riding around for hours looking for spaces.

I feel pissed off when I leave my house 20 minutes before class and end up being 5 minutes late for class. My house is only 10 minutes from campus.

Hard to find a spot.

...

Danger from Other Drivers

Dangerous parking behavior.

People zooming around 100 mph going backwards to get a spot.

Once I followed a guy and out of nowhere, a car zoomed into the spot. I saw a fight.

Anger over being followed to your car by drivers looking for a space; dangerous.

People back up without looking. I beep my horn, but they don't hear me.

Racing to get to a spot before someone else.

Why aren't there more accidents?

...

Poor Design of Parking System Infrastructure

Punitive towing system.

Anger when security tows away your car on the first few days of classes.

During the first couple of weeks at school, my car was towed after searching for a spot for 5–10 minutes; I was forced to park by a curb. There was no sign saying "No Parking."

...

Parking Space Design

Parking spaces too small for large cars.

Parking spaces are too small.

Next, team members organize the raw circumstantial data into major circumstantial themes (e.g., poor design of parking infrastructure), system, and minor circumstantial themes (punitive towing system) for input into technical investigations and lateral thinking sessions to identify focus points (see Table 14.11).

TABLE 14.11   Organization of Circumstantial Data for Analysis

Raw Circumstantial Data	Affinity Diagram Circumstantial Themes and Their Raw Data Points	Focus Points

Focus points are based only on circumstantial data. Product-related data is useful for Level A studies, not for Level B or Level C studies. Therefore, team members put aside product-related data for now and analyze only circumstantial data using technical investigations and lateral thinking methods.

Technical investigations involve team members seeking out experts in the field under study to help them understand the needs and wants (focus points) underlying a circumstantial data point.

Parking Example. A technical investigation of the circumstantial data points "Parking spaces too small for large cars" and "Too small parking spaces" was conducted by team members. The team members met with an expert on parking systems and asked: "From your technical perspective, what underlying needs or wants (focus points) are being broached by these two comments?" The expert thought for a moment and said: "First, these two comments are indicative of 'poor design of parking system infrastructure,' and 'poor parking space design in particular.'" Upon further reflection, he said that: "Poor parking space design is a reflection of the parker's need to be able to park in an environment in which spaces are not designed for different size cars (Miata, Hummer, Van) and spaces are not designed robustly for people who park crooked." At this point, team members had identified two focus points: (1) spaces are not designed for different size cars (Miata, Hummer, Van); and (2) spaces are not designed robustly for people who park crooked.

Lateral thinking [see Reference 2], developed by Edward de Bono, is a process that helps an individual or a group escape from existing thought patterns and generate new thought patterns (ideas or alternative designs). Traditional thinking is very good at improving existing ideas.

Lateral thinking is very good at making new ideas. Both types of thinking are at opposite ends of the same spectrum. Lateral thinking stimulates creative thought and encompasses several techniques [see Reference 3] that PD team members can use to develop focus points. Two of these techniques are "alternatives" and "the concept fan."

"Alternatives" is a method for identifying additional focus points for a circumstantial issue or theme. This search requires a "reference point." A reference point provides clarity to the issue(s) underlying a circumstantial issue or theme. Reference points are identified by asking one or more of the following questions [see Reference 3]:

1. What *alternative ways* of achieving this *purpose* are there?
2. What *alternative ways* of *carrying out* this function are there?
3. What other *things* fit into this *group*?
4. What other *things* look like *this*?
5. What other *things* behave like *this*?

Parking Example 1: *Using Alternatives to Identify Additional Focus Points*. The Director of the Parking Department wanted to find new alternatives for dealing with parking problems. To do this, he worked with team members to develop a reference point on which to focus his search for new alternatives. Together, they developed "fixed spots and variable demand" as a reference point for searching for alternative ways to deal with parking problems. This reference point caused the director and team members to ask the question: "What other industries or organizations experience the problem of fixed spots and variable demand?" The answer included restaurants (fixed seats with variable number of patrons) or emergency medical facilities (fixed number of physicians and variable number of patients). The team members then studied restaurants and medical facilities that had successfully dealt with this issue and benchmarked their processes to discover new alternatives for the parking system. This use of creativity enhancing tools creates options and alternatives appropriate for use in the Analyze Phase of the DMADV model.

Parking Example 2: *Using Alternatives to Identify Additional Focus Points*. The mission of the Parking Department is to provide, maintain, and administer safe, judicious, and attractive parking. One alternative available to the Parking Department to accomplish its mission is to use a "shuttle bus." The "shuttle bus" is an alternative. The reference point behind this alternative is "moving university stakeholders around the campus in a timely and safe manner." Creatively thinking about the reference point can generate new alternatives for the Parking Department. For example, team members asked themselves the question: "What alternative ways of achieving this purpose are there?" Their answer led to the following alternatives: "create a tram service like the one used in the Disney World parking lot system" or "create a shuttle boat service that can be used to move people around campus on the canal system that exists in Coral Gables." Again, this use of creativity enhancing tools creates options and alternatives appropriate for use in the Analyze Phase of the DMADV model.

The concept fan is another technique for finding additional focus points by using reference points. A concept fan has three component parts: alternatives, reference points, and a direction. Alternatives are practical and doable ways of making a reference point actionable. As stated earlier, reference points are general and nonspecific ways of doing things. A direction is the very broadest reference point. The difference between a reference point and a direction is in the broadness of the reference point.

Parking Example. "Shuttle bus service" is an example of an alternative. "Move people around campus" is an example of a reference point. "Provide, maintain, and administer safe, judicious, and attractive parking" is an example of a direction.

A concept fan helps team members start at any existing alternative and move forward to its reference point (see Alternative A to Reference Point 1 in Figure 14.1), or from a reference point to the direction (see Reference Point 1 to Direction in Figure 14.1), or to move backward from the direction to a reference point (see Direction to Reference Point 2 in Figure 14.1), or from a reference point to a new alternative (see Reference Point 2 to Alternative D in Figure 14.1).

Alternative A >

Alternative B   <   **Reference Point 1**   >

Alternative C   <

Alternative D   <

Alternative E   <   Reference Point 2   < Direction

Alternative F   <

Alternative G   <

Alternative H   <   Reference Point 3   <

Alternative I   <

FIGURE 14.1   Concept Fan

In Figure 14.1, Alternative A is used to create Reference Point 1. Reference Point 1 is used to generate Alternatives B and C, and to create the direction. The direction is used to generate Reference Points 2 and 3, which are in turn used to generate Alternatives D, E, F, G, H, and I. You can see how this technique is used to "fan out" new alternatives.

Parking Example. Team members developed a concept fan to create additional alternatives for the Parking Department (see Figure 14.2). The parking example concept fan has five stages and shows the interplay between alternatives, reference points, and the direction. It demonstrates the utility of the concept fan in creating new alternatives in the Analyze Phase of the parking example.

Each critical circumstantial data point was assigned to one or more team members for translation into focus points using technical investigations or lateral thinking techniques. Partial results are shown in Table 14.12.

Step 1 shows team members using the existing "shuttle bus" alternative that was taken from the list of circumstantial data points to create the reference point "move people around the campus."

Step 1

| Alternative A | | Reference point 1 |
| Shuttle bus | > | Move people around campus |

Step 2 shows team members using the "move people around campus" reference point to generate the "tram service" alternative and the "shuttle boat" alternative.

Step 2

Alternative A		Reference point 1
Shuttle bus	>	Move people around campus
Alternative B		
Tram service	<———————⎸	
Alternative C		
Shuttle boat	<———————⎸	

Step 3 shows team members also using the "move people around campus" reference point to create the "provide, maintain, and administer safe, judicious, and attractive parking" direction.

Step 3

Alternative A		Reference point 1		Direction
Shuttle bus	>	Move people around campus	>	Provide, maintain,
Alternative B				and administer
Tram service.	<———————⎸			safe, judicious, and
Alternative C				and attractive parking
Shuttle boat	<———————⎸			

Step 4 shows team members using the "provide, maintain, and administer safe, judicious, and attractive parking" direction to generate the "move people around campus in a timely manner" reference point.

Step 4

Alternative A		Reference point 1		Direction
Shuttle bus	>	Move people around campus	>	Provide, maintain
Alternative B				and administer safe
Tram service.	<———————⎸			judicious, and
Alternative C				attractive parking
Shuttle boat	<———————⎸			
		Move people around campus in a	<———⎸	
		timely manner		

Step 5 shows team members using the "move people around campus in a timely manner" reference point to generate the "schedule the shuttle bus service" and "guarantee on-time delivery to your destination" alternatives.

Step 5

Alternative A		Reference point 1		Direction
Shuttle bus	>	Move people around campus	>	Provide, maintain
Alternative B				and administer safe
Tram service.	<———————⎸			judicious, and
Alternative C				attractive parking
Shuttle boat	<———————⎸			
		Move people around campus in a	<———⎸	
		timely manner		
Alternative D				
Schedule shuttle	<———————⎸			
bus service				
Alternative E				
Guarantee 15 minute				
on-time delivery to				
destination	<———————⎸			

FIGURE 14.2 Revised Concept Fan

TABLE 14.12 Identification of Focus Points

Circumstantial Issue	Initial Focus Point	Final Focus Point
Riding around for hours looking for spaces. I feel pissed off when I leave my house 20 minutes before class and end up being 5 minutes late for class. My house is only 10 minutes from campus. Spend no more than 10 minutes between getting to campus, pulling into a space, and walking to class. Hard to find a spot.	**Parking Creates Feelings of Stress** Anger over time to find a parking space. Fixed spaces and variable demand creates a tense and frustrating environment.	Uncontrolled flow of traffic patterns creates negative environment.
Fear of being late for class. Rushing so I'm late to class. Hassled and hectic people rushing to class. Frustration—confined, rushed, and pressured to get to class.	**Parking Creates Feelings of Stress** Frustration over being late to class.	Everybody knows their class schedule. Have designated spots. Say you have M/W/F classes from 10 to 12; you park in your designated spot.
Riding the shuttle to the garage is time consuming. Shuttle system is slow and inefficient.	**Parking Creates Feelings of Stress** Guaranteed delivery time for shuttle bus.	Guarantee 15-minute delivery from arrival at shuttle to arrival at destination.
Anger when security tows away your car on the first few days of classes, as opposed to a strong warning. During the first couple of weeks at school, my car was towed from the lot behind the Memorial building. After searching for a spot for 5–10 minutes, I was forced to park by a curb. There was no sign saying "No Parking." Also, many other cars were parked in the same place. I had to spend $100 to get my car out. It was an incredible inconvenience. If they had simply given me a ticket I would have gotten the message. The whole thing was absolutely outrageous. Luckily, my friend gave me a lift to get my car.	**Poor Design of Parking System Infrastructure** Punitive towing system.	Towing is one method of dealing with severe parking problems. Look for alternatives to towing (e.g., booting cars).
Parking spaces too small for large cars. Parking spaces too small.	**Poor Design of Parking System Infrastructure** Parking space design.	Spaces are not designed for different size cars (Miata, Hummer, Van). Spaces are not designed robustly for people who park crooked.

STAGE THREE—Step 7: Develop Cognitive Images (CTQs) for Each Focus Point in Each Market Segment

This step actually creates potential innovations by translating focus points (user's underlying and unexpressed needs and wants) into detailed, unambiguous, qualitative statements of needs and wants in the language of design engineers. These statements are called cognitive images (CIs) or CTQs.

The pathways available to translate focus points into cognitive images (CTQs) include: (1) team members restating a focus point into one or more obvious actionable and designable ideas; (2) design engineers using technical knowledge to restate a focus point into one or more obvious actionable and designable ideas; (3) experts in the field under study use their product knowledge to restate a focus point into one or more actionable and designable ideas; and (4) team members use the "alternatives" or "concept fan" techniques to restate a focus point into one or more actionable and designable ideas. The fourth pathway uses each focus point as a reference point to create new alternatives as in Step 6.

An example of team members restating a focus point into one or more obvious actionable and designable ideas (cognitive images) is as follows:

- Focus Point—Encourage people to get to campus other ways (e.g., by bicycle). Lots of students and faculty live within easy cycling distance. But in order for a large number of people to commute by bicycle, some changes would be helpful.

- Cognitive Image—Develop a bicycle-friendly campus (bike pathways and racks, and shower facilities for sweaty bikers).

An example of design engineers using technical knowledge to restate a focus point into one or more obvious actionable and designable ideas (cognitive images) is as follows:

- Focus Point—Uncontrolled flow of traffic patterns create negative environment.

- Cognitive Image 1—Create lots with one entrance and one exit. Install a counter system that adds one car to the count upon admission and subtracts one car from the count upon exiting from the lot.

- Cognitive Image 2—Have electronic signs at lot entrances that show the count statistics with respect to the total spaces available in the lot.

An example of experts in the field under study using their expertise to restate a focus point into one or more actionable and designable ideas (cognitive images) is as follows:

- Focus Point—Use unskilled temporary employees.

- Cognitive Image—Create a "career path" through the Parking Department.

An example of team members using the "alternatives" technique to restate a focus point into one or more actionable and designable ideas is as follows:

- Focus Point—Encourage people to get to campus other ways; e.g., by bicycle. Lots of students and faculty live within easy cycling distance. But in order for a large number of people to commute by bicycle, some changes would be helpful.
- Cognitive Image 1—Develop a bicycle-friendly campus. Developed using Pathway 1 above.
- Cognitive Image 2—Build a covered walkway from the Metrorail station into the campus. Developed using the alternatives technique.

Next, team members developed cognitive images for each focus point using the pathways described earlier (see Table 14.13). The cognitive image column in Table 14.13 refers the reader to the final statement of a cognitive image, or to a continuous improvement activity.

TABLE 14.13 Partial List of Cognitive Images

Circumstantial Issue	Initial Focus Point	Final Focus Point	Cognitive Image
Riding around for hours looking for spaces. I feel pissed off when I leave my house 20 minutes before class and end up being 5 minutes late for class. My house is only 10 minutes from campus. Spend no more than 10 minutes between getting to campus, pulling into a space, and walking to class.	**Parking Creates Feelings of Stress** Anger over time to find a parking space. Fixed spaces and variable demand creates a tense and frustrating environment.	Uncontrolled flow of traffic patterns create negative environment.	Create lots with one entrance and one exit. Install a counter system that adds one car to the count upon admission and subtracts one car from the count upon exiting from the lot. See CI #1. Have electronic signs at lot entrances that show the count statistics in respect to total spaces available in the lot. See CI #1.
Fear of being late for class. Rushing so I'm late to class. Hassled and hectic people rushing to class. Frustration—confined, rushed, and pressured to get to class.	**Parking Creates Feelings of Stress** Frustration over being late to class.	Everybody knows their class schedule. Have designated spots. Say you have M/W/F classes from 10 to 12; you park in your designated spot.	Develop lot and fee systems based on type of usage. See CI #20.

Circumstantial Issue	Initial Focus Point	Final Focus Point	Cognitive Image
Riding the shuttle to the garage is time consuming. People stumble over you and it is crowded on the shuttle. Shuttle system is slow and inefficient.	**Parking Creates Feelings of Stress** Shuttle bus is slow.	Shuttle can't guarantee on-time delivery to destination.	Improve the shuttle system. See CI #6. Guaranteed arrival time at destination by shuttle service. See CI #6.
Anger when security tows away your car on the first few days of classes, as opposed to a strong warning. During the first couple of weeks at school, my car was towed from the lot behind the Memorial building. After searching for a spot for 5–10 minutes, I was forced to park by a curb. There was no sign saying "No Parking." Also, many other cars were parked in the same place. I had to spend $100 to get my car out.	**Poor Design of Parking System Infrastructure** Punitive towing system	Towing is one method of dealing with severe parking problems. Look for alternative methods for parking.	Use a boot with a built-in beeper to call security to release boot. This creates a safe (stay by your car) situation. See CI #8. Develop inter-campus parking agreements. See CI #9.
Parking spaces too small for large cars. Too small parking spaces.	**Poor Design of Parking System Infrastructure** Parking space design.	Spaces are not designed for different size cars (Miata, Hummer, Van). Spaces are not designed robustly for people who park crooked.	Design color-coded spaces for different size cars. See CI #1. Design spaces with rubber poles on white lines to prevent drivers from taking up two spaces. See CI #1.

These cognitive images were clarified, expanded, and reorganized by team members. The revised cognitive images are as follows.

CI #1a: Redesign large student lots. Subdivide large student lots into smaller lots, each with one entrance and one exit. Install a counter system that adds one car to the count upon admission and subtracts one car from the count upon exiting from the lot. When the lot is full, close the front gate. Have electronic signs at lot entrances that show the count statistics with respect to total spaces available in the lot.

CI #1b: Redesign large student lots. Redesign spaces for angle parking (not 90 degrees) for improved visibility when backing out of a space. Design spaces to conform to standards of 9 feet by 19 feet.

CI #1c: Redesign large student lots. Create snake-like traffic flow in lots. Vehicles entering lots must move in a one-way serpentine pattern through the lot. There is only one path through each lot. If the driver knows that three spaces are available upon entering the lot, and passes up all three spaces, she or he must exit the lot. This prevents dangerous competition for a space.

CI #6: Improve the shuttle system. (Guaranteed arrival time at destination.)

1. Improve routing of shuttle buses through the following actions:
   - Establish clockwise and counterclockwise shuttle bus routes around the perimeter of the Coral Gables campus.
   - Establish express bus routes with limited stops during peak hours on the Coral Gables campus. Develop routes and stops.
   - Develop and post bus schedules at each stop.
2. Improve the safety of shuttle bus stops through the following actions:
   - Shuttle drivers take each person directly to her or his car after dark.
   - Number all parking spaces in a lot for quick identification and drop off.
3. Decrease waiting time for pickup by a shuttle bus.
4. Create a campus telephone system between shuttle bus stops (parkers) and a transportation dispatcher *[Dropped by the team because this doesn't solve the parking problem]*.
5. Reconfigure the shuttle buses to decrease on/off time for passengers (i.e., add back door entrances and exits). Study cost. *This is not an issue to be addressed by PD team members.*
6. Guarantee 15 minute or less on-time shuttle delivery to destination.
7. Create a discount rate for U.M. personnel using public transportation.
8. Create off-campus parking with shuttle service (e.g., in Metrorail parking lots).

CI #8: Change the towing system. "No Parking" signs have been removed from the campus due to the decisions of the Beautification Committee. Consequently, it is no longer feasible to tow vehicles that are improperly parked.

1. Develop a "hot list" based towing system. A "hot list" shows chronic parking offenders. When a vehicle cannot be identified due to no permit or decal, the license is placed electronically into the records. After five infringements, the car is automatically eligible for towing.
2. Use a booting system instead of a towing system. Install a beeper on each boot so that the vehicle owner could contact the Parking Department directly without looking for a phone or having to go to a tow lot, both of which can be dangerous.
3. Cease using the services of a towing company that charges an $80 towing fee. Instead, the university could charge a booting fee of $50. This process would have three advantages:

(1) the fees would remain with the University Parking Department, thus increasing revenue; (2) the fee would save the violator money; and (3) there would be less damage to the vehicle (without towing).

STAGE FOUR: Evolve Strategies for New Features

STAGE FOUR—Step 8: Classify Cognitive Images by Kano category and Kano Cost Distribution in Each Market Segment

Kano Categories. There are six Kano category classifications for cognitive images. Figure 14.3 illustrates the first three classifications.

- *One Dimensional (O)*—User satisfaction is proportional to the performance of the feature; the less performance, the less user satisfaction, and the more performance, the more user satisfaction.

- *Must-Be (M)*—User satisfaction is not proportional to the performance of the feature; the less performance, the less user satisfaction to the feature, but high performance creates feelings of indifference to the feature.

- *Attractive (A)*—Again, user satisfaction is not proportional to the performance of the feature. However, in this case, low levels of performance create feelings of indifference to the feature, but high levels of performance create feelings of delight to the feature.

- *Reverse (R)*—The researcher's *a priori* judgment about the user's view of the feature is the opposite of the user's view.

- *Indifferent (I)* —The user is indifferent to the presence and absence of the feature.

- *Questionable (Q)*—There is a contradiction in the user's response to the feature.

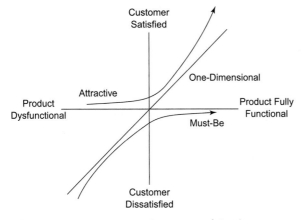

FIGURE 14.3 Kano Features Categories of Quality

Kano Cost Distribution. Kano developed a technique to determine how much regular users desire a new feature (cognitive image) by asking them what percentage increase in costs over current costs they would be willing to accept to have the new feature. There are three "tolerable cost increase" distributions in practice: uniform, triangular, and J-shaped.

The uniform distribution shows that 80% of a market segment will pay at least a 10% cost increase to obtain the feature described by the cognitive image under study (see Figure 14.4). Cognitive images exhibiting this distribution can be used to develop ideas for completely new products.

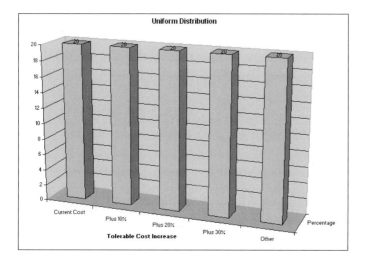

FIGURE 14.4 Uniform Kano Cost Distribution

The triangular distribution shows that 60% of a market segment will pay at least a 10% cost increase to obtain the product feature described by the cognitive image under study (see Figure 14.5). Cognitive images exhibiting this distribution can be used to develop ideas for major new features of existing products.

The J-shaped distribution shows that 10% of a market segment will only pay a 10% cost increase to obtain the product feature described by the cognitive image under study (see Figure 14.6). Cognitive images exhibiting this distribution can be used in Category A studies.

Kano Questionnaire. Team members use a Kano questionnaire to classify each cognitive image into its Kano category and Kano cost distribution. Table 14.14 shows an example of a generic Kano questionnaire. A Kano questionnaire has three questions that are necessary to classify a cognitive image into a Kano category and Kano cost distribution. The first two questions ask how a respondent would feel if the feature (cognitive image) was present or the feature was absent. The third question determines the percentage cost increase over current costs that a respondent would be willing to pay for this CTQ.

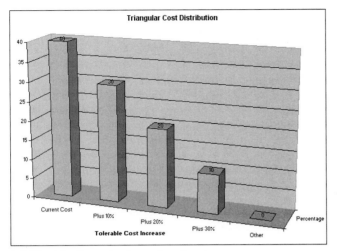

FIGURE 14.5 Triangular Kano Cost Distribution

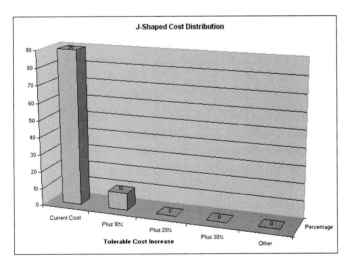

FIGURE 14.6 J-Shaped Kano Cost Distribution

TABLE 14.14   Generic Kano Questionnaire

CTQs	How would you feel if the following CTQ was present in the product?	How would you feel if the CTQ was not present in the product?	What percentage cost increase over current costs would you be willing to pay for this CTQ?
CTQ 1	Delighted [ ] Expect it and like it [ ] No feeling [ ] Live with it [ ] Do not like it [ ] Other [ ]	Delighted [ ] Expect it and like it [ ] No feeling [ ] Live with it [ ] Do not like it [ ] Other [ ]	0% _____ 10% _____ 20% _____ 30% _____ 40% or more _____
. . .			
CTQ 8	Delighted [ ] Expect it and like it [ ] No feeling [ ] Live with it [ ] Do not like it [ ] Other [ ]	Delighted [ ] Expect it and like it [ ] No feeling [ ] Live with it [ ] Do not like it [ ] Other [ ]	0% _____ 10% _____ 20% _____ 30% _____ 40% or more _____

Team members use Table 14.15 to classify each respondent's survey responses for the first two questions, for each cognitive image, into its Kano category.

TABLE 14.15   Kano Classification Table

		Absent Question Response				
		Delighted	Expect it and like it	No feeling	Live with it	Do not like it
Percent Question Response	Delighted	Q	A	A	A	O
	Expect it and like it	R	I	I	I	M
	No feeling	R	I	I	I	M
	Live with it	R	I	I	I	M
	Do not like it	R	R	R	R	Q

Tables 14.16 through Table 14.21 illustrate examples of Kano classifications for the parking example.

One Dimensional (O)—The following response pattern is indicative of a one-dimensional product feature; that is, the greater the performance of the product features, the greater the user satisfaction, and the lower the performance of the product feature, the lower the user satisfaction (see Table 14.16).

TABLE 14.16 One Dimensional Kano Classification

IDEA	How would you feel if the following feature was **present** in the Coral Gables parking system?	How would you feel if the following feature was **not present** in the Coral Gables parking system?
Subdivide large existing lots into smaller lots, each with one entrance and one exit. Install a counter system that adds one car to the count upon admission and subtracts one car from the count upon exiting from the lot. When lot is full, front gate is closed and no more cars are admitted to the lot. Have electronic signs at the entrances of lots that indicate the availability of empty spaces in the lot.	Delighted [X] Expect it and like it [ ] No feeling [ ] Live with it [ ] Do not like it [ ] Other [ ]	Delighted [ ] Expect it and like it [ ] No feeling [ ] Live with it [ ] Do not like it [X] Other [ ]

Must-Be (M)—The following response pattern is indicative of a must-be product feature; that is, the user is less satisfied when the product feature is less functional, but the user is not more satisfied when the product feature is more functional (see Table 14.17).

TABLE 14.17 Must-Be Kano Classification

IDEA	How would you feel if the following feature was **present** in the Coral Gables parking system?	How would you feel if the following feature was **not present** in the Coral Gables parking system?
Subdivide large existing lots into smaller lots, each with one entrance and one exit. Install a counter system that adds one car to the count upon admission and subtracts one car from the count upon exiting from the lot. When lot is full, front gate is closed and no more cars are admitted to the lot. Have electronic signs at the entrances of lots that indicate the availability of empty spaces in the lot.	Delighted [ ] Expect it and like it [ ] No feeling [X] Live with it [ ] Do not like it [ ] Other [ ]	Delighted [ ] Expect it and like it [ ] No feeling [ ] Live with it [ ] Do not like it [X] Other [ ]

Attractive (A)—The following response pattern is indicative of an attractive product feature; that is, the user is more satisfied when the product feature is more functional, but the user is not less satisfied when the product feature is less functional (see Table 14.18).

TABLE 14.18   Attractive Kano Classification

IDEA	How would you feel if the following feature was **present** in the Coral Gables parking system?	How would you feel if the following feature was **not present** in the Coral Gables parking system?
Subdivide large existing lots into smaller lots, each with one entrance and one exit. Install a counter system that adds one car to the count upon admission and subtracts one car from the count upon exiting from the lot. When lot is full, front gate is closed and no more cars are admitted to the lot. Have electronic signs at the entrances of lots that indicate the availability of empty spaces in the lot.	Delighted [**X**] Expect it and like it [ ] No feeling [ ] Live with it [ ] Do not like it [ ] Other [ ]	Delighted [ ] Expect it and like it [ ] No feeling [**X**] Live with it [ ] Do not like it [ ] Other [ ]

Reverse (R)—The following response pattern is indicative of a reverse product feature; that is, the researcher's a priori judgment about the user's view of the product feature is the opposite of the user's view (see Table 14.19).

TABLE 14.19   Reverse Kano Classification

IDEA	How would you feel if the following feature was **present** in the Coral Gables parking system?	How would you feel if the following feature was **not present** in the Coral Gables parking system?
Subdivide large existing lots into smaller lots, each with one entrance and one exit. Install a counter system that adds one car to the count upon admission and subtracts one car from the count upon exiting from the lot. When lot is full, front gate is closed and no more cars are admitted to the lot. Have electronic signs at the entrances of lots that indicate the availability of empty spaces in the lot.	Delighted [ ] Expect it and like it [ ] No feeling [ ] Live with it [ ] Do not like it [**X**] Other [ ]	Delighted [**X**] Expect it and like it [ ] No feeling [ ] Live with it [ ] Do not like it [ ] Other [ ]

Indifferent (I)—The following response pattern is indicative of an indifferent product feature; that is, the user is indifferent to the presence and absence of the product feature (see Table 14.20).

TABLE 14.20   Indifferent Kano Classification

IDEA	How would you feel if the following feature was **present** in the Coral Gables parking system?	How would you feel if the following feature was **not present** in the Coral Gables parking system?
Subdivide large existing lots into smaller lots, each with one entrance and one exit. Install a counter system that adds one car to the count upon admission and subtracts one car from the count upon exiting from the lot. When lot is full, front gate is closed and no more cars are admitted to the lot. Have electronic signs at the entrances of lots that indicate the availability of empty spaces in the lot.	Delighted [ ] Expect it and like it [ ] No feeling [X] Live with it [ ] Do not like it [ ] Other [ ]	Delighted [ ] Expect it and like it [ ] No feeling [X] Live with it [ ] Do not like it [ ] Other [ ]

Questionable (Q)—The following response pattern is indicative of a questionable product feature; that is, there is a contradiction in the user's response to the product feature (see Table 14.21).

TABLE 14.21   Questionable Kano Classification

IDEA	How would you feel if the following feature was **present** in the Coral Gables parking system?	How would you feel if the following feature was **not present** in the Coral Gables parking system?
Subdivide large existing lots into smaller lots, each with one entrance and one exit. Install a counter system that adds one car to the count upon admission and subtracts one car from the count upon exiting from the lot. When lot is full, front gate is closed and no more cars are admitted to the lot. Have electronic signs at the entrances of lots that indicate the availability of empty spaces in the lot.	Delighted [X] Expect it and like it [ ] No feeling [ ] Live with it [ ] Do not like it [ ] Other [ ]	Delighted [X] Expect it and like it [ ] No feeling [ ] Live with it [ ] Do not like it [ ] Other [ ]

The analysis of data from a Kano questionnaire for the purpose of determining the Kano category of a cognitive image is dependent on the level of detail of the study that identified the cognitive image. That is, if the study is conducted at a very general level (for example, a study of innovation in the supermarket industry), data from respondents will provide an excellent vehicle to determine the Kano category of a cognitive image. In this case, the modal Kano category is used to determine the Kano category for the cognitive image; in other words:

Kano category = maximum (*A, O, M, I, Q, R*).

where *A* = Attractive, *O* = One-Way, *M* = Must-Be, *I* = Indifferent, *Q* = Questionable, *R* = Reverse.

On the other hand, if the study is conducted at a very specific level (for example, a study of innovations in the fruit and vegetable department of a supermarket), data from respondents will contain much noise in the form of indifferent ("I") responses, and will not provide a sound vehicle to determine the Kano category for a cognitive image. In this case, there are two steps for reducing noise and determining the Kano category for a cognitive image. The first step is to segment the data by market segments. The second step is to determine the Kano category for a cognitive image, in a particular market segment (or overall), as follows:

If $(A + O + M) \geq (I + R + Q)$, then Kano category = maximum (*A, O, M*).

If $(A + O + M) < (I + R + Q)$, then Kano category = maximum (*I, R, Q*) [see Reference 1].

As with Kano categories, the analysis of cost data from a Kano questionnaire is dependent on the level of detail of the study. If a study is conducted at a very general level, then you use all the data or the data in a particular market segment, to determine the cost distribution type for the cognitive image. On the other hand, if the study is conducted at a very specific level, data from respondents will contain much noise, and will not provide a sound vehicle to determine the cost distribution for a cognitive image. In this case, you determine the cost distribution for a cognitive image, in a particular market segment (or overall), as follows:

If $(A + O + M) \geq (I + R + Q)$, use only the cost data from the respondents who classified the cognitive image in the maximum (*A, O, M*) category.

If $(A + O + M) < (I + R + Q)$, use only the cost data from the respondents who classified the cognitive image in the maximum (*I, R, Q*) category.

One question from the Kano questionnaire is used to illustrate a user response pattern that is illogical. Questionnaires that are illogical should be eliminated from the database. Table 14.22 illustrates one example of an illogical questionnaire.

Occasionally, a product feature related to price will appear on a Kano questionnaire. The cost increase question doesn't seem to make sense for this type of question. In this case, you explain to the respondent that the cost-increase question is being used to get an indication of how he or she feels about the price-related product feature (see Table 14.23).

TABLE 14.22 Response Bias

IDEA	How would you feel if the following feature was **present** in the Coral Gables parking system?	How would you feel if the following feature was **not present** in the Coral Gables parking system?	What percentage cost increase over current costs would you be willing to pay for this feature?
Subdivide large existing lots into smaller lots, each with one entrance and one exit. Install a counter system that adds one car to the count upon admission and subtracts one car from the count upon exiting from the lot. When lot is full, front gate is closed and no more cars are admitted to the lot. Have electronic signs at the entrances of lots that indicate the availability of empty spaces in the lot.	Delighted [ ] Expect it and like it [ ] No feeling [**X**] Live with it [ ] Do not like it [ ] Other [ ]	Delighted [ ] Expect it and like it [ ] No feeling [**X**] Live with it [ ] Do not like it [ ] Other [ ]	0% _____ 10% _____ 20% _____ 30% _____ 40% or more __X__

TABLE 14.23 Price-Related Feature

IDEA	How would you feel if the following feature was **present** in the Coral Gables parking system?	How would you feel if the following feature was **not present** in the Coral Gables parking system?
Create reserved parking spots for a $1,000.00 per year permit fee.	Delighted [ ] Expect it and like it [ ] No feeling [ ] Live with it [ ] Do not like it [ ] Other [ ]	Delighted [ ] Expect it and like it [ ] No feeling [ ] Live with it [ ] Do not like it [ ] Other [ ]

Occasionally, a respondent will ask: "If I check off that I can tolerate a 10% price increase for two questions, does that mean that the price of the entire product will go up 20%?" The answer is: "No, the cost questions are not additive. They are just being used to assess how strongly you feel about product features."

Next, team members sample regular users and tabulate their responses by market segment.

Parking Example. Team members stratified all parking permits issued in 1995 by type (see Table 14.24).

TABLE 14.24 Stratification of Parking Permit Frame

Permit Type	Description	Number	Percent
B	Board of trustees	115	1.001
C	Commuter	5,799	50.452
D	Disabled	22	0.191
E	Staff and Employees	799	6.951
EM	Emeritus	73	0.635
F	N/A	3	0.026
FA	Faculty and Administration	1,476	12.841
G	Reserved: dean, chairman	105	0.914
H	Fraternity house	29	0.252
L	New garage (commuter)	1,022	8.892
M	Motorcycle	58	0.505
R	Residential	1,663	14.468
T	Temporarily disabled	4	0.035
U	Service vehicles	74	0.644
V	Visitor	147	1.279
VN	Vendors	22	0.191
Z	Sticker for different lots (faculty)	40	0.348
X	Carrier pass	<u>43</u>	<u>0.374</u>
	Total:	11,494	100%

Only parking permit types coincident with the market segments described earlier were used in the study. Table 14.25 shows the distribution of permit types by market segment (strata).

TABLE 14.25 1995 Distribution of Parking Permits by Market Segment

Permit Type Market Segment	Frequency	Percentage	Sample Size
Commuter Students	5,799	53.9	118
Staff and Employee	799	7.4	15
Faculty and Administration	1,476	13.7	31
Parking Garage	1,022	9.5	20
Residential Students	<u>1,663</u>	<u>15.5</u>	<u>35</u>
Total	10,759	100%	219

(Visitors were excluded from the sample due to the difficulty of identifying and contacting them at a reasonable cost, and their small proportion of the total parking population. Additionally, all graduating seniors were excluded from the survey.)

A budget of $2,190 was established for a survey of regular users using the Kano questionnaire. Survey planning, execution, and analysis were performed by the author and a graduate student doing an independent study project. All personnel-related costs were considered zero, and all administrative costs were absorbed by the Parking Department. Due to zero personnel and administrative costs, and the $10 credit to each respondent, the maximum sample size is 219 regular users.

The rightmost column in Table 14.25 shows the sample sizes for each type of parking permit required to have a quota sample of 219 regular users. The study budget allows for a sample of 219 users. In this case, the people in each category are selected using convenience or judgment sampling plans.

Next, team members administer the Kano questionnaire according to the sampling plan. Table 14.26 shows a partial listing of the Kano questionnaire used in a survey of 219 regular users of the parking facilities at the University of Miami.

TABLE 14.26 Kano Survey for Parking Survey

PARKING FEATURE Partial Listing of Kano Questionnaire Used in the Parking System Study	How would you feel if the following feature was present in the Coral Gables parking system?	How would you feel if the following feature was not present in the Coral Gables parking system?	What percentage cost increase over current costs would you be willing to pay for this feature?
Subdivide large existing lots into smaller lots, each with one entrance and one exit. Install a counter system that adds one car to the count upon admission and subtracts one car from the count upon exiting from the lot. When lot is full, front gate is closed and no more cars are admitted to the lot. Have electronic signs at the entrances of lots that indicate the availability of empty spaces in the lot.	Delighted [ ] Expect it and like it [ ] No feeling [ ] Live with it [ ] Do not like it [ ] Other [ ]	Delighted [ ] Expect it and like it [ ] No feeling [ ] Live with it [ ] Do not like it [ ] Other [ ]	0% _____ 10% _____ 20% _____ 30% _____ 40% or more _____
Improve shuttle bus service so it can provide on-time arrival to any point on campus if a person arrives at the parking garage 15 minutes before they must reach their destination.	Delighted [ ] Expect it and like it [ ] No feeling [ ] Live with it [ ] Do not like it [ ] Other [ ]	Delighted [ ] Expect it and like it [ ] No feeling [ ] Live with it [ ] Do not like it [ ] Other [ ]	0% _____ 10% _____ 20% _____ 30% _____ 40% or more _____

(continued)

TABLE 14.26   Kano Survey for Parking Survey (Continued)

PARKING FEATURE Partial Listing of Kano Questionnaire Used in the Parking System Study	How would you feel if the following feature was present in the Coral Gables parking system?	How would you feel if the following feature was not present in the Coral Gables parking system?	What percentage cost increase over current costs would you be willing to pay for this feature?
Cease using the services of a towing company that charges an $80 towing fee. Instead, the university could charge a booting fee of $50. This process would have three advantages: (1) the fees would remain with the University Parking Department, thus increasing departmental revenue; (2) the fee would save the violator money; and (3) there would be less damage to the vehicle (without towing).	Delighted [ ] Expect it and like it [ ] No feeling [ ] Live with it [ ] Do not like it [ ] Other [ ]	Delighted [ ] Expect it and like it [ ] No feeling [ ] Live with it [ ] Do not like it [ ] Other [ ]	0% _____ 10% _____ 20% _____ 30% _____ 40% or more _____
Create a Visitor's Center in the Parking Garage. Visitors could park and obtain information about the campus. The facility could also be utilized by other departments, such as Admissions, the bookstore, or food services. Special visitors could be taken by car or shuttle to their destinations from the Visitor's Center. No guests would be lost. No guests would receive parking tickets.	Delighted [ ] Expect it and like it [ ] No feeling [ ] Live with it [ ] Do not like it [ ] Other [ ]	Delighted [ ] Expect it and like it [ ] No feeling [ ] Live with it [ ] Do not like it [ ] Other [ ]	0% _____ 10% _____ 20% _____ 30% _____ 40% or more _____

Table 14.27 shows the Kano categories and cost distributions for each cognitive image, for each market segment, and overall market segments.

TABLE 14.27 Kano Categories and Cost Distributions for the Parking Study

Abbreviated List of Cognitive Images	Overall Market Segments Kano Category Cost Distribution		Commuter Students Kano Category Cost Distribution		Residential Students Kano Category Cost Distribution		Deans Kano Category Cost Distribution	
Improve the shuttle service so it can provide on-time arrival to any point on campus....	A = 43 O = 44 M = 19 I = 99 Q = 1 R = 3	O = 175 5 = 32 10 = 9 20 = 1 30 = 2	A = 26 O = 23 M = 16 I = 48 Q = 0 R = 1	O = 93 5 = 17 10 = 2 20 = 1 30 = 2	A = 7 O = 10 M = 4 I = 17 Q = 0 R = 1	O = 34 5 = 2 10 = 2 20 = 0 30 = 0	A = 1 O = 5 M = 0 I = 0 Q = 0 R = 0	O = 4 5 = 1 10 = 1 20 = 0 30 = 0
Develop a public transportation discount rate with Dade County....							A = 4 O = 2 M = 0 I = 0 Q = 0 R = 0	O = 4 5 = 2 10 = 0 20 = 0 30 = 0
Cease using the services of a towing company that charges an $80 towing fee. Instead, the university could charge a booting fee of $50....			A = 21 O = 30 M = 7 I = 47 Q = 1 R = 5	O = 102 5 = 11 10 = 1 20 = 0 30 = 1	A = 5 O = 13	O = 34 5 = 4		
Create a Visitor's Center parking garage....							A = 3 O = 2 M = 0 I = 1 Q = 0 R = 0	O = 5 5 = 1 10 = 0 20 = 0 30 = 0

Team members drew the following conclusions from the survey data.

- "Improve shuttle bus service so it can provide on-time arrival to any point on campus if a person arrives at the parking garage 15 minutes before they must reach their destination" was considered a one-way feature with a triangular distribution for overall market segments, a one-way feature with a J-distribution to residential students, an attractive feature with a triangular distribution for commuter students, and a one-way feature with a J-distribution for deans (6 of 12 deans responded).

- "Develop a public transportation discount rate with Dade County for members of the university community who come to campus on public transportation with the Dade County Transportation Department (e.g., Metrorail or Metrobus)" was considered an attractive feature with a J-distribution by deans.

- "Cease using the services of a towing company that charges an $80 towing fee. Instead, the University could charge a booting fee of $50. This process would have three advantages: (1) the fees would remain with the University Parking Department, thus increasing departmental revenue; (2) the fee would save the violator money; and (3) there would be less damage to the vehicle (without towing)" was considered a one-way feature with a J-distribution by residential students, and a one-way feature with a J-shaped distribution with commuter students.

- "Create a Visitor's Center in the Parking Garage. Visitors could park and obtain information about the campus. The facility could also be utilized by other departments, such as Admissions, the bookstore, or food services. Special visitors could be taken by car or shuttle to their destinations from the Visitor's Center. No guests would be lost. No guests would receive parking tickets" was considered an attractive feature with a J-distribution by deans.

Dormitory Example. Several key stakeholders of the current housing system at the University of Miami were interviewed to collect preliminary data on the needs of the proposed housing construction, including two former Resident Masters (faculty members who live in apartments inside dormitory buildings); the Facilities Director (maintains existing dormitories); the Director of Residence Halls (coordinates residential assignments, residential policies, and other residential affairs); and the Dean of the Business School. Additionally, data was collected on five-star hotels to address the needs of the executives in the residence market segment.

Two focus groups were conducted that consisted of a mixture of full-time MBA students and undergraduate business students. An example of some of the original raw data collected by stakeholder group from the focus groups is depicted in the first two columns of Table 14.28.

The raw "Voice of the User" data in Column 2 of Table 14.28 was arranged using an affinity diagram and then classified into product and circumstantial data in Column 3 of Table 14.28 [see Reference 4]. Recall, product data identifies the current expectations and perceptions of stakeholders, whereas circumstantial data provides insight into the emotional circumstance in which a product, service, or process is used by a stakeholder.

The circumstantial data was analyzed using an affinity diagram to identify the underlying emotional latent structure, represented by focus points (see Columns 1 and 2 of Table 14.29). These focus points can then be quantified into possible solution modalities called cognitive images, which can be seen in the third column of Table 14.29. Table 14.29 shows how one small section of circumstantial issues from the interviews and focus groups was taken and turned into a cognitive image.

TABLE 14.28   Sample of the Raw Voice of the User Data from Interviews and Focus Groups

Voice of the User (VoU)		
Stakeholder Group	**Raw Data**	**Data Classification**
Undergraduates and MBA Students	Current dorms don't have enough space ... I feel like I'm living in a jail.	Product
	The elevators are slow:	Product
	I want caller ID.	Product
	I don't like it when people move in with roomates.	Circumstantial
Dean, School of Bus. Admin.	I will not allow them to paint the walls ... these rooms will not appeal to everyone by design.	Circumstantial
	Microwaves are a fire hazard.	Product
Resident Master	Grad students are like freshman ... they need to be initiated.	Circumstantial
	We are not in the hotel repair business.	Product
Director, Residence Halls	Pick a neutral color ... let them personalize their rooms with bedspreads etc.	Product
	Give students the opportunity to recycle.	Product
Director, Facilities	Carpet is a disaster.	Product
	Use electronic locks, keys are a nightmare.	Product
Hotel Expert	Closet space is minimal.	Product
	People don't get what they pay for.	Circumstantial

TABLE 14.29   Development of a Cognitive Image

Circumstantial Issue	**Focus Points**	**Cognitive Image(s)**
Something about people that age ... they think everyone wants to hear their music.	People are annoyed by loud music.	Provide an integrated audio system with headphone jacks placed by the bed and at the desk so residents can easily enjoy audio and not disturb their roommates or neighbors.
What good is a quiet area if it's not enforced?	People want quiet time but do not get it.	

Team members developed a Kano survey [see Reference 4] from the cognitive images (a portion is shown in Table 14.30), which was then completed by a quota sample of 295 regular MBA and undergraduate business students collected by class section.

TABLE 14.30 An Excerpt from the Kano Survey

Feature or Service	How would you feel if this feature or service is included in a dormitory residence?	How would you feel if this feature or service is NOT included in a dormitory residence?	What percent increase over the cost of a typical dorm room would you be willing to pay to have this feature or service?	
Single Occupancy Rooms	a) Delighted b) Expect it and like it c) No feeling d) Live with it e) Do not like it f) Other	a) Delighted b) Expect it and like it c) No feeling d) Live with it e) Do not like it f) Other	a) 0% b) 0.5% c) 1% d) 2% e) 3%	f) 5% g) 10% h) 15% i) 20% j) 30% or more
Individual Bathrooms	a) Delighted b) Expect it and like it c) No feeling d) Live with it e) Do not like it f) Other	a) Delighted b) Expect it and like it c) No feeling d) Live with it e) Do not like it f) Other	a) 0% b) 0.5% c) 1% d) 2% e) 3%	f) 5% g) 10% h) 15% i) 20% j) 30% or more
Queen-Size Bed	a) Delighted b) Expect it and like it c) No feeling d) Live with it e) Do not like it f) Other	a) Delighted b) Expect it and like it c) No feeling d) Live with it e) Do not like it f) Other	a) 0% b) 0.5% c) 1% d) 2% e) 3%	f) 5% g) 10% h) 15% i) 20% j) 30% or more

All of the students in the sample surveyed were either in graduate or undergraduate business classes. The professors of these classes administered the surveys. The demographic breakdown of the sample surveyed is shown in Table 14.31.

TABLE 14.31 Kano Survey Sample Demographics

	Freshman	Sophomore	Junior	Senior	Undergraduate Composite	Graduate Students
Count	72	54	44	25	195	96
Percent	25%	19%	15%	9%	67%	33%

Once the data from a Kano questionnaire was compiled, each response was placed in its Kano category. The classification technique for the Kano quality categories used in the dormitory study was developed by the Center for Quality Management [see Reference 1].

$$\text{Kano category} = \max (A, O, M) \text{ if } (A + O + M) \geq (I + Q + R)$$
$$= \max (I, Q, R) \text{ if } (A + O + M) < (I + Q + R)$$

In the event of a tie, you choose the more conservative Kano category. Conservatism is defined as being the most apathetic view of the feature, and as a result, the O-M-A group's most apathetic view is "Must Be" and the most apathetic view of the I-R-Q group is "Indifference."

The percentage increase students are willing to pay is not shown in a conventional format. Instead, it is shown in an expected value format for easier discussion:

Expected Price Increase = Σ (Response Percentage at Each Price Point in Column 4 of Table 14.30) * (Value of the Price Point))

Table 14.32 lists a complete Kano quality categorization of the cognitive images, or features, and their expected percentage price increase for all market segments.

TABLE 14.32 Complete Kano Survey Results from All Market Segments

Cognitive Images	Largest Kano Category	E(Percent Increase in Pay)
Single Occupancy Rooms	One-Way (25.6%)	6.58%
Individual Bathrooms	Attractive (37.5%)	5.75%
Queen-Size Bed	Attractive (56.8%)	2.99%
Broadband Internet	Attractive (36.4%)	1.65%
Integrated Audio System	Indifferent (49.3%)	0.49%
Integrated Headphone Jacks	Indifferent (65.3%)	0.37%
Television	Attractive (54.5%)	1.74%
Telephone	Attractive (34.2%)	0.60%
Cordless Telephone	Attractive (49.3%)	0.66%
Additional Phone Services	Attractive (60.0%)	1.19%
Personal Computer Rental Service	Indifferent (61.8%)	NA
Shared Common Printer	Attractive (44.3%)	0.69%
Large Corner Desk	Attractive (54.8%)	0.53%
Executive Desk Chair	Attractive (53.4%)	0.56%
Additional Desk Chairs	Indifferent (47.1%)	0.42%
Climate Control by Room	Must-Be (43.7%)	3.10%
Full-Size Bathtub	Attractive (29.6%)	1.80%

(continued)

TABLE 14.32   Complete Kano Survey Results from All Market Segments (Continued)

Cognitive Images	Largest Kano Category	E(Percent Increase in Pay)
Microwave	Attractive (31.0%)	1.17%
Small Refrigerator	Attractive (32.4%)	1.61%
Kitchenette	Attractive (45.1%)	3.83%
Appliance Rental Service	Indifferent (47.8%)	NA
VCR	Attractive (40.0%)	0.69%
DVD Player	Attractive (60.3%)	0.49%
Carpet	Attractive (33.3%)	0.69%
Tile	Indifferent (50.7%)	0.59%
Enforced Quiet Areas	Indifferent (46.4%)	0.74%
Vacuum Cleaner Rental Service	Indifferent (50.7%)	NA
Shared Common Vacuum Cleaner	Attractive (39.1%)	0.63%
Accessible Roof	Attractive (42.6%)	1.36%
Security Guard	Must-Be (33.8%)	NA
Laundry Facility by Floor	One-Way (30.4%)	1.11%
Iron and Ironing Board	Indifferent (57.4%)	0.57%
Optional Laundry Service	Attractive (47.8%)	1.36%
Optional Maid Service	Attractive (43.3%)	1.66%
Concierge	Attractive (35.3%)	1.02%
Reserved Convenient Parking Place	Attractive (48.0%)	1.98%
Competitive Admissions (vs. Conventional Assignment)	Indifferent (53.3%)	0.27%
Admission Based on GPA	Indifferent (38.7%)	0.21%
Admissions for Business Students Only	Reverse (25.7%)	0.77%
Admissions for Junior Level and Up Only	Indifferent (43.8%)	0.28%
Segregate Residents by Class Level	Indifferent (44.6%)	0.34%
Armoire	Attractive (43.8%)	NA
Coffee Table	Indifferent (61.6%)	0.36%
High Quality Linens	Indifferent (48.0%)	0.45%
Option to Rent by Semester	One-Way (30.7%)	1.33%

Table 14.33 shows the Kano quality categorizations of the cognitive images by Kano quality category and expected cost increase, for each market segment.

The cognitive images classified into the I-R-Q Kano quality categories do not present any benefit to the market segments. Consequently, they are eliminated from consideration in future designs. The cognitive images classified into the O-M-A Kano quality categories provide an array of features that need to be considered in future designs, as they positively impact the market segments. Recall from Chapter 5 that Figures 5.1 and 5.2 on pages 111-112 present the filtered, reduced set of cognitive images for each market segment. For each market segment, the percentage increase in cost that is acceptable to consumers is shown as a horizontal bar, by A-O-M Kano quality categories. Observe the difference in the scale of the *X*-axis between Figures 5.1 and 5.2.

TABLE 14.33 Kano Survey Results Broken Down by Market Segment

Cognitive Image (Features)	Freshman Kano Quality Category	E(Cost)	Sophomore Kano Quality Category	E(Cost)	Junior Kano Quality Category	E(Cost)	Senior Kano Quality Category	E(Cost)	Undergraduate Composite Kano Quality Category	E(Cost)	Graduate Kano Quality Category	E(Cost)
Single Occupancy Rooms	O	3.6%	O	5.2%	M	5.0%	O	5.5%	O	4.6%	M	10.5%
Individual Bathrooms	O	4.5%	A	3.8%	A	4.9%	A	4.7%	A	4.4%	A	8.5%
Queen-Size Bed	A	2.9%	A	2.6%	A	2.2%	A	1.8%	A	2.5%	A	4.1%
Broadband Internet	A	1.6%	A	1.0%	A	1.0%	O	0.6%	A	1.2%	A	2.7%
Integrated Audio System	A	0.9%	I	0.2%	I	0.3%	I	0.0%	I	0.4%	I	0.6%
Integrated Headphone Jacks	I	0.2%	I	0.3%	I	0.2%	A	0.0%	I	0.2%	I	0.7%
Television	A	2.6%	A	1.0%	I	1.8%	I	0.0%	A	1.7%	A	2.0%
Telephone	A	0.9%	A	0.3%	I	1.3%	M	0.0%	A	0.7%	M	0.4%
Cordless Telephone	A	0.7%	A	0.8%	I	1.1%	A	0.3%	A	0.8%	I	0.4%
Additional Phone Services	A	1.0%	A	2.2%	I	1.0%	A	0.3%	A	1.3%	A	0.9%
Personal Computer Rental Service	I	NA	I	NA	I	NA	A	NA	A	NA	I	NA
Shared Common Printer	A	0.5%	A	0.7%	I	1.3%	A	0.0%	A	0.7%	A	0.7%
Large Corner Desk	A	0.4%	I	0.3%	A	1.4%	A	0.3%	A	0.6%	A	0.5%
Executive Desk Chair	A	0.3%	I	0.4%	I	0.4%	A	0.1%	A	0.3%	A	1.0%
Additional Desk Chairs	A	0.5%	I	0.2%	I	1.3%	A	0.0%	I	0.5%	A	0.2%
Climate Control by Room	M	1.6%	M	4.1%	M	1.0%	M	2.6%	M	2.1%	M	5.6%
Full-Size Bathtub	A	2.0%	A	3.7%	I	1.2%	A	3.9%	A	2.4%	I	0.5%
Microwave	I	0.5%	A	3.5%	I	0.4%	A	2.3%	I	1.3%	A	1.0%
Small Refrigerator	A	0.8%	I	4.7%	I	0.7%	I	2.4%	A	1.7%	A	1.4%
Kitchenette	A	3.2%	A	6.6%	A	1.3%	I	3.4%	A	3.4%	A	5.1%
Appliance Rental Service	I	NA	A	NA	I	NA	I	NA	I	NA	A	NA
VCR	A	0.7%	A	3.8%	I	0.1%	Q	2.5%	I	1.4%	A	0.4%
DVD Player	A	0.9%	A	0.5%	I	0.3%	A	2.6%	A	0.9%	A	0.2%
Carpet	A	1.3%	A	0.7%	A	0.4%	A	3.2%	A	1.3%	A	0.3%
Tile	I	0.2%	I	4.1%	I	0.7%	I	0.8%	I	1.1%	I	1.0%
Enforced Quiet Areas	I	0.3%	I	0.0%	I	0.7%	O	3.6%	I	0.7%	M	1.9%
Vacuum Cleaner Rental Service	M	NA	I	NA	I	NA	I	NA	I	NA	I	NA
Shared Common Vacuum Cleaner	A	0.6%	I	0.4%	A	0.4%	A	0.1%	A	0.4%	A	1.8%
Accessible Roof	A	1.6%	A	0.8%	A	0.9%	A	2.3%	A	1.3%	I	3.4%
Security Guard	I	NA	M	NA	O	NA	M	NA	M	NA	M	NA
Laundry Facility by Floor	O	1.4%	A	1.1%	O	1.1%	O	0.8%	O	1.2%	A	3.2%
Iron and Ironing Board	I	0.2%	I	0.2%	I	0.2%	I	0.0%	I	0.2%	I	1.6%
Optional Laundry Service	A	3.0%	A	2.1%	A	1.2%	A	1.3%	A	2.1%	A	2.7%
Optional Maid Service	A	1.2%	A	1.9%	A	1.5%	A	1.3%	A	1.5%	A	5.0%
Concierge	A	0.4%	I	0.4%	A	1.1%	I	0.6%	I	0.6%	A	4.1%
Reserved Convenient Parking Place	A	3.4%	A	2.4%	A	0.2%	A	3.8%	A	2.6%	A	5.0%
Competitive Admissions (vs. Conventional Assignment)	I	0.7%	I	0.4%	I	0.1%	I	0.3%	I	0.4%	I	0.7%
Admission Based on GPA	R	0.8%	I	0.3%	R	0.1%	R	0.1%	I	0.4%	R	0.4%
Admissions for Business Students Only	R	0.6%	I	0.2%	A	0.2%	R	0.3%	I	0.4%	A	3.3%
Admissions for Junior Level and Up Only	R	0.6%	I	0.1%	A	0.3%	I	0.3%	I	0.4%	R	0.6%
Segregate Residents by Class Level	I	0.1%	R	0.1%	I	0.9%	I	0.4%	I	0.3%	O	1.4%
Armoire	A	NA	A	NA	A	NA	A	NA	A	NA	A	NA
Coffee Table	I	0.5%	I	0.3%	I	0.1%	I	0.1%	I	0.3%	I	0.9%
High Quality Linens	A	0.6%	A	0.8%	A	0.8%	I	0.1%	I	0.6%	I	0.9%
Option to Rent by Semester	A	0.3%	I	1.8%	O	0.9%	I	2.4%	I	1.1%	O	4.2%

STAGE FOUR—Step 9: Develop Strategic Themes for Each Cognitive Image for Selected Market Segments

The cognitive images that are selected in Step 9 are called **strategic themes** and are used in designing products, services, or processes. An assessment of the effectiveness of the strategic themes is done by visiting development engineers or experts and asking them for their opinions of the strategic themes.

Level C Survey—Entirely New Designs

Introduction

The purpose of a Level C study is to invent and innovate an entirely new product, service, or process. There four stages and eight steps in a Level C study (see Table 14.34).

TABLE 14.34 Stages and Steps in a Level C Study

STAGES	STEPS WITHIN STAGES
STAGE ONE Collect Voice of the People (VoP) Data	
	Step 1—Determine an aspect of people's behavior that will create new product opportunities that are congruent with the organizational service or process identity.
	Step 2—Conduct a survey of opinion leaders in the selected market segment to collect "Voice of the People" (VoP) data about the behavior of interest.
	Step 3—Classify Voice of the People data as circumstantial issues or product-related issues.
STAGE TWO Analyze Circumstantial Issues	
	Step 4—Use an affinity diagram to determine the underlying latent categories of circumstantial issues.
STAGE THREE Develop Features of New Product	
	Step 5—Determine the focus point for each circumstantial issue.
	Step 6—Develop cognitive images for each focus point.

STAGES	STEPS WITHIN STAGES
STAGE FOUR Decide Strategic Themes	
	Step 7—Classify each cognitive image into a Kano category and cost distribution.
	Step 8—Develop strategic themes.

STAGE ONE: Collect "Voice of the People" (VoP) Data

STAGE ONE—Step 1: Determine an Aspect of People's Behavior That Will Create New Product/Service/Process Opportunities That Are Congruent with the Organizational Identity

Select the members of the project team.

STAGE ONE—Step 2: Conduct a Survey of Opinion Leaders in the Selected Market Segment to Collect "Voice of the People" (VoP) Data About the Behavior of Interest

"Voice of the People" (VoP) is a phrase used to describe the data that identifies the future needs and wants of users of entirely new products and services. It comes from lead users [see Reference 13]. It cannot come from regular users because they do not yet exist.

Team members conduct a survey of lead users in the selected market segment and ask broad questions to deepen their understanding of the chosen behavior. Survey data should always be kept in the language of the lead user. Two products that emerged from Level C studies are Japanese word processors and Japanese automobile navigation systems.

STAGE ONE—Step 3: Classify Voice of the People Data as Circumstantial Issues or Product-Related Issues

Put aside product-related data and focus on circumstantial data.

STAGE TWO: Analyze Circumstantial Issues

STAGE TWO—Step 4: Use an Affinity Diagram to Determine the Underlying Latent Categories of Circumstantial Issues

If too many circumstantial issues emerge out of Step 3, team members use the affinity diagram to determine the underlying latent circumstantial issues. These latent issues then become the circumstantial data used in the study.

STAGE THREE: Develop Features of New Product

STAGE THREE—Step 5: Determine the Focus Point for Each Circumstantial Issue

For each circumstantial issue highlighted in Step 4, conduct a technical investigation of its cause and determine its focus point(s).

STAGE THREE—Step 6: Develop Cognitive Images for Each Focus Point

Team members develop detailed, unambiguous, and qualitative statements (cognitive images) of customer needs for each focus point.

STAGE FOUR: Decide Strategic Themes

STAGE FOUR—Step 7: Classify Each Cognitive Image into a Kano Category and Cost Distribution

Team members classify each cognitive image (CI) into a Kano category and determine the cost increase that will be acceptable to users. Cognitive images (CIs) that are widely desired and accepted by users are called strategic themes.

STAGE FOUR—Step 8: Develop Strategic Themes

Team members decide which cognitive images (CIs) will become strategic themes to be used in designing products, services, and/or processes. They visit with one or more development engineers or experts to discuss the effectiveness of the strategic themes.

Home Office Example. An example of a Level C study is Home Office Solutions. Home Office Solutions decided to conduct a Level C study to define the characteristics of the "home office of tomorrow." Home Office Solution management hoped that by identifying the characteristics of the office of tomorrow, their engineers would be able to develop an entirely new line of products and/or services that are congruent with their corporate identity.

Option 1: Team members survey and/or observe people (regular users of home office) who work at home and identify the needs and wants (problems) they have that are attributable to the home office. List these needs and wants (problems) and find experts who can identify lead users of home offices who have effectively dealt with one or more of these needs and wants (problems).

Option 2: Team members survey experts to determine the characteristics of lead users of the home office of tomorrow. Next, have the experts identify people who exhibit the lead user characteristics, or conduct a large survey to identify people with the lead user characteristics.

Lead users might be inventive in their methods for caring for a small child, storing files or inventory, arranging for meeting space, obtaining secretarial support, creating human interaction, separating home life and work life, and dealing with lack of prestige caused by not working for a large organization. Additionally, lead users may be inventive in their systems for backing-up computers (response to down time), using office equipment, and interacting with a main office (mail pick-up).

SUMMARY

The focus of this chapter is explaining how PD team members can "hear" well articulated statements of the "voices of the stakeholders" in each of the stakeholder segments of an organization. Stakeholders segments include customer segments, employee segments, investor segments, supplier segments, and regulator segments, to name a few segments. Further, this chapter explains how PD team members can use Kano surveys within each stakeholder segment to identify the Attractive, One-Way, and Must-Be cognitive images (CTQs).

REFERENCES

1. Center for Quality Management, "A Special Issue on: Kano's Methods for Understanding Customer-Defined Quality," *The Center for Quality Management Journal*, vol. 2, no. 4, Fall 1993 (Cambridge, MA), p. 13.

2. E. de Bono, *Lateral Thinking for Management: A Handbook of Creativity*, American Management Association, 1971.

3. E. de Bono, *Serious Creativity: Using the Power of Lateral Thinking to Create New Ideas* (New York, NY: Harper Business, A Division of Harper Collins, 1992).

4. H. Gitlow, "Innovation on Demand," *Quality Engineering*, vol. 11, no. 1, 1998–1999, pp. 79–89.

5. H. Gitlow, and D. Levine, *Six Sigma for Green Belts and Champions* (Upper Saddle River, NJ: Financial Times Prentice Hall, 2005).

6. P. Green, D., Tull, and G. Albaum, *Research for Marketing Decisions*, 5th ed. (Upper Saddle River, NJ: Prentice Hall, 1988).

7. J. Hauser and D. Clausing, "House of Quality," *Harvard Business Review*, May/June 1988, pp. 63–73.

8. B. King, *Better Designs in Half the Time* (Methuen, MA: GOAL/QPC, 1987).

9. M. Liner, E. Loredo, H. Gitlow, and N. Einspruch, "Quality Function Deployment Applied to Electronic Component Design," *Quality Engineering*, vol. 9, no. 2, 1996–97, pp. 237–248.

10. D. Montgomery, *Design and Analysis of Experiments*, 6th ed. (New York: John Wiley, 2005).

11. P. Kotler, *Marketing Management: Analysis, Planning and Control*, 9th ed. (Upper Saddle River, NJ: Prentice Hall, 1999).

12. G. Urban and J. Hauser, *Design and Marketing of New Products*, 2nd ed. (Englewood Cliffs, NJ: Prentice-Hall, 1993).

13. E. Von Hippel, "Lead Users: A Source of Novel Product Concepts," *Management Science*, vol. 32, no. 7, 1986, pp. 791–805.

ENHANCING CREATIVITY TO DEVELOP ALTERNATIVE DESIGNS

SECTIONS

Introduction
15.1 Using de Bono's Thinking Habits and Tools to Generate Alternative Design Concepts
15.2 Using TRIZ to Generate Alternative Design Concepts
15.3 Using Benchmarking to Generate Alternative Design Concepts
Summary
References
Appendix 15.1 Full Contradictions Matrix (See the text web site at `www.prenhall.com/gitlow`)

LEARNING OBJECTIVES

After reading this chapter, you will know how to:

- Use thinking habits and tools to generate alternative high-level design concepts for the CTQs and CTPs.
- Use the Theory of Inventive Problem Solving, called TRIZ, to generate alternative high-level design concepts for the CTQs and CTPs.
- Use Benchmarking to generate alternative high-level design concepts for the CTQs and CTPs.

INTRODUCTION

Creativity is not an innate trait. It can be developed in almost anyone using appropriate thinking styles, tools, and methods. In this chapter, PD team members learn how to use de Bono's thinking habits and tools, TRIZ, and benchmarking to generate alternative high-level design concepts for the critical parameters (CTQs and/or CTPs).

15.1 USING DE BONO'S THINKING HABITS AND TOOLS TO GENERATE ALTERNATIVE DESIGN CONCEPTS

As mentioned in Chapter 6, "Analyze Phase," lateral thinking [see Reference 2] is used to move from established ideas and perceptions to new ideas and perceptions. It is required for creating the ideas and perceptions necessary to generate design concepts. Creative thinking can be used deliberately. You do not need to wait for an inspiration.

Thinking Habits

de Bono [see Reference 2] has developed the thinking habits required for creative thinking: focus and purpose, forward and parallel, perception and logic, values, and outcome and conclusion. For your convenience, each habit is discussed next as it was in Chapter 6.

The **focus and purpose** habit keeps a thinker aimed in the right direction. It stops drift, confusion, and inefficiency in thinking about a topic by asking the following questions:

- What am I looking at (thinking about) right now?
- What am I trying to do?

The **forward and parallel** habit helps a thinker identify the next step in his or her thinking process by asking the following questions:

- Forward—So what follows?
- Sideways—What else might there be?

The **perception and logic** habit helps the thinker see his or her world (perception) and how to utilize his or her perceptions (logic) about the world by asking the following questions:

- Perception (Breadth)—How broad a view am I taking?
- Perception (Change)—In what other ways is it possible to look at things?
- Logic—What follows from this?

The **values** habit determines the "value of an idea" to real life by asking the following questions:

- What are the values involved?
- Who are affected by these values?

The **outcome and conclusion** habit assists the thinker in harvesting the fruit of the thinking effort and feeling achievement in the outcome by asking the following questions:
If you have not succeeded in reaching a conclusion:

- What have I found out?
- What is the sticking point?

If you have succeeded in reaching a conclusion:

- What is my answer?
- Why do I think my answer will work?

The outcome and conclusion habit comes at the end of the thinking effort.

Thinking Tools

de Bono [see Reference 2] has developed several tools to assist individuals or teams to think creatively about a problem—in this case, about a design parameter. According to de Bono, all of us have creative potential and ability.

Recall from Chapter 6, the **CAF (Consider All Factors)** tool is designed to increase the breadth of perception with respect to a topic. It adds to the list of factors relevant to a topic by asking the following questions:

- What has been left out?
- Can you add another factor to the list you have?
- What else must be considered?

Exercise: You are redesigning the "paperwork for obtaining a bank loan." What has been left out? Do a CAF. One of an infinite number of possible answers is: Redesign the paperwork process so one person can do every step in the bank loan process. Consequently, the paperwork does not move at all.

Exercise: You are designing a "pill box" for frail elderly people. What things do you have to keep in mind? Do a CAF. One of an infinite number of possible answers is: Design a pill box that beeps when pills are to be taken by the pill box owner.

The **APC (Alternatives, Possibilities, Choices)** tool is designed to expand the alternatives, possibilities, and choices with respect to a topic by asking the following questions:

- What are alternative ways of looking at this?
- What are alternative actions for doing this?
- What are alternative solutions for this?
- What are alternative approaches for this?
- What are alternative explanations for this?
- What are alternative designs for this?

Exercise: What are alternative ways for arranging furniture in your living room? Do an APC. One of an infinite number of possible answers is: Arrange the furniture to promote conversation and to discourage watching television.

Exercise: List alternative designs for serving ice cream in an ice cream store. Do an APC. One possible example is: Have patrons make their own ice cream desserts and charge them by weight.

The **OPV (Other People's Views)** tool is designed to identify the people affected by a topic (including future generations) and to imagine their views on the topic by asking the following questions:

- Who is affected by this thinking (action)?
- What are the views (thinking) of those affected?

You can use OPV to consider both sides of an argument.

Exercise: A teenager loves listening to extremely loud music. He does not want to use earphones. His parents like peace and quiet. Do an OPV. One of an infinite number of possible answers is: Line the teenager's room with noise-reducing wall and ceiling materials.

The **C&S (Consequences and Sequel)** tool is designed to determine the consequences (immediate, short-term, medium-term, or long-term) of a decision, choice, plan, or action by asking the following questions:

- Will the decision work out?
- What are the benefits of the decision?
- What are the risks of the decision?
  - What might go wrong?
  - What is the worst outcome?
  - What is the best outcome?
  - What is the expected outcome?

- What are the costs of the decision?
- How likely is this outcome?

You must specify a time scale before using the C&S tool.

Exercise: The university has decided to guarantee that the time it takes to get to a destination after the arrival of the bus at the shuttle bus stop will be 15 minutes or less. Will the decision work out? What are the benefits of the decision? What are the risks of the decision? What are the costs of the decision? How likely is 15 minute or less shuttle bus service at the university? Do a C&S. One of an infinite number of possible answers is: Make sure that any alternative considers the needs of handicapped passengers.

The **PMI (Plus, Minus, and Interesting)** tool assists a thinker in scanning (360-degree view around a decision) for plus points, minus points, and interesting points of a decision by asking the following question:

- What would happen if you made this decision?

Exercise: What would happen if the university guaranteed 15 minute or less shuttle bus service from the time of arrival at a shuttle bus stop to the desired destination? Do a PMI. One of an infinite number of solutions is: Students would park on the campus perimeter.

Exercise: Should students give professors a rating every semester? Do a PMI. One of an infinite number of possible answers is: Professors might respond to frequent student evaluations by inflating their grades to ensure that they will receive high student evaluation scores.

The **AGO (Aims, Goals, and Objectives)** tool focuses attention on an aim by asking the following questions:

- What is the aim of your thinking?
- What do you want to end up with?

If an aim is too broad, it can be broken down into sub-aims to assist in reaching the overall aim.

Exercise: What is the aim of guaranteed 15 minute or less shuttle bus service? Do an AGO. One of an infinite number of possible answers is: The goal of 15 minute shuttle bus services is to decrease the number of automobiles in the core parking areas of the university between 10:00 A.M. and 2:00 P.M., Monday through Friday.

The **FIP (First Important Priorities)** tool directs a thinker's attention to the top three to five priorities of the relevant stakeholders of a situation by asking the following questions:

- What are my priorities in this situation?
- What are your priorities in this situation?

Exercise: What are your top priorities for your relationship with a friend? Do a FIP. One of an infinite number of possible answers is: The top priorities for my friendship with my best friend is to "let all of my personality traits hang out" without criticism.

The **Concept Fan** tool moves a thinker back and forth between broad ideas and detailed ideas by asking the following questions:

- What is the broad idea here?
- What detailed ideas emanate from this broad idea?
- This detailed idea is an example of what broad idea?

This tool was discussed and illustrated in the Measure Phase.

Exercise: At the University of Miami, it is difficult to find a parking space between 10:00 A.M. and 2:00 P.M. on Monday through Thursday. You want to improve the situation. What is the broad idea behind the parking problem? How can you use the broad idea to solve the problem? Use a concept fan. One of an infinite number of possible answers is: The broad idea behind parking problems is "fixed spaces and variable demand." Restaurants, hotels, and Disney World all have developed solutions to this problem.

The **UWC (Under What Circumstances)** tool enables a thinker to identify the situations under which something is true by asking the following questions:

- Under what circumstances is this true?
- Under what circumstances will this decision cause harm to a user?

Exercise: Under what circumstances is it dangerous to wear a tie? Do a UWC. One of an infinite number of possible answers is: It can be dangerous to wear a tie in a factory when heavy equipment is being operated.

The **PO (Provocative Operation)** tool is used to provoke (move) a thinker to thinking in new directions. PO precedes a statement. Its purpose is to create a provocative operation on the part of a thinker.

Exercise: PO: Students park anywhere on campus. This PO could cause an individual to think about the creation of a bicycle system that allows students to pick up and drop off university-owned bicycles all around campus. A student may never use the same bicycle twice.

Summary

The creative habits and tools discussed in this section can be very helpful to PD team members when they are trying to think "outside of the box" to generate design concepts. PD team members should not accept existing assumptions, restrictions, and rules because they limit potential options. Team members can choose a design that satisfies the needs of the most demanding stakeholders, and consequently, surpass (delight) the needs of less-stringent stakeholders.

15.2 USING **TRIZ** TO GENERATE ALTERNATIVE DESIGN CONCEPTS

Introduction

Recall from Chapter 6, TRIZ is a method developed by Altshuller [see Reference 1] that uses physics, mathematics, and chemistry to create inventions and innovations to solve real-world problems. TRIZ is an acronym for "The Theory of Inventive Problem Solving," translated from Russian. It is a dramatic improvement over the "trial and error" method for solving problems. TRIZ significantly improves the abilities of PD team members to develop inventive and innovative design concepts. Altshuller studied thousands of patents from many industries and discovered that 90% of the problems have been previously solved elsewhere. He organized the information from the patents into an extensive knowledge base that is independent of industry.

TRIZ is most appropriate for small improvements, major changes, and significant inventions. It is not suitable for solving simple and obvious problems (known by most everyone) and discovering entirely new phenomena (not known in science literature).

The five steps of the TRIZ model for creating inventive and innovative design concepts are as follows:

1. Identify the design problem (your problem).
2. Translate the design problem into a TRIZ problem.
3. Study the TRIZ knowledge base (40 inventive principles of TRIZ).
4. Solve the TRIZ problem using the TRIZ knowledge base.
5. Translate the TRIZ solution into a solution for your design problem.

40 Inventive Principles of TRIZ with Service Examples

Although TRIZ was developed for the improvement, invention, and innovation of products and processes, it is also useful in the improvement, invention, and innovation of services. The 40 inventive principles of TRIZ are presented next with service applications for each physical or technical principle [see Reference 6].

Principle 1—Segmentation

A. *Divide an event into independent parts.* For example, divide a large consumer market into smaller market segments so that the smaller segments can be managed more effectively, or break a complex task into smaller subtasks that are easier for an individual to complete.

B. *Make an event easy to disassemble.* For example, design a service for easy disassembly to satisfy time restrictions.

C. *Increase the degree of fragmentation or segmentation.* For example, describe a large problem as many small problems.

Principle 2—Taking Out

Separate an interfering component or property from an event. Single out the necessary components (or properties) for an event. For example, focus on a particular customer's needs without being distracted by other customers.

Principle 3—Local Quality

A. *Change an event's structure from uniform to nonuniform; change an external environment (or external influence) from uniform to nonuniform.* For example, change from a standardized process to a series of individualized processes to make maximal use of individual's nuances.

B. *Make each part/person/subsystem of an event function in conditions most suitable for its operation.* For example, assign special projects to match an employee's personality type with the task to be performed.

C. *Make each part/person/subsystem of an event fulfill a different and useful function.* For example, break down an operation into its component parts and assign each part to a different employee (specialization of labor).

Principle 4—Asymmetry

A. *Change the shape of an event from symmetrical to asymmetrical.* For example, change a party snack from cashew nuts (symmetrical) to mixed nuts (asymmetrical).

B. *If an event is asymmetrical, increase its degree of asymmetry.* For example, increase the diversity of a marketing department with respect to culture, languages, and ages.

Principle 5—Merging

A. *Bring closer together (or merge) identical or similar events; assemble identical or similar persons/systems to perform parallel operations.* For example, utilize one cashier's office for all cashier functions in an organization with many different departments, each with its own cashier function.

B. *Make operations contiguous or parallel; bring them together in time.* For example, complete tasks in parallel that don't have to be worked on in series.

Principle 6—Universality

Make a person/system or event to perform multiple functions; eliminate the need for other persons. For example, replace a series of individuals, each performing a special function in a bank loan department, with individuals performing all functions.

Principle 7—"Nested Doll"

A. *Place one event inside another event.* For example, insert cheese into the crust of pizza for a cheesier pizza or create a phone answering system with layers of options.

B. *Make one part/person/sub-system of a system pass through a cavity in another part/ person/sub-system of the same system.* For example, utilize an "open door" policy to create multiple communication channels in an organization.

Principle 8—Anti-Weight

A. *Compensate for the weight of an event by merging it with another event that provides lift.* For example, assign student interns to Six Sigma team members who are overburdened with work.

B. *Compensate for the weight of an event by making it interact with its environment.* For example, send competitive employees (event) to an "Outward Bound" program (environment) to teach the benefits of cooperation.

Principle 9—Preliminary Anti-Action

A. *If it will be necessary to do an action with both harmful and useful effects, this action should be replaced with anti-actions to control harmful effects.* For example, health-conscious individuals should take healthy snacks on airplanes to avoid eating unhealthy foods.

B. *Create beforehand stresses in an event that will oppose known undesirable working stresses later on.* For example, utilize a simulation model to train individuals on the stressful realities of a job.

Principle 10—Preliminary Action

A. *Perform the required change of an event (either fully or partially) before it is needed.* For example, anticipate a future decline in staffing requirements by decreasing the workforce through a program of planned attrition.

B. *Pre-arrange events such that they can come into action from the most convenient place and without losing time for their delivery.* For example, switch the movement of work in process in a production facility from moving work to the next station when it has been completed to moving work to the next station when it is requested by the next station.

Principle 11—Beforehand Cushioning

Prepare emergency means beforehand to compensate for the relatively low reliability of an event. For example, develop a contingency plan for a potential problem such as a hurricane.

Principle 12—Equi-Potentiality

Limit changes (e.g., change operating conditions to eliminate the need to raise or lower events to match requirements) in a system. For example, segment a market into customer segments for a service to decrease the need for special attention to a randomly selected customer.

Principle 13—The Other Way Round

A. *Invert the action(s) used to solve the problem (e.g., instead of cooling an event, heat it).* For example, supermarkets make deliveries directly to customer's homes instead of customers going to the supermarket to purchase their groceries.

B. *Make movable elements fixed or make fixed elements movable.* For example, deliver surgical patients to the recovery room when the recovery room has space, not when surgery on the patient has finished.

C. *Turn the event (or process) "upside down."* For example, have customers at the top of the organization chart and the CEO at the bottom.

Principle 14—Spheroidality—Curvature

A. *Move from flat elements to spherical elements or move from cube-shaped elements to ball-shaped elements.* For example, change rigid procedures to flexible procedures; that is, eliminate the sharp edges.

B. *Use rollers, balls, spirals, domes.* For example, employees learn how to speak to irate customers to minimize customer dissatisfaction.

C. *Go from linear to rotary motion or use centrifugal forces.* For example, rotate the position of department manager to all members of the department.

Principle 15—Dynamics

A. *Allow (or design) the characteristics of an element to change to find the optimal operating conditions for the characteristics of the element.* For example, use the PDSA cycle to optimize a process.

B. *Divide an event into elements capable of movement relative to each other.* For example, a Six Sigma project team invites various experts to join the team as temporary members, as needed by the project.

C. *If an element is rigid or inflexible, make it movable or adaptive.* For example, cross train individuals to perform multiple tasks.

Principle 16—Partial or Excessive Actions

If 100 percent of an event is hard to achieve using a given solution method, then use "slightly less" or "slightly more" of the same method instead. For example, use stretch goals as a motivational vehicle to increase output.

Principle 17—Another Dimension

A. *Move an event in two- or three-dimensional space.* For example, look at the consequences of a service interaction in the future or think about a problem from multiple points of view.

B. *Use a multi-story arrangement of events instead of a single-story arrangement.* For example, utilize a policy for outsourcing work to subcontractors.

C. *Tilt or re-orient the event; lay it on its side.* For example, train employees using role reversal activities.

D. *Use "another side" of a given area.* For example, think from the point of view of your competitor.

Principle 18—Mechanical Vibration

A. *Cause an element to oscillate or vibrate.* For example, change best practice methods every year.

B. *Increase the frequency of the oscillation or vibration of an element (even up to the ultrasonic).* For example, change best practice methods every week.

C. *Use an event's resonant frequency.* For example, schedule employees to work according to their circadian clock, not a wall clock.

Principle 19—Periodic Action

A. *Instead of continuous action, use periodic or pulsating actions.* For example, use random eye examinations instead of annual eye examinations of employees performing visual jobs.

B. *If an action is already periodic, change the periodic magnitude or frequency.* For example, switch from an annual performance appraisal system to a monthly performance appraisal system.

C. *Use pauses between impulses to perform a different action.* For example, store clerks in Miami study Spanish in their free time to better interact with Spanish-speaking customers.

Principle 20—Continuity of Useful Action

A. *Carry on work continuously; make all persons/systems of an event work at full load, all the time.* For example, routinely understaff the workforce in a department to create an environment requiring continuous effort.

B. *Eliminate all idle or intermittent actions or work.* For example, use time management to study an individual's allocation of time to eliminate wasted tasks.

Principle 21—Skipping

Perform an action at high speed. For example, run to your next appointment, don't walk; or eliminate nonvalue steps from a process.

Principle 22—"Blessing in Disguise" or "Turn Lemons into Lemonade"

A. *Use harmful factors (particularly, harmful effects of the environment or surroundings) to achieve a positive effect.* For example, make going to your office on the fifth floor an opportunity for exercise, rather than a problem.

B. *Eliminate the primary harmful action by adding it to another harmful action to resolve the problem.* For example, make a team of two dysfunctional individuals whose personalities create a positive synergistic effect.

C. *Amplify a harmful factor to such a degree that it is no longer harmful.* For example, develop a strain of vegetables that smell so bad when they spoil that no one would think they are edible.

Principle 23—Feedback

A. *Introduce feedback (referring back, cross-checking) to improve a process or action.* For example, conduct monthly reviews with employees or conduct tollgate reviews for each phase of the DMADV model.

B. *If feedback is already used, change its magnitude or influence.* For example, switch from a gut-feel feedback system to a data driven feedback system.

Principle 24—Intermediary

A. *Use an intermediary carrier or an intermediary process.* For example, have an ombudsman resolve a conflict between an employee and a manager.

B. *Merge one event temporarily with another (which can be easily removed).* For example, hire student interns to decrease the per-capita workload in a call center.

Principle 25—Self-Service

A. *Make an event serve itself by performing auxiliary helpful functions.* For example, create an ATM system that sells movie tickets to the theater adjacent to its location.

B. *Use waste resources, energy, or substances.* For example, recycle paper to create new paper products.

Principle 26—Copying

A. *Instead of an unavailable, expensive, or fragile event, use simpler and inexpensive copies.* For example, purchase generic drugs instead of brand-name drugs

B. *Replace an event or process with optical copies.* For example, perform selling functions using video conferencing.

Principle 27—Use Cheap Replacement Events

Replace an expensive event with multiple inexpensive events, compromising certain qualities (such as service life) or loyalty. For example, replace expensive senior faculty teaching remedial courses with inexpensive, qualified adjunct professors.

Principle 28—Substitution for Mechanical Means

A. *Replace a mechanical means with sensory (optical, acoustic, taste, or smell) means.* For example, replace face-to-face communications with video phone communications.

B. *Use electric, magnetic, and electromagnetic fields to interact with the event.* For example, re-place in-office psychological counseling with virtual video at-home psychological counseling.

C. *Change from static to movable fields, from unstructured fields to those having structure.* For example, create a mobile library or mobile office in a car.

D. *Use electric, magnetic, and electromagnetic fields in conjunction with field-activated (e.g., ferromagnetic) particles.* For example, mix iron filings with soil and apply an electric cur-rent to create soil conditions of varying hardness to test tractors that will work in different soil conditions around the world.

Principle 29—Pneumatics and Hydraulics

Use gas and liquid elements of an event instead of solid elements of an event (e.g., inflat-able, filled with liquids, air cushion, hydrostatic, hydro-reactive). For example, look at a process as a flow of events instead of a series of interconnected separate steps.

Principle 30—Flexible Shells and Thin Films

A. *Use flexible shells and thin films instead of three-dimensional structures.* For example, use flat organizational structures instead of multi-layered organizational structures.

B. *Isolate the event from the external environment using flexible shells and thin films.* For example, utilize an ombudsman to solve problems between two arguing factions.

C. *Connect an event to its external environment by removing barriers such as shells and films.* For example, use an open-door policy so a CEO can talk directly to line employees to remove the distortion of information created by middle management.

Principle 31—Porous Materials

A. *Make an event porous or add porous elements (inserts, coatings, etc.).* For example, train all employees in creative thinking methods to open them up to different thought patterns.

B. *If an event is already porous, use the pores to introduce a useful substance or function.* For example, if employees are open to change, introduce them to the change concepts through field trips to organizations that possess the change concept.

Principle 32—Color Changes

A. *Change the color of an event or its external environment.* For example, utilize color-coded files to distinguish different type of customers (e.g., geriatric patients get a blue folder and pediatric patients get a green folder).

B. *Change the transparency of an event or its external environment.* For example, create an environment in a hotel where check-in is so pleasant that it is an enjoyable activity (e.g., in some hotels in India, a desk clerk meets the guest at the front door and immediately takes him/her to their room and checks them in from the room).

Principle 33—Homogeneity

Make events interacting with a given event of the same material (or material with identical properties). For example, provide standardized methods for all employees performing a particular function.

Principle 34—Discarding and Recovering

A. *Make portions of an event that have fulfilled their functions go away (discard by dissolving, evaporating, etc.) or modify these directly during operation.* For example, move medicine requiring extreme cold from one location to another by freezing it in a block of ice that melts at the destination.

B. *Conversely, restore consumable elements of an event directly in operation.* For example, restock parts required for an assembly using a Just-In-Time system so that there is no inventory.

Principle 35—Parameter Changes

A. *Change an event's physical state (e.g., to a gas, liquid, or solid).* For example, escalate a situation from an acceptable state to a crisis to change the behavior of people involved in the situation.

B. *Change concentration or consistency.* For example, provide frequent psychological counseling for a troubled employee instead of occasional psychological counseling.

C. *Change the degree of flexibility.* For example, create customer resolution systems that have more flexibility than current systems through empowering employees to make decisions.

D. *Change the temperature.* For example, decrease the temperature in a training room to decrease drowsiness of trainees or turn down the heat of an argument in an attempt to resolve it.

Principle 36—Phase Transitions

Use phenomena occurring during phase transitions (e.g., volume changes, loss or absorption of heat, etc.). For example, utilize the increase in societal empathy during natural disasters to improve emergency response systems.

Principle 37—Thermal Expansion

A. *Use thermal expansion (or contraction) of materials.* For example, shoe stores use a foot cooler to decrease the swelling of feet at the end of the day to create a more accurate fit for new shoes.

B. *If thermal expansion is being used, use multiple materials with different coefficients of thermal expansion.* For example, create teams utilizing a range of personalities to improve performance.

Principle 38—Strong Oxidants

A. *Replace common air with oxygen-enriched air.* For example, create a team of individuals trained in statistical methods instead of creating a team of individuals not trained in statistical methods.

B. *Replace enriched air with pure oxygen.* For example, create a Six Sigma team of green belts instead of creating a team of individuals who are not trained in Six Sigma methods.

Principle 39—Inert Atmosphere

A. *Replace a normal environment with an inert one.* For example, hire employees in a health spa whose personalities exude a relaxed and slow atmosphere.

B. *Add neutral persons, or inert additives to an event.* For example, create buffers between warring departments when allocating resources; or staff the customer service department with patient individuals.

Principle 40—Composite Materials

Change from uniform to composite (multiple) materials. For example, hire employees who can multi-task instead of employees who can only perform one function at a time.

39 Contradictions of TRIZ

A basic principle of TRIZ is that a technical problem is defined by contradictions [see References 4 and 5]. That is, if there are no contradictions, there are no problems. This radical-sounding statement forms the basis for the TRIZ problem-solving methods that are fastest and easiest to learn.

TRIZ defines two kinds of contradictions: "Technical" and "Physical." **Technical contradictions** are the classical engineering "trade-offs." The desired state cannot be reached because something else in the system prevents it. In other words, when something gets better, something else gets worse. Examples include the following:

- The service is more comprehensive (positive), but it takes longer to provide (negative).

- The vehicle has higher horsepower (positive), but uses more fuel (negative).

- A menu has entrées that satisfy specific customer's tastes (positive), but creates increased difficulties for the kitchen staff to provide high-quality entrées (negative).

Physical contradictions are situations where one object has contradictory, opposite requirements. Examples include the following:

- When pouring hot filling into chocolate candy shells, the filling should be hot in order to pour fast, but it should be cold to prevent melting the chocolate.

- Meals should be served fast (to feed hungry patrons), but should be served slow to create a relaxed dining experience.
- Software should be easy to use, but should have many complex features and options.

Many problems can be stated as both physical and technical contradictions. In general, when using the TRIZ research findings, the most comprehensive solutions come from using the physical contradiction formulation, and the most prescriptive solutions come from using the technical contradiction. In terms of learning, people usually learn to solve technical contradictions first, because the method is very concrete. Then, they learn to solve physical contradictions, and then they learn to use both methods interchangeably, depending on the problem.

Resolving Technical Contradictions. The TRIZ patent research classified 39 features for technical contradictions (see Table 15.1). Table 15.2 shows selected two-way combinations of the 39 technical contradictions shown in Table 15.1.

TABLE 15.1 List of 39 Technical Contradictions

Feature Number	Name of Contradiction	Explanation of Contradiction
1	Weight of moving object	The mass of the object in a gravitational field. The force that the body exerts on its support or suspension.
2	Weight of stationary object	The mass of the object in a gravitational field. The force that the body exerts on its support or suspension, or on the surface on which it rests.
3	Length of moving object	Any one linear dimension, not necessarily the longest, is considered a length.
4	Length of stationary object	Same.
5	Area of moving object	A geometrical characteristic described by the part of a plane enclosed by a line. The part of a surface occupied by the object or the square measure of the surface, either internal or external, of an object.
6	Area of stationary object	Same.
7	Volume of moving object	The cubic measure of space occupied by the object. Length × width × height for a rectangular object, height × area for a cylinder, etc.
8	Volume of stationary object	Same.
9	Speed	The velocity of an object; the rate of a process or action in time.
10	Force	Force measures the interaction between systems. In Newtonian physics, force = mass × acceleration. In TRIZ, force is any interaction that is intended to change an object's condition.
11	Stress or pressure	Force per unit area. Also, tension.
12	Shape	The external contours, appearance of a system.

Feature Number	Name of Contradiction	Explanation of Contradiction
13	Stability of the object's composition	The wholeness or integrity of the system; the relationship of the system's constituent elements. Wear, chemical decomposition, and disassembly are all decreases in stability. Increasing entropy is decreasing stability.
14	Strength	The extent to which the object is able to resist changing in response to force. Resistance to breaking.
15	Duration of action by a moving object	The time that the object can perform the action. Service life. Mean time between failures is a measure of the duration of action. Also, durability.
16	Duration of action by a stationary object	Same.
17	Temperature	The thermal condition of the object or system. Loosely includes other thermal parameters, such as heat capacity, that affect the rate of change of temperature.
18	Illumination intensity	Light flux per unit area; also, any other illumination characteristics of the system such as brightness, light quality, etc.
19	Use of energy by moving object	The measure of the object's capacity for doing work. In classical mechanics, energy is the product of force times distance. This includes the use of energy provided by the super-system (such as electrical energy or heat). Energy is required to do a particular job.
20	Use of energy by stationary object	Same.
21	Power	The time rate at which work is performed. The rate of use of energy.
22	Loss of energy	Use of energy that does not contribute to the job being done (see 19). Reducing the loss of energy sometimes requires different techniques from improving the use of energy, which is why this is a separate category.
23	Loss of substance	Partial or complete, permanent or temporary, loss of some of a system's materials, substances, parts, or subsystems.
24	Loss of information	Partial or complete, permanent or temporary, loss of data or access to data in or by a system. Frequently includes sensory data such as aroma, texture, etc.
25	Loss of time	Time is the duration of an activity. Improving the loss of time means reducing the time taken for the activity. "Cycle time reduction" is a common term.
26	Quantity of substance/ the matter	The number or amount of a system's materials, substances, parts, or subsystems that might be changed fully or partially, permanently or temporarily.
27	Reliability	A system's ability to perform its intended functions in predictable ways and conditions.
28	Measurement accuracy	The closeness of the measured value to the actual value of a property of a system. Reducing the error in a measurement increases the accuracy of the measurement.

(continued)

TABLE 15.1   List of 39 Technical Contradictions (Continued)

Feature Number	Name of Contradiction	Explanation of Contradiction
29	Manufacturing precision	The extent to which the actual characteristics of the system or object match the specified or required characteristics.
30	External harm affects the object	Susceptibility of a system to externally generated (harmful) effects.
31	Object-generated harmful factors	A harmful effect is one that reduces the efficiency or quality of the functioning of the object or system. These harmful effects are generated by the object or system, as part of its operation.
32	Ease of manufacture	The degree of facility, comfort, or effortlessness in manufacturing or fabricating the object/system.
33	Ease of operation	Simplicity: The process is *not* easy if it requires a large number of people, large number of steps in the operation, needs special tools, etc. "Hard" processes have low yield and "easy" process have high yield; they are easy to do right.
34	Ease of repair	Quality characteristics such as convenience, comfort, simplicity, and time to repair faults, failures, or defects in a system.
35	Adaptability or versatility	The extent to which a system/object positively responds to external changes. Also, a system that can be used in multiple ways under a variety of circumstances.
36	Device complexity	The number and diversity of elements and element interrelationships within a system. The user may be an element of the system that increases the complexity. The difficulty of mastering the system is a measure of its complexity.
37	Difficulty of detecting and measuring	Measuring or monitoring systems that are complex, costly, require much time and labor to set up and use, or systems that have complex relationships between components or components that interfere with each other all demonstrate "difficulty of detecting and measuring." Increasing cost of measuring to a satisfactory error is also a sign of increased difficulty of measuring.
38	Extent of automation	The extent to which a system or object performs its functions without human interface. The lowest level of automation is the use of a manually operated tool. For intermediate levels, humans program the tool, observe its operation, and interrupt or re-program as needed. For the highest level, the machine senses the operation needed, programs itself, and monitors its own operations.
39	Productivity	The number of functions or operations performed by a system per unit time. The time for a unit function or operation. The output per unit time, or the cost per unit output.

Once a contradiction is expressed in the technical contradiction form (the trade-off), the next step is to locate the features in the Contradiction Matrix (see Appendix 15.1 on the text web site at `www.prenhall.com/gitlow` for the complete Contradictions Matrix or see Table 15.2 below for a portion of the complete matrix).

Worsening Feature → / Improving Feature ↓		Volume of moving object	Speed	Force (Intensity)	Stress or pressure	Shape	Reliability	Object-generated harmful factors	Ease of operation	Ease of repair	Device complexity	Difficulty of detecting and measureing
		7	9	10	11	12	27	31	33	34	36	37
9	Speed	7, 29, 34	+	13, 28, 15, 19	6, 18, 38, 40	35, 15, 18, 34	11, 35, 27, 28	2, 24, 35, 21	32, 28, 13, 12	34, 2, 28, 27	10, 28, 4, 34	3, 34, 27, 16
10	Force (Intensity)	15, 9, 12, 37	13, 28, 15, 12	+	18, 21, 11	10, 35, 40, 34	3, 35, 13, 21	13, 3, 36, 24	1, 28, 3, 25	15, 1, 11	26, 35, 10, 18	36, 37, 10, 19
11	Stress or pressure	6, 35, 10	6, 35, 36	36, 35, 21	+	35, 4, 15, 10	10, 13, 19, 35	2, 33, 27, 18	11	2	19, 1, 35	2, 36, 37
12	Shape	14, 4, 15, 22	35, 15, 34, 18	35, 10, 37, 40	34, 15, 10, 14	+	10, 40, 16	35, 1	32, 15, 26	2, 13, 1	16, 29, 1, 28	15, 13, 39
15	Duration of action of moving object	10, 2, 19, 30	3, 35, 5	19, 2, 16	19, 3, 27	14, 26, 28, 25	11, 2, 13	21, 39, 16, 22	12, 27	29, 10, 27	10, 4, 29, 15	19, 29, 39, 35
33	Ease of operation	1, 16, 35, 15	18, 13, 34	28, 13, 35	2, 32, 12	15, 34, 29, 28	17, 27, 8, 40		+	12, 26, 1, 32	32, 26, 12, 17	

TABLE 15.2 Selected Rows and Columns from the 39 × 39 Contradiction Matrix

To use the compete Contradictions Matrix in Appendix 15.1 on the text web site, find the row that most closely matches the feature or parameter you are improving in your "trade-off" and the column that most closely matches the feature or parameter that degrades. The cell at the intersection of that row and column will have several numbers. These are the identifying numbers for the 40 TRIZ principles that are most likely, based on the TRIZ research, to solve the problem; that is, to lead to a breakthrough solution instead of a trade-off.

For example, suppose a fast food restaurant creates a process to deliver food to hungry patrons in less time (improving [good] feature # 15: duration of action of moving object), but the decreased meal time creates a less-relaxing environment (worsening [bad] feature # 31: object-generated harmful effects). This contradiction is most likely resolved using one or more of the following of the 40 principles (see Table 15.2):

Principle 21—Skipping (perform an action at high speed)

Principle 39—Inert atmosphere

Principle 16—Partial or excessive actions

Principle 22—"Turn lemons into lemonade"

Principle 21 can be utilized by management to create free time for patrons to take a leisurely walk after eating their fast food to help them digest their meals. The inventive concept is a fast food restaurant with a peaceful walking path adjoining it. Principle 39 can be utilized by management to create a relaxed atmosphere by hiring employees who exude relaxation as part of their personalities. Principle 16 can be utilized by management to create a slower paced atmosphere by understaffing bus persons so patron's tables are not cleared quickly, thereby creating a slower pace in the restaurant. Principle 22 can be utilized by management to take advantage of a less-relaxing environment by getting patrons to watch a timed fun/educational video. When the video is done, they leave the restaurant.

Resolving Physical Contradictions. TRIZ has five classical methods for resolving physical contradictions:

- Separation in time and/or space.
- Phase transition (Solid—liquid—gas—plasma).
- Paramagnetic (alignment of a nonmagnetic material with a magnetic field), ferromagnetic (spontaneous magnetization of a material), to name a few.
- Move to the super-system or the sub-system.
- Convert a physical contradiction to a technical contradiction.

Examination of the 39 features of resolving technical contradictions shows extensive overlap with these five methods, because they are based on the same research and on the same collection of innovative solutions to a wide variety of problems. Returning to the fast food example, one dominant physical contradiction for the speed of meal service is: the delivery of meals should be fast (to satisfy hungry patrons) and slow (to create a relaxing meal).

Using the first method for resolving a physical contradiction ("separation in time and/or space") leads to a dual system that provides slow meal delivery for patrons wanting a relaxed meal and provides fast meal delivery for patrons who are hungry. This solution introduces problems of sensor and logic complexity; that is, how do you know what a patron wants?

Using the second method for resolving a physical contradiction ("phase transition") appears unlikely to help in this case, but should not be rejected immediately. Consider the physical state of everything that does harm in the scenario. For example, one form of harm is caused by patrons being hungry while waiting for their meal. The patron is waiting for food in an uncomfortable (hungry) state. The hungry state has been blamed for rude behavior. Could the hunger that harms people be moderated by using some other material? This leads us to the idea of a snack being served immediately as patrons walk in the door of the restaurant.

The third method for resolving physical contradictions ("paramagnetic, ferromagnetic") is not discussed or illustrated in this book [see Reference 1].

Using the fourth method for resolving a contradiction ("move to use the super-system or the sub-system") leads to the ultimate super-system solution of educating all citizens in public school about proper nutrition, the need to eat healthy snacks to stave off harmful hunger, and the need to eat relaxing meals.

A fifth method for resolving a physical contradiction is to convert it into a technical contradiction. The most common technique employed when using this method is to separate the elements of the contradiction and ask: "WHY?" For example, continuing with the fast/slow delivery of meals contradiction:

Why must it be fast? To avoid hungry patrons.
Why must it be slow? To provide relaxing meals.

This leads us to the following technical contradiction: as the delivery of the meal gets faster, the meal becomes less relaxing *and* as the delivery of the meal gets slower, the patron becomes hungrier. This is not just circular logic: It focuses us on the root cause of the problem, the delivery of a pleasant dining experience, and makes it very clear that changing the speed of the delivery of the meal is only a "band-aid" solution to the problem. This is why resolving the physical contradiction is regarded as a more general solution than resolving the technical contradiction. TRIZ does not generate breakthrough solutions by "better brainstorming" or by teaching people to "think creatively." In dealing with contradictions, TRIZ generates breakthrough solutions by giving you the tools to find the root cause(s) behind a problem and to remove the root cause(s).

Conclusion

TRIZ is a powerful technique to utilize when creating inventive and innovative high-level designs for CTQs and CTPs. It takes practice, but is well worth the effort.

15.3 USING BENCHMARKING TO GENERATE ALTERNATIVE DESIGN CONCEPTS

Recall from Chapter 6, **benchmarking** is "a structured approach for identifying the best practices from industry and government, and comparing and adapting them to your organization's operations. It counteracts the 'reinvent the wheel' syndrome. Such an approach is aimed at identifying more efficient and effective processes for achieving intended results, and suggesting ambitious goals for program output, product/service quality, and process improvement." Consequently, benchmarking is a technique that can be used to discover creative solutions to problems discovered by others. The solutions may be used in another organization or industry. Nonetheless, they may be very helpful for creatively solving problems.

Many business processes are common throughout industry. For example, the University of Miami has the same basic Human Resources requirements for hiring and developing employees as Texaco. Xerox has similar customer problem resolution needs as McDonald's. Business processes from many industries are similar and can be benchmarked.

The key to successful benchmarking is to compare your organization's flowchart or process map for the process under study to a best-in-class organization's flowchart or process map, called a "best practice." If its flowchart, or a section of it, makes sense in your organization, you have a potential process improvement or design concept.

SUMMARY

The chapter presented three types of techniques, tools, and methods for enhancing the creative abilities of an individual or a PD team: thinking habits and tools, the Theory of Inventive Problem Solving (TRIZ), and benchmarking. All three methods are extremely useful in the proper circumstances.

REFERENCES

1. G. Altshuller, *And Suddenly the Inventor Appeared: TRIZ, the Theory of Inventive Problem Solving*, 2nd ed. translated by Lev Shulyak (Worcester, MA: Technical Innovation Center, Inc., 1996).

2. E. de Bono, *Teach Your Child How to Think* (New York, NY: Penguin Books, 1992).

3. G. Deiter, *Engineering Design: A Materials and Processing Approach*, 2nd ed. (New York, NY: McGraw-Hill Book Company, 1991).

4. E. Domb, J. Miller, E. MacGran, and M. Slocum, "The 39 Features of Altshuller's Contradiction Matrix," *The TRIZ Journal*, July 1992.

5. E. Domb, "Contradictions: Air Bag Applications," *The TRIZ Journal*, July 1992.

6. J. Terninko, "40 Inventive Principles with Social Examples," *The TRIZ Journal*, June 2001.

APPENDIX 15.1

FULL CONTRADICTIONS MATRIX

The full contradictions matrix can be found on the text web site, located at www.prenhall.com/gitlow.

PROFESSIONAL INTERPERSONAL BEHAVIOR SKILLS, TEAM BEHAVIOR SKILLS, AND SIX SIGMA MANAGEMENT

SECTIONS

LEARNING OBJECTIVES

After reading this chapter, you will:

- Understand assertive behavior and "I" messages.
- Understand how to constructively express anger.
- Understand how to create "win-win" situations.
- Understand how to resolve conflicts and make healthy decisions.
- Understand the psychological needs of individuals met by teamwork.
- Understand the stages in the life of a team.
- Appreciate how decisions are made by teams.
- Understand how to build and manage a Six Sigma PD team.
- Know how to resolve team problems.
- Understand the basics of concurrent engineering PD teams.
- Understand how to conduct and receive Six Sigma tollgate reviews.

INTRODUCTION

It is critical to your professional development that you learn, if you do not already know, appropriate interpersonal behavioral skills. These skills help you handle difficult situations by exercising deliberate conscious control over the outcome of the situation. Professional interpersonal behavior involves recognizing your own weaknesses and working to overcome them, not by changing other people or the environment, but by primarily changing your own behaviors, feelings, skills, cognition (thoughts), or unconscious processes.

Additionally, it is critical to your professional development that you learn, if you do not already know, appropriate team behavior skills. A team is a small group of people with complementary skills who work for a common objective (mission) for which they hold themselves accountable; for example, people working to create a design for a new service. It is critical that you learn how to work effectively and efficiently in a team setting; for example, knowing how to prevent getting stuck doing other team member's work, waiting for habitually late team members, or accepting disruptive behavior in team meetings.

There are many types of teams. In this book, the focus is on DMADV teams. A DMADV team, also called a Product Development team (PD team), is a cross-functional team with the objective of developing a new product, service, or process, or redesigning an existing product, service, or process. PD team members make all decisions about product design, production systems, and field support systems.

16.1 PROFESSIONAL INTERPERSONAL BEHAVIOR SKILLS[1]

Assertive Behavior

People who exhibit assertive behavior stand up for their rights without violating the rights of others. They tactfully, justly, and effectively express needs and wants, and opinions and feelings. They are not passive (weak, compliant, self-sacrificing) or aggressive (self-centered, inconsiderate, hostile, arrogantly demanding).

Frequently, passive people want to be nice and not create trouble. Consequently, they suffer in silence and get frustrated at their lot in life. If a passive person permits an aggressive person to take advantage of him or herself, the passive person is not only cheating him or herself, but is also enabling dysfunctional behavior in the aggressive person.

Purposes. Assertive behavior is frequently helpful in coping with fear, shyness, passivity, and even anger. Consequently, it is appropriate for a broad spectrum of situations. Assertive behavior involves:

---

[1] Source: Dr. Tucker-Ladd has produced a wonderful book on psychological self-help that is available to all on the web; see Reference 10.

- Stating what is on your mind, asking for things, requesting favors, and generally insisting that your rights be respected as a significant, equal human being.
- Stating negative feelings such as complaints, resentment, disagreement, and refusing requests from other people.
- Demonstrating positive feelings such as joy or attraction, and giving compliments.
- Asking why and questioning authority or tradition, not to rebel, but to assume responsibility for asserting your share of control of the situation.
- Starting, participating in, changing, and stopping conversations.
- Resolving irritations before you get angry and feel aggressive.

Steps. The four steps of assertive behavior are discussed in this section.

STEP ONE: Identify Situations in Which You Exhibit Passive or Aggressive Behavior

Recognize that you have the right to change from being a passive or aggressive person to being an assertive person. Answer the following questions:

Do you have difficulty saying "no?" ....(Yes/No)

Do you see yourself as unassertive? ....(Yes/No)

Are you depressed? ....(Yes/No)

Do you have many physical ailments? ....(Yes/No)

Do you complain about work? ....(Yes/No)

If you answered "yes" to one or more of the preceding questions, then you may have difficulty being an assertive person.

You will continue to be an unassertive person until you decide to change your behavior. A common aid for identifying the situations in which you are unassertive (intimidated, compliant, passive), or situations in which others are aggressive (demanding, whiny, bitchy) is to keep an "unassertiveness diary." You can use a c-chart to determine if the number of unassertive episodes per week is stable and predictable, although possibly unacceptable, system of behavior. If it is, then you can use a Pareto diagram to identify the most frequent type of unassertive episode. For example, Marsha keeps a daily diary of her unassertive behavior for a two-week period (see Table 16.1).

Table 16.2 shows the number of unassertive episodes per day taken from Table 16.1 before a change to Marsha's behavioral response to unassertive episodes. Table 16.1 shows a total of 126 episodes of unassertive behavior for the two-week period from January 15 through 28, 2005, with an average of 9 (126/14) episodes per day.

TABLE 16.1   Part of Marsha's Diary of Unassertive Behavior for Two Weeks

Episode #	Date	Description of Unassertive Episode
1	1/15/05	Can't say no.
2	1/15/05	Let my son get away with murder.
3	1/15/05	Can't say no.
4	1/15/05	Can't say no.
5	1/15/05	Can't say no.
6	1/15/05	Can't ask for simple directions.
7	1/15/05	Can't say no.
8	1/15/05	Can't say no.
...		
124	1/28/05	Can't say no.
125	1/28/05	Let my son get away with murder.
126	1/28/05	Can't say no.

TABLE 16.2   Daily Count of Number of Unassertive Episodes

Date	No. Unassertive Episodes
1/15/2005	11
1/16/2005	9
1/17/2005	9
1/18/2005	8
1/19/2005	7
1/20/2005	9
1/21/2005	9
1/22/2005	11
1/23/2005	7
1/24/2005	13
1/25/2005	9
1/26/2005	6
1/27/2005	7
1/28/2005	11
Total	126

Figure 16.1 is a *c*-chart of the number of unassertive episodes per day for the period from January 15 through 28, 2005. It shows that the number of unassertive episodes per day is a stable and predictable process with an average of 9 episodes per day, an upper control limit (UCL) of 18 $(9 + 3\sqrt{9})$ episodes per day, and a lower control limit (LCL) of 0 $(9 - 3\sqrt{9})$ unassertive episodes per day.

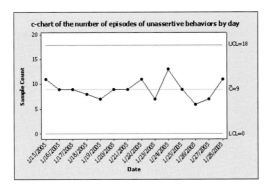

FIGURE 16.1 Minitab *c*-Chart of Marsha's Unassertive Behavior Per Day

Figure 16.2 is a Pareto diagram with type of unassertive episode on the *X*-axis and frequency on the *Y*-axis. The Pareto diagram highlights "can't say no" as the most frequent type of unassertive behavior.

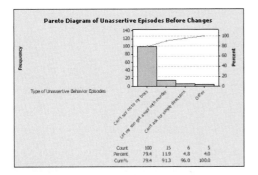

FIGURE 16.2 Minitab Pareto Diagram of Marsha's Unassertive Behavior

Based on the Pareto diagram in Figure 16.2, Marsha decides to use "I" messages (discussed later in this chapter) to improve her ability to appropriately "say no." Figure 16.3 is *c*-chart showing the effectiveness of Marsha's use of the "I" message in the two-week period from January 29–February 11, 2005.

Figure 16.4 shows that Marsha's use of the "I" message seems to be an extremely effective method for reducing the incidences of unassertive episodes in her life. "Can't say no" has shifted to a minor second-place problem. The largest bar in Figure 16.4, "Let my son get away with murder," could also be an example of "Can't say no." Marsha may have to develop a special "I" message for her son.

Most people can provide examples in which they have been aggressive. These examples are frequently used as evidence that the individual is not really unassertive. Frequently, people are unassertive in some way; for example, they can't say no to a co-worker or a boss, they are uncomfortable taking a compliment, they allow a family member to control their life, or they will not say what is on their mind, to name a few examples.

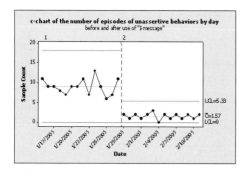

FIGURE 16.3 Marsha's Before and After c-Chart

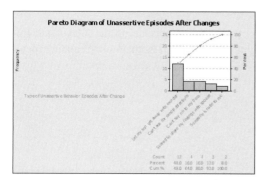

FIGURE 16.4 Marsha's After Pareto Diagram

You may need to deal with the anxiety that frequently goes along with change, to deal with any inconsistencies in your existing belief system, to assess the collateral damage of being assertive, and to prepare others for your new behavior. Talk to others about being assertive in situations that bother you.

Our personal belief system is frequently a major contributor to our unassertive behavior. Some examples of values and beliefs that can be dysfunctional are as follows:

Never be selfish.

Never make mistakes.

Never be emotional.

Never second guess people.

Never interrupt people.

Never complain.

Never brag, and so on.

The preceding values can contribute to being a passive person. No value system is rational in all situations:

Sometimes you can put your needs above the needs of others.

Occasionally you can make mistakes.

Sometimes you can be emotional.

If appropriate, you state your feelings.

If needed, you can ask for help.

Sometimes you can say "no."

Unassertive behavior can do great harm to you and the people that you deal with on a daily basis; for example:

1. You are submissive and lose self-respect.
2. You conceal your true feelings and are dishonest.
3. You are passive and have difficulty being loved.
4. You are manipulative and hide your true feelings.
5. You are compliant and reward your oppressor with your compliance.

On the positive side, assertiveness leads to more self-respect and happiness.

Remember, there are situations in which a sudden change from passive to assertive behavior may be problematic; for example:

- Your boss might be upset and fire you.
- Your spouse might get confused and want a separation or divorce.
- Your best friend might get upset and start to cry.

For the preceding extreme situations, try to develop a plan for a slow and gradual change in your behavior. In any event, you should talk to your family, friends, and associates about your decision to become an assertive person. Surprisingly, the people around you may be supportive of your efforts.

STEP TWO: Prepare Contingency Plans That Utilize Assertive Behavior to Deal with Your Most Common Types of Unassertive Episodes

An effective assertive response contains several parts, as follows:

1. First, it describes (to the other person involved) the unassertive episode from your point of view.
   - Be specific about actions and their consequences.
   - Do not make general accusations like "you're always hostile, late, or busy."

- Be objective.
- Do not say that the other person is "always this" or "always that."

You should focus on the other person's aggressive or passive behavior, not on his/her motives.

2. Second, it describes your feelings (to the other person involved) using an "I" message (discussed in the next section). When you use an "I" message, you are taking responsibility for your feelings.

- Be firm and strong.
- Make eye contact with the other person involved.
- Be objective. Try not to get emotional.

Try to focus on your positive feelings concerning the unassertive episode, not on your negative feelings. It can be helpful to explain your feelings; for example: "I feel _____ because _____."

3. Third, it describes (to the other person involved) the changes you would like to make to resolve the unassertive or aggressive episode. You need to be specific about what action should stop and what action should start.

- Be sure that the changes you would like to occur are reasonable to all parties concerned.
- Think from the perspective of the other people involved in the conflict episode.
- Be willing to change your behavior.

Sometimes, you may have specific consequences in mind if the other person in the conflict episode does not conform to your needs. If so, these should be described to all relevant people. Do not make empty threats. Table 16.3 shows some examples of assertive responses.

TABLE 16.3 Examples of Assertive Responses

Situation:	Your co-worker always complains about the boss's behavior, day after day.
Assertive Response:	"Every day for the past two years, you have been complaining about our boss. I like talking with you, but I get frustrated with hearing the same facts stated over and over. I wish we could talk about fun things."
Poor Responses:	An unassertive person would suppress his/her feelings. An aggressive person would call his/her co-worker names and tell him/her to shut up.
Situation:	A co-worker is repeatedly late for meetings.
Assertive Response:	"When we set times to meet and you arrive late, as you've done two out of the last three times, I feel frustrated because it wastes my time. I could be getting other work done. Besides, I start to think that you don't really don't care about our work. In the future, I'd like you to tell me at least an hour in advance if you are going to be late. Please do that?"
Poor Responses:	Let it go, fearing the co-worker will get mad. Or, tell the co-worker how inconsiderate he/she is and that it is amazing he/she hasn't been fired.

STEP THREE: Practice Giving Assertive Responses to Your Most Common Types of Unassertive or Aggressive Episodes

Workshop: Select a problem situation in which you are repetitively passive or aggressive. Write out an "I" message for responding to the situation. For example, "I feel frustrated because you have shown up late to two of our last three meetings. Please show up on time for our meetings in the future. Thank you."

Practice your "I" messages with a friend using role play for your most common unassertive or aggressive episodes. You will quickly find out regardless of how calm and tactful you are, your new assertive behavior will sometimes be viewed as an attack on the other person involved. You should prepare yourself for possible strong reactions to your assertive behavior; for example, the other person involved may do the following:

- Get angry at you.

- Say nasty things to you.

- Counterattack and criticize you.

- Seek revenge against you.

- Become sick or cry to evoke your feelings of guilt.

- Suddenly become passive with you.

If you choose to practice "I" messages with a friend, ask them to act out the more likely reactions. Frequently, explaining your behavior to the other person involved and being firm about your new assertive behavior will probably handle the situation. However, if explaining your new behavior to the other person involved and being firm do not resolve the unassertive or aggressive episode, then you can use several techniques for responding to criticism when the episode is not going well.

You may find yourself falling into old passive or aggressive behaviors when you are criticized for your assertive behavior; for example, you may:

- Be sarcastic.

- Procrastinate.

- Get mad.

- Be slow to get work done or be late for appointments.

- Get quiet.

- Be whiny.

- Criticize back.

- Do anything that drives him/her up a wall ("Oh, I didn't know that was bothering you").

Try not to behave in an "I count, you don't count" position because it is aggressive behavior. Also, try not to behave in a "You count, I don't count" position because that is passive behavior. Attempt to behave in a "we both count equally" position. A "we both count equally" position includes the following elements:

- Listen carefully, and ask for clarification, until you understand the other person's views. Focus your comments on his/her main point(s), and ask: "What is it that bothers you about...?"

- If the criticism is true, acknowledge the criticism. You can give honest explanations ("I was stuck in traffic," if it is true), but do not make excuses ("I was stuck in traffic," if it is not true).

If part of the criticism is true, acknowledge that part of the criticism. For example, "You could be right about that part of what you said," or "I understand how you feel about that part of what you said." These last two comments are avoiding the basic unassertive or aggressive episode.

Some people will not accept your saying "no" as an answer; that is, they refuse to acknowledge your reasonable assertive behavior. Sometimes you have to repeat a message many times to increase the likelihood that the other person involved in the unassertive episode will hear it. Sometimes you can use the "broken record" technique to be heard by the other person. For example, you calmly and firmly repeat a concise statement multiple times until the other person understands your message, for example:

- "I want you to arrive at the meeting at 1:00 P.M."
- "I am not happy with my new sport jacket; I want to return it for a complete refund."
- "I don't want to go out tonight; I want to stay home."

Repeat the same statement until the other person involved in the unassertive or aggressive episode leaves you alone, regardless of the excuses, diversions, or arguments.

There are two additional techniques that are useful when confronting difficult situations and people. You use these techniques when the communication is breaking down; for example:

- The topic has shifted to something other than resolving the unassertive or aggressive episode at hand.
- Both participants in the unassertive or aggressive episode are losing control of their emotions.
- Both participants in the unassertive or aggressive episode cannot resolve the episode.

Techniques for dealing with these situations are as follows:

1. Shift the focus from the unassertive or aggressive episode at hand to what is currently happening between you and the other person; for example:
    *   "We are both getting upset; let's try to stay reasonable."
    *   "We have drifted off the subject, can we go back to ____?"
2. Delay the time for dealing with the unassertive or aggressive episode at hand by taking a break:
    *   "That's an important point; give me a chance to mull it over. Can we take a half hour break?"
    *   "I need to sleep on that; can we talk tomorrow at lunch?"

STEP FOUR: Use Assertive Behavior in Actual Unassertive or Aggressive Episodes

Begin using assertive behavior in the situations you have practiced with your role-playing friend. As you become more confident, you can attempt to deal with more stressful situations. Modify your assertive behavior as appropriate. You might consider keeping a diary of your unassertive or aggressive episodes and analyze it with a *c*-chart and Pareto diagram.

"I" Messages

Definition. An "I" message is one of the most important techniques you can use to promote assertive behavior. It is used to help people accept responsibility for their feelings. A useful rule is: "If you are confronted with an unassertive or aggressive episode, use an "I" message."

An "I" message has two to four parts:

1. It states "I," "me," or "my."
2. It expresses a feeling.
3. It may describe the other person's behavior that is related to your feelings.
4. It may indicate what you would like to see changed.

A typical format for an "I" message is: "I feel *(your emotional state)* when *(the condition(s) that creates your emotional state)* please *(desired outcome)*."

You must do several things to effectively communicate your feelings about an unassertive or aggressive episode using an "I" message, as follows:

1. You must recognize the unassertive or aggressive episode.
2. You must interpret the situation. (What is going on?)
3. You must understand your feelings about the episode.
4. You must make an "I" message about the episode.

You may decide to hide, reject, deny, or transform into physical symptoms your feelings about the unassertive or aggressive episode. Or, you may decide to blame another person for a particular unassertive or aggressive episode and demand that he or she change his or her behavior. On the other hand, if you do not like how you feel with respect to an unassertive or aggressive episode, you can attempt to change your feelings.

Some common problems caused by not expressing your feelings about an unassertive or aggressive episode are the following:

1. Anger and fighting.
2. Distorted perception and blind spots.
3. Dishonesty.

"I" messages will help you express your feelings and avoid the preceding problems. "I" messages do not judge, blame, or threaten the other people involved in the conflict episode. "I" messages present your feelings that are rarely challengeable. "I" messages leave the other person involved in an unassertive or aggressive episode free to decide if he or she will change to accommodate your feelings.

Purpose. "I" messages are helpful in any of the following situations:

- You want to share your feelings in an honest and unthreatening manner.
- You are feeling stress in a relationship.
- You are hearing a lot of "you" (blaming, critical) statements.

Steps. There are three steps in delivering an "I" message.

STEP ONE: Understand the Proper Use of an "I" Message

If you are unaware of your feelings concerning an unassertive or aggressive episode and/or are not able to express your feelings, then you are likely to use a "you" statement. Table 16.4 shows some examples of "you" and "I" messages.

TABLE 16.4   *Examples of "You" and "I" Messages*

"You" statements	"I" messages
Blaming: "You make me so frustrated."	"I feel frustrated when you...."
Judging or labeling: "You are an idiot."	"I feel foolish when you criticize me in public."
Accusing: "You hate me!"	"I feel neglected when you speak to me in that tone of voice."
Ordering: "You shut up!"	"I feel annoyed when you call me names and make fun of me."
Questioning: "Why did you do that?"	"I feel bad when you do that."
Arguing: "You don't know what you are talking about."	"I feel convinced it is this way."

"You" statements	**"I" messages**
Sarcasm: "Of course, you are an expert!"	"I would like you a lot more if you were a bit more humble."
Approving: "You're an expert."	"I am impressed with your knowledge."
Disapproving: "You are a rotten person."	"I feel crushed when you seem only interested in spending my money."
Threatening: "You better........."	"I'd like it if you'd...."
Moralizing: "You should........"	"I think it would be fair for you to...."
Treating: "You need to rest and..."	"I'd like to be helpful to you."
Supporting: "It will get better."	"I'm sorry you feel...."
Analyzing: "You can't stand to leave your mother!"	"I'm disappointed that you are so reluctant to leave...."

Many "you" messages are used to control, intimidate, or deprecate another person. They are not statements made by assertive people; they are messages sent by manipulative people.

If you use "we," "it," or "they" messages to depersonalize your comment and/or vaguely conceal your feelings, you are avoiding personal responsibility for a situation (see Table 16.5). For example, you are not taking personal responsibility for your feelings if you use "we" to create the impression that other people share your view of a situation, when in fact, no one has authorized you to speak for them.

Table 16.5 shows examples of "we" and "I" messages.

TABLE 16.5 *Examples of "We" and "I" Messages*

"We," "it," "they" statements	**"I" messages**
"The team doesn't think...."	"I don't think the team believes...."
"The team is attempting to help you with your problem."	"I want to help you with your problem, but I'm having a hard time understanding the problem."
"This restaurant is depressing me."	"I am depressed."
"This movie is a waste of my time."	"I feel I am wasting my time."

The last example shows that your *personal opinions can sound like facts* if you use "am" or "is;" for example, "You are____," or "It is____". Additionally, "am" or "is" messages imply the whole person is a certain way, forever. For example: "You are a moron" says that the person has no intelligence at all. This is an overgeneralization. It would be better to say, "I resent it when you make plans without asking me what I want to do."

STEP TWO: Seek Out Situations in Which You Can Use "I" Messages

You may want to use your unassertiveness diary to identify situations in which you can use "I" messages. Once you find a situation, construct an "I" message for use in the future.

STEP THREE: Practice Using "I" Messages

You may find it difficult to use an "I" message at first, but keep on practicing. You will get better at it with practice and your behavior will seem natural after awhile.

You may discover that some people will ask you to stop using assertive behavior because it makes them uncomfortable. For example, if you say "I get angry when you do that," the person may say, "Back off."

Creating "No Lose" or "Win-Win" Solutions to Conflicts

Introduction. Conflict is part of the human condition. However, conflicts do not have to end with someone winning and someone losing. Assertive people can resolve conflicts with all participants still respecting each other.

There are five conflict resolution styles, as follows:

1. **Avoiding or denying a situation to stop conflict.** This is a bad approach.
2. **Giving in to stop conflict.** This is another bad approach.
3. **Blaming the other person to stop conflict.** This is also a bad approach.
4. **Compromising to stop conflict.** This is a good approach if it creates a "no lose" solution at worst, or a "win-win" solution at best. However, if it creates a "win-lose" solution, it is a bad approach.
5. **Integrating all participant's differences and similarities to stop conflict.** An integrative solution is built on the similarities of all participants. All participants are open and honest, not deceptive and manipulative. They build trust to develop a wise and workable solution. It is not easy, but this is a good approach.

There are many conflicts not subject to integrative solutions; for example, buying a used car. The salesperson wants a high price and you want a low price, the two of you bargain, and then you may never see each other again. This kind of tough, unsympathetic, self-centered, often manipulative, deceptive, and hostile negotiating involves great skills. However, they are not the skills discussed in this chapter.

Purpose. Integrative solutions resolve conflicts fairly and peacefully, if possible. They may involve parent-child or marital conflicts, disagreements at work, business transactions, and many other situations.

Steps. There are six steps for creating an integrative solution to a conflict.

STEP ONE: View the Participants in the Conflict as Equals Trying to Solve a Problem to Their Mutual Advantage

"No lose" or "win-win" conflict resolution strategies require that the participants enter the conflict as equals trying to identify a solution that both are happy with, or at least that neither is dissatisfied with. The participants should not think in terms of "win-lose" solutions. Conflict doesn't necessarily imply anger at each other. Conflict can provide an opportunity to strengthen a relationship and make all participants winners.

STEP TWO: Identify the Viewpoints of All Participants of the Conflict

The participants in a conflict should accept all the other participant's points of view as being valid. Each participant should enter the conflict with a respectful, open, and honest attitude. No one should campaign for his or her point of view, at the expense of another participant's point of view. Finally, all participants should recognize that it is possible that not everyone can have everything they want, but all the participants should still try to develop a "win-win" solution to the conflict.

The participants in a conflict should collect information from each other to clarify the exact nature of the conflict. The golden rule of collecting data to find a positive solution to a conflict is: listen, listen, and listen. Do not begin by offering solutions, just listen and get all the facts. Do not assess blame. Be empathic and sympathetic. Be careful not to use offensive language. Describe the benefits and costs of a solution to the conflict to all participants. Consider past efforts to resolve the conflict. Consider the difference between what the other participant's need (their "position") and what they really want (their "interest"). For example, suppose an employee asks for a pay raise (his or her "position"), but the company cannot afford the pay raise. If you collected data and discovered that the employee likes his or her job, but his or her "interest" was to get transportation for his/her family, the company may be able to find a vehicle for the employee. Stating different demands or "positions" does not mean that your basic "interests" are irreconcilable.

Frequently, there are several solutions that will satisfy all the different interests of the participants of a conflict. Participants should avoid thinking in terms of only one solution. Also, participants should avoid feeling competitive. All of this takes time.

STEP THREE: Develop Alternative Solutions for the Conflict That Result in "Win-Win" Situations, or at Least a "No Lose" Situations

All the participants of the conflict should study the viewpoints and data concerning the conflict. They should try to create alternative solutions to the conflict that result in "win-win" situations, or at least a "no lose" situation.

Creating "Win-Win" Solutions to Conflict. People use their values and beliefs to define a problem and develop a range of alternative solutions to a conflict. Consider including the following four values and beliefs into your decision-making process because they encourage "win-win" solutions to conflicts:

Improve the process that makes results; do not just demand results.

Balance intrinsic and extrinsic motivators; do not just use extrinsic motivators.

Cooperate, do not compete, if the aim of the system is not to win.

Optimize the whole system, not just your component of the system.

These values and beliefs are examined because they form the core assumptions of Six Sigma management. They have been proven successful in many Six Sigma endeavors.

Improve the Process to Get Results. Manage by improving processes to get results (process and results management). Do not manage just to get results (results-only management). Process and results management promotes improvement and innovation of organizational processes. Highly capable processes facilitate prediction of the near future, and consequently, a higher likelihood of achieving desired results. Results-only management causes people to abuse processes to get their desired results, and ultimately, things get worse. For example, don't just demand better grades from your child; rather, help your child figure out how to improve his or her studying process. As another example, don't just demand more productivity from your subordinate; rather, help your subordinate improve the process he or she used to generate results using the DMAIC or DMADV model.

Balance Intrinsic and Extrinsic Motivation. Manage to create a balance between intrinsic and extrinsic motivation for each individual. Do not rely only on extrinsic motivation to stimulate people. Intrinsic motivation comes from the sheer joy of doing an act; for example, the joy from a job well done. It releases human energy that can be focused on the improvement and innovation of a system. Intrinsic motivation cannot be given to an individual. It comes entirely from within the person experiencing it. Extrinsic motivation comes from desire for reward or fear of punishment; for example, the feelings stimulated by receiving a bonus. It comes from someone else, not the individual experiencing it. Frequently, extrinsic motivation can restrict the release of energy from intrinsic motivation by judging and policing an individual.

Managers can create a fertile environment for others to experience intrinsic motivation in two ways. First, managers can promote joy in work by empowering employees to improve and innovate the processes in which they work using the PDSA cycle or the DMAIC/DMADV models. Second, managers can hire and assign people into job positions that suit their personality and abilities. People are more likely to experience intrinsic motivation if they are performing a job for which they are suited. For example, help your child figure out how to improve his or her study habits to get good grades using the PDSA cycle or the DMAIC/DMADV models. Don't just punish your child for poor grades or reward your child for good grades. Another example, help your subordinates improve the processes they use to generate results through application of the PDSA cycle or the DMAIC/DMADV models. Don't just demand more productivity from your subordinate.

Promote Cooperation. Manage to promote cooperation, not competition, if the aim of the system is not to win. In a competitive environment, most people lose. The costs resulting from competition are unknown and unknowable, but they are huge. For example, cooperate with your spouse by sharing techniques for parenting which create healthy, positive experiences for your child. Don't compete with your spouse over who is the "good" parent. As another example, create an environment in which your sales people cooperate and share "selling tips." Don't use sales contests to promote competition because they will stifle cooperation and sharing information.

Optimize the Whole System. Manage to optimize the whole system, not just your components of the system. The whole system includes the interdependent system of stakeholders of an organization. Some stakeholders are investors, customers, employees, divisions, departments and areas within departments, suppliers, subcontractors, regulators, the community, and the environment. Intersystem competition causes individuals, subsystems, or stakeholders to optimize their own efforts at the expense of other stakeholders. This form of optimization seriously erodes overall system performance. For example, investors demanding a downsizing of employees in a year of record profit, or one department demanding resources that it knows could be better used in another department.

The preceding four values and beliefs frequently provide a different lens for viewing many conflicts and create the opportunity to develop "win-win" solutions to such conflicts. However, if these four values and beliefs do not generate one or more "win-win" solutions to a conflict, then the people involved must fall back to the development of "no lose" solutions to conflicts.

Creating "No Lose" Solutions to Conflict. Each participant in a conflict should describe the solution she or he wants, very specifically. Each potential solution should be specific and not contain vague comments; for example: "I want to be closer." A more specific solution is: "I want to spend at least 30 minutes together every day so we can share our lives and learn more about each other." Do not insult or criticize the other participants, for example: "You are so uncommunicative." Do not push for solutions that are very difficult or impossible for the other participants in the conflict to live with, such as a change of feelings: "Accept watching me flirt with other women."

STEP FOUR: All Participants in the Conflict Review the "Win-Win" Solutions, or Negotiate the Differences in Their Solutions to Create "No Lose" Solutions, to the Conflict

"Win-win" solutions to a conflict do not require much discussion before they can be implemented due to their nature. However, "no lose" solutions to a conflict do require discussion of the different viewpoints present before they are implemented. A few good rules you can use to develop and select a "no lose" solution to a conflict episode include the following:

1. Be open and willing to modify your solution(s).
2. Be clear about the rationale behind your solution(s).
3. Consider the needs and wants of all participants in your solution(s).
4. State your proposed solution(s) so they are as pleasant as possible for the other participants to hear.
5. Each participant presents his or her two best solutions and asks the other participants which solution they like best, or if they can improve one of the solutions. If another participant seems dissatisfied with one of your solutions, ask: "What would you do if you were me?"

STEP FIVE: Avoid the Common Pitfalls of "No Lose" Solutions

If a "win-win" solution is not possible, then the first common pitfall is to assume that there is one best "no lose" solution (usually yours) to the conflict. In most situations, a good "no lose" (compromise) solution benefits all participants in some way. The second common pitfall is not establishing a process for making decisions. If the participants in a conflict episode do not have a clear process for making decisions, then it is likely that they will resort to their old aggressive or passive behaviors. The third common pitfall is to misjudge the personality of one or more of the participants of the conflict episode. For example, you assume that you are dealing with a reasonable and dependable person who is willing to develop a "no lose" (compromise) solution, but discover too late that he or she is a manipulative shark. The fourth common pitfall is losing your patience with the process for developing a "no lose" solution.

STEP SIX: Try Out the "Win-Win" Solution, or the "No Lose" Solution, for a Limited Time Period

Participants in the conflict episode develop a plan for executing the solution. This means they identify who does what, where, when, and how. Once the plan is developed, it can be put into action for a trial time period, and then it can be re-evaluated, as needed.

16.2 PROFESSIONAL TEAM BEHAVIOR SKILLS

Psychology of Teams

No two people are exactly alike. People are different from each other in many ways. Some people are tall, others are short; some people are fat, others are skinny; some people respond well to authority, others act out; some people like math, others like language, and others like both; some learn quickly, and others learn slowly; some learn by reading, others by watching, and others by doing.

A manager of people must understand the significance of these differences and use them when creating teams. Relevant individual differences are a necessary ingredient for a mature full-functioning team because the team works under the assumption that the abilities of its members are complementary, not redundant. For example, it is desirable that a Six Sigma project team have an expert in the theory and practice of the process under study, an expert in Six Sigma theory and tools, an expert in the political and resource issues relevant to the process under study, an expert in information technology, an expert in finance, and an appropriate number of Six Sigma savvy team members.

Most people need other people to fulfill their desire for relationships, companionship, camaraderie, love, and esteem, to name a few of the needs of the human condition. Human beings are a gregarious species. The need for affiliation is one of the main reasons why people join groups and work in teams.

People are born with the innate desire to learn. Learning is a source of growth, change, and innovation. Teams are important vehicles for people to satisfy their desire to learn, grow, and change. For example, a person may join a charitable organization (team) with the intention of learning about the plight of others and changing their world for the better. In the process, the person may discover a previously neglected part of themselves that now grows from the experience.

In consideration of the preceding information, managers can use teams to promote the intrinsic motivation of their people. Teams are an important forum for the turning of the PDSA cycle or the DMAIC/DMADV cycle.

Stages in the Life of Teams

The life of a team follows a prescribed cycle. The first stage in the life of a team is **forming**. Forming is the stage in which members get to know each other and seek to establish ground rules. This stage finishes with the awareness of being a group member. The second stage in the life of a team is **storming**. Storming is the stage in which members may have conflicting views of team goals, priorities, and how to move forward. Sometimes this manifests itself when team members resist direction by the group leader and show hostility. This stage finishes when conflicts are eliminated or resolved and members agree to an overall direction for the team facilitated by the team leader. The third stage of team development is **norming**. Norming is the stage in which team members begin to work together and develop interdependence for achieving the task and become more cohesive. This stage finishes when expectations are set regarding ways of doing things. The fourth stage in the life of a team is **performing**. Performing is the stage in which team members' energy is devoted to getting the job done and the team is functioning very well in accomplishing its agreed activities. The final stage in the life of a team is **adjourning**. Adjourning is the stage in which team members disband voluntarily or because the work is done. A well-structured and facilitated team expends most of its time and energy in the performing stage, not the forming, storming, norming, or adjourning stages.

Individual Versus Team Decision Making

The available literature is unclear on the superiority of individual or group decision making. As a general rule, decisions made by individuals are better when problems demand innovative solutions or original insights, or when time and technical constraints are a limiting factor. Conversely, decisions made by a group are usually better when problem solving demands a diversity of skills and viewpoints, and there is a need for broad-based acceptance. Design for Six Sigma (DFSS) projects are usually of the later variety because they require diverse skills and viewpoints, and the results of such projects must be widely accepted throughout the stakeholders of the organization. For example, the development of global positioning systems (GPS) required diverse skills (computer engineering, geography, psychology, marketing, and sales) and points of view (military use, commercial use, and personal use).

Building a Successful Six Sigma Project Team

Several steps are required to build a successful Six Sigma project team. First, the members of the executive committee and the champion communicate a draft business case about a potential Six Sigma project selected from the organizational dashboard to a team leader (black belt) and process owner. Second, the champion, team leader, and process owner clarify the Six Sigma project charter (Define Phase). Third, the team leader, champion, and process owner identify team members (e.g., team members, master black belt, Information Technology Department representative, and Finance Department representative), and clarify their roles and expectations. Fourth, team members prepare a draft project charter (i.e., business case, roles and responsibilities, timelines, etc.) for all relevant persons (e.g., team members, executive committee, relevant suppliers, relevant customers). Fifth, the team leader promotes functional and healthy team behavior (e.g., focused, consensual, polite, open minded, nonpolitical, stress-free, clearly defined ground rules for meetings and team work, etc.) that uses consensual and data-based methods for making decisions, and creates balanced participation and workloads for team members. Finally, the team leader uses the DMAIC/DMADV models for accomplishing the project objective.

Characteristics of a Team Leader

A professional leader has three critical traits: (1) knowledge of the process (political, process, and technical knowledge); (2) personality with charisma; and (3) formal authority (power). The key components of knowledge are listed next [see Reference 2].

First, a leader sees the group as a system of interrelated components, each with an aim, but all focused collectively to support the aim of the group. This type of focus may require sub-optimization of some system components. A leader uses his knowledge of the interactions between the components of a system to minimize interpersonal conflicts among team members.

Second, a leader uses graphical and statistical methods, with knowledge of special and common causes of variation, to try to understand both his performance and that of his people.

Third, a leader knows when employees are experiencing problems that make their performance fall outside of the system, and leaders treat the problems as special causes of variation. These problems could be common causes to the individual (e.g., long-term alcoholism), but special causes to the system (an alcoholic works differently from his peers).

Fourth, a leader must understand that experience without theory does not facilitate prediction of future events. For example, a team leader cannot predict how a person will perform in a new job based solely on experience in the old job. A leader must have a theory to predict how an individual will perform in a new job.

Fifth, a leader must be able to predict the future to plan the actions necessary to pursue the organization's aim. Prediction of future events requires that the leader continuously work to create stable processes with low variation to facilitate rational prediction.

Sixth, a leader does not expect perfection from his people or processes, but constantly works toward perfection.

Seventh, a leader endures over the life of a project and does not give up on people.

Eight, a leader communicates with all relevant stakeholders as much as is needed to move a system toward its mission; these communications are with team members, the champion, the process owner, and customers and suppliers of the process.

Guidelines for Reacting to Team Problems

Team leaders have a tough job because they must anticipate and prevent team problems whenever possible. They have a range of possible responses to team-related problems originating from an individual, such as the following:

- Slacker team member (shoddy work product, failure to provide timely work product).
- Dominating team member (doesn't stop talking, over-controlling personality).
- Argumentative team member.
- Tardy team member.
- Hostile team member.
- Passive team member.
- Inept team member (inability to perform needed work).
- Offensive team member (language, behavior, hygiene).

A team leader has several escalating types of responses to the preceding categories of problems:

- **Do nothing (nonintervention).** Doing nothing is generally a bad way to proceed. It sets the stage for increasingly dysfunctional behavior on the part of the difficult team member.

- **Offline private conversation (minimal intervention).** An offline private conversation requires that the team leader be assertive, not passive-aggressive. An assertive team leader uses an "**I**" message to make a point. For example, "**I** am concerned about **your tardiness** to the team meetings because it makes me feel that you **don't respect** the value of the team member's time. Please **be on time** from now on." A passive-aggressive team leader will let the problem go unresolved until it is so troublesome that it explodes in the team's face.

- **Impersonal group time (low intervention).** Impersonal group time utilizes a "**we**" message in a team meeting. A "**we**" message is just like an "**I**" message except that it comes from the entire team. For example, "**We** are concerned about **your tardiness** to our team meetings because it makes us feel that you **don't respect** the value of our time. Please **be on time** from now on."

- **Offline confrontation (medium intervention).** An offline confrontation by a team leader to a difficult team member reiterates the problem and solution, but it clearly states (politely with no sugar added to avoid confusion) the consequences of not conforming to the team's request. For example, "**We** are frustrated about **your repeated tardiness** to our team meetings because it makes us feel that you **don't respect** the value of our time. If you are not **on time from now on**, we will **document your behavior in our team minutes for distribution to the champion and process owner.**"

- **Expulsion from the group (Do not use this option!).** Expulsion from a group is a severe option and carries unknown consequences for the difficult employee and the team members. It is difficult to foresee how expelling a team member may play out years in the future.

Regardless of the response to an individual or the group, it is imperative that the team leader does not over- or underreact to a problem. This requires an understanding of special and common causes of variation.

Creative Techniques to Resolve Team Problems

Background. The team leader must encourage all team members to think of each problem relating to the team as the team's problem, not an individual's problem. This may be a bitter pill for some team members to swallow, especially if one individual is causing problems for the team.

Edward de Bono developed many creative techniques which may be helpful to team members when pursuing their charters (see Chapter 15, "Enhancing Creativity to Develop Alternative Designs"). Examples of team issues that are amenable to creative techniques include resolving issues concerning difficult team members, creating alternatives avenues for studying a problem, and developing options for solving a defined problem. Three of de Bono's creative techniques are reiterated and illustrated next. They are: Consequences & Sequel (C&S), Other People's Views (OPV), and Alternatives, Possibilities, Choices (APC).

Consequences and Sequel (C&S). C&S determines the consequences of a decision by asking the following questions:

- Will the decision work out?
- What are the benefits of the decision?
- What are the risks of the decision?
- What is the worst outcome?
- What is the best outcome?
- What is the expected outcome?
- What are the costs of the decision?
- How likely is this outcome?

You must specify a time scale before using the C&S tool.

For example, team members have a budget of $150,000 to complete a Six Sigma project. As they move into the Improve Phase, they realize that they can meet their project objective, but if they obtain an additional $100,000, they can double the hard revenue benefits of the project beyond what is expected from the Define Phase. They want the additional funds, but are fearful of asking for them. They wonder if they should just do what is expected and forget going for the potentially dangerous home run. The team used C&S to resolve their problem by asking, "What is the risk of asking for more resources?"

Answer: Team members decide that the worst possible outcome of asking for more resources is that they will all get fired, or at least never promoted. Having verbalized their worst fear among themselves, they all realize that they are being irrational, especially given that the additional resources will double the results of their project. Next, the team members decide that the best possible outcome is that the champion and process owner are thrilled at the opportunity to double the results of the project with the additional expense. Further, as a result of their project work, they all get a bonus and a promotion. Finally, team members realize the most realistic outcome is much closer to the best possible outcome than the worst possible outcome. They decide to request the additional fund. The champion and process owner are delighted at the prospect of the additional results. Problem solved!

Other People's Views (OPV). OPV is designed to identify the people affected by a topic (including future generations) and to imagine their views on the topic by asking the following questions:

- Who is affected by this thinking (action)?
- What are the viewpoints of those affected by this thinking (action)?

OPV can be used to consider both sides of an argument. For example, a team is experiencing disruptions caused by a difficult team member.

Answer: The team leader asks, "What is the viewpoint of the difficult team member, OPV?" It is recognized that the difficult team member's boss is putting tremendous pressure on her to meet a quarterly sales quota. Fear of the quota is causing the team member to be stressed and resentful of any activity that takes her away from generating new sales. The team members recognize and empathize with her problem and help her to meet her goal by pointing out sales opportunities she had not thought of due to her stressed condition. She makes enough sales and is appreciative of her team members. She begins to be a positive source of energy for the team.

Alternatives, Possibilities, Choices (APC). APC is a creative technique designed to expand the alternatives, possibilities, and choices with respect to a topic by asking the following questions:

- What are alternative ways of looking at this (APC)?
- What are alternative actions for doing this?
- What are alternative solutions for this?
- What are alternative approaches for this?
- What are alternative explanations for this?
- What are alternative designs for this?

For example, the members of a Six Sigma project team have identified the percentage of abandoned calls by month for the Accounts Receivable Department as a CTQ. They know that the relevant process is the phone-answering process, but they are experiencing great difficulty thinking of alternative designs for the phone answering process that would reduce the percentage of abandoned calls by month. They have studied data on the Xs in the process to no avail, and the same is the case for benchmarking other Accounts Receivable Departments. Their frustration led them to a list of 70 possible generic ideas for improving a process [see Reference 6]. Team members found that one of the 70 items was "Shift Demand." The team members know from studying demand patterns that most of the abandoned calls occur between 10:00 A.M. and 2:00 P.M., Monday through Friday. The team members thought about how they could shift demand to a less busy time. The team leader asked two questions:

1. On average, how many times per year does a student telephone the accounts receivable office? Answer: "About 10 times per year."
2. Do most students call 10 times per year, or do most call 0 times and a few call 30 or 40 times per year? "Answer: The latter."

Answer: At this point, the team members decided to install a system that required every clerk to enter the university student identification number into the computer. If a particular university student identification number showed more than three calls in any given month, team members felt confident that they had identified a frequent caller. Consequently, they preemptively called the person at 8:00 A.M. to resolve any possible problems. Team members had shifted a sizeable portion of the calls away from busy times, and subsequently, the "percentage of abandoned calls by month" dropped off precipitously. Problem solved!

16.3 PRODUCT DEVELOPMENT TEAM BASICS

Concurrent Engineering[2]

Introduction. Concurrent engineering is a business strategy that replaces the traditional product development process with a product development process in which tasks are done in parallel and cooperatively, and there is an early consideration for every aspect of a product's development process. This strategy focuses on the optimization and distribution of a firm's resources in the design and development process to ensure a rapid, effective, and efficient product development process.

In traditional engineering, the development of a product, service, or process is accomplished through the Plan-Do-Adjust cycle. In concurrent engineering, the development of a product, service, or process is accomplished through the Plan-Do-Study-Act cycle. This occurs when appropriate areas are committed to interactively and cooperatively identify, clarify, approve, develop, and implement products, services, or processes that surpass predetermined customer specifications. Concurrent engineering requires far fewer design changes over the life cycle of a product, service, or process than traditional engineering

Commitment and Leadership. Concurrent engineering requires strong commitment from the firm's leadership to mandate the required organizational changes from the top down needed to create the cooperative and collaborative environment necessary for concurrent engineering. Concurrent engineering without leadership may be disastrous.

Communication and Collaboration. Concurrent engineering begins by creating a corporate environment that facilitates communication and collaboration, not just between individuals, but also between departments and divisions within the firm. This may entail major structural changes, reeducation of the existing workforce, and/or restructuring of the development process.

Principles

The 10 basic principles of concurrent engineering married into the DFSS context are listed next.

1. Senior management must have a burning desire to utilize concurrent engineering. This is the most important principle. Without senior management commitment, concurrent engineering will fail. Senior management must make concurrent engineering a strategic priority.

---

[2] Slightly modified from `http://best.me.berkeley.edu/~pps/pps/concurrent.html`.

2. Senior management must establish an organizational environment that is conducive to concurrent engineering.

3. PD team members develop a clear project objective that considers multi-generational issues.

4. PD team members prepare a detailed product development plan early in the process.

5. The champion and process owners are very involved in tollgate reviews at each stage of the product development process.

6. The PD team leader should be a Six Sigma black belt or green belt, according to the complexity of the product, service, or process being developed.

7. The PD team should strictly follow the DMADV model.

8. The PD team should take special care in the Measure Phase of the DMADV model to identify the market/customer segments for the product, service, or process being developed.

9. Six Sigma metrics are used by PD team members, and eventually appropriate process owners, to track the product through its entire life cycle.

10. PD team members collectively work on all parts of the PD project in parallel.

Benefits

The benefits of concurrent engineering are as follows:

- Decreased time to market.
- Increased market share.
- Decreased production costs.
- Decreased rework, scrap, and defect rates.
- Increased quality of products.
- Increased productivity.
- Increased competitive advantage in world markets.
- Decreased variation in all related processes.
- Increased predictability of outcomes.
- Increased ability to plan, schedule, set timelines, and budgets.
- Increased reliability in the PD process.
- Increased effectiveness in transferring technology.
- Increased customer satisfaction.
- Increased ability to execute high-level and complex projects with minimum difficulty.
- Decreased design and development time.
- Decreased time for execution of a project.

- Increased return on investments.
- Decreased number of design changes and reengineering efforts in the PD process.
- Decreased labor and resource requirements for the PD process.
- Increased creativity by all PD team members.
- Increased cooperation and cohesiveness within the firm.
- Increased communication between individuals and departments within the firm.
- Decreased implementation risks.
- Decreased reaction time in responding to the rapidly changing market.

Model of Concurrent Engineering[3]

A typical model for a concurrent engineering (CE) team considers the total life cycle of a product, service, or process, from birth to death and disposal. Such a team brings together all of the relevant functions of an organization; for example, top management, purchasing, design, marketing, engineering, manufacturing, inventory, and shipping, to name a few.

Specific Issues of Product Development Teams (PD Teams)

Definition. A Product Development (PD) team is a multifunctional team whose objective is to develop a new product, service, or process or redesign an existing product, service, or process. PD team members make all decisions about design, production/delivery systems, and field-support systems. PD teams are concurrent engineering teams.

Functions of the Members of a PD Team. PD team members have several responsibilities to their DMADV project. First, they contribute their knowledge about the product, service, or process, relevant theory, appropriate technology, practical matters, relevant experiences, and political savvy to the design effort. Second, PD team members study the "voices of stakeholders" to quantify the nominal values and specification limits for the CTQs relevant to the design. Third, they communicate information about the design to each other, and with the other stakeholders of the design; for example, customers, employees, distributors, suppliers, and regulators. Fourth, PD team members maintain their function's commitment to the design effort, not just their function's support of the design effort. Fifth, they are committed to utilizing the results of their efforts when making decisions about the design.

Functions of the Team Leader of a PD Team. PD team leaders need certain attributes to be effective in addition to the attributes of a leader discussed earlier in this chapter. First, they need broad knowledge of the product, service, or process that the DMADV team is designing. Second, a PD team leader must be responsible for the specifications, costs, and schedules of the design effort. Finally, the PD team leader must endure as the leader for the entire life of the DMADV project.

Characteristics of a Well-Functioning PD Team. If the leader and members of a PD team are properly selected and trained, then there is a high likelihood that members of the team will exhibit the following characteristics:

---

[3] Slightly modified from `http://www.ece.msstate.edu/~hagler/Aug1996/030/cd/main.htm`.

- Keep open minds.
- Keep a balance between individual and group work.
- Communicate, formally and informally.
- Respect each other and can work together.
- Look out for the welfare of all stakeholders, not just their area.
- Develop designs that all stakeholders understand and accept.
- Use the DMADV model.
- Are current with relevant new developments.
- Spread information throughout the organization, if appropriate.

Management Reviews of Six Sigma Team Projects

Introduction. Six Sigma teams present their projects to their champion and the process owner for approval in **tollgate** reviews. A tollgate review involves comparing the actual results generated by applying a set of methods with the targets established, allocating resources to optimize the organization's progress toward its aim; and finding opportunities to improve and innovate methods. Tollgate reviews are utilized at the end of each stage in the DMAIC and DMADV models to ensure that objectives for each stage have been completed. If some objectives have not been completed, then additional work on the activities associated with that stage may be required or the team may have identified barriers to completing that stage whose removal requires the assistance of their champion.

Three critical inputs are required for a management review. They are a well-researched methods (called a best practice method), a target established to allocate resources to optimize the organization toward its aim, and an actual result. The development of the first and second inputs requires that a manager have a deep and thorough understanding of the method being studied; a firm grasp on where the method stands with respect to process capability and environment; knowledge of the aim of the organization to determine appropriate methods to get there; the realization that a method is used to predict a result; recognition that a method should yield a high likelihood of achieving a target before it is implemented; and understanding that targets are vehicles for allocating resources between methods.

A set of suggested questions that can form the basis of a management review of a project team appears next. These questions will help all stakeholders involved in the management review focus on opportunities for improvement and innovation of methods. These questions are only suggestions. Management reviews have natural flows. A manager can use preset questions, but also needs to go with the rhythm of the review to accomplish its purpose.

1. What is your group's first priority method?
2. Are you (as an individual) or your group working on improvement or innovation of your first priority method?
3. How do you measure the performance of the first priority method?

4. What is your group's target for this method? Monthly? Yearly?

5. Did you study this method last year? How have you incorporated the results of that study into your current method?

6. What is the status of your group's method to date?

7. Are methods yielding targets? Monthly? Yearly?

8. If targets are not being achieved, what countermeasures have your team members taken, and what actions will prevent the same situation from recurring in the future?

A management review probes the root cause(s) of the differences between actual results and targets without tampering with methods.

Variation Analysis

Management reviews should be conducted in accordance with the principles of Six Sigma management. Not all sources of variation are due to special causes. A manager using the principles of Six Sigma management does not tamper with processes under her control. Instead, causes of variation are separated into common and special sources by statistical methods. Then, employees work to resolve special sources of variation, and management works to remove common sources of variation by modifying methods.

The management review focuses on whether the actual method used by an employee follows the best practice method. Table 16.6 shows the relationship between following methods and achieving targets.

TABLE 16.6   Relationship Between Following Methods and Achieving Targets

	Attain Target	Fail to Attain Target
Follow Method	Cell 1	Cell 3
Fail to Follow Method	Cell 2	Cell 4

Cell 1 shows the outcome of an employee following a best practice method as the attainment of a target.

Cell 4 shows the outcome of an employee not following a best practice method as the failure to attain a target. To reverse this failure, the employee follows the best practice method. In this case, the management review determines answers to the following questions:

1. What best practice method was not followed?

2. Who failed to follow the best practice method? Note: The focus is on system problems, not on the individual. This will help promote joy in work and pride in the outcome.

3. Why did the employee not follow the best practice method? Was it due to ignorance, misunderstanding, lack of training, negligence, problems with a machine, or problems with raw materials?

4. Should the best practice method be changed to resolve problems due to ignorance, misunderstanding, lack of training, negligence, problems with a machine, or problems with raw materials?

Cell 2 shows the outcome of an employee not following a best practice method as the attainment of a target. In this case, depending on prevailing pressures, the employee may adopt a slower pace when determining why the method used yielded the target.

Cell 3 shows the outcome of an employee following the best practice method as the failure to attain a target. In this case, the best practice method is improved or innovated, and/or a change is made in the target; the employee is not blamed. This change is accomplished by asking the following questions proposed by Kano:

1. What best practice method missed its target?
2. How can the best practice method be changed to attain its target?
3. Must the best practice method be changed to resolve problems due to ignorance, misunderstanding, lack of training, problems with a machine, or problems with raw materials?
4. What target was missed?
5. How much was the target missed over time? Is the process under study stable? Will adjustment of the target result in tampering with the best practice method?
6. Why was the target missed? Was the target set incorrectly due to ignorance, lack of training, problems with a machine, problems with raw materials, management, or by guesswork?

Once these questions are answered, the necessary information may be available for improvement or innovation of the best practice method or change of the target. These questions focus on improvement and innovation of the best practice method, not on blaming the individual.

Frequently, it is not possible to investigate the negative scenarios presented in cells 2, 3, or 4 on a daily basis. One day may not provide enough time to perform all four stages of the PDSA cycle to achieve the desired improvement and/or innovation.

SUMMARY

This chapter discusses the role that behavior plays in Six Sigma projects in general, and DMADV projects in particular. First, the chapter discusses the interpersonal skills necessary for professional behavior, such as assertiveness and conflict resolution. Second, this chapter explains the needs of individuals that are fulfilled by team work. Then, the life cycle stage of teams is discussed. The chapter explains how decisions are made by teams. Fourth, the chapter discusses how to build and manage a Six Sigma project team, and how to resolve team problems. Finally, the chapter explains the basics of concurrent engineering PD teams.

References

1. de Bono, E., *Teach Your Child How to Think* (New York: Penguin Group, 1992).

2. Deming, W. E., *The New Economics: For Industry, Government, Education*, (Cambridge, MA: M.I.T. Center for Advanced Engineering Study,1994).

3. Gitlow, H., A. Oppenheim, R. Oppenheim, and D. Levine, *Quality Management*, 3rd ed. (New York: McGraw-Hill Irwin, 2005).

4. Katzenbach, J., and D. Smith, *The Wisdom of Teams* (New York: Harper Business, 1993).

5. Kohn, A., *No Contest* (Boston, MA: Houghton-Mifflin, 1992).

6. Langley, J., K. Nolan, T. Nolan, C. Norman, and L. Provost, *The Improvement Guide* (San Francisco, CA: Jossey-Bass Publishers, 1996).

7. Maier, N., "Assets and Liabilities in Group Problem Solving," *Psychology Review*, vol. 74 (1967), pp. 239–249.

8. McNary, L. and H. Gitlow, "Creating Integrative Solutions in Conflict Episodes," *Quality Engineering*, vol. 14, no. 4, 2002, pp. 581–588.

9. Scholtes, P., *The Team Handbook* (Madison, WI: Joiner Associates, 1988).

10. Tucker-Ladd, C., *Psychological Self-Help* (Springfield, IL:Clayton Tucker-Ladd & the Self-Help Foundation, 1996–2000) `http://mentalhelp.net/psyhelp/chap13/chap13f.htm`.

DESIGN FOR SIX SIGMA CASE STUDY

Six Sigma DMADV Case Study[1]

SECTIONS

LEARNING OBJECTIVES

After reading this chapter, you will appreciate the structure and intricacies of performing a Six Sigma DMADV project.

INTRODUCTION

This chapter provides a detailed expose of a successful Six Sigma DMADV project in a service environment. It is hoped that reading a detailed case study will enhance your appreciation of, and ability to perform, a Six Sigma DMADV project.

---

[1] This chapter was contributed by Jodan Ledford, Ameena Shrestha, and Amy Qun Zuo.

17.1 BACKGROUND

The University of Miami School of Business Administration's Department of Management Science decided to consider expanding the educational opportunities offered to its MBA students and MS in Management Science students by offering Six Sigma courses and certification "for academic credit." This Six Sigma DMADV project is the result of that decision.

17.2 DEFINE PHASE

Recall, the Define Phase of a DMADV project has five parts.

Part 1: Develop the Business Case. The first step of the Define Phase is to develop the business case for the design under study. The rationale for the project usually appears in the right-most column of the dashboard for the organization; for example, see "Optimize MAS academic and executive courseware project" in Table 17.1. This table is a partial dashboard for the Department of Management Science, in the School of Business Administration, at the University of Miami.

TABLE 17.1   Partial Dashboard for the Department of Management Science

MAS Department Mission Statement:

1. Attract the "best and brightest" to our program.
2. Staff the management science courses with talented, dedicated faculty.
3. Provide the concepts, knowledge, and skills necessary to be successful in management science.
4. Create a real-world connection for students through classroom materials and the use of guest lecturers.
5. Provide a management science foundation for nonmanagement science graduates.
6. Provide fully qualified graduates capable of tackling the most challenging positions.
7. Assist students in obtaining positions in the field of management science.

MAS Department Chairman		MAS Department Faculty and Staff		Potential Six Sigma Projects
Key Objectives	**Key Indicators**	**Faculty and Staff Objectives**	**Faculty and Staff Indicators**	
Improve research output of the faculty in the MAS department.	# of juried articles published by all MAS faculty by year.	Improve research output of faculty member i.	# of juried articles published by faculty member i by year.	Quality and quantity of research project.
	% of juried articles published by all MAS faculty in "A" journals by year.		% of juried articles published by faculty member i in "A" journals by year.	

MAS Department Chairman		MAS Department Faculty and Staff		Potential Six Sigma Projects
Key Objectives	**Key Indicators**	**Faculty and Staff Objectives**	**Faculty and Staff Indicators**	
Improve quality of teaching of the faculty in the MAS department.	Interdepartmental ranking of MAS student evaluation scores for Question 1 by semester.	Improve quality of teaching of faculty member *i*.	Interdepartmental ranking of faculty member *i*'s student evaluation scores for Question 1 by semester.	Quality of teaching skills project.
Optimize the courseware of the MAS department.	Survey of stakeholders of the MAS department every other year.	Develop MAS academic and executive courseware.	Gantt chart for development program.	Optimize MAS academic and executive education courseware projects: • White belt project • Green belt project
		Promote MAS academic and executive courseware.	Gantt chart for promotional program.	
		Schedule and staff MAS courseware.	List of courseware offerings by faculty by year.	
			# of sections by courseware offering by semester.	
			# of students by courseware offering by semester.	
		Phase out MAS courseware.	List of courseware phased out by year.	

Once potential Six Sigma projects have been identified on the organizational dashboard, the Executive Committee of an organization constructs a Project Priority matrix. The purpose of this matrix is to rank all potential Six Sigma projects for their contribution to the President's Key Objectives, as weighted by the Finance Department. Table 17.2 is a partial listing of the project prioritization matrix for the Department of Management Science. As you can see, "Optimize

MAS academic and executive courseware project" was selected as the highest-priority project with a weighted average of 4.9.

TABLE 17.2   Project Priority Matrix and Select the Highest-Priority Six Sigma Project

				Potential Six Sigma Projects				
				Quality and quantity of research project	Quality of teaching project	Enhancement of service project	Improvement of high-priority MAS dept. systems project	Optimize academic and executive education MAS courseware project
Chairman's Key Objectives	Improve research output of the faculty in the MAS department.	Weights	.40	9	3	1	0	1
	Improve quality of teaching of the faculty in the MAS department.		.10	1	9	1	0	9
	Improve service of MAS Department to the School of Business, the university, and the community.		.10	1	0	9	0	9
	Manage the MAS department.		.05	0	0	0	9	0
	Improve the management systems of the MAS department.		.05	0	0	0	9	0
	Optimize the courseware of the MAS department.		.30	0	1	3	0	9
Weighted Average of Potential Six Sigma Projects				3.8	2.4	2.3	0.9	4.9

Now that a project has been selected for entry into the Define Phase, the Six Sigma team members answer the following partially redundant questions:

- Why do the highest project at all? The MAS department needs a source of energy and excitement to keep it vibrant and on its current positive trajectory. Students need a competitive edge in the job market. Employers want to hire students who can "hit the ground running."
- Why should team members do the highest priority project now? The MAS department is moving on a positive trajectory, and the faculty and students want to keep up the momentum.

- What are the consequences of not doing the highest-priority project? The MAS department could slip back to its former state, exhibiting low energy and low productivity.
- What business objectives are supported by the highest-priority project? The "improve teaching" and "improve courseware" objectives are strongly supported by the "optimize courseware project."

Next, team members prepare the opportunity statement for the project. The opportunity statement answers the question: What is the pain? The pain is the MAS department sinking back into low energy and low productivity.

Then, team members develop the initial project objective. A project objective describes the following:

1. Product, service, or process being designed with relevant market segment(s).
   - MBA specialization in MAS
   - MS in MAS
   - Executive Education MAS Certificate Programs
2. Measure(s) of success [market share, sales, ROI, etc.] for the design.
   - # of students enrolled in MBA specialization in MAS
   - # of students enrolled in MS in MAS
   - # of students enrolled in Executive Education MAS Certificate Programs
3. Direction of success for the design.
   - Increase
4. Target measure for the design.
   - # of students enrolled in MBA specialization in MAS > 50 per year
   - # of students enrolled in MS in MAS > 25 per year
   - # of students enrolled in Exec Ed MAS Certificate Programs > 100 per year
5. Deadline for the design.
   - September 30, 2005

After team members develop the initial project objective(s), they develop the project scope. The scope details the Multi-Generation Product Plan, the obstacles, and constraints of the project. Table 17.3 shows the MGPP for the project under study.

Next, team members identify all the constraints placed upon the design; for example, design boundaries and resource limitations.

- MAS departmental offerings must meet with the approval of: MAS faculty, SBA Council, Vice Dean, Dean, and university.
- MAS departmental offerings must fit into the structure of one or more of the following structures: MBA specialization in MAS or Executive Education Six Sigma programs.

- No budgetary constraints.
- Limited faculty to teach courseware.

TABLE 17.3   MGPP for the Project

Generation	Generation 1	Generation 2	Generation 3
Vision	Stop bleeding in existing market(s).	*Take offensive action by filling unmet needs of existing market(s)—* Employers want to hire students who can immediately perform on the job without additional training.	Take leadership position in new market(s).
Product/Service Generations	Improved or less-expensive existing features.	*New major features—* Academic-based courseware design based on input from the Voice of the Stakeholder.	New products or services or processes.
Product/Service Technologies and Platforms	Current technology.	*Current technology with relevant technological enhancements, if any—* Current technology used for all courseware with computer-based platforms.	Current technology plus new technology, if possible.

Additionally, team members list all the obstacles to completion of the design. In this case, no obstacles exist.

Next, team members develop a Gantt chart for the project. Table 17.4 shows the Gantt chart for the project under study.

Finally, team members develop a document control system for the potential new design. The following checklist reflects suggested minimum requirements for a document control system.

- All documents are marked with creation date.   (Yes)
- All documents are assigned control numbers.   (Yes)
- All documents are backed up in a central repository.   (Yes)
- All documents have proper access controls.   (Yes)

TABLE 17.4 Gantt Chart

TASKS	Resp.	Aug	Sep	Oct	Nov	Dec	Jan	Feb	Mar	Apr	May	Jun	Jul	Aug	Sep	COM-MENTS
Define	Team	X	X	X	X	X										
Measure	Team						X	X								
Analyze	Team								X	X						
Design	Team										X	X				
Validate	Team												X	X	X	

Part 2: Assess the Benefits of the Potential Six Sigma Project. The second part of the Define Phase involves estimating the soft and hard benefits of doing the proposed Six Sigma project. The soft benefits include the following:

- MAS faculty teach advanced courses creating joy in work.
- MAS students receive an education that provides a competitive edge in the job market.
- Employers getting a better trained and educated workforce.
- UM fulfills the needs of the community and the nation for a well-trained workforce.
- A source of revenue to UM.
- A tool of promotion for UM's reputation as an innovative academic institution.
- UM introduces a new certification in Six Sigma Education to the market/business world.
- Enhance awareness of Six Sigma management in the international market.
- Provide UM MBA and MS in MAS students knowledge of Six Sigma management.

The hard benefits and costs of the potential Six Sigma project are presented in Table 17.5. As you can see, a sensitivity analysis was performed for 20, 30, 40 50, 60, 80, and 100 students/enrollees. Table 17.5 shows that academic programs are far more profitable at each level of enrollment.

Part 3: Assess the Risks to the Project's Success. A hazard analysis and risk abatement plan identified the risks associated with realizing the project's findings. Table 17.6 shows the hazard analysis for the project. The hazard analysis shows that the riskiest elements involve Six Sigma Executive Education opportunities. Further, the MBA with a specialization in MAS is the least-risky option, as well as the most profitable option (see Table 17.6).

TABLE 17.5   Hard Benefits of the Project

Hard Benefits Analysis

Revenue Analysis

Academic Programs	Revenue Retriever	# of Courses	Cost per Credit	# of Students						
				20	30	40	50	60	80	100
MBA with MAS Concentration	UM, SBA	8	$1,000	$160,000	$240,000	$320,000	$400,000	$480,000	$640,000	$800,000
MS in MAS Program	UM, SBA	22	$1,000	$440,000	$660,000	$880,000	$1,100,000	$1,320,000	$1,760,000	$2,200,000
Revenue from Academic Programs				$600,000	$900,000	$1,200,000	$1,500,000	$1,800,000	$2,400,000	$3,000,000

Six Sigma Certification Program in Exec Ed	Exec Ed, MAS, UMISQ	# of Courses	Cost per Course	# of Students						
				20	30	40	50	60	80	100
	Champion Certification	1	$3,000	$60,000	$90,000	$120,000	$150,000	$180,000	$240,000	$300,000
	Green Belt Certification	1	$3,000	$60,000	$90,000	$120,000	$150,000	$180,000	$240,000	$300,000
	Black Belt Certification (Same students as in GB certification)	3	$3,000	$180,000	$270,000	$360,000	$450,000	$540,000	$720,000	$900,000

Six Sigma Projects in Exec Ed	Exec Ed, MAS, UMISQ	# of Projects	Cost per Project	# of Students						
				20	30	40	50	60	80	100
	Green Belt Certification	1	$2,000	$40,000	$60,000	$80,000	$100,000	$120,000	$160,000	$200,000
	Black Belt Certification (Same students as in GB certification)	1	$2,000	$40,000	$60,000	$80,000	$100,000	$120,000	$160,000	$200,000

Note: Champion certification is the prerequisite for Green Belt certification. Green Belt certification is the prerequisite for Black Belt certification.

Revenue from Exec Ed Six Sigma Program	$380,000	$570,000	$760,000	$950,000	$1,140,000	$1,520,000	$1,900,000

Cost Analysis

	# of Faculty per Course	Cost per Course	# of Courses						
			4	4	4	4	4	4	4
Faculty (MBA with MAS Concentration)	1	$8,666	$34,664	$34,664	$34,664	$34,664	$34,664	$34,664	$34,664
	# of Faculty per Course	Cost per Course	# of Courses						
			11	11	11	11	11	11	11
Faculty (MS in MAS Program)	1	$8,666	$95,326	$95,326	$95,326	$95,326	$95,326	$95,326	$95,326
Cost of Academic Programs			$129,990	$129,990	$129,990	$129,990	$129,990	$129,990	$129,990

	# of Faculty per Course	Cost per Course	# of Courses						
			5	5	5	5	5	5	5
Faculty (Exec Ed Six Sigma Program)	1	$13,000	$65,000	$65,000	$65,000	$65,000	$65,000	$65,000	$65,000
	# of Faculty per Project	Cost per Project	# of Projects (2 projects each student)						
			40	60	80	100	120	160	200
Faculty (Exec Ed Six Sigma Program)	1	$2,000	$80,000	$120,000	$160,000	$200,000	$240,000	$320,000	$400,000
	# of Days per Course	Cost per Day	# of Courses						
			5	5	5	5	5	5	5
Classroom	5	$250	$6,250	$6,250	$6,250	$6,250	$6,250	$6,250	$6,250
	# of Days per Course	Cost per Lunch	# of Students						
			20	30	40	50	60	80	100
Lunch	5	$20	$10,000	$15,000	$20,000	$65,000	$65,000	$65,000	$65,000
	# of Breaks per Day	Cost per Break	# of Students						
			20	30	40	50	60	80	100
Coffee Break	2	$10	$10,000	$15,000	$20,000	$25,000	$30,000	$40,000	$50,000
	# of Material	Cost per Student	# of Students						
			20	30	40	50	60	80	100
Materials (Book, CD, software, etc.) Champion Certification	1	$50	$1,000	$1,500	$2,000	$2,500	$3,000	$4,000	$5,000
Green Belt Certification	1	$50	$1,000	$1,500	$2,000	$2,500	$3,000	$4,000	$5,000
Black Belt Certification	1	$200	$4,000	$6,000	$8,000	$10,000	$12,000	$16,000	$20,000
Cost of Exec Ed Six Sigma Program			$97,250	$110,250	$123,250	$136,250	$149,250	$175,250	$201,250

Profit Analysis

Profits from Academic Programs	$470,010	$770,010	$1,070,010	$1,370,010	$1,670,010	$2,270,010	$2,870,010
Profits from Exec Ed Six Sigma Program	$282,750	$459,750	$636,750	$813,750	$990,750	$1,344,750	$1,698,750
Total Profits	$752,760	$1,229,760	$1,706,760	$2,183,760	$2,660,760	$3,614,760	$4,568,760

TABLE 17.6 Hazard Analysis of Risk Elements

1	2	3	4	5	6	7
Process, Product, or Service Under Study	Risk Element	Hazard (Potential Source of Harm)	Harm (Physical Injury to Person and/or Damage to Property)	Likelihood 1 = low 5 = high	Severity 1 = low 5 = high	Risk Element Score 1 to 8 = low 9 to 15 = medium 16 to 25 = high
MBA specialization in MAS.	Faculty availability.	Unavailable faculty.	Student has to revise his or her schedule.	3	2	6
	Student demand.	Insufficient enrollment.	Student has to revise his or her schedule.	2	2	4
	Employer acceptance.	Fail to place students in jobs.	Student doesn't reap benefit of education.	2	2	4
MS in MAS.	Faculty availability.	Unavailable faculty.	Student has to revise his or her schedule.	3	2	6
	Student demand.	Insufficient enrollment.	Student has to revise his or her schedule.	2	2	4
	Employer acceptance.	Fail to place students in jobs.	Student doesn't reap benefit of education.	3	5	15
Exec Ed Six Sigma courses.	Faculty availability.	Unavailable faculty.	No revenue.	5	5	25
	Student demand.	Insufficient enrollment.	No revenue.	5	5	25
	Employer acceptance.	Fail to find employers willing to pay for participants.	No revenue.	4	5	20

Next, team members construct a risk abatement plan for the academic Six Sigma program option. Table 17.7 shows part of the risk abatement plan.

TABLE 17.7 Partial Risk Abatement Plan

1	2	3		4	5	6
Potential Risk Elements for Academic Six Sigma Option	Potential Harm for the Risk Elements from Process *i*	Risk Element Score		Countermeasure (Risk Abatement Plan)	Risk Owner	Completion Date for Countermeasure
		Before	After			
Unavailable faculty.	Fail to offer courses required for certification.	Likelihood = 5, so Risk Element Score = 5 × 5 = 25.	Likelihood goes from 5 to 1, so Risk Element Score = 1 × 5 = 5.	Identify and train two or three faculty to teach Six Sigma course.	MAS faculty, UMISQ	9-30-2005
Insufficient enrollment.	Fail to offer courses required for certification.	Likelihood = 5, so Risk Element Score = 5 × 5 = 25.	Likelihood goes from 5 to 2, so Risk Element Score = 2 × 5 = 10.	Develop promotional program for Six Sigma certifications to individuals and companies.	MAS faculty, UMISQ	9-30-2005
Fail to find employers willing to hire students with Six Sigma certifications.	Fail to place students in jobs.	Likelihood = 4, so Risk Element Score = 4 × 5 = 20.	Likelihood goes from 4 to 2, so Risk Element Score = 2 × 5 = 10.	(1) Develop promotional program for Six Sigma-certified MBAs. (2) Develop a warranty program for free additional training if MBAs fail to adequately perform Six Sigma duties in the eyes of the employer (unrealistic at this time).	UMISQ	9-30-2005

Part 4: Activating a DFSS Product Development Team. The fourth part of the Define Phase is to create and empower the Six Sigma team. Table 17.8 shows the project team members for the project under study.

TABLE 17.8 DFSS Product Development Team

Role	Responsibility	Signature	Date	Supervisor's Signature	Address
Champion	HG	HG	8/15/04		Room 411 K/E, SBA
Process Owner	AM	AM	8/15/04		
Training BB	JL	JL	8/15/04		
Training BB	AS	AS	8/15/04		
Training BB	QZ	QZ	8/15/04		
Master Black Belt	HG	HG	8/15/04		Room 411 K/E, SBA

Part 5: Finalize the Project Objective(s). The final step of the Define Phase is to state the finalized project objective. Recall that there were three possible objectives:

1. Increase (direction) the number of students enrolled (measure) in the MBA specialization in MAS (process) from 25 to 50 students (target) per year by 9/30/2005 (deadline).
2. Increase (direction) the number of students enrolled (measure) in the MS in MAS (process) from 10 to 25 students (target) per year by 9/30/ 2005 (deadline).
3. Increase (direction) the number of students enrolled (measure) in Executive Education Six Sigma programs (process) from 0 to 100 student equivalents (target) per year by 9/30/2005 (deadline).

It was decided only to pursue objective 1 at the current time, because objectives 2 and 3 are riskier and result in less potential revenue.

Define Phase Tollgate Review Process. Finally, team members go through a Define Phase tollgate review. The tollgate review by the project's champion, process owner, and master black belt were successful.

17.3 MEASURE PHASE

The Measure Phase has three parts. Each part is presented in this section.

Part 1: Prioritize and Select the Market Segments. A SIPOC analysis was used to segment the market for academic Six Sigma education and certification. Table 17.9 shows the SIPOC analysis for this project.

TABLE 17.9   SIPOC Analysis

Supplier Segments	Suppliers	>	Inputs (Xs)	>	Process (Xs)	>	Outputs (CTQs)	>	Customer (Market) Segments
Academic Suppliers	MBA program		Students		Insert flowchart of MAS Dept. Education and Training Process (Figure 17.1)		List of courses with number of sections and number of students and participants by semester		Students • MBA specialization in MAS • MS in MAS • Exec Ed Six Sigma Programs
							# of MBAs specializing in MAS by semester		
	MS in MAS program		Students				# of MS in MAS majors by semester		Employers
	MAS Dept.		Faculty Admin. Support Marketing Support				# of companies recruiting MAS specialists at UM		
			Course-ware				Skills taught (# of different management approaches to problems)		

Supplier Segments	Suppliers	>	Inputs (Xs)	>	Process (Xs)	>	Outputs (CTQs)	>	Customer (Market) Segments
Infrastructure Suppliers	SBA		Classrooms				Average % pay increase after program completion		
					Insert flowchart of MAS Dept. Education and Training Process (Figure 17.1)		Skills learned (# projects done; % on standardized tests)		
Organizational Suppliers	Employers		Curriculum Requirements				# of projects done by year		
			Job Opportunities				# of projects done by students for community and/or UM by year		

Part 2: Select the Design Strategy (Level B Survey). The second part of the Measure Phase is to conduct a Kano analysis to determine the cognitive features for the proposed design. Recall, a Level B Kano survey has four stages with a total of nine steps.

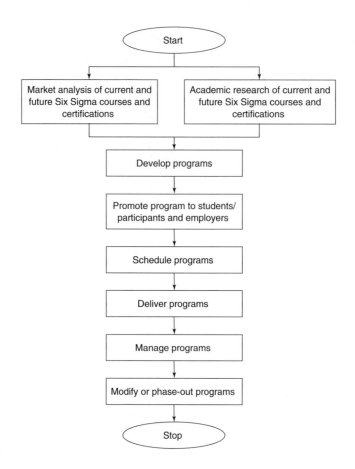

FIGURE 17.1   MAS Dept. Education and Training Process

STAGE ONE: Collect "Voice of the User" and "Voice of the Customer" Data

STAGE ONE—Step 1: Select a product, service, or process in a given market segment(s) to serve as the subject of a DFSS project. The service selected for this project is providing academic Six Sigma courses and certification to MBA students. The stakeholder segments for the service are students, employers, and faculty, as shown in Table 17.10.

STAGE ONE—Step 2: Identify lead users and heavy users. Team members identified the characteristics of lead and heavy users by market segment, and identify contact information for individuals in each cell. Team members surveyed all of the individuals listed in Table 17.11 for "Voice of the Customer" data concerning the proposed Six Sigma specialization in the MBA program.

TABLE 17.10 Market Segmentation Matrix

Market Segments	Product or Service	Detailed Product Line
Students	MBA specialization in MAS	*Champion Belt* MAS 633: Introduction to Quality Management MAS 634: Administrative Systems of Quality Management *Green Belt* MAS 635: Design of Experiments MAS 636: SPC and Reliability *Black Belt* MAS 637: Applied Regression Analysis and Forecasting MAS 639: Project Management (under development)
	MS in MAS	Above courses plus: MAS 638: MAS Consulting MAS 696: Independent Study (Projects) MAS 699: Independent Study (Internship) Other MAS courses MGT 622: High Performance Teams Industrial Engineering courses Psychology courses Biostatistics courses Epidemiology courses
Employers	Provide new employees for employers. Provide current employees with skills for future jobs.	High-caliber employees who "can hit the ground running."
Faculty	Provide rewarding teaching experiences.Provide additional sources of income.	Varied

TABLE 17.11 Partial "Lead User and Heavy User Characteristics by Market Segment" Matrix

Characteristics of Lead or Heavy Users for the MBA Specialization in MAS	Students	Employers	Faculty
Heavily involved in designing courseware	Names	Names	Names
Heavily involved in using Six Sigma	Names	Names	Names
Heavily involved in Six Sigma training	Empty Segment	Names	Names
Heavily involved in promoting Six Sigma	Empty Segment	Names	Names

STAGE ONE—Step 3: Collect "Voice of the Stakeholder" circumstantial data from lead users and heavy users. Team members collected "Voice of the Stakeholder" data from each market segment. Selected portions of the raw "Voice of the Stakeholder" data are shown in Table 17.12.

TABLE 17.12   Select Raw "Voice of the Stakeholder" Data

Selected Market Segment(s)	Select Abstracts from the Raw "Voice of the User" and "Voice of the Customer" Data (in the Language of Respondent)
Student	MBA seeking black belt should get technical course. Statistics is very important. If you don't have statistical basics, then you'll get lost.
	I also feel there should be courses that hit on the three main subject areas: DMAIC models, DMADV models, and Deming theory, the three main tools of Six Sigma.
	As far as projects go, if you have students who want to certify in Six Sigma, it is important to get them certified. Making money while working on projects is nice, but being able to certify rapidly would be more beneficial. I think they should allocate projects that aid in certification to those who want to certify and allow others who don't want to certify the ability to gain paid experience in the other types of projects.
	I think a student should have to do a simple project that covers all of the steps and see it to completion, so that out on a live project, you aren't learning on the job.
	I wish to get internship opportunities.
Employers	I need black belts who can lead teams, work with managers and supervisors to effect the changes inherent in any improvement initiative, find and analyze all the data needed to make the chain of evidence ironclad, and build understanding of the entire cause system.
	I need a set of teachable, accessible tools that work in my environment, with my data.
	You need to adapt the management techniques you learned at the University of Miami and change organizations, change processes, and just change the way people think.
	I want certification that applies to my environment. If I'm in healthcare, I need someone who understands healthcare problems, metrics, and data. If I'm in banking, I want someone who understands banking metrics and problems.
	I want employees who are not only trained in technical skills but in project management skills too.
Faculty	Six Sigma gives me an opportunity to impact student's lives by giving them various opportunities, such as networking and practical experience.
	The specific sequence of courses that are required for the Six Sigma program is important.
	For sustaining the program, we need the involvement of other companies for internships/projects, and more participation from other faculty to be involved in those projects.

STAGE TWO: Analyze "Voice of the Stakeholder" Data

STAGE TWO—Step 4: Classify "Voice of the User" and "Voice of the Customer" data as circumstantial or product-related data. Team members classified the "Voice of the Stakeholder" data into either circumstantial or product-related data. Table 17.13 shows selected examples of "Voice of the Stakeholder" data by market segment.

TABLE 17.13 Selected "Voice of the Stakeholder" Data by Stakeholder Segment

Selected Stakeholder Segment(s)	Raw "Voice of the Stakeholder" Data (in the Language of Respondent)	Data Classification (Product or Circumstantial)
Student	MBA seeking black belt should get technical course. Statistics is very important. If you don't have statistical basics, then you'll get lost.	C
	I also feel there should be courses that hit on the three main subject areas: DMAIC models, DMADV models, and Deming theory, the three main tools of Six Sigma.	P
	As far as projects go, if you have students who want to certify in Six Sigma, it is important to get them certified. Making money while working on projects is nice, but being able to certify rapidly would be more beneficial. I think they should allocate projects that aid in certification to those who want to certify and allow others who don't want to certify the ability to gain paid experience in the other types of projects.	C
	I think a student should have to do a simple project that covers all of the steps and see it to completion, so that out on a live project, you aren't learning on the job.	P
	I wish to get internship opportunities.	C
Employers	I need black belts who can lead teams, work with managers and supervisors to effect the changes inherent in any improvement initiative, find and analyze all the data needed to make the chain of evidence ironclad, and build understanding of the entire cause system.	C
	I need a set of teachable, accessible tools that work in my environment, with my data.	P
	You need to adapt the management techniques you learned at the University of Miami and change organizations, change processes, and just change the way people think.	C
	I want certification that applies to my environment. If I'm in healthcare, I need someone who understands healthcare problems, metrics, and data. If I'm in banking, I want someone who understands banking metrics and problems.	P
	I want employees who are not only trained in technical skills but in project management skills too.	C

(continued)

TABLE 17.13 Selected "Voice of the Stakeholder" Data by Stakeholder Segment (Continued)

Selected Stakeholder Segment(s)	Raw "Voice of the Stakeholder" Data (in the Language of Respondent)	Data Classification (Product or Circumstantial)
Faculty	Six Sigma gives me an opportunity to impact student's lives by giving them various opportunities, such as networking and practical experience.	C
	The specific sequence of courses that are required for a Six Sigma program is important.	P
	For sustaining the program, we need the involvement of other companies for internships/projects, and more participation from other faculty to be involved in those projects.	C

STAGE TWO—Step 5: Determine the critical circumstantial issues or themes to regular users. Step 5 creates a survey that is given to a large sample of regular users to identify which circumstantial issues are critical to them. Step 5 was not conducted in this application, because we concentrated on improving the new features.

STAGE THREE: Develop New Features

STAGE THREE—Step 6: Determine the focus point for each circumstantial issue or theme. Focus points are the underlying needs and wants upon which circumstantial issues or themes are based. Table 17.14 presents the affinity diagram used to develop the focus points for the circumstantial "Voice of the Stakeholder" data.

STAGE THREE—Step 7: Develop cognitive images for each focus point. Team members develop cognitive images from the focus points. Table 17.15 presents selected cognitive images developed from the focus points.

TABLE 17.14 Selected Elements from the Affinity Diagram of Circumstantial Raw Data

Raw "Voice of the User" and "Voice of the Customer" Data	Affinity Diagram Circumstantial Themes and Their Raw Data Points	Focus Points
You need to adapt the management techniques you learned at the University of Miami and change organizations, change processes, and just change the way people think. I need black belts who can lead teams, work with managers and supervisors to effect the changes inherent in any improvement initiative, find and analyze all the data needed to make the chain of evidence ironclad, and build understanding of the entire cause system. Statistics is very important. If you don't have statistical basics, then you'll get lost. I want employees who are not only trained in technical skills but in project management skills too.	Content (skill set, techniques)	Bridge between theory and practice
Six Sigma gives me an opportunity to impact student's lives by giving them various opportunities, such as networking, practical experience. I wish to get paid internship opportunities. I want black belts who have experience in working on real-life projects.	Outcome (experience, reputation)	Experience and Internship

TABLE 17.15 Selected List of Cognitive Image

Circumstantial Issue	Focus Point	Cognitive Image(s)
Student: "I wish to get paid internship opportunities."	Experience/Internship	Acquire paid internships for students.
Faculty: "Six Sigma gives me an opportunity to impact student's lives by giving them various opportunities, such as networking and practical experience." *For sustaining the program, we need the involvement of other companies for internships/projects.*	Experience/Internship	
Employer: "I want employees who are not only trained in technical skills, but in project management skills too."	Bridge between theory and practice.	

STAGE FOUR: Evolve Strategies for New Features

STAGE FOUR—Step 8: Classify cognitive images by Kano category and Kano cost distribution. Team members construct a Kano survey to test the stakeholder segments on their attitudes for the cognitive images; see Table 17.16 for a portion of the Kano survey.

TABLE 17.16   Partial Kano Questionnaire

CTQs	How would you feel if you were paid to work on Six Sigma certification projects?	How would you feel if you were not paid to work on Six Sigma certification projects?	What percentage tuition fee increase, over current fee, would you be willing to pay for paid Six Sigma certification projects?
Acquire paid internship for students.	Delighted [ ] Expect it and like it [ ] No feeling [ ] Live with it [ ] Do not like it [ ] Other [ ]	Delighted [ ] Expect it and like it [ ] No feeling [ ] Live with it [ ] Do not like it [ ] Other [ ]	0% _____ 10% _____ 20% _____ 30% _____ 40% or more _____

A Kano survey conducted by the Six Sigma team members yielded the Kano classifications shown in Table 17.17.

TABLE 17.17   Classification of Cognitive Images by Kano Category

Market Segment	Cognitive Images	Kano Quality Category
Student*		
(S1)	1. Increase number of job offers due to Six Sigma certification.	O
(S2)	2. Increase starting salary of job offers due to Six Sigma certification.	O
(S3)	3. Increase salary due to Six Sigma certification.	A
(S4)	4. Increase "joy in work" due to Six Sigma management style.	O
	5. Definite structured Six Sigma certification program.	I
	6. Standardized certification projects.	I
(S5)	7. Provide a technical vs. non-technical course route.	R
	8. Involve students in one certification project at a time.	I
(S6)	9. Acquire paid internships for students.	A

Market Segment	Cognitive Images	Kano Quality Category
(S7)	10. Mandatory statistical software packages course.	A
Employer (E1)	1. Hire employees who have already been trained in Six Sigma management.	O
(E2)	2. Hire employees who have already been trained in project management skills.	O
Faculty Involved in Six Sigma (F1)	1. Increase extra pay due to Six Sigma teaching and research.	A
(F2)	2. Increase research output due to Six Sigma projects.	A
(F3)	3. Improve international image of MAS department.	O
(F4)	4. Increase "joy in work" due to Six Sigma projects.	A
(F5)	5. Increase # of Juried Articles published by faculty member (i) per year.	O
(F6)	6. Increase percentage of juried articles published by faculty in "A" journals per year.	O
(F7)	7. Improve MAS courseware through standardization of syllabi with Six Sigma applications and case studies, and using Minitab 14 as the departmental standard for statistical software applications.	O
(F8)	8. Increase interdepartmental ranking of faculty member (i)'s student evaluation scores.	O

STAGE FOUR—Step 9: Develop strategic themes for each cognitive image by market segment. The cognitive images that are selected in step 8 are called strategic themes and are inputs into a QFD matrix to determine the CTQs for the project.

Part 3: Convert Cognitive Images into CTQs. A Quality Function Deployment (QFD) matrix was used to convert the cognitive image into CTQs by stakeholder segment. Table 17.18 shows the QFD matrix. The cognitive images are in the rows and the CTQs are in the columns.

TABLE 17.18   QFD Table

Market Segment	Market Sub-Segment	Critical to Quality (CTQs) / Cognitive Images	Kano Category	Increase number of job offers	Increase starting salary of job offers	Increase overall salary	Increase "joy in work"	Provide technical and nontechnical course routes (DELETED DUE TO KANO CATEGORY = Reverse)	Acquire paid internships for students	Mandatory statistical software packages course	Hire employees trained in Six Sigma Management	Attain employees already trained in project management	Increase extra pay due to Six Sigma teaching and research	Increase research output due to Six Sigma Research	Improve international image of MAS department	Increase "joy in work" due to Six Sigma projects	Increase # of juried articles published by faculty member(i) per year	Increase % of juried articles published in "A" journals	Improve courseware by standardizing syllabi with Six Sigma applications and case studies using Minitab 14	Increase interdepartmental ranking of faculty members based on student evaluations	Score Column
				Students							Employers		Faculty Involved with Six Sigma								
Students	MBA Students Specializing in MAS	Increase number of job offers due to Six Sigma Certification	O	45	45	45	5	45	45	45	45	45	45	45	45	15	45	45	45	15	5
		Increase starting salary of job offers due to Six Sigma certifications	O	45	45	45	15	45	45	45	45	45	5	5	45	15	45	45	45	5	5
		Increase salary due to Six Sigma certifications	A	36	36	36	12	36	36	36	36	36	4	4	36	12	36	36	36	4	4
		Increase "joy in work" due to Six Sigma management style	O	5	15	15	45	45	45	5	45	45	5	5	5	45	15	15	45	45	5
		Provide a technical vs. nontechnical course route (DELETED DUE TO KANO CATEGORY = Reverse)	R	9	9	9	9	9	9	9	9	9		3	3	9	1	0	0	9	1
		Acquire paid internships for students.	A	36	36	36	36	36	36	36	36	36	36	36	36	4	36	36	12	0	4
		Mandatory Statistical Software Packages Course	A	36	36	36	12	36	36	36	36	4	4	4	36	36	0	0	36	0	4
Faculty	Faculty Involved with Six Sigma	Increase extra pay due to Six Sigma teaching and research	A	36	4	4	4	12	36	4	0	0	36	36	12	36	36	12	12	36	4
		Increase research output due to Six Sigma projects	A	36	4	4	4	12	36	4	0	0	36	36	12	36	36	36	36	12	4
		Improve international image of MAS department	O	45	45	45	5	45	45	45	0	0	15	15	45	45	45	45	45	15	5
		Increase "joy in work" due to Six Sigma projects	A	12	12	12	36	4	4	36	0	0	36	36	36	36	36	36	36	36	4
		Increase # of juried articles published by faculty member (i) per year	O	45	45	45	15	0	45	0	0	0	45	45	45	45	45	45	45	15	5
		Increase percentage of juried articles published by faculty in "A" journals per year	O	45	45	45	15	0	45	0	0	0	15	45	45	45	45	45	45	15	5

Employers	CTQ		More job offers	Increased starting salary	Increased overall salary	Normative improvement	Multiple versions of courses	Varied internships	SAS, Minitab, SPSS	At least minimal certification	Certified (Y/N)	Increased overall salary		Improve int. rankings (publications)	Normative Improvement	More published research	Greater percentage of articles	Offer improved courseware	Improve rankings of faculty	
	Improve courseware	O	45	45	45	45	45	45	45	45	15	45	45	45	5	15	5	5	45	5
	Increase interdepartmental ranking of faculty member (i)'s student evaluation scores	O	15	5	5	45	0	0	0	0	0	45	15	15	45	15	15	15	45	5
	Hire employees who are already trained in Six Sigma management (decrease training costs)	O	45	45	45	45	45	45	45	45	0	0	0	0	0	0	0	0	5	0	5
	Receive employees who are already trained in project management skills.	O	45	45	45	15	15	45	5	15	45	0	0	0	0	0	0	0	45	0	5
			581	517	517	363	430	598	396	357	274	375	375	467	421	450	416	517	288	7342
	Normalized weights		0.079	0.07	0.07	0.049	0.059	0.081	0.054	0.049	0.037	0.051	0.051	0.064	0.057	0.061	0.057	0.07	0.039	

Figure 17.2 shows a Pareto diagram of the CTQs ordered by their unnormalized weights from Table 17.18.

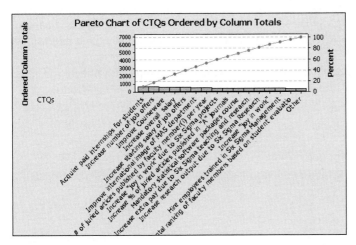

FIGURE 17.2 Minitab Pareto Diagram of CTQs

Figure 17.3 shows a *c*-chart of the CTQs ordered by unnormalized weights from Table 17.18. Although a *c*-chart is not a completely appropriate tool for the data type used in the Pareto diagram, it is used here to give a sense to which CTQs are more or less significant to the high-level design.

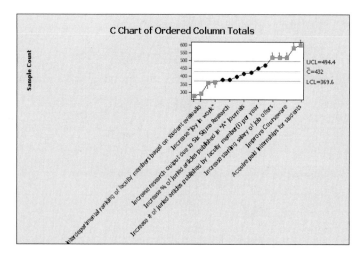

FIGURE 17.3   Minitab c-Chart of Ordered CTQs by Total Column Score

Select Final Set of CTQs

Table 17.19 shows that the first four ordered CTQs are less important and the last five ordered CTQs are statistically more important that the rest of the ordered CTQs from Figure 17.3. Consequently, the last five CTQs will play an important role in defining the new design for the MBA specialization in MAS. They are increase starting salary of job offers, increase overall salary, improve courseware, increase number of job offers, and acquire paid internships for students.

All CTQs will be used in the high-level design, with special emphasis on the five CTQs listed previously.

TABLE 17.19   CTQs Ordered by Column Totals

Attain employees already trained in project management.	274
Increase interdepartmental ranking of faculty members based on student evaluation.	288
Hire employees trained in Six Sigma management.	357
Increase "joy in work."	363
Increase extra pay due to Six Sigma teaching and research.	375
Increase research output due to Six Sigma research.	375
Mandatory statistical software packages course.	396
Increase % of juried articles published in "A" journals.	416
Increase "joy in work" due to Six Sigma projects.	421
Increase # of juried articles published by faculty member(i) per year.	450
Improve international image of MAS department.	467
Increase starting salary of job offers.	517

Develop a Design Scorecard

Team members developed a design score card for the CTQs. Only nominal values are stated due to the nature of all CTQs (see Table 17.20).

TABLE 17.20 Design Scorecard

Scorecard—Part A (Voice of the Customer)					Scorecard—Part B (Predicted Voice of the Process)					
CTQ	Target (Nominal)	LSL	USL	Sigma Target	Stable (Y/N)	Shape	Mean	Std. Dev.	DPU	Predicted Process Sigma
Increase number of job offers.	More job offers.	N/A	N/A	N/A						
Increase starting salary of job offers.	Increased starting salary.	N/A	N/A	N/A						
Increase overall salary.	Increased overall salary.	N/A	N/A	N/A						
Increase "joy in work."	Normative improvement.	N/A	N/A	N/A						
Acquire paid internships for students.	Varied internships.	N/A	N/A	N/A						
Mandatory statistical software packages course.	Minitab 14.	N/A	N/A	N/A						
Hire employees trained in Six Sigma management.	At least minimal certification.	N/A	N/A	N/A						

(continued)

TABLE 17.20 Design Scorecard (Continued)

Scorecard—Part A (Voice of the Customer)					Scorecard—Part B (Predicted Voice of the Process)					
CTQ	Target (Nominal)	LSL	USL	Sigma Target	Stable (Y/N)	Shape	Mean	Std. Dev.	DPU	Predicted Process Sigma
Attain employees already trained in project management.	Certified (Y/N).	N/A	N/A	N/A						
Increase extra pay due to Six Sigma teaching and research.	Increased overall salary.	N/A	N/A	N/A						
Increase research output due to Six Sigma Research.	More research projects.	N/A	N/A	N/A						
Improve international image of MAS department.	Improve int. rankings (publications).	N/A	N/A	N/A						
Increase "joy in work" due to Six Sigma projects.	Normative Improvement.	N/A	N/A	N/A						
Increase # of juried articles published by faculty member (*i*) per year.	More published research.	N/A	N/A	N/A						
Increase % of juried articles published in "A" journals.	Greater percentage of articles.	N/A	N/A	N/A						
Improve courseware.	Offer improved courseware.	N/A	N/A	N/A						

Scorecard—Part A (Voice of the Customer)					Scorecard—Part B (Predicted Voice of the Process)					
CTQ	Target (Nominal)	LSL	USL	Sigma Target	Stable (Y/N)	Shape	Mean	Std. Dev.	DPU	Predicted Process Sigma
Increase interdepartmental ranking of faculty members based on student evaluation.	Improve rankings of faculty.	N/A	N/A	N/A						

Review Intellectual Property Issues

It is critically important that team members seek the counsel of a competent patent attorney and/or trademark attorney. Patent law is a specialized area of the law with its own bar examination. A review of the literature on universities offering Six Sigma and education and training yielded an article in *Quality Progress* magazine from October 2004 titled, "Colleges and University Programs in Quality," by Valerie Funk. The article listed over 100 colleges and universities offering courses, degrees, or programs in quality or related subjects. The paper covered all 50 states, Canada, Ireland, Korea, Mexico, Puerto Rico, and Sweden. The following four-year colleges and universities were listed as having some form of Six Sigma education or training:

California State University at Fullerton	Certification
University of Miami	Academic Certification
Southwestern College Professional Studies & SC Online	Certification
Loyola University, New Orleans	Certification
University of Minnesota, Carlson School (Juran Institute)	Certification
University of St. Thomas, St. Paul, Minnesota	Certification
North Carolina State University (Engineering Extension)	C.E. credit
Weber State University	Course

From our cursory review, the University of Miami seems to be the only four-year academic institution that offers a range of Six Sigma courses that lead to Six Sigma certification *and* a specialization in the MBA program for academic credit.

17.4 ANALYZE PHASE

Introduction

The Analyze Phase contains four parts: design generation, design analysis, risk analysis, and design model. Each part is presented next.

Part 1: Design Generation (Generating Design Concepts for Critical Parameters)

Breaking Down CTQs into High-Level CTPs. PD team members use a systematic (tree) diagram to decompose each CTQ into high-level CTPs (critical to process characteristics). Columns 1 through 5 of Table 17.21 show the tree diagram of the relationships between the CTQs and the high-level CTPs by stakeholder segment. Further, PD team members added eight columns to the right side of Table 17.21 (see columns 6-13), creating a matrix of possible high-level design concepts.

TABLE 17.21   CTQ and CTP Relationships for Stakeholder Segments

System	Level	CTQ	Nominal Values for the CTQs	High-Level CTPs	Base Design	Concept 2	3	4	5	6	7	8
MBA w/ MAS Concentration and Six Sigma Program	Students	Increase # of job offers due to Six Sigma Certification.	More job offers.	≥ 3 Offers	★			X	X	X		X	X
				< 3 Offers	★	X					X		X
		Increase starting salary of job offers due to Six Sigma Certification.	Increase starting salary.	≥$5,000	★			X	X	X		X	
				< $5,000	★	X					X		X
		Increase overall salary due to Six Sigma Certification.	Increased overall salary.	≥ $10,000				X	X	X		X	
				< $10,000	★	X					X		X
		Increase "joy in work" due to Six Sigma management.	Normative improvement.	No post student survey	★					X			
				< 1 yr post student survey		X		X			X		X
				1 < 5 yr student survey				X				X	

System	Level	CTQ	Nominal Values for the CTQs	High-Level CTPs	Base Design	Concept 2	3	4	5	6	7	8
MBA w/ MAS Concentration and Six Sigma Program	Faculty Involved with Six Sigma	Acquire paid internships.	Varied internships.	$13/hr	★	X	X			X		X
				$25/hr				X	X		X	
		Mandatory statistical software packages course.	Varied statistical packages.	Minitab	★			X	X		X	
				Minitab, SPSS, SAS		X		X		X		X
		Increase extra pay due to Six Sigma teaching and research.	Increase overall salary.	≤$10,000	★			X		X		X
				>$10,000					X	X		X
		Increase research output due to Six Sigma projects.	More research projects.	≤ 2 projects	★				X		X	
				> 2 projects			X	X		X		X
		Improve international image of MAS department.	Improvement in international rankings.	Local Placement of Students	★	X			X			
				National Placement of Students				X			X	X
				International Placement of Students					X		X	
		Increase "joy in work" due to Six Sigma projects.	Normative improvement.	No post student survey	★						X	
				< 1 yr post student survey			X	X			X	
				1 < 5 yr student survey				X	X			X
		Increase # of juried articles published by faculty member (*i*) per year.	More published research.	1 article	★	X			X		X	
				>1 article				X	X		X	X

(continued)

TABLE 17.21   CTQ and CTP Relationships for Stakeholder Segments (Continued)

System	Level	CTQ	Nominal Values for the CTQs	High-Level CTPs	Base Design	Concept 2	3	4	5	6	7	8
MBA w/ MAS Concentration and Six Sigma Program	Faculty Involved with Six Sigma	Increase % of juried articles published by faculty in "A" journals per year.	Greater percentage of articles selected.	≤20%	★	X			X		X	
				>20%			X	X		X	X	
		Improve courseware.	Offer improved courses and courseware.	Standardize syllabi without Six Sigma applications and case studies.	★	X			X		X	
				Standardize syllabi with Six Sigma applications and case studies using Minitab 14.		X		X		X		X
		Increase interdepartmental ranking of faculty member (i)'s student evaluation scores.	Improve rankings of faculty.	≤ 20% improvement	★	X	X		X		X	
				>20% Improvement				X		X		X
	Employers	New employees trained in Six Sigma management.	Champion									
			Green Belt	Non-Technical Service GB	★		X		X		X	
				Technical MFG GB		X		X		X		X
			Black Belt	Non-Technical Service BB	★			X		X		X
				Technical MFG BB		X		X		X		X

System	Level	CTQ	Nominal Values for the CTQs	High-Level CTPs	Base Design	Concept 2	3	4	5	6	7	8
MBA w/ MAS Concentration and Six Sigma Program	Employers	New employees trained in project management.	Champion	w/o certificate, trained in project mgmt.	★	X	X		X		X	
				w/ certificate				X		X		X
			Green Belt	w/o certificate, trained in project mgmt.	★	X	X		X		X	
				w/ certificate				X		X		X
			Black Belt	w/o certificate, trained in project mgmt.	★	X	X		X		X	
				w/ certificate				X		X	X	

Part 2: Design Analysis (Alternative Design Concepts for Critical Parameters)

Concept 4 is the best design according to the criteria in the Pugh Matrix in Table 17.22. It has 4 positives (the highest number), 1 negative (tied for the lowest number), and 0 sames.

TABLE 17.22   Pugh Matrix of Alternative High-Level Designs

1 Criteria to Evaluate Concepts (Set by PD Team Members)	2 Concept 1 (Baseline Concept)	3 Concept 2	4 Concept 3	5 Concept 4	6 Concept 5	7 Concept 6	8 Concept 7	9 Concept 8
Benefit/cost of concept.	All concepts are evaluated with respect to the baseline concept.	-	+	+	+	-	+	-
Time required to realize the concept.		S	-	-	-	S	-	S
Organization's ability to realize concept.		S	-	+	S	+	-	+
Effect of concept on organization's strategy.		S	+	+	S	+	-	S
Political ramifications of concept.		S	+	+	S	+	-	+
Sum of "Positives"		0	3	4	1	3	1	2
Sum of "Negatives"		1	2	1	1	1	4	1
Sum of "Sames"		4	0	0	3	1	0	2

The CTPs, and their selected levels, for concept 4 are presented next by stakeholder segment. CTPs that must be designed into the MBA specialization in MAS are shown in regular font. *CTPs that are a result of an effective design (yet require action such as advertising, but are not formally part of the design) are shown in italic font.*

Student level

- *Increase number of job offers due to Six Sigma Certification* ➔ *at least three offers.*
- *Increase starting salary of job offers due to Six Sigma Certification* ➔ *at least $5,000.*
- *Increase overall salary due to Six Sigma Certification* ➔ *at least $10,000.*
- *Increase "joy in work" due to Six Sigma management* ➔ *1~5 year student survey.*
- Acquire paid internships ➔ at least $25/hour.
- Mandatory statistical software packages course ➔ Minitab 14.

Faculty level

- *Increase extra pay due to Six Sigma teaching and research* ➔ *higher than $10,000.*
- Increase research output due to Six Sigma projects ➔ more than 2 projects.
- *Improve international image of MAS department* ➔ *international placement of students.*
- *Increase "joy in work" due to Six Sigma management* ➔ *1–5 year student survey.*
- *Increase number of juried articles published by faculty member* (i) *per year* ➔ *more than 1 article.*
- *Increase % of juried articles published by faculty in "A" journals per year* ➔ *more than 20% articles.*
- Improve courseware ➔ standardize syllabi with Six Sigma applications and case studies using Minitab 14.
- *Increase interdepartmental ranking of faculty member*(i)*'s student evaluation scores* ➔ *higher than 20% improvement.*

Employers level

- New employees trained in Six Sigma management ➔ technical manufacturing Green Belt or Black Belt.
- New employees trained in project management ➔ Champion, Green Belt, or Black Belt with project management skills.

Part 3: Risk Analysis (Assessing Risk of the "Best" Design Concept)

Team members performed an FMEA on the CTPs, and their levels, in the best design from the Pugh Matrix (see Table 17.22). The FMEA is shown in Table 17.23.

TABLE 17.23 FMEA of High-Level CTPs

16	**Notes**	Long-term network with Six Sigma companies build up trust between each other, which increases no. of job offers.	Long-term network with Six Sigma companies build up trust between each other, which ensures the payment for student internship.	Long-term network with Six Sigma companies and high qualification of students build up trust between each other, which helps to increase students starting salary.
16	**R P N**	18	24	36
#	**Detection**	3	4	4
#	**Occurrence**	2	2	3
#	**Severity**	3	3	3
12	**Action Taken**	01/20/05	01/20/05	01/20/05
11	**Resp. and Target Date**	HSG 05/05/05	HSG 05/05/05	HSG 05/05/05
10	**Recommended Action**	Build up long-term network with Six Sigma companies.	Build up long-term network with Six Sigma companies nationwide.	Build up long-term network with Six Sigma companies.
9	**R P N**	150	175	225
8	**Detection**	5	7	9
7	**Current Controls**	Less frequent contact with Six Sigma companies.	Network in Miami only.	Six Sigma companies have fewer job offers for new graduates.
6	**Occurrence**	5	5	5
5	**Potential Causes**	Job market is not better for our students.	Company's budget constraints.	Not a Six Sigma company.
4	**Severity**	6	5	5
3	**Potential Failure Effect**	Students become upset.	Students become upset.	Students become upset.
2	**Potential Failure Mode**	Fewer than three job offers.	Nonpaid internship, or internship pay < $25/hr.	Starting salary increase does not exceed $5,000 even with Six Sigma certification.
1	**Critical Parameter (CTPs)**	# of job offers due to Six Sigma certification ≥ 3 offers.	Paid internship ≥ $25/hr.	Starting salary of job offers due to Six Sigma Certification ≥ $5,000.
	Level	Students		

	Notes	Top mgmt with more Six Sigma knowledge increases the opportunity of higher overall salary of students with Six Sigma certification.	Top mgmt with more Six Sigma knowledge increases the satisfaction level of both students and themselves.
16	**R P N**	30	12
#	**Detection**	5	3
#	**Occurrence**	2	2
#	**Severity**	3	2
12	**Action Taken**	01/20/05	01/20/05
11	**Resp. and Target Date**	HSG 05/05/05	HSG 05/05/05
10	**Recommended Action**	Train top management in Six Sigma module or methodologies.	Train top management in Six Sigma module or methodologies.
9	**R P N**	200	140
8	**Detection**	8	7
7	**Current Controls**	Top management not/less trained (educated) in Six Sigma methodologies.	Top management not/less trained (educated) in Six Sigma methodologies.
6	**Occurrence**	5	4
5	**Potential Causes**	Top management not committed to Six Sigma quality management style.	Students could not find "joy in work."
4	**Severity**	5	5
3	**Potential Failure Effect**	Students become upset.	Students become upset and frustrated.
2	**Potential Failure Mode**	Overall salary increase does not exceed $10,000 even with Six Sigma Certification.	Fewer students participate in the survey.
1	**Critical Parameter (CTPs)**	Overall salary increase due to Six Sigma Certification ≥$10,000.	Normative improvement: 1–5 yr student survey.
	Level	Students	

(continued)

TABLE 17.23   FMEA of High-Level CTPs (Continued)

	Notes	More alternatives in choosing courseware and the opportunity of learning technical applications increase the competitiveness of students at looking for a job.	Proficiency in statistical software packages increases students' competitiveness in the field.
16	**R P N**	27	18
#	**Detection**	3	3
#	**Occurrence**	3	2
#	**Severity**	3	3
12	**Action Taken**	01/20/05	01/20/05
11	**Resp. and Target Date**	HSG 05/05/05	HSG 05/05/05
10	**Recommended Action**	Offer at least two versions of a class, featured technical application, and courses on project management skills.	Offer user-friendly statistical software packages course.
9	**R P N**	125	150
8	**Detection**	5	5
7	**Current Controls**	Only one version of a class featured technical applications; no course on project management skills.	No statistical software packages course offered currently.
6	**Occurrence**	5	6
5	**Potential Causes**	Companies require technical applications and project management skills.	Mandatory statistical software package not user-friendly; students' math background not strong enough.
4	**Severity**	5	5
3	**Potential Failure Effect**	Students and companies become upset.	Students cannot gain learning experience in statistical software.
2	**Potential Failure Mode**	Only one version of class, without technical applications.	No mandatory statistical software package course.
1	**Critical Parameter (CTPs)**	Provide more than one version of a class; featured technical applications.	Mandatory statistical software packages course: Minitab, SPSS, SAS.
	Level		

	Notes	More budget in the MAS helps to motivate faculty involved in the Six Sigma teaching with extra pay.	Six Sigma network brings more challenging projects, which motivates faculty in doing their Six Sigma-related research.	Six Sigma network brings more challenging projects and support, which motivates faculty in doing their Six Sigma related research.
16	**R P N**	24	36	36
#	**Detection**	3	4	4
#	**Occurrence**	4	3	3
#	**Severity**	2	3	3
12	**Action Taken**	01/20/05	01/20/05	01/20/05
11	**Resp. and Target Date**	HSG 05/05/05	HSG 05/05/05	HSG 05/05/05
10	**Recommended Action**	Get faculty involved in the consulting job in Six Sigma companies.	Build up network with Six Sigma companies.	Build up network with Six Sigma companies.
9	**R P N**	180	180	150
8	**Detection**	6	6	5
7	**Current Controls**	No extra pay due to Six Sigma teaching.	Fewer challenging research projects in Six Sigma field.	Fewer challenging research projects in Six Sigma field.
6	**Occurrence**	6	6	6
5	**Potential Causes**	No budget in the MAS department.	Time constraints of the faculty.	No motivation.
4	**Severity**	5	5	5
3	**Potential Failure Effect**	Faculty become upset and less involved in Six Sigma projects.	Faculty become upset and less involved in Six Sigma projects.	Faculty become upset and less involved in Six Sigma projects.
2	**Potential Failure Mode**	Overall salary increase does not exceed $10,000, even with Six Sigma teaching and research.	No research projects related with Six Sigma.	No juried articles published by faculty member due to Six Sigma experience.
1	**Critical Parameter (CTPs)**	Extra pay due to Six Sigma teaching and research > $10,000.	Research output due to Six Sigma projects > 2 projects.	# of juried articles published by faculty member (i) per year > 1 article.
	Level	Faculty Involved with Six Sigma		

(continued)

TABLE 17.23   FMEA of High-Level CTPs (Continued)

16	**Notes**	Six Sigma network brings more challenging projects and financial support, which motivates faculty in doing their Six Sigma related research.	More positive students survey motivates faculty into searching and getting involved in challenging Six Sigma projects.	With more budget and promotion activity, international placement of students increases and international image of MAS improves, which attracts excellent faculty candidates.
16	**R P N**	27	27	36
#	**Detection**	3	3	3
#	**Occurrence**	3	3	4
#	**Severity**	3	3	3
12	**Action Taken**	01/20/05	01/20/05	01/20/05
11	**Resp. and Target Date**	HSG 05/05/05	HSG 05/05/05	HSG 05/05/05
10	**Recommended Action**	Build up network with Six Sigma companies.	Build up network with Six Sigma companies.	Get more involved in the international Six Sigma quality management conference/events.
9	**R P N**	150	150	150
8	**Detection**	5	5	5
7	**Current Controls**	Fewer challenging research projects in Six Sigma field.	Fewer challenging research projects in Six Sigma field.	No promotion activity.
6	**Occurrence**	6	6	6
5	**Potential Causes**	No motivation.	No motivation.	No budget in the MAS department.
4	**Severity**	5	5	5
3	**Potential Failure Effect**	Faculty become upset and less involved in Six Sigma projects.	Faculty become upset and less involved in Six Sigma projects.	Less attractiveness for potential talented faculty candidates.
2	**Potential Failure Mode**	No juried articles published in "A" journals by faculty member due to Six Sigma experience.	Fewer students participate in the survey.	No improvement in international image of MAS department.
1	**Critical Parameter (CTPs)**	% of juried articles published by faculty in "A" journals per year > 20%.	Normative improvement: 1–5 yr student survey.	Improve international image by international placement of students.
	Level			

	Notes	With more faculty involved in designing courseware, the courseware is more diverse, which generates more choices for students.	Courseware improvement gains students' satisfaction, which accordingly increases faculty evaluation scores.
16	**R P N**	18	12
#	**Detection**	3	3
#	**Occurrence**	2	2
#	**Severity**	3	2
12	**Action Taken**	01/20/05	01/20/05
11	**Resp. and Target Date**	HSG 5/05/05	HSG 05/05/05
10	**Recommended Action**	Improve courseware based on feedback from the students and faculty, identify trend of Six Sigma companies' employment requirements.	Improve courseware based on feedback from the students and faculty, improve faculty interaction/communication.
9	**R P N**	150	150
8	**Detection**	5	5
7	**Current Controls**	Courseware not changing fast enough.	Courseware not changing fast enough.
6	**Occurrence**	6	5
5	**Potential Causes**	Time constraints of the faculty; fewer faculty involved in the courseware design.	No improvement in the courseware or professor's teaching skills.
4	**Severity**	5	6
3	**Potential Failure Effect**	Students become upset.	Faculty get upset or disappointed.
2	**Potential Failure Mode**	Offer only one courseware and it is not improving (out-of-date).	No or few improvement of interdepartmental ranking.
1	**Critical Parameter (CTPs)**	Improve courseware by offering more diverse options for applying Six Sigma to a degree.	Improvement of interdepartmental ranking of faculty member (i)'s student evaluation scores > 20%.
	Level		

(continued)

TABLE 17.23 FMEA of High-Level CTPs (Continued)

	Notes	Students get started in Six Sigma projects earlier and get correct certification before/at graduation, which helps them in looking for a job, which greatly increases students' and employers' satisfaction level.	Students get started in Six Sigma projects earlier and get correct certification before/at graduation, which helps them in looking for a job, which greatly increases students' and employers' satisfaction level.
16	**R P N**	24	24
#	**Detection**	4	4
#	**Occurrence**	2	2
#	**Severity**	3	3
12	**Action Taken**	01/20/05	01/20/05
11	**Resp. and Target Date**	HSG 05/05/05	HSG 05/05/05
10	**Recommended Action**	Enroll students in the Six Sigma projects as soon as possible.	Enroll students in the Six Sigma projects as soon as possible.
9	**R P N**	180	180
8	**Detection**	6	6
7	**Current Controls**	Students cannot get GB certification before graduation.	Students cannot get BB certification before graduation.
6	**Occurrence**	6	6
5	**Potential Causes**	Employer wants employees educated with Six Sigma GB certificate at hiring.	Employer wants employees educated with Six Sigma BB certificate at hiring.
4	**Severity**	5	5
3	**Potential Failure Effect**	Employer becomes upset.	Employer becomes upset.
2	**Potential Failure Mode**	New employees not trained in Six Sigma management.	New employees not trained in Six Sigma management.
1	**Critical Parameter (CTPs)**	New employees trained with technical MFG GB.	New employees trained with technical MFG BB.
	Level	Employers	

	Notes	Students graduate with Champion certificate and project management skills, which meets employer's requirement.	Students graduate with GB certificate and project management skills, which meets employer's requirement. It increases satisfaction level of both employer and students.
16	**R P N**	18	18
#	**Detection**	3	3
#	**Occurrence**	2	2
#	**Severity**	3	3
12	**Action Taken**	01/20/05	01/20/05
11	**Resp. and Target Date**	HSG 05/05/05	HSG 05/05/05
10	**Recommended Action**	Offer courses on project management skills.	Enroll students in the Six Sigma projects as soon as possible; offer courses on project management skills.
9	**R P N**	180	180
8	**Detection**	6	6
7	**Current Controls**	No project management skills course offered currently.	Students cannot get GB certification before graduation; no project management skills course offered currently.
6	**Occurrence**	6	6
5	**Potential Causes**	Employer wants employees with project management skills at hiring.	Employer wants employees educated with Six Sigma GB certificate and trained with project management skills at hiring.
4	**Severity**	5	5
3	**Potential Failure Effect**	Employer becomes upset.	Employer becomes upset.
2	**Potential Failure Mode**	New employees not trained in project management.	New employees not trained in Six Sigma GB; no project management training either.
1	**Critical Parameter (CTPs)**	New employees trained with Champion certification project management certificate.	New employees trained with technical MFG GB and project management certificate.
	Level	Employers	

(continued)

TABLE 17.23   FMEA of High-Level CTPs (Continued)

	Notes	Students graduate with BB certificate and project management skills, which meets employer's requirement. It increases satisfaction level of both employer and students.
16	**R P N**	24
#	**Detection**	4
#	**Occurrence**	2
#	**Severity**	3
12	**Action Taken**	01/20/05
11	**Resp. and Target Date**	HSG 05/05/05
10	**Recommended Action**	Enroll students in the Six Sigma projects as soon as possible; offer courses on project management skills.
9	**R P N**	180
8	**Detection**	6
7	**Current Controls**	Students cannot get BB certification before graduation; no project management skills course offered currently.
6	**Occurrence**	6
5	**Potential Causes**	Employer wants employees educated with Six Sigma BB certificate and trained with project management skills at hiring.
4	**Severity**	5
3	**Potential Failure Effect**	Employer becomes upset.
2	**Potential Failure Mode**	New employees not trained in Six Sigma BB; no project management training either.
1	**Critical Parameter (CTPs)**	New employees trained with technical MFG BB and project management certificate.
	Level	

Optimizing the Total Life Cycle Cost (TLCC) of the Design

Table 17.24 shows a total life cycle cost (TLCC) analysis of the selected high-level design. The analysis reveals a cost-effective design.

TABLE 17.24 Total Life Cycle Costs

	Direct Costs	**Residual Cost**	**Fixed Costs**	**Variable Cost**
Concept	Project team	-	-	-
Six Sigma Green Belt courseware	$16,000	-	-	-
Prototype	Project team	-	-	-
Six Sigma Green Belt courseware design	$9,000	-	-	-
Production	-	-	Faculty & Admin	Classroom
Six Sigma Green Belt courseware pilot test	-	-	$18,832	0
Field Use	-	-	Faculty & Admin	Classroom
Six Sigma Green Belt courseware adopted in the MBA program	-	-	$36,164	0
Disposal & Environment	-	MAS image	-	-
Consequence of stopping Six Sigma program in the MBA program	-	Priceless	-	-

Concept:	Project team: 2 students *$10/hr *10hr/week * 20 weeks = $4,000
	Faculty: $600/hr * 1hr/week * 20 weeks = $12,000
Prototype:	Project team: 3 students *$10/hr *10hr/week * 10 weeks = $3,000
	Faculty: $600/hr * 10weeks = $6,000
Production:	Faculty salary: 2 courses * $8,666/course = $17,332
	Administrative cost: 3 terms * $500/term = $1,500
	Classroom: 0
Field Use:	Faculty salary: 4 courses * $8,666/course = $34,664
	Administrative cost: 3 terms * $500/term = $1,500
	Classroom: 0

Part 4: Design Model (Develop a High-Level Model for the Design)

The high-level design includes the following elements:

1. Ad for *Quality Progress* magazine (placed every three months).
2. MAS syllabi with Six Sigma applications and case studies using Minitab 14.
3. Project Gantt chart.
4. Client internship form.
5. List of journals.
6. Student satisfaction survey.
7. UM bulletin revision.
8. MAS brochures.

17.5 DESIGN PHASE

Identify the Detailed CTPs Using QFD

The CTPs, and their selected levels, for concept 4 are presented in Table 17.25 by stakeholder segment. Recall, CTPs that must be designed into the MBA specialization in MAS are shown in regular font. *CTPs that are a result of an effective design (yet require action such as advertising, but are not formally part of the design) are shown in italic font.* Column 1 lists the high-level CTPs, and their levels in concept 4, while column 2 lists the detailed CTPs associated with each high-level CTP in column 1.

Table 17.26 shows the QFD matrix constructed from Table 17.25. Also, Table 17.26 shows which detailed CTPs are the most important; see the bottom row for CTPs with weighted averages of 45 or more.

TABLE 17.25 Flow Down of High-Level CTPs to Detailed-Level CTPs

High-Level CTPs with Levels	Detailed CTPs with Levels
Students level	
Increase number of job offers due to Six Sigma Certification ➜ at least three offers.	Place quarterly advertisement in *Quality Progress* magazine listing contact information on each Six Sigma graduate.
Increase starting salary of job offers due to Six Sigma Certification ➜ at least $5,000.	Place quarterly advertisement in *Quality Progress* magazine listing contact information on each Six Sigma graduate.
Increase overall salary due to Six Sigma Certification ➜ at least $10,000.	Place quarterly advertisement in *Quality Progress* magazine listing contact information on each Six Sigma graduate.
Increase "joy in work" due to Six Sigma management ➜ 1 and 5 year student surveys.	Conduct a former student satisfaction survey with occupational preparation and performance.
Acquire paid internships ➜ at least $25/hour.	Place quarterly advertisement in *Quality Progress* magazine announcing students available for internships and salary expectations.
Mandatory statistical software packages course ➜ Minitab14 and SigmaFlow.	Minitab 14 Statistical Software Package. SigmaFlow Simulation Software Package.
Faculty level	
Increase extra pay due to Six Sigma teaching and research ➜ higher than $10,000.	Out of bounds at the current time.
Increase research output due to Six Sigma projects ➜ more than two projects.	Utilize existing Gantt chart tracking system of all Six Sigma projects by faculty member.
Improve international image of MAS department ➜ international placement of students.	Place quarterly advertisement in *Quality Progress* magazine listing contact information on each Six Sigma graduate.
Increase "joy in work" due to Six Sigma management ➜ 1 and 5 year student survey.	Conduct a former student satisfaction survey with occupational preparation and performance.
Increase no. of juried articles published by faculty member (*i*) per year ➜ more than 1 article.	Create a list of Six Sigma friendly journals and develop relationships with the editors. Get MAS faculty on journal's Editorial Review Boards.
Increase % of juried articles published by faculty in "A" journals per year ➜ more than 20% articles.	Create a list of "A" level Six Sigma friendly journals and develop relationships with the editors. Get MAS faculty on journal's Editorial Review Boards.
Improve courseware ➜ standardize syllabi with Six Sigma applications and case studies using Minitab 14.	Standardize syllabi with Six Sigma applications and case studies using Minitab 14.

(continued)

TABLE 17.25   Flow Down of High-Level CTPs to Detailed-Level CTPs (Continued)

High-Level CTPs with Levels	Detailed CTPs with Levels
Faculty Level	
Increase interdepartmental ranking of faculty member (*i*)'s student evaluation scores ➔ higher than 20% improvement.	Place quarterly advertisement in *Quality Progress* magazine listing contact information on each Six Sigma graduate. (Note: Students' view this free advertisement as a positive feature of MBA concentration in MAS.)
Employers level	
New employees trained in Six Sigma management ➔ technical manufacturing green belt or black belt.	*Place quarterly advertisement in* Quality Progress *magazine listing contact information on each Six Sigma graduate.*
New employees trained in project management ➔ champion, green belt, or black belt with project management skills.	*Place quarterly advertisement in* Quality Progress *magazine listing contact information on each Six Sigma graduate.*

TABLE 17.26 QFD Matrix

QFD Matrix With High-Level CTPs and Detailed CTPs			Detailed CTPs with Levels								
			Place quarterly advertisement in _Quality Progress_ magazine listing contact information on each Six Sigma graduate	**_Conduct a former student satisfaction survey with occupational preparation and performance_**	**Place quarterly advertisement in _Quality Progress_ magazine announcing students availability for internships with rates**	**Standardize syllabi with Six Sigma applications and case studies using Minitab 14**	**_Minitab 14 Statistical Software Package_**	**Utilize existing Gantt chart tracking system of all Six Sigma projects by faculty**	**Create a list of Six Sigma friendly journals and develop relationships**	**Create a list of "A" level Six Sigma friendly journals and develop relationships**	**_Out of bounds at the current time_**
High-Level CTPs with Levels	**Students**	Increase no. of job offers due to Six Sigma Certification → at least three offers.	9	0	9	0	0	0	0	0	0
		Increase starting salary of job offers due to Six Sigma Certification → at least $5,000.	9	0	9	0	0	0	0	0	0
		Increase overall salary due to Six Sigma Certification → at least $10,000.	9	0	9	0	0	0	0	0	0
		Increase "joy in work" due to Six Sigma management → 1 and 5 year student surveys.	0	9	0	0	0	0	0	0	0

(continued)

TABLE 17.26   QFD Matrix (Continued)

QFD Matrix With High-Level CTPs and Detailed CTPs			Detailed CTPs with Levels									
			Place quarterly advertisement in *Quality Progress* magazine listing contact information on each Six Sigma graduate	Conduct a former student satisfaction survey with occupational preparation and performance	Place quarterly advertisement in *Quality Progress* magazine announcing students availability for internships with rates	Standardize syllabi with Six Sigma applications and case studies using Minitab 14	*Minitab 14 Statistical Software Package*	Utilize existing Gantt chart tracking system of all Six Sigma projects by faculty	Create a list of Six Sigma friendly journals and develop relationships	Create a list of "A" level Six Sigma friendly journals and develop relationships	*Out of bounds at the current time*
High-Level CTPs with Levels	Students	Acquire paid internships → at least $25/hour.	9	0	9	0	0	0	0	0	0
		Provide technical vs. non-technical course routes → more than one version of a course.	0	0	0	0	0	0	0	0	0
		Mandatory statistical software packages course → Minitab14 and SigmaFlow.	0	0	0	9	9	0	0	0	0
	Faculty	Increase extra pay due to Six Sigma teaching and research → higher than $10,000.	0	0	0	0	0	0	9	9	0

High-Level CTPs with Levels											
Faculty	Increase research output due to Six Sigma projects → more than two projects.	0	0	0	0	0	9	9	9	0
	Improve international image of MAS department → international placement of students.	9	0	9	0	0	0	9	9	0
	Increase "joy in work" due to Six Sigma management → 1–5 year student survey.	0	9	3	0	0	9	9	9	0
	Increase no. of juried articles published by faculty member (i) per year → more than 1 article.	0	0	0	0	0	9	9	9	0
	Increase % of juried articles published by faculty in "A" journals per year → more than 20% articles.	0	0	0	0	0	9	3	9	0
	Improve courseware by standardizing syllabi with Six Sigma applications and case studies using Minitab 14.	0	0	0	9	0	0	0	0	0
	Increase interdepartmental ranking of faculty member (i)'s student evaluation scores → higher than 20% improvement.	9	0	9	0	0	0	9	9	0
Employers	New employees trained in Six Sigma management with a technical manufacturing green belt.	0	0	0	0	9	9	0	0	0
	New employees trained in project management for champion, green belt, and black belt levels.	0	0	0	0	0	0	0	0	0
	TOTALS	54	18	57	18	18	45	57	63	0

Create Operational Definition for Each CTQ and CTP

An operational definition contains three parts: a criterion to be applied to an object or group, a test of the object or group, and a decision as to whether the object or group met the criterion. Table 17.27 shows the operational definitions for each detailed CTP.

TABLE 17.27   Operational Definitions

Operational Definition of the Detailed CTPs	Criteria	Test	Decision
Place quarterly advertisement in *Quality Progress* magazine listing contact information on each Six Sigma graduate. Place quarterly advertisement in *Quality Progress* magazine announcing students availability for internships with rates.	Place an advertisement in *QP* magazine every quarter listing Six Sigma graduates with contact information and a list of students available for paid internships at a rate of $25/hour.	Copy editing for advertisement is received 1 month before publication date of *QP* magazine.	If copy editing is received and acknowledged by UMISQ, then advertisement is acceptable. If copy editing is not received or acknowledged by UMISQ, then advertisement is not acceptable.
Conduct a former student satisfaction survey with occupational preparation and performance.	Develop and distribute survey instrument, deal with nonresponse bias and analyze the survey data, draw conclusions, and change Six Sigma strategy.	Develop a frame of former students. Either census former students or select a random sample of former students.	If sample results indicate positive career impact from the Six Sigma program, then the MBA with a Six Sigma specialization is effective. If sample results do not indicate positive career impact from the Six Sigma program, then the MBA with a Six Sigma specialization is not effective.
Improve courseware by standardizing syllabi with Six Sigma applications and case studies using Minitab 14.	Standardized syllabi exist for MAS 633-MAS639.	Select a particular year.	If standardized syllabi with Six Sigma applications and case studies using Minitab 14 exist for MAS 633-639, the syllabi are acceptable. If standardized syllabi with Six Sigma applications and case studies using Minitab 14 does not exist for MAS 633-639, then the syllabi are not acceptable.

Operational Definition of the Detailed CTPs	Criteria	Test	Decision
Minitab 14 Statistical Software Package.	Determine if Minitab 14 is the statistical software package listed on each MAS elective syllabus.	View each MAS elective syllabus each year.	If each syllabus lists Minitab 14, then the department is using Minitab. If each syllabus does not list Minitab 14, then the department is not using Minitab.
Utilize existing Gantt chart tracking system of all Six Sigma projects by faculty.	Project Gantt chart is updated on a weekly basis.	Select a particular week.	If Gantt chart is updated on a weekly basis, then Gantt chart is being used to track Six Sigma projects. If Gantt chart is not updated on a weekly basis, then Gantt chart is not being used to track Six Sigma projects.
Create a list of Six Sigma friendly journals and develop relationships.	Contact chairs of all SBA departments for a list of journals. Contact journal editors for each listed journal and determine if they are interested in Six sigma articles.	Faculty member sends a Six Sigma article to editor of a Six Sigma friendly journal.	If article is given extra consideration due to Six Sigma content, then the journal is Six Sigma friendly. If article is given no extra consideration due to Six Sigma content, then the journal is not Six Sigma friendly.
Create a list of "A" level Six Sigma friendly journals and develop relationships.	Contact chairs of all SBA departments for a list of "A" journals. Contact "A" journal editors for each listed journal and determine if they are interested in Six sigma articles.	Faculty member sends a Six Sigma article to editor of a Six Sigma friendly "A" journal.	If article is given extra consideration due to Six Sigma content, then the "A" journal is Six Sigma friendly. If article is given no extra consideration due to Six Sigma content, then the "A" journal is not Six Sigma friendly.

Validate the Measurement System for CTQs and CTPs (N/A for the GB project)

Measurement Systems Analyses (MSAs) were not possible for the CTPs because of their present or absent nature.

Establish Baseline Capability for the Detailed Design (N/A for the GB project)

Estimating the baseline capabilities of the CTPs was not possible due to their present or absent nature.

Estimate the Capability of the Detailed Design (N/A for the GB project)

Estimating the capability of the detailed design was not possible because it was not a reality or a simulated model at this point in time.

Estimate the Risks of the Detailed Design

PDT members use FMEA to identify, estimate, prioritize, and reduce the risk of failure of the CTPs in the detailed design through the development of actions (process changes on the Xs) and contingency plans (just-in-case plans based on Xs).

Develop a Detailed Design Scorecard for the Detailed Design

Table 17.28 shows a design scorecard for the selected detailed design.

TABLE 17.28 Design Scorecard for CTPs

The second QFD matrix is used to identify the CTPs from CTQs.					Capability analysis using discrete event simulation is used to predict the performance of the CTPs in the detailed design.			
Scorecard—Part A (Voice of the CTP)					**Scorecard—Part B (Predicted Voice of the CTP)**			
CTP	Target (Nominal)	LSL	USL	Sigma Target	Mean	Standard Deviation	DPMO	Predicted Sigma
Place quarterly advertisement in *Quality Progress* magazine listing contact information on each Six Sigma graduate.	1/qtr	N/A	N/A	N/A	1/qtr	N/A	N/A	N/A
Place quarterly advertisement in *Quality Progress* magazine announcing students availability for internships with rates.	1/qtr	N/A	N/A	N/A	1/qtr	N/A	N/A	N/A

The second QFD matrix is used to identify the CTPs from CTQs.					Capability analysis using discrete event simulation is used to predict the performance of the CTPs in the detailed design.			
Scorecard—Part A (Voice of the CTP)					**Scorecard—Part B** (Predicted Voice of the CTP)			
CTP	Target (Nominal)	LSL	USL	Sigma Target	Mean	Standard Deviation	DPMO	Predicted Sigma
Conduct a former student satis-faction survey with occupa-tional preparation and performance.	5/yr	N/A	N/A	N/A	5/yr	N/A	N/A	N/A
Standardize syllabi with Six Sigma applications and case studies using Minitab 14.	2 versions per course				2 versions per course			
Minitab 14 Statistical Soft-ware Package.	All rele-vant courses	N/A	N/A	N/A	All rele-vant courses	N/A	N/A	N/A
Utilize existing Gantt chart tracking system of all Six Sigma projects by faculty.	1/wk	N/A	N/A	N/A	1/wk	N/A	N/A	N/A
Create a list of Six Sigma-friendly journals and develop relationships.	3/yr	N/A	N/A	N/A	3/yr	N/A	N/A	N/A
Create a list of "A" level Six Sigma-friendly journals and develop relationships.	3/yr	N/A	N/A	N/A	3/yr	N/A	N/A	N/A

Conduct an Accounting Analysis of the Detailed Design

An accounting analysis of the detailed design revealed a profitable new specialization for the MAS department (see Table 17.29).

TABLE 17.29   Accounting Analysis

	Accounting Analysis	

(With 30 students enrolled in the Six Sigma Concentration in the MBA program each semester, 4 courses are required frfor the GB project)

		Notes:
Sales Revenue	$240,000	8 credits with $1,000 per credit → 4 courses
Less: Costs of Goods Sold		
Faculty Salary	34,664	4 courses with $8,666 per course
Gross Profit	205	
Less: Operating Expenses		
Administrative Expenses	1,500	3 terms with $500 per term
Income Before Income Taxes	203,836	
Less: Income Tax Expense	57,074	Tax rate at 28%
Net Income	$148,762	

Mistake-Proof the Detailed Design

An FMEA of the detailed design is presented in Table 17.30.

TABLE 17.30   FMEA of the Detailed Design

1	2	3	4	5	6	7	8	9	10	11	12	13	14	15	16
Critical Parameter	Potential Failure Mode	Potential Failure Effect	Severity	Potential Causes	Occurrence	Current Controls	Detection	RPN	Recommend. Action	Responsibility and Target Date	Action Taken	Severity	Occurrence	Detection	RPN
Place quarterly advertisement in *Quality Progress* magazine listing contact information on each Six Sigma graduate.	Ad not placed in QP on time for publication.	Six Sigma grads don't receive job offers.	10	Lack of attention	5	None	1	50	MAS secretary uses recurrence feature in the departmental Microsoft calendar.	8/05	Yes	10	1	1	10
Place quarterly advertisement in *Quality Progress* magazine announcing students availability for internships with rates.	Ad not placed in QP on time for publication.	Six Sigma grads don't receive job offers.	10	Lack of attention.	5	None	1	50	MAS secretary uses recurrence feature in the departmental Microsoft calendar.	8/05	Yes	10	1	1	10

1	2	3	4	5	6	7	8	9	10	11	12	13	14	15	16
Critical Parameter	Potential Failure Mode	Potential Failure Effect	Severity	Potential Causes	Occurrence	Current Controls	Detection	RPN	Recommend. Action	Responsibility and Target Date	Action Taken	Severity	Occurrence	Detection	RPN
Conduct a former student satisfaction survey with occupational preparation and performance.	Negative response from the former student survey.	Faculty get upset.	7	Courseware not designed to the employment trends.	5	None	1	35	Conduct former student satisfaction survey and get feedback	8/05	Yes	3	1	1	3
Standardize syllabi with Six Sigma applications and case studies using Minitab 14.	Minitab 14 not in use for MAS633-639.	Students no knowledge of Minitab 14.	7	Not included in the courseware design.	5	Minitab is used in courseware, but not heavily used.	1	35	Involve Minitab 14 in every chapter study.	8/05	Yes	2	1	1	2
Minitab 14 Statistical Software Package.	Minitab 14 not used in the courseware.	Students no knowledge of Minitab 14.	7	Not included in the courseware design.	5	Minitab is used in courseware, but not heavily used.	1	35	Involve Minitab 14 in every chapter study.	8/05	Yes	2	1	1	2
Utilize existing Gantt chart tracking system of all Six Sigma projects by faculty.	Gantt chart not updated weekly.	Six Sigma projects not done on schedule.	7	Lack of commitment from process owners.	6	Gantt chart is reviewed on a weekly basis.	2	84	Train process owners Six Sigma knowledge and management skills.	8/05	Yes	2	1	1	2
Create a list of Six Sigma friendly journals and develop relationships.	No extra consideration for Six Sigma content articles.	Faculty get upset and less involved in the Six Sigma projects.	7	Lack of attention.	5	None	1	35	MAS secretary creates the list and develops relationships.	8/05	Yes	2	1	1	2
Create a list of "A" level Six Sigma friendly journals and develop relationships.	No extra consideration for Six Sigma content articles.	Faculty get upset and less involved in the Six Sigma projects.	7	Lack of attention.	5	None	1	35	MAS secretary creates the list and develops relationships.	8/05	Yes	2	1	1	2
				Before RPN =							After RPN =				

Conduct a Tollgate Review of the Design Phase

The Design Phase tollgate review was successfully completed.

TABLE 17.31 Partial Control and Verification Plan

Documentation of the Detailed Design	List of CTPs	Targets (Nominal Values) for CTPs	USL for CTPs	LSL for CTPs	Sampling Plan for CTPs	Data Analysis Plan for CTPs	Actions for CTPs	
							Short Term	Long Term
Place quarterly advertisement in *Quality Progress* magazine listing contact information on each Six Sigma graduate and announcing students availability for internships with rates. (See advertisement.) Note: ads are paid for by internship program.	Place quarterly advertisement in *Quality Progress* magazine listing contact information on each Six Sigma graduate.	1/qtr	Not relevant					
	Place quarterly advertisement in *Quality Progress* magazine announcing students availability for internships with rates.	1/qtr	Not relevant					
See student satisfaction survey with sampling and analysis plan	*Conduct a former student satisfaction survey with occupational preparation and performance.*	5/yr	Not relevant					
	Standardize syllabi with Six Sigma applications and case studies using Minitab 14.	Flow up is accomplished by setting course dates for topics to ensure that all topics can be covered in the semester (see example for MAS 636); for MAS 635, MAS 636, MAS 637 and MAS 638, see the example for MAS 636 on pages 619-622.						
See syllabi with Minitab 14 as statistical software package	*Minitab 14 Statistical Software Package.*	Two versions per course	Not relevant					

Documentation of the Detailed Design	List of CTPs	Targets (Nominal Values) for CTPs	USL for CTPs	LSL for CTPs	Sampling Plan for CTPs	Data Analysis Plan for CTPs	Actions for CTPs	
							Short Term	Long Term
See Gantt chart and internship form for corporate clients specifying fees.	Utilize existing Gantt chart tracking system of all Six Sigma projects by faculty.	1/week	Not relevant					
See list of Six Sigma friendly journals with tickler file for updating every three years.	Create a list of Six Sigma friendly journals and develop relationships.	3/yr	Not relevant					
	Create a list of "A" level Six Sigma friendly journals and develop relationships.	3/yr	Not relevant					

Prepare a Control and Verification Plan

A control and verification plan for the detailed design is presented in Table 17.31.

For example, MAS 636: Statistical Process Control and Reliability is a two-credit course that is taught in 24 classroom contact hours. The 24 hours must be flowed up from the topic modules such that the sum of the topic modules does not exceed 24 hours. This is accomplished as follows:

> Assume the 24-hour upper specification limit (high-level CTP) is flowed up from the topic modules (detailed CTPs). It is important to realize that 24 hours is an upper specification limit (USL), not a desired nominal level. Consequently, it is wise to set the average less than 24 hours and fill in more examples to attain the 24 hour objective without going over. The nominal time allocations for the course modules are as follows:

Topics:
Introduction   (2 hours)
Review of Basic Probability and Statistics   (2 hours)
Introduction to Control Charts   (1 hour)
Attribute Control Charts   (2 hours)

(continued)

Variables Control Charts	(3 hours)
Out of Control Patterns	(1 hour)
Diagnosing a Process	(8 hours)
Process Capability and Improvement Studies	(2 hours)
Reliability	(3 hours)

Because Overall Delivery Time for the Course = Introduction + Review of probability and Statistics + ⋯ + Reliability, the transfer functions for the flow-down mean and standard deviation are:

$$M_{Overall} = f(M_{Introduction}, M_{Review\ of\ Probability\ and\ Statistics}, \ldots, M_{Reliability})$$

$$= M_{Introduction} + M_{Review\ of\ Probability\ and\ Statistics} + \cdots + M_{Reliability}$$

$$S_{Overall} = \sqrt{(Variance_{Introduction} + \cdots + Variance_{Reliability})}$$

In this example, for the purpose of simplicity, team members assumed equal variances for the time to complete each topic module. Normally, team members would not assume equal variances for the cycle time data for each topic module. The reader should realize that it is very common for time data with large means to have large variances, and time data with small means to have smaller variances.

In any event, given the preceding assumption:

$$Variance_{Introduction} = Variance_{Review\ of\ Probability\ and\ Statistics} = \cdots = Variance_{Reliability}, \text{ therefore,}$$

Overall Process Variance $= 9 * Variance_{Introduction}$

Because the USL is 24 hours, team members choose a nominal value for the length of each topic module based on the variations in each module, so that the entire course time is less than 24 hours. Additionally, team members want to design the total course time at a Six Sigma level; that is, time for the entire course does not surpass 24 hours more than 3.4 times per million.

As a point of interest, team members explained the variation in total class time (CTQ) from semester to semester by considering differences in instructors, differences between students, logistics and classroom environment, unforeseen events (e.g., school shutdown due to natural events [weather] or fire alarms), or time of day.

If the team members designed each topic module to be at their nominal values, with the total equaling 24 hours, it implies that 50% of the course offerings would exceed 24 hours. Team members assumed all courses are independent of each other; that is, the instructors do not review what other instructors actually covered or did not cover in previous course modules because they assume the course syllabus was completed. If team members establish a plus or minus 1 hour tolerance around 24 hours—that is, 23 to 25 hours—then $6*S_{ST} = 1$ hour at the Six Sigma level of performance for the course time. Because $S^2_{ST} = 9* Variance_{Introduction}$ (assuming the variances are the same for each topic module), then

$$S_{ST} = \sqrt{(9 * Variance_{Introduction})} = 3 * S_{Introduction}$$

Therefore, $6*S_{ST} = 1$ hour $= 6(3*S_{Introduction}) = 18*S_{Introduction}$, which implies that we need $S_{Introduction} = 1/18$ hour $\equiv .056$ hour $= 3.33$ minutes. This also implies that $S_{ST} = 1/6$ hour. However, this option would exceed the 24-hour time constraint on the length of the course 50% of the time.

If team members do not wish to exceed 24 hours, at a Six Sigma rate of performance, then they need to set the nominal level for the entire course time at, say, 1 hour less than 24 hours, or 23 hours. To accomplish this, team members design each module to produce a standard deviation of no more than 3.33 minutes per topic module. Therefore, each step in all topic modules should have a distribution to completion with an average of the hours listed previously and a standard deviation of 3.33 minutes per course. The overall cycle time for MAS 636 is a serial process; hence, the Introduction must be completed before the Review of Probability and Statistics, etc. Consequently, Overall Cycle Time for MAS 636, as listed below will have a mean of 24 hours with a standard deviation of 9.5 minutes ($\sqrt{9*3.333^2} = \sqrt{90} \cong 9.5$).

Design trade-offs must be made among the topic modules to achieve the design and/or budgetary targets for all CTQs and high-level CTPs. Design trade-offs answer the question: Can flow-down targets and tolerances achieve higher-level targets and tolerances? For example, suppose PD team members determined that the means for each topic module are:

Introduction	(2 hours)
Review of Basic Probability and Statistics	(2 hours)
Introduction to Control Charts	(1 hour)
Attribute Control Charts	(2 hours)
Variables Control Charts	(3 hours)
Out of Control Patterns	(1 hour)
Diagnosing a Process	(8 hours)
Process Capability and Improvement Studies	(2 hours)
Reliability	(3 hours)

Team members must determine if the course modules meet the specifications for the Overall Course Cycle Time (CTQ). In other words, do all nine steps flow-up to the requirements of Overall Cycle Time for MAS 636?

The mean for the Overall Cycle Time for MAS 636 is as follows:

$$M_{Overall} = M_{Introduction} + \cdots + M_{Reliability} = 23 \text{ hours}$$

If the standard deviation of each module is less than 3.33 minutes, say 2 minutes, then the overall average time can be moved close to 24 hours, say 23 hours and 24 minutes as the overall standard deviation would be 6 minutes, so 6 standard deviations to the limit of 24 hours is 36 minutes.

This meets the flow-up target (nominal value) for the Overall Cycle Time for the Design Delivery process mean.

Suppose you learn that another version of MAS 636 was designed and *Variance*$_{Introduction}$ was found to be 16 hours^2, an absurdly high number. What would that imply for the overall cycle time standard deviation if the other version's modules had similar variances? You compute the standard deviation for Overall Cycle Time for MAS 636 as follows:

$$S_{Overall} = \sqrt{(9*16 \text{ hours}^2)} = \sqrt{(144 \text{ hours}^2)} = 12 \text{ hours}$$

In this case, the detailed CTP tolerances did not flow up because 12 hours is much greater than 1/6 hours. Thus, PD team members may have to make process improvements to reduce the variation in how the courses are designed and presented to reduce the inconsistency in coverage time as evidenced by the variation. Of course, you have the option to decide upon trade-offs between flow-down targets and/or tolerances.

The preceding flow-up analysis lead the PD team to realize that if the sum of the mean times for all course modules in each course is 24 hours, then any variation would cause a violation of the flow-up USL of 24 hours. Consequently, PD team members decided to redesign each course module to consist of 50% lecture material and 50% unstructured material, such as questions and answers or workshops, thereby creating flexibility in module means to allow for variation. In this redesigned model, the Overall Cycle Time for MAS 636 is computed as follows:

$$M_{Overall} = M_{Introduction} + \cdots + M_{Reliability} = 12.0 \text{ hours using only the lecture component of each}$$
module. This meets the flow-up target (nominal value) for the Overall Cycle Time for MAS 636 of 12 hours.

Further, suppose team members are able to cut the standard deviation for each module by a factor of 100 by using the following process improvements: [a] deliver of topic modules with large cycle time standard deviations through e-learning, thereby eliminating much of the variation created by face-to-face instruction, and [b] combine topic modules to reduce the number of components of a course, thereby reducing the variation caused by the addition of independent components. Given the preceding changes to MAS 636, PD team members computed the standard deviation for Overall Cycle Time for MAS 636 as follows:

$$S_{Overall} = 0.12 \text{ hours. (Note: 0.12 hours is 1% of 12 hours, or a 100 fold reduction in}$$
standard deviation.)

In this case, the detailed CTP tolerances did flow up because 0.12 hours < 1/6 hours for the overall course.

17.6 Verify/Validate Phase

Build a Prototype of the Detailed Design

1. **Ad for *Quality Progress* magazine (placed every 3 months; see Table 17.32).**

    The University of Miami is proud to announce that the following MBA students have graduated with Six Sigma certifications. If you are interested in contacting any of our students, please call the Ziff Placement Center at 305 284-6905.

TABLE 17.32 Ad for *Quality Progress* Magazine

Certification Level for January – July 2005	Names	Languages Spoken in Addition to English
Green Belt		
Black Belt		
Master Black Belt		

The Green Belt, Black Belt, and Master Black Belt certifications require Six Sigma project work. Our students are available for internships at various times of year for locations around the globe. Some examples of organizations that have hosted internships include: Johnson & Johnson, General Electric, Boca Raton Community Hospital, Jackson Memorial Hospital, Bascom Palmer Eye Hospital, Florida Power & Light Corporation, University of Miami, University of Cincinnati, City of Coral Gables, and the United States Marine Corp. As of 2006, the University charges $50 per hour, plus expenses, for student internships and a University of Miami Master Black Belt supervision fee of $600 per hour or $250 per hour depending on the seniority of the faculty member.

2. **MAS 633-MAS 639 syllabi with Six Sigma applications and case studies.**

   Integrated syllabi have been developed for all of the academic courses that support Six Sigma education and certification. All courses integrate Six Sigma theory, tools, and methods into their topics, exams, papers, and workshops. Additionally, all courses utilize the Minitab 14 statistical software package. The courses are as follows:

   MAS 633: Introduction to Quality Management—Participants in this course will be introduced to the major elements of Dr. Deming's theory of management, as well as Six Sigma theory, tools, and methods. These tools and methods have been adopted with great success by many of the largest organizations in the world; for example, General Electric, Allied Signal, Dupont, American Express, and J.P. Morgan, to name a few. Additionally, the course is a prerequisite for the Six Sigma Champion and Green Belt certification examinations.

   MAS 634: Administrative Systems for Quality Management—This course presents a model to pursue Quality Management that features the administrative systems and structures necessary for Six Sigma management. The administrative systems and structures presented in this course are required to sit for the Six Sigma management Champion and Green Belt certification examination.

   MAS 635: Design of Experiments for Business Decision Making—This course presents the tools and methods for conducting experiments, including an overall approach to obtaining and analyzing experimental data, the advantages of using structured multifactor experiments to screen for important factors, ways of minimizing the number of data points needed to obtain desired information, and how to identify values of experimental factors that optimize the value of measured responses. Factorial designs, fractional factorial designs, screening designs, and response surface designs will be presented. Emphasis will be on the knowledge required for proper application of these methods through many examples in business and quality management.

MAS 636: Statistical Process Control and Reliability for Business Decision Making—This course introduces the fundamental concepts of statistical process control and reliability in the context of Quality Management. The course focuses on control charts and other process improvement tools, including several tools and techniques of reliability theory. All the tools and techniques discussed are used by Quality Management systems such as Total Quality Management (TQM) and Six Sigma Management (6σ) to monitor and improve processes in service and manufacturing organizations, educational institutions, governments, and healthcare organizations. Many real-life case studies will be examined to enhance the student's learning experience. MAS 636 is required to sit for a Six Sigma Green Belt certification.

MAS 637: Applied Regression Analysis and Forecasting—This course aims to familiarize the student with statistical prediction. It covers simple and multiple regression methods, as well as time series and forecasting models in business. Instead of theoretical development, the course emphasizes the application of these methods in business systems analysis and improvement. MAS 637 is required to sit for Six Sigma Black Belt certification.

MAS 638: Management Science Consulting—The purpose of this course is to enhance students' consulting skills in management science. In addition to skills of modeling and choosing appropriate tools for analysis, these include the communication skills of presenting quantitative and analytical material in business settings. The course is structured around a set of case studies that are based on real applications of management science models and methods discussed in Basic Statistics (MAS 631), Operations Research, (MAS 632), and MAS 633. Several of the case studies are related to Six Sigma management. MAS 638 is required to sit for Six Sigma Black Belt certification.

3. **Gantt chart.**

   A Gantt chart is used to monitor progress of all Six Sigma projects. Notes are inserted into the Gantt chart indicating activities to be completed or revised for the next weekly meeting for each project. More advanced students are encouraged to mentor less senior students.

4. **Client internship form.**

   A letter of understanding between the MBA Six Sigma internship program, the student intern, the supervising faculty member, and the client is used to clarify all expectations for an internship. The items addressed in the letter are: corporate contact information, corporate GB/BB/MBB supervisor, corporate project champion, corporate process owner, university MBB supervisor, name of project, description of project, roles and responsibilities for MBA intern, deliverables from the project, time frame for project, fees and charges, and terms and conditions, such as interns will be constantly supervised by University MBB, interns will regularly present the progress of the project to Corporate Project Champion, interns will work for 20 hr/week, interns will fill out the time sheet for the number of hours they have worked, and payments will be made on bi-weekly basis.

5. **Sample list of Six Sigma-friendly journals.**

    A list of Six Sigma-friendly journals should be developed and submitted to faculty. This will help direct their Six Sigma research efforts. The journals listed are a function of what each department and college considers acceptable outlets for publications.

6. **Student satisfaction survey.**

    An "Alumni Satisfaction Survey for MBAs Specializing in Six Sigma Management" was developed to determine the success of the Six Sigma specialization in the MBA program. The survey includes the following questions: (1) When did you receive your MBA?; (2) In your opinion, did your Six Sigma certification increase the number of job offers you received upon graduation from the MBA program? (Yes or No); (3) If yes, did your Six Sigma certification help you obtain a higher starting salary than you would have received without it? (Yes or No); (4) If yes, how much higher in dollars? ($_____); (5) Is your current job related to Six Sigma management? (Yes or No); (6) If yes, please explain how?; (7) What is your current job title?; (8) What is your current yearly compensation including bonuses?; (9) What MBA subject matter is most helpful to your current position?

7. **UM bulletin.**

    Please go to `www.miami.edu/umbulletin/grad/bus/man.htm` for the text of the university bulletin relevant to the Management Science department.

8. **MAS brochures.**

    The Management Science department has a brochure that explains its three tracks: (1) Six Sigma management, (2) Applied Statistics, and (3) Applied Operations Research.

Pilot Test the Prototype of the Detailed Design

PDT members prepared a plan for a pilot test of the new design for a sample of experts and MBA students. All individuals surveyed were delighted with the new design for the MBA specialization in MAS.

Conduct Design Reviews Using Design Scorecards

PDT members conduct a design review for the CTQs of the new design using a design scorecard (see Table 17.33).

TABLE 17.33   Selected Portions of the Design Scorecard for CTPs

The second QFD matrix is used to identify the CTPs from CTQs.					Guesstimated performance of the CTPs in the detailed design.				
Scorecard—Part A (Voice of the CTP)					Scorecard—Part B (Predicted Voice of the CTP)				
CTP	Target (Nominal)	LSL	USL	Sigma Target	Mean	Std Dev	DPMO	Predicted Sigma
Place quarterly advertisement in *Quality Progress* magazine listing contact information on each Six Sigma graduate.	1/qtr	Not relevant						
Place quarterly advertisement in *Quality Progress* magazine announcing students availability for internships with rates.	1/qtr	Not relevant						
Conduct a former student satisfaction survey with occupational preparation and performance.	5/yr	Not relevant						
Standardize syllabi with Six Sigma applications and case studies using Minitab 14.	2 versions per course	Not relevant						
Use 50% lecture and 50% unstructured format with Power Point slides for all MAS 633 course modules.	12	12 − 3 (0.12) = 11.64	12 + 3 (0.12) = 12.36	6	12	0.12 hour	3.4	6
Use 50% lecture and 50% unstructured format with Power Point slides for all MAS 634 course modules.	12	12 − 3 (0.12) = 11.64	12 + 3 (0.12) = 12.36	6	12	0.12 hour	3.4	6
Use 50% lecture and 50% unstructured format with Power Point slides for all MAS 635 course modules.	12	12 − 3 (0.12) = 11.64	12 + 3 (0.12) = 12.36	6	12	0.12 hour	3.4	6

The second QFD matrix is used to identify the CTPs from CTQs.					Guesstimated performance of the CTPs in the detailed design.			
Scorecard—Part A (Voice of the CTP)					**Scorecard—Part B (Predicted Voice of the CTP)**			
CTP	**Target (Nominal)**	**LSL**	**USL**	**Sigma Target**	**Mean**	**Std Dev**	**DPMO**	**Predicted Sigma**
Use 50% lecture and 50% unstructured format with Power Point slides for all MAS 636 course modules.	12	12 – 3 (0.12) = 11.64	12 + 3 (0.12) = 12.36	6	12	0.12 hour	3.4	6
Use 50% lecture and 50% unstructured format with Power Point slides for all MAS 637 course modules.	12	12 – 3 (0.12) = 11.64	12 + 3 (0.12) = 12.36	6	12	0.12 hour	3.4	6
Use 50% lecture and 50% unstructured format with Power Point slides for all MAS 638 course modules.	12	12 – 3 (0.12) = 11.64	12 + 3 (0.12) = 12.36	6	12	0.12 hour	3.4	6
Minitab 14 Statistical Software Package.	All relevant courses	Not relevant						
Utilize existing Gantt chart tracking system of all Six Sigma projects by faculty.	1/wk	Not relevant						
Create a list of Six Sigma-friendly journals and develop relation-ships.	3/yr	Not relevant						
Create a list of "A" level Six Sigma friendly jour-nals and develop rela-tionships.	3/yr	Not relevant						

Part A presents the Voice of the Customer for selected detailed CTPs. The detailed CTPs listed in Part A are frequently an output of the second QFD matrix discussed on pages 609-611. The Voice of the Customer for each detailed CTP includes the nominal value, the upper and/or lower specification limit(s), and a flow-down process sigma target. Part B of the design scorecard presents the guesstimated statistics for each detailed CTP; that is, the mean, standard deviation, DPMO (using the USL and LSL), and the predicted process sigma for the detailed design.

Decide Whether or Not to Scale-Up Design

After the design review has been conducted and the design scorecards have been prepared, PD team members made a GO (scale-up the design to full-scale production of products or delivery of services) decision.

Build and Operate Full-Scale Process

Done.

Decide if Full-Scale Process Is Meeting Business Objectives

One of the final tasks of the PD team is to study the dashboard associated with the new design; that is, are key objectives, as measured by their key indicators, being met in full-scale production of the product or delivery of the service. There are four aspects of the design that must be considered when evaluating its contribution to an organization, as follows:

- Financial objectives and indicators.   (Yes)
- Process objectives and indicators.   (Yes)
- Customer objectives and indicators.   (Yes)
- Employee objectives and indicators.   (Yes)

Document the Full-Scale Process

See the prototype of full-scale design discussed previously.

Transition Full-Scale Process to Owners with a Control Plan

PDT members create a list of questions they must answer to ensure a smooth transition of the new design to the Operations and Marketing departments. The list should address the following issues:

- Has the design been successfully pilot tested by PDT members?   (Yes)
- Is the full-scale process up and running?   (Yes)

- Does the full-scale process have a functioning control plan? (Yes)
- Has the full-scale system been documented? (Yes)
- Has all training been conducted for process stakeholders? (Yes)
- Does the full-scale process result in the desired business objectives? (Yes)
- Will the outputs of the full-scale process satisfy (delight) stakeholders? (Yes)
- Have process owners bought into the next generation of the MGPP? (Yes)

Because the answers to all the preceding questions are yes, then the full-scale version of the design is ready to be transferred to its process owners.

Close the DMADV Project

PD team members closed the DMADV project on time and within budget.

Transfer the Lessons Learned from the Project

This paper was made available to all relevant University of Miami personnel.

SUMMARY

This chapter presented a DMADV case study. It presented the launch of a very successful academic Six Sigma green belt training and certification program.

PART V

DESIGN FOR SIX SIGMA CERTIFICATION

CHAPTER 18 DFSS CHAMPION AND GREEN BELT CERTIFICATION AT THE UNIVERSITY OF MIAMI

DFSS CHAMPION AND GREEN BELT CERTIFICATION AT THE UNIVERSITY OF MIAMI

SECTIONS

LEARNING OBJECTIVES

After reading this chapter, you will be able to:

* Understand the procedure for obtaining Design for Six Sigma champion and green belt training and certification at the University of Miami.
* Be able to study sample questions and answers for the DFSS champion and green belt examination.

INTRODUCTION

At this point, you are probably interested in becoming certified as a Design for Six Sigma champion or Design for Six Sigma green belt. This chapter provides information on one course of action that you can follow to attain Design for Six Sigma champion or green belt certification.

18.1 CERTIFICATION AT THE UNIVERSITY OF MIAMI

You can obtain Design for Six Sigma certification through a few certificate programs given by universities and many other organizations. This chapter details the certification program at the University of Miami, the one that the authors are most familiar with.

The Department of Management Science, the Institute for the Study of Quality, and the McLamore Executive Education Center, all of the University of Miami, jointly offer Six Sigma education, training, and certification. The objective of the University of Miami is to provide a comprehensive, fair, and independent source for academically based Six Sigma education and training, certification examinations, dossier reviews, and ultimately, Six Sigma certifications. You can obtain information about Six Sigma programs at the University of Miami by contacting Vanessa Ferguson at `vferguson@miami.edu`.

There are three types of Design for Six Sigma certifications offered through the University of Miami:

- DFSS champion
- DFSS yellow belt
- DFSS green belt

The University of Miami does not offer DFSS black belt certification at the current time. However, it is expected that this certification will be offered in the future.

A **champion** is an individual who wishes to become aware of the theory and practice of Design for Six Sigma project teams, while being able to adequately review projects, remove impediments, and secure adequate resources and support. A **yellow belt** is an individual who is aware of the theory and practice of Design for Six Sigma and can provide support to team members (for example, data collection), but is not sufficiently trained in statistical methods to perform the duties of a Six Sigma team member. A yellow belt has passed the Design for Six Sigma champion and green belt certification examinations, but has not completed a Design for Six Sigma project. A **green belt** is an individual who understands statistical methods and is a member of one or more Design for Six Sigma teams. She or he is not sufficiently trained to lead a complex Design for Six Sigma team, but is trained to lead a simple Design for Six Sigma project. A green belt has passed the Design for Six Sigma champion and yellow/green belt certification examinations and has completed at least one Design for Six Sigma project.

You need to be aware that champion, yellow belt, and green belt do not specify hierarchy on the organizational charts. A senior executive might do well to be Design for Six Sigma yellow or green belt certified. In fact, this would be a good goal for all executives, and have Design for Six Sigma black belts, master black belts, and/or champions reporting to them. This chapter is concerned with Design for Six Sigma champion and yellow/green belt certification.

18.2 DFSS CERTIFICATION EXAMINATIONS

Certification examinations are offered for Design for Six Sigma champion and yellow/green belt to interested individuals and organizations at secure remote locations. You will have to work with University of Miami personnel to find an approved secure location for your examination; for example, a local university or high school. These examinations are open to anyone wishing certification.

It is strongly suggested that you study Chapters 1 through 8 and Chapters 17 and 18 (only questions for champion examination) in this book before sitting for the DFSS champion certification examination, and all the chapters before sitting for the DFSS yellow/green belt certification examination. A laptop computer with Minitab 14 or JMP 6 statistical software packages and Microsoft Word is required to sit for the DFSS yellow/green belt certification examination.

All participants are expected to score 100% on a certification examination. A passing grade of 80% is required on the first pass of the examination to take a follow-up examination covering only the parts of the first examination that were answered incorrectly. If a participant fails to achieve a grade of 80% or better on the first pass, or fails to attain a grade of 100% on the second pass, then he or she is required to begin the certification process from the beginning, and incur all costs.

All persons interested in sitting for the DFSS yellow/green belt examination must first pass the Six Sigma champion examination at the University of Miami. A DFSS green belt is awarded after passing the DFSS green belt certification examination and successfully completing a DFSS Six Sigma project.

18.3 COSTS FOR DFSS CERTIFICATION EXAMINATIONS

The cost in 2005 (subject to change) for sitting for the champion examination is $3,000 per examination. This cost includes all materials. The cost for sitting for the DFSS yellow/green belt examination is an additional $1,500 per examination. Sitting for the green belt examination requires that you have already passed the champion examination.

18.4 APPLICATION PROCESS

The University of Miami actively seeks participants who demonstrate seriousness of educational purpose. Admission is selective, and is offered to those applicants whose credentials are academically sound and whose work experience reflects interest in Six Sigma management.

To receive a complete application packet, contact: Vanessa Ferguson, Department of Management Science, School of Business Administration, University of Miami, Coral Gables, FL, 33124 (305-284-6595) or send email to `vferguson@miami.edu`.

18.5 SAMPLE DFSS CERTIFICATION EXAMINATION REVIEW QUESTIONS WITH ANSWERS

The following questions pertain to the champion certification examination.

QUESTION: Explain the origin of 3.4 DPMO. Draw a picture using normal distributions and specification limits.

Answer: If a process generates output that is stable, normally distributed, and centered on the nominal value that occupies only one half the distance allowed by specifications (see center normal distribution), then the process will produce only 2 defective parts per billion opportunities. If the process mean drifts 1.5 standard deviations in either direction for the above process (see the normal distributions on the right and the left), then the process will produce 3.4 defects per million opportunities at the closest specification limit; see Figure 18.1.

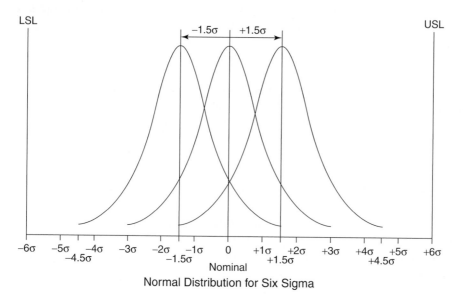

FIGURE 18.1 Technical Definition of 3.4 DPMO

QUESTION: A service has 10 steps and each step has only one defect opportunity. If the DPMO is 2,700 for each step, then what is Rolled Throughput Yield of the final service? What is the process sigma for the final service?

Answer: Yield at each step = 0.9973, RTY = (0.9973)^{10} = 0.973326, DPO = 1 – RTY = 0.026674, DPMO = 26,674, Process sigma = between 3.4 and 3.5.

QUESTION: Define special causes of variation. Who is responsible for a special cause of variation?

Answer: Special causes of variation are due to factors that are external to the system. Workers and engineers on the line are initially responsible for finding and correcting special causes of variation.

QUESTION: Define common causes of variation. Give a few examples. Who is responsible for common causes of variation?

Answer: Common causes of variation are due to the system itself. Examples include: hiring, training, and supervisory practices, management style, and stress level. Management is responsible for common causes of variation because they are responsible for the system. The system defines common variation.

QUESTION: Explain the Taguchi Loss Function view of quality. Draw a picture.

Answer: Dr. Genichi Taguchi developed the continuous improvement view of quality when he invented the Taguchi Loss Function. The Taguchi Loss Function explains that losses begin to accrue as soon as a product or service deviates from nominal. Under his Loss Function, the never-ending reduction of process variation around nominal without capital investment makes sense.

Losses incurred from unit-to-unit variation before process improvement (see distribution A in Figure 18.2) is greater than the losses incurred from unit-to-unit variation after process improvement (see distribution B in Figure 18.2). As shown in Figure 18.2, the Taguchi Loss Function promotes the continual reduction of variation of the output of a process around the nominal value, absent capital investment.

QUESTION: Explain the origin of the 1.5 sigma shift on the process mean to the definition of Six Sigma management.

Answer: Through experience, managers have discovered that it is typical for process variation to increase over time. This variation increase has been shown to be similar to a process mean that shifts between 1 and 2 sigma over time. Hence, 1.5 sigma has been established as an industrial standard for describing typical process shift.

QUESTION: Explain how the DMADV model promotes Six Sigma management.

Answer: The DMADV model is a roadmap for innovating a product, service, or process. It is used to determine the major new features of existing products, services, or processes, or entirely products, services, or processes to surpass the needs and wants of customers in the future. In a limited sense, DMAIC is concerned with today and DMADV is concerned with tomorrow.

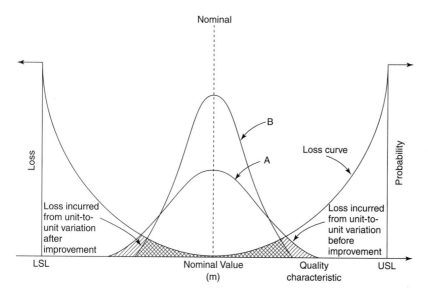

The Taguchi Loss Function

FIGURE 18.2   Taguchi Loss Function

QUESTION: Construct a dashboard explaining the relationship between the mission statement and Six Sigma projects. Make sure you include objectives and indicators in your answer. Insert an example into your dashboard.

Answer: See Table 18.1.

QUESTION: Construct a table that shows how to prioritize potential Strategic Six Sigma projects based on their relationships with business objectives. Explain how the table functions to accomplish its aim.

Answer: See Table 18.2.

- W_is are developed by the Finance Department. The sum of W_i = 1.0.
- Cell values are determined by team members with the strong guidance of the finance department (1 = weak, 2 = moderate, 3 = strong).

The weighted averages that are shown in the last row are ranked from smallest to largest. The largest average is considered the highest priority project (1 = weak, 2 = moderate, 3 = strong).

TABLE 18.1 Six Sigma Dashboard

Mission: To be A, B, and C						
President		Vice Presidents (V.P.)		Direct Reports (D.R.)		
Business Objectives	Business Indicators	V.P. Business Objectives	V.P. Business Indicators	D.R. Business Objectives	D.R. Business Indicators	DMAIC DMADV Projects
A	A1	A11	A111			
	A2	A21	A211			
			A212			
		A22	A221			
B	B1					
C = Increase World-Wide Sales	C1= $ World-Wide Sales by Month	Increase Latin American Sales	$ Latin American Sales by Month	Increase Peruvian Sales	$ Peruvian Sales by Month	DFSS New Service Projects

TABLE 18.2 Six Sigma Project Prioritization Matrix

				Six Sigma Project			
				Project 1	Project 2		Project 11
B O	BO1	W E I G H T S	W1				
	BO2		W2				
	BOm		Wm				
Weighted Average of CTQs							

QUESTION: Define and explain the purpose of DFSS.

Answer: Design for Six Sigma (DFSS) is the method used by a Six Sigma project team to invent and innovate products, services, and processes. It can be used to design entirely new products, services, and processes, or major new features of existing products, services, or processes that are consistently reliable and manufacturable, and uniformly surpass customer requirements. Additionally, DFSS creates designs that are: (1) based on stakeholder needs and want; (2) resource efficient; (3) minimal in complexity; (4) capable of generating high yields; (5) robust to process variation; and (6) quick to generate a profit.

QUESTION: List the steps of the Define Phase of the DMADV model.

Answer: The Define Phase of the DMADV model has five components: establish the background and business case, assess the risks and benefits of the project, form the team, develop the project plan, and write the project objective.

QUESTION: List the steps of the Measure Phase of the DMADV model.

Answer: The Measure Phase of a Design for Six Sigma Project has three steps: segmenting the market, designing and conducting a Kano Survey, and finally, using the Kano survey results as Quality Function Deployment inputs to find critical-to-quality characteristics (CTQs).

QUESTION: List the steps of the Analyze Phase of the DMADV model.

Answer: The Analyze Phase contains four steps: design generation, design analysis, risk analysis, and design model. The aim of the four steps in the Analyze Phase is to develop high-level designs. In addition to this, the designs will be evaluated per risk assessments. Finally, nominal values are established for all CTQs in the Analyze Phase for the "best" design.

QUESTION: List the steps of the Design Phase of the DMADV model.

Answer: The Design Phase of a Design for Six Sigma Project has three steps: construct a detailed design of the "best" design from the Analyze Phase, develop and estimate the capabilities of the critical-to-process elements (CTPs) in the design, and prepare a verification plan to enable a smooth transition among all affected departments.

QUESTION: List the steps of the Verify/Validate Phase of the DMADV model.

Answer: The intent of the Verify/Validate Phase is to facilitate buy-in of process owners, to design a control and transition plan, and to conclude the DMADV project.

QUESTION: Prepare a sample project objective.

Answer: To create a high-end living facility at the University of Miami that encourages learning and community (service) aimed at executives in residence, MBAs, and junior and senior undergraduate business students (market segments). It should increase (direction) the number of on-campus residents (measure) by 200 students (target) no later than July 15, 2003 (deadline).

QUESTION: Define the term market segmentation.

Answer: Market segmentation is the process of dividing a market into homogeneous subsets of customers such that the customers in any subset will respond similarly to a marketing mix established for them, and differently from the customers in another subset. A marketing mix is a combination of product, service, or process features, a price structure, a place (distribution) strategy, and a promotional strategy.

QUESTION: Discuss three common market segmentation strategies.

Answer: The three market segmentation strategies are:

1. *Undifferentiated market segmentation is a strategy in which all market segments receive the same marketing mix.*

2. *Differentiated market segmentation is a strategy in which each market segment receives its own unique marketing mix.*

3. *Concentrated market segmentation is a strategy in which only selected market segments receive a unique marketing strategy to maximize sales within those markets.*

QUESTION: Describe why a SIPOC analysis can be used to segment a market.

Answer: A SIPOC analysis is a simple tool for identifying the Suppliers and their Inputs into a process, the high-level steps of a Process, the Outputs of the process, and the Customer (market) segments interested in the outputs. The format of a SIPOC analysis is shown in Table 18.3.

TABLE 18.3 Format for a SIPOC Analysis

Suppliers		Inputs (Xs)		Process (Xs)		Outputs (CTQs)		Customer (Market) Segments
	>		>		>		>	

QUESTION: Describe the purposes of Kano Level A, B, and C surveys.

Answer: Level A surveys are used to improve existing products, services, or processes or to create less-expensive versions of existing products, services, or processes. Level B surveys are used to create major new features for existing products, services, or processes. Level C surveys are used to invent and innovate an entirely new product, service, or process.

QUESTION: Define the three major Kano quality categories. Draw a graph.

Answer: One Dimensional quality is when user satisfaction is proportional to the performance of the feature; the less performance, the less user satisfaction, and the more performance, the more user satisfaction. Must-Be quality is when user satisfaction is not proportional to the performance of the feature; the less performance, the less user satisfaction to the feature, but high performance creates feelings of indifference to the feature. Attractive quality is when user satisfaction is not proportional to the performance of the feature; however, in this case, low levels of performance create feelings of indifference to the feature, but high levels of performance create feelings of delight to the feature (see Figure 18.3).

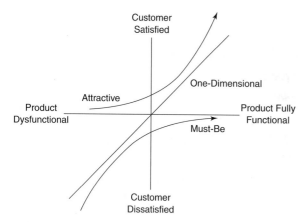

FIGURE 18.3   Kano Quality Categories

QUESTION: Explain the purpose of Quality Function Deployment.

Answer: Quality Function Deployment (QFD) is a method of building the demands of customers into the development of product/service features, characteristics, and specifications, as well as the selection and development of process equipment, methods, and control systems. It is a series of matrices and charts that deploys customer's demands and technical requirements into critical-to-product, service, or process (CTP) characteristics, such as all phases of design, planning, production or service, and delivery. For example, QFD clarifies the relationships between the following dimensions:

1. *Cognitive Images and CTQs, called Product Planning.*
2. *CTQs and Service Steps and/or Parts Characteristics (CTPs), called Parts Deployment.*
3. *Service Steps and/or Parts Characteristics and Manufacturing Operations (more detailed CTPs), called Process Planning.*
4. *Manufacturing Operations and Production Requirements (even more detailed CTPs), called Production Planning.*

The first QFD matrix (Cognitive Images by CTQs) is called the "House of Quality" (see Table 18.4).

TABLE 18.4   House of Quality

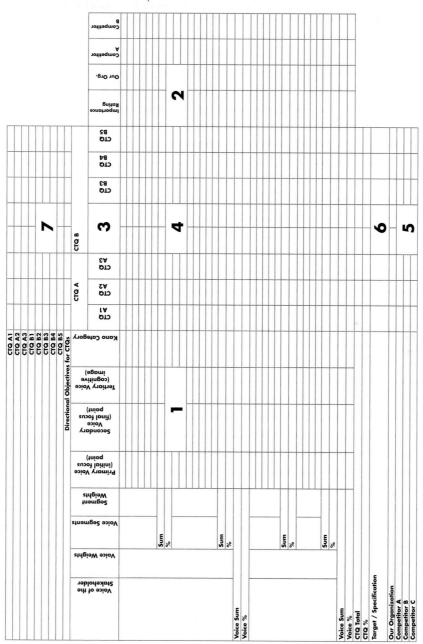

QUESTION: Construct a mock design scorecard. Make sure to include parts A and B of the scorecard. Provide an example of one CTQ across all the columns of the scorecard matrix.

Answer: See Table 18.5.

TABLE 18.5   Generic Design Scorecard

Scorecard—Part A (Voice of the Customer)					Scorecard—Part B (Predicted Voice of the Process)					
CTQ	Target (Nominal)	LSL	USL	Process Sigma Target	Stable (Y/N)	Shape	Mean	Standard Deviation	DPMO	Predicted Process Sigma
Days early or late for a service	0 days	-3 days	+3 days	6.0	Yes	Normal	0 days	1 day	66,807	3.00

QUESTION: Show the structure of a Pugh Matrix.
    Answer: See Table 18.6.

QUESTION: Explain the purpose of a failure modes and effects analysis.

Answer: Failure Mode and Effects Analysis (FMEA) is a tool used to identify, estimate, prioritize, and reduce the risk of failure in CTQs through the development of actions (process changes and innovations) and contingency plans based on CTPs.

QUESTION: Define CAD.

Answer: Computer Aided Design (CAD) can be defined as any design activity that involves the effective use of the computer to create, modify, or document an engineering design. CAD is most associated with the use of an interactive computer graphics system, referred to as a CAD system.

TABLE 18.6 Structure of a Pugh Matrix

1	2	3	4	5	6	7	8
Criteria to Evaluate Concepts	**Concept 1 (Baseline Concept)**	**Concept 2**	**Concept 3**	**Concept 4**	**Concept 5**	**Concept 6**	**Concept 7**
Benefit/ cost of concept		+	+	S	S	+	-
Time required to realize the concept		S	+	S	-	-	S
Organization's ability to realize concept		+	S	+	S	S	S
Effect of concept on organization's strategy		+	-	S	+	S	S
Legal/regulatory impact of concept	All concepts are evaluated with respect to the baseline concept	+	+	+	+	+	+
Safety impact of concept on stakeholders		S	+	+	-	-	S
Political ramifications of concept		+	-	-	-	+	+
Sum of Positives		5	4	3	2	3	2
Sum of Negatives		0	2	1	3	2	1
Sum of Sames		2	1	3	1	2	4

QUESTION: Define rapid prototyping. Give an example of its application.

Answer: Rapid prototyping is a method that creates a physical model of a design using a Computer Aided Design (CAD) model. Rapid prototyping can turn a conceptual design into a working physical model in minutes or hours, thereby promoting visualization and concept verification of the design. Rapid prototypes can serve as final products, given suitable materials (e.g., medical orthotics, such as false legs). Additionally, rapid prototyping can be used to produce tools for manufacturing.

QUESTION: Explain the purpose of a pilot test

Answer: A pilot test is simply a dry run of a design in a laboratory, controlled setting, or in actual use, but on a small scale and for a limited time frame. Pilot tests confirm that the design CTQs and CTPs surpass the design input requirements. It is important to remember to calibrate and control all appropriate verification and validation activities.

QUESTION: List and briefly discuss the five objectives of a pilot test.

Answer: There are five objectives for a pilot test: transferring the design, collecting data, creating buy-in, eliminating risks, and decreasing capital investment.

1. *Transferring the design ensures that a complete set of specifications are deployed to all stakeholders of the design in multiple locations.*
2. *Collecting data provides repeatable and reproducible information (data) on the performance of a design from multiple locations.*
3. *Creating buy-in promotes acceptance from stakeholders of the design.*
4. *Eliminating risk reduces failure and error modes.*
5. *Decreasing capital investment reduces the financial requirements by testing the design in a realistic setting.*

QUESTION: Define and explain the purposes of a design review.

Answer: A design review is a type of management review that is a well-documented, comprehensive, and systematic examination of a design with the following purposes:

- *Evaluate the adequacy of the design with respect to each detailed CTP, CTP and CTQ stability, distributional shape, variability, and mean.*
- *Evaluate the capability of the design to meet these requirements with respect to specification limits, nominal values, DPMOs, and process sigmas for the detailed CTPs, CTPs, and CTQs.*
- *Decide if the design is "ready" (perhaps at risk) for full-scale implementation.*
- *Assign responsibilities for necessary actions.*

QUESTION: List the issues a product development team must consider when conducting a design review.

Answer: The seven issues product development team members must consider are:

- *Identification of the process to be validated.*
- *Identification of products or services to be generated using this process.*
- *Criteria for a successful design review.*
- *Identification of the operating conditions of the process.*

- *Development of a detailed flowchart of the process with specifications.*
- *Identifying the parameters to be controlled and monitored, and the statistical methods for controlling and monitoring them.*
- *Definition of nonconformance for parameters.*

QUESTION: What questions should the product development team know the answers to in order to ensure a smooth transition of the new design to the Operations and Marketing departments?

Answer:

- *Has the design been successfully pilot tested by PD team members?*
- *Is the full-scale process up and running?*
- *Does the full-scale process have a functioning control plan?*
- *Has the full-scale system been documented?*
- *Has all training been conducted for process stakeholders?*
- *Does the full-scale process result in the desired business objectives?*
- *Will the outputs of the full-scale process satisfy (delight) stakeholders?*
- *Have process owners bought-into the next generation of the MGPP?*

QUESTION: What is the key to the successful transfer of ideas within an organization?

Answer: The main ingredient of a successful diffusion of an idea is the identification of "opinion leaders" to the promotion of the idea. Additional ingredients include the following:

1. *To develop the learning capacity of potential adopters of an innovation.*
2. *To improve management's understanding of the factors that affect the success and or failure of the innovation and improving management's ability to communicate these factors to potential adopters.*
3. *To increase the level of intimacy between potential adopters and diffusers of an idea.*

QUESTION: Describe the five adopter categories.

Answer: All potential adopters fall into one of five categories.

1. *Innovators are frequently the gatekeepers of new ideas into their system. However, they may not be respected by the members of their system because they are considered unreliable due to their attraction to new things.*
2. *Early adopters are respected by their peers, have a local network of contacts, are opinion leaders, and are role models for other members of their system.*

3. *Early majority deliberate for some time before adopting new ideas and interact frequently with their peers.*

4. *Late majority require peer pressure to adopt an innovation.*

5. *Laggards are suspicious of innovation and their reference point is in the past.*

QUESTION: Which adopter category is the key to diffusing an innovation? Why?

Answer: Early adopters (opinion leaders) are the key to the diffusion process. Early adopters command the respect and admiration of their peers necessary to diffuse an innovation.

The following questions pertain only to the yellow/green belt certification examination. However, the yellow/green belt certification examination is a cumulative examination and includes questions from the champion examination.

QUESTION: Describe the characteristics of the three types of multi-generational product plans (MGPPs).

Answer: See Table 18.7.

TABLE 18.7   Characteristics of MGPPs

Generation	Generation 1	Generation 2	Generation 3
Vision	Stop bleeding in existing market(s).	Take offensive action by filling unmet needs of existing market(s).	Take leadership position in new market(s).
Product/Service Generations	Improved or less-expensive existing features.	New major features.	New products, services, or processes.
Product/Service Technologies and Platforms	Current technology.	Current technology with relevant technological enhancements, if any.	Current technology plus new technology, if possible.

QUESTION: Explain the function of a document control system.

Answer: A document control system is needed to manage design changes when individuals and sub-teams are working concurrently on a Six Sigma project.

QUESTION: Describe the minimum requirements for a document control system.

Answer: The minimum requirements of a document control system are as follows:

- *All documents are marked with creation date.*
- *All documents are assigned control numbers.*

- *All documents are backed up in a central repository.*
- *All documents have proper access controls.*

QUESTION: Show the format of a risk abatement plan.

Answer: See Table 18.8.

TABLE 18.8   Format for a Risk Abatement Plan

1	2	3		4	5	6
Potential Risk Elements for Process *i*	Potential Harm for the Risk Elements from Process *i*	Risk Element Score		Countermeasure (Risk Abatement Plan)	Risk Owner	Completion Date for Countermeasure
		Before	After			

QUESTION: Define lead user. Why are lead users important to Level B Kano surveys?

Answer: Lead users are consumers of a product, service, or process that are months or years ahead of regular users in their use of the item and will benefit greatly by an innovation. For example, a lead user of a hair dryer may attach a portable battery pack and use it as a body warmer at football games played in cold weather. Lead users are useful for identifying the unknown needs and wants of regular users necessary for creating innovative new features of existing products, services, or processes. Heavy users are useful for identifying the needs and wants of regular users necessary for improving existing products, services, or processes

QUESTION: Describe Kano's method for translating circumstantial, lead, and heavy user data into cognitive images.

Answer: Classifying "Voice of the Customer" data as product-related or circumstantial takes practice; see Table 18.9.

Focus points are the underlying needs and wants upon which circumstantial issues or themes are based. They are identified by team members using affinity diagrams, technical investigations, and lateral thinking. Team members translate focus points into detailed, unambiguous, qualitative statements of needs and wants in the language of design engineers, called cognitive images (CIs).

TABLE 18.9 Classification Matrix by Market Segment

Selected Market Segment(s)	Raw "Voice of the User" and "Voice of the Customer" data (in the language of respondent)	Data Classification (Product or Circumstantial)
Segment A		
High-Priority Customer A1	Comment A11	P
	Comment A12	P
	Comment A13	C
Lead User A2	Comment A21	C
	Comment A22	P
Segment B		
Lead User B1	Comment B11	C
High-Priority Customer B2	Comment B21	C
	Comment B22	P
Lead User B3	Comment B31	C
	Comment B32	C
Segment C		
High-Priority Customer C1	Comment C11	C
	Comment C12	P
	Comment C13	P

QUESTION: Construct a sample Kano questionnaire for a cognitive image.

Answer: See Table 18.10.

TABLE 18.10   Kano Questionnaire

Cognitive Image	How would you feel if the following CTQ was present in the product?	How would you feel if the CTQ was not present in the product?	What percentage cost increase, over current costs, would you be willing to pay for this CTQ?
CTQ 1	Delighted [ ] Expect it and like it [ ] No feeling [ ] Live with it [ ] Do not like it [ ] Other [ ]	Delighted [ ] Expect it and like it [ ] No feeling [ ] Live with it [ ] Do not like it [ ] Other [ ]	0% _____ 10% _____ 20% _____ 30% _____ 40% or more _____

QUESTION: A Kano survey of 800 regular users revealed the following data:

Attractive = 750

One-Way = 50

Must-Be = Indifferent = Reverse = Questionable = 0

0% = 20

10% = 20

20% = 20

30% = 20

40+% = 20

Interpret the preceding data.

Answer: The cognitive image is an attractive Kano quality characteristic that 80% of the market is willing to pay at least 10% more for. It is a characteristic that will delight customers and create a competitive advantage for the organization.

QUESTION: Explain the purpose of Room 1.

Answer: Room 1 is used to identify, list, and weight primary, secondary, and tertiary "Voice of the Stakeholder" data and benchmark data, by stakeholder segment. Examples of stakeholder segments are the following:

- *"Voice of the Customer" by market segment.*
- *"Voice of the Employee" by employee segment.*
- *"Voice of the Investor" by investor segment.*
- *"Voice of the Supplier" by type of supplier.*

- *"Voice of the Sub-contractor" by type of sub-contractor.*
- *"Voice of the Regulator" by regulator.*
- *"Voice of the Environment."*
- *"Voice of the Community."*

QUESTION: Explain the purpose of room 2.

Answer: Room 2 compares your organization with best-in-class organizations with respect to each cognitive image. Room 2 is not always appropriate in a House of Quality; for example, a new product, service, or process might not have any competition.

QUESTION: Explain the purpose of room 3.

Answer: Room 3 is used to translate each cognitive image into one or more product, service, or process CTQs. CTQs are identified using:

- *Product, service, or process knowledge.*
- *Benchmark information.*
- *Data from existing QFD tables for similar designs.*

QUESTION: Explain the purpose of room 4.

Answer: Room 4 is used to prioritize the CTQs. An empty row indicates a stakeholder voice that is not being serviced by any CTQ. This represents the opportunity to fill an unmet stakeholder need or want. An empty column indicates a CTQ that is not related to any stakeholder need or want. This represents an opportunity to eliminate an unnecessary CTQ.

QUESTION: Explain the purpose of room 5.

Answer: Room 5 is used to compare your organization with best-in-class organizations, with respect to each CTQ (use internal experts and benchmarking to make the comparisons). You use room 5 to uncover perceptual problems with your product, service, or process, rather than technical problems.

QUESTION: Explain the purpose of room 6.

Answer: Room 6 is used to set target (nominal values) and specification limits for each CTQ. Team members establish targets (nominal values) and specification limits for each CTQ using product, service, or process knowledge and technical expertise. Also, team members should not set specifications just to meet the performance levels of best-in-class competitors; rather, they should be set to surpass the needs and wants of relevant stakeholder segments.

QUESTION: Describe a method for establishing two-sided customer based specification limits. Illustrate your explanation with a chart.

Answer: A two-sided specification limit is an upper and lower boundary on the acceptable performance of a quality characteristic (CTQ or CTP). In its simplest form, it is determined by

constructing a questionnaire. Table 18.11 shows how to identify the upper and lower specification limits for acceptable waiting times for the delivery of perishable materials.

TABLE 18.11 Questionnaire for Constructing a Two-Sided Specification Limit for Waiting Time
for Perishable Materials

Waiting Time	Very Satisfied (1)	Satisfied (2)	Neutral (3)	Dissatisfied (4)	Very Dissatisfied (5)
4 days early					
3 days early					
2 days early					
1 day early					
On time					
1 day late					
2 days late					
3 days late					
4 days late					

Team members select a sample of patients waiting for perishable materials, say 100, and
administer the questionnaire. The results of the survey are shown in Table 18.12.

TABLE 18.12 Survey Results for Acceptable Waiting Time for Perishable Materials

Waiting Time	Very Satisfied (1)	Satisfied (2)	Neutral (3)	Dissatisfied (4)	Very Dissatisfied (5)
4 days early	0	0	0	0	100
3 days early	0	25	50	25	0
2 days early	60	40	0	0	0
1 day early	98	2	0	0	0
On time	100	0	0	0	0
1 day late	95	5	0	0	0
2 days late	50	50	0	0	0
3 days late	0	25	50	25	0
4 days late	0	0	0	0	100

Team members select a sample of patients waiting for perishable materials, say 100, and
the bar chart on page 654 indicates that 1 day early is the LSL and 1 day late is the USL on number of days a delivery can be off target before there is serious erosion in the level of customer dissatisfaction. A stricter interpretation may indicate that only on-time delivery (0 days early or
late) is acceptable to customers. The specification depends on what the company is trying to
achieve with the product, service, or process (see Figure 18.4).

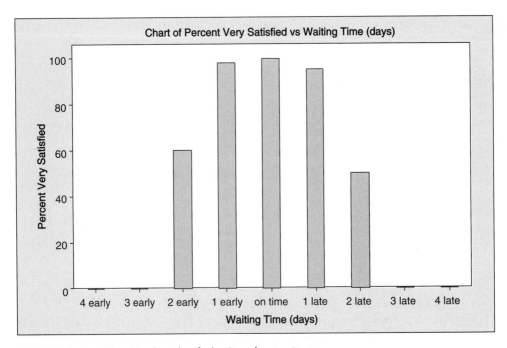

FIGURE 18.4 Bar Chart Used to Identify the Specification Limit

QUESTION: Explain the purpose of room 7.

Answer: Team members use room 7 to quantify and study the relationships among the CTQs and to create tradeoffs among the CTQs. Customer's needs and wants, not organizational constraints, should be considered when creating tradeoffs between negatively related CTQs. For example, "speed of service" and "maintenance of service area" are negatively related. Increasing "speed of service" causes additional cost in "maintenance of service area."

QUESTION: Create a list of the different types of CTPs that are defined in the second QFD house.

Answer: For services, CTPs need to be developed for the following aspects of the product, service, or process being designed:

- *Product or service detailed CTPs.*
- *Process detailed CTPs.*
- *Human system detailed CTPs.*
- *Information system detailed CTPs.*
- *Equipment and tools detailed CTPs.*

- *Material and supply detailed CTPs.*
- *Buildings and grounds detailed CTPs.*

QUESTION: Describe the purpose and components of a measurement system analysis.

Answer: A measurement system analysis involves the following tasks:

1. *Description of the ideal measurement system (flowchart the process).*
2. *Description of the actual measurement system (flowchart the process).*
3. *Identification of the causes of the differences between the ideal and actual measurement systems.*
4. *Identification of the accuracy (bias) and precision (repeatability) of the measurement system.*
5. *Estimation of the proportion of observed variation due to unit-to-unit variation and R&R variation.*

QUESTION: Use a concept fan to create ideas for "moving people around a college campus."

Answer: Step 1 shows team members using the existing "shuttle bus" alternative that was taken from the list of circumstantial data points to create the reference point "move people around the campus."

Step 1

Alternative A	*Reference point 1*
Shuttle bus >	*Move people around campus*

Step 2 shows team members using the "move people around campus" reference point to generate the "tram service" alternative and the "shuttle boat" alternative.

Step 2

Alternative A	*Reference point 1*
Shuttle bus >	*Move people around campus*
Alternative B	
Tram service	*<————-|*
Alternative C	
Shuttle boat	*<————-|*

Step 3 shows team members also using the "move people around campus" reference point to create the "provide, maintain, and administer safe, judicious, and attractive parking" direction.

Step 3

Alternative A	Reference point 1	Direction
Shuttle bus >	Move people around campus >	Provide, maintain,
Alternative B		and administer
Tram service.	<————⏐	safe, judicious, and
Alternative C		and attractive parking
Shuttle boat	<————⏐	

Step 4 shows team members using the "provide, maintain, and administer safe, judicious, and attractive parking" direction to generate the "move people around campus in a timely manner" reference point.

Step 4

Alternative A	Reference point 1	Direction
Shuttle bus >	Move people around campus >	Provide, maintain
Alternative B		and administer safe
Tram service.	<————⏐	judicious, and
Alternative C		attractive parking
Shuttle boat	<————⏐	

Move people around campus in a <————⏐
timely manner

Step 5 shows team members using the "move people around campus in a timely manner" reference point to generate the "schedule the shuttle bus service" and "guarantee on-time delivery to your destination" alternatives.

Step 5

Alternative A	Reference point 1	Direction
Shuttle bus >	Move people around campus >	Provide, maintain
Alternative B		and administer safe
Tram service.	<————⏐	judicious, and
Alternative C		attractive parking
Shuttle boat	<————⏐	

Move people around campus in a <————⏐
timely manner

Alternative D

Schedule shuttle bus service   <————|

Alternative E

Guarantee 15 minute on-time delivery to destination   <————|

QUESTION: The university has decided to guarantee 15 or less minute service to a destination from arrival at a shuttle bus stop. Do a C&S.

Answer: What are the benefits of the decision? Students will be happier because they will not have to hunt for a parking space, waste time, and be late for class. Students will park on the perimeter of campus freeing up core parking spaces. Fewer students will be driving within the core areas of the university campus.

What are the costs of the decision? Parking fees for core parking will get more expensive. The university will have to purchase and manage one additional shuttle bus.

QUESTION: Explain the purpose of TRIZ. Provide an example of TRIZ being applied to solve a service problem.

Answer: TRIZ Principle 7: "Nested doll."

A. *Place one event inside another event; for example, insert cheese into the crust of pizza for a cheesier pizza or create a phone-answering system with layers of options.*

B. *Make one part/person/sub-system of a system pass through a cavity in another part/ person/sub-system of the same system; for example, allow anyone in an organization to communicate directly to any higher level.*

QUESTION: Explain the structure of an FMEA.

*Answer: There are 10 steps in conducting an FMEA. First, team members identify the critical parameters and their potential failure modes for each CTP (or X) identified through the type of analysis shown in Table 18.13; that is, ways in which the process step (CTP or X) might fail (columns 1 and 2). Second, team members identify the potential effect of each failure (consequences of that failure) and rate its severity (columns 3 and 4). Third, team members identify causes of the effects and rate their likelihood of occurrence (columns 5 and 6). Fifth, team members identify the current controls for detecting each failure mode and rate the organization's ability to detect each failure mode (columns 7 and 8). Sixth, team members calculate the **RPN** (**Risk Priority Number**) for each failure mode by multiplying the values in columns 4, 6, and 8 (column 9). Seventh, and very importantly, team members identify the action(s), contingency plans, persons responsible, and target completion dates for reducing or eliminating the RPN for each failure mode (columns 10 and 11). Actions are the process changes needed to reduce the severity and likelihood of occurrence, and increase the likelihood of detection, of a potential failure mode. **Contingency plans** are the alternative actions immediately available to a process owner when a failure mode occurs, in spite of process improvement actions. A contingency plan might include a contact name and phone number in case of a failure mode. Eight, team members identify the date the action was taken to reduce or eliminate each failure mode (column 12).*

Ninth, team members rank the severity (column 13), occurrence (column 14), and detection (column 15) of each failure mode after the recommended action (column 10) has been put into motion. Tenth, team members multiple the values in columns 13, 14, and 15 to re-calculate the RPN (Risk Priority Number) for each failure mode after the recommended action (column 16) has been put into motion.

TABLE 18.13   Format for an FMEA

1	2	3	4	5	6	7	8	9	10	11	12	13	14	15	16
Critical Parameter	Potential Failure Mode	Potential Failure Effect	Severity	Potential Causes	Occurrence	Current Controls	Detection	Before RPN	Recommended Action	Responsibility and Target Date	Counter Measure (Action Taken)	Severity	Occurrence	Detection	After RPN

QUESTION: Present a format for a hazard analysis.

Answer: See Table 18.14.

TABLE 18.14   Generic Hazard Matrix

Item	Function	Hazard	Cause	Effect (Harm)	Hazard Severity	Corrective or Preventive Measure

QUESTION: Explain the different taxonomies of simulation models.

Answer: The first taxonomy is a static model versus a dynamic model. A static model is one in which events are repeated independent of time. A dynamic model is one in which events are run over time. The second taxonomy is a deterministic model versus a probabilistic model. In a deterministic model, each parameter has constant values. In a probabilistic model, each parameter has a distribution. The third taxonomy is a continuous model versus a discrete model. A continuous model continuously runs a clock over all events. A discrete model advances a clock discretely to the next event. The fourth taxonomy is a Monte Carlo simulation model versus a discrete event simulation model. A Monte Carlo simulation advances time by a clock. A discrete event simulation advances time by events.

QUESTION: List the steps in conducting a discrete event simulation.

Answer: There are nine steps in performing a discrete event simulation.

> **Step 1**: *Define the idea, product, service, or process to be simulated from the perspective of all relevant stakeholders with a timeline.*
>
> **Step 2**: *Study the real-world system, identify its CTQs and CTPs, and develop a realistic flowchart of it. Determine if the flowchart is sufficiently similar to the real-world system, and if necessary, revise the flowchart.*
>
> **Step 3**: *Collect the data needed to define the parameters of the simulation model, they include arrival patterns, service times, resource requirements, transfer times between activities, storage and wait time statistics, and the control logic of the system.*
>
> **Step 4**: *Develop a computer model for the system under study using a discrete event simulation software package.*
>
> **Step 5**: *Run and validate the simulation model against the real system.*
>
> **Step 6**: *Plan one or more experiments to identify the optimal configuration of the system (best levels for the CTPs to obtain the best statistics for the CTQs).*
>
> **Step 7**: *Run, record, and analyze the experimental alternatives using the computer simulation model.*
>
> **Step 8**: *Study the results and select the best high-level route design.*
>
> **Step 9**: *Recommend the best high-level design concept.*

QUESTION: A tooth pick has an average length of 40 mm with a standard deviation of 0.010 mm and a cocktail sandwich has an average thickness of 27 mm with a standard deviation of 0.008 mm.

What is the average projection of the toothpick *through the cocktail sandwich?*

What is the standard deviation of the tooth pick projection through the cocktail sandwich?

Answer: average =13 mm = [40 mm – 27 mm]

Answer: standard deviation = $\sqrt{(0.01)^2 + (0.008)^2}$ = 0.0128

QUESTION: If there are three independent methods to accomplish a task and each method has 99% reliability, what is the overall reliability of the task?

Answer: [1.0 − (1 − 0.99)(1 − 0.99)(1 − 0.99)] = 1.0 − 0.000001 = 0.999999

QUESTION: If there are four independent methods to accomplishing a task and the task requires that at least two of the four methods work, and each method is 92% reliable, what is the overall system reliability?

Answer: M = 4 methods, N = 2 at least methods must work (i.e., 2 or 3 or 4), R_2 of 4 = 6(0.92)^2(0.08)^2 = 0.0325, R_3 of 4 = 4(0.92)^3(0.08)^1 = 0.2492, R_4 of 4 = 1(0.92)^4(0.08)^0 = 0.7164, R_{system} = 0.9981

QUESTION: List and describe several rapid prototyping methods useful for services.

Answer: Eight prototyping methods for services are described next:

1. *Scenarios. Product development team members create alternative applications for the design that demonstrate its use under a variety of conditions (scenarios).*

2. *Videography. Product development team members use videography to create short movies depicting the consumer's experience with the product, service, or process.*

3. *Role play. Product development team members ask different types of customers (market segments) to role play their use of the design.*

4. *Tagging the whales. Product development team members select a particular user (with permission) and observe his or her habits in using the product, service, or process.*

5. *Behavioral mapping. Product development team members can photograph or video a user's experience with a product, service, or process. Behavioral mapping is a combination of videography and tagging the whales.*

6. *Consumer journal. Product development team members ask selected users of the design to record their experiences with the design in a journal.*

7. *Storytelling. Product development team members ask users of the design to tell personal stories of their experiences with the design.*

8. *Intellectuals SWOT team. Product development team members assemble a team of people with extremely diverse theoretical views of life, and consequently the design.*

QUESTION: Describe the rules when rapidly prototyping services.

Answer: Three rules are used by product development team members when prototyping designs.

1. *Simplicity. Team members should create simple mock-ups of the service design. Frills should be ignored at this stage to prevent hang-ups and delays.*

2. *Speed. Team members should create simple mock-ups quickly, again to prevent hang-ups and delays.*

3. *Inclusion. Team members should create mock-ups whenever you can for services, products, or processes.*

QUESTION: What is a Device Master Record?

Answer: A Device Master Record (DMR) is a data file that contains all of the routine documentation required to generate products or deliver services in accordance with the specifications and nominal values for all CTQs and CTPs. The final design CTQs and CTPs form the contents of the DMR. A DMR documents the methods and specifications for a product, service, or process.

QUESTION: Describe Rogers' five perceived attributes of innovations

Answer: Rogers' five perceived attributes of innovations are: relative advantage, compatibility, complexity, trial-ability, and observe-ability.

1. *Relative advantage is the degree to which an innovation is perceived as being better than the idea it supersedes.*

2. *Compatibility is the degree to which an innovation is perceived as consistent with the existing values, past experiences, and needs of potential adopters*

3. *Complexity is the degree to which an innovation is perceived as relatively difficult to understand and use by the potential adopter.*

4. *Trial-ability is the degree to which a potential adopter can experiment with an innovation.*

5. *Observe-ability is the degree to which the results of an innovation are visible to potential adopters.*

QUESTION: Describe the five stages of the innovation-decision process.

Answer: The innovation-decision process is how a decision-making unit passes from first knowledge of an innovation, to forming an attitude about the innovation, to a decision to adopt or reject the innovation, to implementation of the innovation, and to confirmation of the innovation decision. The innovation-decision process consists of five stages: knowledge stage, persuasion stage, decision stage, implementation stage, and confirmation stage.

1. *The knowledge stage occurs when a decision-making unit (individual or group) is exposed to an innovation's existence and gains some understanding of how it functions.*

2. *The persuasion stage occurs when a decision-making unit forms a favorable or unfavorable attitude (feeling) toward the innovation.*

3. *The decision stage occurs when a decision-making unit engages in the activities that lead to a choice to adopt or reject the innovation.*

4. *The implementation stage occurs when a decision-making unit actually uses the innovation.*

5. *The confirmation stage occurs when a decision-making unit seeks reinforcement of an innovation-decision already made, or reverses a previous decision to adopt or reject the innovation if exposed to conflicting messages about the innovation.*

QUESTION: Describe the organizational factors that are important to a diffusion strategy.

Answer: Three organizational factors key to a diffusion strategy are as follows:

1. *Develop the learning capacity of potential adopters of an innovation.*
2. *Improve management's understanding of the factors that affect the success and/or failure of the innovation and their ability to communicate these factors to potential adopters.*
3. *Increase the level of intimacy between potential adopters and the diffusers of an innovation.*

18.6 DFSS Green Belt Project

Prepare the Define Phase of your project and submit it for review to: Dr. Howard Gitlow at hgitlow@miami.edu. Once your project passes the Define Phase tollgate review, you can proceed onto the Measure Phase using the same critiquing procedure, and so on, until you complete your project. Once you successfully complete your project, you will be awarded a "DFSS Green Belt Certification of Achievement" by the Executive Education Center of the School of Business Administration of the University of Miami. The cost for the critiquing process is between $250 and $600 per hour, depending on the level of expertise required. Please contact hgitlow@miami.edu to establish a critiquing process contract. Usually, DFSS green belts do not require more than two or three hours of consultation.

Summary

This chapter describes the protocol for achieving DFSS champion and yellow/green belt certification from the University of Miami. Good luck in your DFSS Six Sigma journey!

SUMMATION NOTATION

Because the operation of addition occurs so frequently in statistics, the special symbol Σ is used to mean "take the sum of." If there is a set of n values for a variable labeled X, the expression $\sum_{i=1}^{n} X_i$ means that these n values are to be added together from the first value to the last (n^{th}) value. Thus,

$$\sum_{i=1}^{n} X_i = X_1 + X_2 + X_3 + \cdots + X_n$$

To illustrate summation notation, suppose there are five values for a variable X:

$$X_1 = 2, X_2 = 0, X_3 = -1, X_4 = 5, \text{ and } X_5 = 7$$

For these data,

$$\sum_{i=1}^{n} X_i = X_1 + X_2 + X_3 + X_4 + X_5$$
$$= 2 + 0 + (-1) + 5 + 7 = 13$$

In statistics, it is also often necessary to sum the squared values of a variable. Using summation notation, the sum of the squared X's is written as:

$$\sum_{i=1}^{n} X_i^2 = X_1^2 + X_2^2 + X_3^2 + \cdots + X_n^2$$

Using the preceding data,

$$\sum_{i=1}^{n} X_i^2 = X_1^2 + X_2^2 + X_3^2 + X_4^2 + X_5^2$$
$$= 2^2 + 0^2 + (-1)^2 + 5^2 + 7^2$$
$$= 4 + 0 + 1 + 25 + 49$$
$$= 79$$

It is important to understand that $\sum_{i=1}^{n} X_i^2$, the sum of the squares, is *not* the same as $\left(\sum_{i=1}^{n} X_i\right)$, the square of the sum.

$$\sum_{i=1}^{n} X_i^2 \neq \left(\sum_{i=1}^{n} X_i\right)^2$$

In the preceding example, the sum of the squares, $\sum_{i=1}^{n} X_i^2$, equals 79. That is not equal to the square of the sum, $\left(\sum_{i=1}^{n} X_i\right)^2$, which is $(13)^2 = 169$.

Another frequently used operation involves summing the product of two variables, called the *cross product*. This operation involves two variables, X and Y, each having n values. Then,

$$\sum_{i=1}^{n} X_i Y_i = X_1 Y_1 + X_2 Y_2 + X_3 Y_3 + \cdots + X_5 Y_5$$

Continuing with the preceding data, suppose that a second variable, Y, has the following five values: $Y_1 = 1$, $Y_2 = 3$, $Y_3 = -2$, $X_4 = 4$, and $X_5 = 3$. Then,

$$\sum_{i=1}^{n} X_i Y_i = X_1 Y_1 + X_2 Y_2 + X_3 Y_3 + X_4 Y_4 + X_5 Y_5$$
$$= (2)(1) + (0)(3) + (-1)(-2) + (5)(4) + (7)(3)$$
$$= 2 + 0 + 2 + 20 + 21$$
$$= 45$$

In computing $\sum_{i=1}^{n} X_i Y_i$, the first value of X is multiplied by the first value of Y, the second value of X is multiplied by the second value of Y, and so on. These cross products are then summed. Observe that the sum of the cross products is *not* equal to the product of the individual sums; that is,

$$\sum_{i=1}^{n} X_i Y_i \neq \left(\sum_{i=1}^{n} X_i\right)\left(\sum_{i=1}^{n} Y_i\right)$$

Using the preceding data, $\sum_{i=1}^{n} X_i = 13$ and $\sum_{i=1}^{n} Y_i = 1 + 3 + (-2) + 4 + 3 = 9$, so that

$$\left(\sum_{i=1}^{n} X_i\right)\left(\sum_{i=1}^{n} Y_i\right) = (13)(9) = 117$$

This is not the same as $\sum_{i=1}^{n} X_i Y_i$, which equals 45.

The four basic rules of summation notation are as follows:

Rule 1: The sum of the values of two different variables is equal to the sum of the values of each variable.

$$\sum_{i=1}^{n}(X_i + Y_i) = \sum_{i=1}^{n} X_i + \sum_{i=1}^{n} Y_i$$

Thus, for the preceding data,

$$\sum_{i=1}^{n}(X_i + Y_i) = (2+1) + (0+3) + (-1+(-2)) + (5+4) + (7+3)$$

$$= 3 + 3 + (-3) + 9 + 10$$

$$= 22 = \sum_{i=1}^{5} X_i + \sum_{i=1}^{5} Y_i = 13 + 9 = 22$$

Rule 2: The sum of the difference between the values of two variables is equal to the difference between the sum of the two variables.

$$\sum_{i=1}^{n}(X_i - Y_i) = \sum_{i=1}^{n} X_i - \sum_{i=1}^{n} Y_i$$

Using the preceding data,

$$\sum_{i=1}^{n}(X_i - Y_i) = (2-1) + (0-3) + (-1-(-2)) + (5-4) + (7-3)$$

$$= 1 + (-3) + 1 + 1 + 4$$

$$= 4 = \sum_{i=1}^{5} X_i - \sum_{i=1}^{5} Y_i = 13 - 9 = 4$$

Rule 3: The sum of a constant multiplied by a variable is equal to the constant multiplied by the sum of the values of the variable:

$$\sum_{i=1}^{n} cX_i = c\sum_{i=1}^{n} X_i$$

where c is a constant.

Thus, if $c = 2$,

$$\sum_{i=1}^{5} cX_i = 2\sum_{i=1}^{5} X_i = (2)(2) + 2(0) + (2)(-1) + (2)(5) + (2)(7)$$

$$= 4 + 0 + (-2) + 10 + 14$$

$$= 26 = 2\sum_{i=1}^{5} X_i = (2)(13) = 26$$

Rule 4: A constant summed n times is equal to n multiplied by the value of the constant.

$$\sum_{i=1}^{n} c = nc$$

where c is a constant. Thus, if the constant $c = 2$ is summed five times,

$$\sum_{i=1}^{n} c = 2 + 2 + 2 + 2 + 2$$

$$= 10 = (5)(2) = 10$$

REFERENCES

1. Bashaw, W. L., *Mathematics for Statistics* (New York: Wiley, 1969).
2. Lanzer, P., *Video Review of Arithmetic* (Hickville, NY: Video Aided Instruction, 1999).
3. Levine, D., *The MBA Primer: Business Statistics* (Cincinnati, OH: Southwestern Publishing, 2000).
4. Levine, D., *Video Review of Statistics* (Hickville, NY: Video Aided Instruction, 1989).
5. Shane, H., *Video Review of Elementary Algebra* (Hickville, NY: Video Aided Instruction, 1996).

STATISTICAL TABLES

TABLE B.1 The Cumulative Standardized Normal Distribution

*Each entry represents an area under the cumulative standardized
normal distribution from −∞ to Z.*

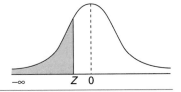

z	0.00	0.01	0.02	0.03	0.04	0.05	0.06	0.07	0.08	0.09
-3.9	0.00005	0.00005	0.00004	0.00004	0.00004	0.00004	0.00004	0.00004	0.00003	0.00003
-3.8	0.00007	0.00007	0.00007	0.00006	0.00006	0.00006	0.00006	0.00005	0.00005	0.00005
-3.7	0.00011	0.00010	0.00010	0.00010	0.00009	0.00009	0.00008	0.00008	0.00008	0.00008
-3.6	0.00016	0.00015	0.00015	0.00014	0.00014	0.00013	0.00013	0.00012	0.00012	0.00011
-3.5	0.00023	0.00022	0.00022	0.00021	0.00020	0.00019	0.00019	0.00018	0.00017	0.00017
-3.4	0.00034	0.00032	0.00031	0.00030	0.00029	0.00028	0.00027	0.00026	0.00025	0.00024
-3.3	0.00048	0.00047	0.00045	0.00043	0.00042	0.00040	0.00039	0.00038	0.00036	0.00035
-3.2	0.00069	0.00066	0.00064	0.00062	0.00060	0.00058	0.00056	0.00054	0.00052	0.00050
-3.1	0.00097	0.00094	0.00090	0.00087	0.00084	0.00082	0.00079	0.00076	0.00074	0.00071
-3.0	0.00135	0.00131	0.00126	0.00122	0.00118	0.00114	0.00111	0.00107	0.00103	0.00100
-2.9	0.0019	0.0018	0.0018	0.0017	0.0016	0.0016	0.0015	0.0015	0.0014	0.0014
-2.8	0.0026	0.0025	0.0024	0.0023	0.0023	0.0022	0.0021	0.0021	0.0020	0.0019
-2.7	0.0035	0.0034	0.0033	0.0032	0.0031	0.0030	0.0029	0.0028	0.0027	0.0026
-2.6	0.0047	0.0045	0.0044	0.0043	0.0041	0.0040	0.0039	0.0038	0.0037	0.0036
-2.5	0.0062	0.0060	0.0059	0.0057	0.0055	0.0054	0.0052	0.0051	0.0049	0.0048
-2.4	0.0082	0.0080	0.0078	0.0075	0.0073	0.0071	0.0069	0.0068	0.0066	0.0064
-2.3	0.0107	0.0104	0.0102	0.0099	0.0096	0.0094	0.0091	0.0089	0.0087	0.0084
-2.2	0.0139	0.0136	0.0132	0.0129	0.0125	0.0122	0.0119	0.0116	0.0113	0.0110
-2.1	0.0179	0.0174	0.0170	0.0166	0.0162	0.0158	0.0154	0.0150	0.0146	0.0143
-2.0	0.0228	0.0222	0.0217	0.0212	0.0207	0.0202	0.0197	0.0192	0.0188	0.0183
-1.9	0.0287	0.0281	0.0274	0.0268	0.0262	0.0256	0.0250	0.0244	0.0239	0.0233
-1.8	0.0359	0.0351	0.0344	0.0336	0.0329	0.0322	0.0314	0.0307	0.0301	0.0294
-1.7	0.0446	0.0436	0.0427	0.0418	0.0409	0.0401	0.0392	0.0384	0.0375	0.0367
-1.6	0.0548	0.0537	0.0526	0.0516	0.0505	0.0495	0.0485	0.0475	0.0465	0.0455
-1.5	0.0668	0.0655	0.0643	0.0630	0.0618	0.0606	0.0594	0.0582	0.0571	0.0559
-1.4	0.0808	0.0793	0.0778	0.0764	0.0749	0.0735	0.0721	0.0708	0.0694	0.0681
-1.3	0.0968	0.0951	0.0934	0.0918	0.0901	0.0885	0.0869	0.0853	0.0838	0.0823
-1.2	0.1151	0.1131	0.1112	0.1093	0.1075	0.1056	0.1038	0.1020	0.1003	0.0985
-1.1	0.1357	0.1335	0.1314	0.1292	0.1271	0.1251	0.1230	0.1210	0.1190	0.1170
-1.0	0.1587	0.1562	0.1539	0.1515	0.1492	0.1469	0.1446	0.1423	0.1401	0.1379
-0.9	0.1841	0.1814	0.1788	0.1762	0.1736	0.1711	0.1685	0.1660	0.1635	0.1611
-0.8	0.2119	0.2090	0.2061	0.2033	0.2005	0.1977	0.1949	0.1922	0.1894	0.1867
-0.7	0.2420	0.2388	0.2358	0.2327	0.2296	0.2266	0.2236	0.2206	0.2177	0.2148
-0.6	0.2743	0.2709	0.2676	0.2643	0.2611	0.2578	0.2546	0.2514	0.2482	0.2451
-0.5	0.3085	0.3050	0.3015	0.2981	0.2946	0.2912	0.2877	0.2843	0.2810	0.2776
-0.4	0.3446	0.3409	0.3372	0.3336	0.3300	0.3264	0.3228	0.3192	0.3156	0.3121
-0.3	0.3821	0.3783	0.3745	0.3707	0.3669	0.3632	0.3594	0.3557	0.3520	0.3483
-0.2	0.4207	0.4168	0.4129	0.4090	0.4052	0.4013	0.3974	0.3936	0.3897	0.3859
-0.1	0.4602	0.4562	0.4522	0.4483	0.4443	0.4404	0.4364	0.4325	0.4286	0.4247
-0.0	0.5000	0.4960	0.4920	0.4880	0.4840	0.4801	0.4761	0.4721	0.4681	0.4641

TABLE B.1 The Cumulative Standardized Normal Distribution
(Continued)

Each entry represents an area under the cumulative standardized
normal distribution from $-\infty$ to Z.

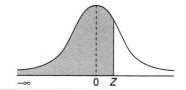

Z	0.00	0.01	0.02	0.03	0.04	0.05	0.06	0.07	0.08	0.09
0.0	0.5000	0.5040	0.5080	0.5120	0.5160	0.5199	0.5239	0.5279	0.5319	0.5359
0.1	0.5398	0.5438	0.5478	0.5517	0.5557	0.5596	0.5636	0.5675	0.5714	0.5753
0.2	0.5793	0.5832	0.5871	0.5910	0.5948	0.5987	0.6026	0.6064	0.6103	0.6141
0.3	0.6179	0.6217	0.6255	0.6293	0.6331	0.6368	0.6406	0.6443	0.6480	0.6517
0.4	0.6554	0.6591	0.6628	0.6664	0.6700	0.6736	0.6772	0.6808	0.6844	0.6879
0.5	0.6915	0.6950	0.6985	0.7019	0.7054	0.7088	0.7123	0.7157	0.7190	0.7224
0.6	0.7257	0.7291	0.7324	0.7357	0.7389	0.7422	0.7454	0.7486	0.7518	0.7549
0.7	0.7580	0.7612	0.7642	0.7673	0.7704	0.7734	0.7764	0.7794	0.7823	0.7852
0.8	0.7881	0.7910	0.7939	0.7967	0.7995	0.8023	0.8051	0.8078	0.8106	0.8133
0.9	0.8159	0.8186	0.8212	0.8238	0.8264	0.8289	0.8315	0.8340	0.8365	0.8389
1.0	0.8413	0.8438	0.8461	0.8485	0.8508	0.8531	0.8554	0.8577	0.8599	0.8621
1.1	0.8643	0.8665	0.8686	0.8708	0.8729	0.8749	0.8770	0.8790	0.8810	0.8830
1.2	0.8849	0.8869	0.8888	0.8907	0.8925	0.8944	0.8962	0.8980	0.8997	0.9015
1.3	0.9032	0.9049	0.9066	0.9082	0.9099	0.9115	0.9131	0.9147	0.9162	0.9177
1.4	0.9192	0.9207	0.9222	0.9236	0.9251	0.9265	0.9279	0.9292	0.9306	0.9319
1.5	0.9332	0.9345	0.9357	0.9370	0.9382	0.9394	0.9406	0.9418	0.9429	0.9441
1.6	0.9452	0.9463	0.9474	0.9484	0.9495	0.9505	0.9515	0.9525	0.9535	0.9545
1.7	0.9554	0.9564	0.9573	0.9582	0.9591	0.9599	0.9608	0.9616	0.9625	0.9633
1.8	0.9641	0.9649	0.9656	0.9664	0.9671	0.9678	0.9686	0.9693	0.9699	0.9706
1.9	0.9713	0.9719	0.9726	0.9732	0.9738	0.9744	0.9750	0.9756	0.9761	0.9767
2.0	0.9772	0.9778	0.9783	0.9788	0.9793	0.9798	0.9803	0.9808	0.9812	0.9817
2.1	0.9821	0.9826	0.9830	0.9834	0.9838	0.9842	0.9846	0.9850	0.9854	0.9857
2.2	0.9861	0.9864	0.9868	0.9871	0.9875	0.9878	0.9881	0.9884	0.9887	0.9890
2.3	0.9893	0.9896	0.9898	0.9901	0.9904	0.9906	0.9909	0.9911	0.9913	0.9916
2.4	0.9918	0.9920	0.9922	0.9925	0.9927	0.9929	0.9931	0.9932	0.9934	0.9936
2.5	0.9938	0.9940	0.9941	0.9943	0.9945	0.9946	0.9948	0.9949	0.9951	0.9952
2.6	0.9953	0.9955	0.9956	0.9957	0.9959	0.9960	0.9961	0.9962	0.9963	0.9964
2.7	0.9965	0.9966	0.9967	0.9968	0.9969	0.9970	0.9971	0.9972	0.9973	0.9974
2.8	0.9974	0.9975	0.9976	0.9977	0.9977	0.9978	0.9979	0.9979	0.9980	0.9981
2.9	0.9981	0.9982	0.9982	0.9983	0.9984	0.9984	0.9985	0.9985	0.9986	0.9986
3.0	0.99865	0.99869	0.99874	0.99878	0.99882	0.99886	0.99889	0.99893	0.99897	0.99900
3.1	0.99903	0.99906	0.99910	0.99913	0.99916	0.99918	0.99921	0.99924	0.99926	0.99929
3.2	0.99931	0.99934	0.99936	0.99938	0.99940	0.99942	0.99944	0.99946	0.99948	0.99950
3.3	0.99952	0.99953	0.99955	0.99957	0.99958	0.99960	0.99961	0.99962	0.99964	0.99965
3.4	0.99966	0.99968	0.99969	0.99970	0.99971	0.99972	0.99973	0.99974	0.99975	0.99976
3.5	0.99977	0.99978	0.99978	0.99979	0.99980	0.99981	0.99981	0.99982	0.99983	0.99983
3.6	0.99984	0.99985	0.99985	0.99986	0.99986	0.99987	0.99987	0.99988	0.99988	0.99989
3.7	0.99989	0.99990	0.99990	0.99990	0.99991	0.99991	0.99992	0.99992	0.99992	0.99992
3.8	0.99993	0.99993	0.99993	0.99994	0.99994	0.99994	0.99994	0.99995	0.99995	0.99995
3.9	0.99995	0.99995	0.99996	0.99996	0.99996	0.99996	0.99996	0.99996	0.99997	0.99997
4.0	0.99996832									
4.5	0.99999660									
5.0	0.99999971									
5.5	0.99999998									
6.0	0.99999999									

TABLE B.2   Critical Values of *t*

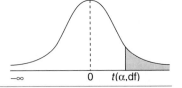

For a particular number of degree of freedom, each entry represents the critical value of t corresponding to a specified upper-tail area (α).

	Upper-Tail Areas					
Degrees of Freedom	**0.25**	**0.10**	**0.05**	**0.025**	**0.01**	**0.005**
1	1.0000	3.0777	6.3138	12.7062	31.8207	63.6574
2	0.8165	1.8856	2.9200	4.3027	6.9646	9.9248
3	0.7649	1.6377	2.3534	3.1824	4.5407	5.8409
4	0.7407	1.5332	2.1318	2.7764	3.7469	4.6041
5	0.7267	1.4759	2.0150	2.5706	3.3649	4.0322
6	0.7176	1.4398	1.9432	2.4469	3.1427	3.7074
7	0.7111	1.4149	1.8946	2.3646	2.9980	3.4995
8	0.7064	1.3968	1.8595	2.3060	2.8965	3.3554
9	0.7027	1.3830	1.8331	2.2622	2.8214	3.2498
10	0.6998	1.3722	1.8125	2.2281	2.7638	3.1693
11	0.6974	1.3634	1.7959	2.2010	2.7181	3.1058
12	0.6955	1.3562	1.7823	2.1788	2.6810	3.0545
13	0.6938	1.3502	1.7709	2.1604	2.6503	3.0123
14	0.6924	1.3450	1.7613	2.1448	2.6245	2.9768
15	0.6912	1.3406	1.7531	2.1315	2.6025	2.9467
16	0.6901	1.3368	1.7459	2.1199	2.5835	2.9208
17	0.6892	1.3334	1.7396	2.1098	2.5669	2.8982
18	0.6884	1.3304	1.7341	2.1009	2.5524	2.8784
19	0.6876	1.3277	1.7291	2.0930	2.5395	2.8609
20	0.6870	1.3253	1.7247	2.0860	2.5280	2.8453
21	0.6864	1.3232	1.7207	2.0796	2.5177	2.8314
22	0.6858	1.3212	1.7171	2.0739	2.5083	2.8188
23	0.6853	1.3195	1.7139	2.0687	2.4999	2.8073
24	0.6848	1.3178	1.7109	2.0639	2.4922	2.7969
25	0.6844	1.3163	1.7081	2.0595	2.4851	2.7874
26	0.6840	1.3150	1.7056	2.0555	2.4786	2.7787
27	0.6837	1.3137	1.7033	2.0518	2.4727	2.7707
28	0.6834	1.3125	1.7011	2.0484	2.4671	2.7633
29	0.6830	1.3114	1.6991	2.0452	2.4620	2.7564
30	0.6828	1.3104	1.6973	2.0423	2.4573	2.7500
31	0.6825	1.3095	1.6955	2.0395	2.4528	2.7440
32	0.6822	1.3086	1.6939	2.0369	2.4487	2.7385
33	0.6820	1.3077	1.6924	2.0345	2.4448	2.7333
34	0.6818	1.3070	1.6909	2.0322	2.4411	2.7284
35	0.6816	1.3062	1.6896	2.0301	2.4377	2.7238
36	0.6814	1.3055	1.6883	2.0281	2.4345	2.7195
37	0.6812	1.3049	1.6871	2.0262	2.4314	2.7154
38	0.6810	1.3042	1.6860	2.0244	2.4286	2.7116
39	0.6808	1.3036	1.6849	2.0227	2.4258	2.7079
40	0.6807	1.3031	1.6839	2.0211	2.4233	2.7045
41	0.6805	1.3025	1.6829	2.0195	2.4208	2.7012
42	0.6804	1.3020	1.6820	2.0181	2.4185	2.6981
43	0.6802	1.3016	1.6811	2.0167	2.4163	2.6951
44	0.6801	1.3011	1.6802	2.0154	2.4141	2.6923
45	0.6800	1.3006	1.6794	2.0141	2.4121	2.6896
46	0.6799	1.3022	1.6787	2.0129	2.4102	2.6870
47	0.6797	1.2998	1.6779	2.0117	2.4083	2.6846
48	0.6796	1.2994	1.6772	2.0106	2.4066	2.6822
49	0.6795	1.2991	1.6766	2.0096	2.4049	2.6800
50	0.6794	1.2987	1.6759	2.0086	2.4033	2.6778
51	0.6793	1.2984	1.6753	2.0076	2.4017	2.6757
52	0.6792	1.2980	1.6747	2.0066	2.4002	2.6737

TABLE B.2 Critical Values of t (Continued)

For a particular number of degree of freedom, each entry represents the critical value of t corresponding to a specified upper-tail area (α).

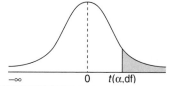

$-\infty$ 0 $t(\alpha, df)$

			Upper-Tail Areas			
Degrees of Freedom	0.25	0.10	0.05	0.025	0.01	0.005
53	0.6791	1.2977	1.6741	2.0057	2.3988	2.6718
54	0.6791	1.2974	1.6736	2.0049	2.3974	2.6700
55	0.6790	1.2971	1.6730	2.0040	2.3961	2.6682
56	0.6789	1.2969	1.6725	2.0032	2.3948	2.6665
57	0.6788	1.2966	1.6720	2.0025	2.3936	2.6649
58	0.6787	1.2963	1.6716	2.0017	2.3924	2.6633
59	0.6787	1.2961	1.6711	2.0010	2.3912	2.6618
60	0.6786	1.2958	1.6706	2.0003	2.3901	2.6603
61	0.6785	1.2956	1.6702	1.9996	2.3890	2.6589
62	0.6785	1.2954	1.6698	1.9990	2.3880	2.6575
63	0.6784	1.2951	1.6694	1.9983	2.3870	2.6561
64	0.6783	1.2949	1.6690	1.9977	2.3860	2.6549
65	0.6783	1.2947	1.6686	1.9971	2.3851	2.6536
66	0.6782	1.2945	1.6683	1.9966	2.3842	2.6524
67	0.6782	1.2943	1.6679	1.9960	2.3833	2.6512
68	0.6781	1.2941	1.6676	1.9955	2.3824	2.6501
69	0.6781	1.2939	1.6672	1.9949	2.3816	2.6490
70	0.6780	1.2938	1.6669	1.9944	2.3808	2.6479
71	0.6780	1.2936	1.6666	1.9939	2.3800	2.6469
72	0.6779	1.2934	1.6663	1.9935	2.3793	2.6459
73	0.6779	1.2933	1.6660	1.9930	2.3785	2.6449
74	0.6778	1.2931	1.6657	1.9925	2.3778	2.6439
75	0.6778	1.2929	1.6654	1.9921	2.3771	2.6430
76	0.6777	1.2928	1.6652	1.9917	2.3764	2.6421
77	0.6777	1.2926	1.6649	1.9913	2.3758	2.6412
78	0.6776	1.2925	1.6646	1.9908	2.3751	2.6403
79	0.6776	1.2924	1.6644	1.9905	2.3745	2.6395
80	0.6776	1.2922	1.6641	1.9901	2.3739	2.6387
81	0.6775	1.2921	1.6639	1.9897	2.3733	2.6379
82	0.6775	1.2920	1.6636	1.9893	2.3727	2.6371
83	0.6775	1.2918	1.6634	1.9890	2.3721	2.6364
84	0.6774	1.2917	1.6632	1.9886	2.3716	2.6356
85	0.6774	1.2916	1.6630	1.9883	2.3710	2.6349
86	0.6774	1.2915	1.6628	1.9879	2.3705	2.6342
87	0.6773	1.2914	1.6626	1.9876	2.3700	2.6335
88	0.6773	1.2912	1.6624	1.9873	2.3695	2.6329
89	0.6773	1.2911	1.6622	1.9870	2.3690	2.6322
90	0.6772	1.2910	1.6620	1.9867	2.3685	2.6316
91	0.6772	1.2909	1.6618	1.9864	2.3680	2.6309
92	0.6772	1.2908	1.6616	1.9861	2.3676	2.6303
93	0.6771	1.2907	1.6614	1.9858	2.3671	2.6297
94	0.6771	1.2906	1.6612	1.9855	2.3667	2.6291
95	0.6771	1.2905	1.6611	1.9853	2.3662	2.6286
96	0.6771	1.2904	1.6609	1.9850	2.3658	2.6280
97	0.6770	1.2903	1.6607	1.9847	2.3654	2.6275
98	0.6770	1.2902	1.6606	1.9845	2.3650	2.6269
99	0.6770	1.2902	1.6604	1.9842	2.3646	2.6264
100	0.6770	1.2901	1.6602	1.9840	2.3642	2.6259
110	0.6767	1.2893	1.6588	1.9818	2.3607	2.6213
120	0.6765	1.2886	1.6577	1.9799	2.3578	2.6174
∞	0.6745	1.2816	1.6449	1.9600	2.3263	2.5758

TABLE B.3 Critical Values of *F*

For a particular combination of numerator and denominator degrees of freedom, each entry represents the critical values of F corresponding to a specified upper-tail area (α).

Denominator df_2	**Numerator, df_1**								
	1	**2**	**3**	**4**	**5**	**6**	**7**	**8**	**9**
1	161.40	199.50	215.70	224.60	230.20	234.00	236.80	238.90	240.50
2	18.51	19.00	19.16	19.25	19.30	19.33	19.35	19.37	19.38
3	10.13	9.55	9.28	9.12	9.01	8.94	8.89	8.85	8.81
4	7.71	6.94	6.59	6.39	6.26	6.16	6.09	6.04	6.00
5	6.61	5.79	5.41	5.19	5.05	4.95	4.88	4.82	4.77
6	5.99	5.14	4.76	4.53	4.39	4.28	4.21	4.15	4.10
7	5.59	4.74	4.35	4.12	3.97	3.87	3.79	3.73	3.68
8	5.32	4.46	4.07	3.84	3.69	3.58	3.50	3.44	3.39
9	5.12	4.26	3.86	3.63	3.48	3.37	3.29	3.23	3.18
10	4.96	4.10	3.71	3.48	3.33	3.22	3.14	3.07	3.02
11	4.84	3.98	3.59	3.36	3.20	3.09	3.01	2.95	2.90
12	4.75	3.89	3.49	3.26	3.11	3.00	2.91	2.85	2.80
13	4.67	3.81	3.41	3.18	3.03	2.92	2.83	2.77	2.71
14	4.60	3.74	3.34	3.11	2.96	2.85	2.76	2.70	2.65
15	4.54	3.68	3.29	3.06	2.90	2.79	2.71	2.64	2.59
16	4.49	3.63	3.24	3.01	2.85	2.74	2.66	2.59	2.54
17	4.45	3.59	3.20	2.96	2.81	2.70	2.61	2.55	2.49
18	4.41	3.55	3.16	2.93	2.77	2.66	2.58	2.51	2.46
19	4.38	3.52	3.13	2.90	2.74	2.63	2.54	2.48	2.42
20	4.35	3.49	3.10	2.87	2.71	2.60	2.51	2.45	2.39
21	4.32	3.47	3.07	2.84	2.68	2.57	2.49	2.42	2.37
22	4.30	3.44	3.05	2.82	2.66	2.55	2.46	2.40	2.34
23	4.28	3.42	3.03	2.80	2.64	2.53	2.44	2.37	2.32
24	4.26	3.40	3.01	2.78	2.62	2.51	2.42	2.36	2.30
25	4.24	3.39	2.99	2.76	2.60	2.49	2.40	2.34	2.28
26	4.23	3.37	2.98	2.74	2.59	2.47	2.39	2.32	2.27
27	4.21	3.35	2.96	2.73	2.57	2.46	2.37	2.31	2.25
28	4.20	3.34	2.95	2.71	2.56	2.45	2.36	2.29	2.24
29	4.18	3.33	2.93	2.70	2.55	2.43	2.35	2.28	2.22
30	4.17	3.32	2.92	2.69	2.53	2.42	2.33	2.27	2.21
40	4.08	3.23	2.84	2.61	2.45	2.34	2.25	2.18	2.12
60	4.00	3.15	2.76	2.53	2.37	2.25	2.17	2.10	2.04
120	3.92	3.07	2.68	2.45	2.29	2.17	2.09	2.02	1.96
∞	3.84	3.00	2.60	2.37	2.21	2.10	2.01	1.94	1.88

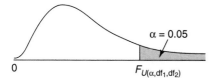

				Numerator, df_1					
10	**12**	**15**	**20**	**24**	**30**	**40**	**60**	**120**	**∞**
241.90	243.90	245.90	248.00	249.10	250.10	251.10	252.20	253.30	254.30
19.40	19.41	19.43	19.45	19.45	19.46	19.47	19.48	19.49	19.50
8.79	8.74	8.70	8.66	8.64	8.62	8.59	8.57	8.55	8.53
5.96	5.91	5.86	5.80	5.77	5.75	5.72	5.69	5.66	5.63
4.74	4.68	4.62	4.56	4.53	4.50	4.46	4.43	4.40	4.36
4.06	4.00	3.94	3.87	3.84	3.81	3.77	3.74	3.70	3.67
3.64	3.57	3.51	3.44	3.41	3.38	3.34	3.30	3.27	3.23
3.35	3.28	3.22	3.15	3.12	3.08	3.04	3.01	2.97	2.93
3.14	3.07	3.01	2.94	2.90	2.86	2.83	2.79	2.75	2.71
2.98	2.91	2.85	2.77	2.74	2.70	2.66	2.62	2.58	2.54
2.85	2.79	2.72	2.65	2.61	2.57	2.53	2.49	2.45	2.40
2.75	2.69	2.62	2.54	2.51	2.47	2.43	2.38	2.34	2.30
2.67	2.60	2.53	2.46	2.42	2.38	2.34	2.30	2.25	2.21
2.60	2.53	2.46	2.39	2.35	2.31	2.27	2.22	2.18	2.13
2.54	2.48	2.40	2.33	2.29	2.25	2.20	2.16	2.11	2.07
2.49	2.42	2.35	2.28	2.24	2.19	2.15	2.11	2.06	2.01
2.45	2.38	2.31	2.23	2.19	2.15	2.10	2.06	2.01	1.96
2.41	2.34	2.27	2.19	2.15	2.11	2.06	2.02	1.97	1.92
2.38	2.31	2.23	2.16	2.11	2.07	2.03	1.98	1.93	1.88
2.35	2.28	2.20	2.12	2.08	2.04	1.99	1.95	1.90	1.84
2.32	2.25	2.18	2.10	2.05	2.01	1.96	1.92	1.87	1.81
2.30	2.23	2.15	2.07	2.03	1.98	1.91	1.89	1.84	1.78
2.27	2.20	2.13	2.05	2.01	1.96	1.91	1.86	1.81	1.76
2.25	2.18	2.11	2.03	1.98	1.94	1.89	1.84	1.79	1.73
2.24	2.16	2.09	2.01	1.96	1.92	1.87	1.82	1.77	1.71
2.22	2.15	2.07	1.99	1.95	1.90	1.85	1.80	1.75	1.69
2.20	2.13	2.06	1.97	1.93	1.88	1.84	1.79	1.73	1.67
2.19	2.12	2.04	1.96	1.91	1.87	1.82	1.77	1.71	1.65
2.18	2.10	2.03	1.94	1.90	1.85	1.81	1.75	1.70	1.64
2.16	2.09	2.01	1.93	1.89	1.84	1.79	1.74	1.68	1.62
2.08	2.00	1.92	1.84	1.79	1.74	1.69	1.64	1.58	1.51
1.99	1.92	1.84	1.75	1.70	1.65	1.59	1.53	1.47	1.39
1.91	1.83	1.75	1.66	1.61	1.55	1.50	1.43	1.35	1.25
1.83	1.75	1.67	1.57	1.52	1.46	1.39	1.32	1.22	1.00

(continued)

TABLE B.3 Critical Values of F (Continued)

For a particular combination of numerator and denominator degrees of freedom, each entry represents the critical values of F corresponding to a specified upper-tail area (α).

Denominator df_2	Numerator, df_1								
	1	**2**	**3**	**4**	**5**	**6**	**7**	**8**	**9**
1	647.80	799.50	864.20	899.60	921.80	937.10	948.20	956.70	963.30
2	38.51	39.00	39.17	39.25	39.30	39.33	39.36	39.39	39.39
3	17.44	16.04	15.44	15.10	14.88	14.73	14.62	14.54	14.47
4	12.22	10.65	9.98	9.60	9.36	9.20	9.07	8.98	8.90
5	10.01	8.43	7.76	7.39	7.15	6.98	6.85	6.76	6.68
6	8.81	7.26	6.60	6.23	5.99	5.82	5.70	5.60	5.52
7	8.07	6.54	5.89	5.52	5.29	5.12	4.99	4.90	4.82
8	7.57	6.06	5.42	5.05	4.82	4.65	4.53	4.43	4.36
9	7.21	5.71	5.08	4.72	4.48	4.32	4.20	4.10	4.03
10	6.94	5.46	4.83	4.47	4.24	4.07	3.95	3.85	3.78
11	6.72	5.26	4.63	4.28	4.04	3.88	3.76	3.66	3.59
12	6.55	5.10	4.47	4.12	3.89	3.73	3.61	3.51	3.44
13	6.41	4.97	4.35	4.00	3.77	3.60	3.48	3.39	3.31
14	6.30	4.86	4.24	3.89	3.66	3.50	3.38	3.29	3.21
15	6.20	4.77	4.15	3.80	3.58	3.41	3.29	3.20	3.12
16	6.12	4.69	4.08	3.73	3.50	3.34	3.22	3.12	3.05
17	6.04	4.62	4.01	3.66	3.44	3.28	3.16	3.06	2.98
18	5.98	4.56	3.95	3.61	3.38	3.22	3.10	3.01	2.93
19	5.92	4.51	3.90	3.56	3.33	3.17	3.05	2.96	2.88
20	5.87	4.46	3.86	3.51	3.29	3.13	3.01	2.91	2.84
21	5.83	4.42	3.82	3.48	3.25	3.09	2.97	2.87	2.80
22	5.79	4.38	3.78	3.44	3.22	3.05	2.93	2.84	2.76
23	5.75	4.35	3.75	3.41	3.18	3.02	2.90	2.81	2.73
24	5.72	4.32	3.72	3.38	3.15	2.99	2.87	2.78	2.70
25	5.69	4.29	3.69	3.35	3.13	2.97	2.85	2.75	2.68
26	5.66	4.27	3.67	3.33	3.10	2.94	2.82	2.73	2.65
27	5.63	4.24	3.65	3.31	3.08	2.92	2.80	2.71	2.63
28	5.61	4.22	3.63	3.29	3.06	2.90	2.78	2.69	2.61
29	5.59	4.20	3.61	3.27	3.04	2.88	2.76	2.67	2.59
30	5.57	4.18	3.59	3.25	3.03	2.87	2.75	2.65	2.57
40	5.42	4.05	3.46	3.13	2.90	2.74	2.62	2.53	2.45
60	5.29	3.93	3.34	3.01	2.79	2.63	2.51	2.41	2.33
120	5.15	3.80	3.23	2.89	2.67	2.52	2.39	2.30	2.22
∞	5.02	3.69	3.12	2.79	2.57	2.41	2.29	2.19	2.11

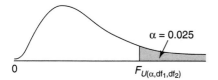

α = 0.025

$F_{U(\alpha, df_1, df_2)}$

0

Numerator, df_1

10	12	15	20	24	30	40	60	120	∞
968.60	976.70	984.90	993.10	997.20	1,001.00	1,006.00	1,010.00	1,014.00	1,018.00
39.40	39.41	39.43	39.45	39.46	39.46	39.47	39.48	39.49	39.50
14.42	14.34	14.25	14.17	14.12	14.08	14.04	13.99	13.95	13.90
8.84	8.75	8.66	8.56	8.51	8.46	8.41	8.36	8.31	8.26
6.62	6.52	6.43	6.33	6.28	6.23	6.18	6.12	6.07	6.02
5.46	5.37	5.27	5.17	5.12	5.07	5.01	4.96	4.90	4.85
4.76	4.67	4.57	4.47	4.42	4.36	4.31	4.25	4.20	4.14
4.30	4.20	4.10	4.00	3.95	3.89	3.84	3.78	3.73	3.67
3.96	3.87	3.77	3.67	3.61	3.56	3.51	3.45	3.39	3.33
3.72	3.62	3.52	3.42	3.37	3.31	3.26	3.20	3.14	3.08
3.53	3.43	3.33	3.23	3.17	3.12	3.06	3.00	2.94	2.88
3.37	3.28	3.18	3.07	3.02	2.96	2.91	2.85	2.79	2.72
3.25	3.15	3.05	2.95	2.89	2.84	2.78	2.72	2.66	2.60
3.15	3.05	2.95	2.84	2.79	2.73	2.67	2.61	2.55	2.49
3.06	2.96	2.86	2.76	2.70	2.64	2.59	2.52	2.46	2.40
2.99	2.89	2.79	2.68	2.63	2.57	2.51	2.45	2.38	2.32
2.92	2.82	2.72	2.62	2.56	2.50	2.44	2.38	2.32	2.25
2.87	2.77	2.67	2.56	2.50	2.44	2.38	2.32	2.26	2.19
2.82	2.72	2.62	2.51	2.45	2.39	2.33	2.27	2.20	2.13
2.77	2.68	2.57	2.46	2.41	2.35	2.29	2.22	2.16	2.09
2.73	2.64	2.53	2.42	2.37	2.31	2.25	2.18	2.11	2.04
2.70	2.60	2.50	2.39	2.33	2.27	2.21	2.14	2.08	2.00
2.67	2.57	2.47	2.36	2.30	2.24	2.18	2.11	2.04	1.97
2.64	2.54	2.44	2.33	2.27	2.21	2.15	2.08	2.01	1.94
2.61	2.51	2.41	2.30	2.24	2.18	2.12	2.05	1.98	1.91
2.59	2.49	2.39	2.28	2.22	2.16	2.09	2.03	1.95	1.88
2.57	2.47	2.36	2.25	2.19	2.13	2.07	2.00	1.93	1.85
2.55	2.45	2.34	2.23	2.17	2.11	2.05	1.98	1.91	1.83
2.53	2.43	2.32	2.21	2.15	2.09	2.03	1.96	1.89	1.81
2.51	2.41	2.31	2.20	2.14	2.07	2.01	1.94	1.87	1.79
2.39	2.29	2.18	2.07	2.01	1.94	1.88	1.80	1.72	1.64
2.27	2.17	2.06	1.94	1.88	1.82	1.74	1.67	1.58	1.48
2.16	2.05	1.94	1.82	1.76	1.69	1.61	1.53	1.43	1.31
2.05	1.94	1.83	1.71	1.64	1.57	1.48	1.39	1.27	1.00

(continued)

TABLE B.3 Critical Values of *F* (Continued)

For a particular combination of numerator and denominator degrees of freedom, each entry represents the critical values of F corresponding to a specified upper-tail area (α).

	Numerator, df_1								
Denominator df_2	**1**	**2**	**3**	**4**	**5**	**6**	**7**	**8**	**9**
1	4,052.00	4,999.50	5,403.00	5,625.00	5,764.00	5,859.00	5,928.00	5,982.00	6,022.00
2	98.50	99.00	99.17	99.25	99.30	99.33	99.36	99.37	99.39
3	34.12	30.82	29.46	28.71	28.24	27.91	27.67	27.49	27.35
4	21.20	18.00	16.69	15.98	15.52	15.21	14.98	14.80	14.66
5	16.26	13.27	12.06	11.39	10.97	10.67	10.46	10.29	10.16
6	13.75	10.92	9.78	9.15	8.75	8.47	8.26	8.10	7.98
7	12.25	9.55	8.45	7.85	7.46	7.19	6.99	6.84	6.72
8	11.26	8.65	7.59	7.01	6.63	6.37	6.18	6.03	5.91
9	10.56	8.02	6.99	6.42	6.06	5.80	5.61	5.47	5.35
10	10.04	7.56	6.55	5.99	5.64	5.39	5.20	5.06	4.94
11	9.65	7.21	6.22	5.67	5.32	5.07	4.89	4.74	4.63
12	9.33	6.93	5.95	5.41	5.06	4.82	4.64	4.50	4.39
13	9.07	6.70	5.74	5.21	4.86	4.62	4.44	4.30	4.19
14	8.86	6.51	5.56	5.04	4.69	4.46	4.28	4.14	4.03
15	8.68	6.36	5.42	4.89	4.56	4.32	4.14	4.00	3.89
16	8.53	6.23	5.29	4.77	4.44	4.20	4.03	3.89	3.78
17	8.40	6.11	5.18	4.67	4.34	4.10	3.93	3.79	3.68
18	8.29	6.01	5.09	4.58	4.25	4.01	3.84	3.71	3.60
19	8.18	5.93	5.01	4.50	4.17	3.94	3.77	3.63	3.52
20	8.10	5.85	4.94	4.43	4.10	3.87	3.70	3.56	3.46
21	8.02	5.78	4.87	4.37	4.04	3.81	3.64	3.51	3.40
22	7.95	5.72	4.82	4.31	3.99	3.76	3.59	3.45	3.35
23	7.88	5.66	4.76	4.26	3.94	3.71	3.54	3.41	3.30
24	7.82	5.61	4.72	4.22	3.90	3.67	3.50	3.36	3.26
25	7.77	5.57	4.68	4.18	3.85	3.63	3.46	3.32	3.22
26	7.72	5.53	4.64	4.14	3.82	3.59	3.42	3.29	3.18
27	7.68	5.49	4.60	4.11	3.78	3.56	3.39	3.26	3.15
28	7.64	5.45	4.57	4.07	3.75	3.53	3.36	3.23	3.12
29	7.60	5.42	4.54	4.04	3.73	3.50	3.33	3.20	3.09
30	7.56	5.39	4.51	4.02	3.70	3.47	3.30	3.17	3.07
40	7.31	5.18	4.31	3.83	3.51	3.29	3.12	2.99	2.89
60	7.08	4.98	4.13	3.65	3.34	3.12	2.95	2.82	2.72
120	6.85	4.79	3.95	3.48	3.17	2.96	2.79	2.66	2.56
∞	6.63	4.61	3.78	3.32	3.02	2.80	2.64	2.51	2.41

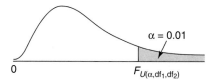

$\alpha = 0.01$

0 $F_{U(\alpha, df_1, df_2)}$

Numerator, df_1

10	12	15	20	24	30	40	60	120	∞
6,056.00	6,106.00	6,157.00	6,209.00	6,235.00	6,261.00	6,287.00	6,313.00	6,339.00	6,366.00
99.40	99.42	99.43	94.45	99.46	99.47	99.47	99.48	99.49	99.50
27.23	27.05	26.87	26.69	26.60	26.50	26.41	26.32	26.22	26.13
14.55	14.37	14.20	14.02	13.93	13.84	13.75	13.65	13.56	13.46
10.05	9.89	9.72	9.55	9.47	9.38	9.29	9.20	9.11	9.02
7.87	7.72	7.56	7.40	7.31	7.23	7.14	7.06	6.97	6.88
6.62	6.47	6.31	6.16	6.07	5.99	5.91	5.82	5.74	5.65
5.81	5.67	5.52	5.36	5.28	5.20	5.12	5.03	4.95	4.86
5.26	5.11	4.96	4.81	4.73	4.65	4.57	4.48	4.40	4.31
4.85	4.71	4.56	4.41	4.33	4.25	4.17	4.08	4.00	3.91
4.54	4.40	4.25	4.10	4.02	3.94	3.86	3.78	3.69	3.60
4.30	4.16	4.01	3.86	3.78	3.70	3.62	3.54	3.45	3.36
4.10	3.96	3.82	3.66	3.59	3.51	3.43	3.34	3.25	3.17
3.94	3.80	3.66	3.51	3.43	3.35	3.27	3.18	3.09	3.00
3.80	3.67	3.52	3.37	3.29	3.21	3.13	3.05	2.96	2.87
3.69	3.55	3.41	3.26	3.18	3.10	3.02	2.93	2.81	2.75
3.59	3.46	3.31	3.16	3.08	3.00	2.92	2.83	2.75	2.65
3.51	3.37	3.23	3.08	3.00	2.92	2.84	2.75	2.66	2.57
3.43	3.30	3.15	3.00	2.92	2.84	2.76	2.67	2.58	2.49
3.37	3.23	3.09	2.94	2.86	2.78	2.69	2.61	2.52	2.42
3.31	3.17	3.03	2.88	2.80	2.72	2.64	2.55	2.46	2.36
3.26	3.12	2.98	2.83	2.75	2.67	2.58	2.50	2.40	2.31
3.21	3.07	2.93	2.78	2.70	2.62	2.54	2.45	2.35	2.26
3.17	3.03	2.89	2.74	2.66	2.58	2.49	2.40	2.31	2.21
3.13	2.99	2.85	2.70	2.62	2.54	2.45	2.36	2.27	2.17
3.09	2.96	2.81	2.66	2.58	2.50	2.42	2.33	2.23	2.13
3.06	2.93	2.78	2.63	2.55	2.47	2.38	2.29	2.20	2.10
3.03	2.90	2.75	2.60	2.52	2.44	2.35	2.26	2.17	2.06
3.00	2.87	2.73	2.57	2.49	2.41	2.33	2.23	2.14	2.03
2.98	2.84	2.70	2.55	2.47	2.39	2.30	2.21	2.11	2.01
2.80	2.66	2.52	2.37	2.29	2.20	2.11	2.02	1.92	1.80
2.63	2.50	2.35	2.20	2.12	2.03	1.94	1.84	1.73	1.60
2.47	2.34	2.19	2.03	1.95	1.86	1.76	1.66	1.53	1.38
2.32	2.18	2.04	1.88	1.79	1.70	1.59	1.47	1.32	1.00

(continued)

TABLE B.3 Critical Values of *F* (Continued)

For a particular combination of numerator and denominator degrees of freedom, each entry represents the critical values of F corresponding to a specified upper-tail area (α).

					Numerator, df_1				
Denominator df_2	**1**	**2**	**3**	**4**	**5**	**6**	**7**	**8**	**9**
1	16,211.00	20,000.000	21,615.00	22,500.00	23,056.00	23,437.00	23,715.00	23,925.00	24,091.00
2	198.50	199.00	199.20	199.20	199.30	199.30	199.40	199.40	199.40
3	55.55	49.80	47.47	46.19	45.39	44.84	44.43	44.13	43.88
4	31.33	26.28	24.26	23.15	22.46	21.97	21.62	21.35	21.14
5	22.78	18.31	16.53	15.56	14.94	14.51	14.20	13.96	13.77
6	18.63	14.54	12.92	12.03	11.46	11.07	10.79	10.57	10.39
7	16.24	12.40	10.88	10.05	9.52	9.16	8.89	8.68	8.51
8	14.69	11.04	9.60	8.81	8.30	7.95	7.69	7.50	7.34
9	13.61	10.11	8.72	7.96	7.47	7.13	6.88	6.69	6.54
10	12.83	9.43	8.08	7.34	6.87	6.54	6.30	6.12	5.97
11	12.23	8.91	7.60	6.88	6.42	6.10	5.86	5.68	5.54
12	11.75	8.51	7.23	6.52	6.07	5.76	5.52	5.35	5.20
13	11.37	8.19	6.93	6.23	5.79	5.48	5.25	5.08	4.94
14	11.06	7.92	6.68	6.00	5.56	5.26	5.03	4.86	4.72
15	10.80	7.70	6.48	5.80	5.37	5.07	4.85	4.67	4.54
16	10.58	7.51	6.30	5.64	5.21	4.91	4.69	4.52	4.38
17	10.38	7.35	6.16	5.50	5.07	4.78	4.56	4.39	4.25
18	10.22	7.21	6.03	5.37	4.96	4.66	4.44	4.28	4.14
19	10.07	7.09	5.92	5.27	4.85	4.56	4.34	4.18	4.04
20	9.94	6.99	5.82	5.17	4.76	4.47	4.26	4.09	3.96
21	9.83	6.89	5.73	5.09	4.68	4.39	4.18	4.02	3.88
22	9.73	6.81	5.65	5.02	4.61	4.32	4.11	3.94	3.81
23	9.63	6.73	5.58	4.95	4.54	4.26	4.05	3.88	3.75
24	9.55	6.66	5.52	4.89	4.49	4.20	3.99	3.83	3.69
25	9.48	6.60	5.46	4.84	4.43	4.15	3.94	3.78	3.64
26	9.41	6.54	5.41	4.79	4.38	4.10	3.89	3.73	3.60
27	9.34	6.49	5.36	4.74	4.34	4.06	3.85	3.69	3.56
28	9.28	6.44	5.32	4.70	4.30	4.02	3.81	3.65	3.52
29	9.23	6.40	5.28	4.66	4.26	3.98	3.77	3.61	3.48
30	9.18	6.35	5.24	4.62	4.23	3.95	3.74	3.58	3.45
40	8.83	6.07	4.98	4.37	3.99	3.71	3.51	3.35	3.22
60	8.49	5.79	4.73	4.14	3.76	3.49	3.29	3.13	3.01
120	8.18	5.54	4.50	3.92	3.55	3.28	3.09	2.93	2.81
∞	7.88	5.30	4.28	3.72	3.35	3.09	2.90	2.74	2.62

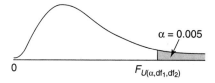

$\alpha = 0.005$

$F_{U(\alpha, df_1, df_2)}$

			Numerator, df_1						
10	**12**	**15**	**20**	**24**	**30**	**40**	**60**	**120**	**∞**
24,224.00	24,426.00	24,630.00	24,836.00	24,910.00	25,044.00	25,148.00	25,253.00	25,359.00	25,465.00
199.40	199.40	199.40	199.40	199.50	199.50	199.50	199.50	199.50	199.50
43.69	43.39	43.08	42.78	42.62	42.47	42.31	42.15	41.99	41.83
20.97	20.70	20.44	20.17	20.03	19.89	19.75	19.61	19.47	19.32
13.62	13.38	13.15	12.90	12.78	12.66	12.53	12.40	12.27	12.11
10.25	10.03	9.81	9.59	9.47	9.36	9.24	9.12	9.00	8.88
8.38	8.18	7.97	7.75	7.65	7.53	7.42	7.31	7.19	7.08
7.21	7.01	6.81	6.61	6.50	6.40	6.29	6.18	6.06	5.95
6.42	6.23	6.03	5.83	5.73	5.62	5.52	5.41	5.30	5.19
5.85	5.66	5.47	5.27	5.17	5.07	4.97	4.86	4.75	1.61
5.42	5.24	5.05	4.86	4.75	4.65	4.55	4.44	4.34	4.23
5.09	4.91	4.72	4.53	4.43	4.33	4.23	4.12	4.01	3.90
4.82	4.64	4.46	4.27	4.17	4.07	3.97	3.87	3.76	3.65
4.60	4.43	4.25	4.06	3.96	3.86	3.76	3.66	3.55	3.41
4.42	4.25	4.07	3.88	3.79	3.69	3.58	3.48	3.37	3.26
4.27	4.10	3.92	3.73	3.64	3.54	3.44	3.33	3.22	3.11
4.14	3.97	3.79	3.61	3.51	3.41	3.31	3.21	3.10	2.98
4.03	3.86	3.68	3.50	3.40	3.30	3.20	3.10	2.89	2.87
3.93	3.76	3.59	3.40	3.31	3.21	3.11	3.00	2.89	2.78
3.85	3.68	3.50	3.32	3.22	3.12	3.02	2.92	2.81	2.69
3.77	3.60	3.43	3.24	3.15	3.05	2.95	2.84	2.73	2.61
3.70	3.54	3.36	3.18	3.08	2.98	2.88	2.77	2.66	2.55
3.64	3.47	3.30	3.12	3.02	2.92	2.82	2.71	2.60	2.48
3.59	3.42	3.25	3.06	2.97	2.87	2.77	2.66	2.55	2.43
3.54	3.37	3.20	3.01	2.92	2.82	2.72	2.61	2.50	2.38
3.49	3.33	3.15	2.97	2.87	2.77	2.67	2.56	2.45	2.33
3.45	3.28	3.11	2.93	2.83	2.73	2.63	2.52	2.41	2.29
3.41	3.25	3.07	2.89	2.79	2.69	2.59	2.48	2.37	2.25
3.38	3.21	3.04	2.86	2.76	2.66	2.56	2.45	2.33	2.21
3.34	3.18	3.01	2.82	2.73	2.63	2.52	2.42	2.30	2.18
3.12	2.95	2.78	2.60	2.50	2.40	2.30	2.18	2.06	1.93
2.90	2.74	2.57	2.39	2.29	2.19	2.08	1.96	1.83	1.69
2.71	2.54	2.37	2.19	2.09	1.98	1.87	1.75	1.61	1.43
2.52	2.36	2.19	2.00	1.90	1.79	1.67	1.53	1.36	1.00

TABLE B.4 Control Chart Constants

Number of Observations in Subgroup, n	A_2	A_3	B_3	B_4	c_4	d_2	d_3	D_3	D_4	E_2
2	1.880	2.659	0.000	3.267	0.7979	1.128	0.853	0.000	3.267	2.660
3	1.023	1.954	0.000	2.568	0.8862	1.693	0.888	0.000	2.574	1.772
4	0.729	1.628	0.000	2.266	0.9213	2.059	0.880	0.000	2.282	1.457
5	0.577	1.427	0.000	2.089	0.9400	2.326	0.864	0.000	2.114	1.290
6	0.483	1.287	0.030	1.970	0.9515	2.534	0.848	0.000	2.004	1.184
7	0.419	1.182	0.118	1.882	0.9594	2.704	0.833	0.076	1.924	1.109
8	0.373	1.099	0.185	1.815	0.9650	2.847	0.820	0.136	1.864	1.054
9	0.337	1.032	0.239	1.761	0.9693	2.970	0.808	0.184	1.816	1.010
10	0.308	0.975	0.284	1.716	0.9727	3.078	0.797	0.223	1.777	0.975
11	0.285	0.927	0.321	1.679	0.9754	3.173	0.787	0.256	1.744	
12	0.266	0.886	0.354	1.646	0.9776	3.258	0.778	0.283	1.717	
13	0.249	0.850	0.382	1.618	0.9794	3.336	0.770	0.307	1.693	
14	0.235	0.817	0.406	1.594	0.9810	3.407	0.762	0.328	1.672	
15	0.223	0.789	0.428	1.572	0.9823	3.472	0.755	0.347	1.653	
16	0.212	0.763	0.448	1.552	0.9835	3.532	0.749	0.363	1.637	
17	0.203	0.739	0.466	1.534	0.9845	3.588	0.743	0.378	1.622	
18	0.194	0.718	0.482	1.518	0.9854	3.640	0.738	0.391	1.608	
19	0.187	0.698	0.497	1.503	0.9862	3.689	0.733	0.403	1.597	
20	0.180	0.680	0.510	1.490	0.9869	3.735	0.729	0.415	1.585	
21	0.173	0.663	0.523	1.477	0.9876	3.778	0.724	0.425	1.575	
22	0.167	0.647	0.534	1.466	0.9882	3.819	0.720	0.434	1.566	
23	0.162	0.633	0.545	1.455	0.9887	3.858	0.716	0.443	1.557	
24	0.157	0.619	0.555	1.445	0.9892	3.895	0.712	0.451	1.548	
25	0.153	0.606	0.565	1.435	0.9896	3.931	0.709	0.459	1.541	
More than 25	$3/\sqrt{n}$		$1 - 3/\sqrt{2n}$	$1 + 3/\sqrt{2n}$						

Source: A_2, A_3, B_3, B_4, c_4, d_2, d_3, D_3, D_4, E_2 reprinted with permission from ASTM Manual on the Presentation of Data and Control Chart Analysis (Philadelphia, PA: ASTM, 1976), pp. 134–36. Copyright ASTM.

DOCUMENTATION OF DATA FILES

The following is an alphabetical listing and description of all the Minitab and JMP files found on the text web site located at `www.prenhall.com/gitlow/designforsixsigma`. The icons that appear throughout the text identify these files.

BANK   Waiting time.

BANKTIME   Waiting times of four bank customers per day for 20 days.

BREAKFAST   Delivery time difference, menu choice, and desired time.

BREAKFAST2   Delivery time difference, menu choice, and desired time.

CAKE   Flour, shortening, egg powder, oven temperature, baking time, and rating score.

DEFECTIVES   Number of defective entries.

DINNER   Delivery time, complexity, elevator, and order volume.

ERWAITING   Emergency room waiting time (in minutes) at the main facility, satellite 1, satellite 2, and satellite 3.

FIGURE12-1   Minitab entries for cause-and-effect diagram of Figure 12.1.

GAGER&R1   Random order, standard order, patient, psychologist, and score.

MOVING   Labor hours, cubic feet, number of large pieces of furniture, and availability of an elevator.

PREPARATION   Preparation time, dessert, side dishes, potato, and entrée.

PREPARATION2   Preparation time, entrée, beverage, order volume, dessert, and complexity.

PROCESSING1   Total time; record pull time.

PROCESSING2   Total time; record pull time, before (=1) and after (=2).

SATISFACTION   Satisfaction, delivery time difference, and previous stay at hotel.

SERVICETIME   Run number, people, strategy, time, cycle time, and throughput.

STANDBY   Standby hours, staff, remote hours, Dubner hours, and labor hours.

THICKNESS   Thickness.

INDEX

A

Accessibility, 458
Accounting analysis, 244–245
Additive flag diagram, 59
Adopter categories, 269–270
Affinity diagram, 398
AGO, 513
Agreement, 150
Alias, 329
Analytic studies, 287
Analyze phase, 590–606
   inputs, 159
   steps, 158–159
APC, 512, 553
Assertive behavior, 532–533
Assumptions of regression, 355
Attribute check sheet, 404
Attribute data, 287
Attribute indicators, 57

B

Background variable, 298
Behavioral mapping, 254
Benchmarking, 166, 529
Best subsets regression, 375–379
Binary indicators, 58
Black belt, 35–36
Brainstorming, 394
   procedure, 395–396
   rules, 396
Business market segments, 462
Business objectives, 56
Business prioritization matrix, 81

C

C&S, 512, 552
Calibration, 138
Cause-and-effect diagram, 402
Cause-and-effect matrix, 403
Champion, 33, 634
Check sheets, 404–405
Cluster analysis, 466
Coefficient of correlation (r), 354
Coefficient of determination (r^2), 354
Coefficient of multiple determination, 361
Collinearity, 370–371
Compatibility, 269
Complexity, 269
Component dimensions, 213–214
Concept fan, 478
Concentrated market segmentation, 463
Concurrent engineering
   benefits, 555–556
   principles, 554–555
Confidence interval estimate for the slope, 365
Confirmation stage, 271
Consider all factors (CAF), 511
Consumer journal, 254
Consumer market segments, 459
Contingency plans, 95
Continuous event, 424
Continuous model, 196
Control chart factors table, 680
Control charts, 68
Cost benefits formula, 88
C_p statistic, 378
Critical-to-process (CTP), 212–213, 223–224, 297
   flow-down CTPs, 217–223
   flow-up CTPs, 213–217
Critical-to-quality (CTQ), 38, 212, 298
Cross-product term. *See* Interaction term
Customer satisfaction key objectives, 57

683

Discover the power of SigmaFlow...

Congratulations! Purchasing this book has entitled you to a complimentary license of SigmaFlow's powerful software suite. We specialize in software solutions for best practice and project life-cycle management that deliver outstanding results.

Your CD contains these robust SigmaFlow applications:

FREE SOFTWARE LICENSE INCLUDED!

Turn the page and learn more!

SigmaFlow Coach

Coach makes it easy to create, standardize and replicate the execution of best practice methodologies and processes. *Coach* compresses the learning curve and makes practitioners self-sufficient. Enabling capabilities include:

- Graphical roadmap illustrates when and how to apply methods and tools
- Reference materials at your fingertips
- Special file management features to streamline project replication
- Project financials, dashboard review and drill-downs

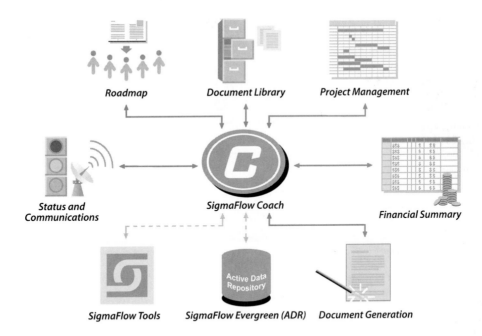

| Roadmap | Document Library | Project Management |

Status and Communications — SigmaFlow Coach — Financial Summary

SigmaFlow Tools — SigmaFlow Evergreen (ADR) — Document Generation

SigmaFlow Tools

With *Modeler*, experiment 'risk free'... at virtually no cost, and in a fraction of the time otherwise required.

- Study process designs prior to piloting
- Eliminate unforeseen barriers, bottlenecks and design flaws
- Optimize resource allocation and priority

Welcome to the power of SigmaFlow...

SigmaFlow VSM

VSM combines multi-level value stream mapping with process benchmarking, data collection and what-if improvement analysis. *VSM* is the only value stream mapping application that offers an integrated Lean/Six Sigma toolkit.

Benchmarking
Quickly assess whether the process is Lean or Fat.

Multi-level Value Stream Maps
Create value stream sub-processes and hierarchy with automatic data roll-up.

Data Collection
Better understand your process variability.

Standard Calculations
Eliminate cumbersome Excel import and export.

Scorecards
Experiment with and understand the vital improvement levers through what-if analysis.

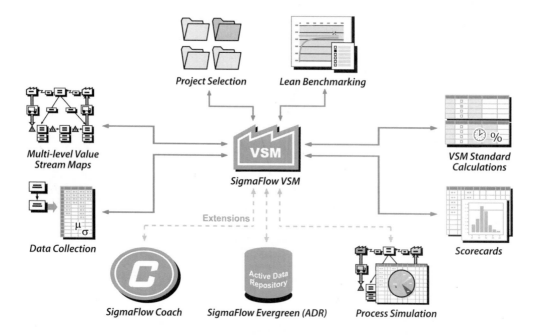

◀ *VSM is just one of SigmaFlow's powerful software tools. Learn more on the previous page!*

Installing Your CD

1 | To extend your default 14-day trial license period, refer to the ReadMe file on the CD to get a License ID and Password for each of applications you want to continue using.

2 | The CD is designed to auto-run when loaded. If it does not load automatically, go to your CD drive and install it from the directory.

3 | If you have trouble installing the software, email us at *support@sigmaflow.com*.

To more information and purchase a license, visit us at www.sigmaflow.com